DRAGON BALL

BALL FULL COLOR FREEZA ARC

1

STORY AND ART BY

AKIRA TORIYAMA

DRAGON BALL
FULL COLOR FREEZA ARC

CONTENTS

DRAGON BALL FULL COLOR FREEZA ARC

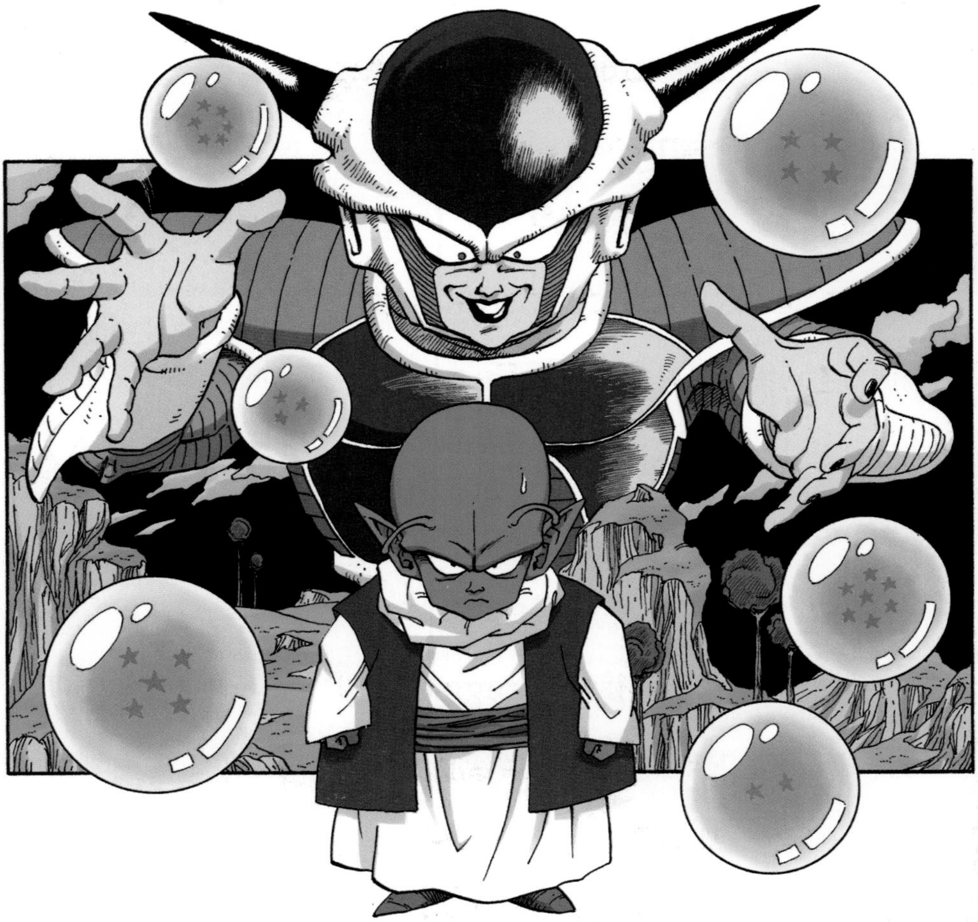

Chapter 1 • The Return of Vegeta

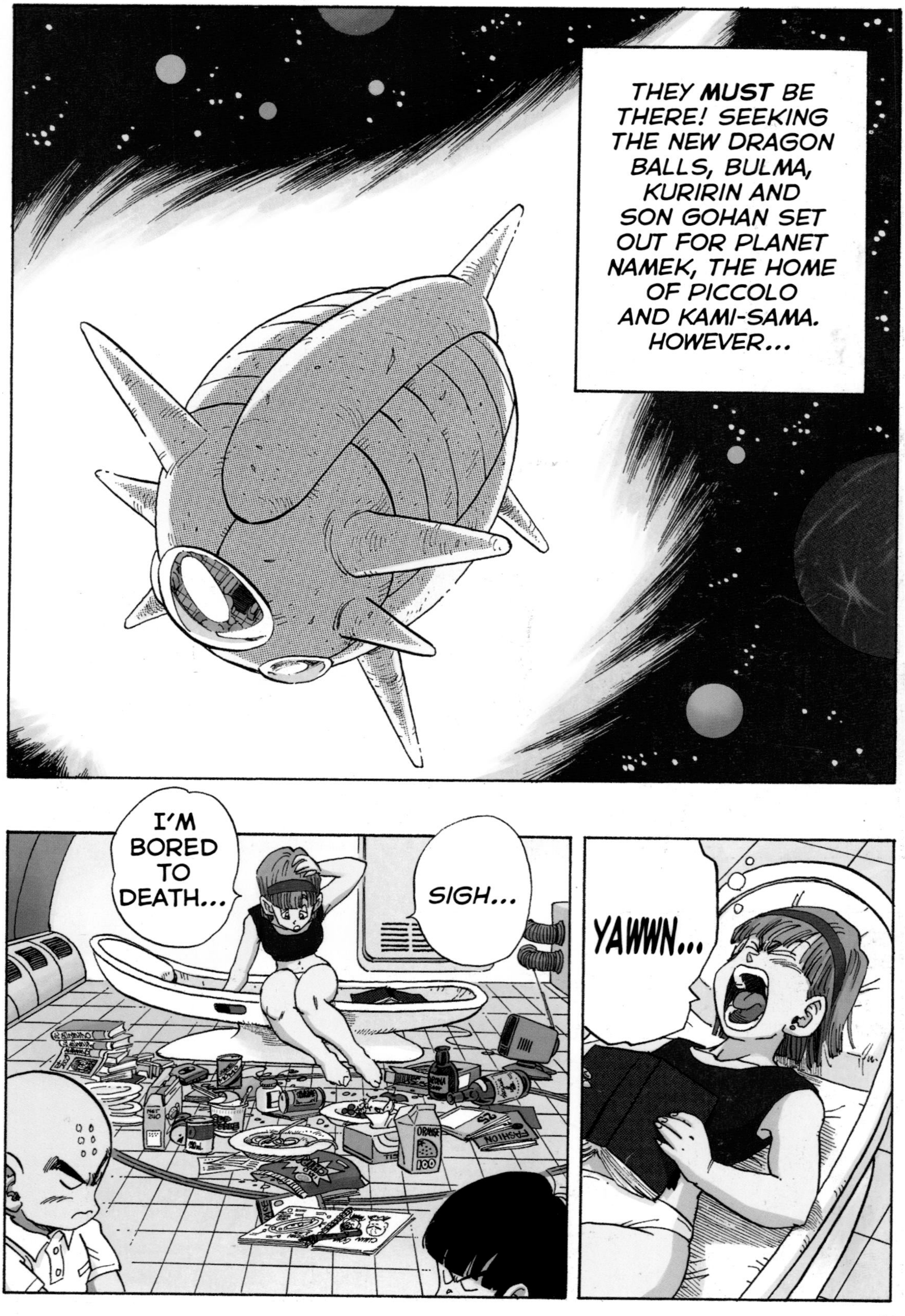
THEY **MUST** BE THERE! SEEKING THE NEW DRAGON BALLS, BULMA, KURIRIN AND SON GOHAN SET OUT FOR PLANET NAMEK, THE HOME OF PICCOLO AND KAMI-SAMA. HOWEVER...
YAWWN...
I'M BORED TO DEATH...
SIGH...

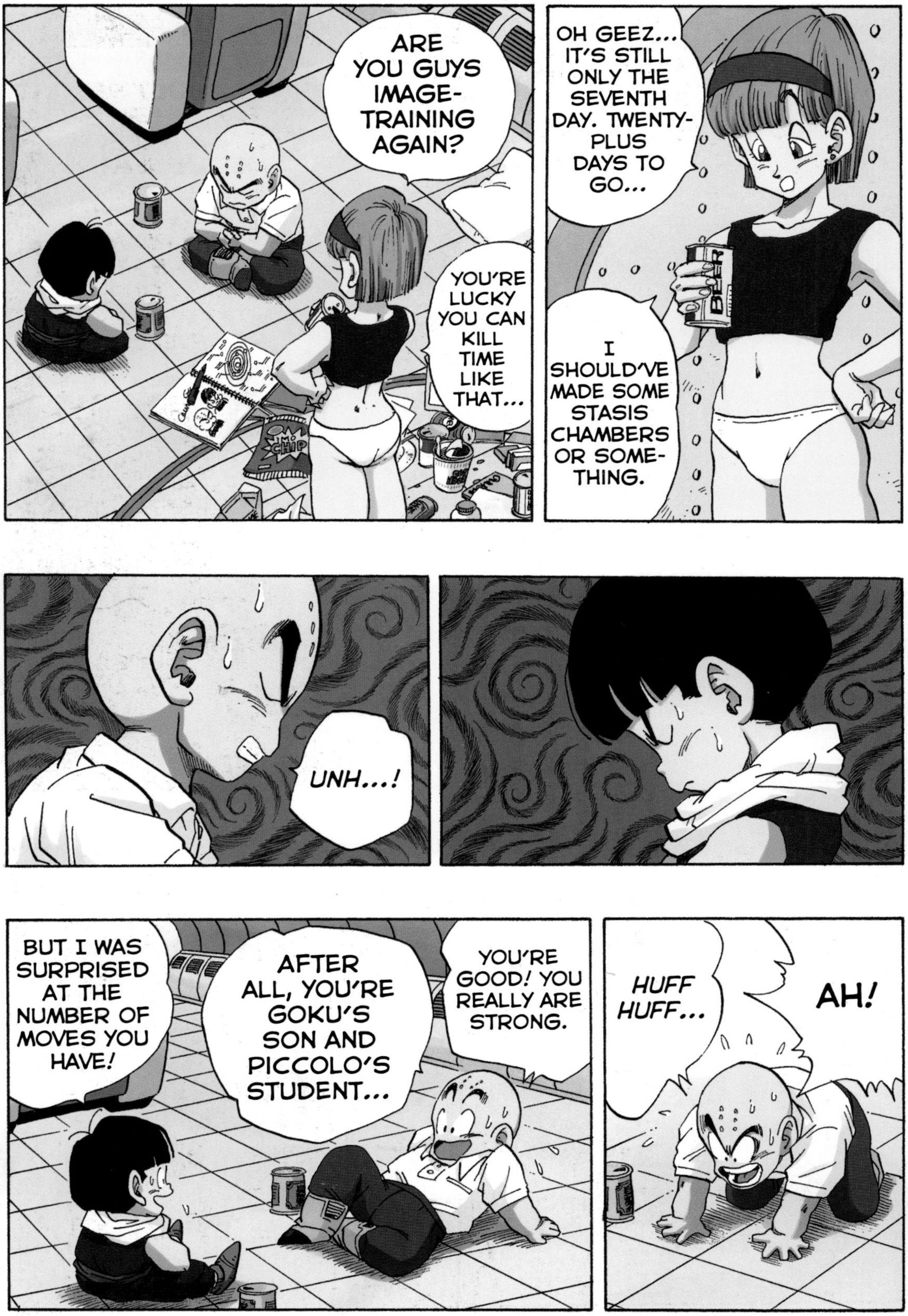
OH GEEZ... IT'S STILL ONLY THE SEVENTH DAY. TWENTY-PLUS DAYS TO GO...
I SHOULD'VE MADE SOME STASIS CHAMBERS OR SOME-THING.
ARE YOU GUYS IMAGE-TRAINING AGAIN?
YOU'RE LUCKY YOU CAN KILL TIME LIKE THAT...
UNH...!
AH!
HUFF HUFF...
YOU'RE GOOD! YOU REALLY ARE STRONG.
AFTER ALL, YOU'RE GOKU'S SON AND PICCOLO'S STUDENT...
BUT I WAS SURPRISED AT THE NUMBER OF MOVES YOU HAVE!

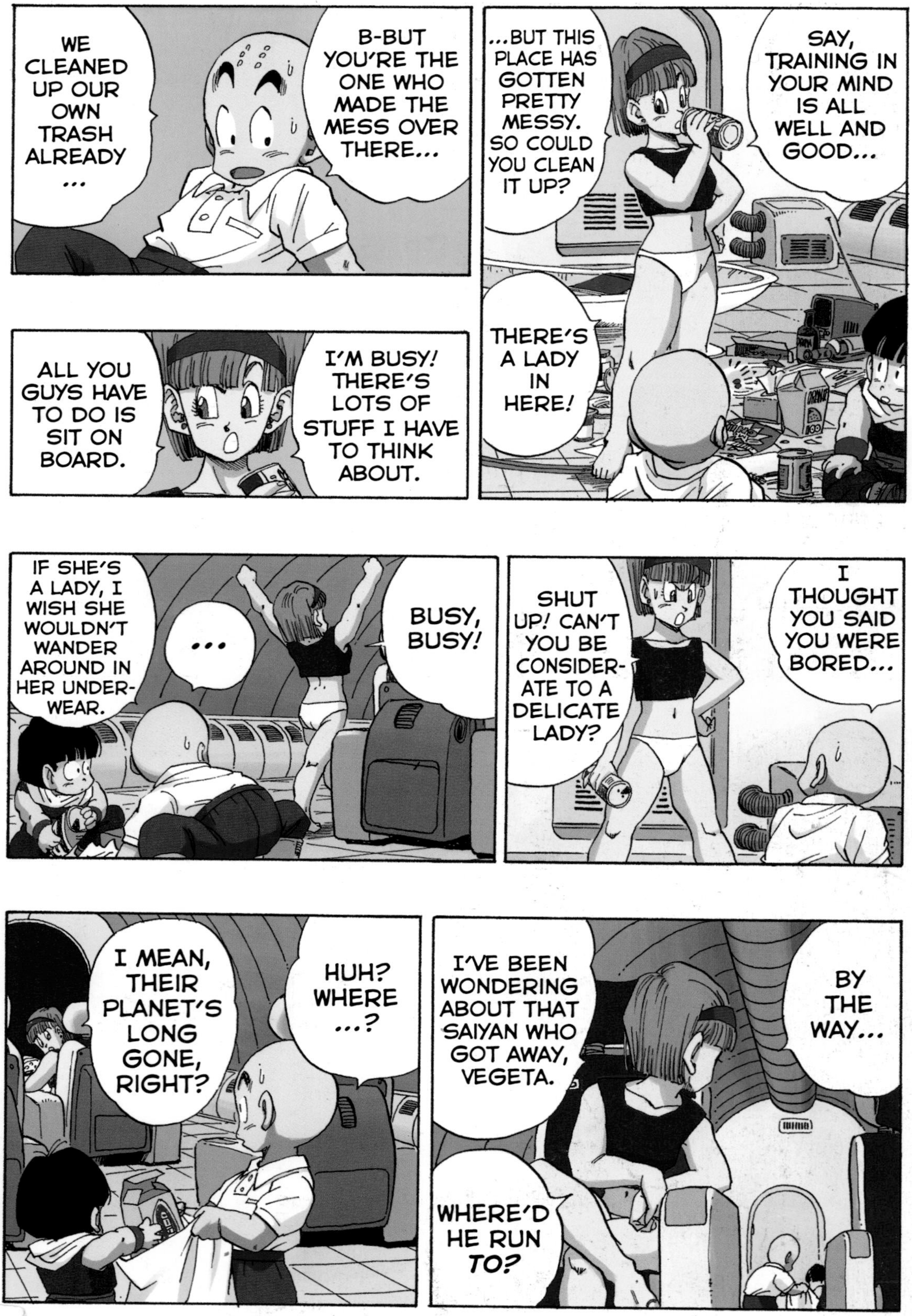
SAY, TRAINING IN YOUR MIND IS ALL WELL AND GOOD...
...BUT THIS PLACE HAS GOTTEN PRETTY MESSY. SO COULD YOU CLEAN IT UP?
THERE'S A LADY IN HERE!
B-BUT YOU'RE THE ONE WHO MADE THE MESS OVER THERE...
WE CLEANED UP OUR OWN TRASH ALREADY ...
I'M BUSY! THERE'S LOTS OF STUFF I HAVE TO THINK ABOUT.
ALL YOU GUYS HAVE TO DO IS SIT ON BOARD.
I THOUGHT YOU SAID YOU WERE BORED...
SHUT UP! CAN'T YOU BE CONSIDER-ATE TO A DELICATE LADY?
BUSY, BUSY!
...
IF SHE'S A LADY, I WISH SHE WOULDN'T WANDER AROUND IN HER UNDER-WEAR.
BY THE WAY...
I'VE BEEN WONDERING ABOUT THAT SAIYAN WHO GOT AWAY, VEGETA.
WHERE'D HE RUN *TO?*
HUH? WHERE ...?
I MEAN, THEIR PLANET'S LONG GONE, RIGHT?

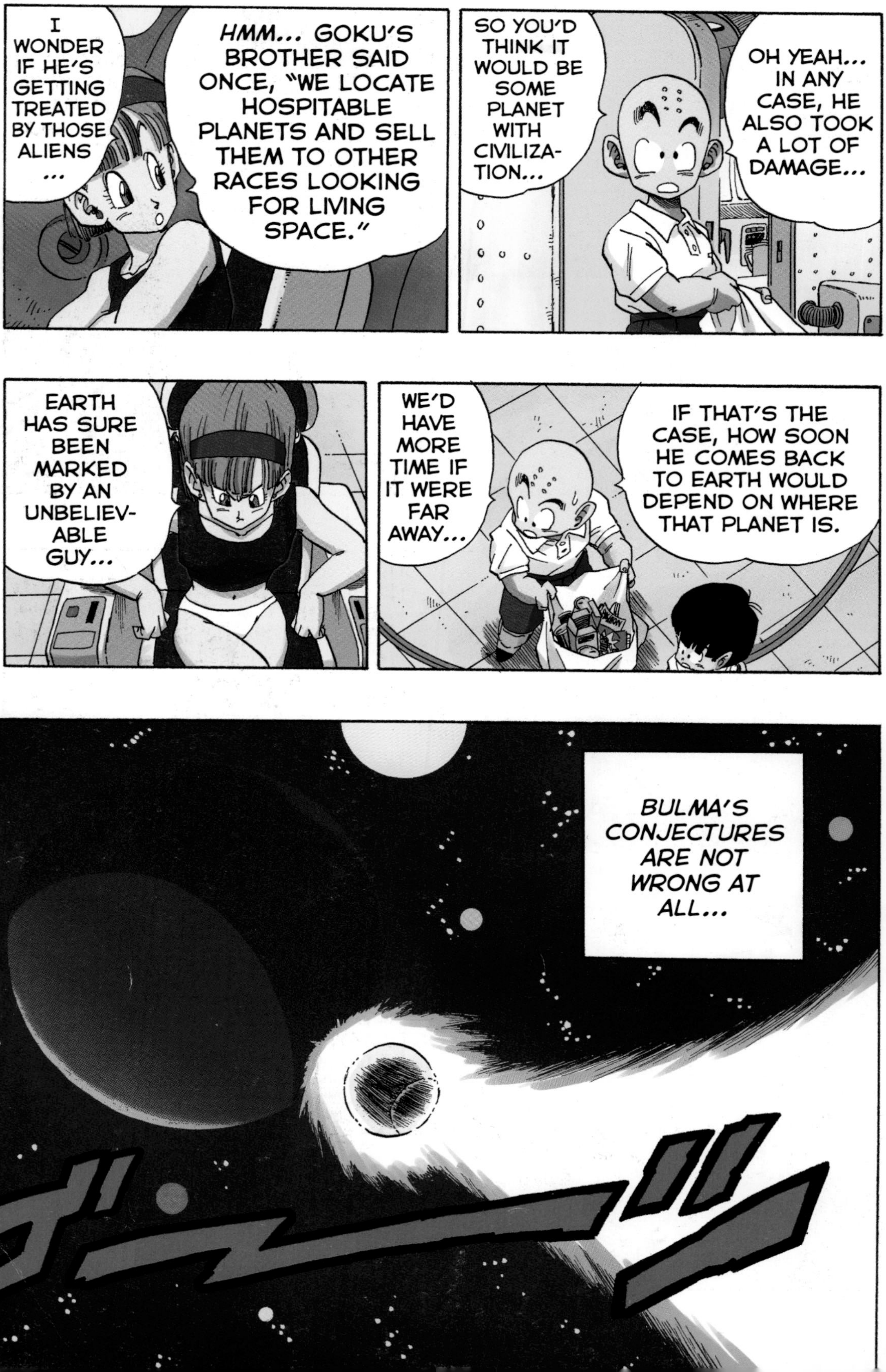
OH YEAH... IN ANY CASE, HE ALSO TOOK A LOT OF DAMAGE...
SO YOU'D THINK IT WOULD BE SOME PLANET WITH CIVILIZATION...
HMM... GOKU'S BROTHER SAID ONCE, "WE LOCATE HOSPITABLE PLANETS AND SELL THEM TO OTHER RACES LOOKING FOR LIVING SPACE."
I WONDER IF HE'S GETTING TREATED BY THOSE ALIENS...
IF THAT'S THE CASE, HOW SOON HE COMES BACK TO EARTH WOULD DEPEND ON WHERE THAT PLANET IS.
WE'D HAVE MORE TIME IF IT WERE FAR AWAY...
EARTH HAS SURE BEEN MARKED BY AN UNBELIEVABLE GUY...
BULMA'S CONJECTURES ARE NOT WRONG AT ALL...

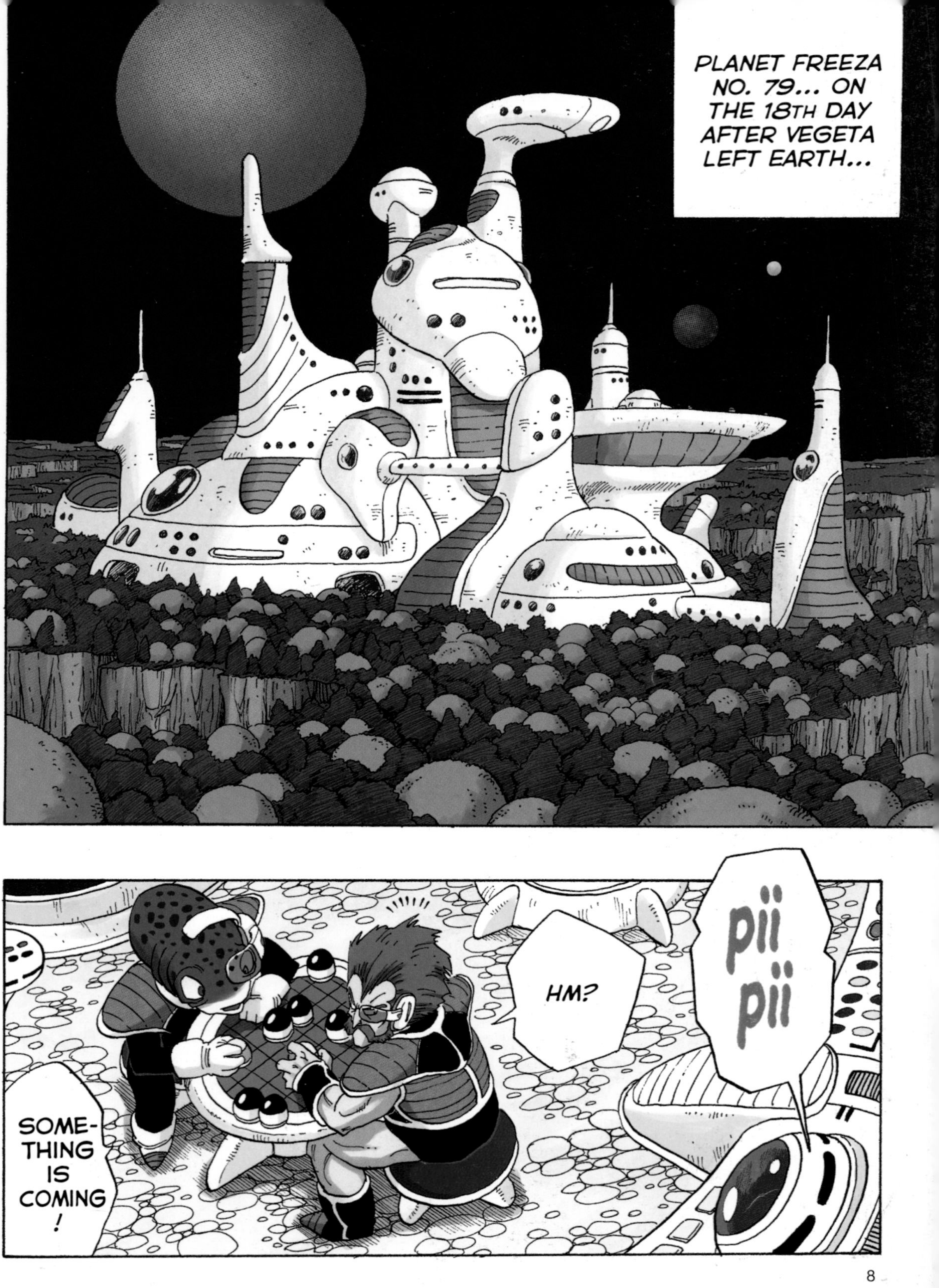
PLANET FREEZA NO. 79... ON THE 18TH DAY AFTER VEGETA LEFT EARTH...
pii pii
HM?
SOME-THING IS COMING!

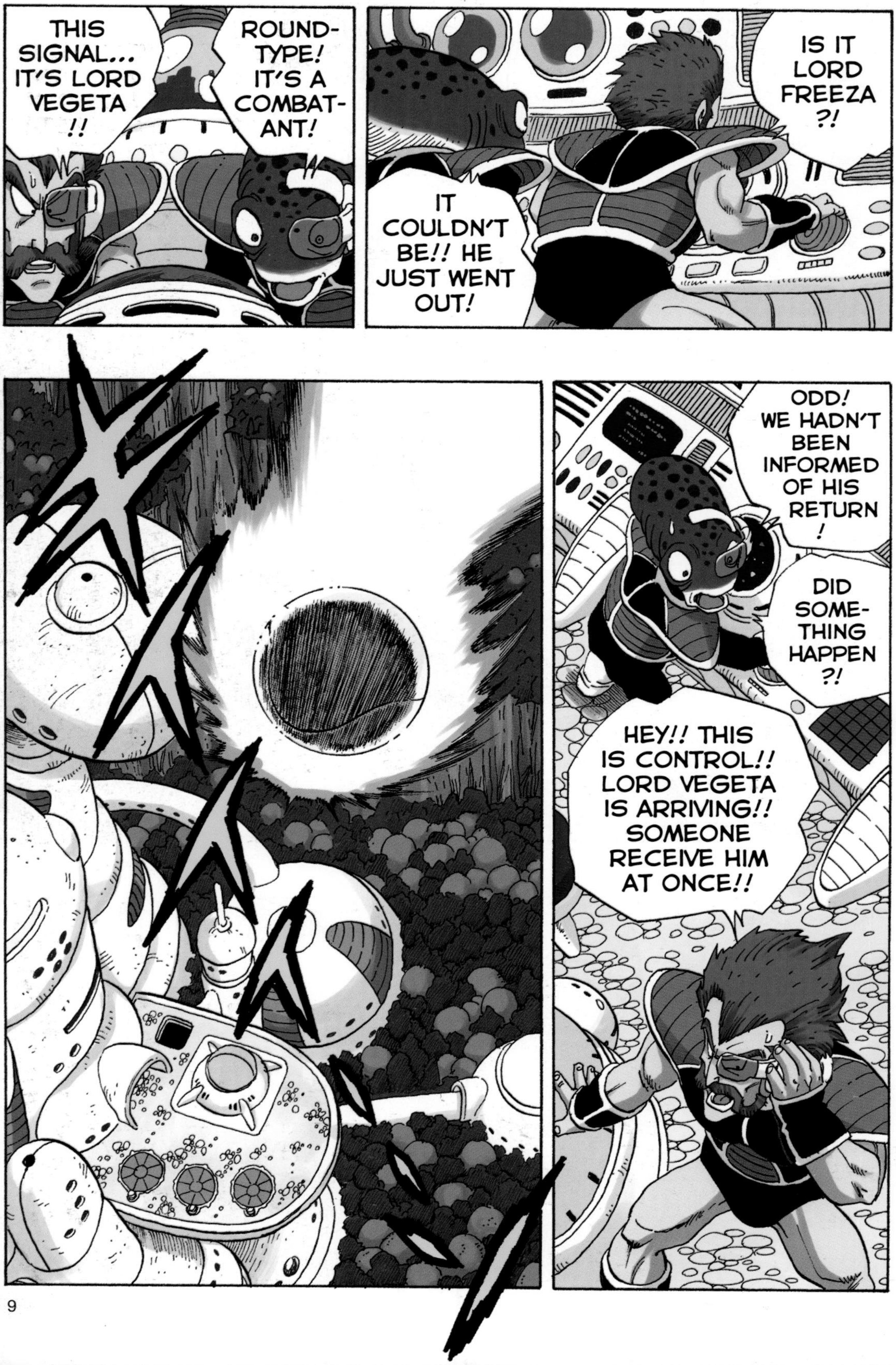
IS IT LORD FREEZA?!
IT COULDN'T BE!! HE JUST WENT OUT!
ROUND-TYPE! IT'S A COMBATANT!
THIS SIGNAL... IT'S LORD VEGETA!!
ODD! WE HADN'T BEEN INFORMED OF HIS RETURN!
DID SOMETHING HAPPEN?!
HEY!! THIS IS CONTROL!! LORD VEGETA IS ARRIVING!! SOMEONE RECEIVE HIM AT ONCE!!

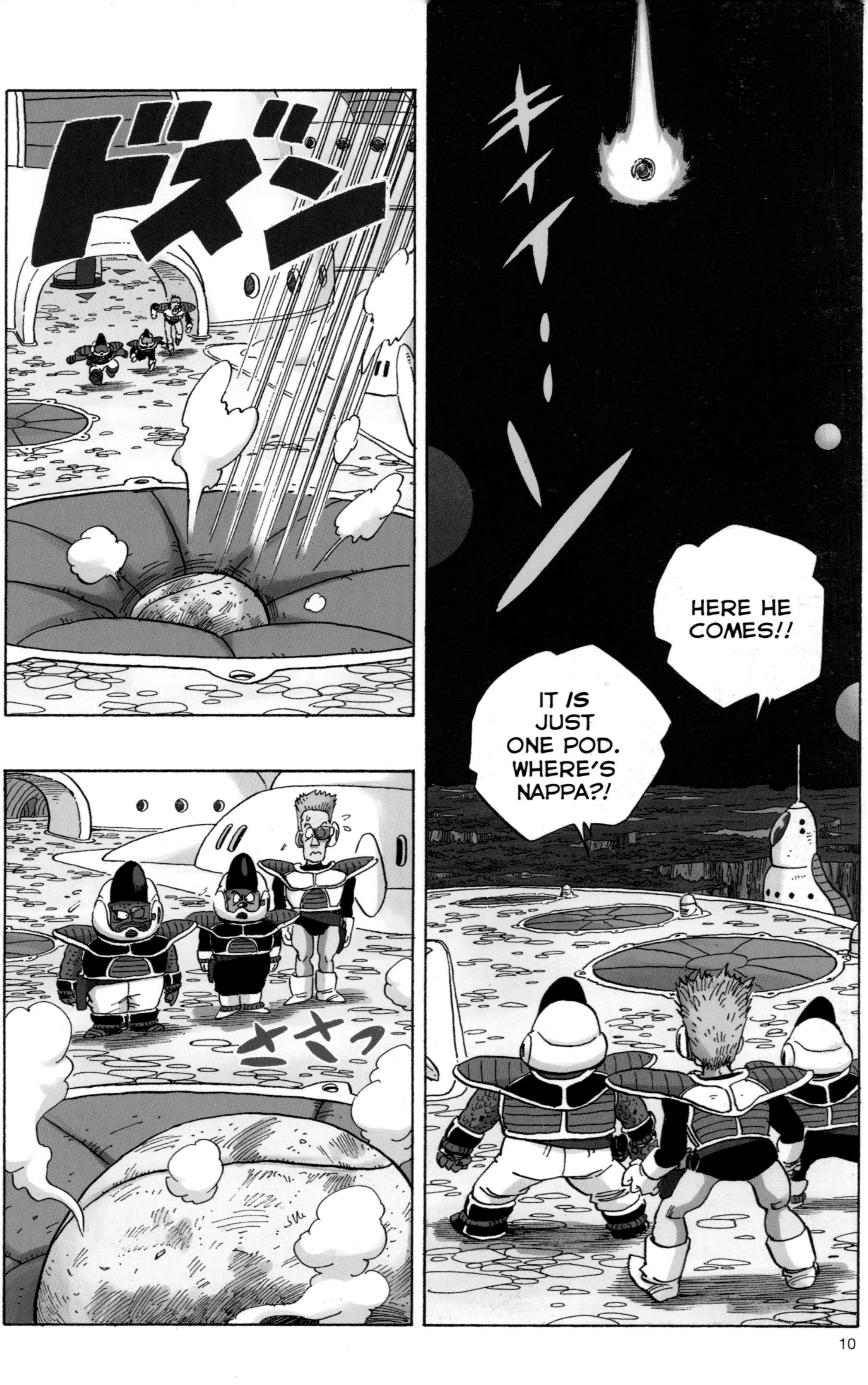
キイイ…ン
HERE HE COMES!!
IT *IS* JUST ONE POD. WHERE'S NAPPA?!
ドズン
ささっ

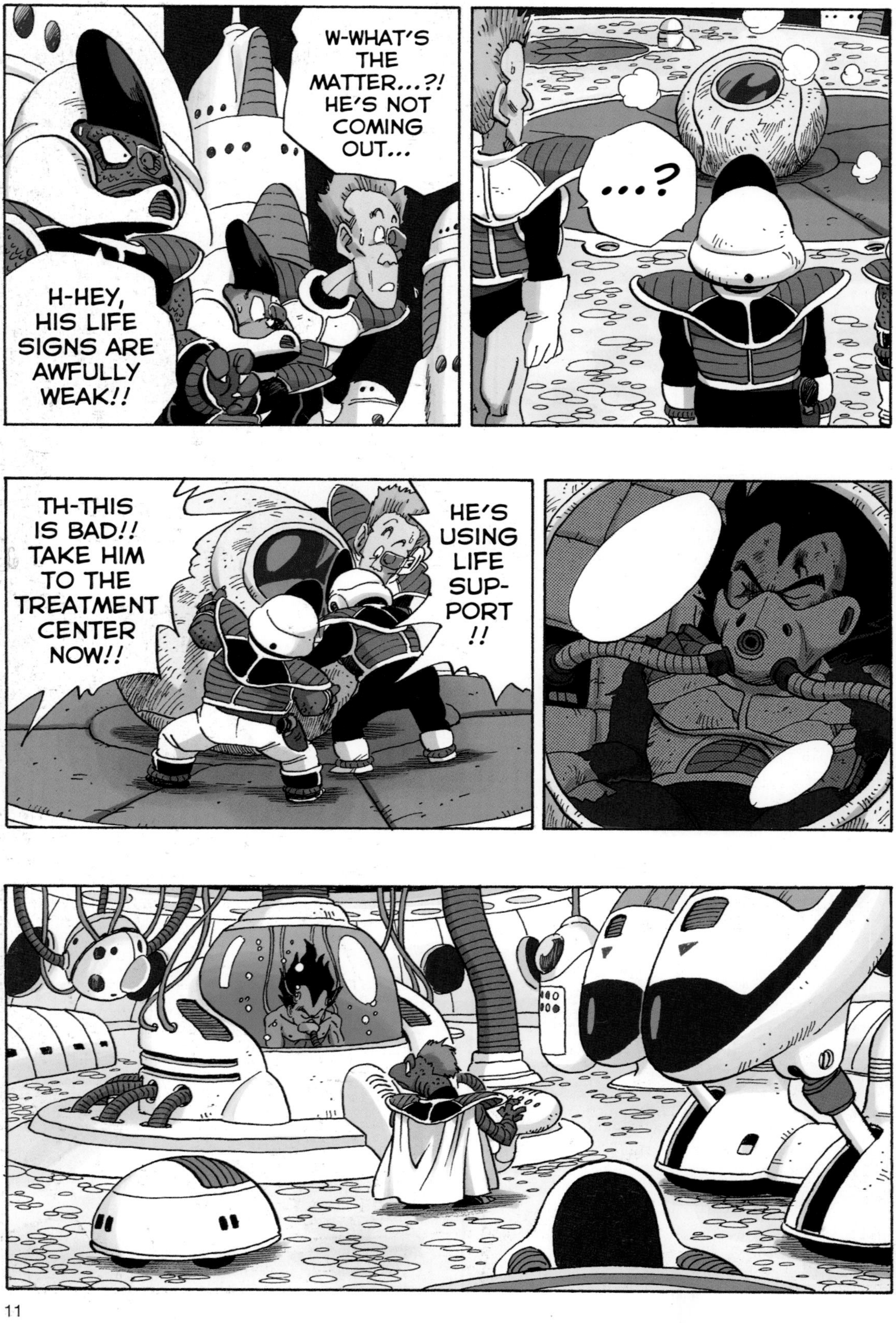
...?
W-WHAT'S THE MATTER...?! HE'S NOT COMING OUT...
H-HEY, HIS LIFE SIGNS ARE AWFULLY WEAK!!
HE'S USING LIFE SUP-PORT!!
TH-THIS IS BAD!! TAKE HIM TO THE TREATMENT CENTER NOW!!

SHHK

GLUG GLUG

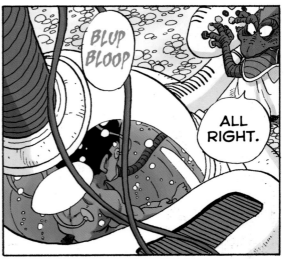

BLUP BLOOP

ALL RIGHT.

YOU'RE HEALED. YOU MAY OPEN YOUR EYES NOW.

UNFORTU-NATELY, YOUR TAIL COULD NOT BE REGENER-ATED...

NO MATTER, IT'LL GROW BACK AGAIN.

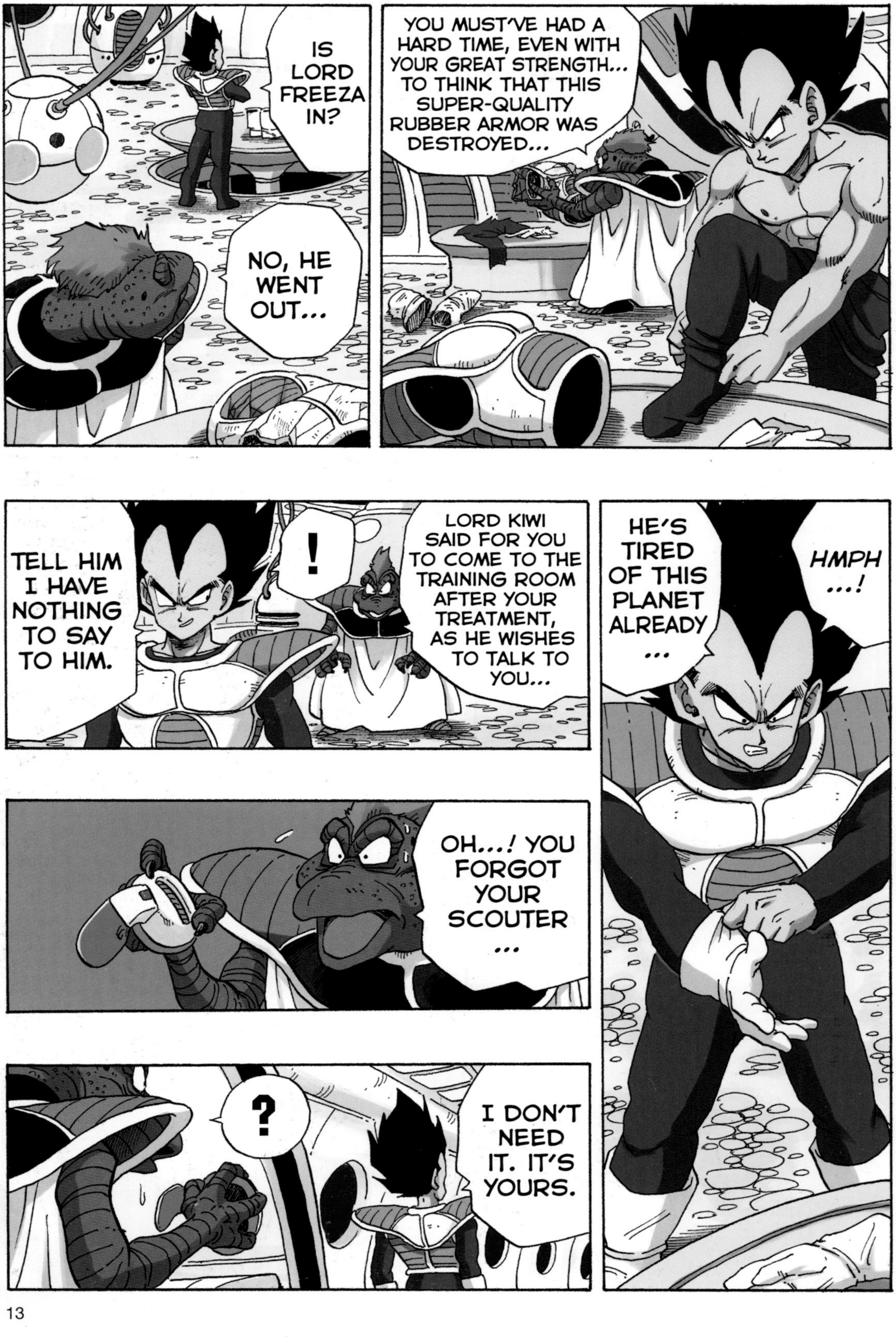
YOU MUST'VE HAD A HARD TIME, EVEN WITH YOUR GREAT STRENGTH... TO THINK THAT THIS SUPER-QUALITY RUBBER ARMOR WAS DESTROYED...
IS LORD FREEZA IN?
NO, HE WENT OUT...
HMPH ...!
HE'S TIRED OF THIS PLANET ALREADY ...
LORD KIWI SAID FOR YOU TO COME TO THE TRAINING ROOM AFTER YOUR TREATMENT, AS HE WISHES TO TALK TO YOU...
!
TELL HIM I HAVE NOTHING TO SAY TO HIM.
OH...! YOU FORGOT YOUR SCOUTER ...
I DON'T NEED IT. IT'S YOURS.
?

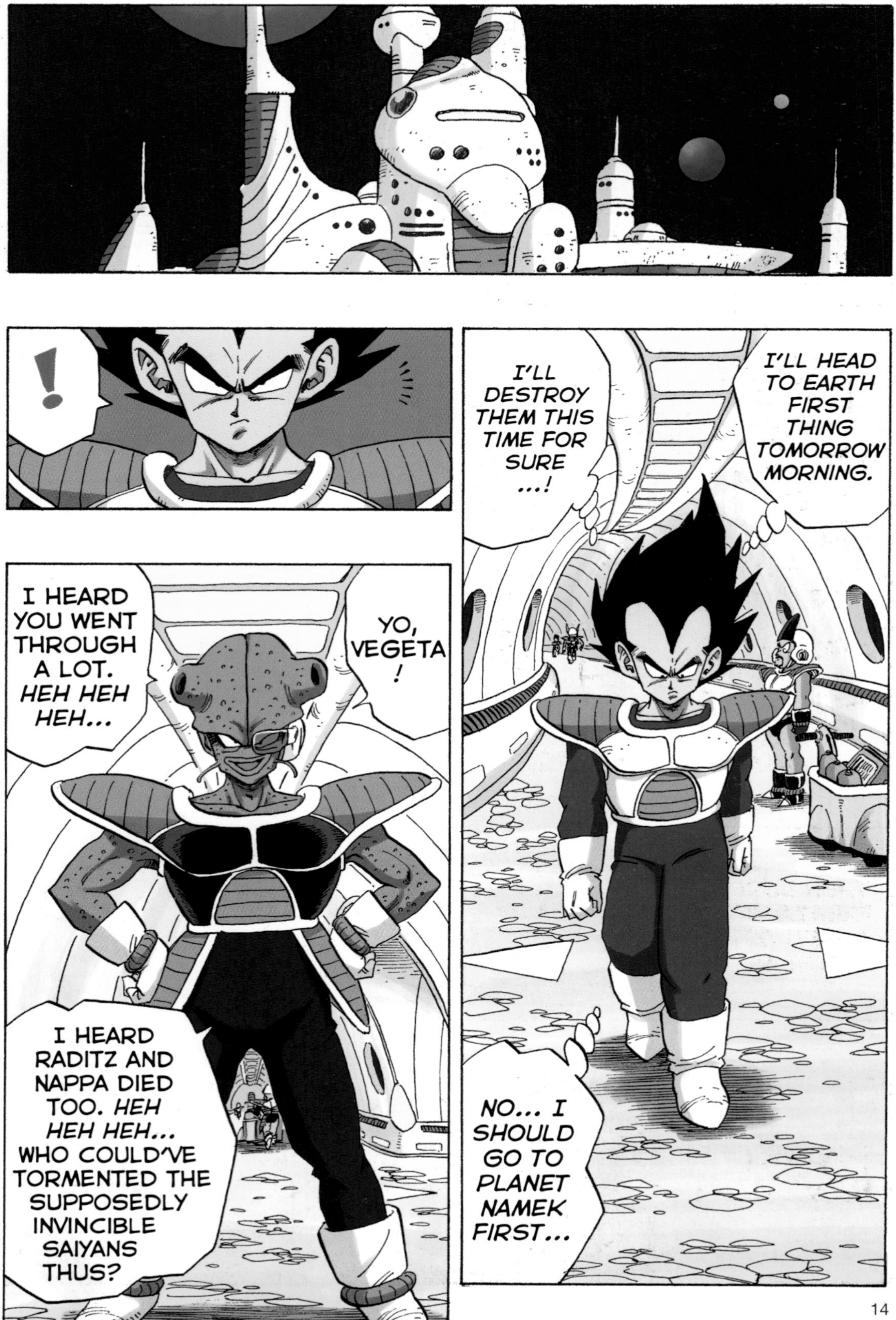
I'LL HEAD TO EARTH FIRST THING TOMORROW MORNING.
I'LL DESTROY THEM THIS TIME FOR SURE ...!
NO... I SHOULD GO TO PLANET NAMEK FIRST...
!
YO, VEGETA!
I HEARD YOU WENT THROUGH A LOT. HEH HEH HEH...
I HEARD RADITZ AND NAPPA DIED TOO. HEH HEH HEH... WHO COULD'VE TORMENTED THE SUPPOSEDLY INVINCIBLE SAIYANS THUS?

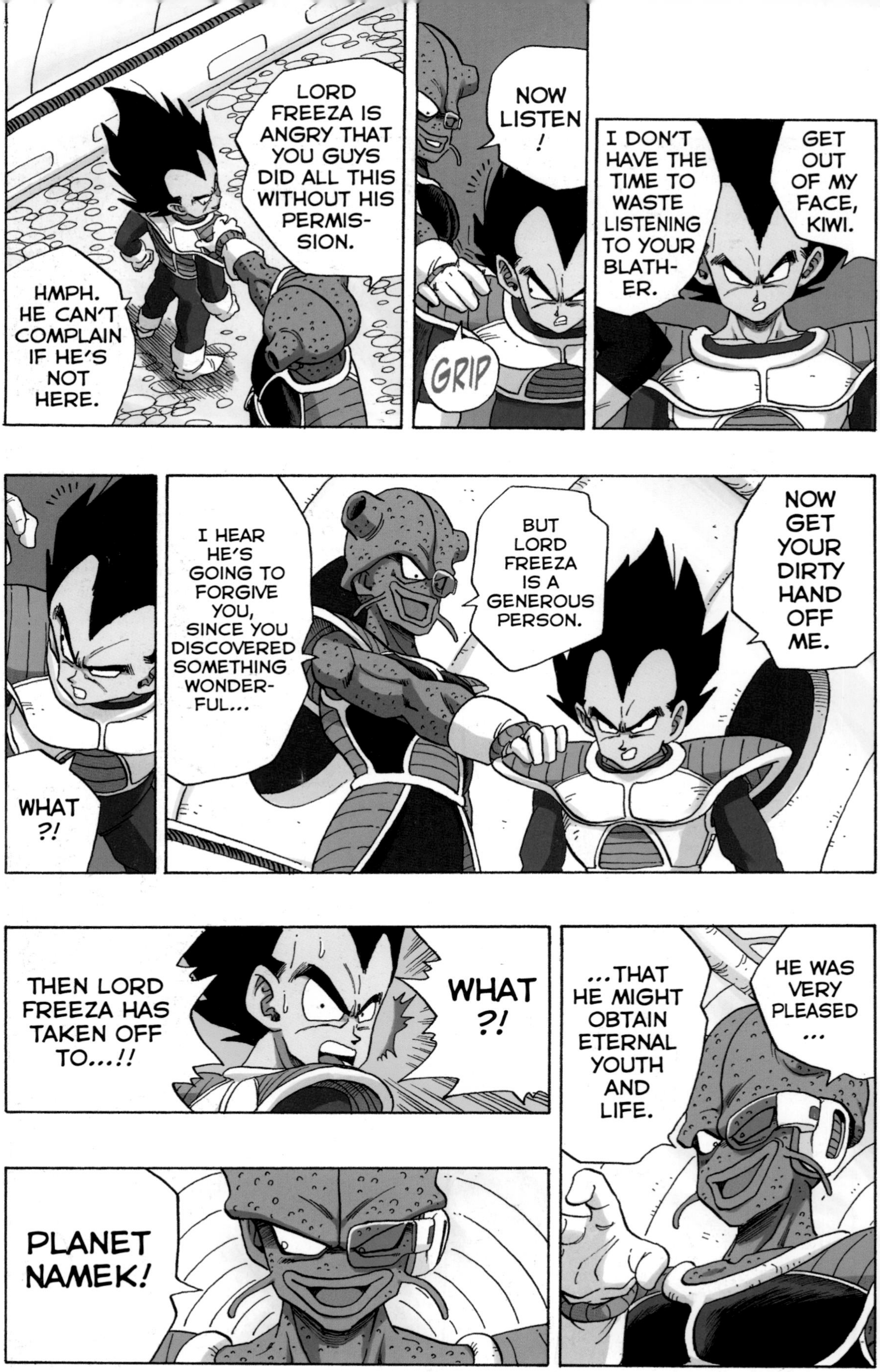
GET OUT OF MY FACE, KIWI.
I DON'T HAVE THE TIME TO WASTE LISTENING TO YOUR BLATHER.
NOW LISTEN!
GRIP
LORD FREEZA IS ANGRY THAT YOU GUYS DID ALL THIS WITHOUT HIS PERMISSION.
HMPH. HE CAN'T COMPLAIN IF HE'S NOT HERE.
NOW GET YOUR DIRTY HAND OFF ME.
BUT LORD FREEZA IS A GENEROUS PERSON.
I HEAR HE'S GOING TO FORGIVE YOU, SINCE YOU DISCOVERED SOMETHING WONDERFUL...
WHAT?!
HE WAS VERY PLEASED...
...THAT HE MIGHT OBTAIN ETERNAL YOUTH AND LIFE.
WHAT?!
THEN LORD FREEZA HAS TAKEN OFF TO...!!
PLANET NAMEK!

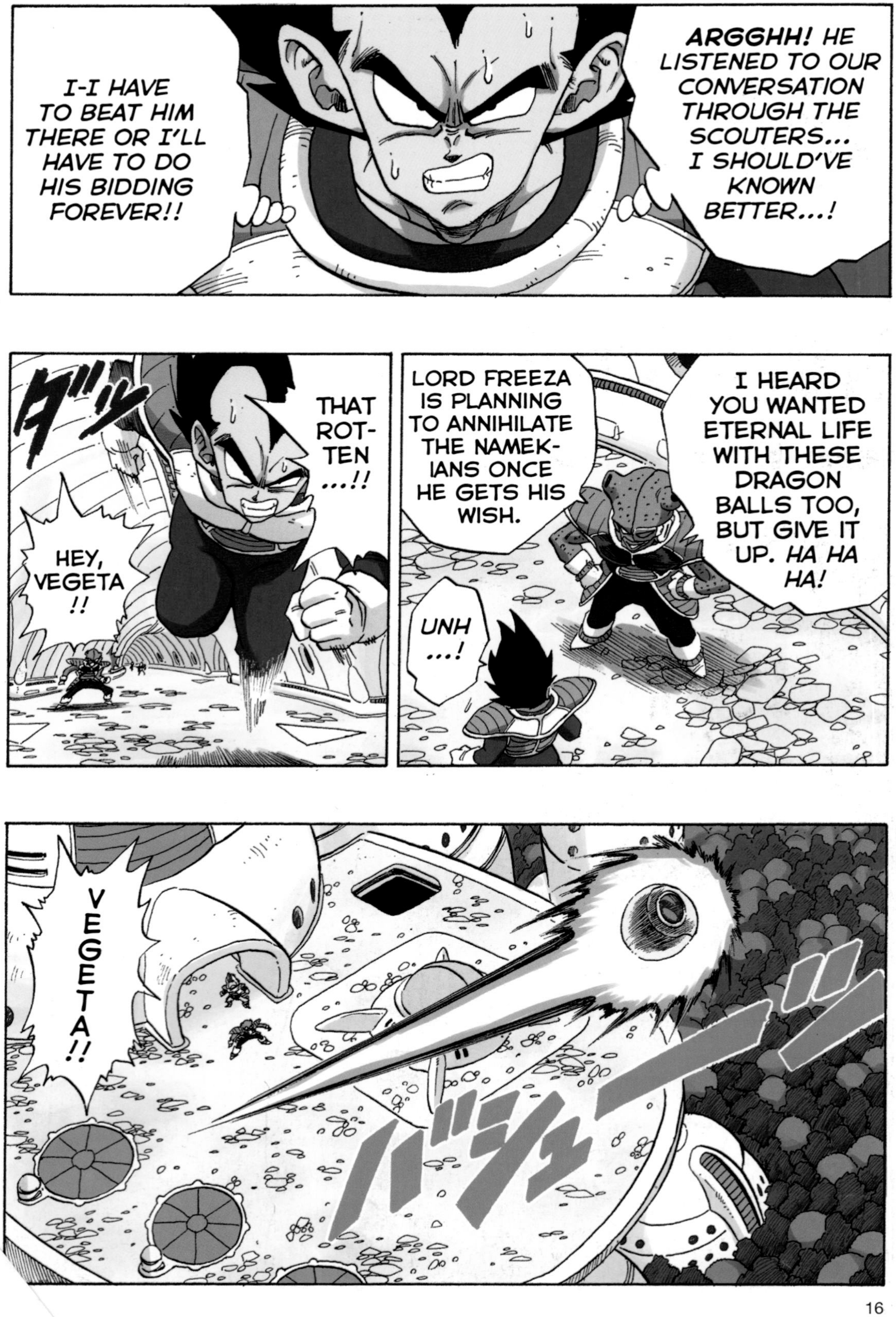
ARGGHH! HE LISTENED TO OUR CONVERSATION THROUGH THE SCOUTERS... I SHOULD'VE KNOWN BETTER...!
I-I HAVE TO BEAT HIM THERE OR I'LL HAVE TO DO HIS BIDDING FOREVER!!
I HEARD YOU WANTED ETERNAL LIFE WITH THESE DRAGON BALLS TOO, BUT GIVE IT UP. HA HA HA!
LORD FREEZA IS PLANNING TO ANNIHILATE THE NAMEK-IANS ONCE HE GETS HIS WISH.
UNH...!
ダッ
THAT ROT-TEN...!!
HEY, VEGETA!!
VEGETA!!
バシューッ

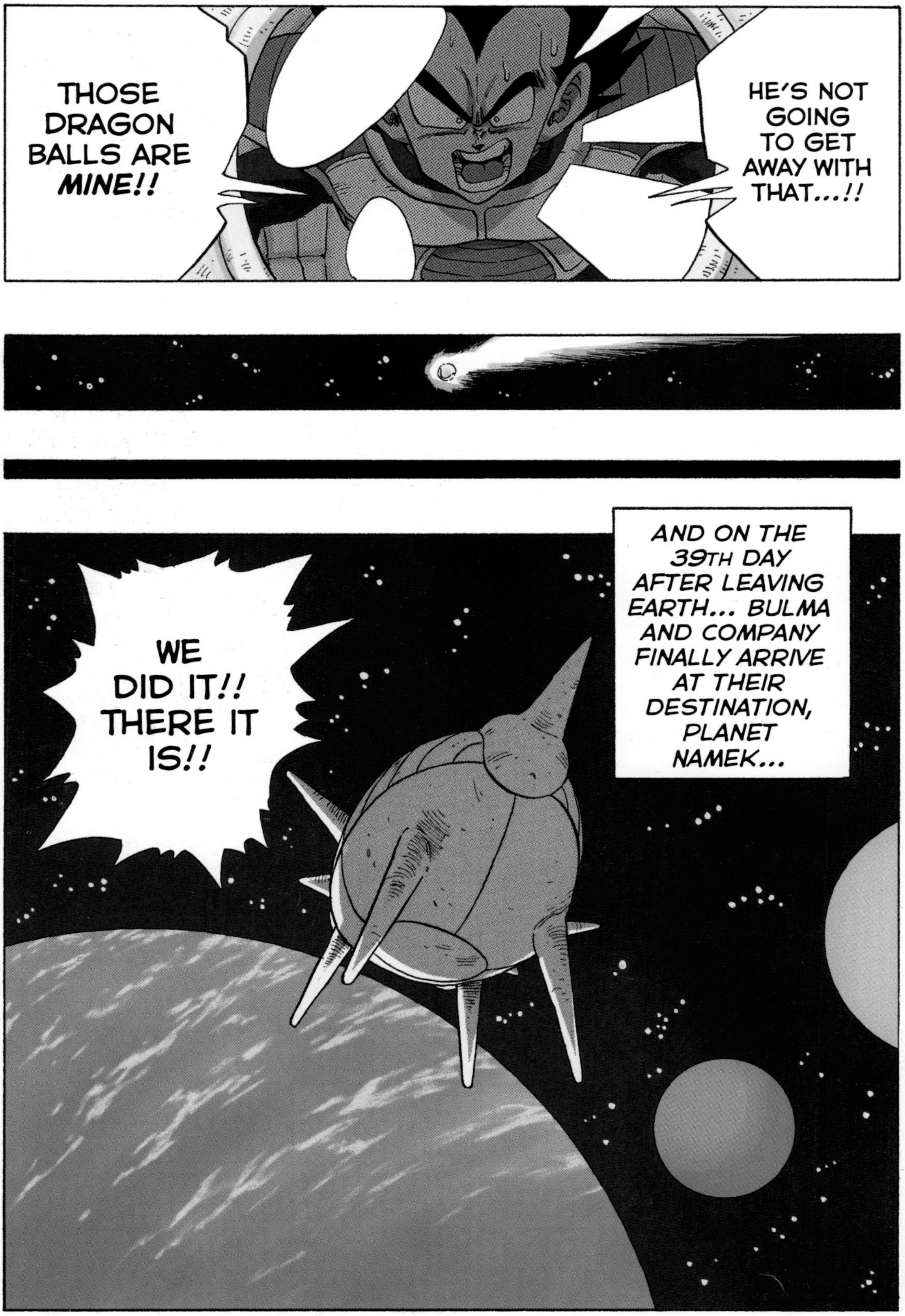
HE'S NOT GOING TO GET AWAY WITH THAT...!!
THOSE DRAGON BALLS ARE MINE!!
AND ON THE 39TH DAY AFTER LEAVING EARTH... BULMA AND COMPANY FINALLY ARRIVE AT THEIR DESTINATION, PLANET NAMEK...
WE DID IT!! THERE IT IS!!

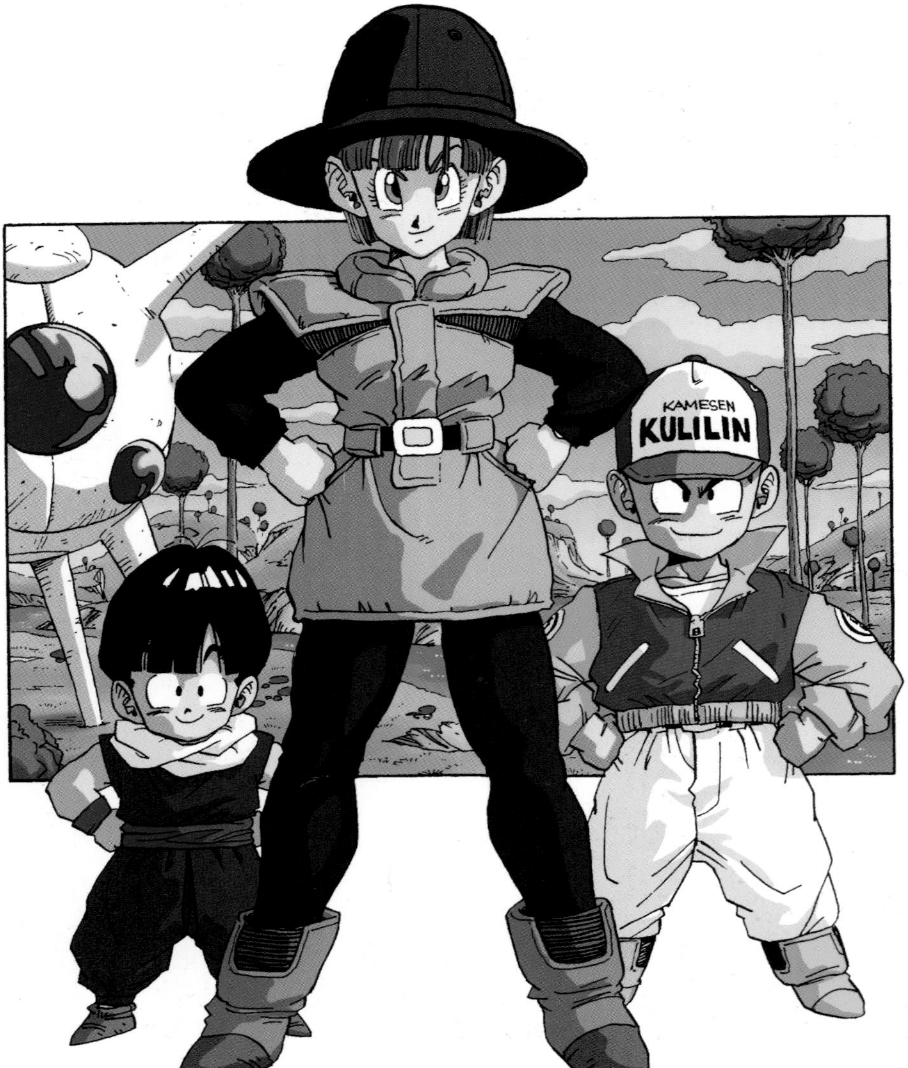

DRAGON BALL FULL COLOR FREEZA ARC

Chapter 2 • Planet Namek, Cold and Dark

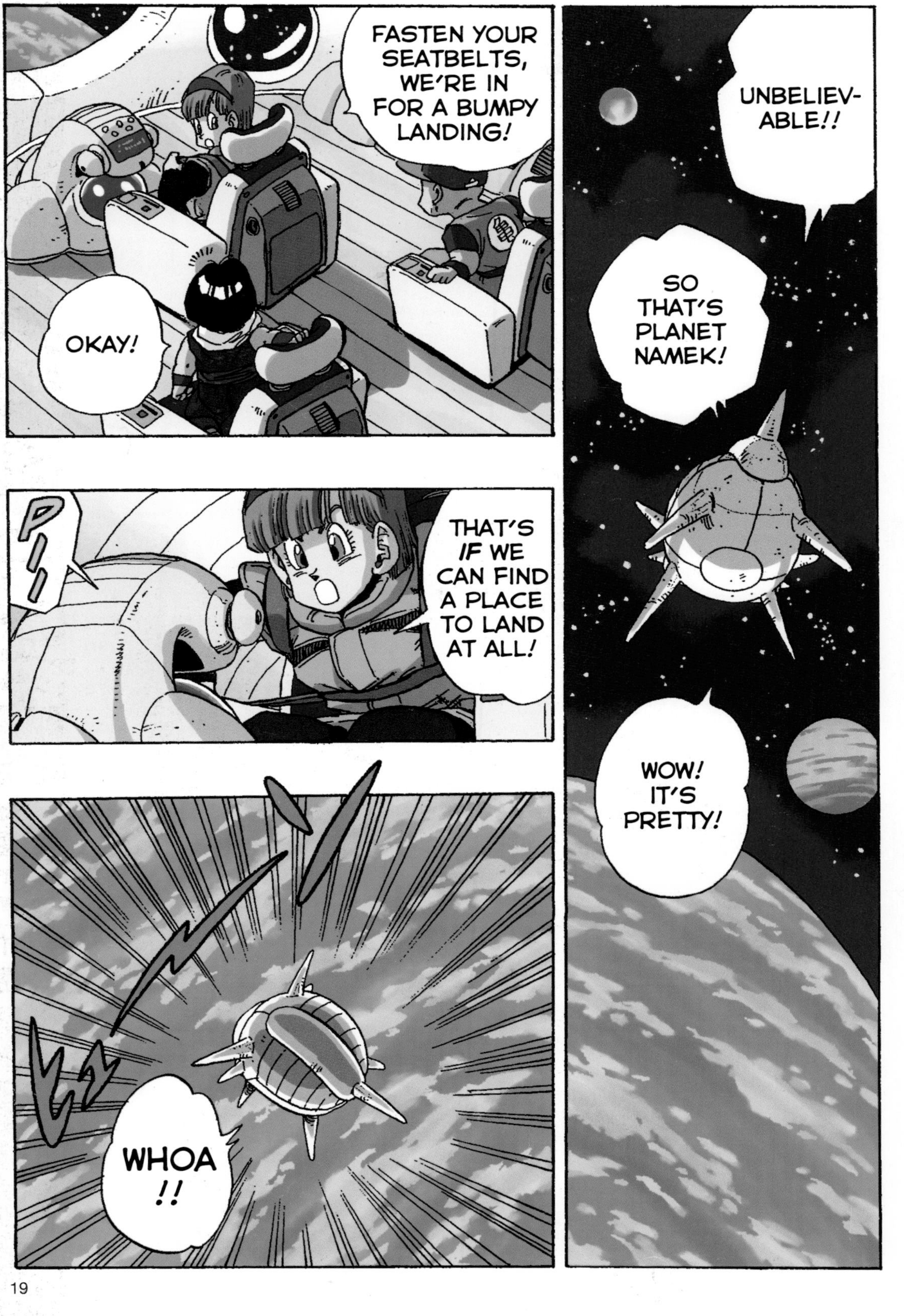
UNBELIEVABLE!!
SO THAT'S PLANET NAMEK!
WOW! IT'S PRETTY!
FASTEN YOUR SEATBELTS, WE'RE IN FOR A BUMPY LANDING!
OKAY!
THAT'S IF WE CAN FIND A PLACE TO LAND AT ALL!
PII
WHOA!!

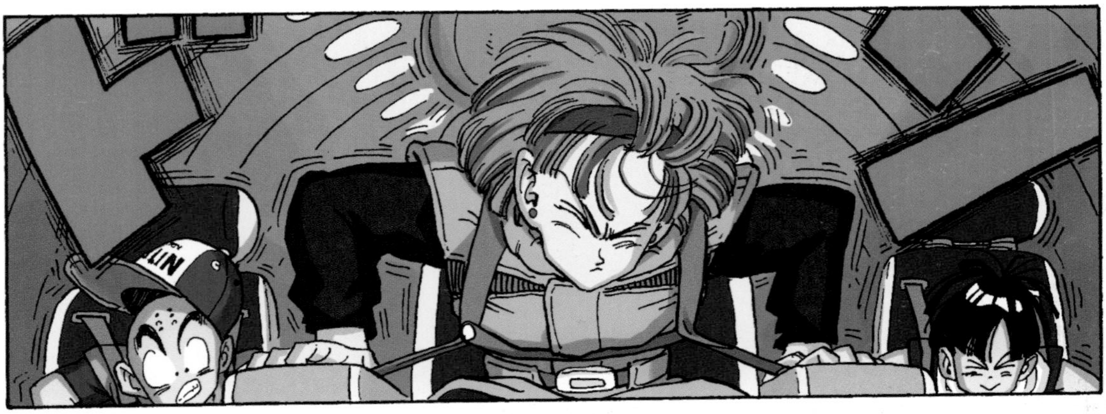

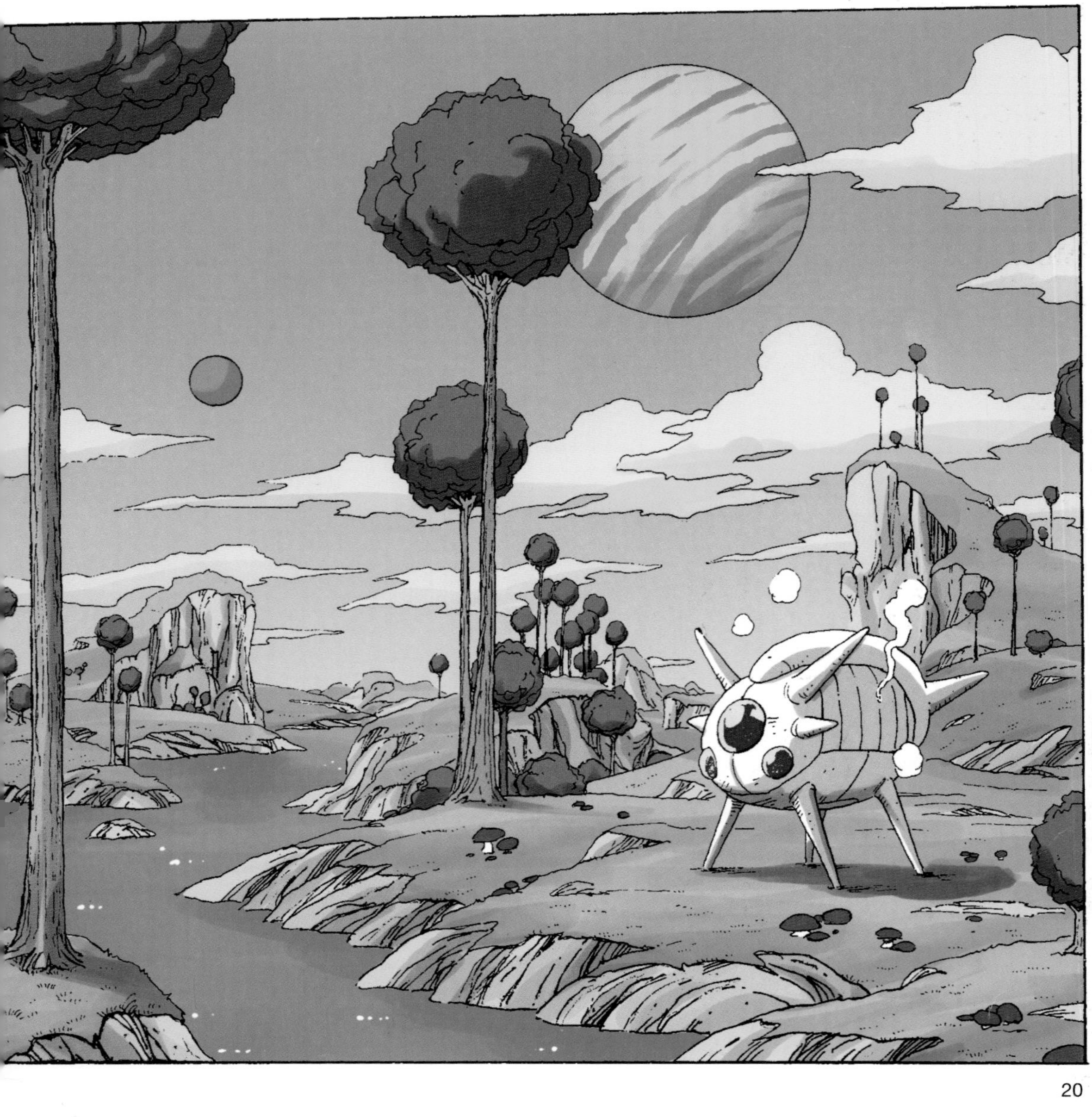

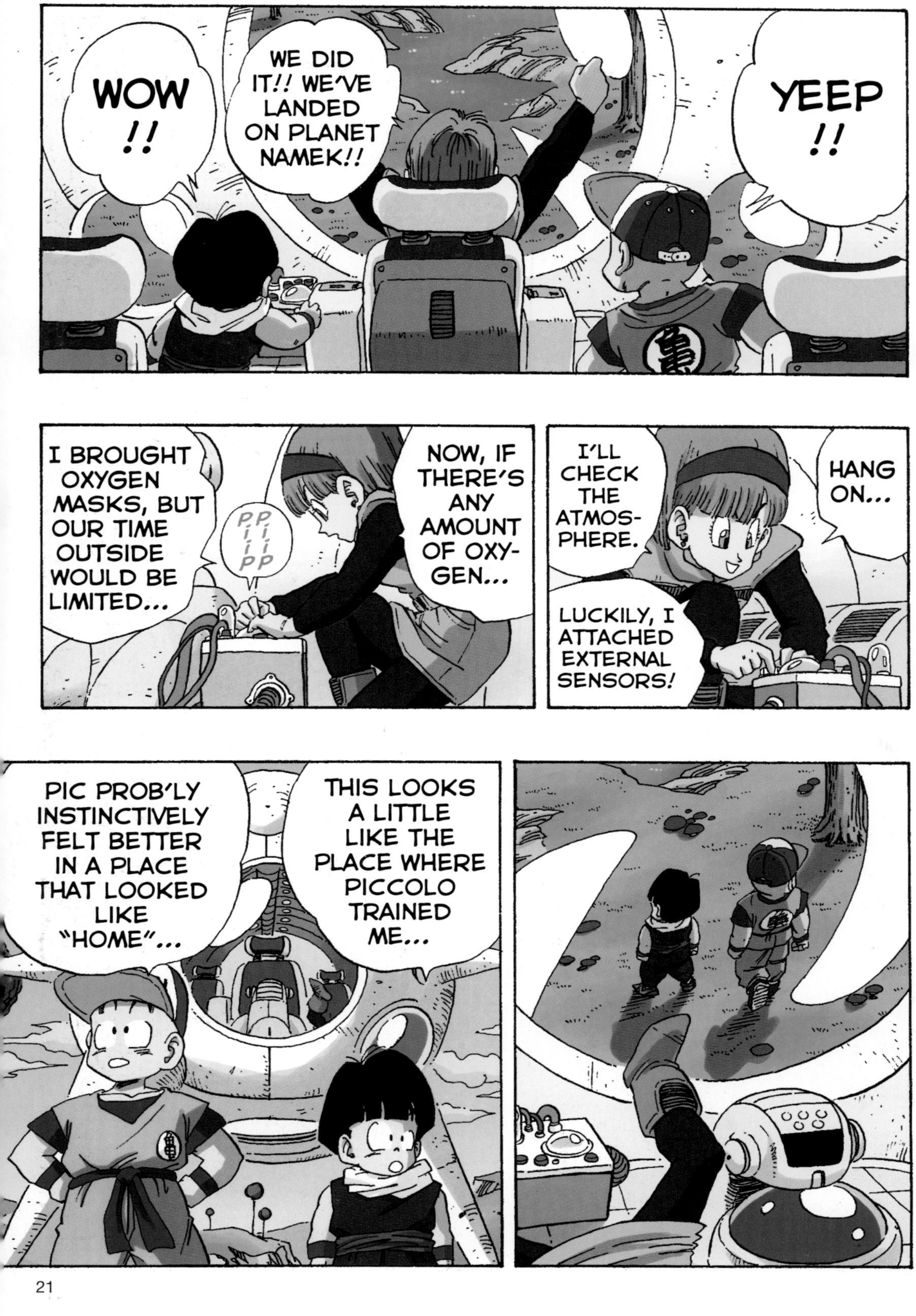
YEEP!!
WE DID IT!! WE'VE LANDED ON PLANET NAMEK!!
WOW!!
HANG ON...
I'LL CHECK THE ATMOS-PHERE.
LUCKILY, I ATTACHED EXTERNAL SENSORS!
NOW, IF THERE'S ANY AMOUNT OF OXY-GEN...
PIPIPIPIPIP
I BROUGHT OXYGEN MASKS, BUT OUR TIME OUTSIDE WOULD BE LIMITED...
THIS LOOKS A LITTLE LIKE THE PLACE WHERE PICCOLO TRAINED ME...
PIC PROB'LY INSTINCTIVELY FELT BETTER IN A PLACE THAT LOOKED LIKE "HOME"...

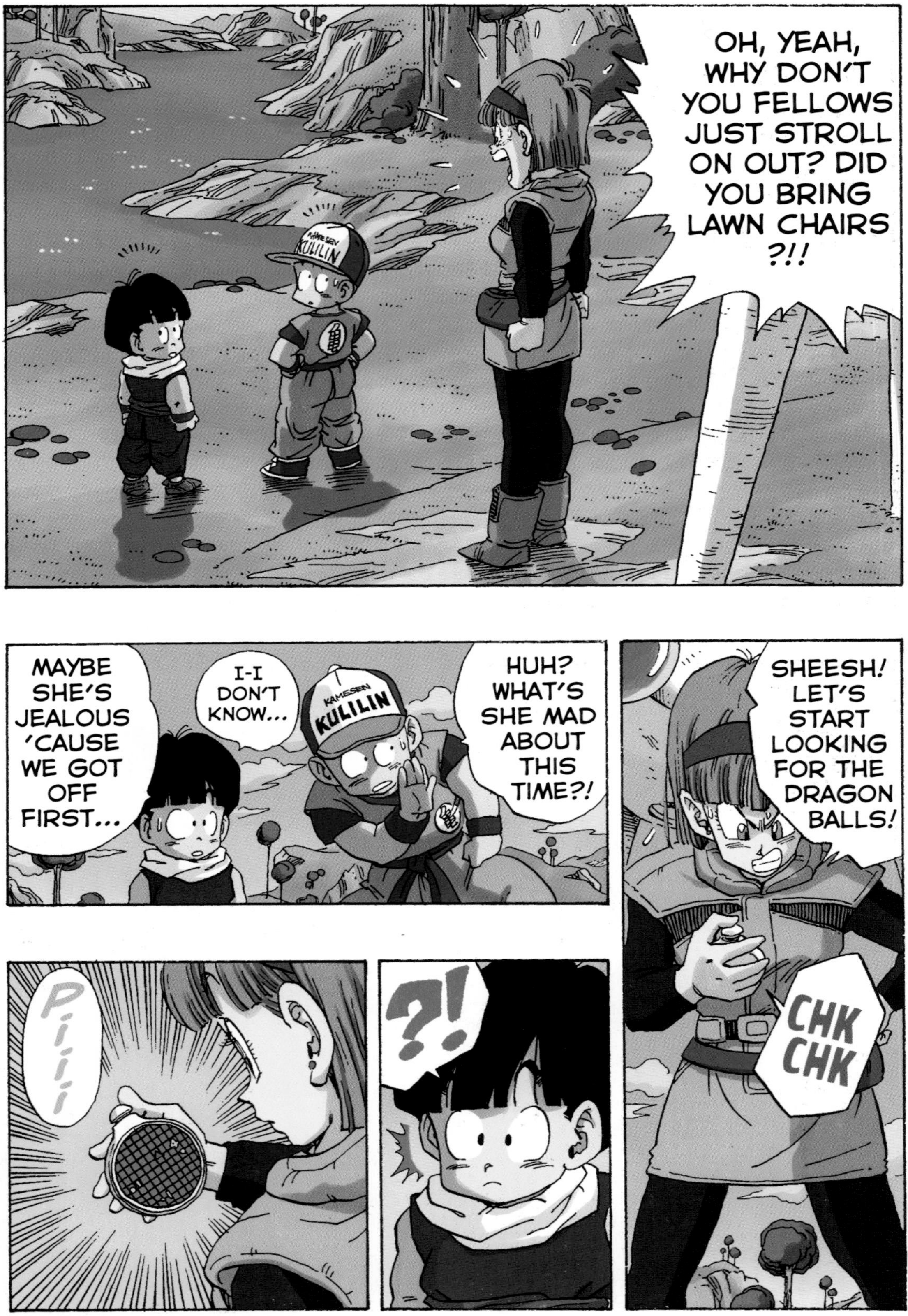
OH, YEAH, WHY DON'T YOU FELLOWS JUST STROLL ON OUT? DID YOU BRING LAWN CHAIRS ?!!
KAMESEN KULILIN
SHEESH! LET'S START LOOKING FOR THE DRAGON BALLS!
CHK CHK
HUH? WHAT'S SHE MAD ABOUT THIS TIME?!
I-I DON'T KNOW...
MAYBE SHE'S JEALOUS 'CAUSE WE GOT OFF FIRST...
KAMESEN KULILIN
?!
Piiii

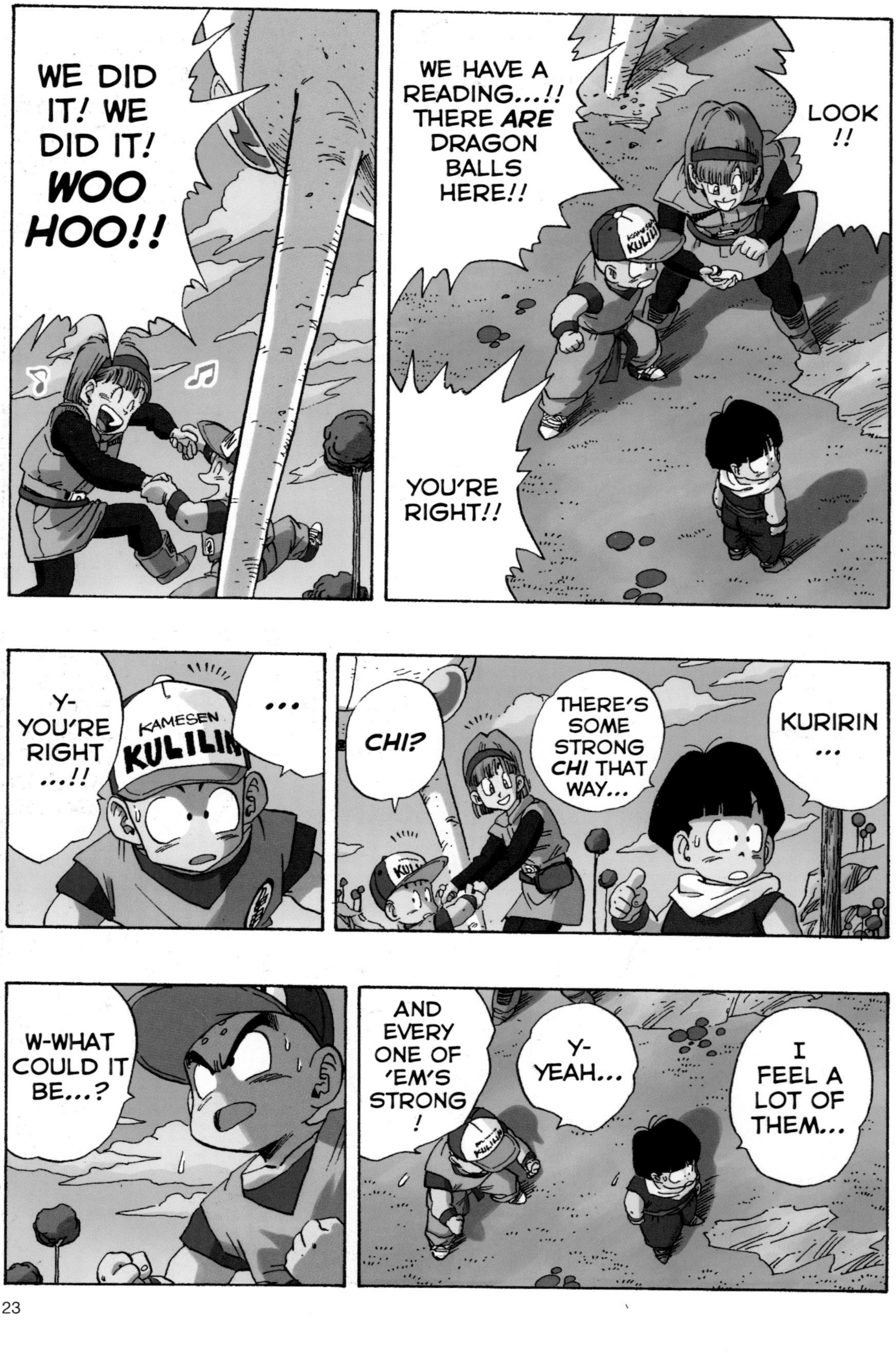
LOOK!!
WE HAVE A READING...!! THERE *ARE* DRAGON BALLS HERE!!
YOU'RE RIGHT!!
WE DID IT! WE DID IT! ***WOO HOO!!***
KURIRIN...
THERE'S SOME STRONG *CHI* THAT WAY...
CHI?
...
Y- YOU'RE RIGHT...!!
KAMESEN KULILIN
I FEEL A LOT OF THEM...
Y- YEAH...
AND EVERY ONE OF 'EM'S STRONG!
W-WHAT COULD IT BE...?

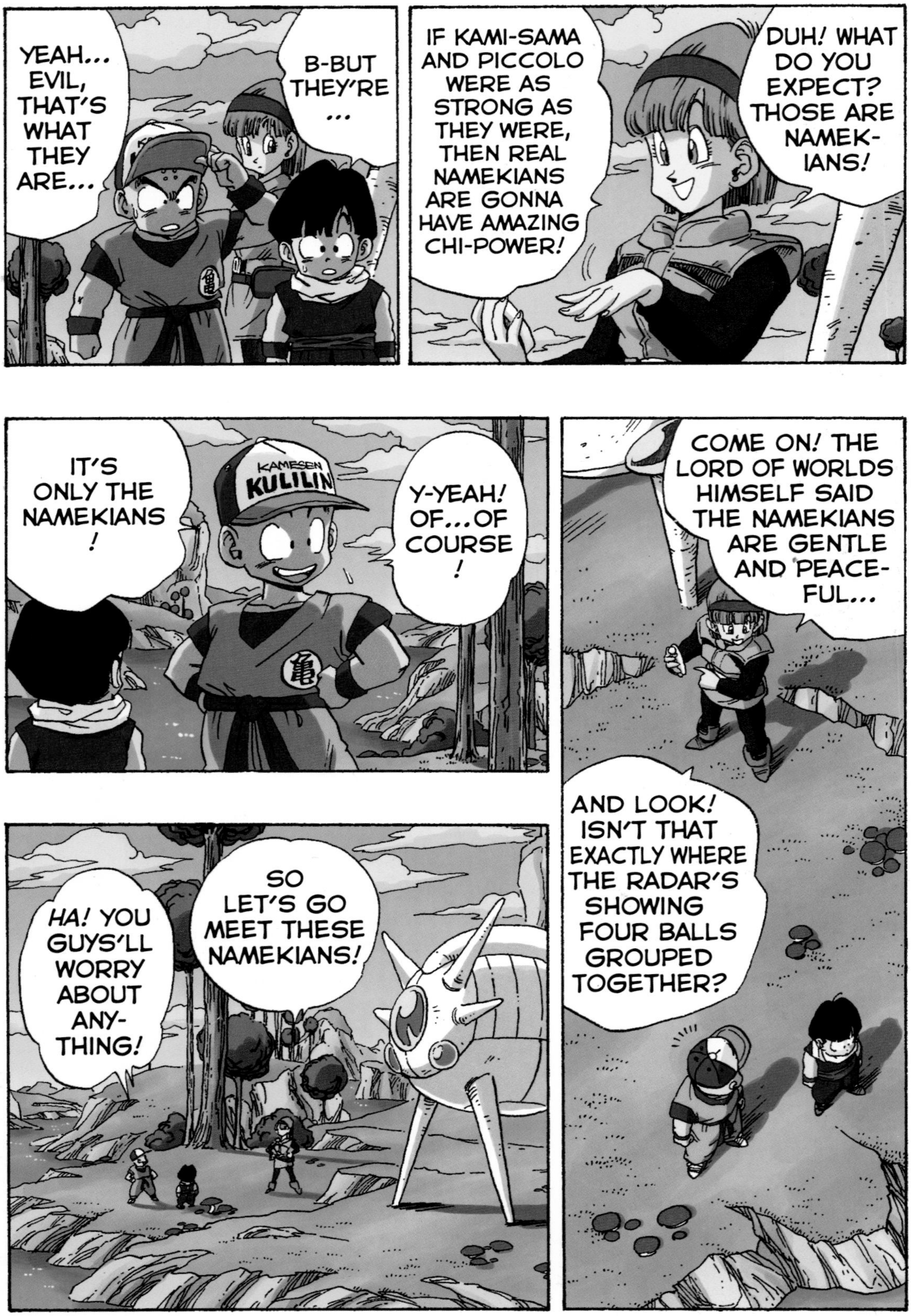
DUH! WHAT DO YOU EXPECT? THOSE ARE NAMEKIANS!
IF KAMI-SAMA AND PICCOLO WERE AS STRONG AS THEY WERE, THEN REAL NAMEKIANS ARE GONNA HAVE AMAZING CHI-POWER!
B-BUT THEY'RE ...
YEAH... EVIL, THAT'S WHAT THEY ARE...
COME ON! THE LORD OF WORLDS HIMSELF SAID THE NAMEKIANS ARE GENTLE AND PEACEFUL...
AND LOOK! ISN'T THAT EXACTLY WHERE THE RADAR'S SHOWING FOUR BALLS GROUPED TOGETHER?
Y-YEAH! OF...OF COURSE!
KAMESEN KULILIN
IT'S ONLY THE NAMEKIANS!
SO LET'S GO MEET THESE NAMEKIANS!
HA! YOU GUYS'LL WORRY ABOUT ANYTHING!

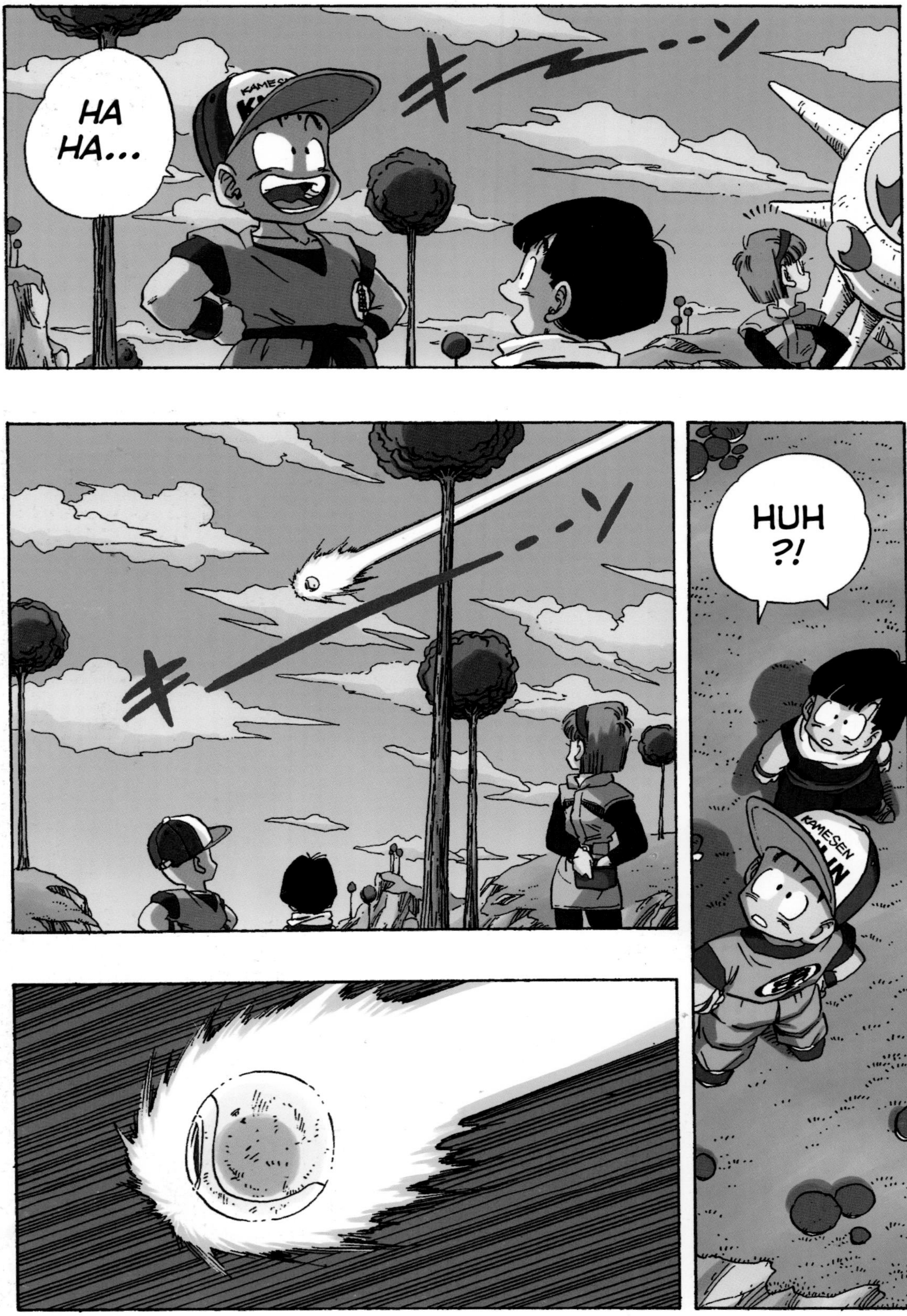
HA HA...
HUH ?!

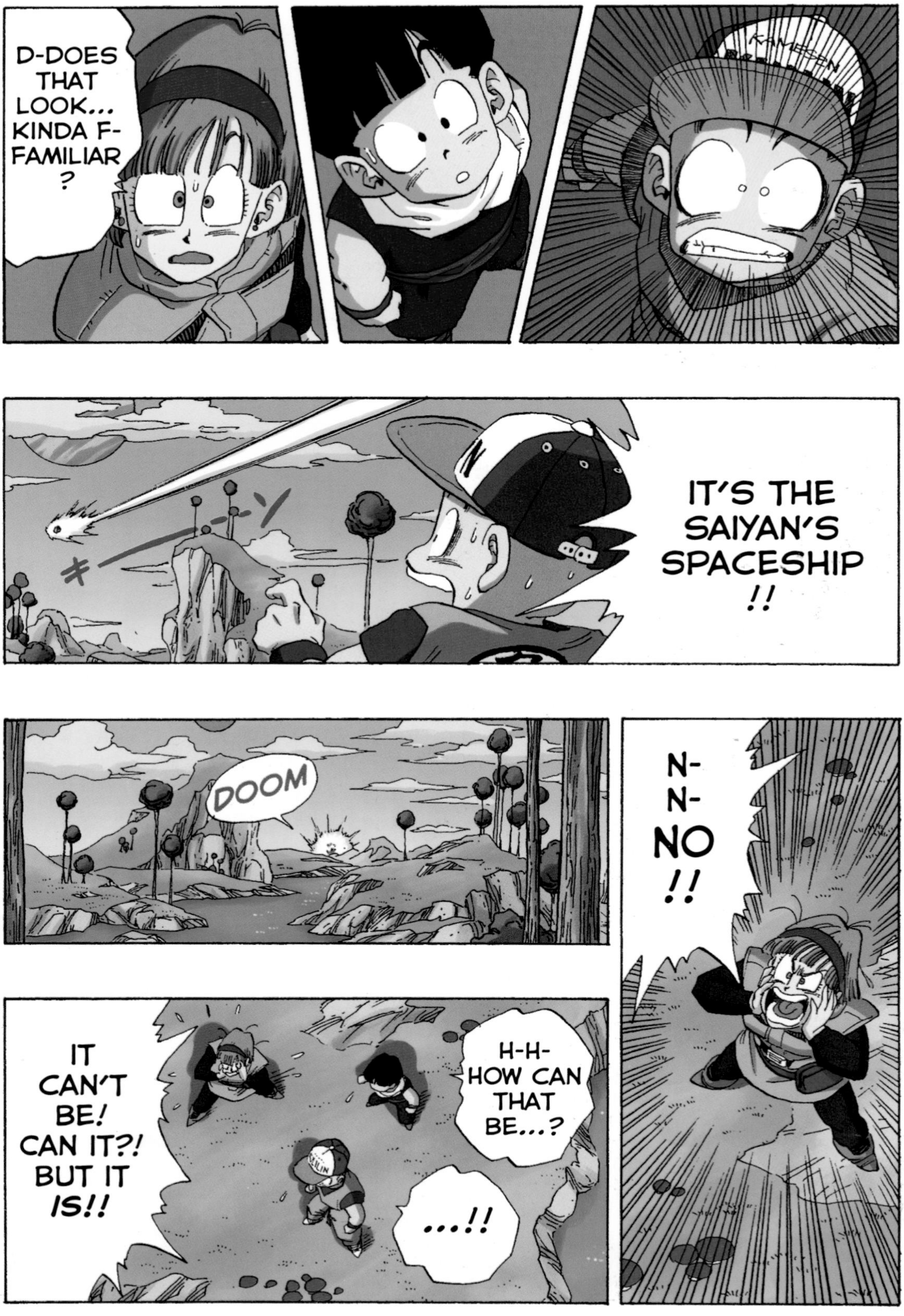
D-DOES THAT LOOK... KINDA F-FAMILIAR?
IT'S THE SAIYAN'S SPACESHIP!!
N-N-NO!!
DOOM
H-H-HOW CAN THAT BE...?
IT CAN'T BE! CAN IT?! BUT IT IS!!
...!!

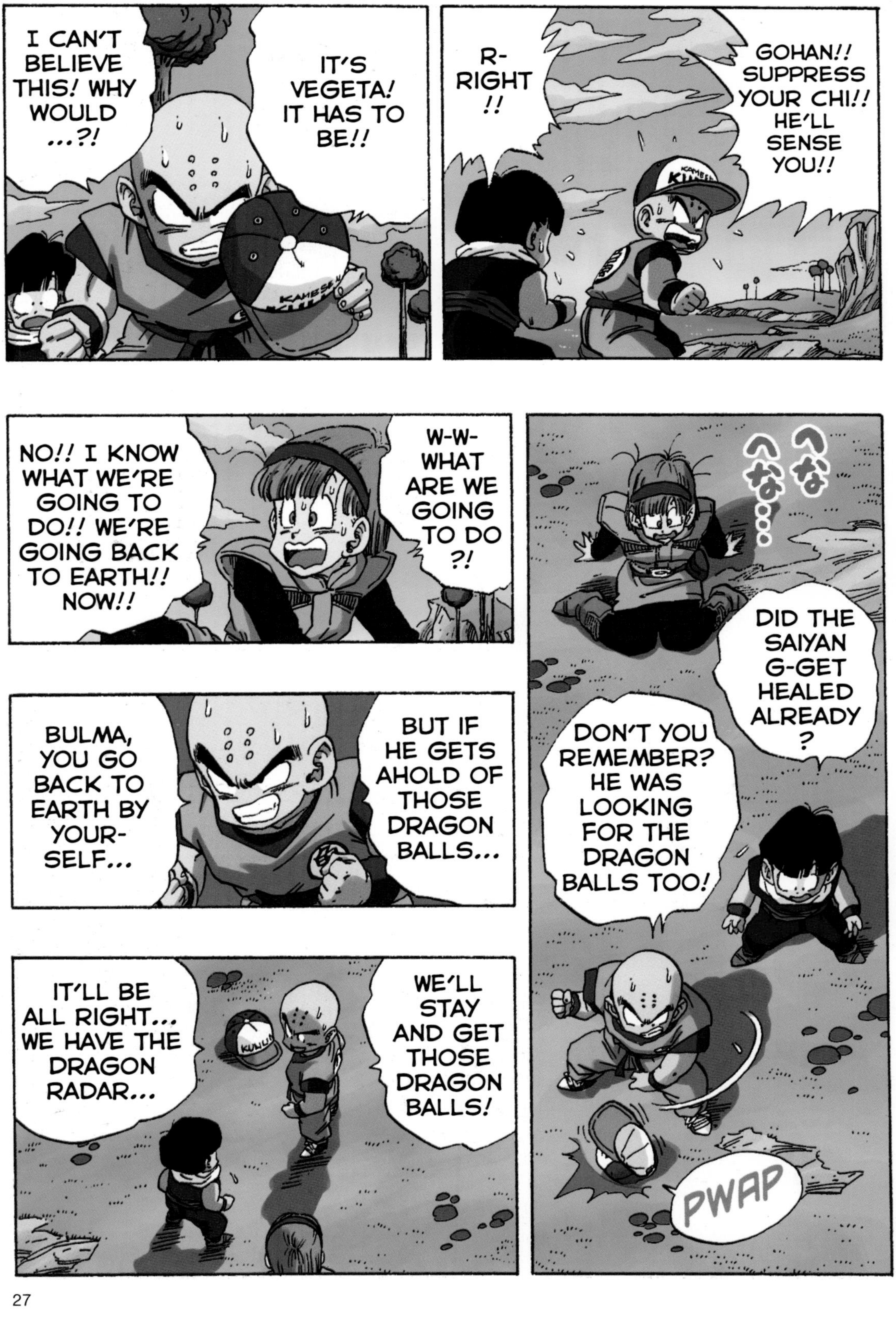
GOHAN!! SUPPRESS YOUR CHI!! HE'LL SENSE YOU!!
R-RIGHT!!
IT'S VEGETA! IT HAS TO BE!!
I CAN'T BELIEVE THIS! WHY WOULD ...?!
へなへな…
DID THE SAIYAN G-GET HEALED ALREADY?
DON'T YOU REMEMBER? HE WAS LOOKING FOR THE DRAGON BALLS TOO!
PWAP
W-W-WHAT ARE WE GOING TO DO?!
NO!! I KNOW WHAT WE'RE GOING TO DO!! WE'RE GOING BACK TO EARTH!! NOW!!
BUT IF HE GETS AHOLD OF THOSE DRAGON BALLS...
BULMA, YOU GO BACK TO EARTH BY YOURSELF...
WE'LL STAY AND GET THOSE DRAGON BALLS!
IT'LL BE ALL RIGHT... WE HAVE THE DRAGON RADAR...

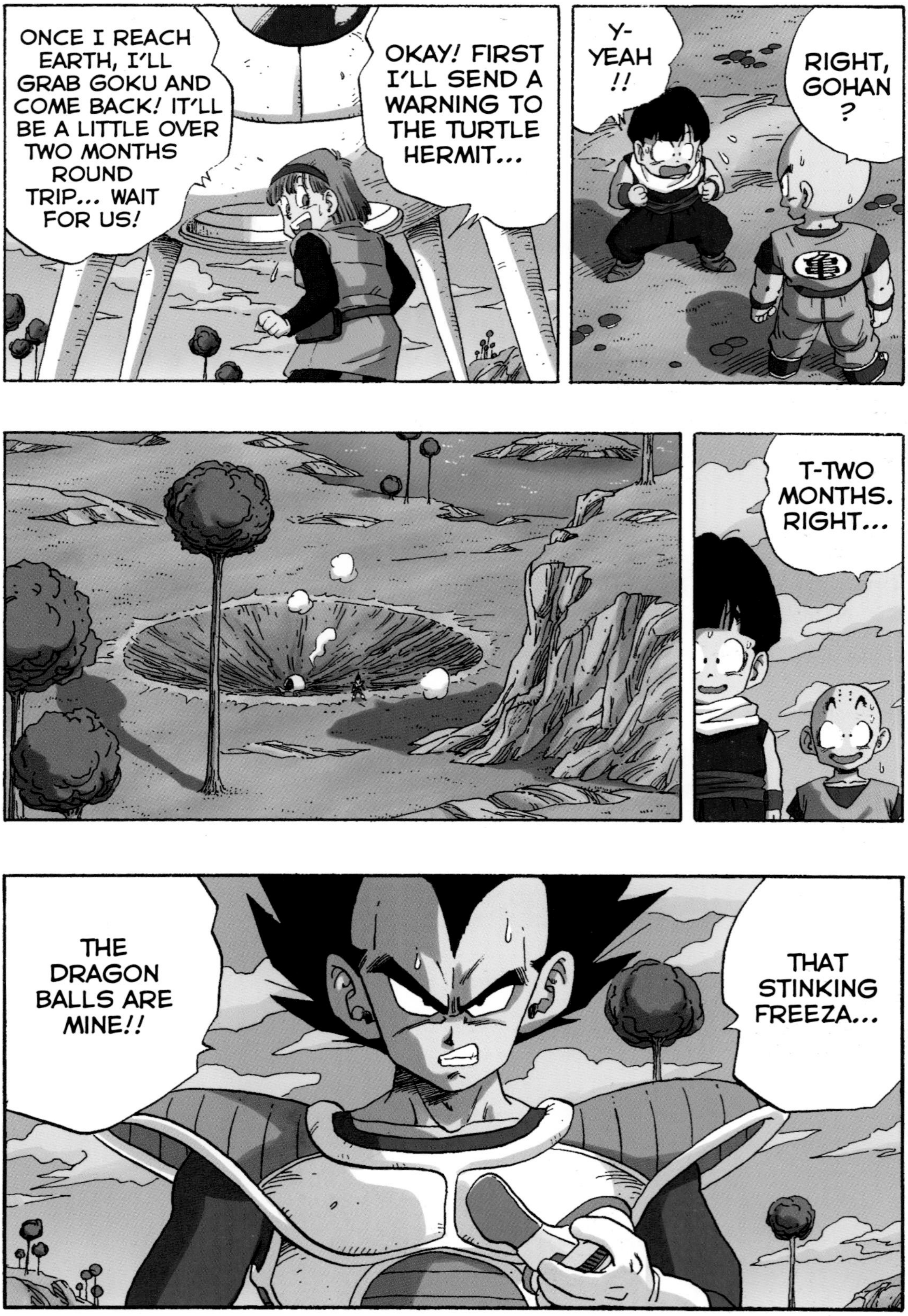
RIGHT, GOHAN?
Y-YEAH!!
OKAY! FIRST I'LL SEND A WARNING TO THE TURTLE HERMIT...
ONCE I REACH EARTH, I'LL GRAB GOKU AND COME BACK! IT'LL BE A LITTLE OVER TWO MONTHS ROUND TRIP... WAIT FOR US!
T-TWO MONTHS. RIGHT...
THAT STINKING FREEZA...
THE DRAGON BALLS ARE MINE!!

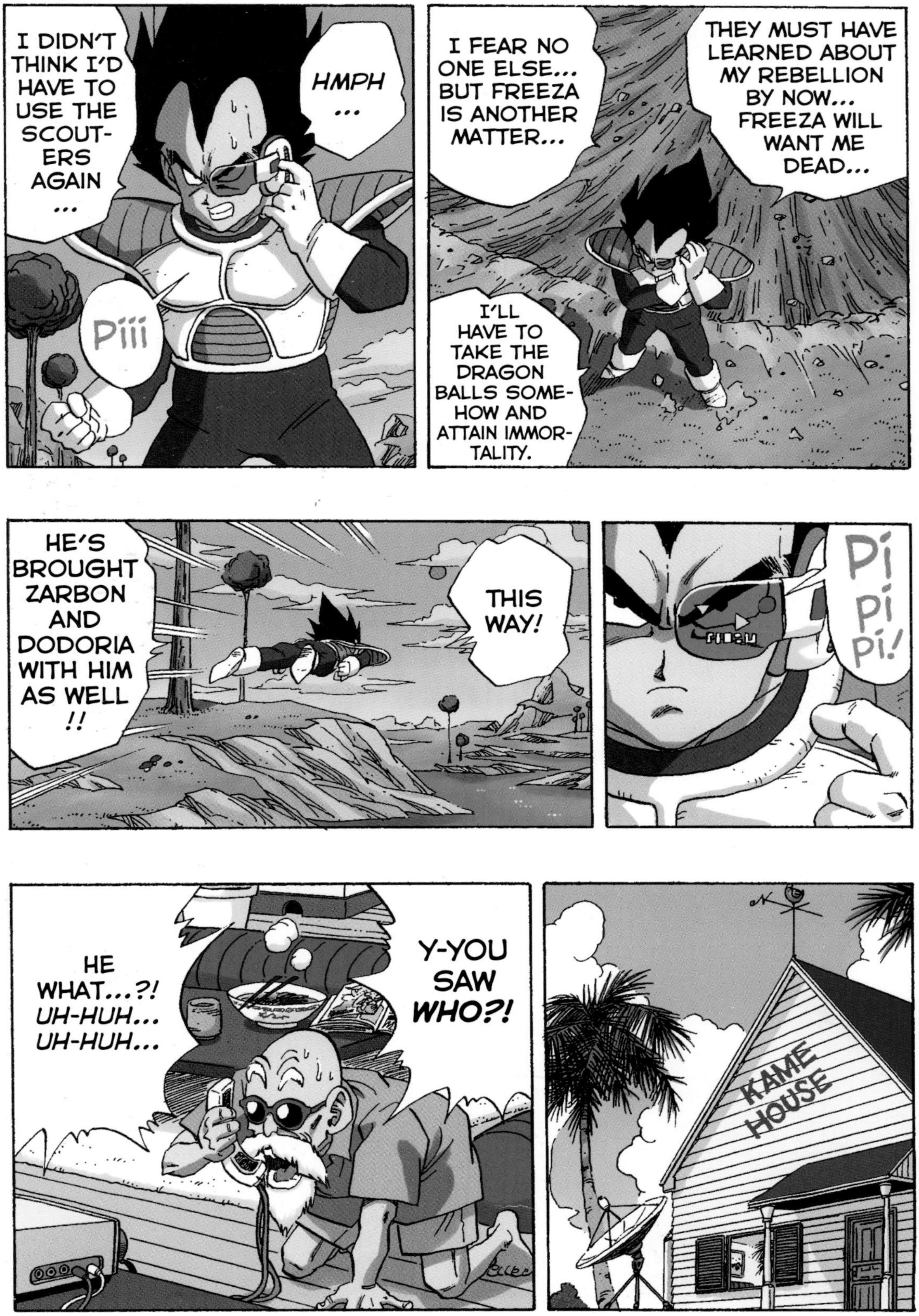
THEY MUST HAVE LEARNED ABOUT MY REBELLION BY NOW... FREEZA WILL WANT ME DEAD...
I FEAR NO ONE ELSE... BUT FREEZA IS ANOTHER MATTER...
I'LL HAVE TO TAKE THE DRAGON BALLS SOMEHOW AND ATTAIN IMMORTALITY.
HMPH ...
I DIDN'T THINK I'D HAVE TO USE THE SCOUTERS AGAIN ...
Piii
Pi Pi Pi!
THIS WAY!
HE'S BROUGHT ZARBON AND DODORIA WITH HIM AS WELL !!
KAME HOUSE
Y-YOU SAW WHO?!
HE WHAT...?! UH-HUH... UH-HUH...

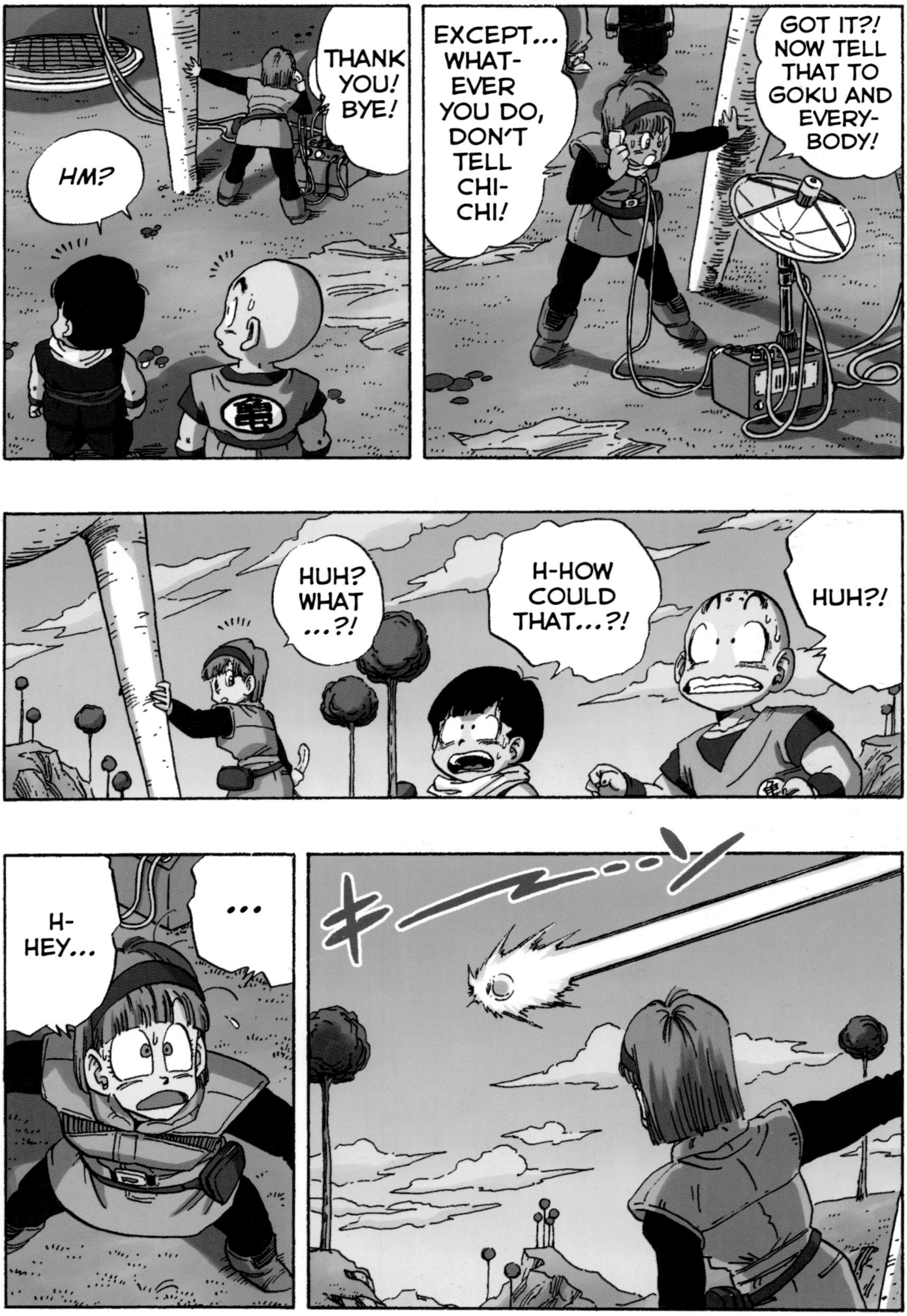
GOT IT?! NOW TELL THAT TO GOKU AND EVERY-BODY!
EXCEPT... WHAT-EVER YOU DO, DON'T TELL CHI-CHI!
THANK YOU! BYE!
HM?
HUH?!
H-HOW COULD THAT...?!
HUH? WHAT ...?!
...
H-HEY...

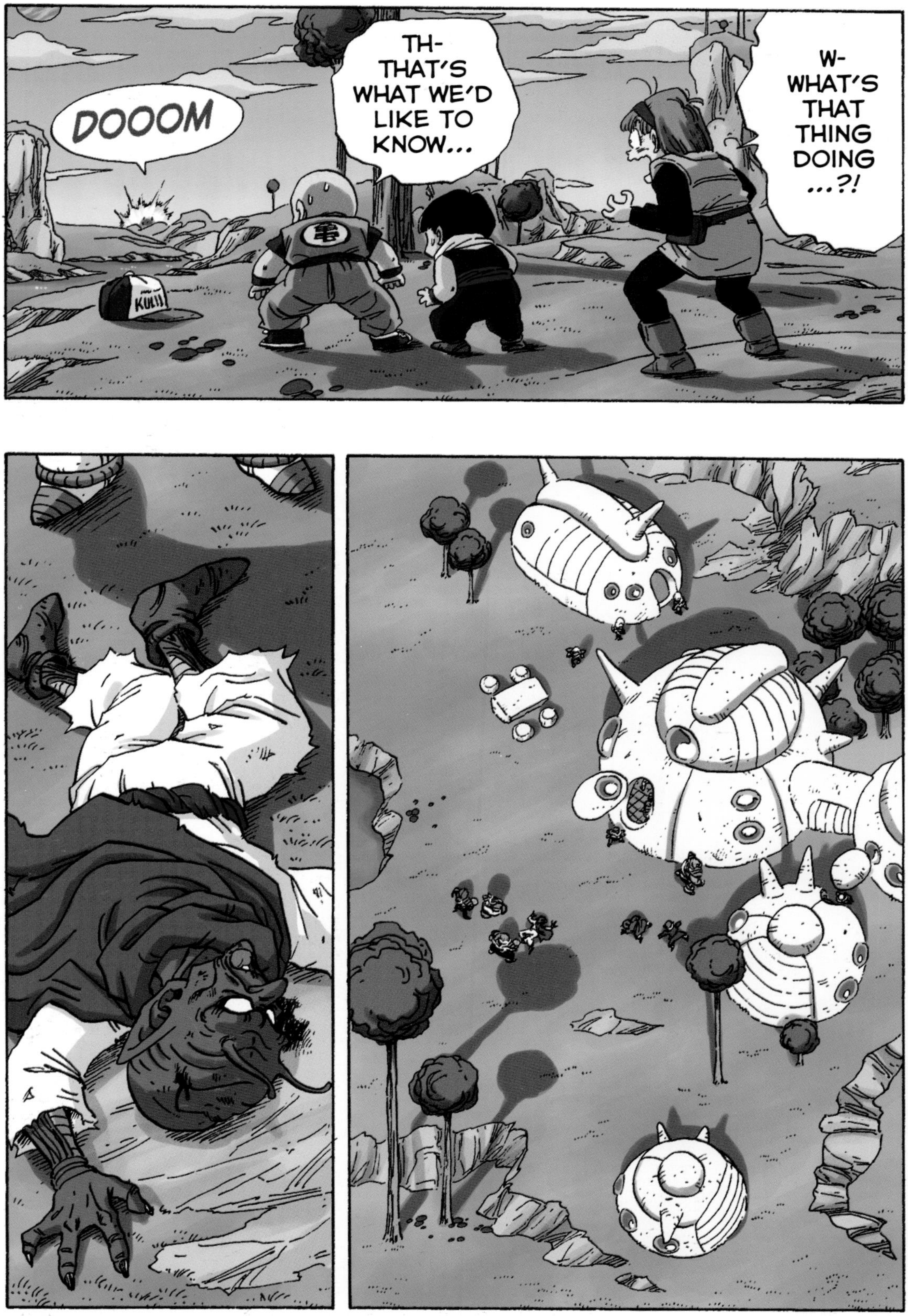
W- WHAT'S THAT THING DOING ...?!
TH- THAT'S WHAT WE'D LIKE TO KNOW...
DOOOM

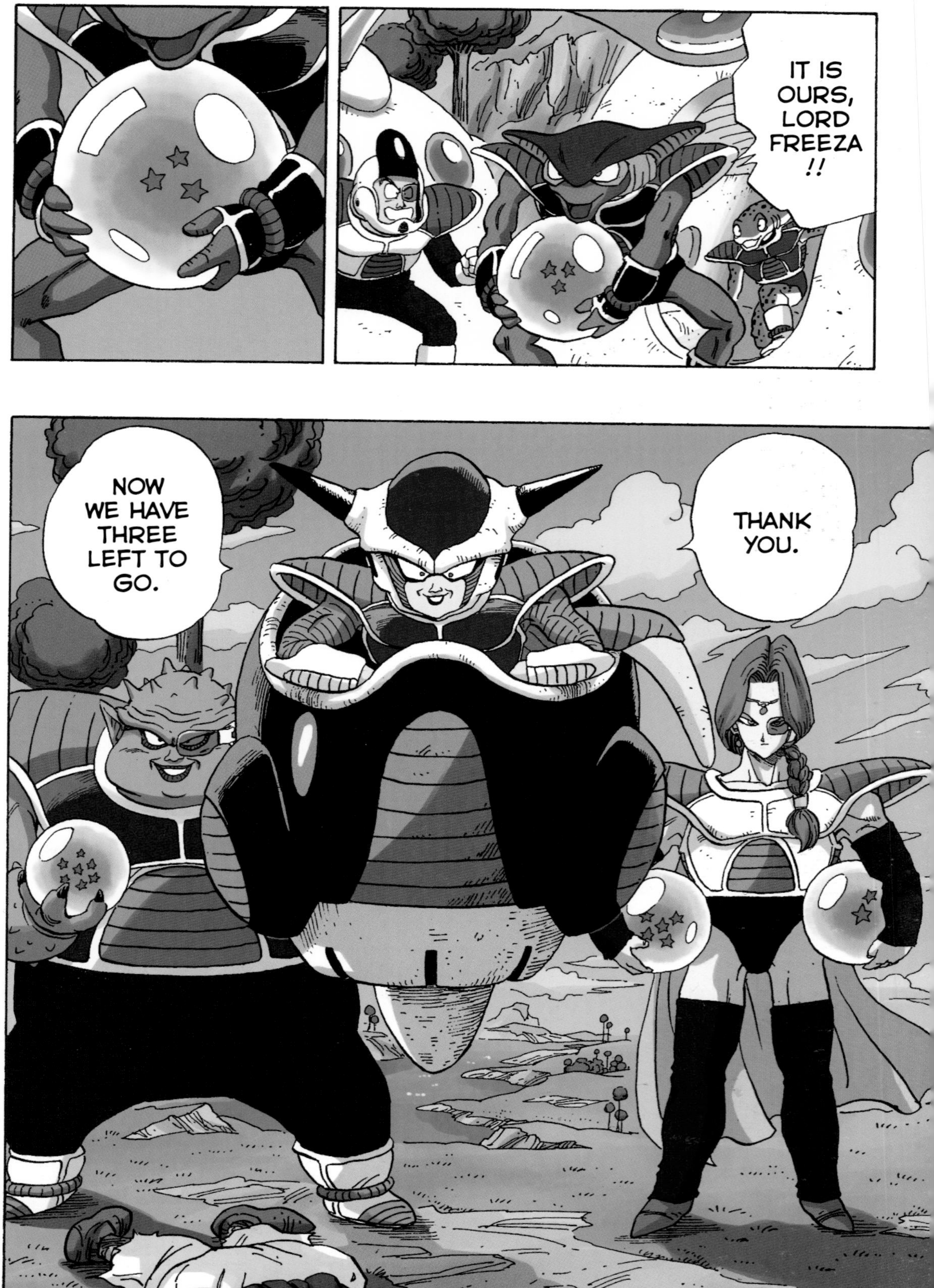
IT IS OURS, LORD FREEZA!!
THANK YOU.
NOW WE HAVE THREE LEFT TO GO.

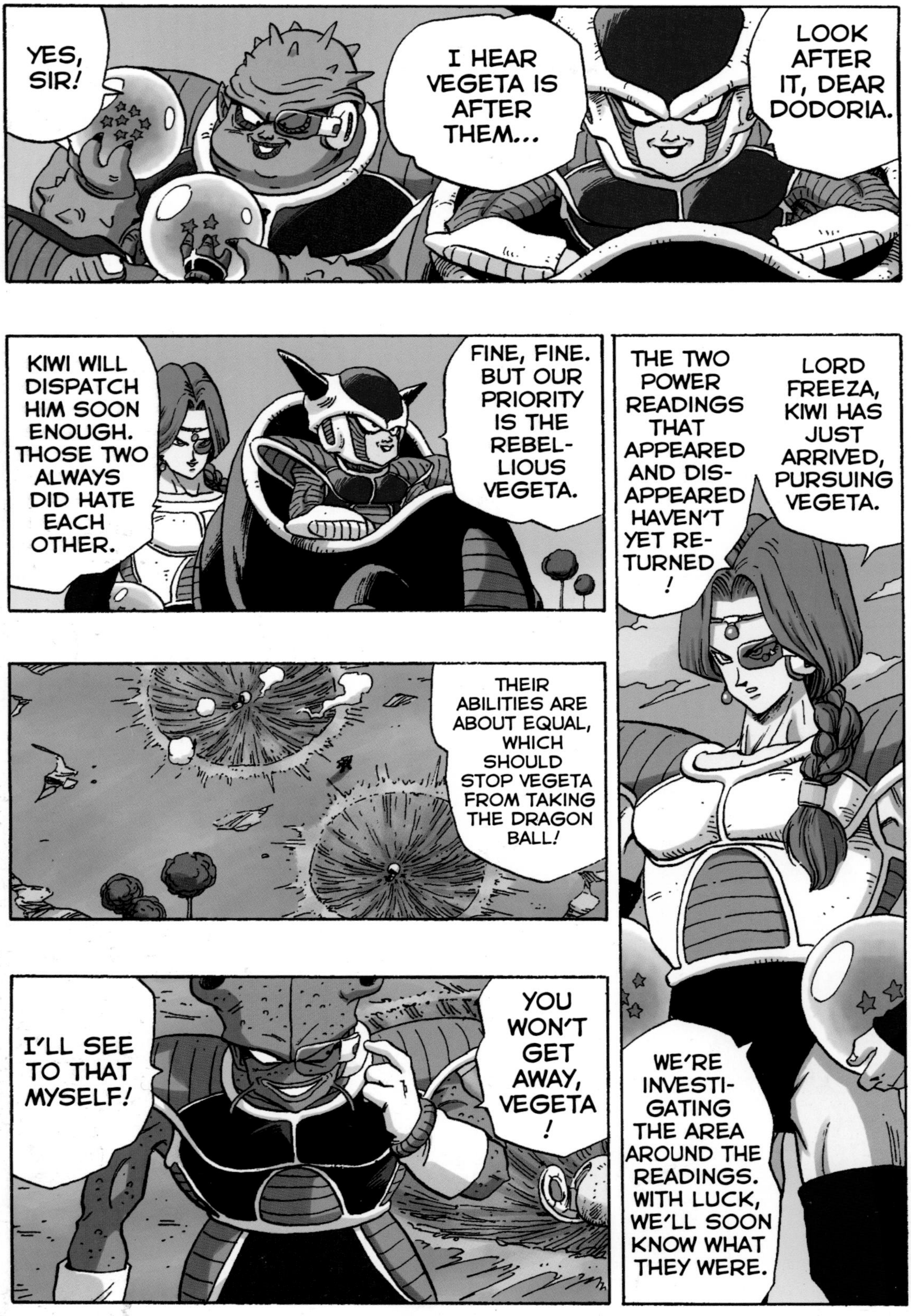
LOOK AFTER IT, DEAR DODORIA.
I HEAR VEGETA IS AFTER THEM...
YES, SIR!
LORD FREEZA, KIWI HAS JUST ARRIVED, PURSUING VEGETA.
THE TWO POWER READINGS THAT APPEARED AND DISAPPEARED HAVEN'T YET RETURNED!
WE'RE INVESTIGATING THE AREA AROUND THE READINGS. WITH LUCK, WE'LL SOON KNOW WHAT THEY WERE.
FINE, FINE. BUT OUR PRIORITY IS THE REBELLIOUS VEGETA.
KIWI WILL DISPATCH HIM SOON ENOUGH. THOSE TWO ALWAYS DID HATE EACH OTHER.
THEIR ABILITIES ARE ABOUT EQUAL, WHICH SHOULD STOP VEGETA FROM TAKING THE DRAGON BALL!
YOU WON'T GET AWAY, VEGETA!
I'LL SEE TO THAT MYSELF!

Chapter 3 • The Mysterious Strangers

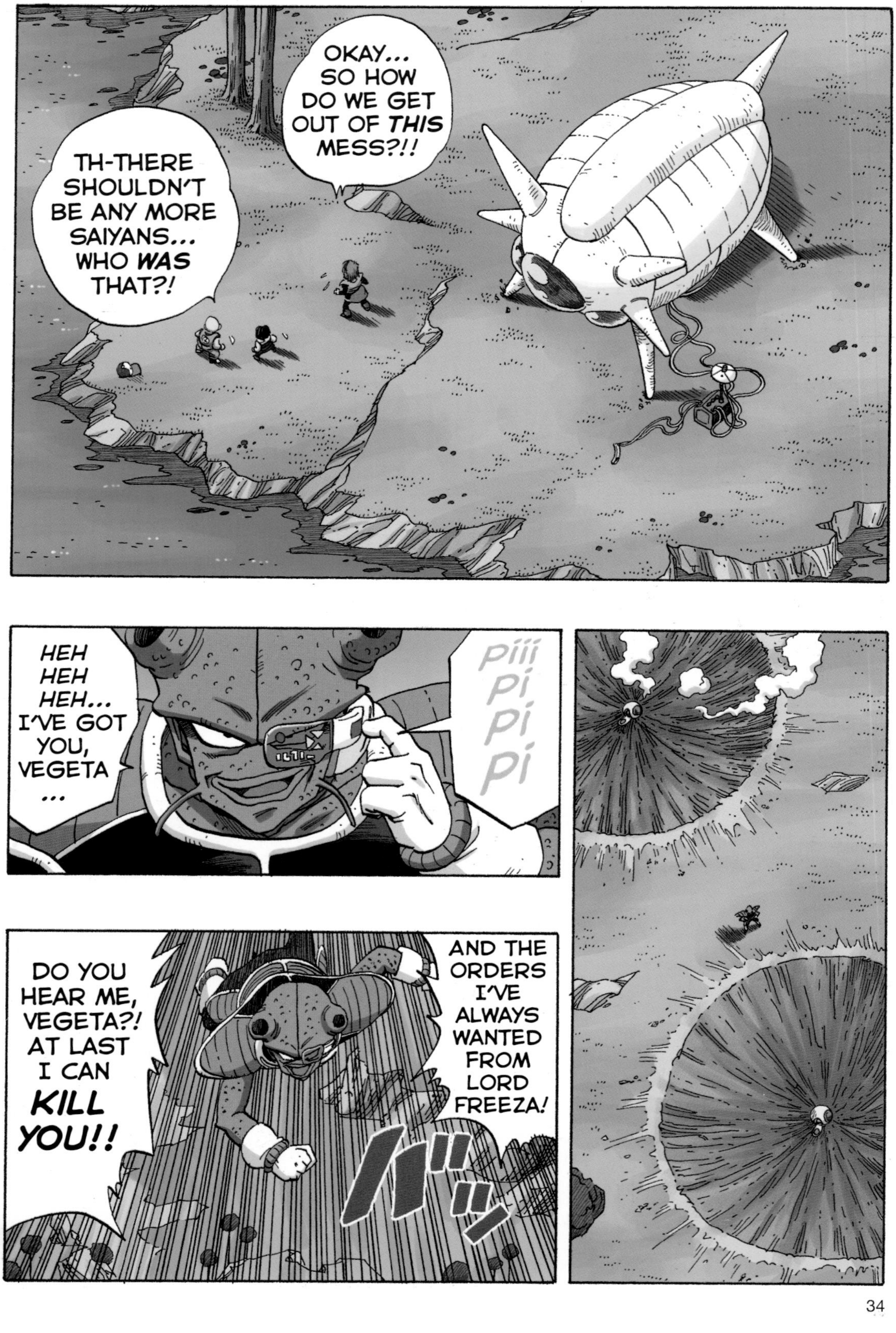
OKAY... SO HOW DO WE GET OUT OF *THIS* MESS?!!
TH-THERE SHOULDN'T BE ANY MORE SAIYANS... WHO *WAS* THAT?!
piii pi pi pi
HEH HEH HEH... I'VE GOT YOU, VEGETA...
AND THE ORDERS I'VE ALWAYS WANTED FROM LORD FREEZA!
DO YOU HEAR ME, VEGETA?! AT LAST I CAN **KILL YOU!!**
バッ

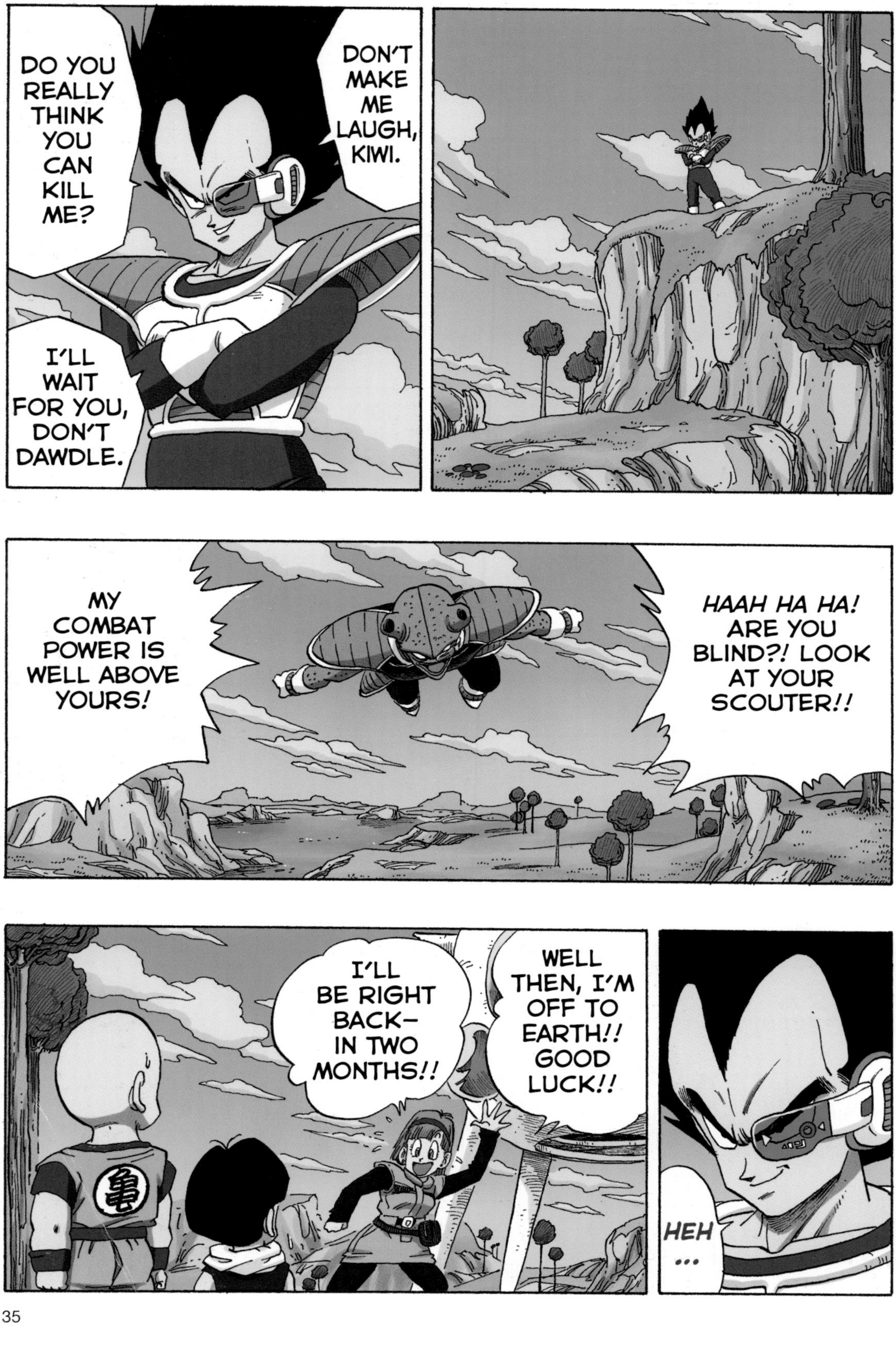
DON'T MAKE ME LAUGH, KIWI.
DO YOU REALLY THINK YOU CAN KILL ME?
I'LL WAIT FOR YOU, DON'T DAWDLE.
HAAH HA HA! ARE YOU BLIND?! LOOK AT YOUR SCOUTER!!
MY COMBAT POWER IS WELL ABOVE YOURS!
HEH ...
WELL THEN, I'M OFF TO EARTH!! GOOD LUCK!!
I'LL BE RIGHT BACK— IN TWO MONTHS!!

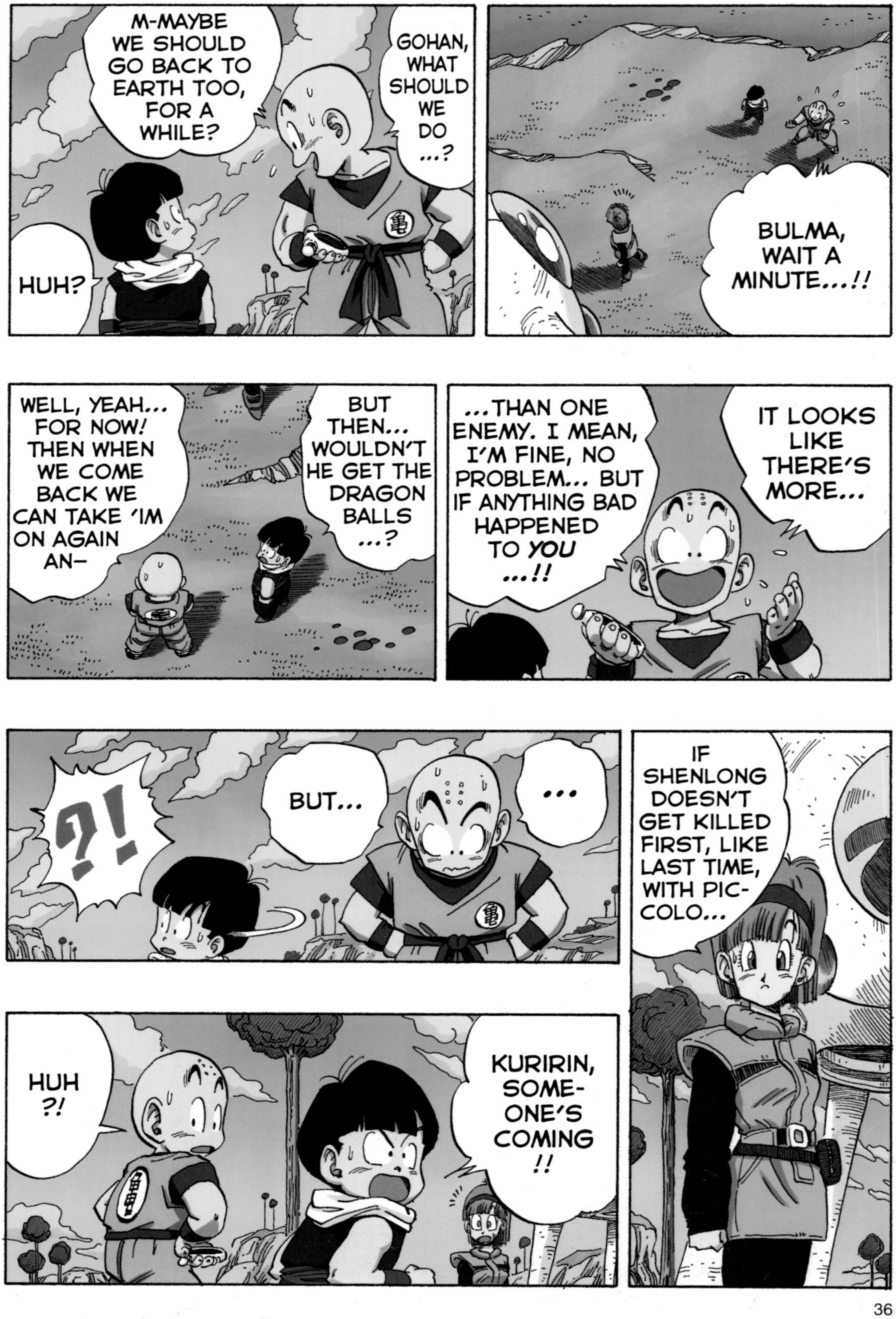
BULMA, WAIT A MINUTE...!!
GOHAN, WHAT SHOULD WE DO...?
M-MAYBE WE SHOULD GO BACK TO EARTH TOO, FOR A WHILE?
HUH?
IT LOOKS LIKE THERE'S MORE...
...THAN ONE ENEMY. I MEAN, I'M FINE, NO PROBLEM... BUT IF ANYTHING BAD HAPPENED TO *YOU*...!!
BUT THEN... WOULDN'T HE GET THE DRAGON BALLS...?
WELL, YEAH... FOR NOW! THEN WHEN WE COME BACK WE CAN TAKE 'IM ON AGAIN AN–
IF SHENLONG DOESN'T GET KILLED FIRST, LIKE LAST TIME, WITH PIC-COLO...
...
BUT...
?!
KURIRIN, SOME-ONE'S COMING!!
HUH?!

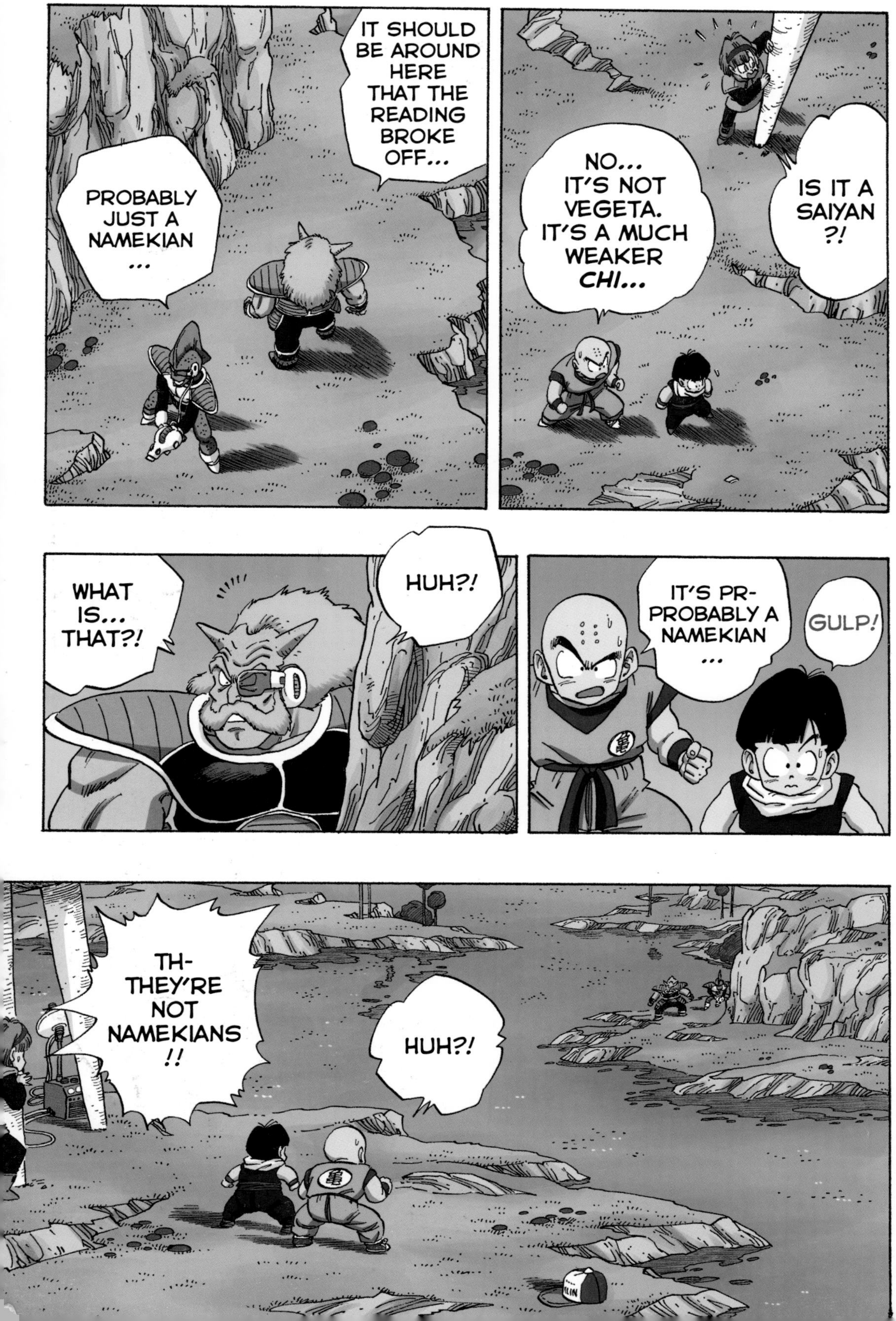
IS IT A SAIYAN ?!
NO... IT'S NOT VEGETA. IT'S A MUCH WEAKER *CHI*...
IT SHOULD BE AROUND HERE THAT THE READING BROKE OFF...
PROBABLY JUST A NAMEKIAN ...
IT'S PR- PROBABLY A NAMEKIAN ...
GULP!
HUH?!
WHAT IS... THAT?!
HUH?!
TH- THEY'RE NOT NAMEKIANS !!

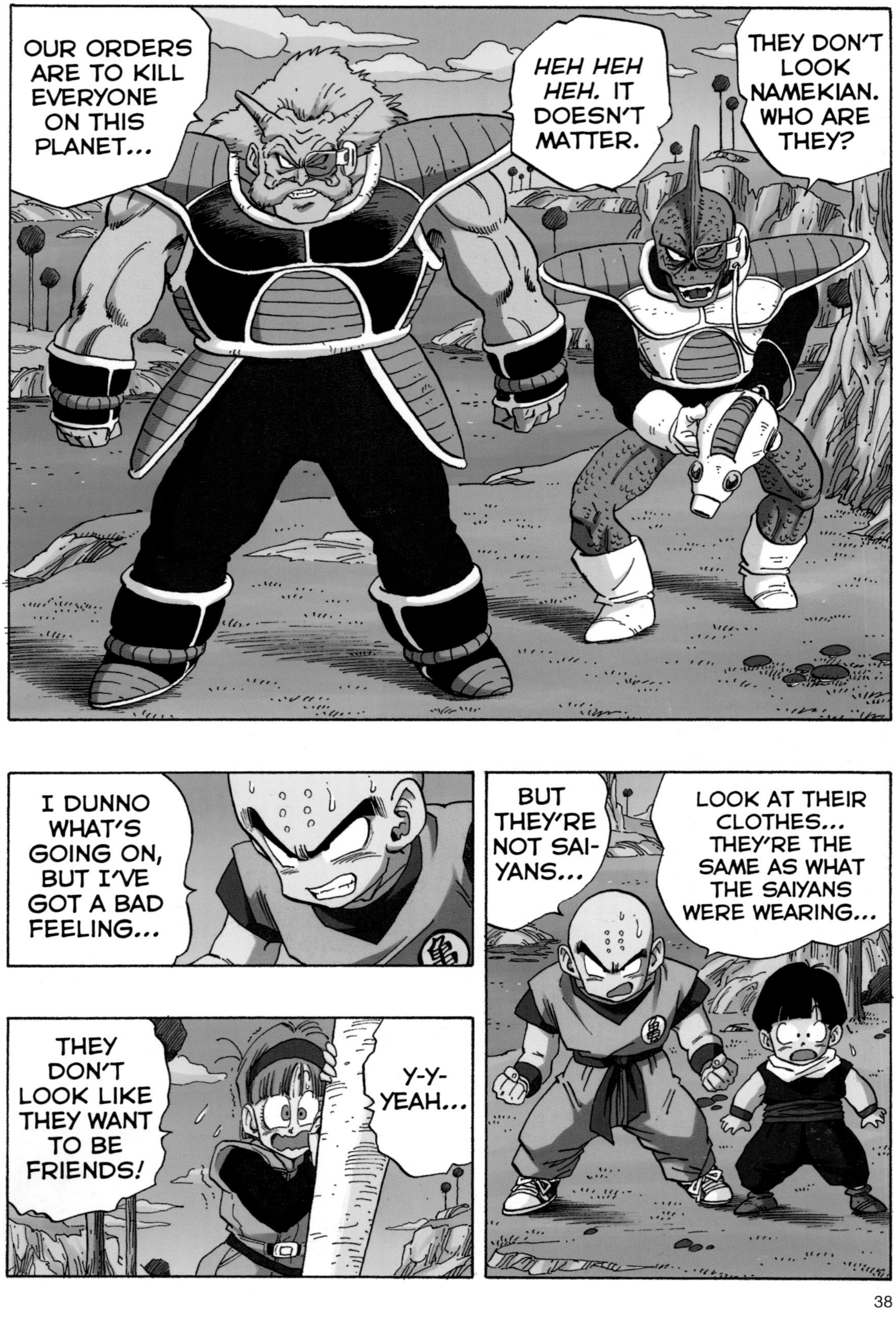
THEY DON'T LOOK NAMEKIAN. WHO ARE THEY?
HEH HEH HEH. IT DOESN'T MATTER.
OUR ORDERS ARE TO KILL EVERYONE ON THIS PLANET...
LOOK AT THEIR CLOTHES... THEY'RE THE SAME AS WHAT THE SAIYANS WERE WEARING...
BUT THEY'RE NOT SAI-YANS...
I DUNNO WHAT'S GOING ON, BUT I'VE GOT A BAD FEELING...
Y-Y-YEAH...
THEY DON'T LOOK LIKE THEY WANT TO BE FRIENDS!

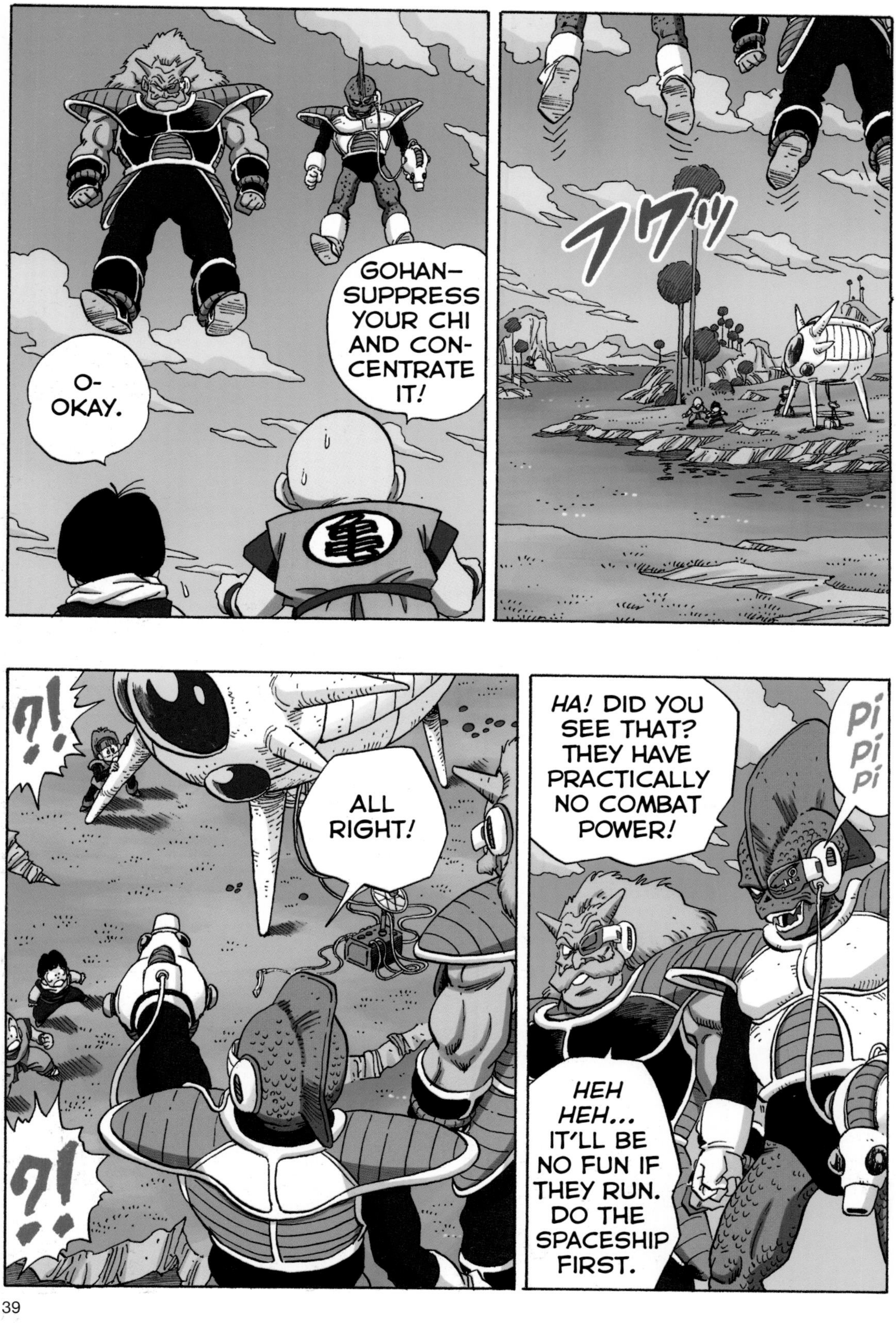
フワッ
GOHAN— SUPPRESS YOUR CHI AND CON- CENTRATE IT!
O- OKAY.
HA! DID YOU SEE THAT? THEY HAVE PRACTICALLY NO COMBAT POWER!
Pi pi pi
HEH HEH... IT'LL BE NO FUN IF THEY RUN. DO THE SPACESHIP FIRST.
?!
ALL RIGHT!
?!

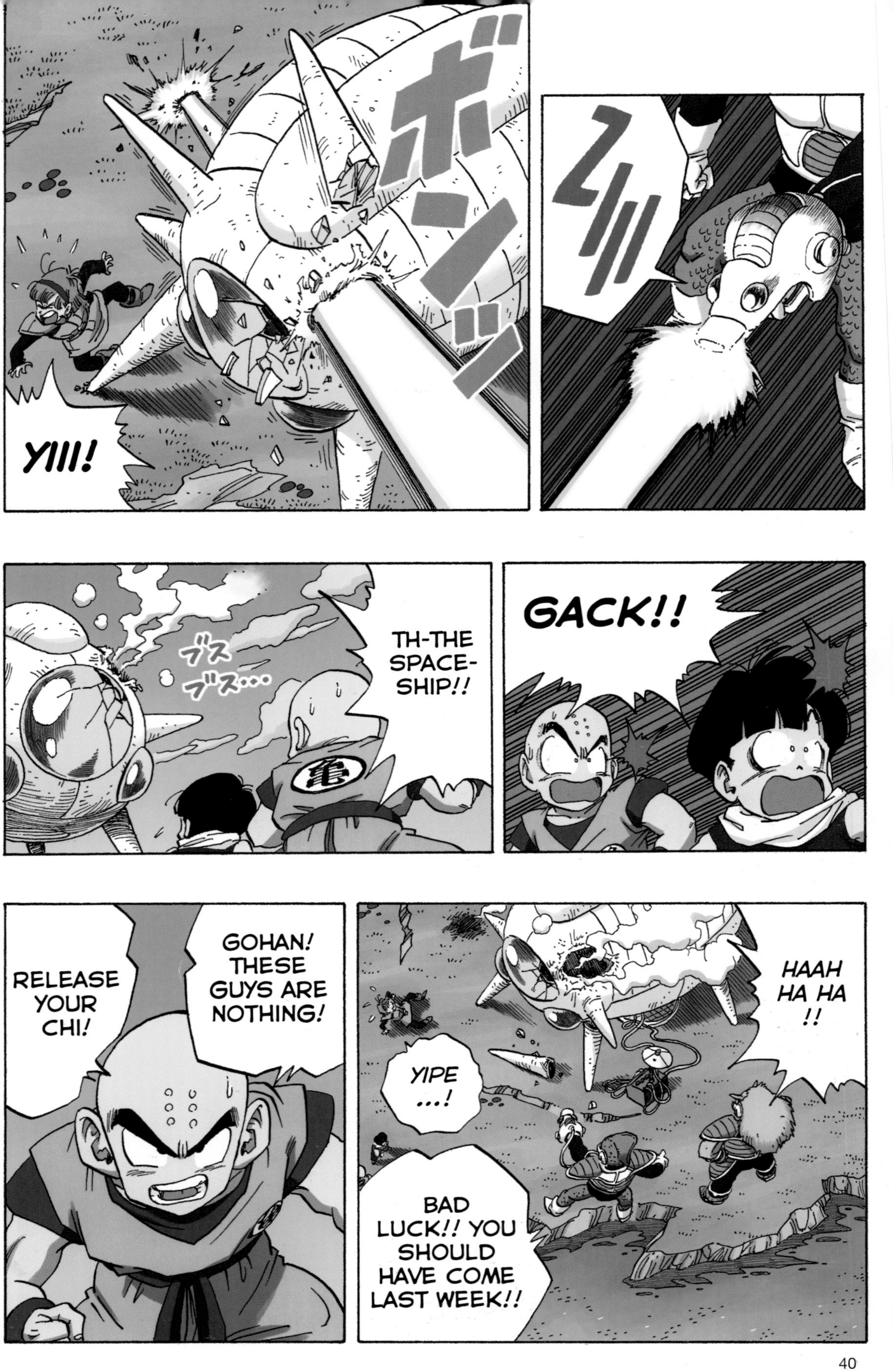
ボンッ
YIII!
GACK!!
TH-THE SPACE-SHIP!!
ブスブス…
HAAH HA HA!!
YIPE ...!
BAD LUCK!! YOU SHOULD HAVE COME LAST WEEK!!
GOHAN! THESE GUYS ARE NOTHING!
RELEASE YOUR CHI!

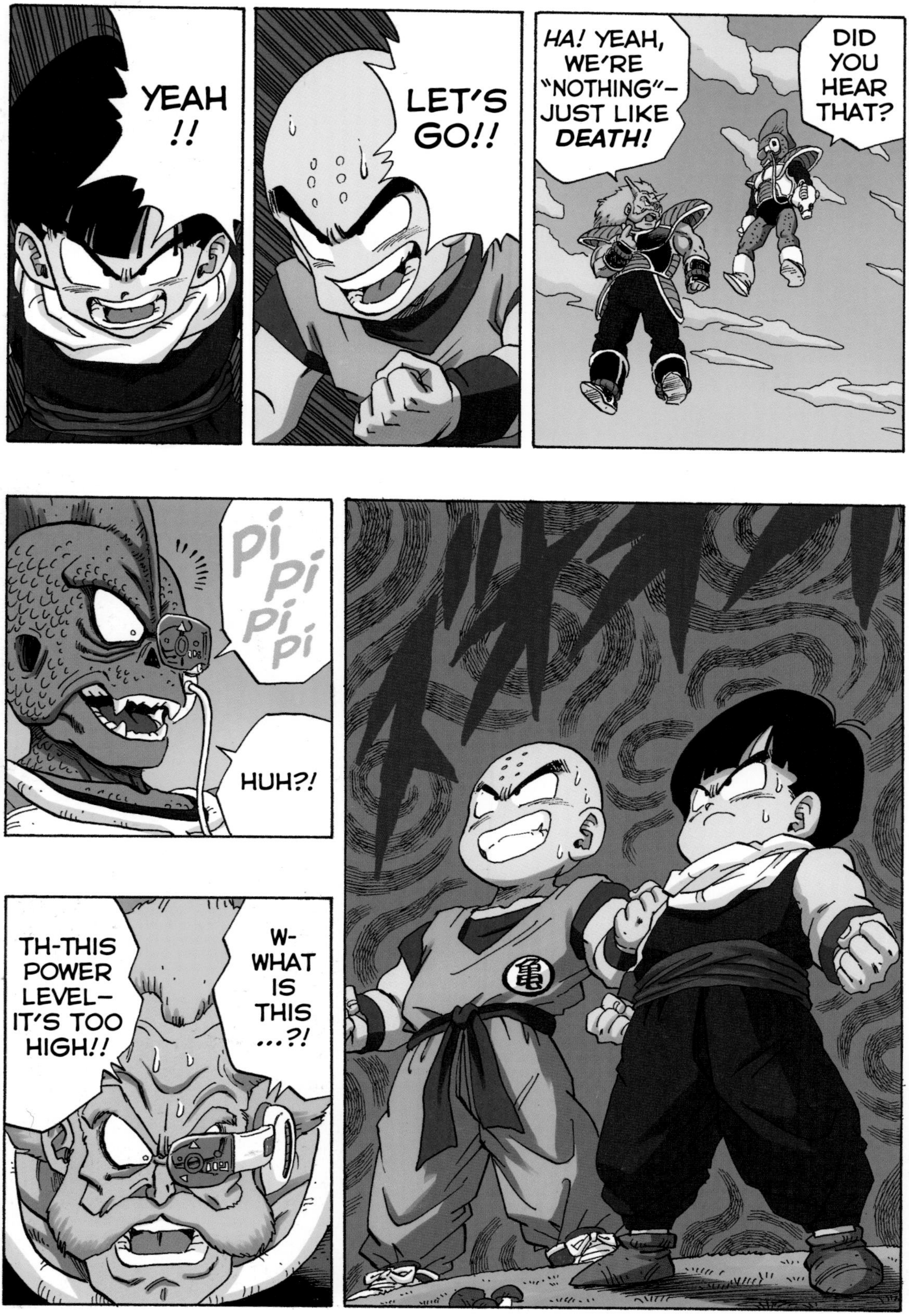

DID YOU HEAR THAT?
HA! YEAH, WE'RE "NOTHING"— JUST LIKE DEATH!
LET'S GO!!
YEAH!!
pi pi pi pi
HUH?!
W-WHAT IS THIS...?!
TH-THIS POWER LEVEL— IT'S TOO HIGH!!

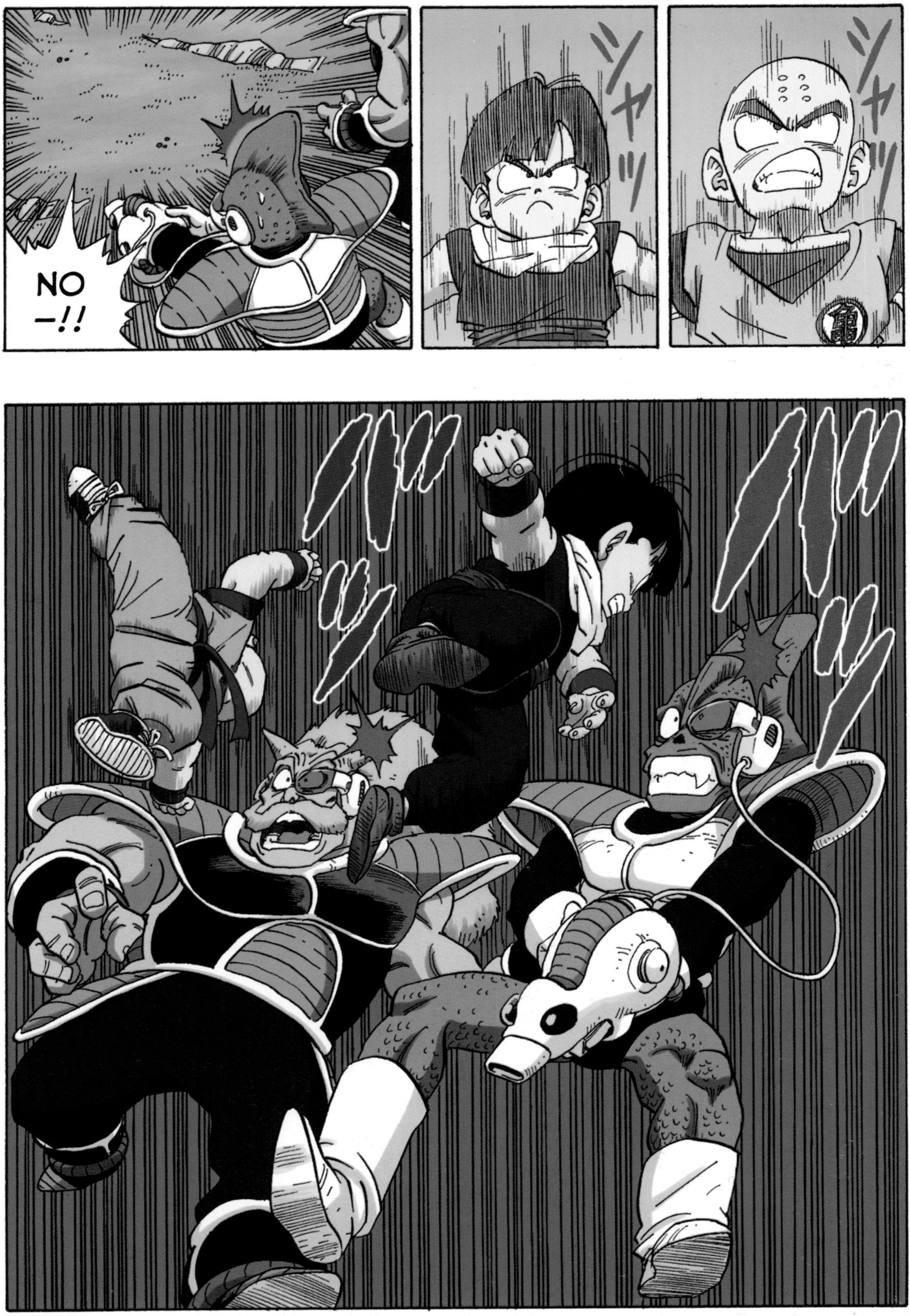
シャッ
シャッ
NO
—!!

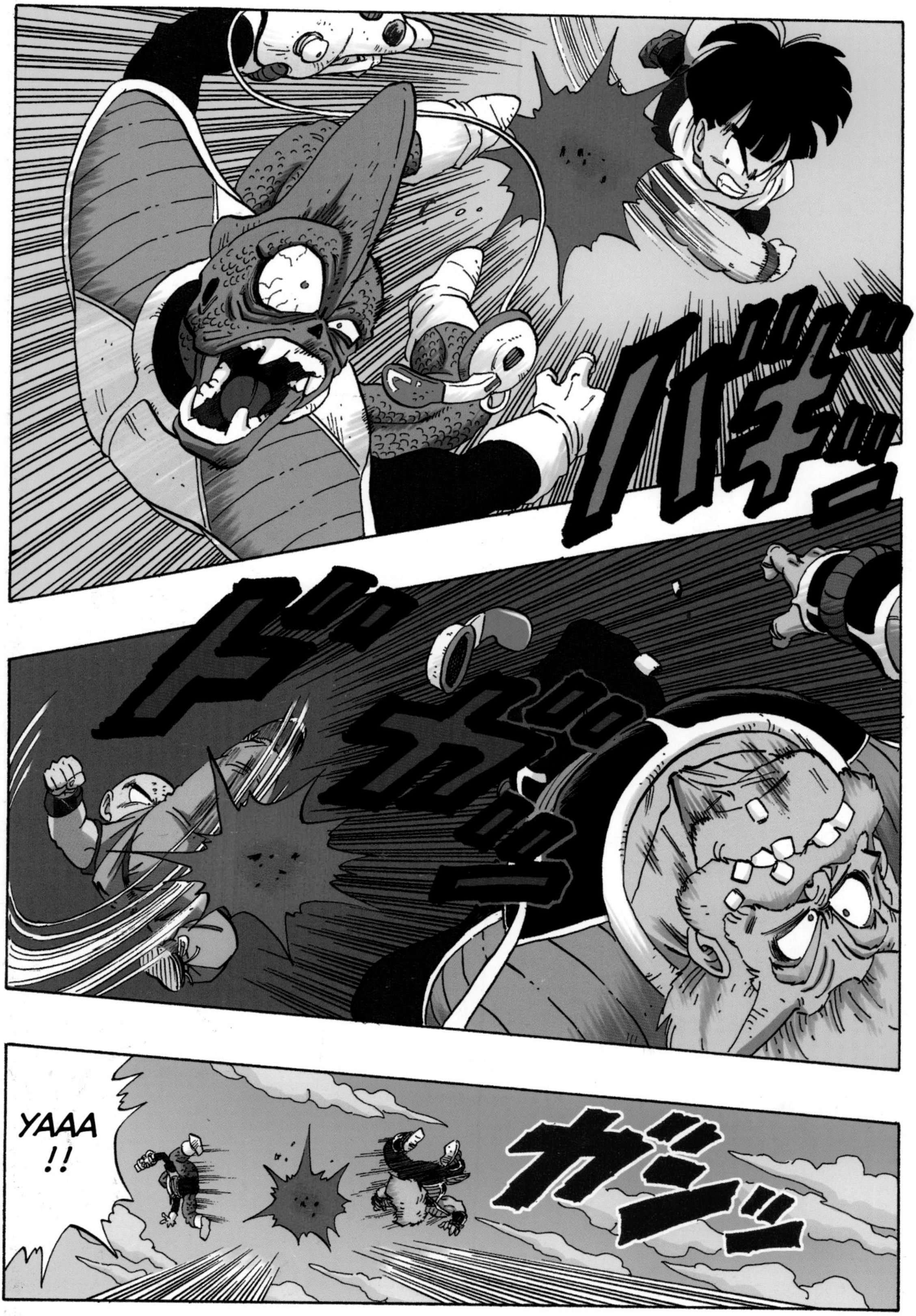
バギッ
ドガッ
ガシッ
YAAA
!!

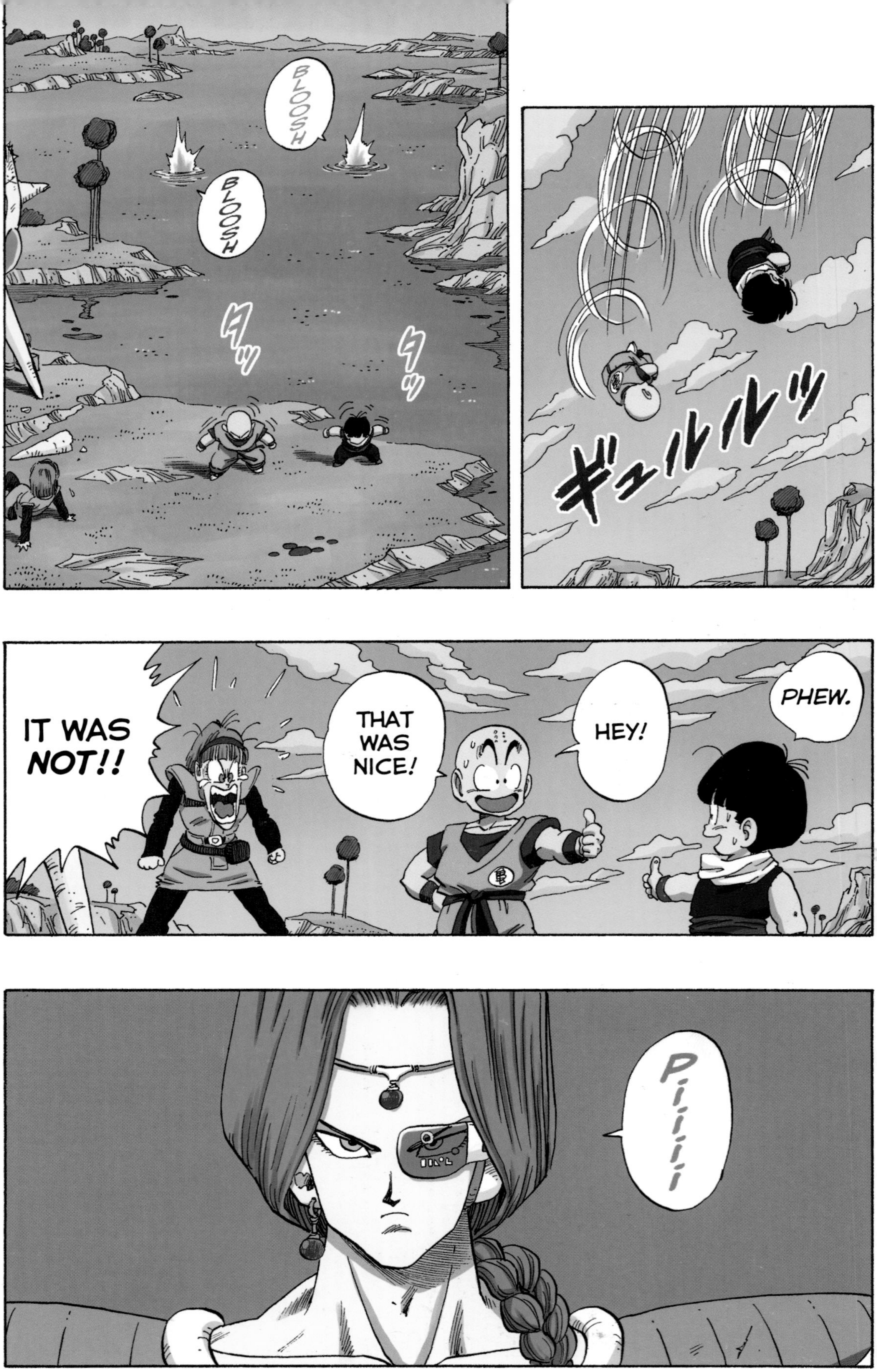
ギュルルッ
BLOOSH
BLOOSH
タッ
タッ
PHEW.
HEY!
THAT WAS NICE!
IT WAS NOT!!
Piiii

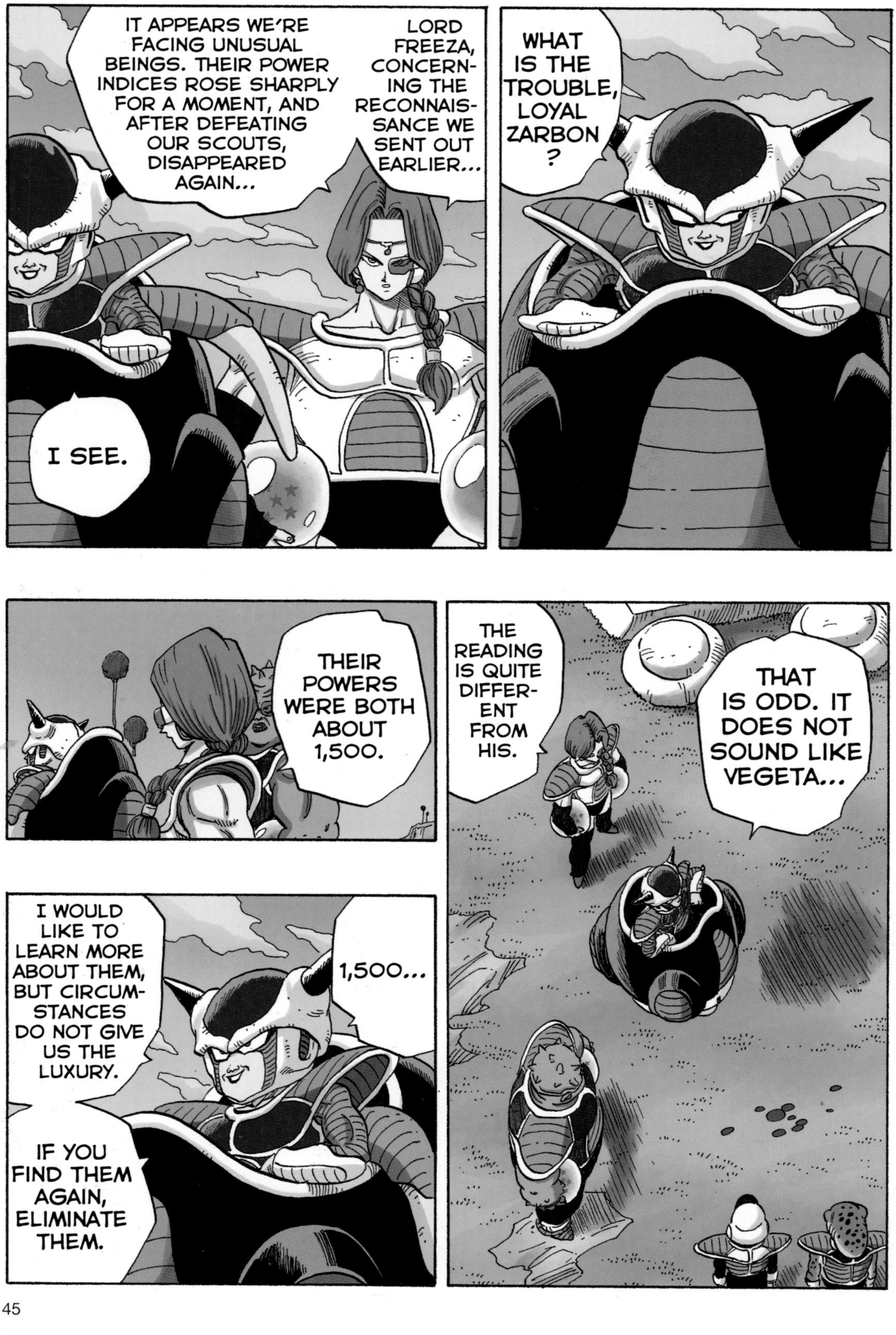
WHAT IS THE TROUBLE, LOYAL ZARBON ?
LORD FREEZA, CONCERNING THE RECONNAISSANCE WE SENT OUT EARLIER...
IT APPEARS WE'RE FACING UNUSUAL BEINGS. THEIR POWER INDICES ROSE SHARPLY FOR A MOMENT, AND AFTER DEFEATING OUR SCOUTS, DISAPPEARED AGAIN...
I SEE.
THAT IS ODD. IT DOES NOT SOUND LIKE VEGETA...
THE READING IS QUITE DIFFERENT FROM HIS.
THEIR POWERS WERE BOTH ABOUT 1,500.
1,500...
I WOULD LIKE TO LEARN MORE ABOUT THEM, BUT CIRCUMSTANCES DO NOT GIVE US THE LUXURY.
IF YOU FIND THEM AGAIN, ELIMINATE THEM.

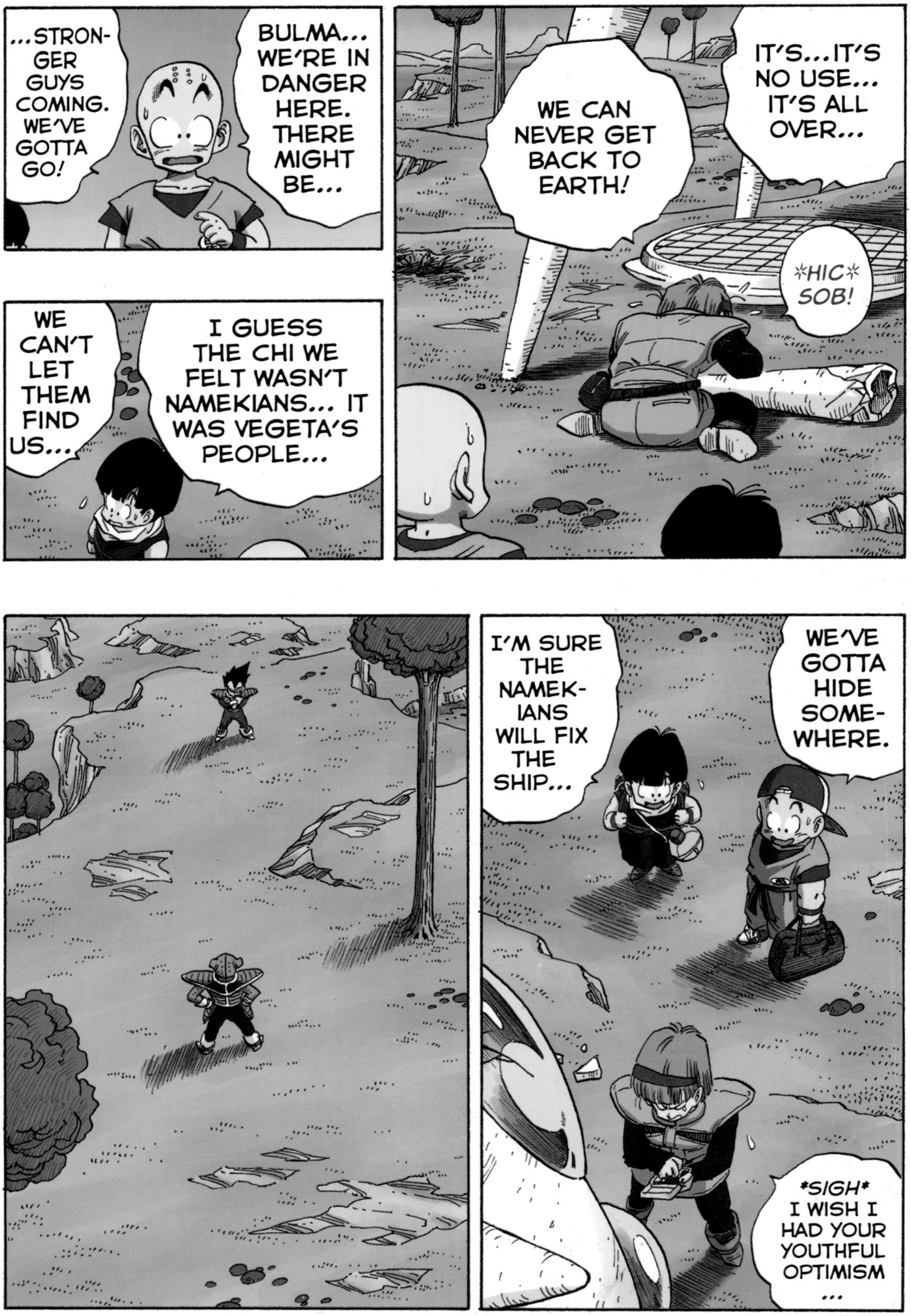
IT'S...IT'S NO USE... IT'S ALL OVER...
WE CAN NEVER GET BACK TO EARTH!
HIC SOB!
BULMA... WE'RE IN DANGER HERE. THERE MIGHT BE...
...STRONGER GUYS COMING. WE'VE GOTTA GO!
I GUESS THE CHI WE FELT WASN'T NAMEKIANS... IT WAS VEGETA'S PEOPLE...
WE CAN'T LET THEM FIND US...
WE'VE GOTTA HIDE SOMEWHERE.
I'M SURE THE NAMEKIANS WILL FIX THE SHIP...
SIGH I WISH I HAD YOUR YOUTHFUL OPTIMISM ...

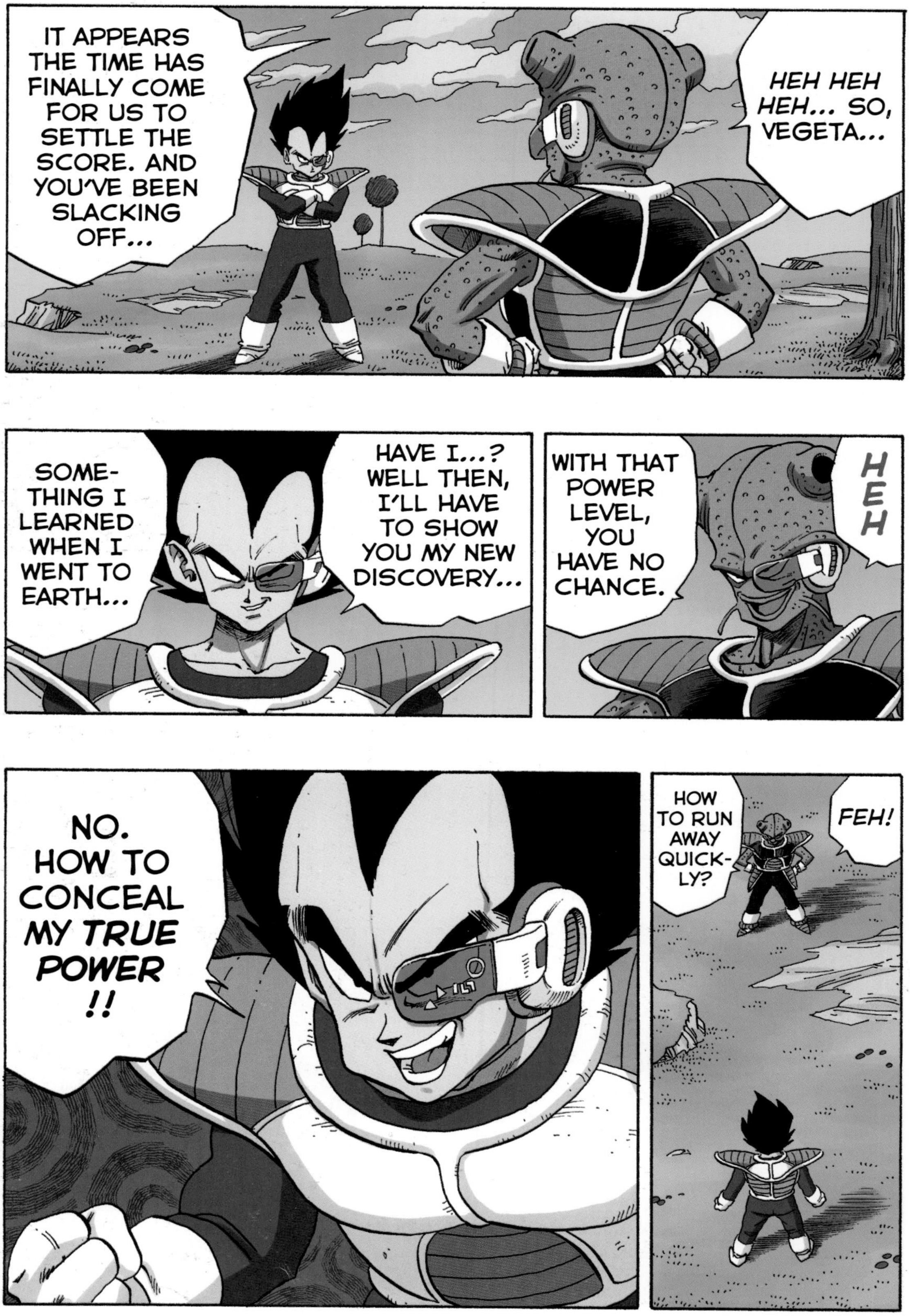
HEH HEH HEH... SO, VEGETA...
IT APPEARS THE TIME HAS FINALLY COME FOR US TO SETTLE THE SCORE. AND YOU'VE BEEN SLACKING OFF...
HEH HEH
WITH THAT POWER LEVEL, YOU HAVE NO CHANCE.
HAVE I...? WELL THEN, I'LL HAVE TO SHOW YOU MY NEW DISCOVERY...
SOME-THING I LEARNED WHEN I WENT TO EARTH...
FEH!
HOW TO RUN AWAY QUICK-LY?
NO. HOW TO CONCEAL MY TRUE POWER!!

Chapter 4 • Vegeta's True Power!

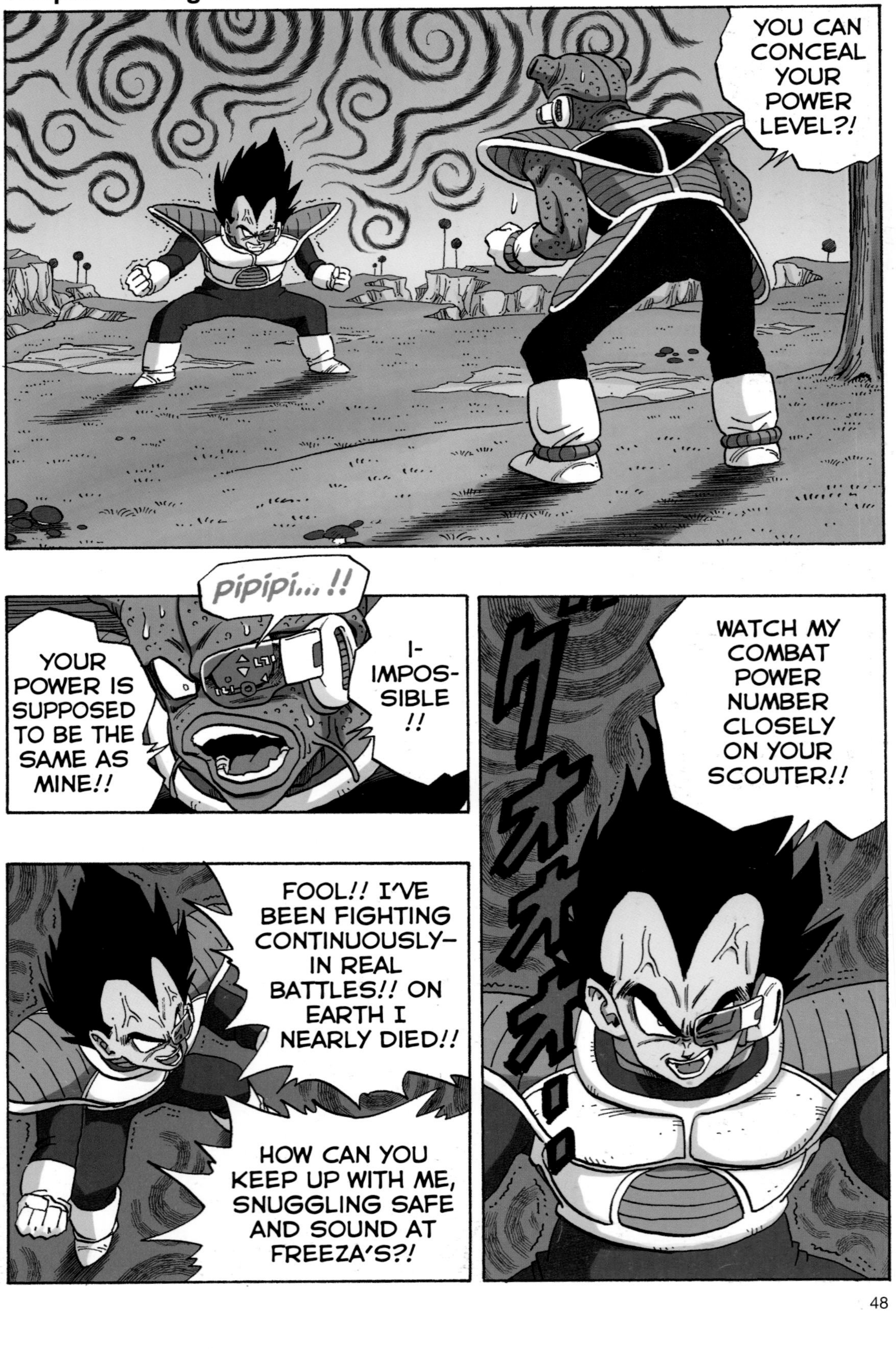

YOU CAN CONCEAL YOUR POWER LEVEL?!
WATCH MY COMBAT POWER NUMBER CLOSELY ON YOUR SCOUTER!!
pipipi...!!
I- IMPOS- SIBLE!!
YOUR POWER IS SUPPOSED TO BE THE SAME AS MINE!!
FOOL!! I'VE BEEN FIGHTING CONTINUOUSLY— IN REAL BATTLES!! ON EARTH I NEARLY DIED!!
HOW CAN YOU KEEP UP WITH ME, SNUGGLING SAFE AND SOUND AT FREEZA'S?!

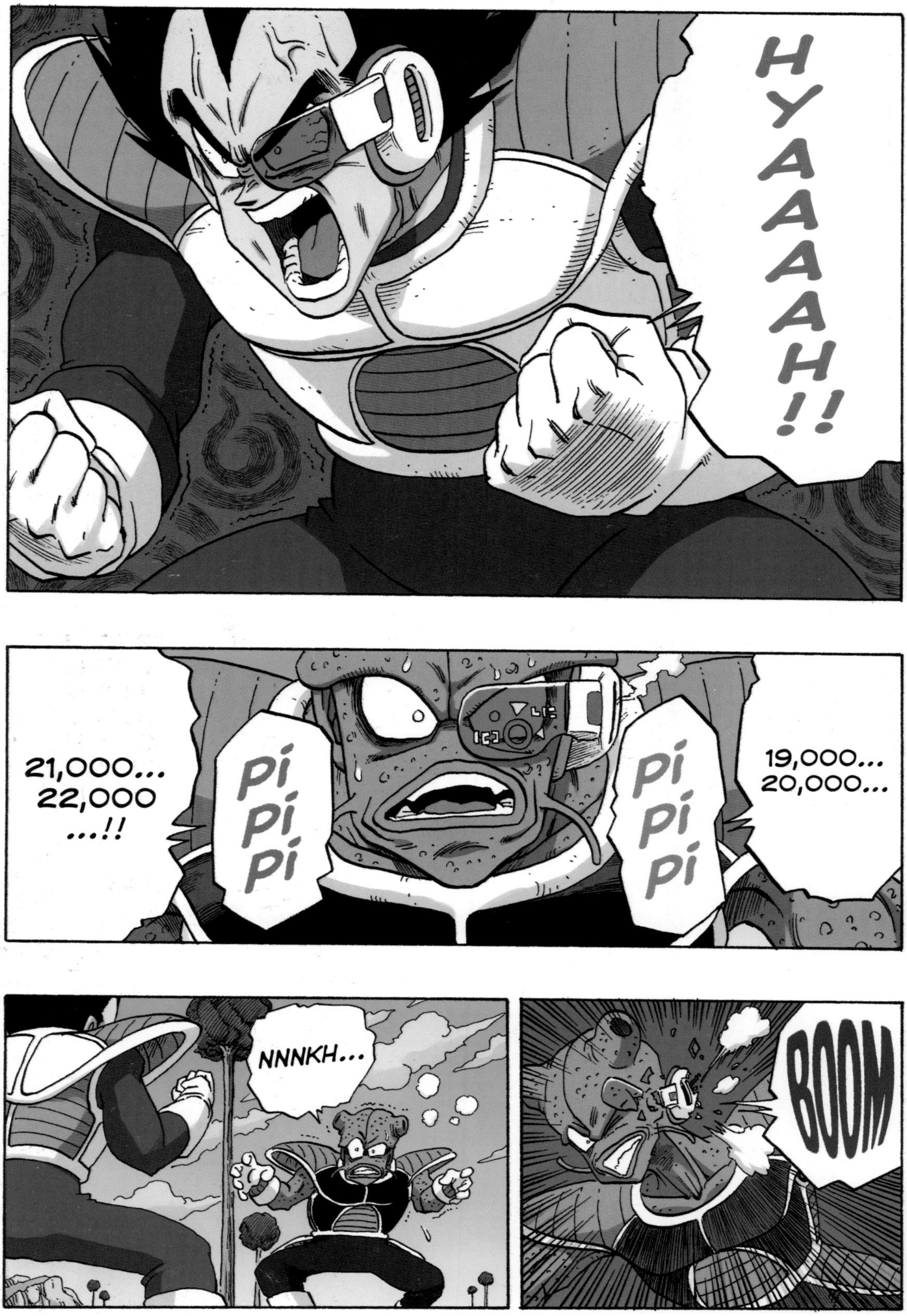
HYAAAAH!!
19,000... 20,000...
Pi Pi Pi
Pi Pi Pi
21,000... 22,000 ...!!
BOOM
NNNKH...

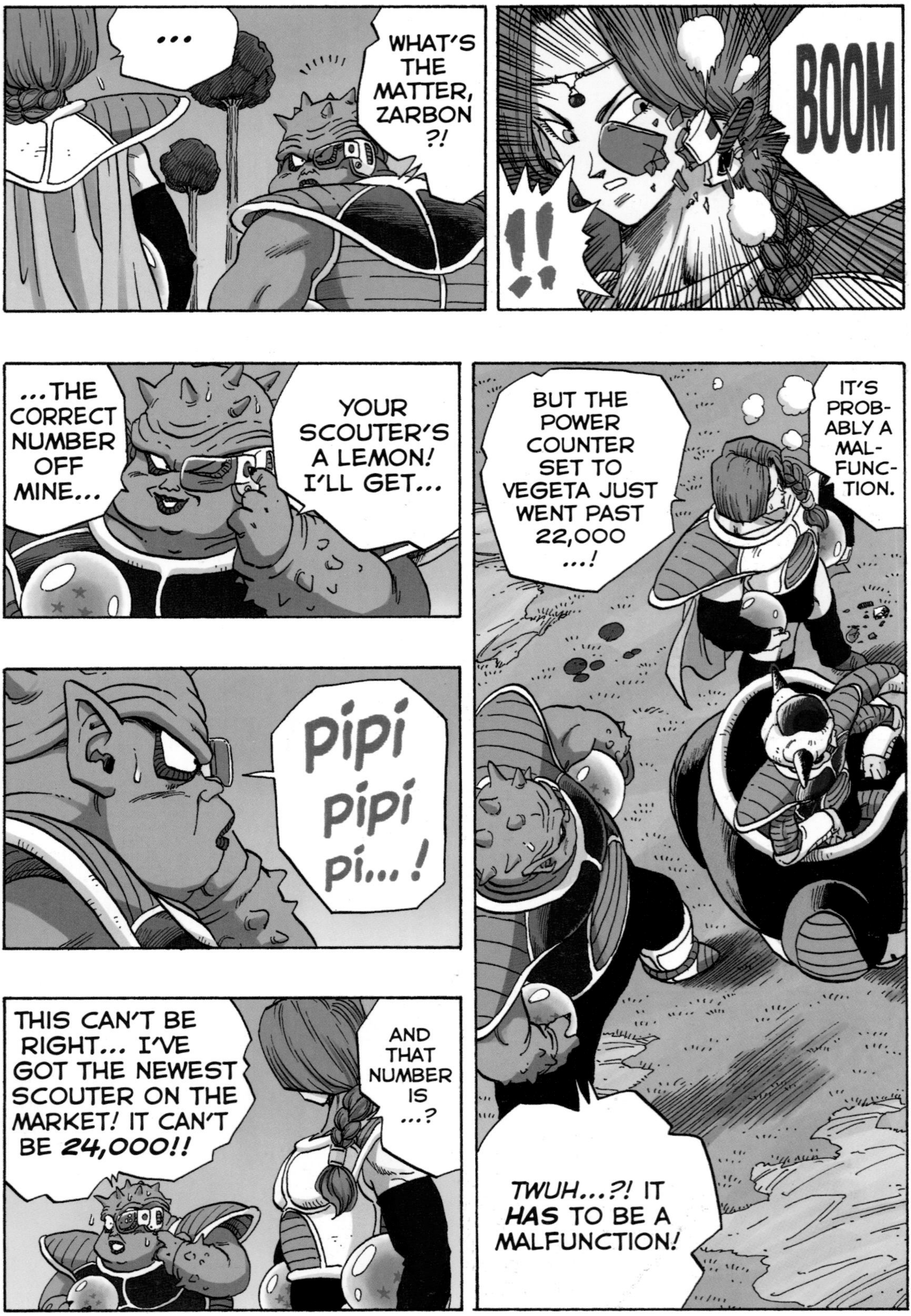
BOOM
!!
WHAT'S THE MATTER, ZARBON ?!
...
IT'S PROBABLY A MALFUNCTION.
BUT THE POWER COUNTER SET TO VEGETA JUST WENT PAST 22,000 ...!
TWUH...?! IT HAS TO BE A MALFUNCTION!
YOUR SCOUTER'S A LEMON! I'LL GET...
...THE CORRECT NUMBER OFF MINE...
pipi pipi pi...!
AND THAT NUMBER IS ...?
THIS CAN'T BE RIGHT... I'VE GOT THE NEWEST SCOUTER ON THE MARKET! IT CAN'T BE 24,000!!

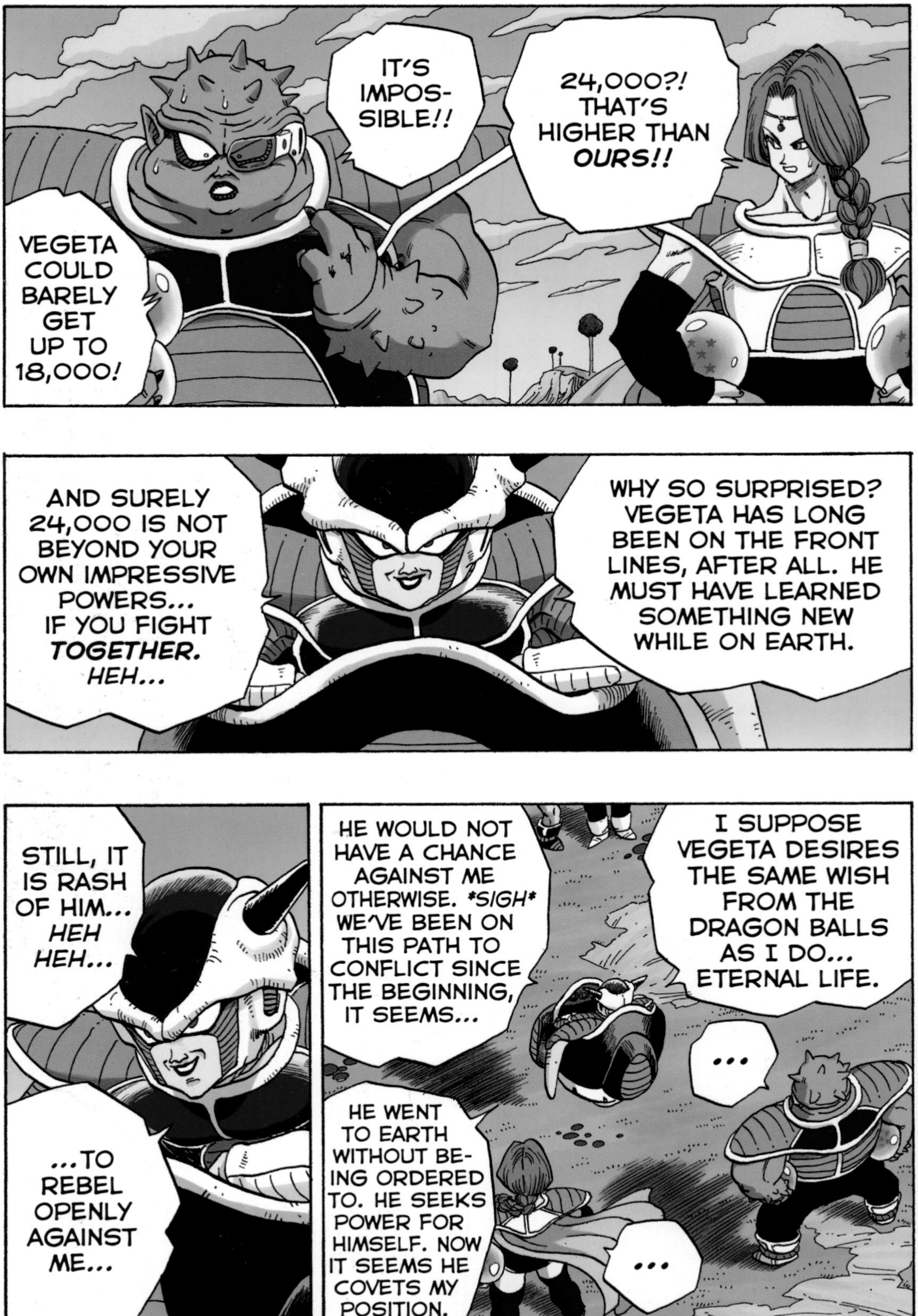
24,000?! THAT'S HIGHER THAN *OURS!!*
IT'S IMPOSSIBLE!!
VEGETA COULD BARELY GET UP TO 18,000!
WHY SO SURPRISED? VEGETA HAS LONG BEEN ON THE FRONT LINES, AFTER ALL. HE MUST HAVE LEARNED SOMETHING NEW WHILE ON EARTH.
AND SURELY 24,000 IS NOT BEYOND YOUR OWN IMPRESSIVE POWERS... IF YOU FIGHT *TOGETHER. HEH...*
I SUPPOSE VEGETA DESIRES THE SAME WISH FROM THE DRAGON BALLS AS I DO... ETERNAL LIFE.
HE WOULD NOT HAVE A CHANCE AGAINST ME OTHERWISE. *SIGH* WE'VE BEEN ON THIS PATH TO CONFLICT SINCE THE BEGINNING, IT SEEMS...
...
HE WENT TO EARTH WITHOUT BEING ORDERED TO. HE SEEKS POWER FOR HIMSELF. NOW IT SEEMS HE COVETS MY POSITION.
...
STILL, IT IS RASH OF HIM... *HEH HEH...*
...TO REBEL OPENLY AGAINST ME...

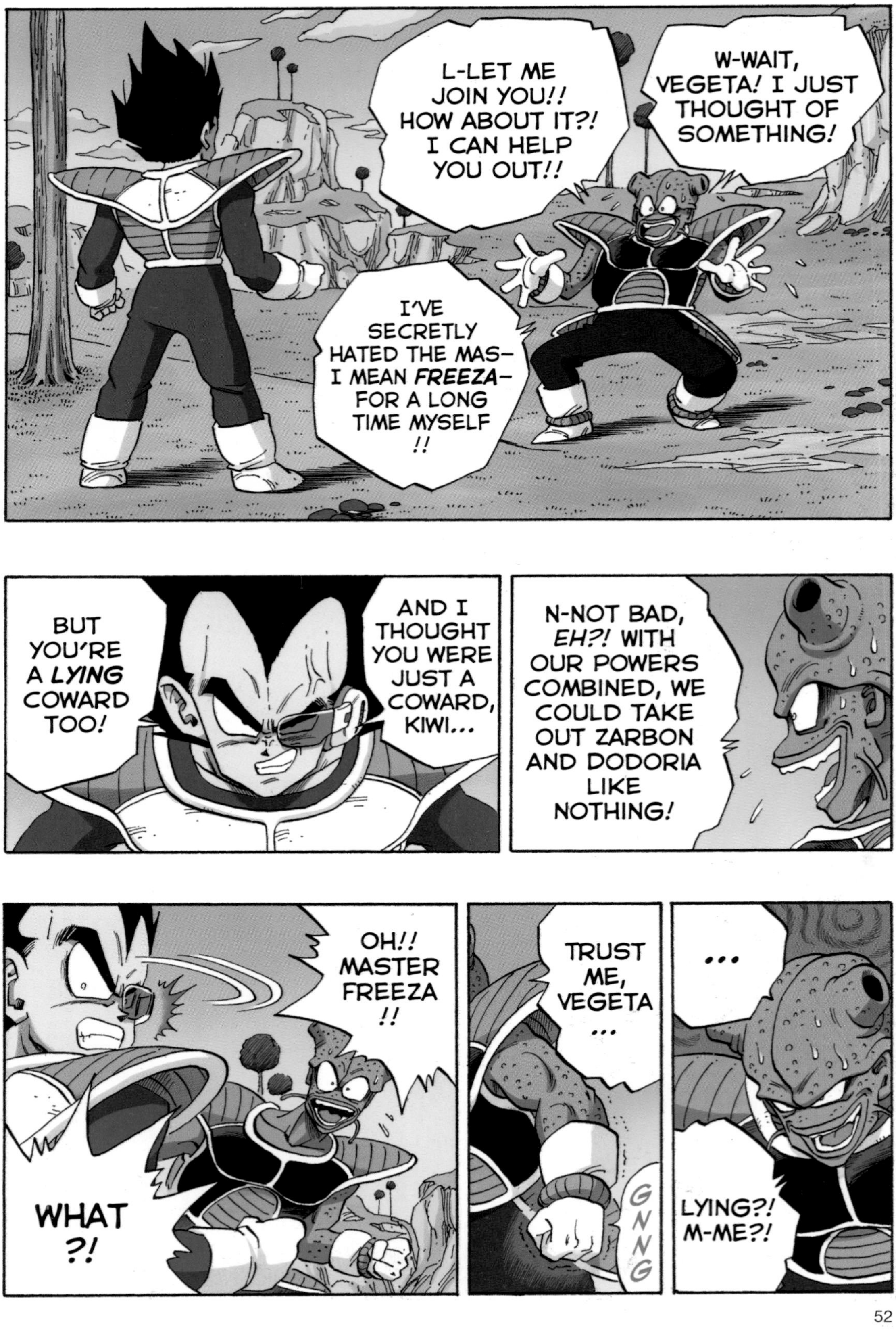
W-WAIT, VEGETA! I JUST THOUGHT OF SOMETHING!
L-LET ME JOIN YOU!! HOW ABOUT IT?! I CAN HELP YOU OUT!!
I'VE SECRETLY HATED THE MAS– I MEAN FREEZA– FOR A LONG TIME MYSELF!!
N-NOT BAD, EH?! WITH OUR POWERS COMBINED, WE COULD TAKE OUT ZARBON AND DODORIA LIKE NOTHING!
AND I THOUGHT YOU WERE JUST A COWARD, KIWI...
BUT YOU'RE A LYING COWARD TOO!
...
LYING?! M-ME?!
TRUST ME, VEGETA...
GNNG
OH!! MASTER FREEZA!!
WHAT?!

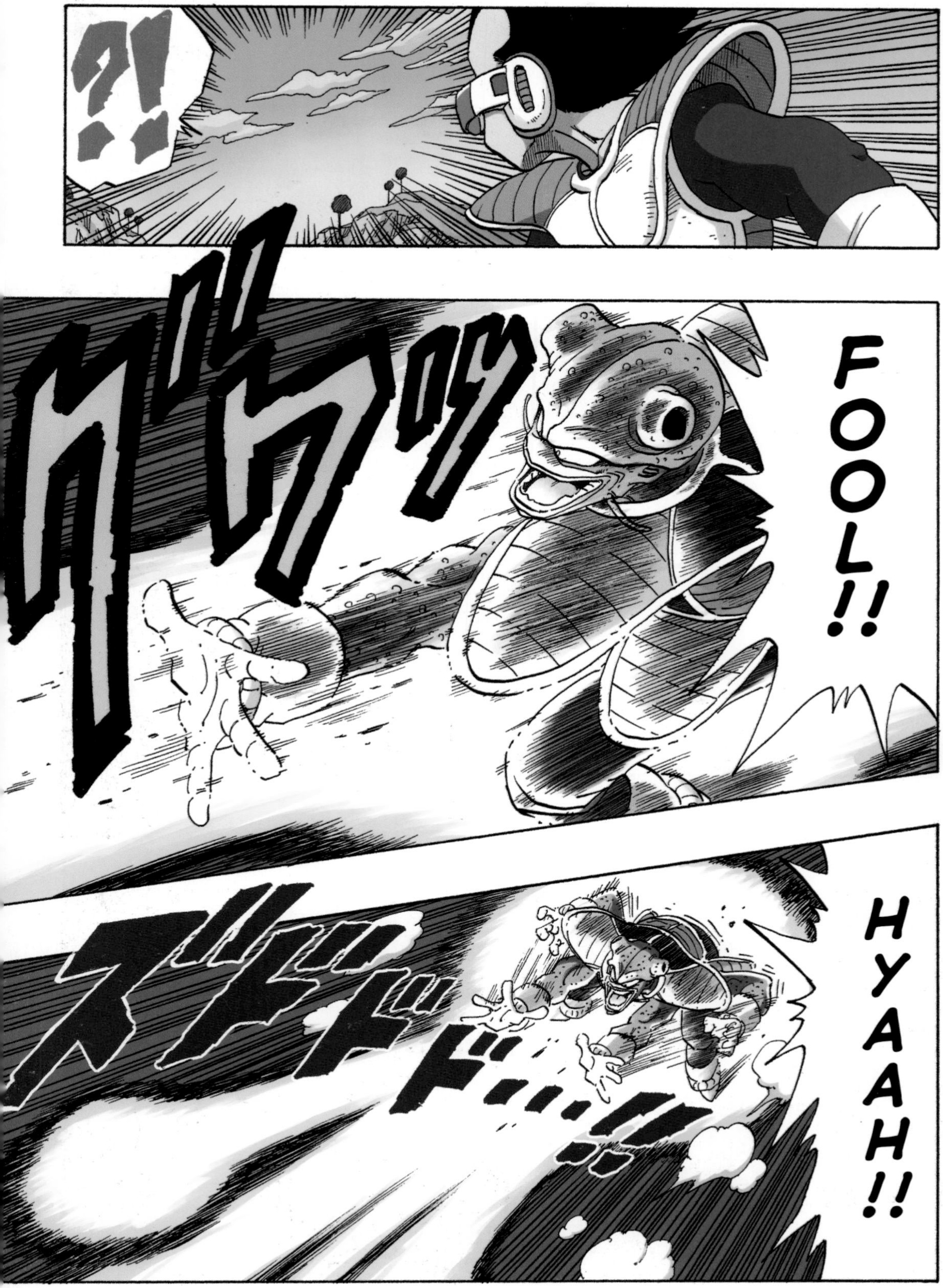
?!
FOOL!!
HYAAH!!

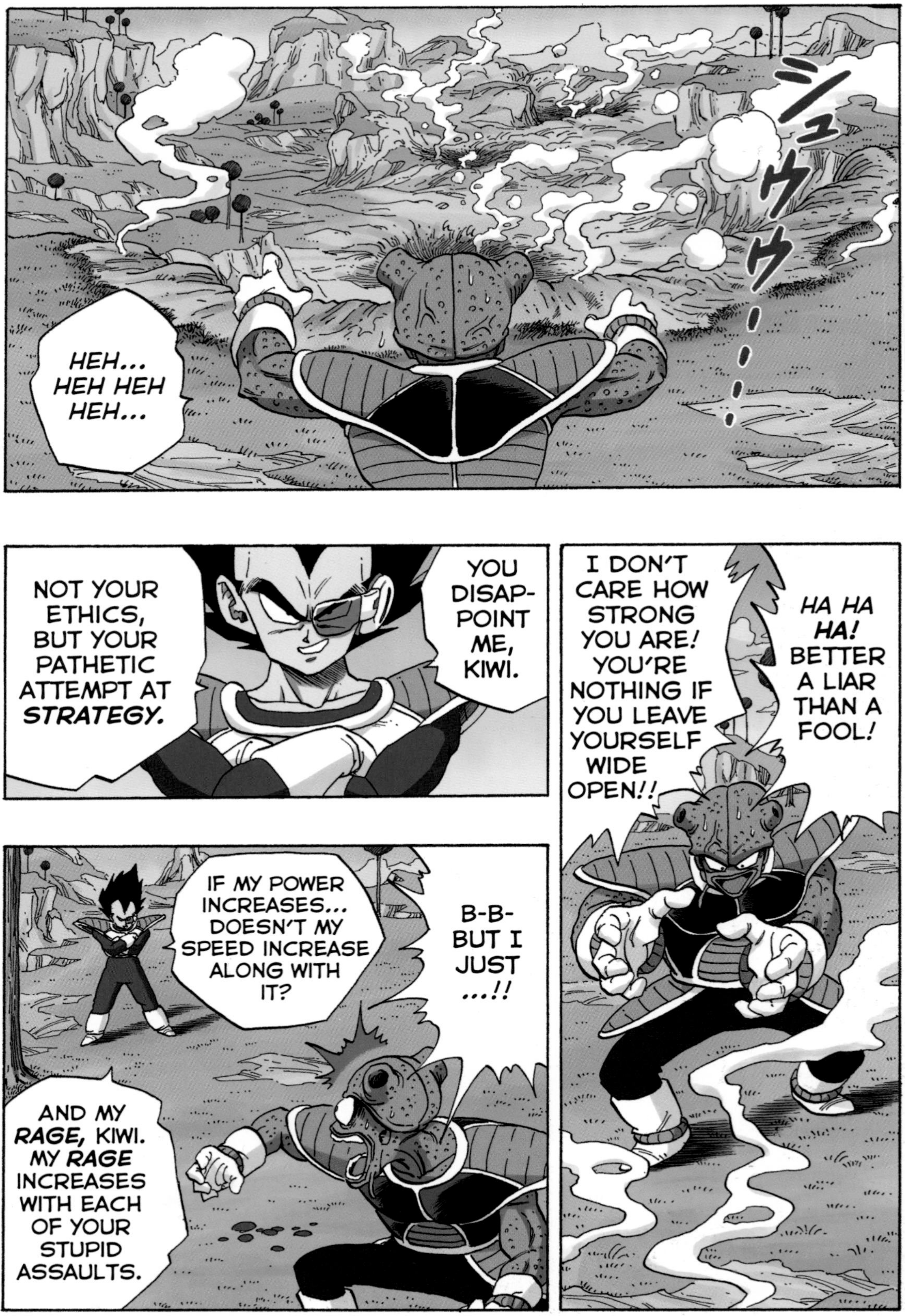
シュウウゥ・・・
HEH... HEH HEH HEH...
HA HA HA! BETTER A LIAR THAN A FOOL!
I DON'T CARE HOW STRONG YOU ARE! YOU'RE NOTHING IF YOU LEAVE YOURSELF WIDE OPEN!!
YOU DISAPPOINT ME, KIWI.
NOT YOUR ETHICS, BUT YOUR PATHETIC ATTEMPT AT STRATEGY.
B-B-BUT I JUST ...!!
IF MY POWER INCREASES... DOESN'T MY SPEED INCREASE ALONG WITH IT?
AND MY RAGE, KIWI. MY RAGE INCREASES WITH EACH OF YOUR STUPID ASSAULTS.

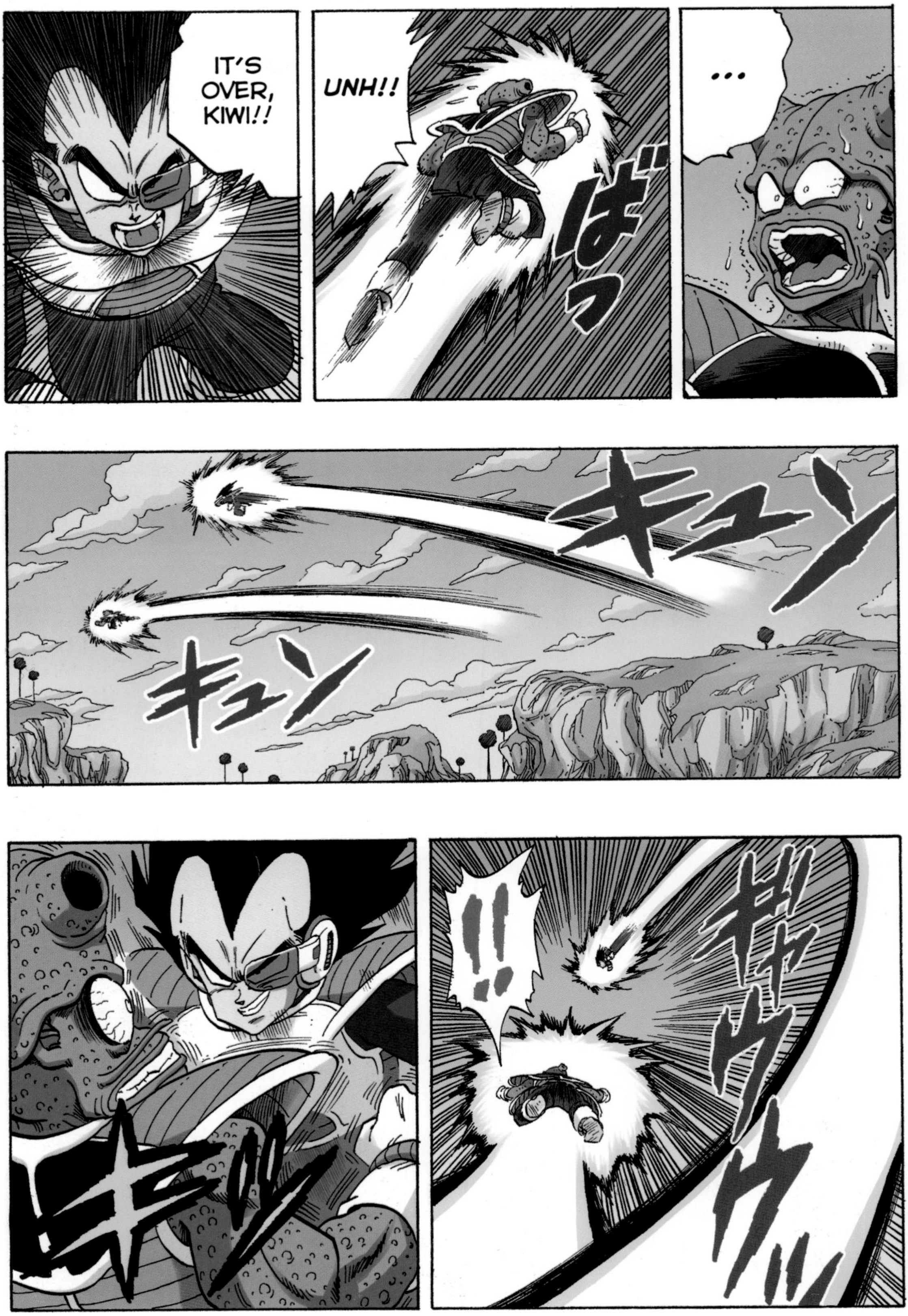
...
UNH!!
ばっ
IT'S OVER, KIWI!!
キュン
キュン
!!
ギャウウッ
キッ

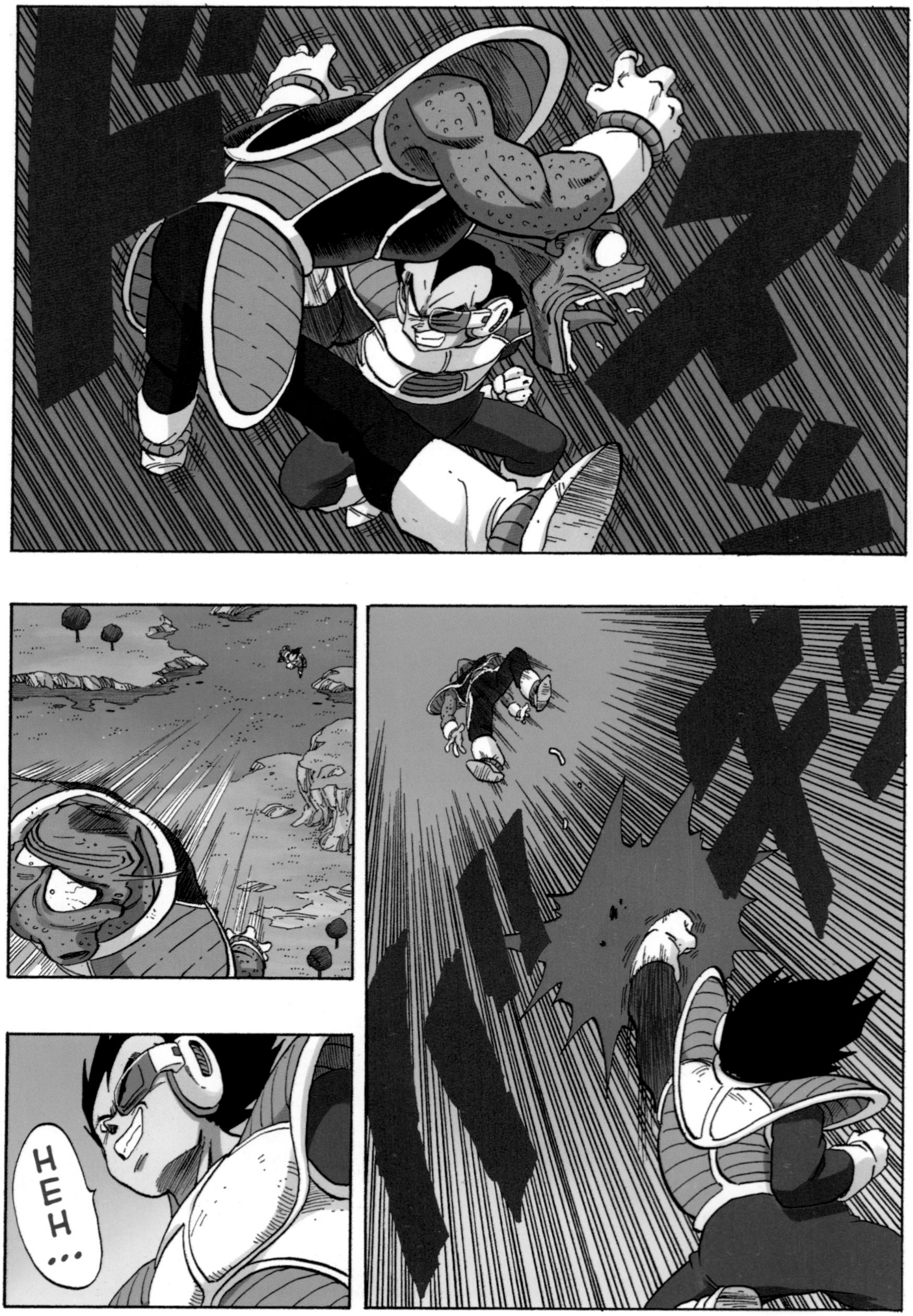
HEH...

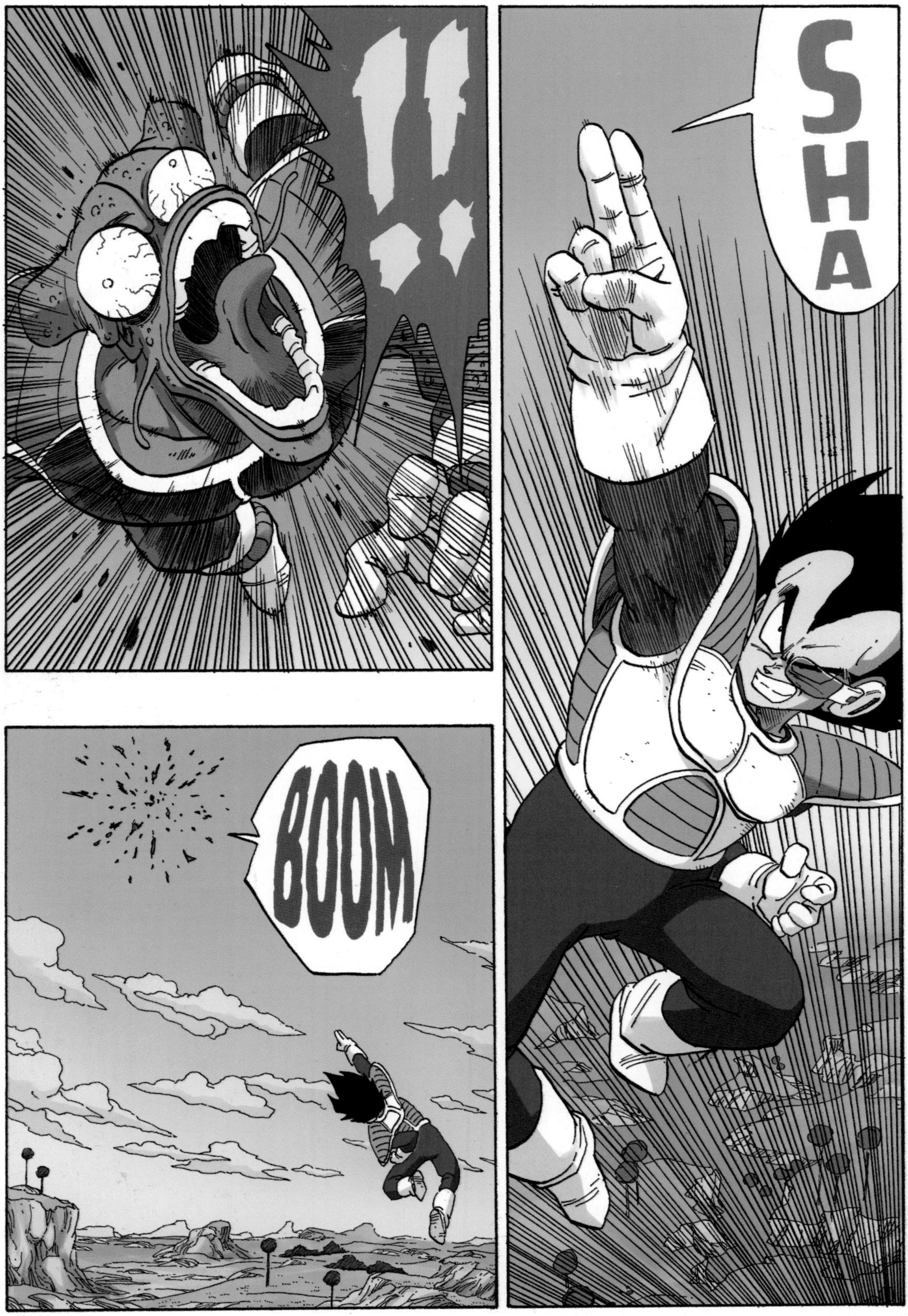
SHA
!!
BOOM

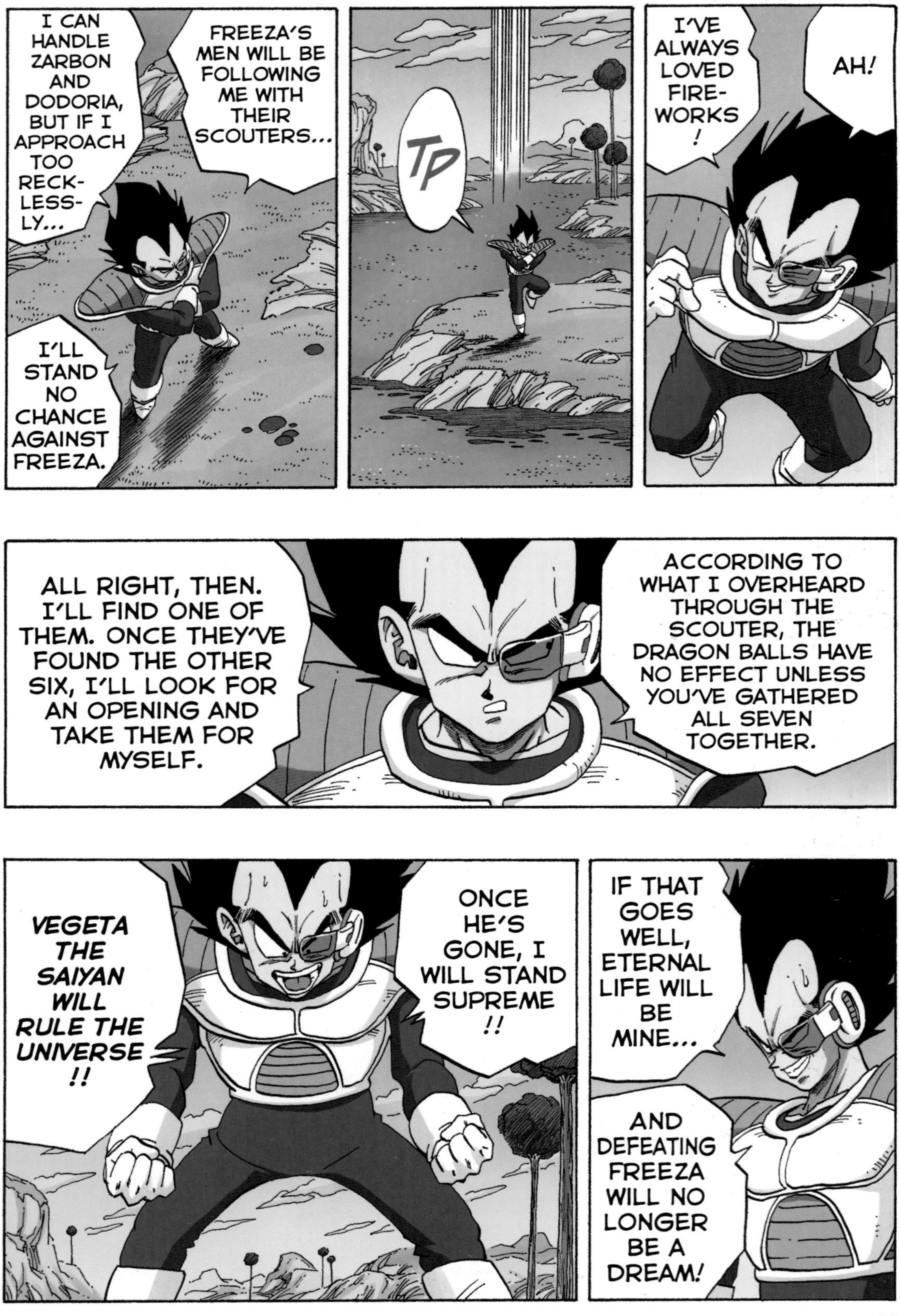
AH!
I'VE ALWAYS LOVED FIRE-WORKS!
TP
FREEZA'S MEN WILL BE FOLLOWING ME WITH THEIR SCOUTERS...
I CAN HANDLE ZARBON AND DODORIA, BUT IF I APPROACH TOO RECK-LESS-LY...
I'LL STAND NO CHANCE AGAINST FREEZA.
ACCORDING TO WHAT I OVERHEARD THROUGH THE SCOUTER, THE DRAGON BALLS HAVE NO EFFECT UNLESS YOU'VE GATHERED ALL SEVEN TOGETHER.
ALL RIGHT, THEN. I'LL FIND ONE OF THEM. ONCE THEY'VE FOUND THE OTHER SIX, I'LL LOOK FOR AN OPENING AND TAKE THEM FOR MYSELF.
IF THAT GOES WELL, ETERNAL LIFE WILL BE MINE...
AND DEFEATING FREEZA WILL NO LONGER BE A DREAM!
ONCE HE'S GONE, I WILL STAND SUPREME!!
VEGETA THE SAIYAN WILL RULE THE UNIVERSE!!

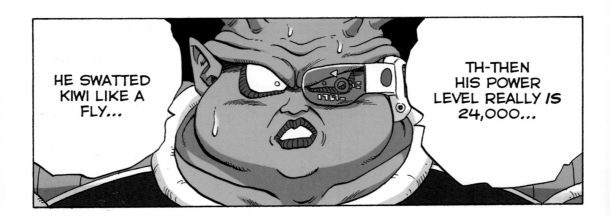

HE SWATTED KIWI LIKE A FLY...

TH-THEN HIS POWER LEVEL REALLY *IS* 24,000...

I HAVE A READING OF TEN OR SO NAMEKIANS IN THAT DIRECTION.

EXCELLENT. LET'S HOPE THEY HAVE THE DRAGON BALLS, MM?

NO MATTER. LET US GO LOOK...

...FOR THE FIFTH DRAGON BALL, SHALL WE?

THERE APPEAR TO BE OTHER STRANGE BEINGS OUT THERE...

IN THE MEANTIME, LET NONE OF US LET DOWN HIS GUARD.

LET US BE OFF!

YES, MAS-TER.

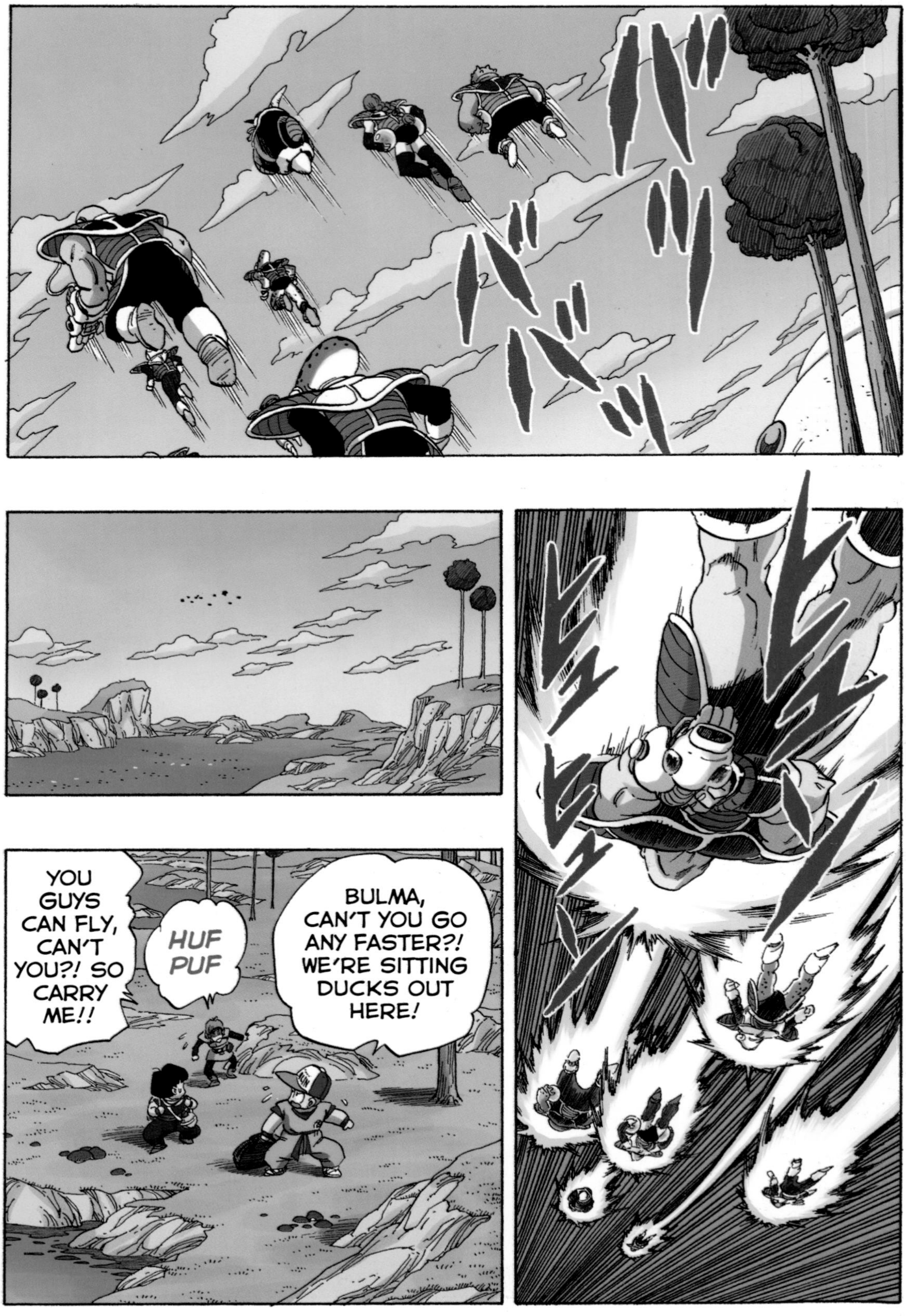
BULMA, CAN'T YOU GO ANY FASTER?! WE'RE SITTING DUCKS OUT HERE!
HUF PUF
YOU GUYS CAN FLY, CAN'T YOU?! SO CARRY ME!!

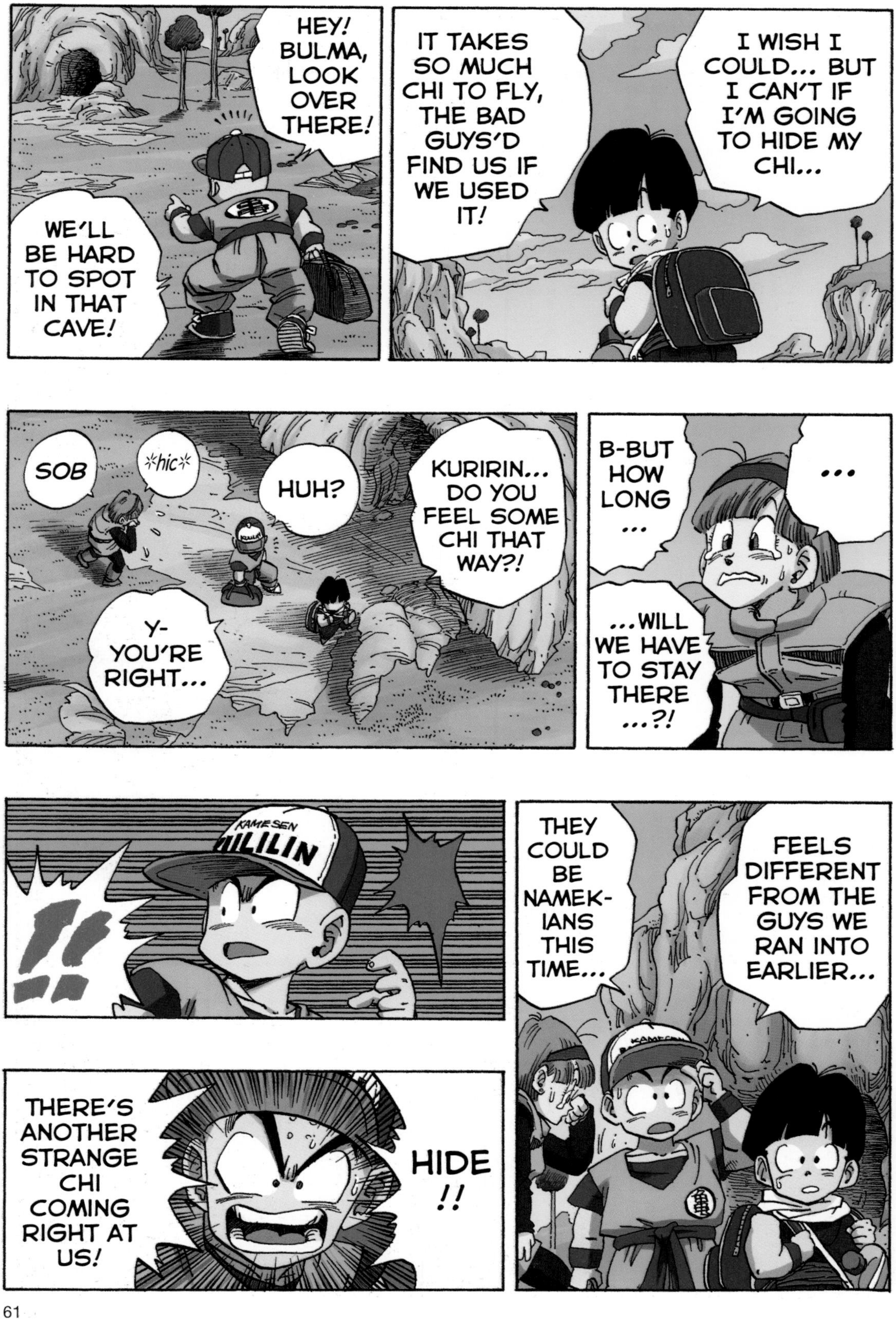
I WISH I COULD... BUT I CAN'T IF I'M GOING TO HIDE MY CHI...
IT TAKES SO MUCH CHI TO FLY, THE BAD GUYS'D FIND US IF WE USED IT!
HEY! BULMA, LOOK OVER THERE!
WE'LL BE HARD TO SPOT IN THAT CAVE!
...
B-BUT HOW LONG ...
...WILL WE HAVE TO STAY THERE ...?!
KURIRIN... DO YOU FEEL SOME CHI THAT WAY?!
HUH?
hic
SOB
Y-YOU'RE RIGHT...
FEELS DIFFERENT FROM THE GUYS WE RAN INTO EARLIER...
THEY COULD BE NAMEK-IANS THIS TIME...
KAMESEN KILILIN
!!
HIDE !!
THERE'S ANOTHER STRANGE CHI COMING RIGHT AT US!

Chapter 5 • Goku Returns! Again!

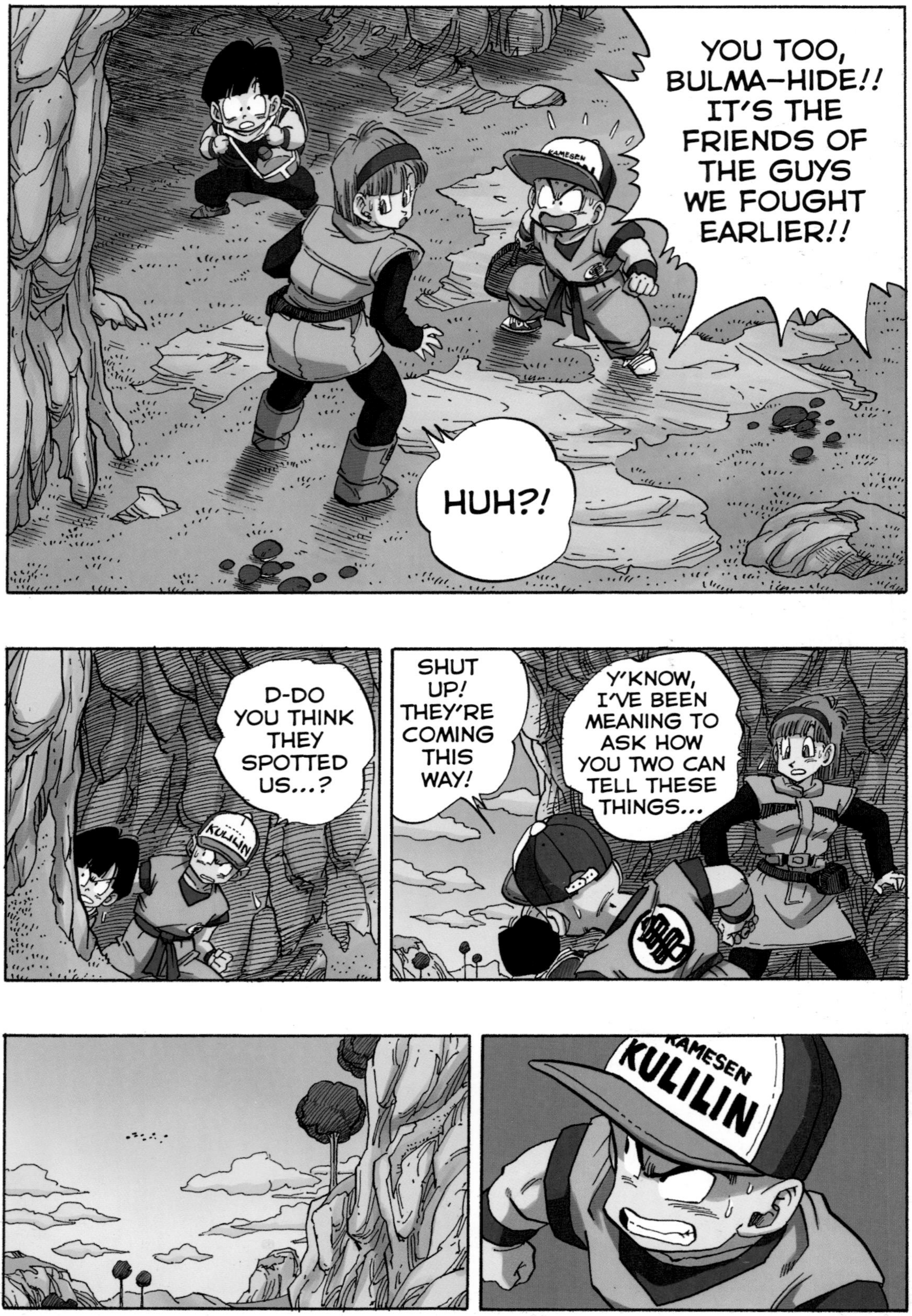
YOU TOO, BULMA-HIDE!! IT'S THE FRIENDS OF THE GUYS WE FOUGHT EARLIER!!
KAMESEN
HUH?!
Y'KNOW, I'VE BEEN MEANING TO ASK HOW YOU TWO CAN TELL THESE THINGS...
SHUT UP! THEY'RE COMING THIS WAY!
D-DO YOU THINK THEY SPOTTED US...?
KULILIN
KAMESEN KULILIN

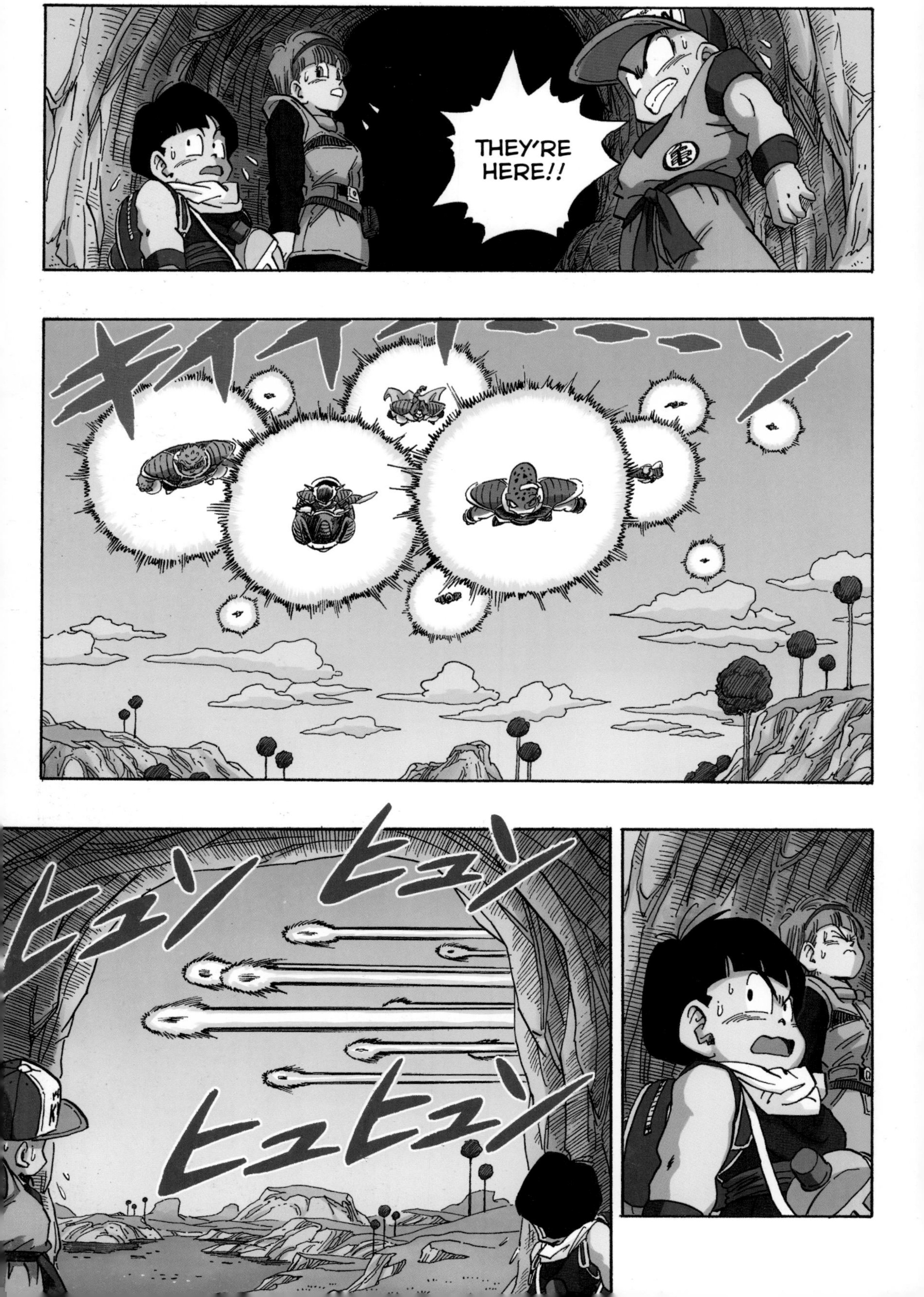
THEY'RE HERE!!
ヒュン
ヒュン
ヒュヒュン

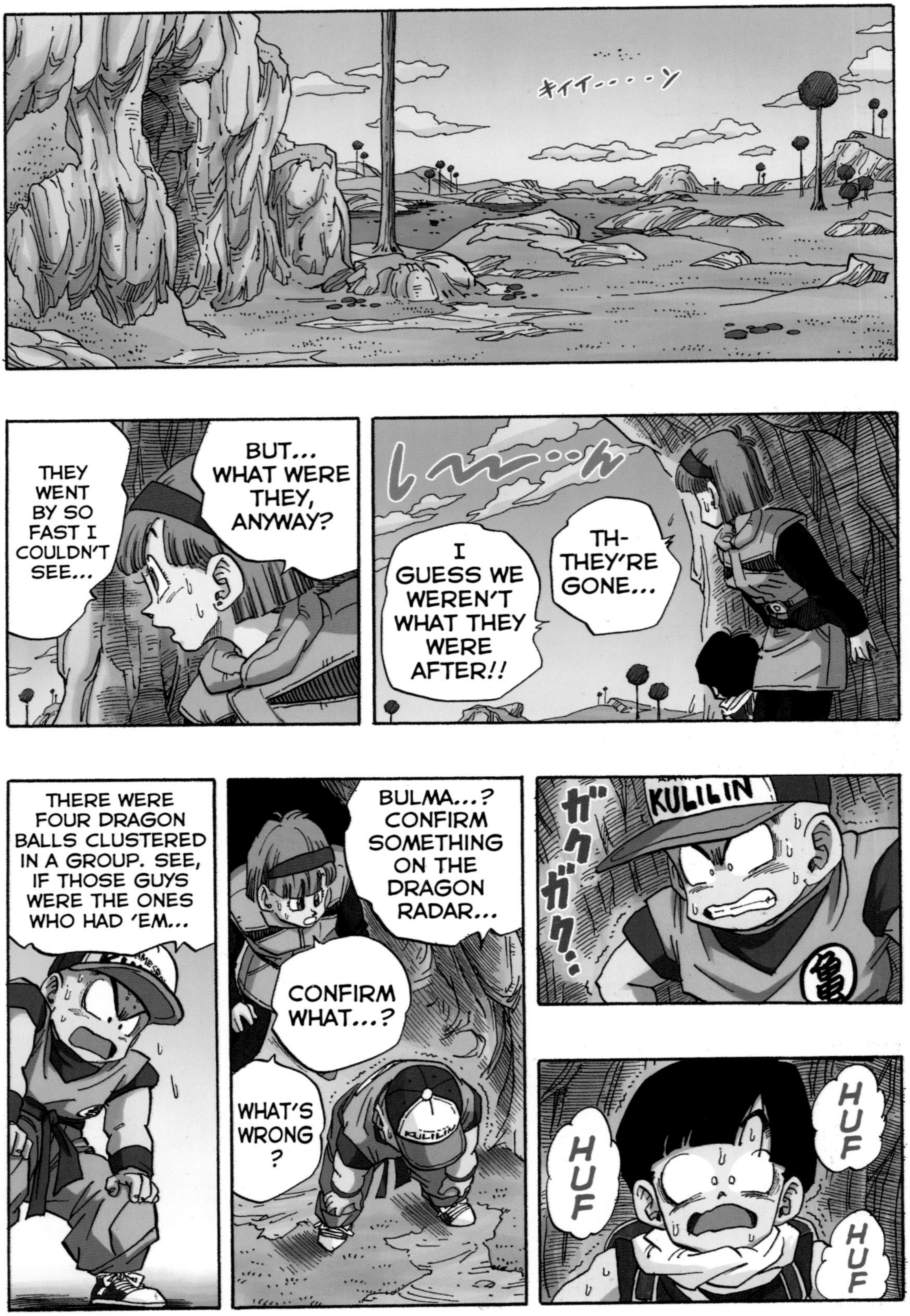
キイイー・・・ン
TH- THEY'RE GONE...
I GUESS WE WEREN'T WHAT THEY WERE AFTER!!
BUT... WHAT WERE THEY, ANYWAY?
THEY WENT BY SO FAST I COULDN'T SEE...
ガクガク・・
HUF
HUF
HUF
HUF
BULMA...? CONFIRM SOMETHING ON THE DRAGON RADAR...
CONFIRM WHAT...?
WHAT'S WRONG?
THERE WERE FOUR DRAGON BALLS CLUSTERED IN A GROUP. SEE, IF THOSE GUYS WERE THE ONES WHO HAD 'EM...

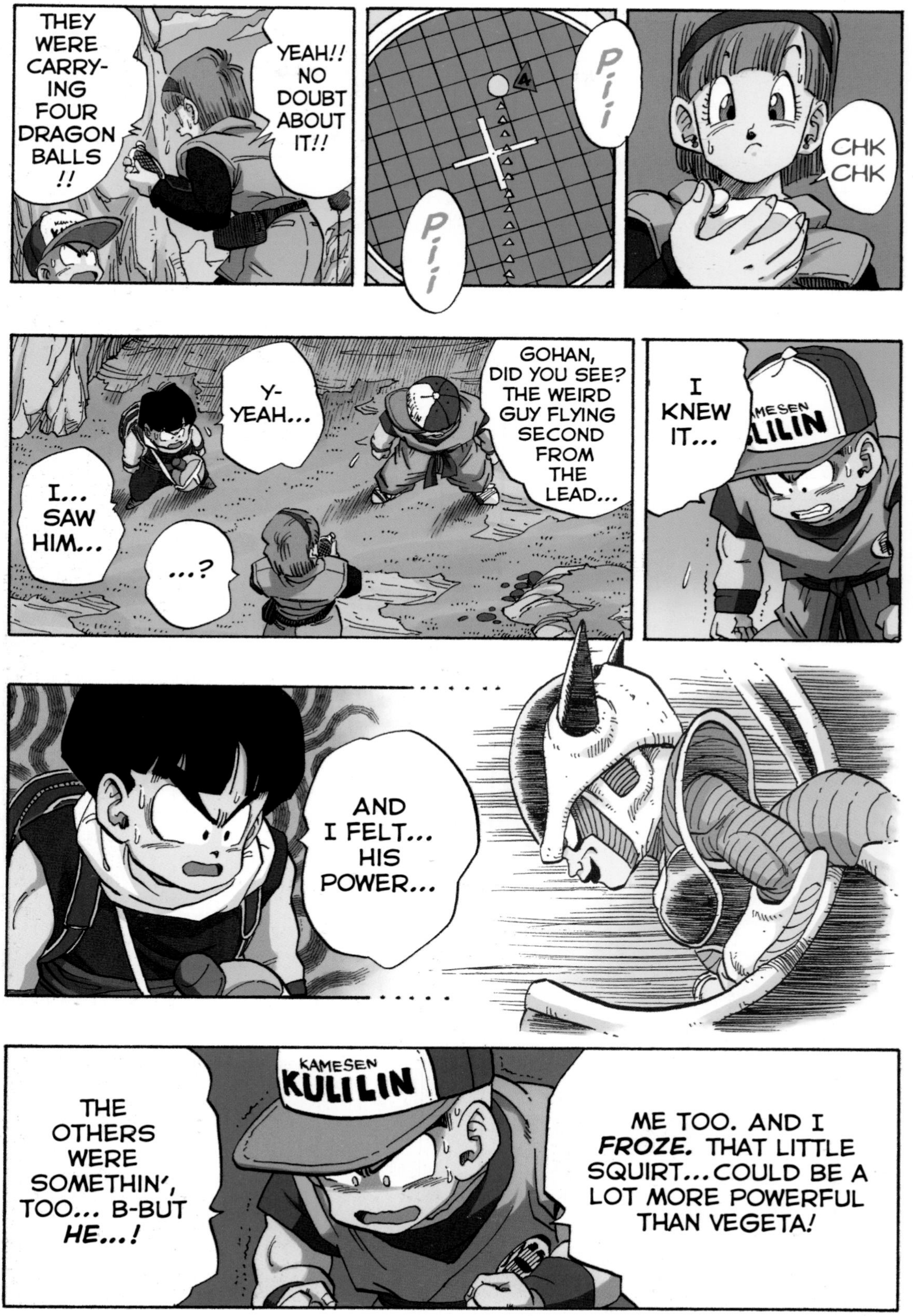
CHK CHK
Pii
Pii
YEAH!! NO DOUBT ABOUT IT!!
THEY WERE CARRYING FOUR DRAGON BALLS!!
I KNEW IT...
KAMESEN KULILIN
GOHAN, DID YOU SEE? THE WEIRD GUY FLYING SECOND FROM THE LEAD...
Y-YEAH...
I... SAW HIM...
...?
AND I FELT... HIS POWER...
KAMESEN KULILIN
ME TOO. AND I *FROZE.* THAT LITTLE SQUIRT...COULD BE A LOT MORE POWERFUL THAN VEGETA!
THE OTHERS WERE SOMETHIN', TOO... B-BUT *HE*...!

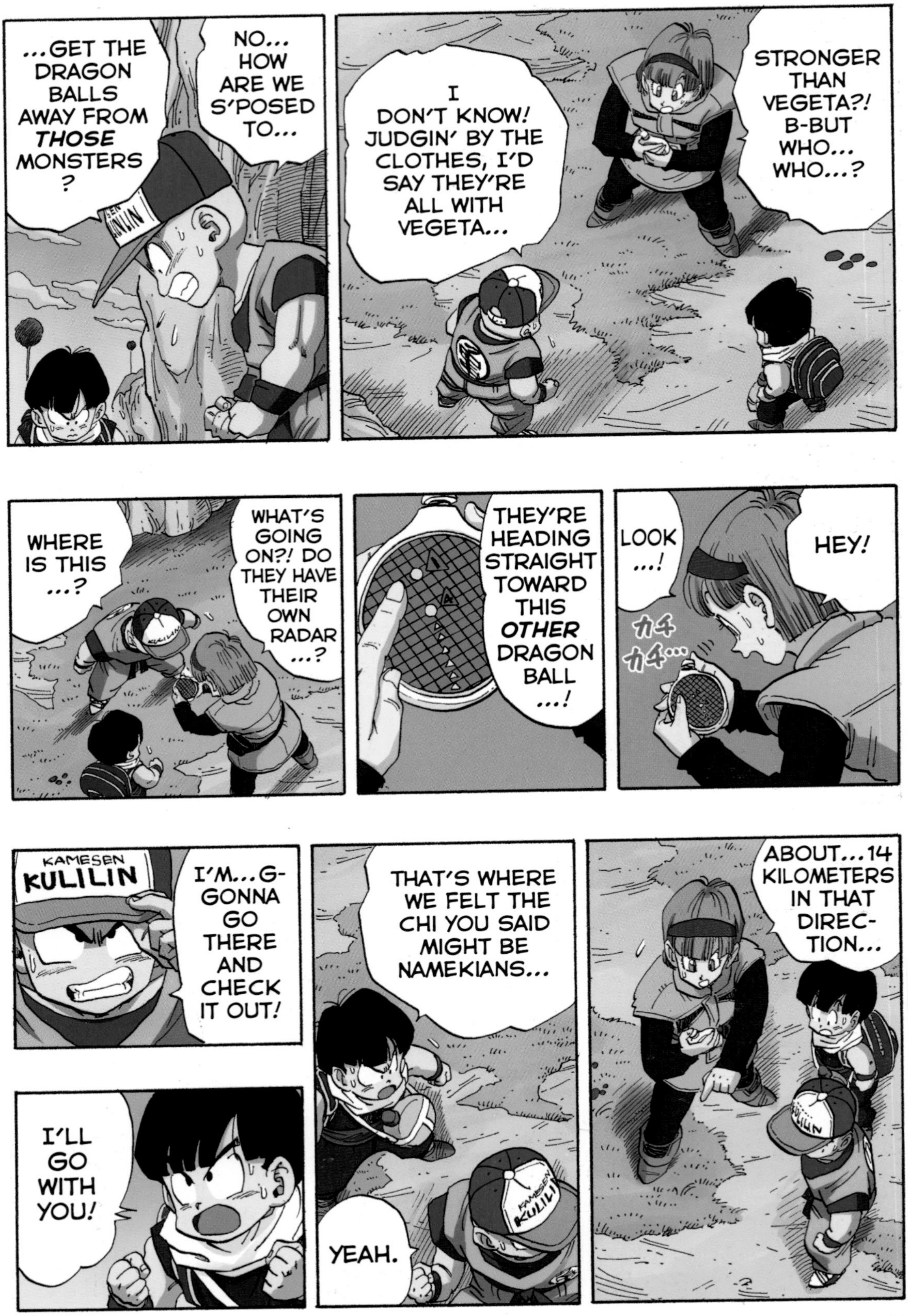
STRONGER THAN VEGETA?! B-BUT WHO... WHO...?
I DON'T KNOW! JUDGIN' BY THE CLOTHES, I'D SAY THEY'RE ALL WITH VEGETA...
NO... HOW ARE WE S'POSED TO...
...GET THE DRAGON BALLS AWAY FROM *THOSE* MONSTERS?
HEY!
LOOK...!
カチ カチ...
THEY'RE HEADING STRAIGHT TOWARD THIS *OTHER* DRAGON BALL...!
WHAT'S GOING ON?! DO THEY HAVE THEIR OWN RADAR...?
WHERE IS THIS...?
ABOUT...14 KILOMETERS IN THAT DIREC-TION...
THAT'S WHERE WE FELT THE CHI YOU SAID MIGHT BE NAMEKIANS...
YEAH.
KAMESEN KULILIN
I'M...G-GONNA GO THERE AND CHECK IT OUT!
I'LL GO WITH YOU!

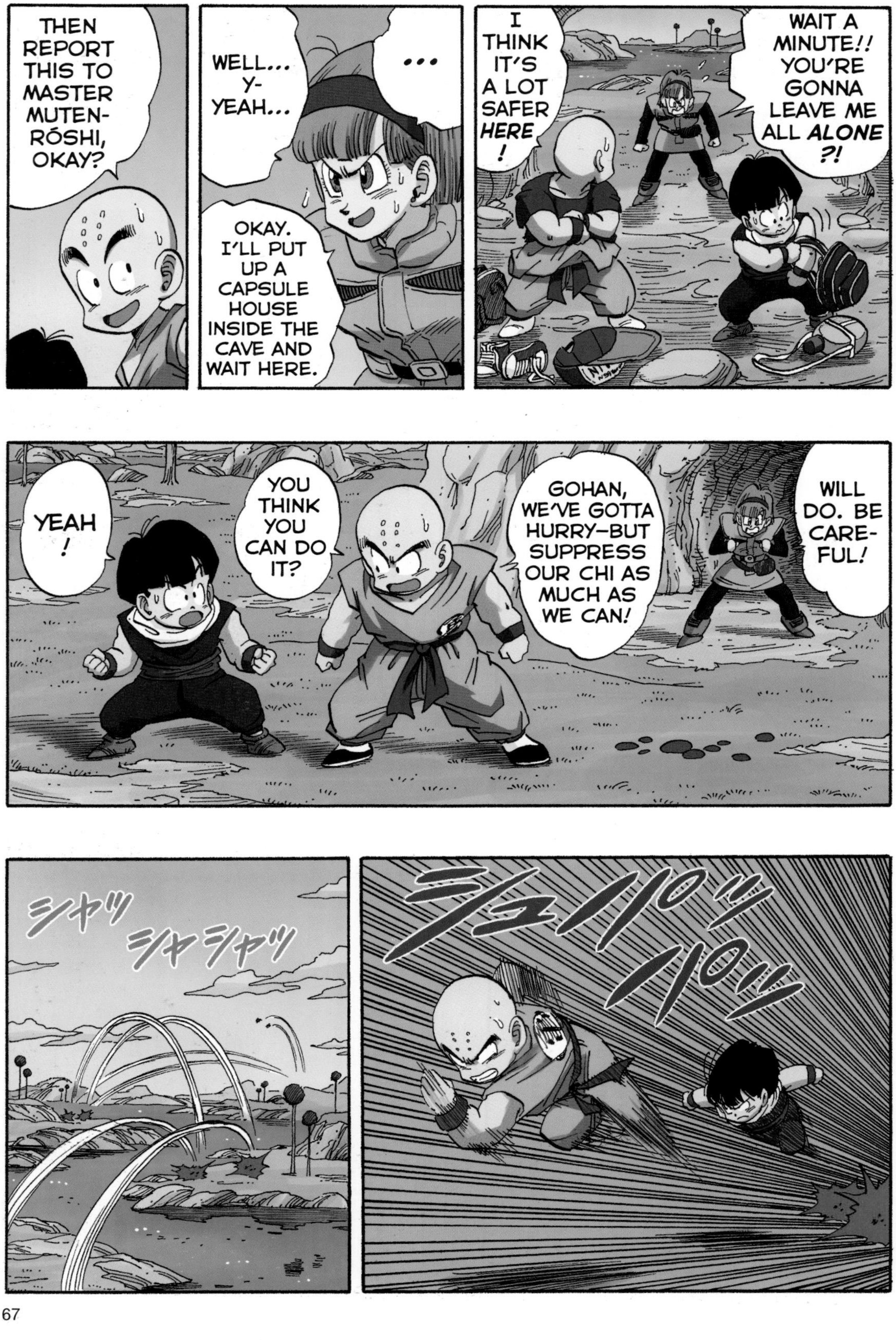
WAIT A MINUTE!! YOU'RE GONNA LEAVE ME ALL *ALONE* ?!
I THINK IT'S A LOT SAFER *HERE*!
...
WELL... Y-YEAH...
OKAY. I'LL PUT UP A CAPSULE HOUSE INSIDE THE CAVE AND WAIT HERE.
THEN REPORT THIS TO MASTER MUTEN-RÓSHI, OKAY?
WILL DO. BE CARE-FUL!
GOHAN, WE'VE GOTTA HURRY—BUT SUPPRESS OUR CHI AS MUCH AS WE CAN!
YOU THINK YOU CAN DO IT?
YEAH!
シュパッ
パッ
シャッ
シャシャッ

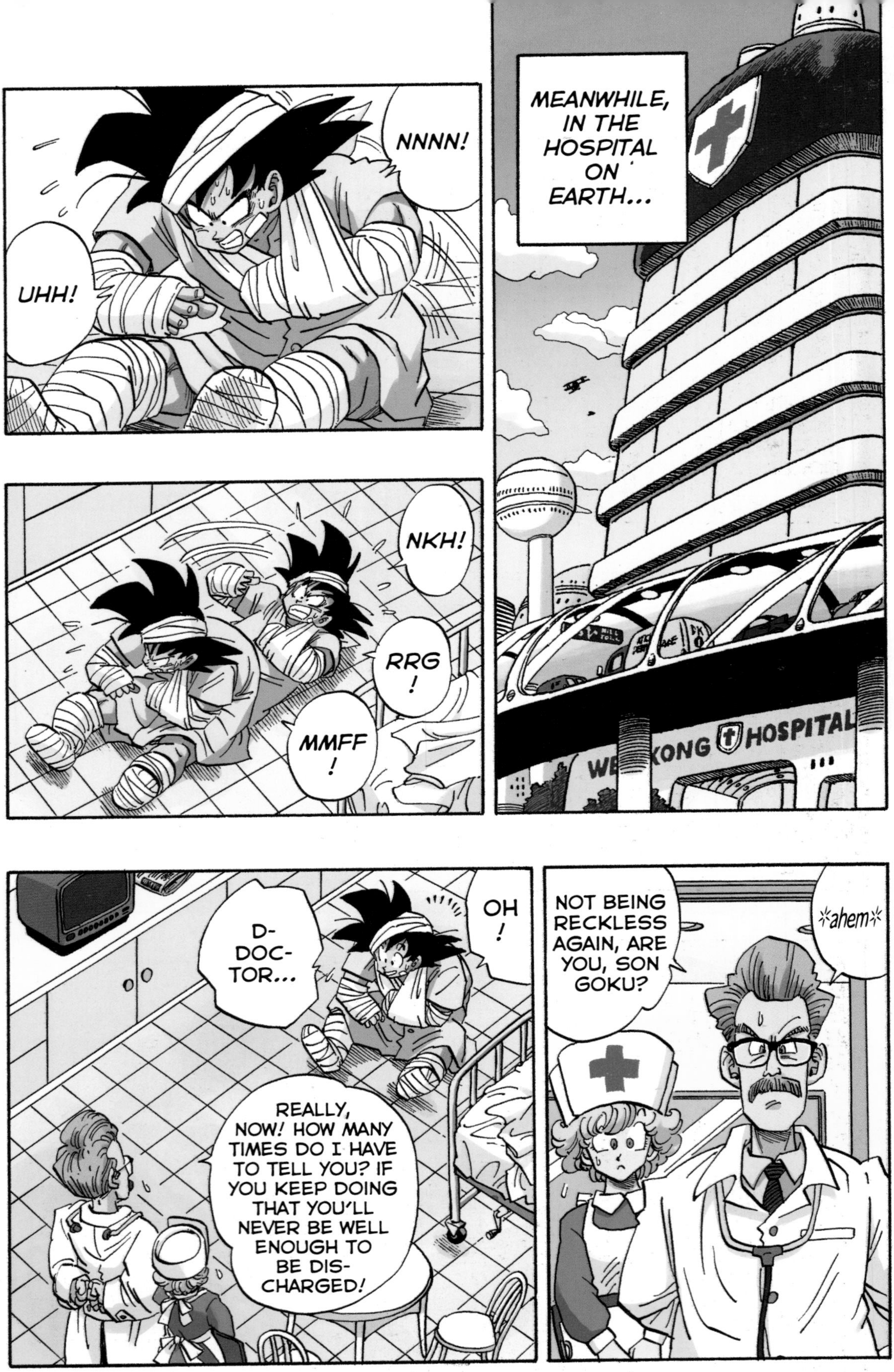
MEANWHILE, IN THE HOSPITAL ON EARTH...
NNNN!
UHH!
NKH!
RRG!
MMFF!
ahem
NOT BEING RECKLESS AGAIN, ARE YOU, SON GOKU?
OH!
D-DOCTOR...
REALLY, NOW! HOW MANY TIMES DO I HAVE TO TELL YOU? IF YOU KEEP DOING THAT YOU'LL NEVER BE WELL ENOUGH TO BE DISCHARGED!

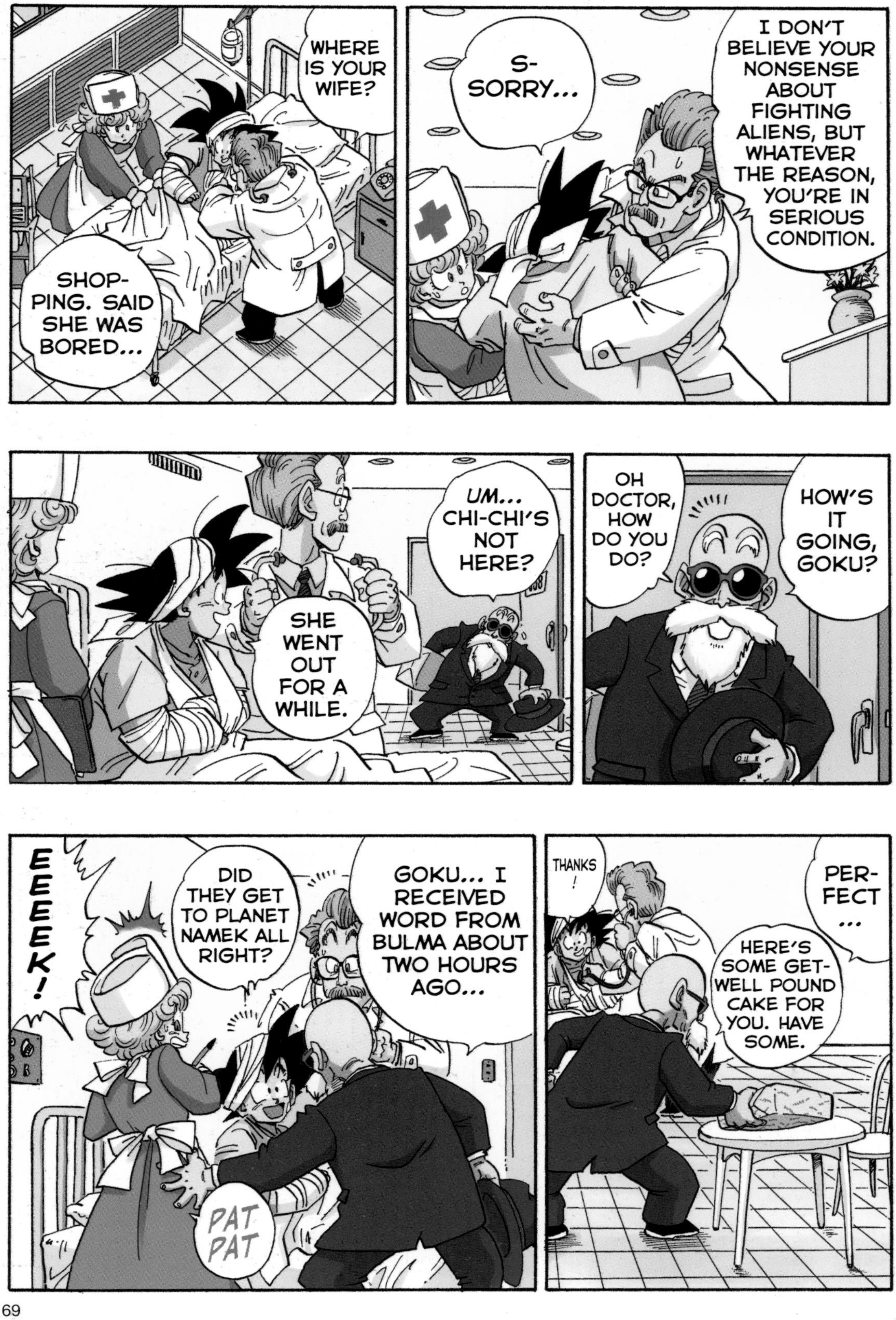
I DON'T BELIEVE YOUR NONSENSE ABOUT FIGHTING ALIENS, BUT WHATEVER THE REASON, YOU'RE IN SERIOUS CONDITION.
S-SORRY...
WHERE IS YOUR WIFE?
SHOP-PING. SAID SHE WAS BORED...
HOW'S IT GOING, GOKU?
OH DOCTOR, HOW DO YOU DO?
UM... CHI-CHI'S NOT HERE?
SHE WENT OUT FOR A WHILE.
PER-FECT...
THANKS!
HERE'S SOME GET-WELL POUND CAKE FOR YOU. HAVE SOME.
GOKU... I RECEIVED WORD FROM BULMA ABOUT TWO HOURS AGO...
DID THEY GET TO PLANET NAMEK ALL RIGHT?
EEEEEK!
PAT PAT

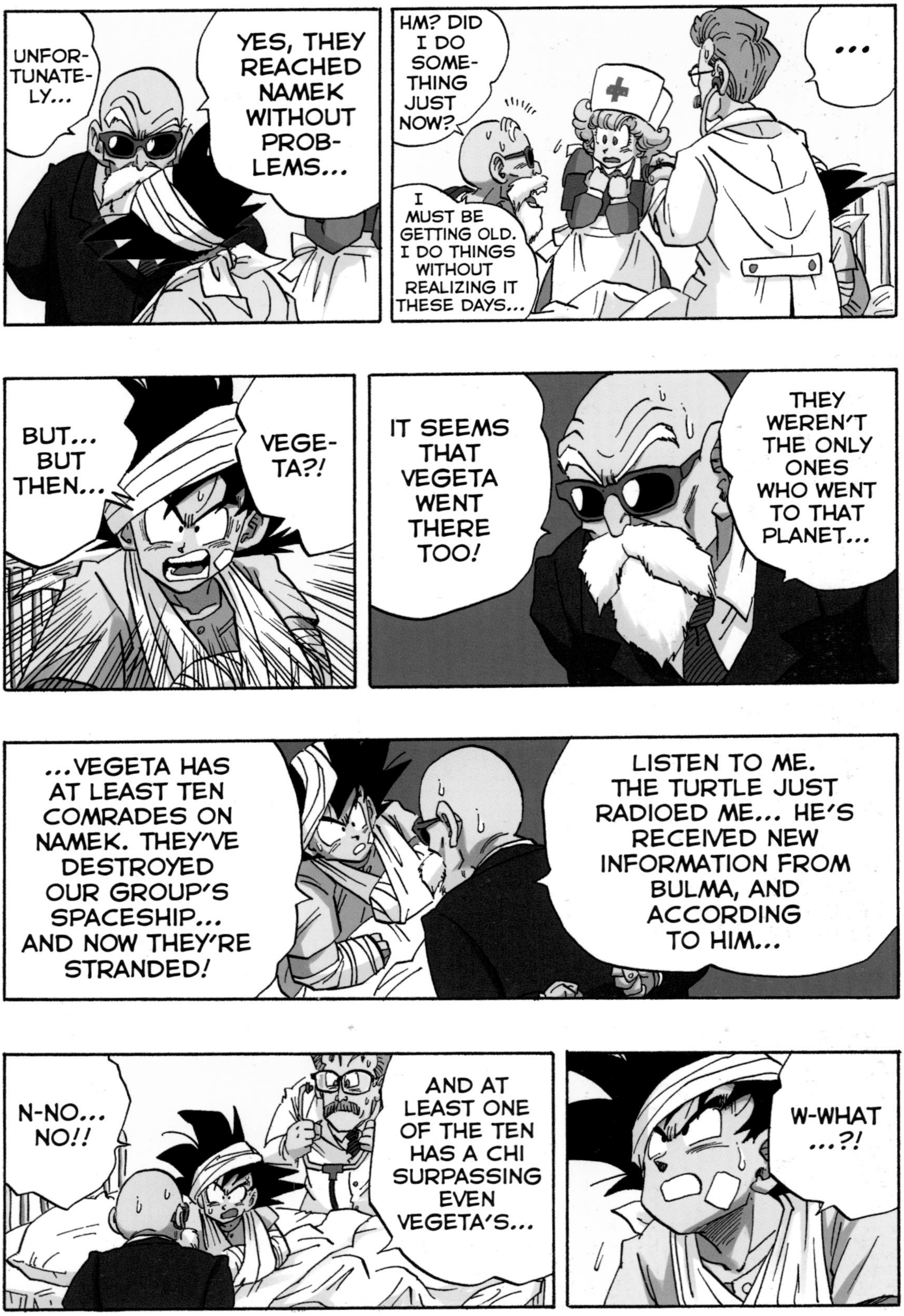
...
HM? DID I DO SOMETHING JUST NOW?
I MUST BE GETTING OLD. I DO THINGS WITHOUT REALIZING IT THESE DAYS...
YES, THEY REACHED NAMEK WITHOUT PROBLEMS...
UNFORTUNATELY...
THEY WEREN'T THE ONLY ONES WHO WENT TO THAT PLANET...
IT SEEMS THAT VEGETA WENT THERE TOO!
VEGETA?!
BUT... BUT THEN...
LISTEN TO ME. THE TURTLE JUST RADIOED ME... HE'S RECEIVED NEW INFORMATION FROM BULMA, AND ACCORDING TO HIM...
...VEGETA HAS AT LEAST TEN COMRADES ON NAMEK. THEY'VE DESTROYED OUR GROUP'S SPACESHIP... AND NOW THEY'RE STRANDED!
W-WHAT...?!
AND AT LEAST ONE OF THE TEN HAS A CHI SURPASSING EVEN VEGETA'S...
N-NO... NO!!

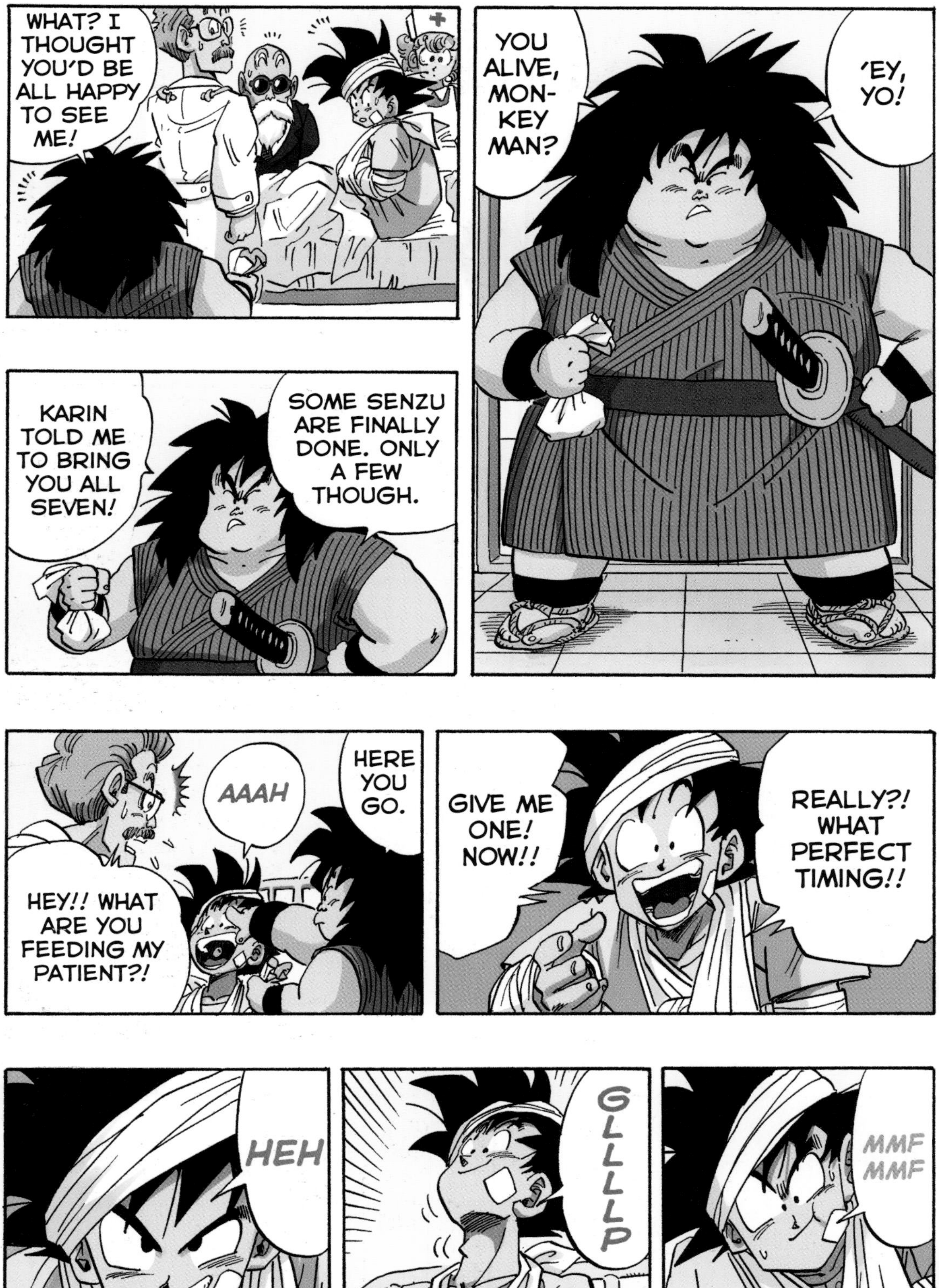
'EY, YO!
YOU ALIVE, MON-KEY MAN?
WHAT? I THOUGHT YOU'D BE ALL HAPPY TO SEE ME!
SOME SENZU ARE FINALLY DONE. ONLY A FEW THOUGH.
KARIN TOLD ME TO BRING YOU ALL SEVEN!
REALLY?! WHAT PERFECT TIMING!!
GIVE ME ONE! NOW!!
HERE YOU GO.
AAAH
HEY!! WHAT ARE YOU FEEDING MY PATIENT?!
MMF MMF
GLLLLP
HEH

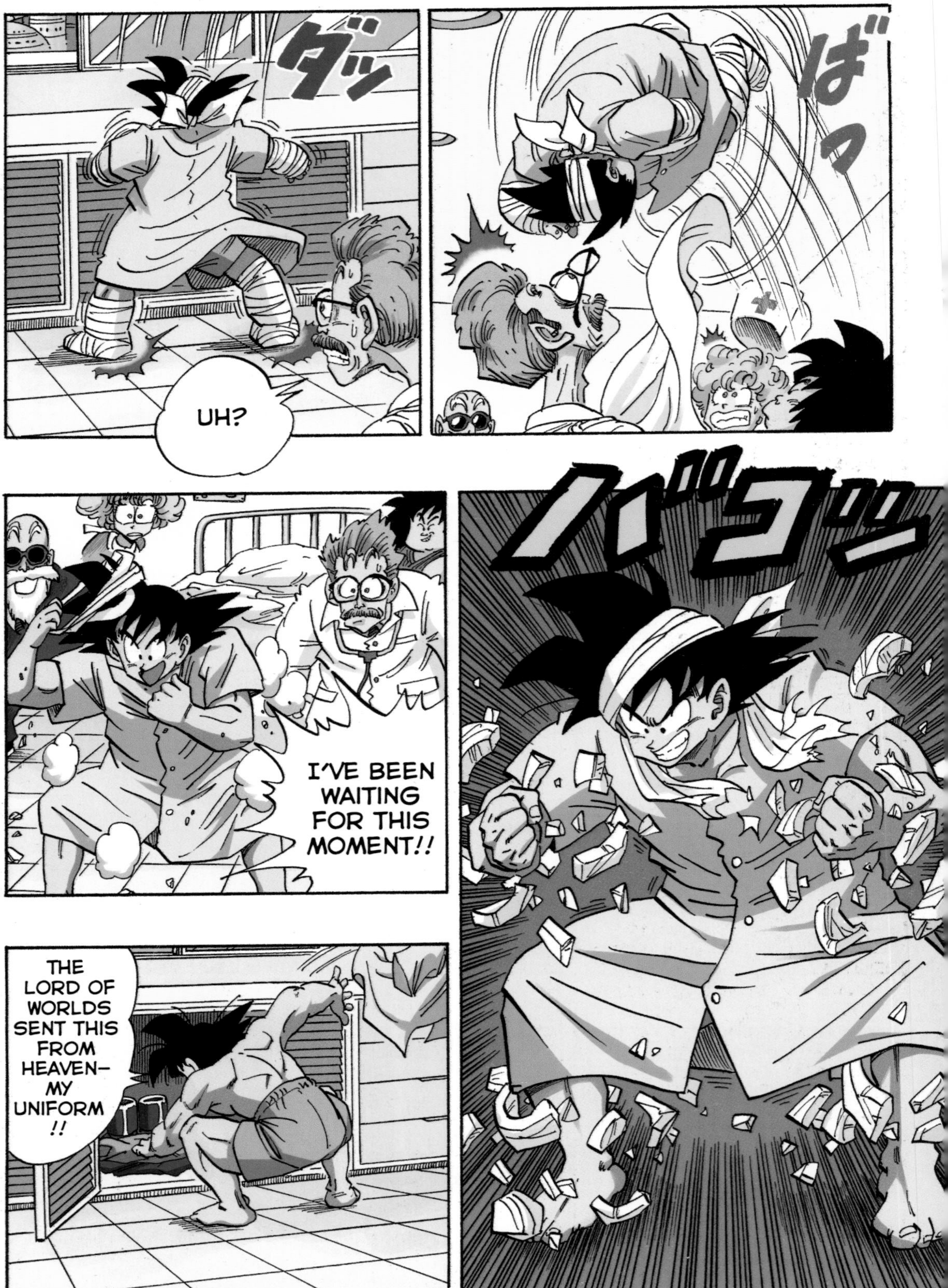

ばっ
ダッ
UH?
バゴッ
I'VE BEEN WAITING FOR THIS MOMENT!!
THE LORD OF WORLDS SENT THIS FROM HEAVEN— MY UNIFORM!!

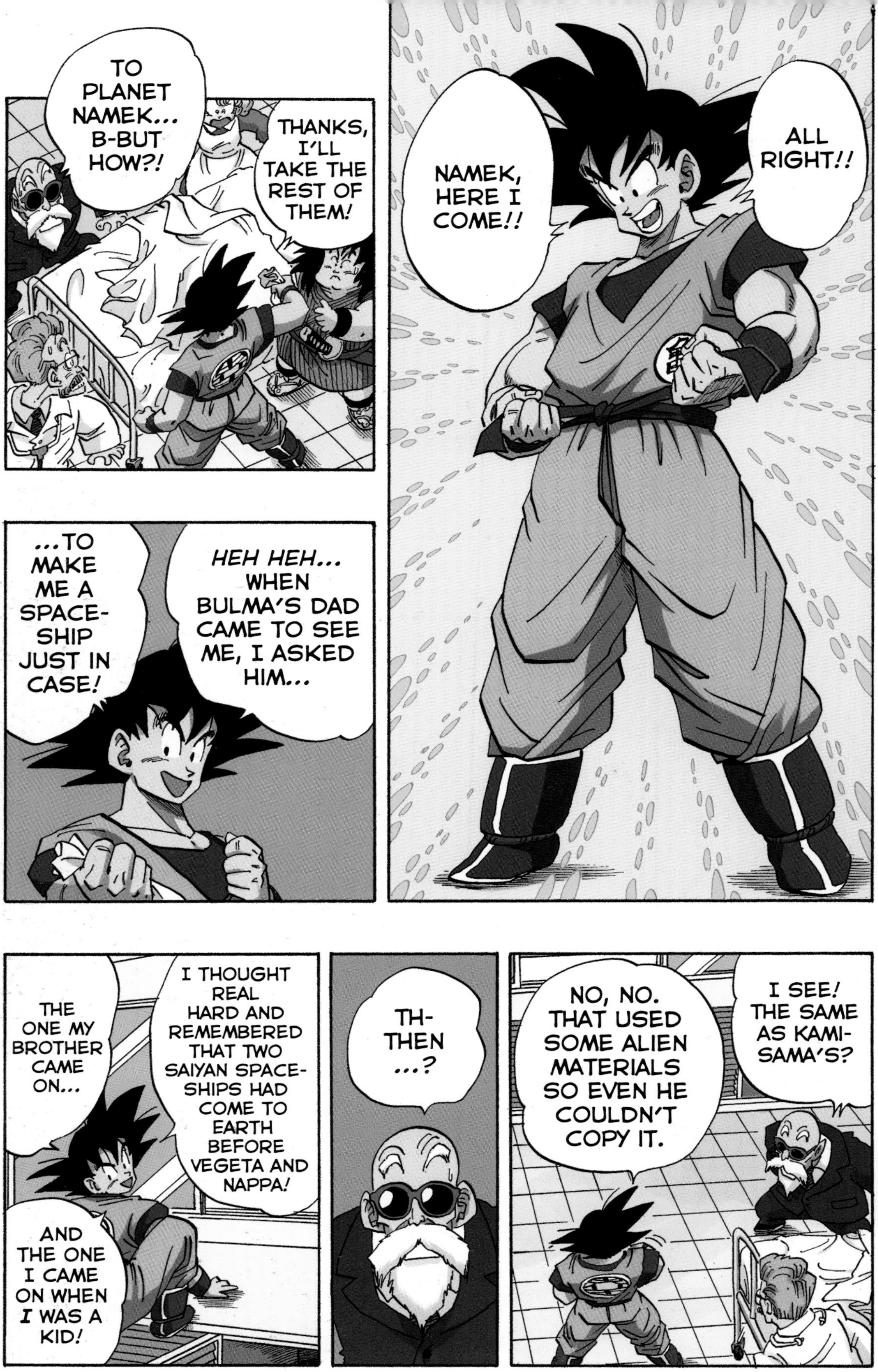
ALL RIGHT!!
NAMEK, HERE I COME!!
THANKS, I'LL TAKE THE REST OF THEM!
TO PLANET NAMEK... B-BUT HOW?!
HEH HEH... WHEN BULMA'S DAD CAME TO SEE ME, I ASKED HIM...
...TO MAKE ME A SPACE-SHIP JUST IN CASE!
I SEE! THE SAME AS KAMI-SAMA'S?
NO, NO. THAT USED SOME ALIEN MATERIALS SO EVEN HE COULDN'T COPY IT.
TH-THEN...?
I THOUGHT REAL HARD AND REMEMBERED THAT TWO SAIYAN SPACE-SHIPS HAD COME TO EARTH BEFORE VEGETA AND NAPPA!
THE ONE MY BROTHER CAME ON...
AND THE ONE I CAME ON WHEN I WAS A KID!

...I CAN GET TO PLANET NAMEK IN SIX DAYS!

WITH THAT...

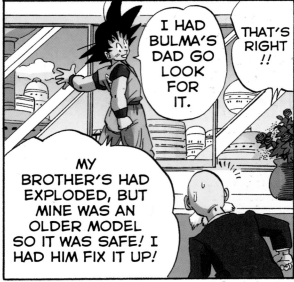

I HAD BULMA'S DAD GO LOOK FOR IT.

THAT'S RIGHT!!

MY BROTHER'S HAD EXPLODED, BUT MINE WAS AN OLDER MODEL SO IT WAS SAFE! I HAD HIM FIX IT UP!

EEEEK!!

WELL, I'M OFF TO SAVE 'EM!!

KINTO'UN!!

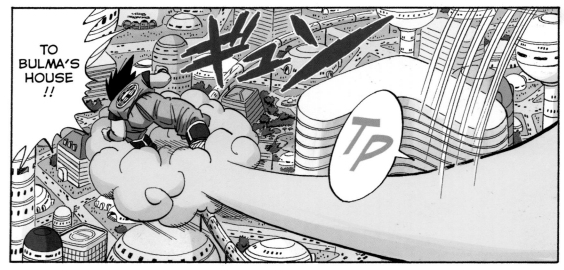

TO BULMA'S HOUSE!!

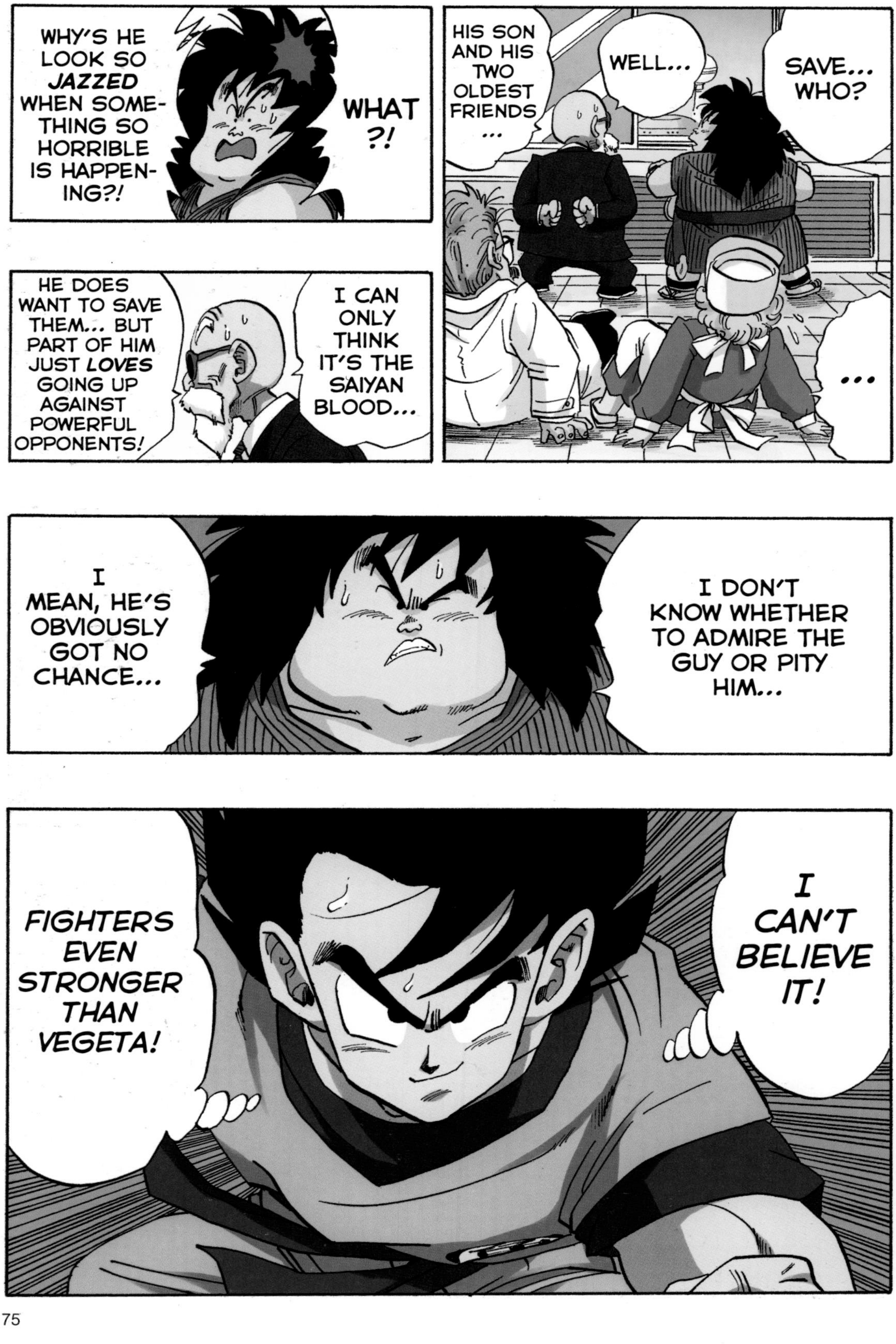

SAVE... WHO?
WELL...
HIS SON AND HIS TWO OLDEST FRIENDS ...
...
WHAT ?!
WHY'S HE LOOK SO *JAZZED* WHEN SOMETHING SO HORRIBLE IS HAPPENING?!
I CAN ONLY THINK IT'S THE SAIYAN BLOOD...
HE DOES WANT TO SAVE THEM... BUT PART OF HIM JUST *LOVES* GOING UP AGAINST POWERFUL OPPONENTS!
I DON'T KNOW WHETHER TO ADMIRE THE GUY OR PITY HIM...
I MEAN, HE'S OBVIOUSLY GOT NO CHANCE...
I CAN'T BELIEVE IT!
FIGHTERS EVEN STRONGER THAN VEGETA!

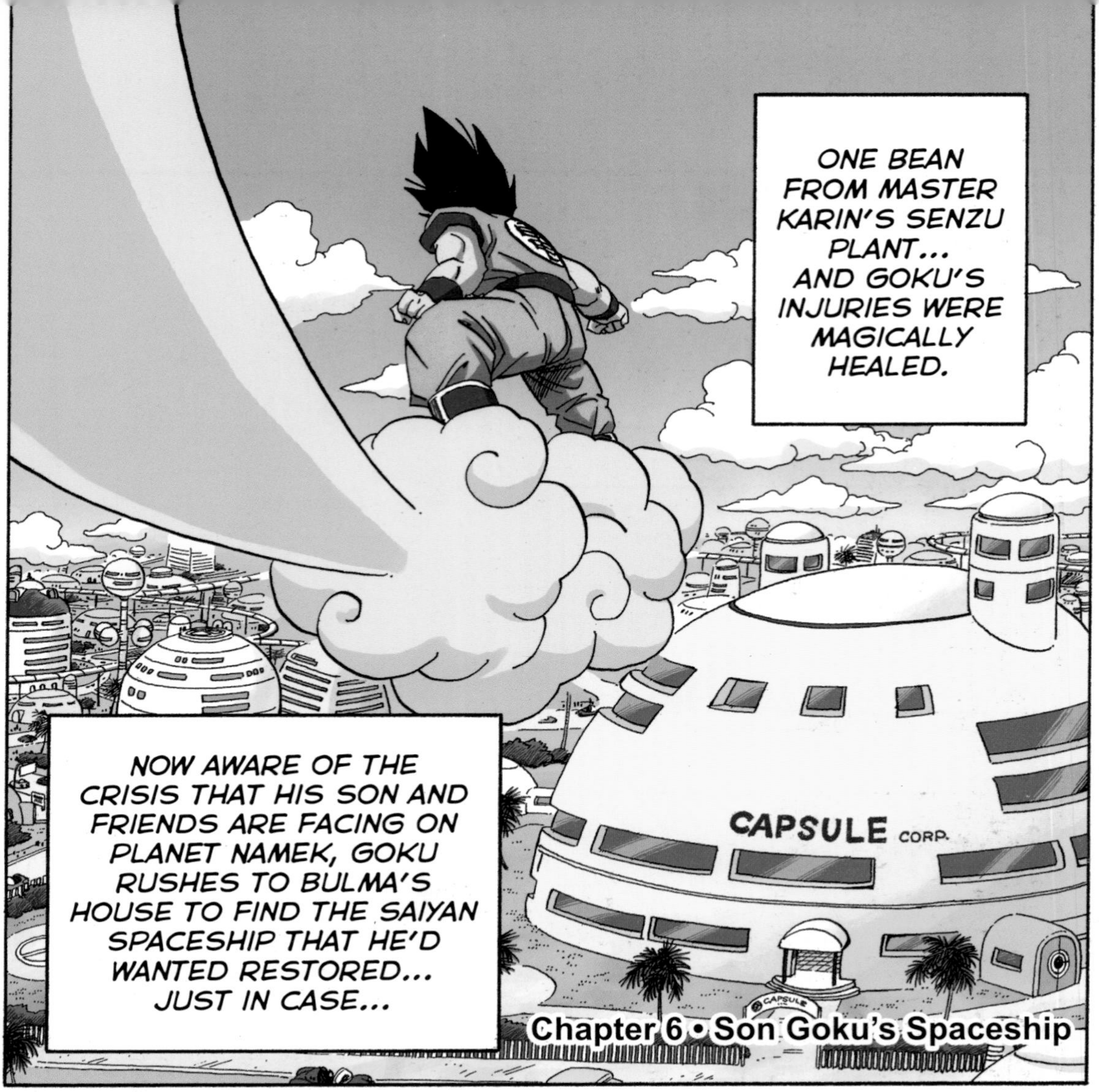
ONE BEAN FROM MASTER KARIN'S SENZU PLANT... AND GOKU'S INJURIES WERE MAGICALLY HEALED.
CAPSULE CORP.
NOW AWARE OF THE CRISIS THAT HIS SON AND FRIENDS ARE FACING ON PLANET NAMEK, GOKU RUSHES TO BULMA'S HOUSE TO FIND THE SAIYAN SPACESHIP THAT HE'D WANTED RESTORED... JUST IN CASE...
Chapter 6 • Son Goku's Spaceship

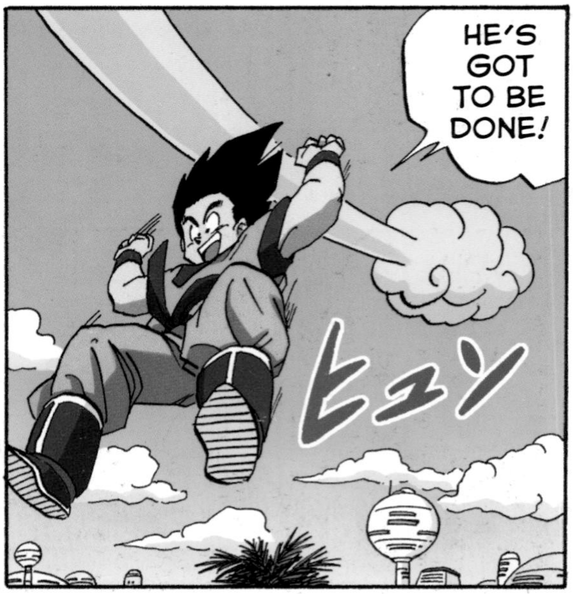
HE'S GOT TO BE DONE!
ヒュン

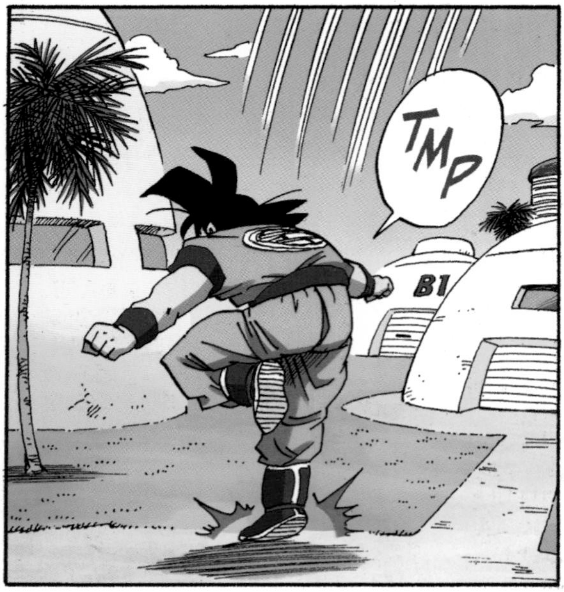
TMP
B1

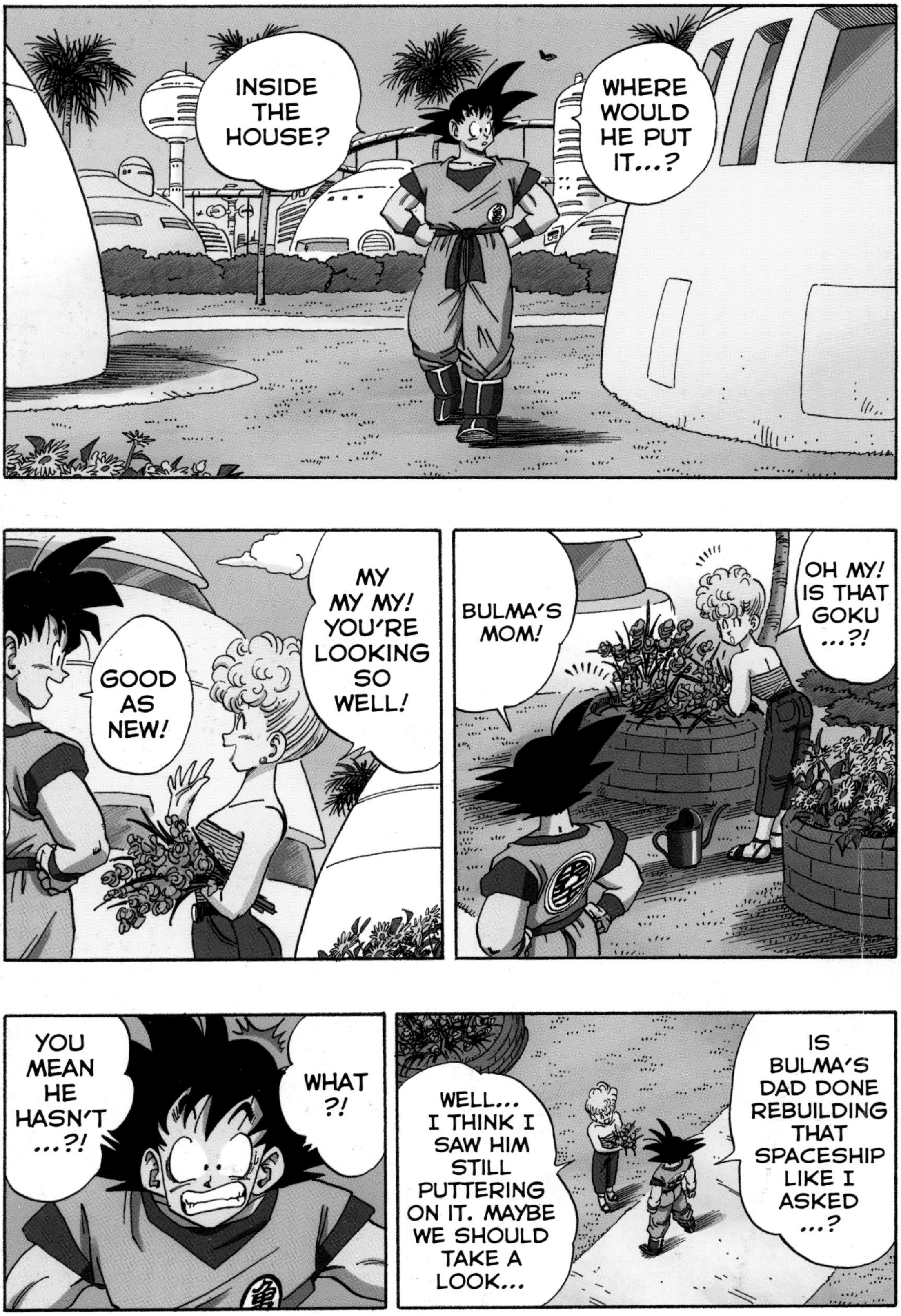
WHERE WOULD HE PUT IT...?
INSIDE THE HOUSE?
OH MY! IS THAT GOKU ...?!
BULMA'S MOM!
MY MY MY! YOU'RE LOOKING SO WELL!
GOOD AS NEW!
IS BULMA'S DAD DONE REBUILDING THAT SPACESHIP LIKE I ASKED ...?
WELL... I THINK I SAW HIM STILL PUTTERING ON IT. MAYBE WE SHOULD TAKE A LOOK...
WHAT ?!
YOU MEAN HE HASN'T ...?!

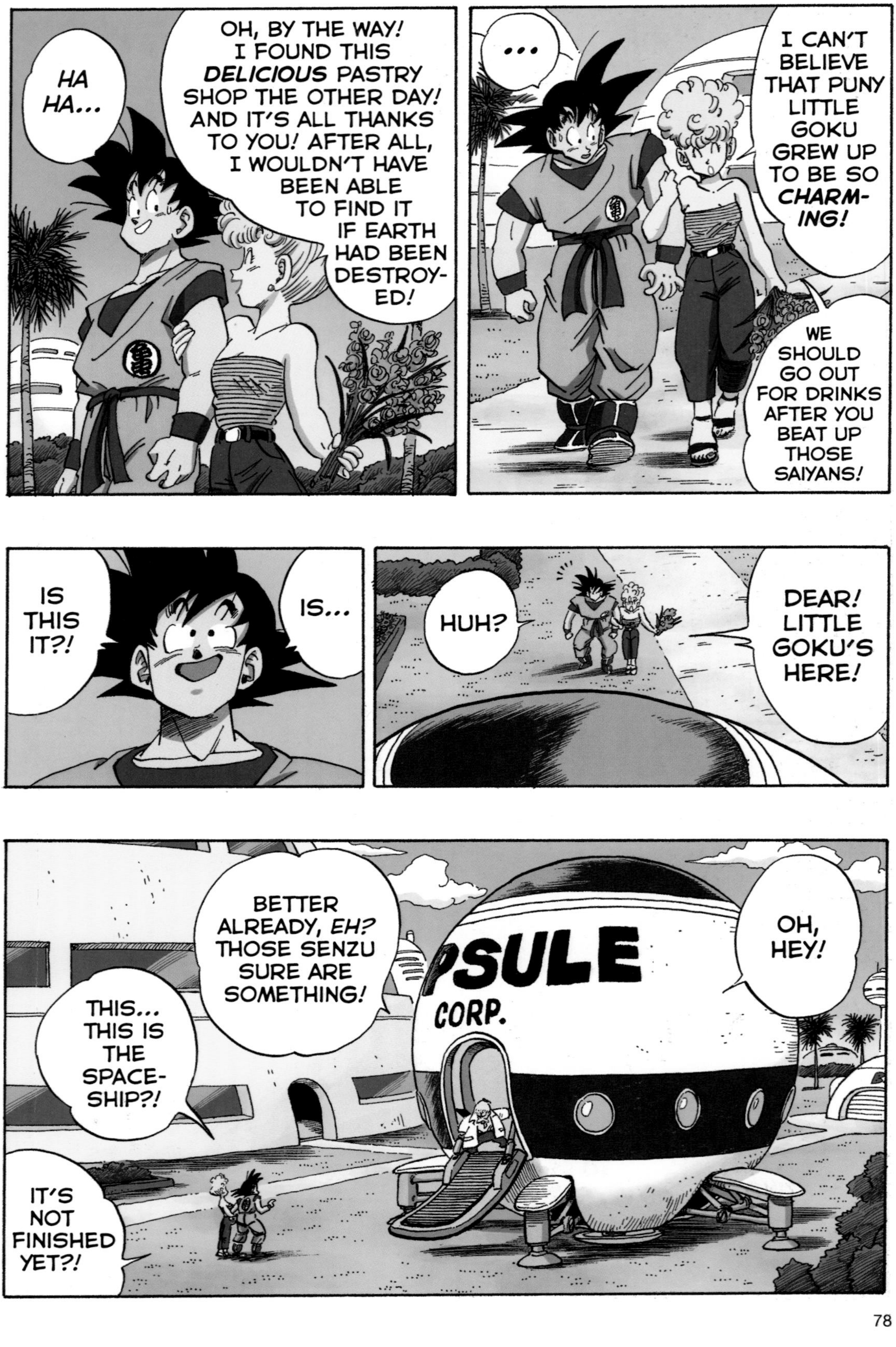
I CAN'T BELIEVE THAT PUNY LITTLE GOKU GREW UP TO BE SO *CHARMING!*
...
WE SHOULD GO OUT FOR DRINKS AFTER YOU BEAT UP THOSE SAIYANS!
OH, BY THE WAY! I FOUND THIS ***DELICIOUS*** PASTRY SHOP THE OTHER DAY! AND IT'S ALL THANKS TO YOU! AFTER ALL, I WOULDN'T HAVE BEEN ABLE TO FIND IT IF EARTH HAD BEEN DESTROYED!
HA HA...
DEAR! LITTLE GOKU'S HERE!
HUH?
IS...
IS THIS IT?!
OH, HEY!
BETTER ALREADY, *EH?* THOSE SENZU SURE ARE SOMETHING!
PSULE
CORP.
THIS... THIS IS THE SPACESHIP?!
IT'S NOT FINISHED YET?!

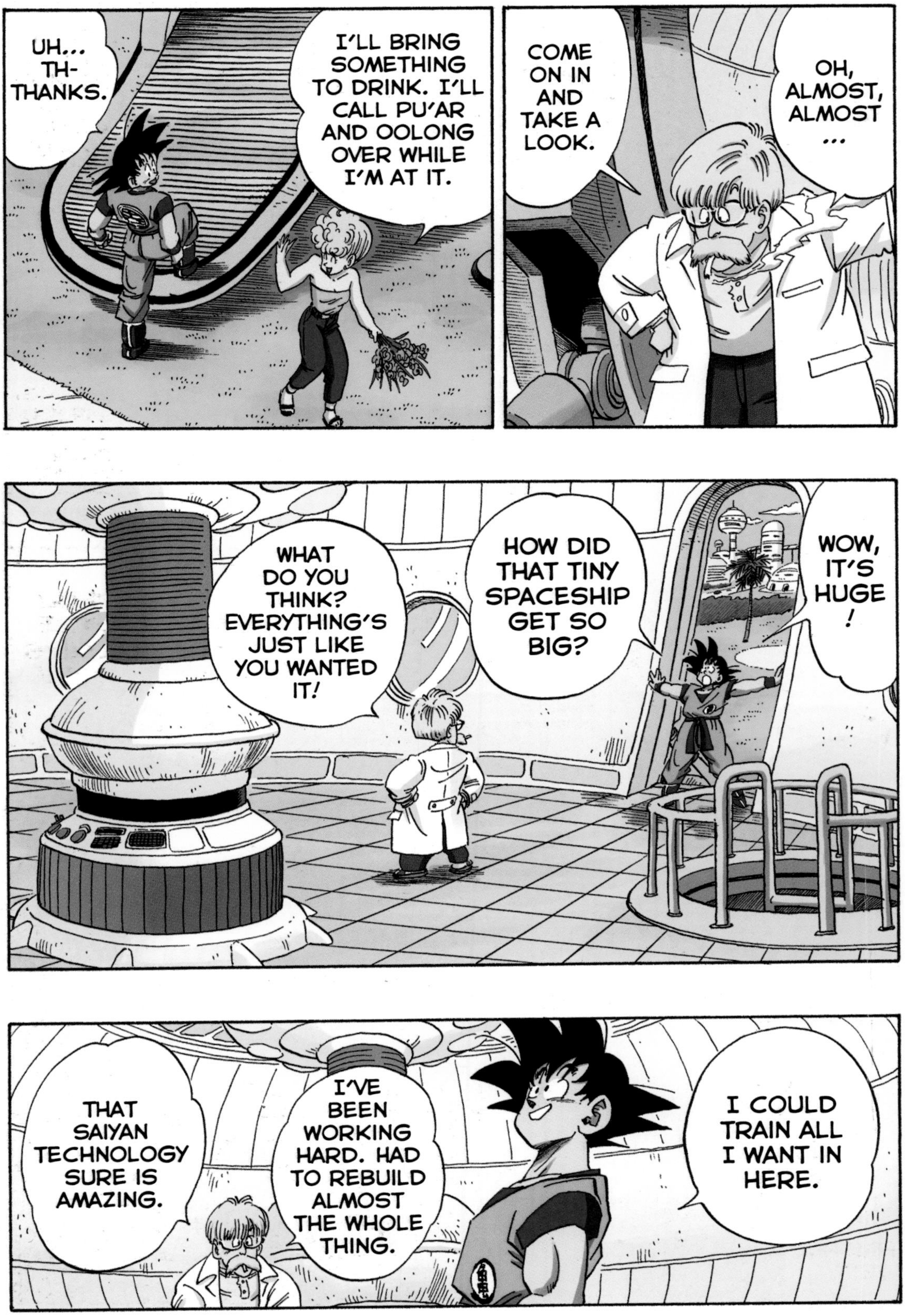
OH, ALMOST, ALMOST ...
COME ON IN AND TAKE A LOOK.
I'LL BRING SOMETHING TO DRINK. I'LL CALL PU'AR AND OOLONG OVER WHILE I'M AT IT.
UH... TH-THANKS.
WOW, IT'S HUGE!
HOW DID THAT TINY SPACESHIP GET SO BIG?
WHAT DO YOU THINK? EVERYTHING'S JUST LIKE YOU WANTED IT!
I COULD TRAIN ALL I WANT IN HERE.
I'VE BEEN WORKING HARD. HAD TO REBUILD ALMOST THE WHOLE THING.
THAT SAIYAN TECHNOLOGY SURE IS AMAZING.

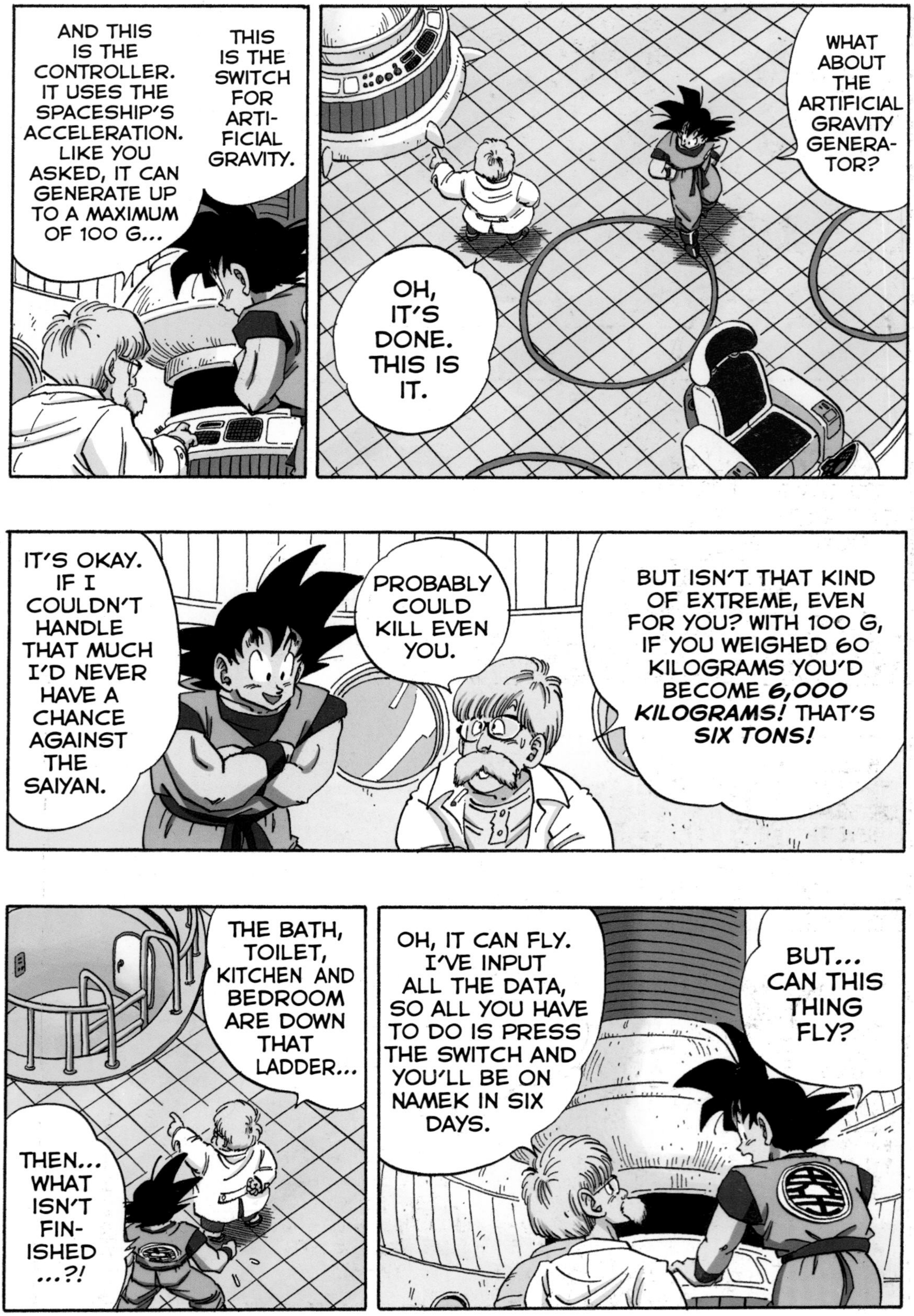
WHAT ABOUT THE ARTIFICIAL GRAVITY GENERATOR?
OH, IT'S DONE. THIS IS IT.
THIS IS THE SWITCH FOR ARTIFICIAL GRAVITY.
AND THIS IS THE CONTROLLER. IT USES THE SPACESHIP'S ACCELERATION. LIKE YOU ASKED, IT CAN GENERATE UP TO A MAXIMUM OF 100 G...
BUT ISN'T THAT KIND OF EXTREME, EVEN FOR YOU? WITH 100 G, IF YOU WEIGHED 60 KILOGRAMS YOU'D BECOME ***6,000 KILOGRAMS!*** THAT'S ***SIX TONS!***
PROBABLY COULD KILL EVEN YOU.
IT'S OKAY. IF I COULDN'T HANDLE THAT MUCH I'D NEVER HAVE A CHANCE AGAINST THE SAIYAN.
BUT... CAN THIS THING FLY?
OH, IT CAN FLY. I'VE INPUT ALL THE DATA, SO ALL YOU HAVE TO DO IS PRESS THE SWITCH AND YOU'LL BE ON NAMEK IN SIX DAYS.
THE BATH, TOILET, KITCHEN AND BEDROOM ARE DOWN THAT LADDER...
THEN... WHAT ISN'T FINISHED ...?!

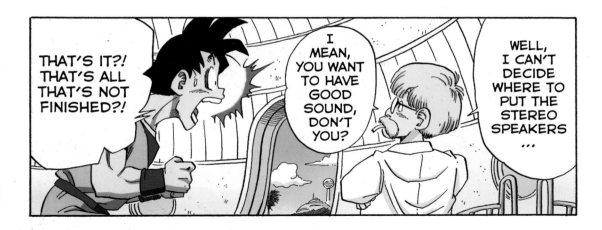

WELL, I CAN'T DECIDE WHERE TO PUT THE STEREO SPEAKERS...
I MEAN, YOU WANT TO HAVE GOOD SOUND, DON'T YOU?
THAT'S IT?! THAT'S ALL THAT'S NOT FINISHED?!
"THAT'S ALL," HE SAYS!
POSITIONING SPEAKERS FOR THE BEST POSSIBLE SOUND IS AN ART FORM, I'LL HAVE YOU KNOW! WHEN YOU CONSIDER THE ACOUSTICS OF...
I DON'T CARE ABOUT THE STEREO!! I'M IN A HURRY!!
I'M GOING TO TAKE OFF RIGHT NOW!!
WHAT COULD BE SO IMPORTANT THAT YOU DON'T CARE ABOUT THE STEREO?
I GOT WORD FROM YOUR DAUGHTER AND MY SON!! THEIR SPACESHIP HAS BEEN DESTROYED!! AND THE SAIYAN AND HIS GANG ARE ON NAMEK WITH THEM!!
MY GOODNESS...!
WELL, THAT IS URGENT, ISN'T IT?
TEACH ME HOW TO FLY THIS THING, NOW!!
ALL RIGHT! BUT YOU KNOW, ALL I NEED IS A FEW HOURS WITH THE SPEAKERS...

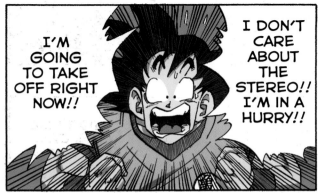

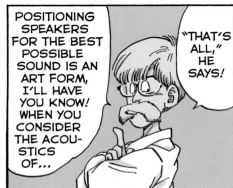

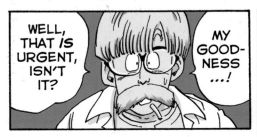

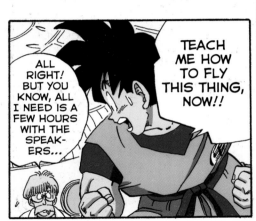

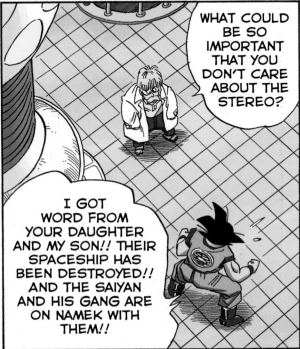

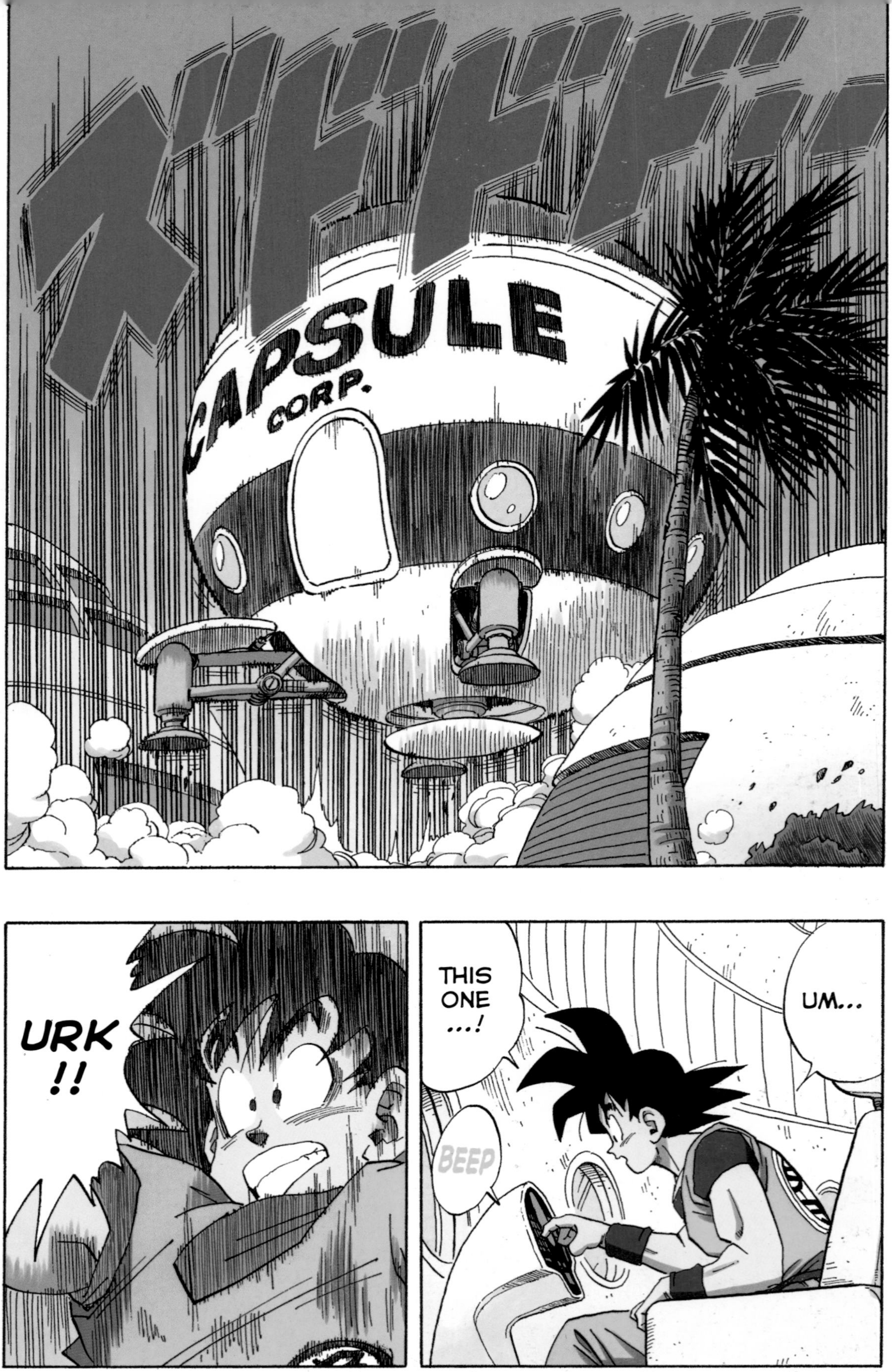
CAPSULE CORP.
UM...
THIS ONE ...!
BEEP
URK !!

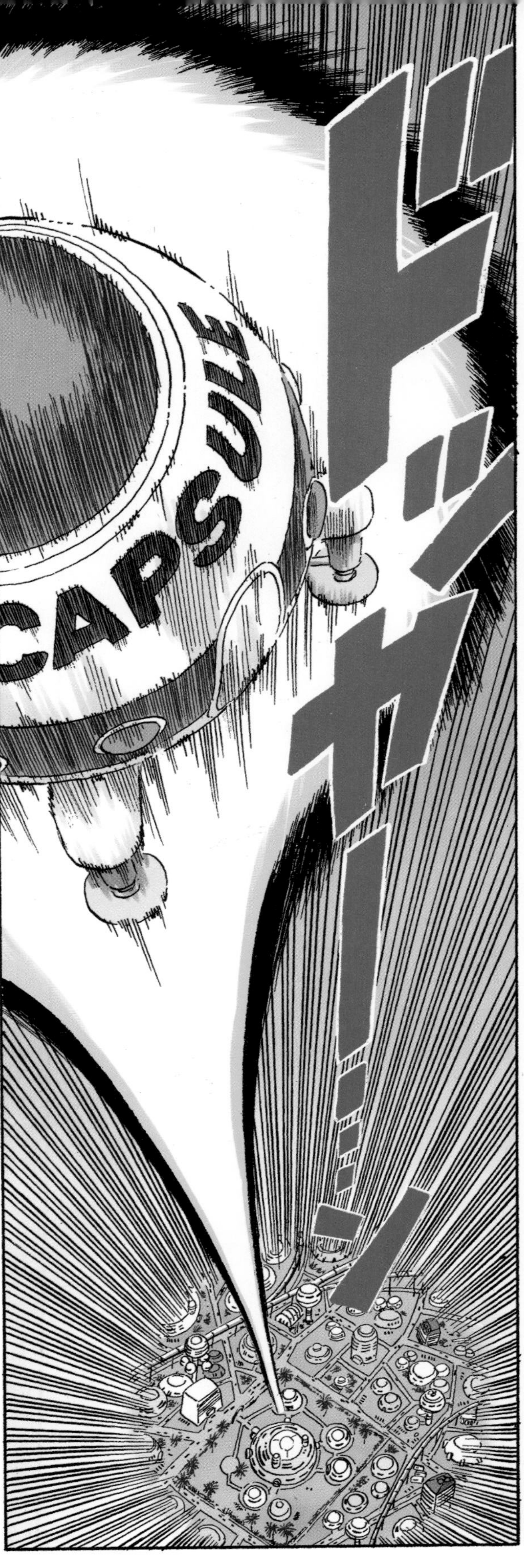
CAPSULE

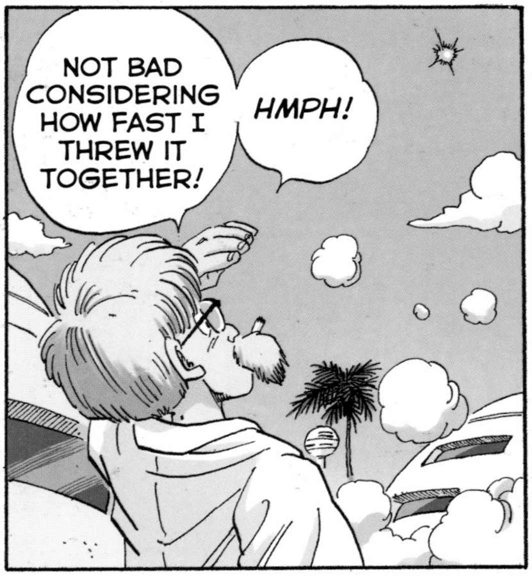
HMPH!
NOT BAD CONSIDERING HOW FAST I THREW IT TOGETHER!

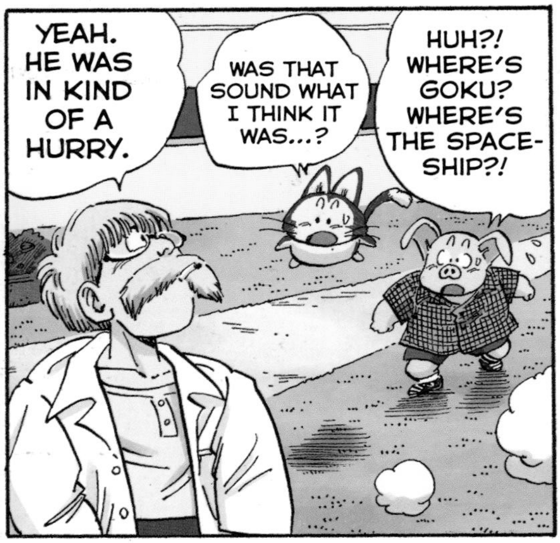
HUH?! WHERE'S GOKU? WHERE'S THE SPACE-SHIP?!
WAS THAT SOUND WHAT I THINK IT WAS...?
YEAH. HE WAS IN KIND OF A HURRY.

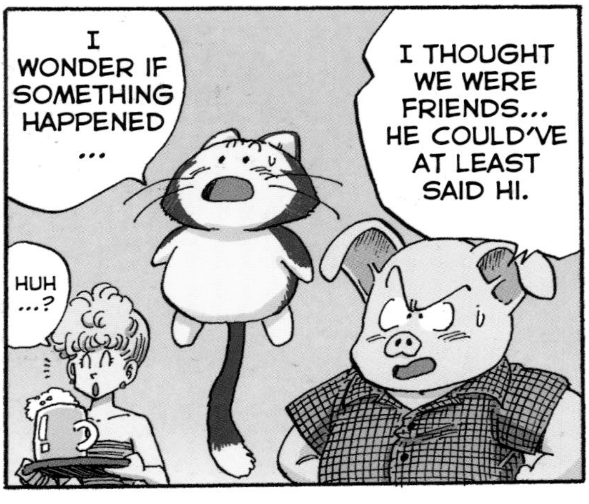
I THOUGHT WE WERE FRIENDS... HE COULD'VE AT LEAST SAID HI.
I WONDER IF SOMETHING HAPPENED...
HUH ...?

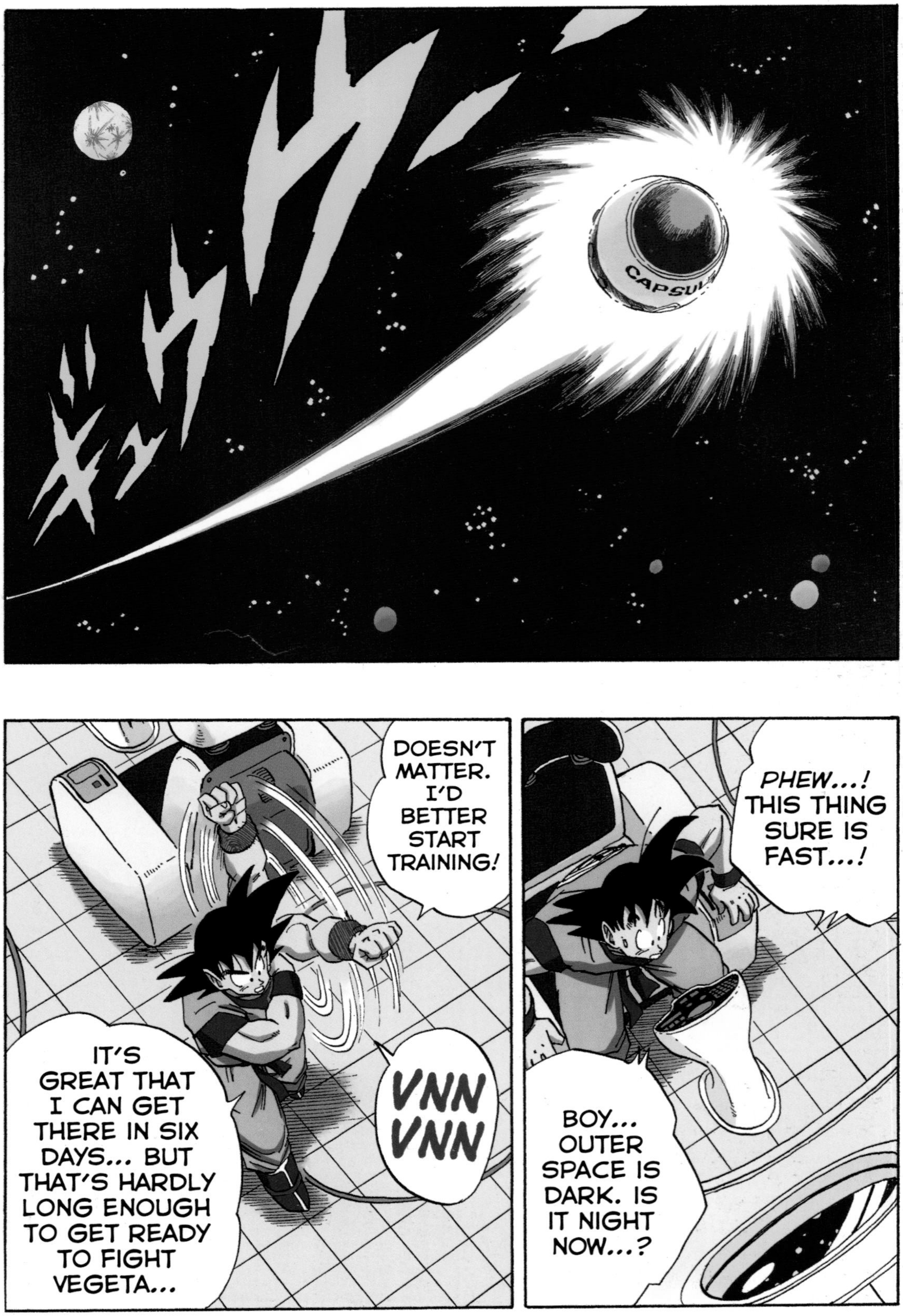
PHEW...! THIS THING SURE IS FAST...!
BOY... OUTER SPACE IS DARK. IS IT NIGHT NOW...?
IT'S GREAT THAT I CAN GET THERE IN SIX DAYS... BUT THAT'S HARDLY LONG ENOUGH TO GET READY TO FIGHT VEGETA...
VNN VNN
DOESN'T MATTER. I'D BETTER START TRAINING!

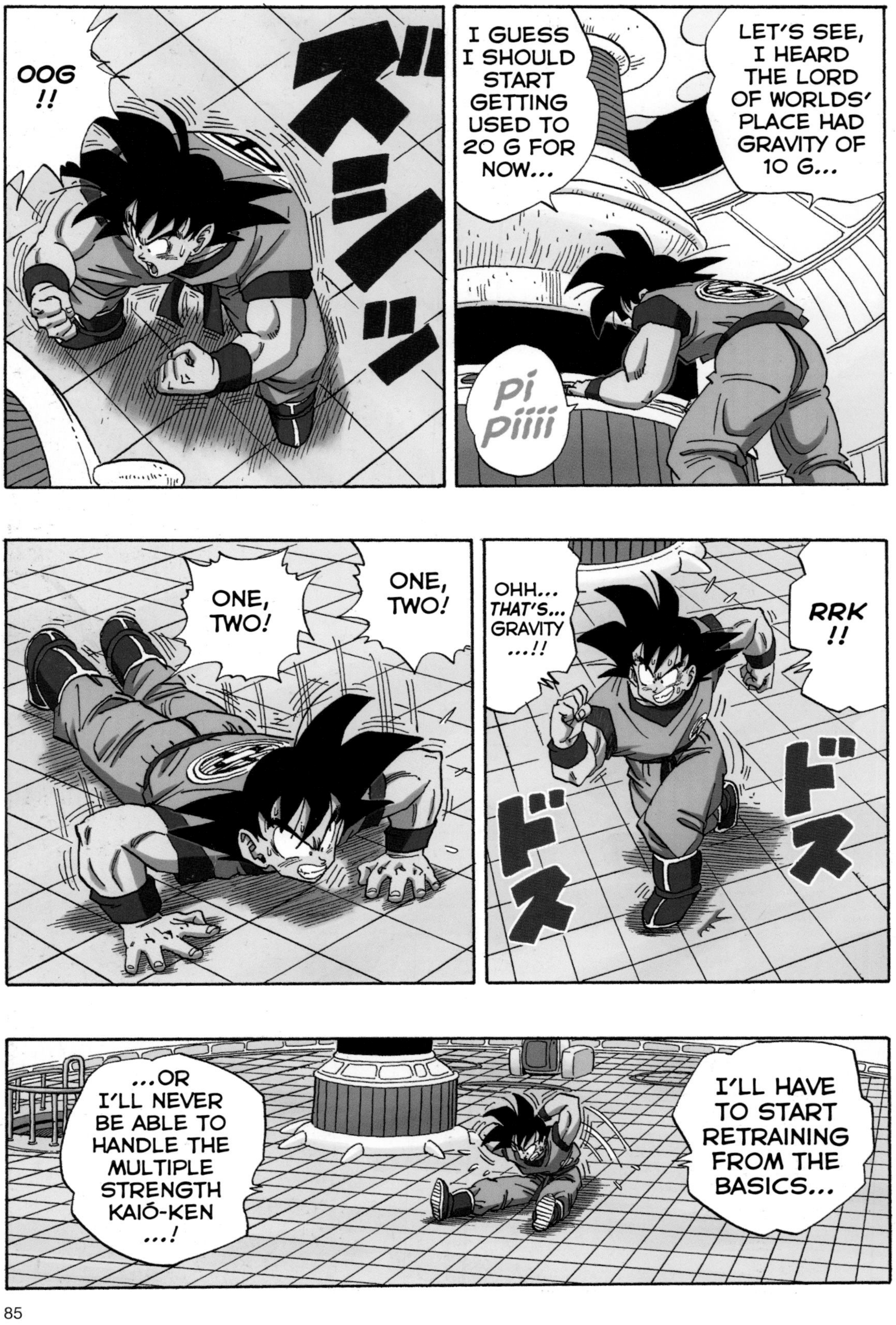
LET'S SEE, I HEARD THE LORD OF WORLDS' PLACE HAD GRAVITY OF 10 G...
I GUESS I SHOULD START GETTING USED TO 20 G FOR NOW...
Pi Piiii
OOG !!
RRK !!
OHH... THAT'S... GRAVITY ...!!
ドス
ドス
ONE, TWO!
ONE, TWO!
I'LL HAVE TO START RETRAINING FROM THE BASICS...
...OR I'LL NEVER BE ABLE TO HANDLE THE MULTIPLE STRENGTH KAIÓ-KEN ...!

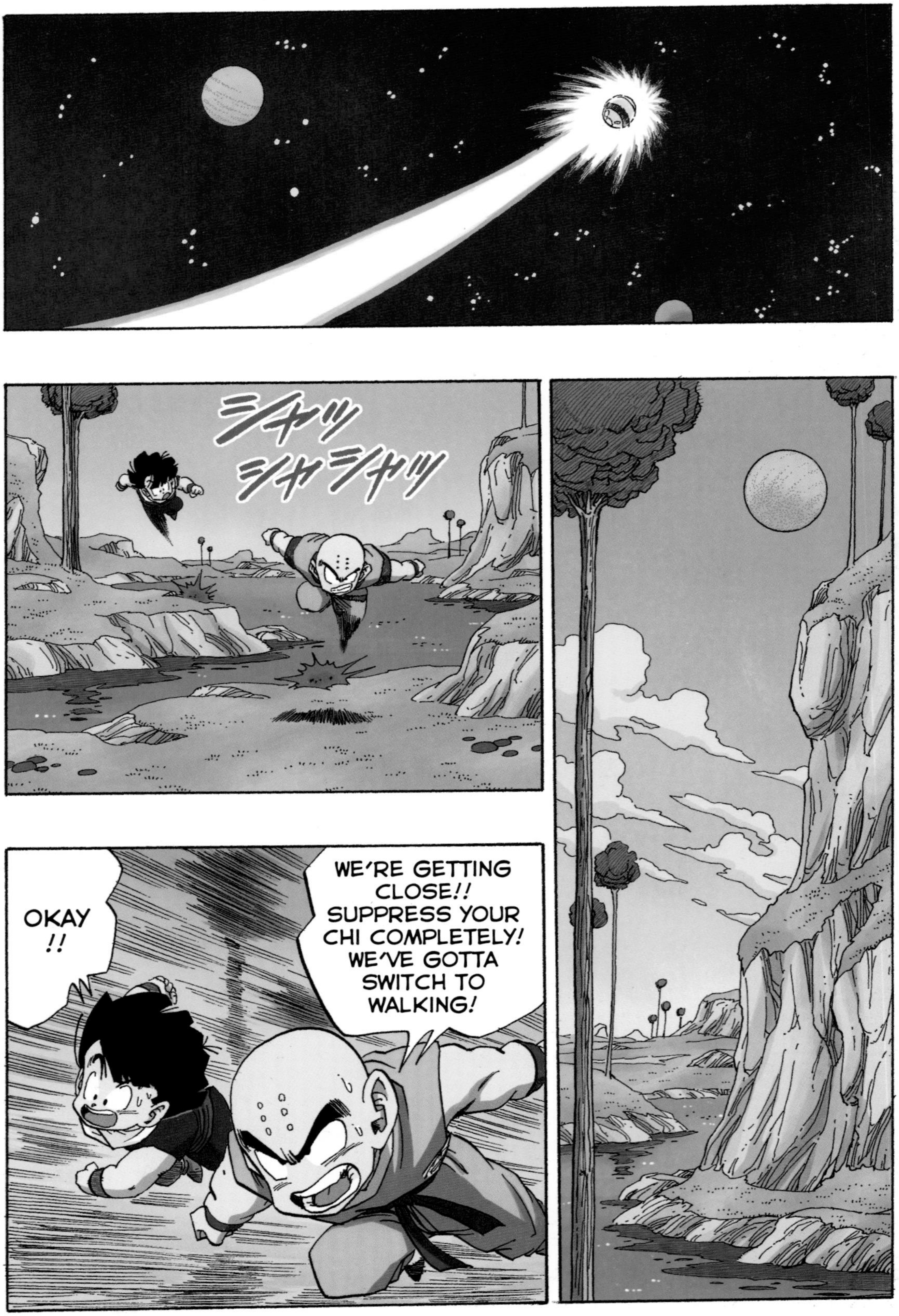
シャッ
シャシャッ
WE'RE GETTING CLOSE!! SUPPRESS YOUR CHI COMPLETELY! WE'VE GOTTA SWITCH TO WALKING!
OKAY !!

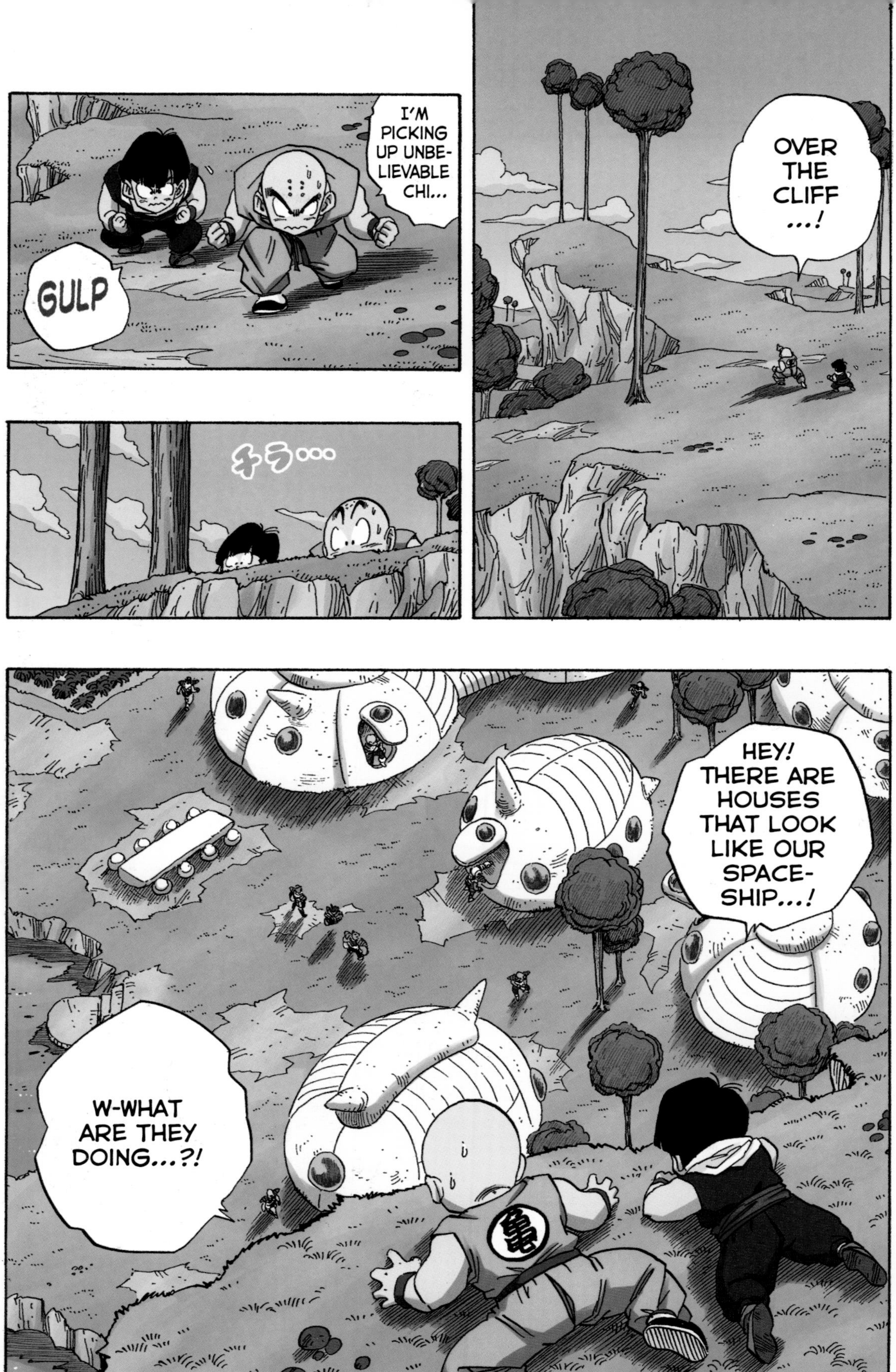
OVER THE CLIFF ...!
I'M PICKING UP UNBE-LIEVABLE CHI...
GULP
チラ…
HEY! THERE ARE HOUSES THAT LOOK LIKE OUR SPACE-SHIP...!
W-WHAT ARE THEY DOING...?!

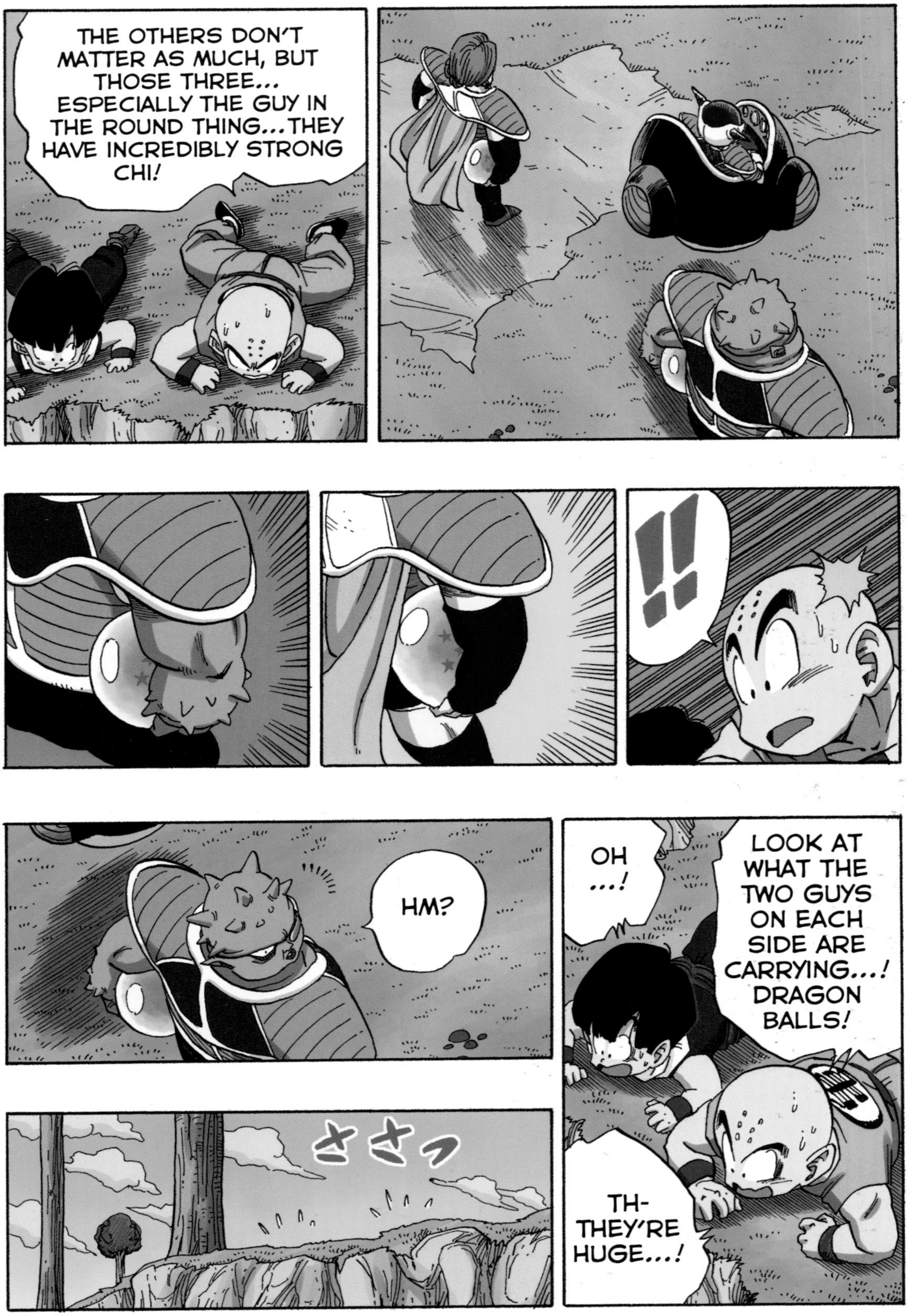
THE OTHERS DON'T MATTER AS MUCH, BUT THOSE THREE... ESPECIALLY THE GUY IN THE ROUND THING... THEY HAVE INCREDIBLY STRONG CHI!
!!
LOOK AT WHAT THE TWO GUYS ON EACH SIDE ARE CARRYING...! DRAGON BALLS!
OH ...!
TH- THEY'RE HUGE...!
HM?
ささっ

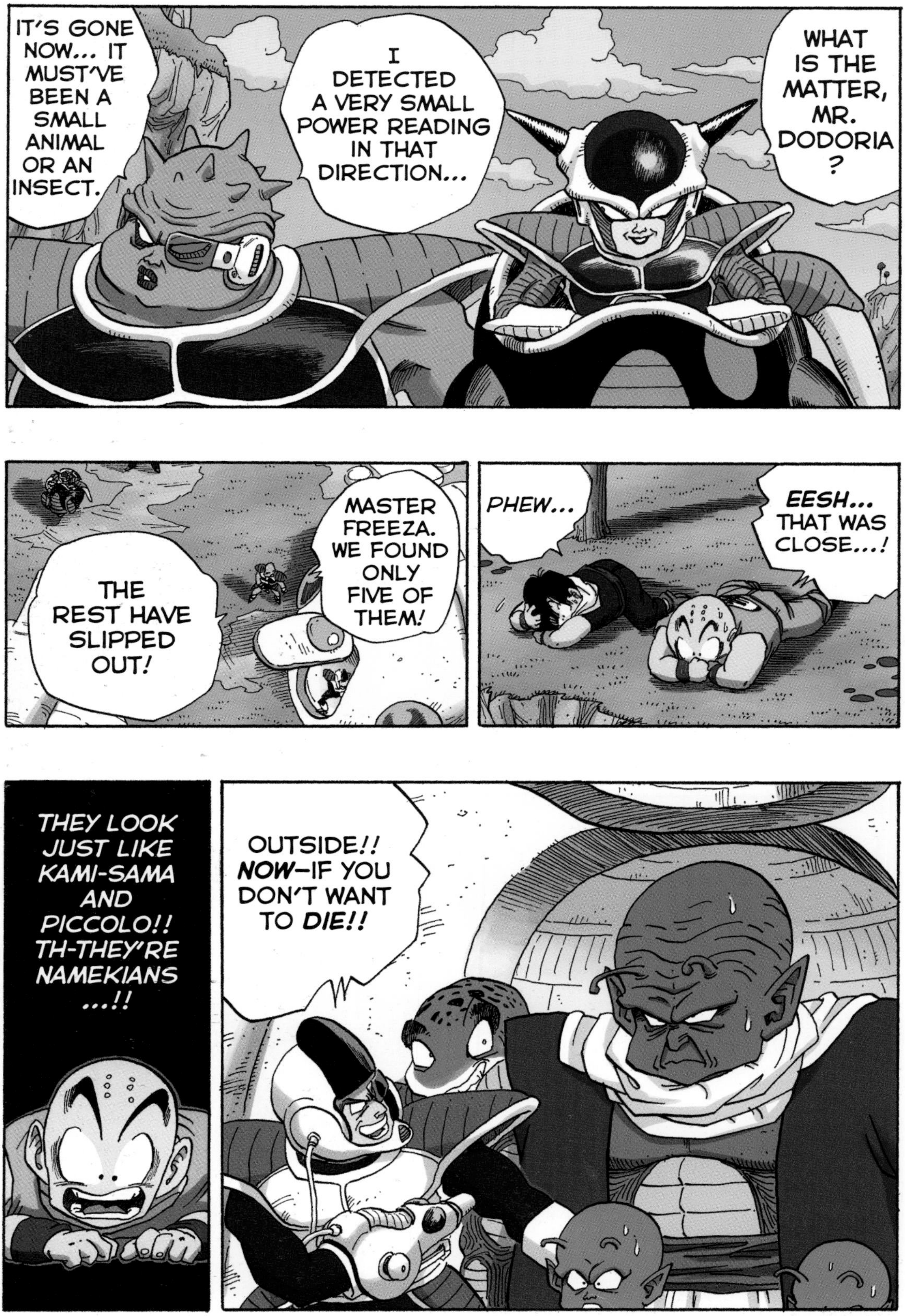

WHAT IS THE MATTER, MR. DODORIA?
I DETECTED A VERY SMALL POWER READING IN THAT DIRECTION...
IT'S GONE NOW... IT MUST'VE BEEN A SMALL ANIMAL OR AN INSECT.
EESH... THAT WAS CLOSE...!
PHEW...
MASTER FREEZA. WE FOUND ONLY FIVE OF THEM!
THE REST HAVE SLIPPED OUT!
OUTSIDE!! NOW—IF YOU DON'T WANT TO DIE!!
THEY LOOK JUST LIKE KAMI-SAMA AND PICCOLO!! TH-THEY'RE NAMEKIANS...!!

Chapter 7 • Namekian Fear

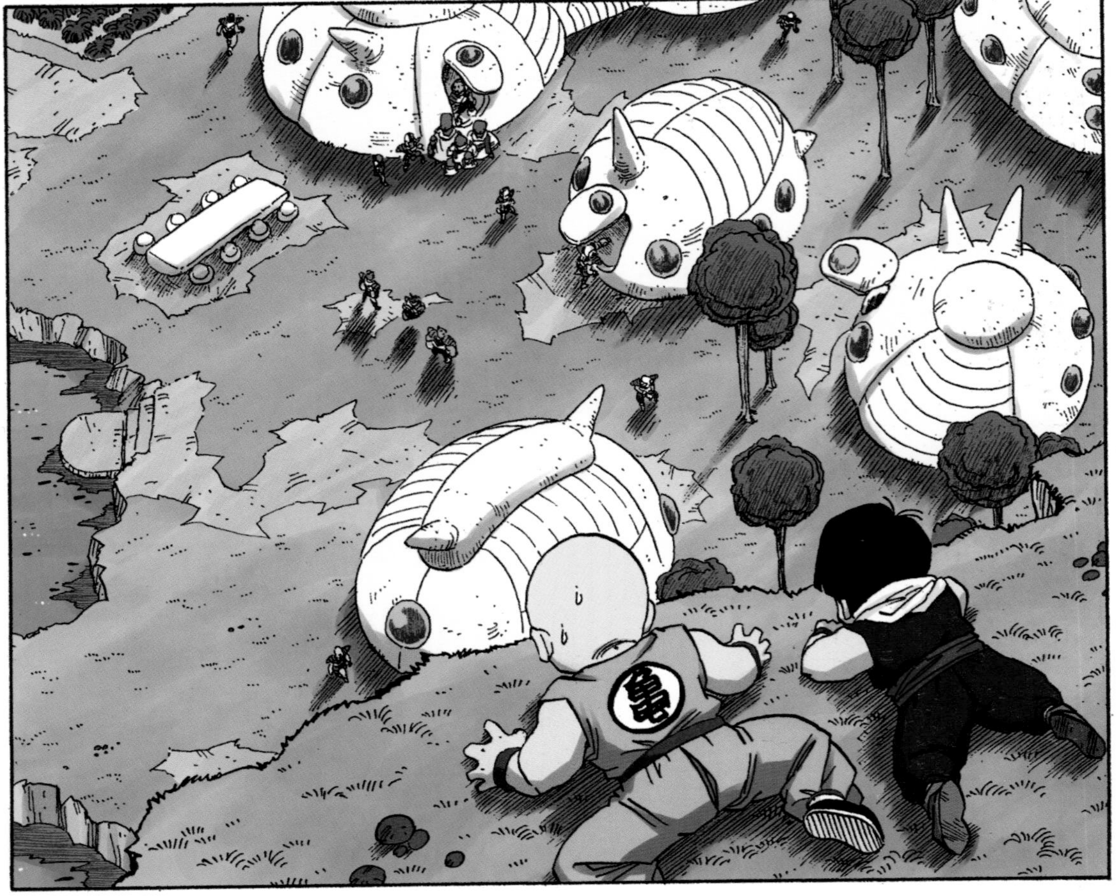

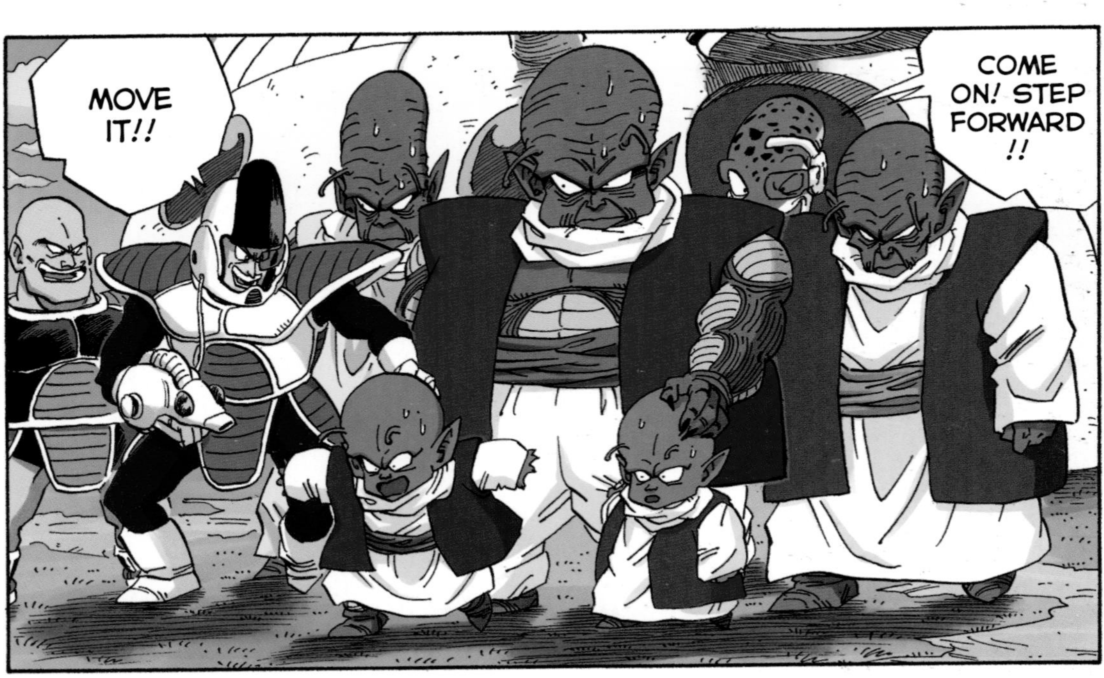
COME ON! STEP FORWARD !!
MOVE IT!!

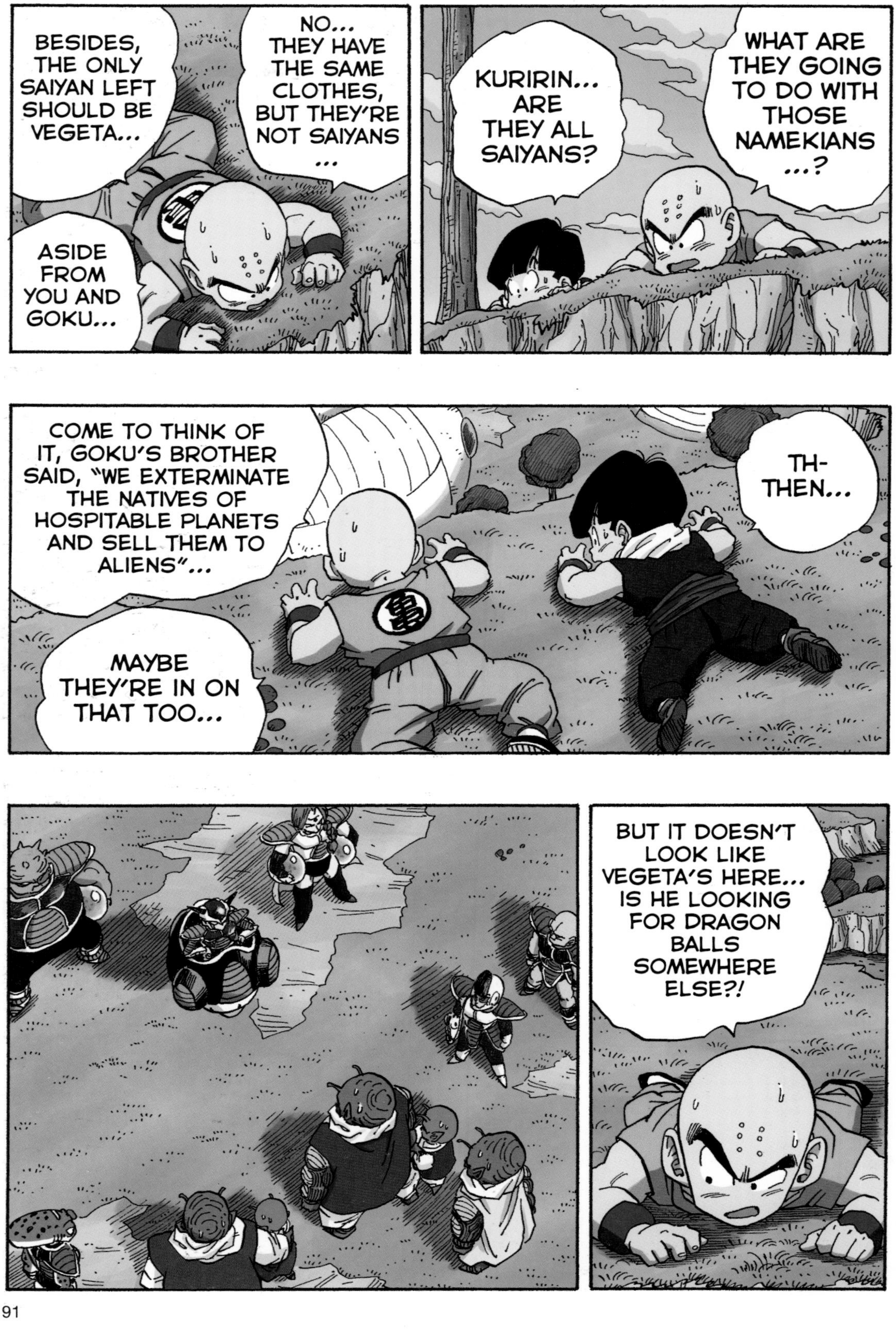
BESIDES, THE ONLY SAIYAN LEFT SHOULD BE VEGETA...
NO... THEY HAVE THE SAME CLOTHES, BUT THEY'RE NOT SAIYANS ...
ASIDE FROM YOU AND GOKU...
KURIRIN... ARE THEY ALL SAIYANS?
WHAT ARE THEY GOING TO DO WITH THOSE NAMEKIANS ...?
COME TO THINK OF IT, GOKU'S BROTHER SAID, "WE EXTERMINATE THE NATIVES OF HOSPITABLE PLANETS AND SELL THEM TO ALIENS"...
TH- THEN...
MAYBE THEY'RE IN ON THAT TOO...
BUT IT DOESN'T LOOK LIKE VEGETA'S HERE... IS HE LOOKING FOR DRAGON BALLS SOMEWHERE ELSE?!

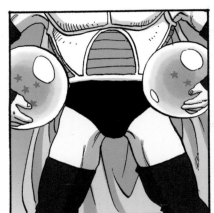

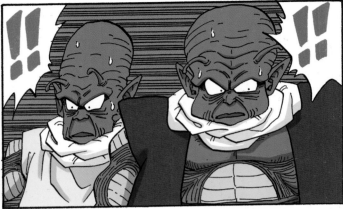

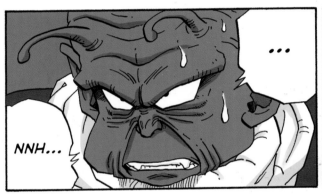

!!
!!
...
NNH...
I AM CALLED FREEZA. AS YOU CAN SEE, I AM COLLECTING YOUR DRAGON BALLS.
WHERE ARE THE OTHERS, BY THE WAY? WE HAD NOTED THAT THERE WERE TEN OF YOU...

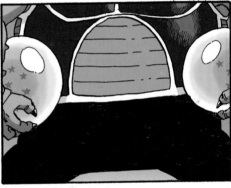

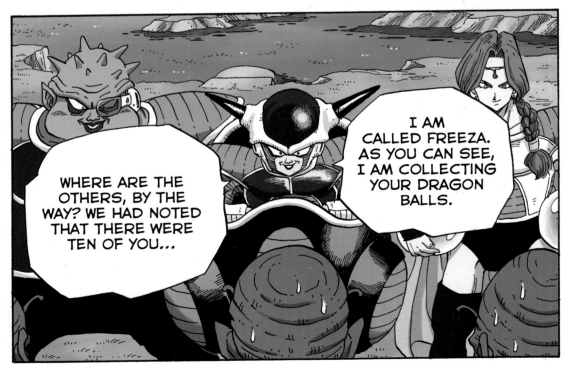

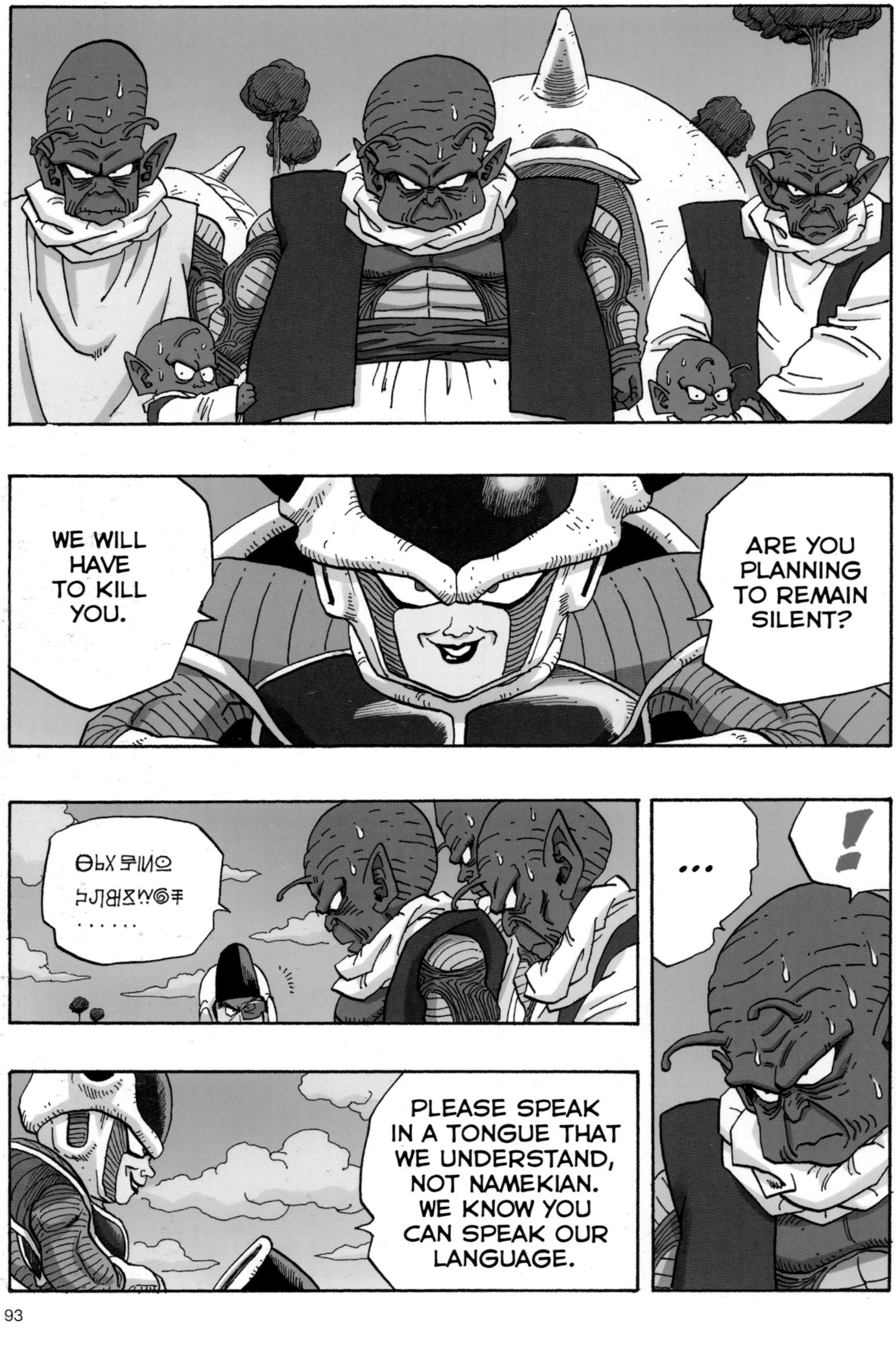
ARE YOU PLANNING TO REMAIN SILENT?
WE WILL HAVE TO KILL YOU.
...
!
PLEASE SPEAK IN A TONGUE THAT WE UNDERSTAND, NOT NAMEKIAN. WE KNOW YOU CAN SPEAK OUR LANGUAGE.

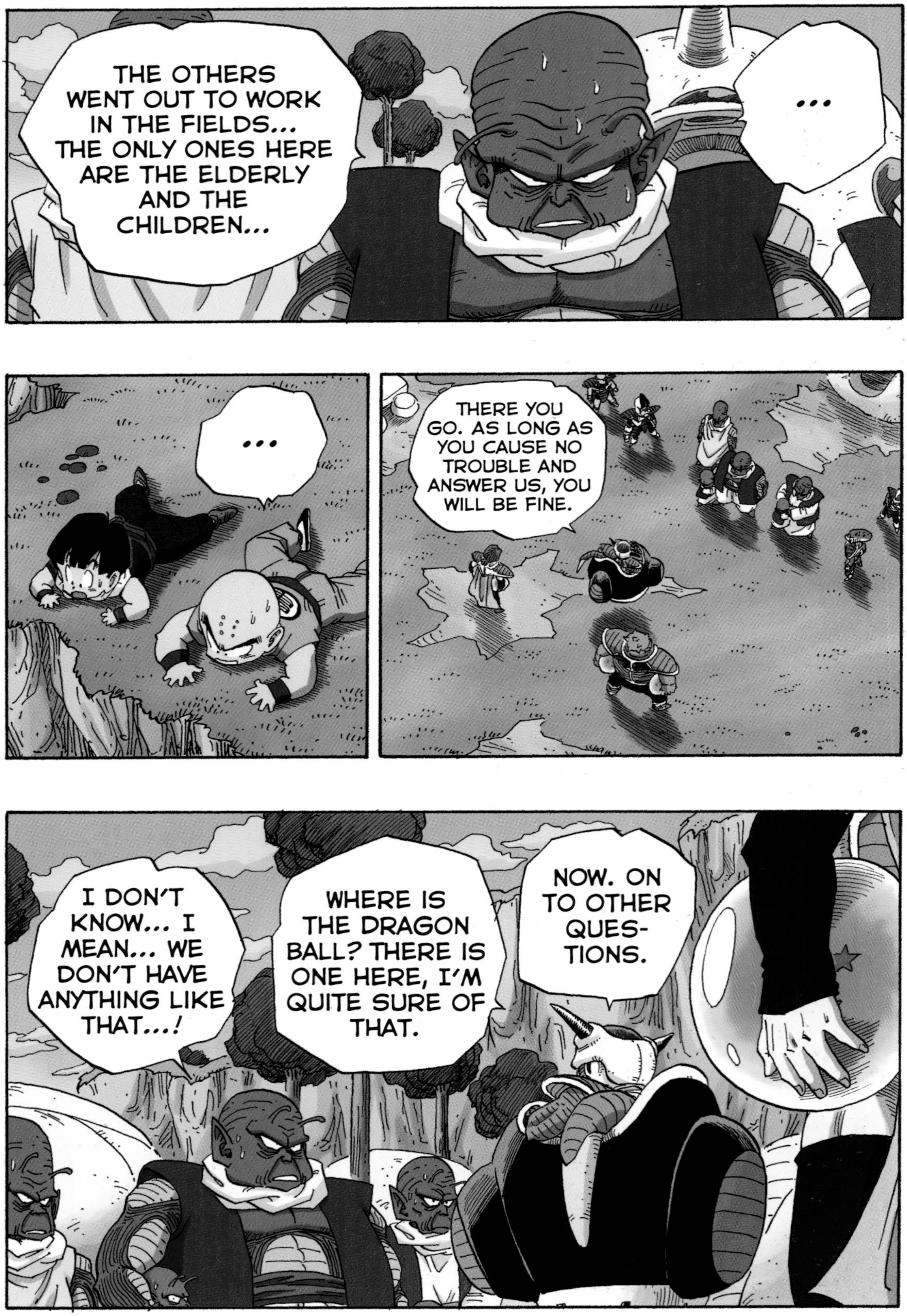
...
THE OTHERS WENT OUT TO WORK IN THE FIELDS... THE ONLY ONES HERE ARE THE ELDERLY AND THE CHILDREN...
THERE YOU GO. AS LONG AS YOU CAUSE NO TROUBLE AND ANSWER US, YOU WILL BE FINE.
...
NOW. ON TO OTHER QUES-TIONS.
WHERE IS THE DRAGON BALL? THERE IS ONE HERE, I'M QUITE SURE OF THAT.
I DON'T KNOW... I MEAN... WE DON'T HAVE ANYTHING LIKE THAT...!

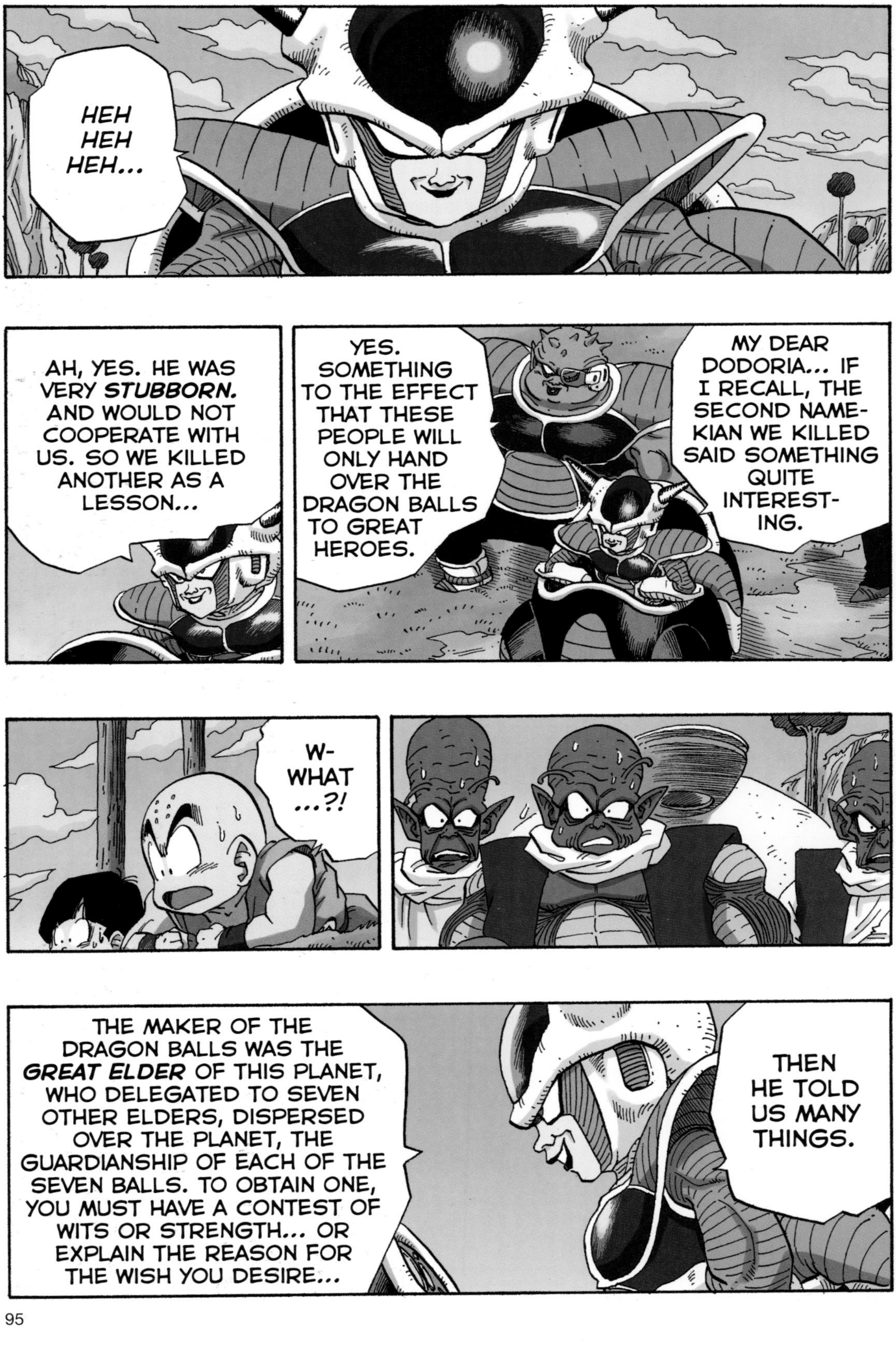
HEH HEH HEH...
MY DEAR DODORIA... IF I RECALL, THE SECOND NAME-KIAN WE KILLED SAID SOMETHING QUITE INTEREST-ING.
YES. SOMETHING TO THE EFFECT THAT THESE PEOPLE WILL ONLY HAND OVER THE DRAGON BALLS TO GREAT HEROES.
AH, YES. HE WAS VERY STUBBORN. AND WOULD NOT COOPERATE WITH US. SO WE KILLED ANOTHER AS A LESSON...
W-WHAT ...?!
THEN HE TOLD US MANY THINGS.
THE MAKER OF THE DRAGON BALLS WAS THE GREAT ELDER OF THIS PLANET, WHO DELEGATED TO SEVEN OTHER ELDERS, DISPERSED OVER THE PLANET, THE GUARDIANSHIP OF EACH OF THE SEVEN BALLS. TO OBTAIN ONE, YOU MUST HAVE A CONTEST OF WITS OR STRENGTH... OR EXPLAIN THE REASON FOR THE WISH YOU DESIRE...

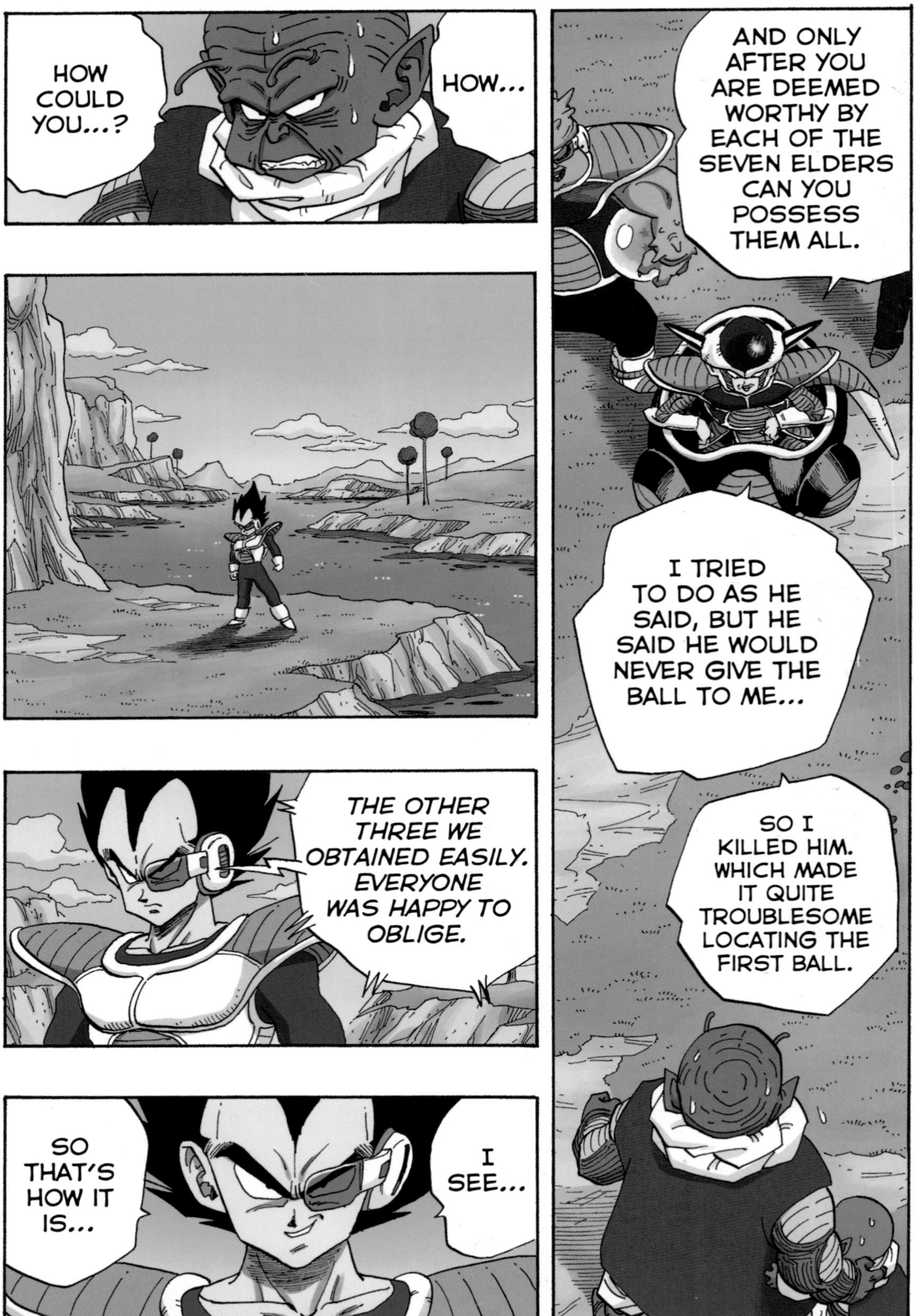
AND ONLY AFTER YOU ARE DEEMED WORTHY BY EACH OF THE SEVEN ELDERS CAN YOU POSSESS THEM ALL.
I TRIED TO DO AS HE SAID, BUT HE SAID HE WOULD NEVER GIVE THE BALL TO ME...
SO I KILLED HIM. WHICH MADE IT QUITE TROUBLESOME LOCATING THE FIRST BALL.
HOW...
HOW COULD YOU...?
THE OTHER THREE WE OBTAINED EASILY. EVERYONE WAS HAPPY TO OBLIGE.
I SEE...
SO THAT'S HOW IT IS...

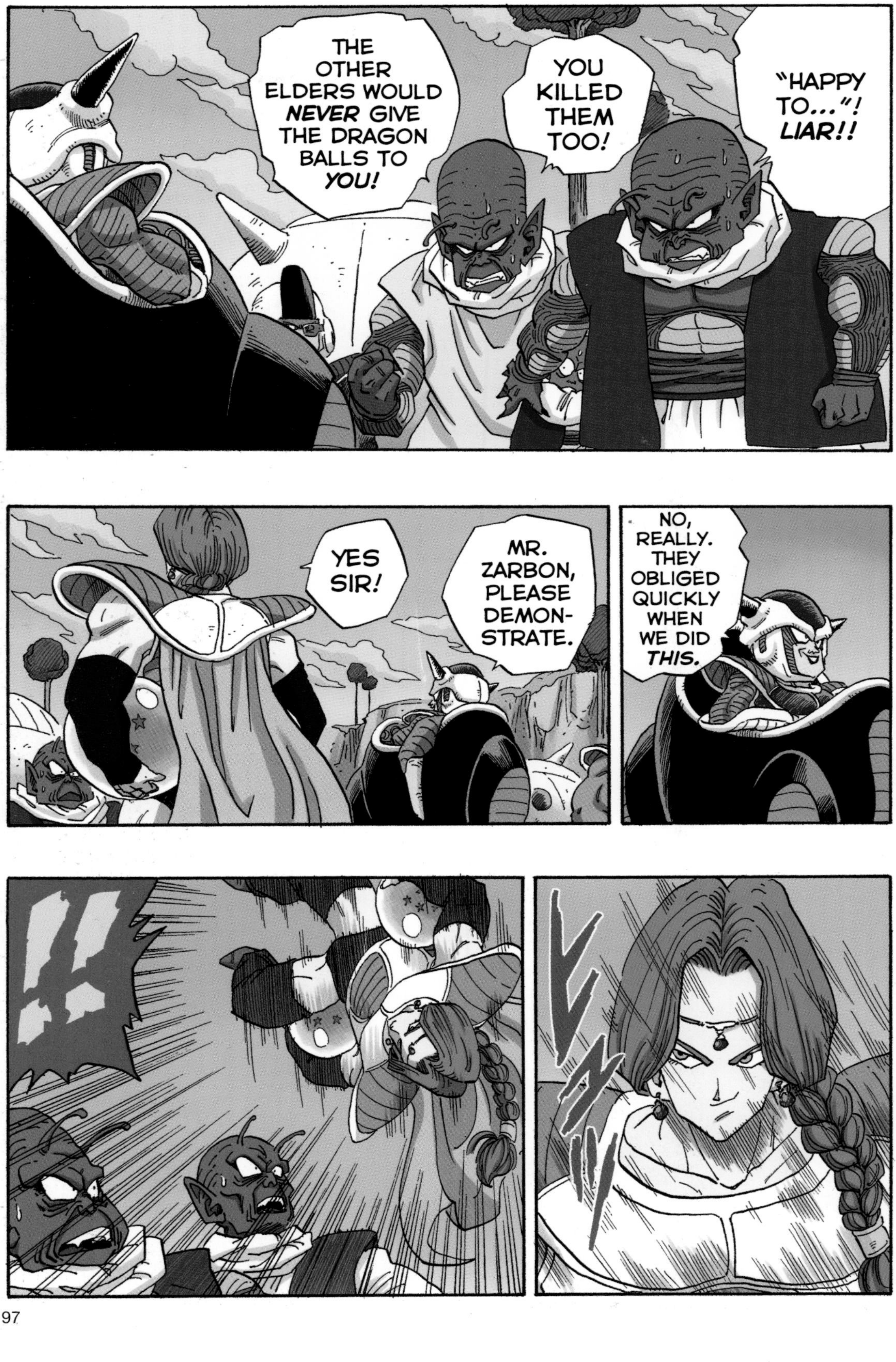
"HAPPY TO..."! LIAR!!
YOU KILLED THEM TOO!
THE OTHER ELDERS WOULD NEVER GIVE THE DRAGON BALLS TO YOU!
NO, REALLY. THEY OBLIGED QUICKLY WHEN WE DID THIS.
MR. ZARBON, PLEASE DEMONSTRATE.
YES SIR!
!!

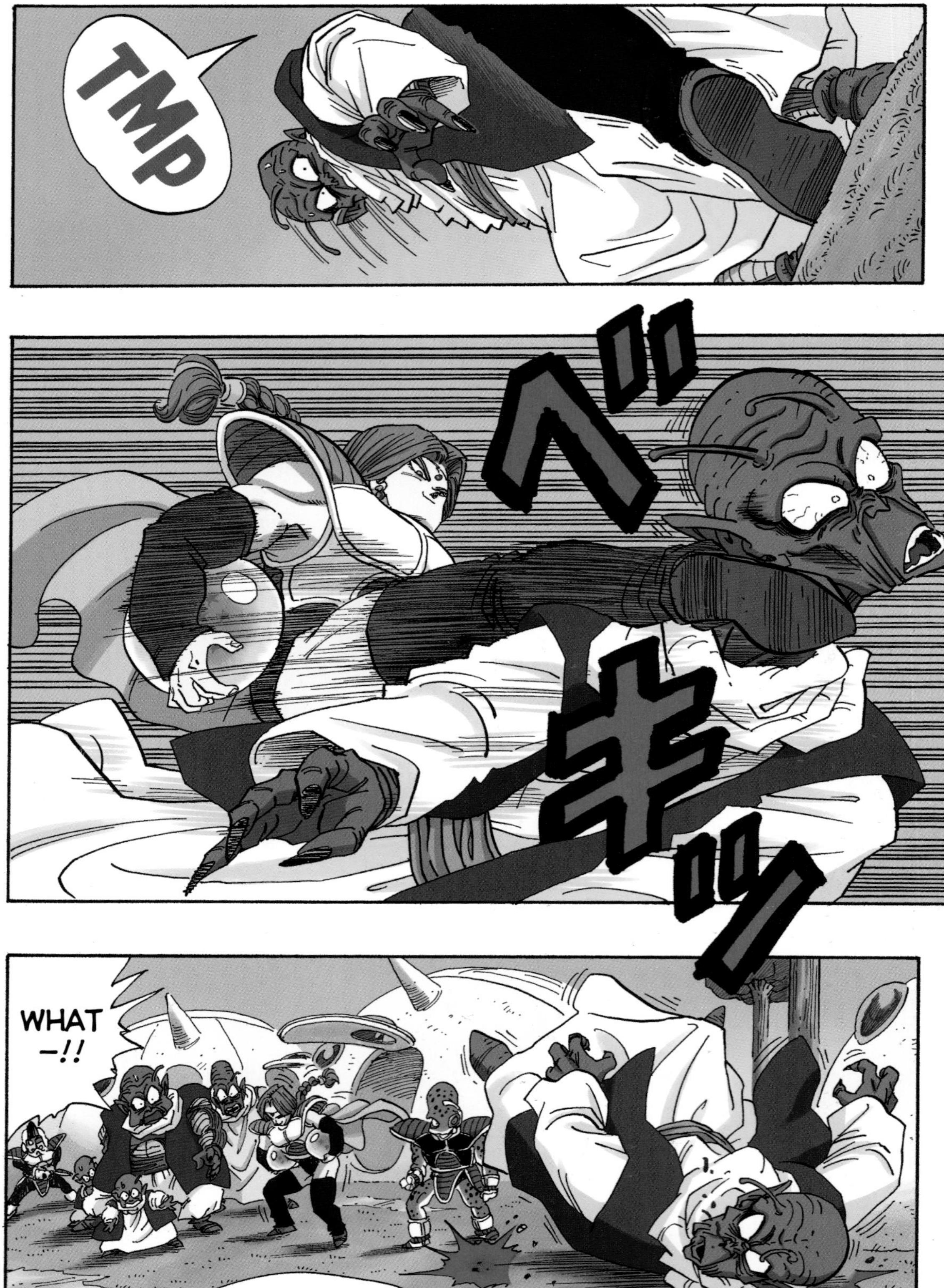
TMP
ベキッ
WHAT
—!!
DOMP

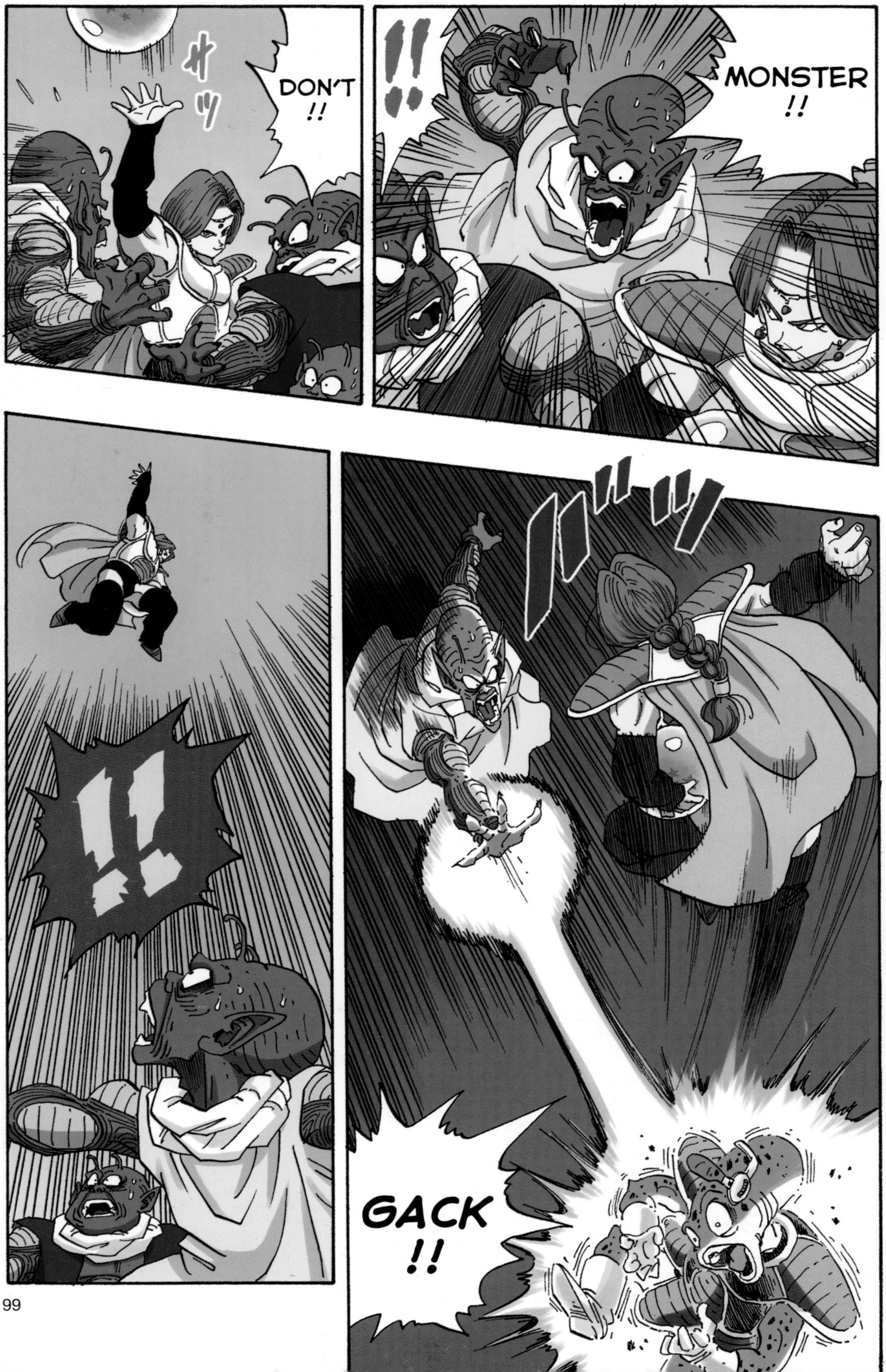
!!
MONSTER !!
DON'T !!
GACK !!
!!

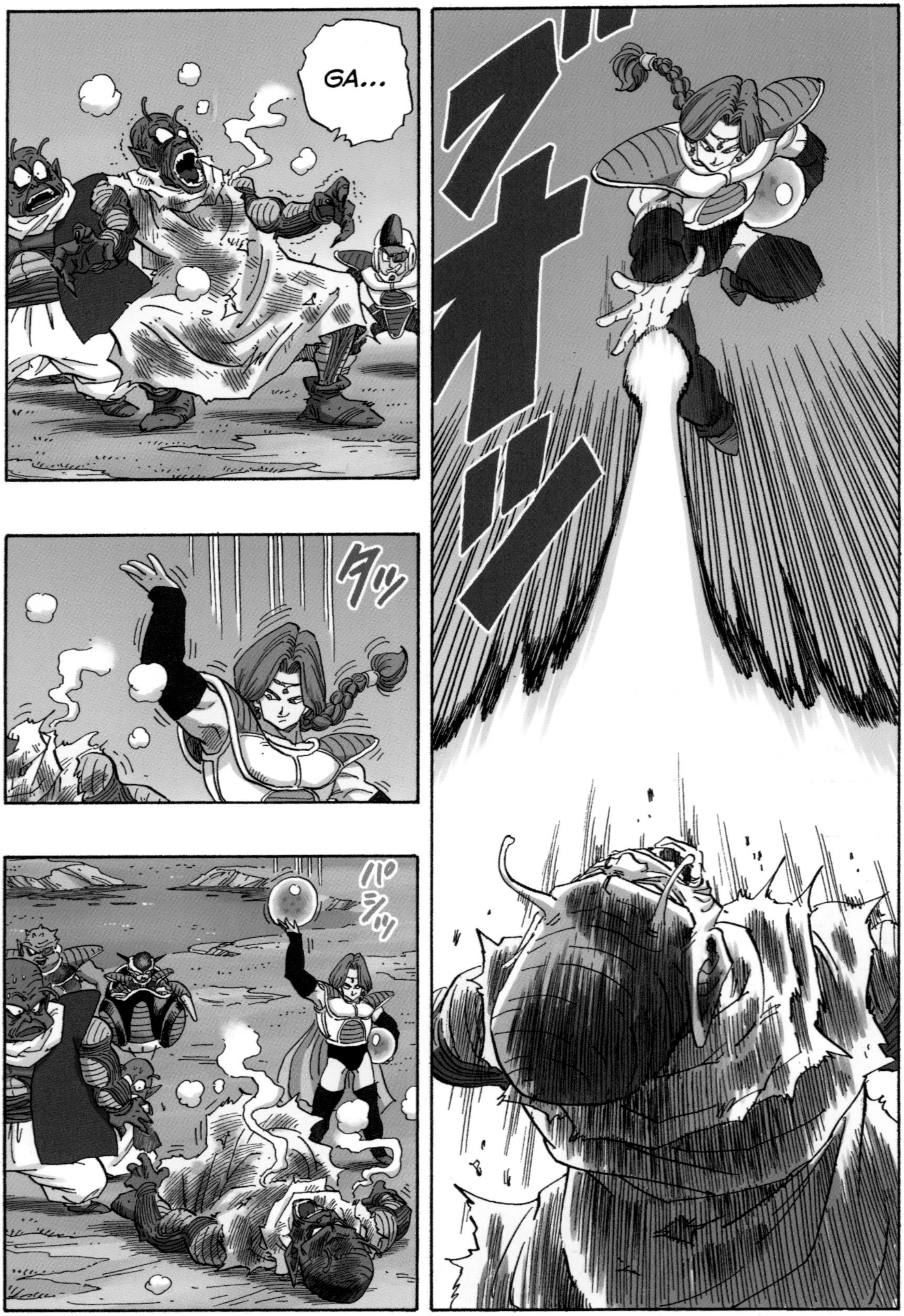
ブオッ
GA...
タッ
パシッ

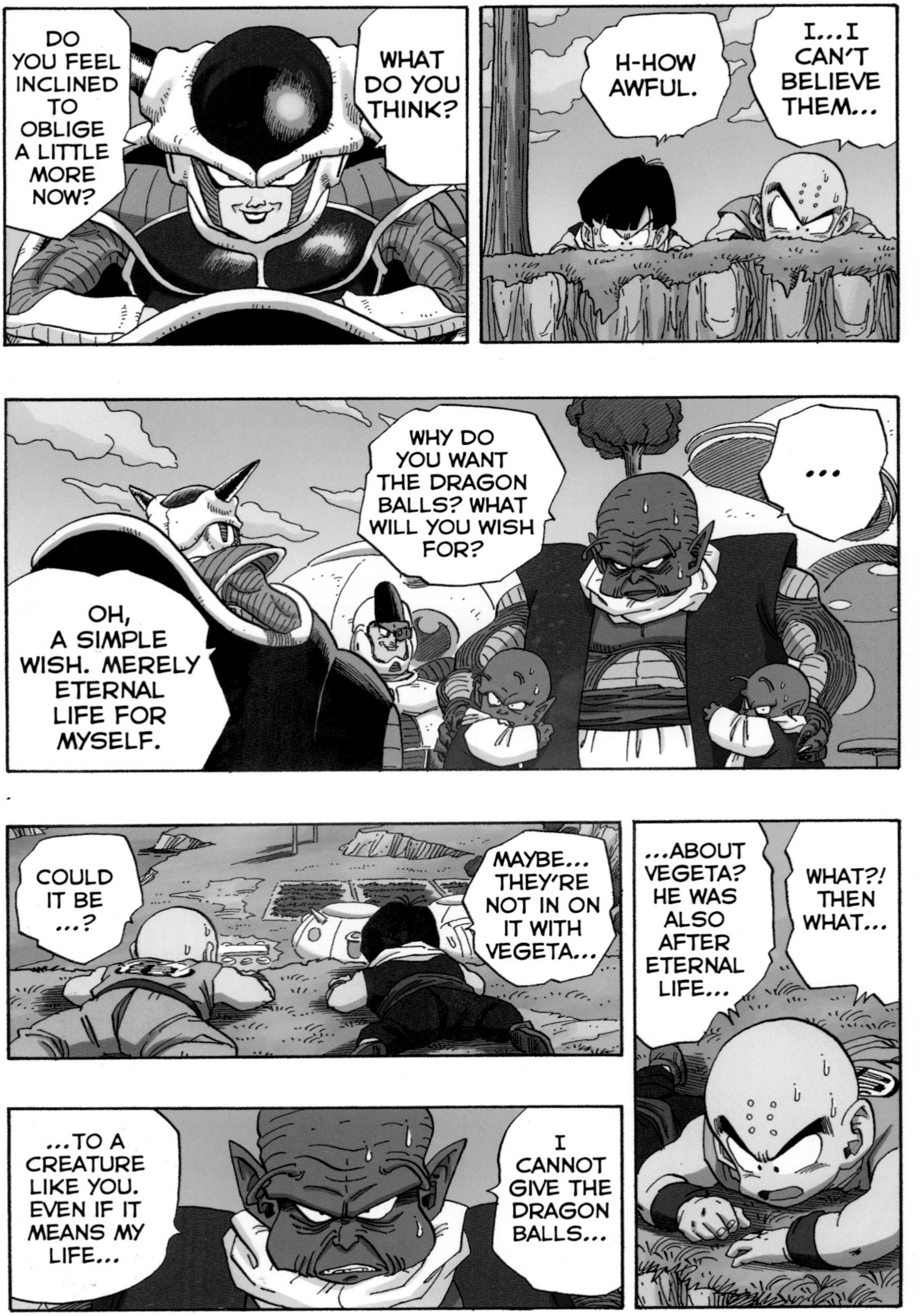
I...I CAN'T BELIEVE THEM...
H-HOW AWFUL.
WHAT DO YOU THINK?
DO YOU FEEL INCLINED TO OBLIGE A LITTLE MORE NOW?
...
WHY DO YOU WANT THE DRAGON BALLS? WHAT WILL YOU WISH FOR?
OH, A SIMPLE WISH. MERELY ETERNAL LIFE FOR MYSELF.
WHAT?! THEN WHAT...
...ABOUT VEGETA? HE WAS ALSO AFTER ETERNAL LIFE...
MAYBE... THEY'RE NOT IN ON IT WITH VEGETA...
COULD IT BE ...?
I CANNOT GIVE THE DRAGON BALLS...
...TO A CREATURE LIKE YOU. EVEN IF IT MEANS MY LIFE...

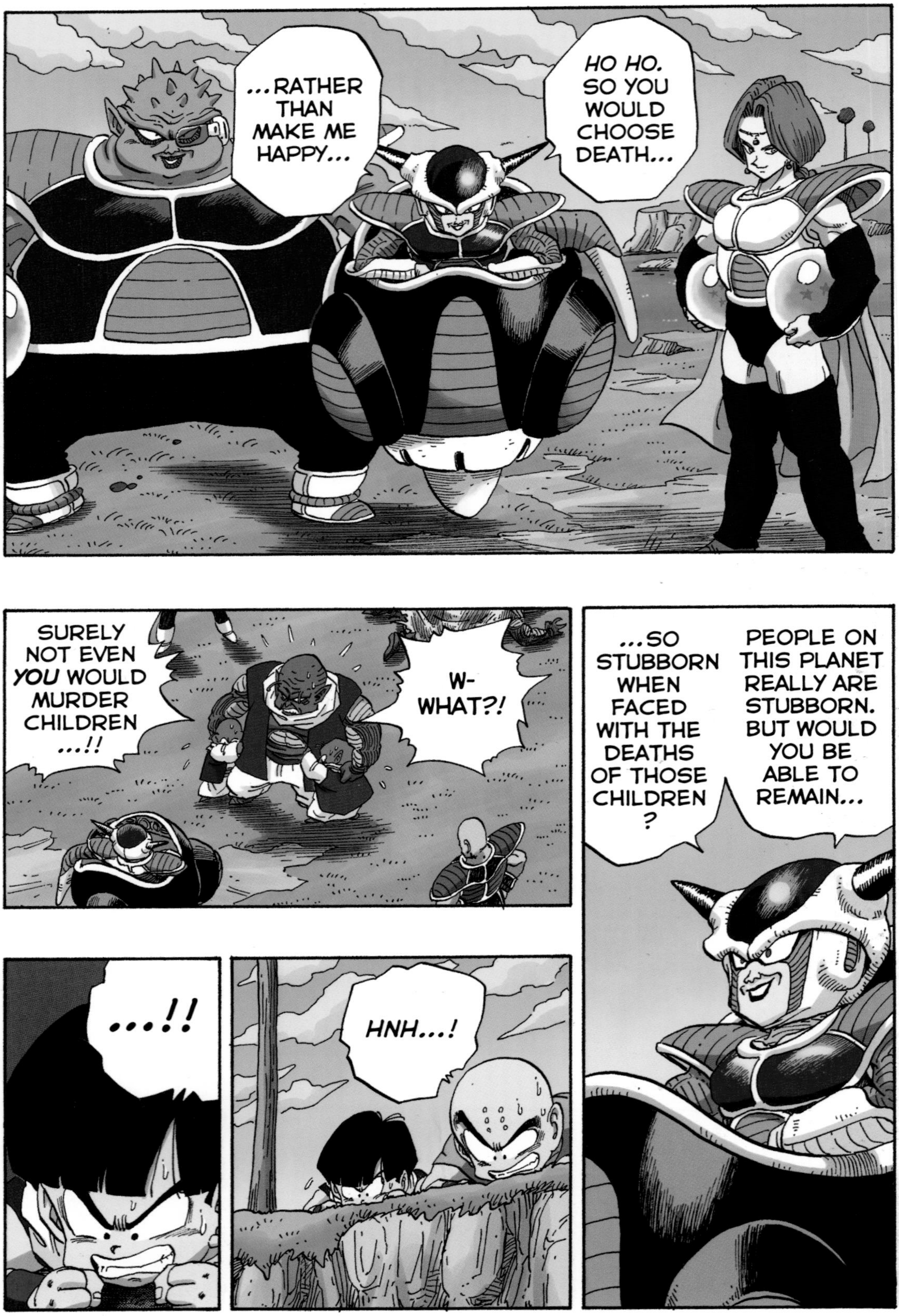
HO HO. SO YOU WOULD CHOOSE DEATH...
...RATHER THAN MAKE ME HAPPY...
PEOPLE ON THIS PLANET REALLY ARE STUBBORN. BUT WOULD YOU BE ABLE TO REMAIN...
...SO STUBBORN WHEN FACED WITH THE DEATHS OF THOSE CHILDREN?
W-WHAT?!
SURELY NOT EVEN *YOU* WOULD MURDER CHILDREN ...!!
HNH...!
...!!

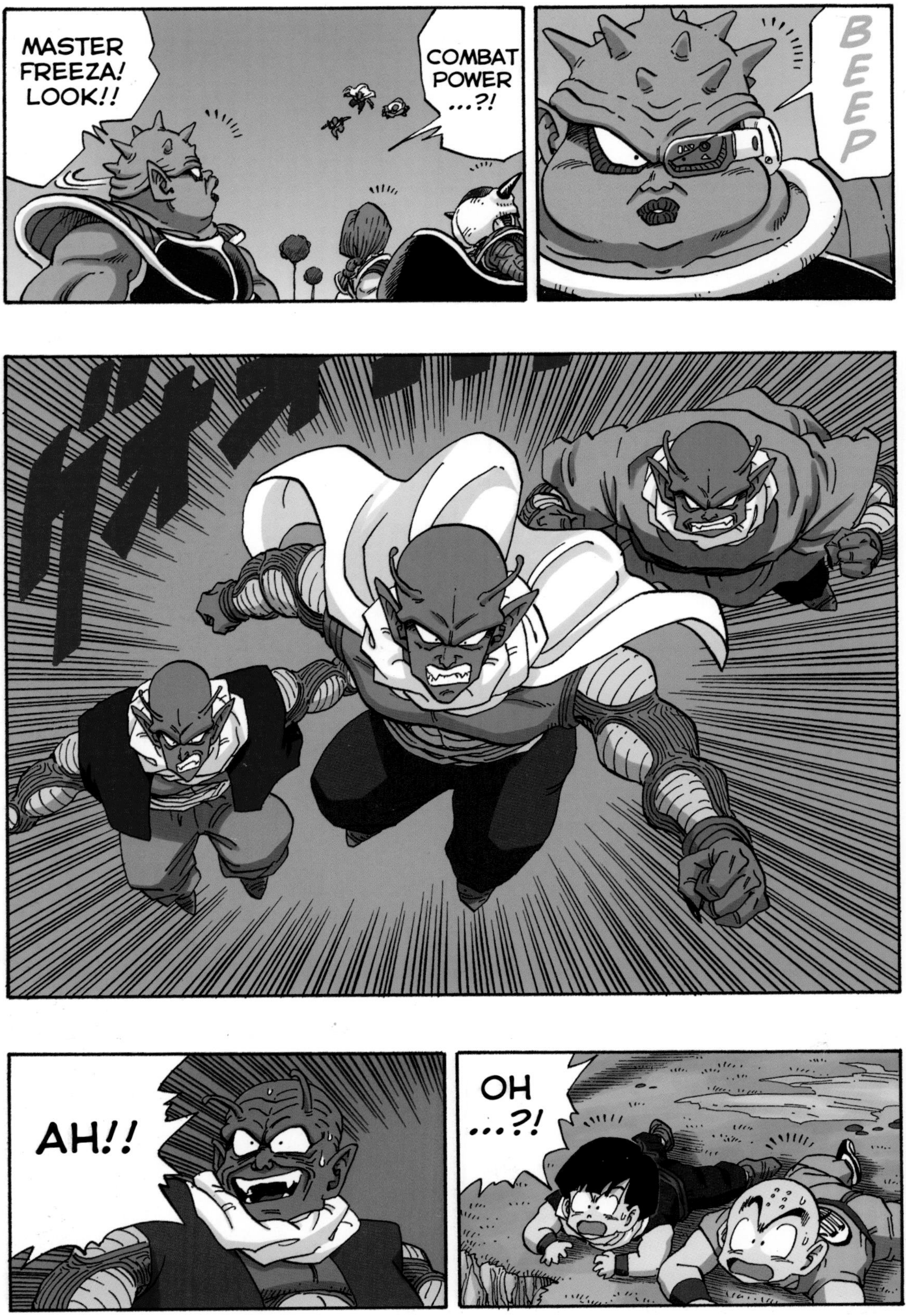

BEEP
COMBAT POWER ...?!
MASTER FREEZA! LOOK!!
OH ...?!
AH!!

Chapter 8 • Showdown!

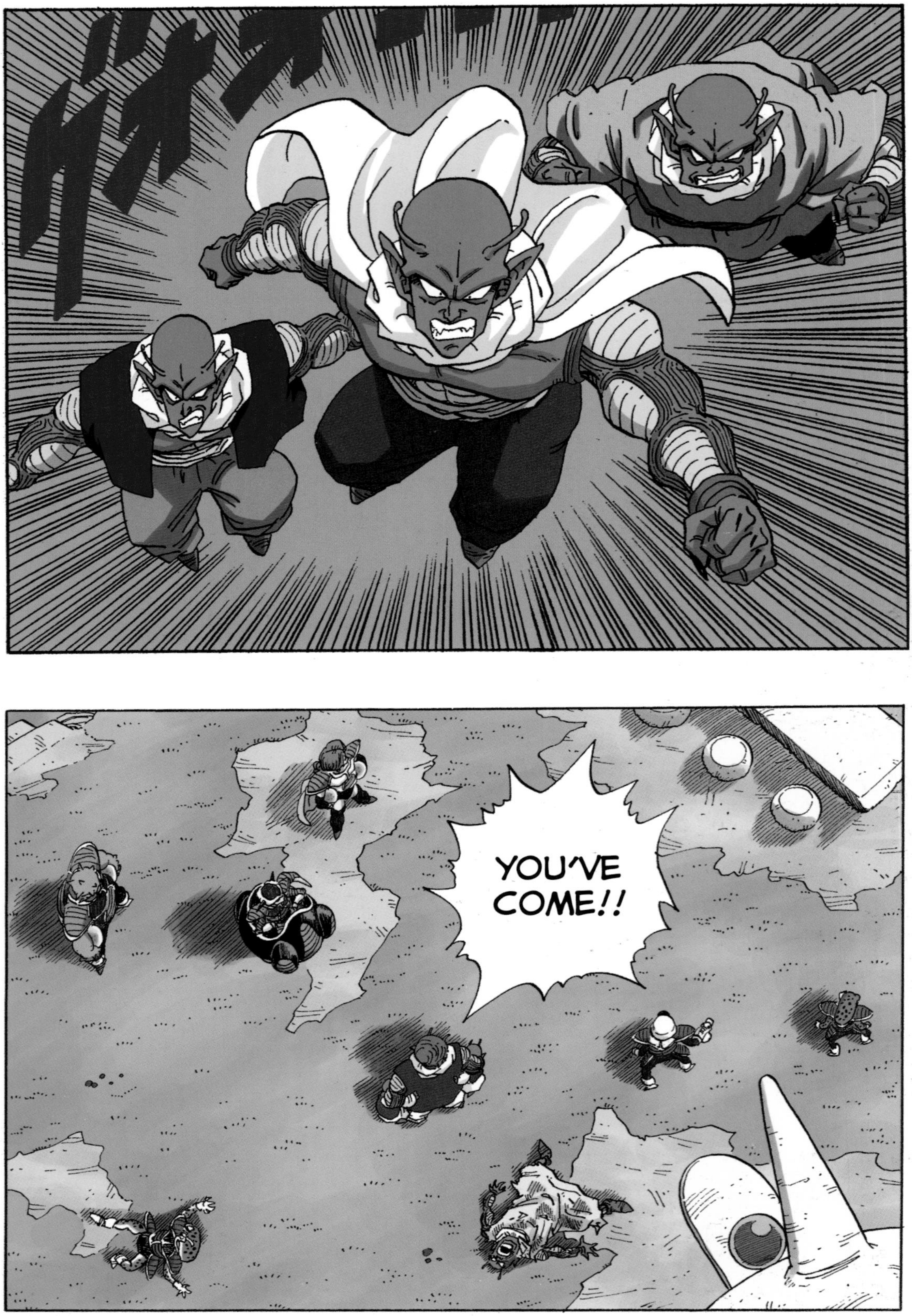
YOU'VE COME!!

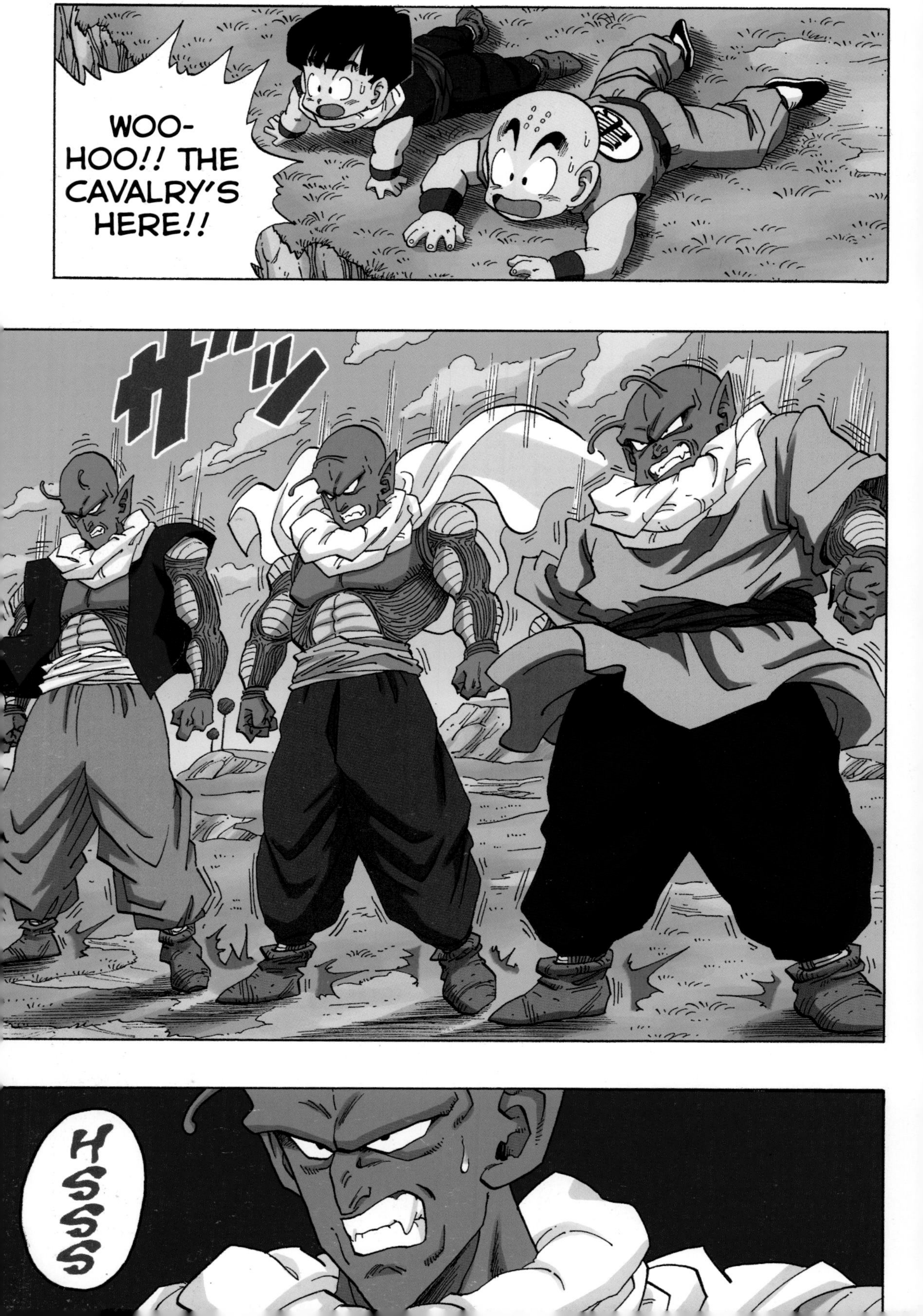
WOO-HOO!! THE CAVALRY'S HERE!!
HSSS

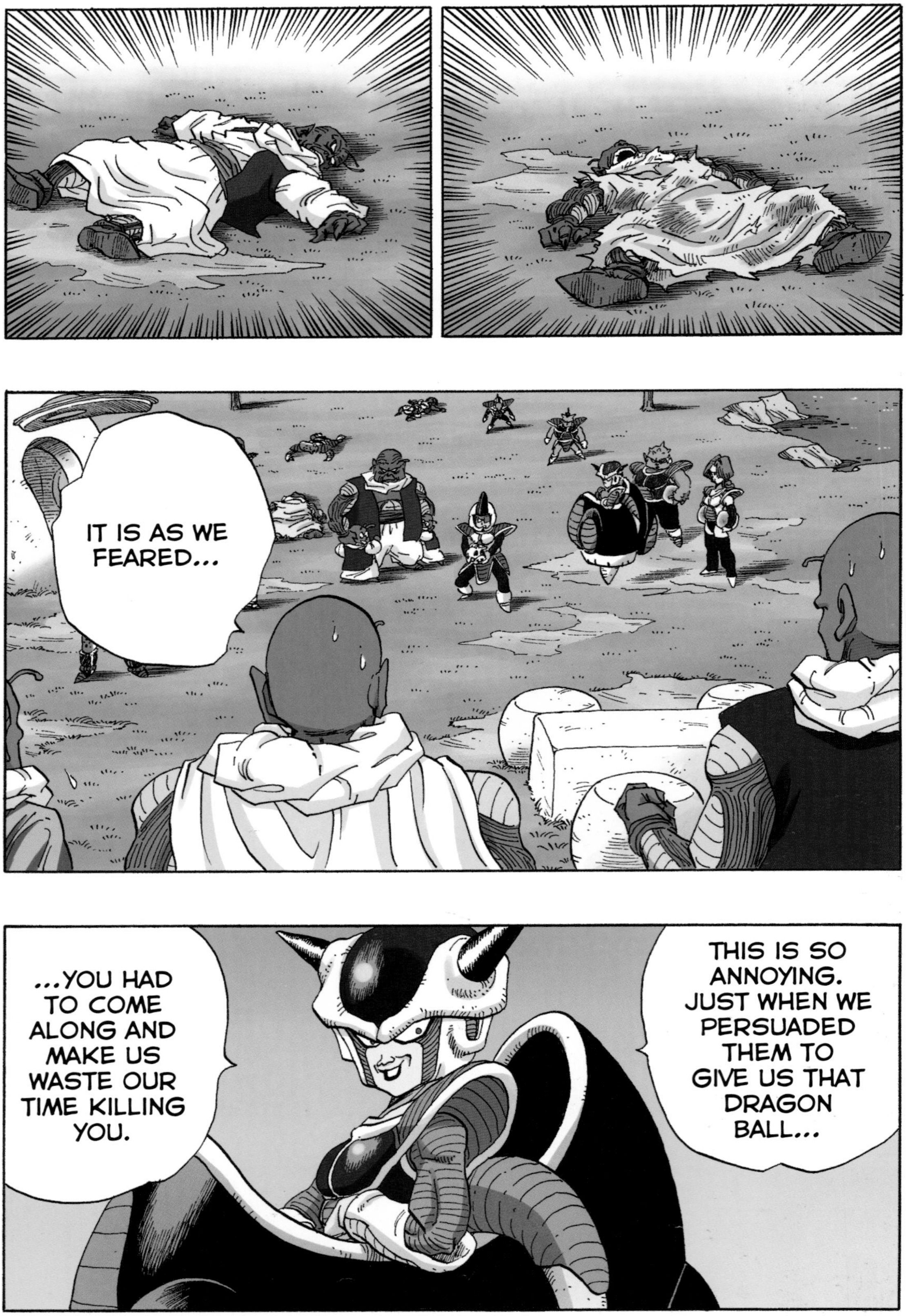
IT IS AS WE FEARED...
THIS IS SO ANNOYING. JUST WHEN WE PERSUADED THEM TO GIVE US THAT DRAGON BALL...
...YOU HAD TO COME ALONG AND MAKE US WASTE OUR TIME KILLING YOU.

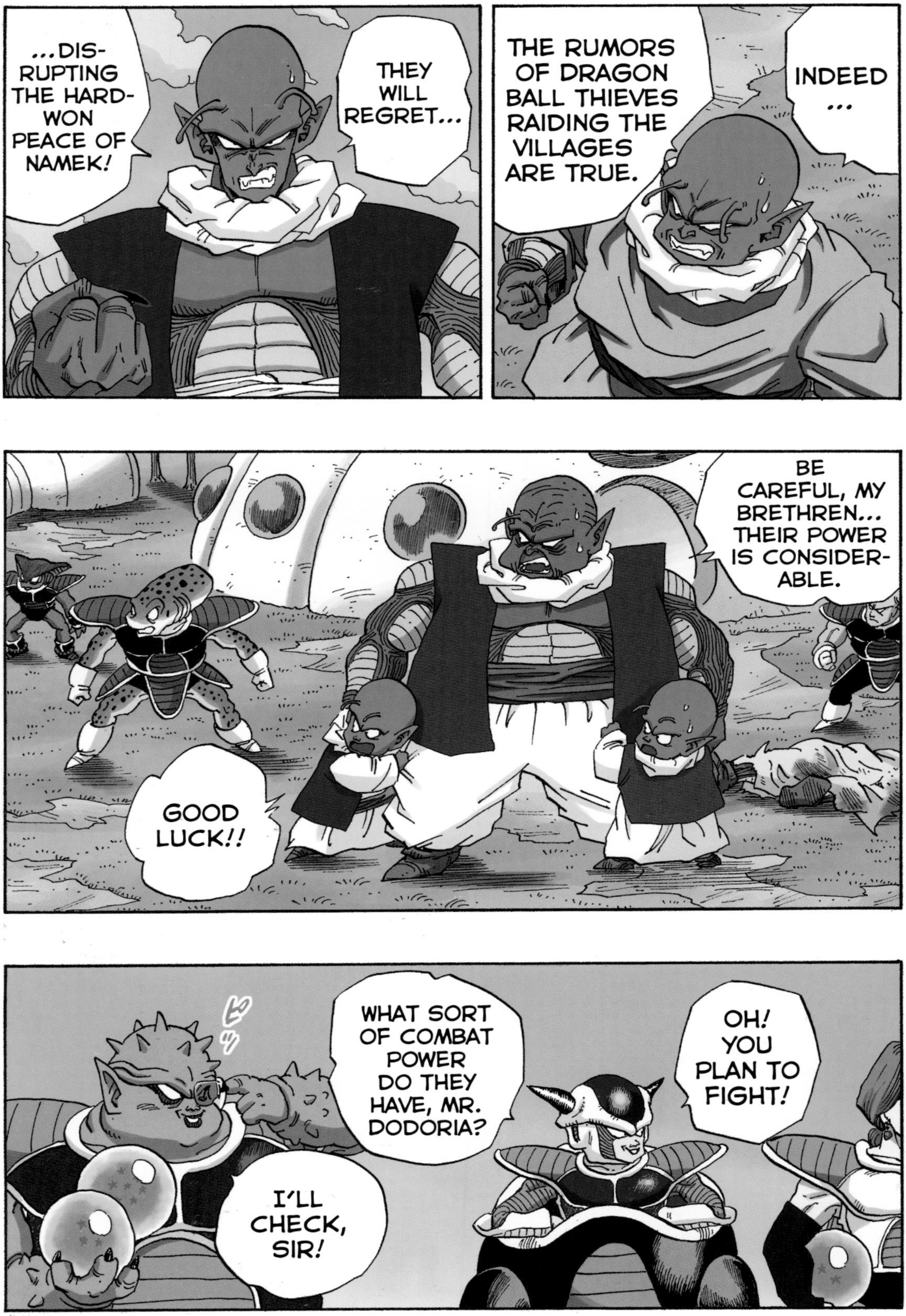
INDEED...
THE RUMORS OF DRAGON BALL THIEVES RAIDING THE VILLAGES ARE TRUE.
THEY WILL REGRET...
...DISRUPTING THE HARD-WON PEACE OF NAMEK!
BE CAREFUL, MY BRETHREN... THEIR POWER IS CONSIDERABLE.
GOOD LUCK!!
OH! YOU PLAN TO FIGHT!
WHAT SORT OF COMBAT POWER DO THEY HAVE, MR. DODORIA?
ピッ
I'LL CHECK, SIR!

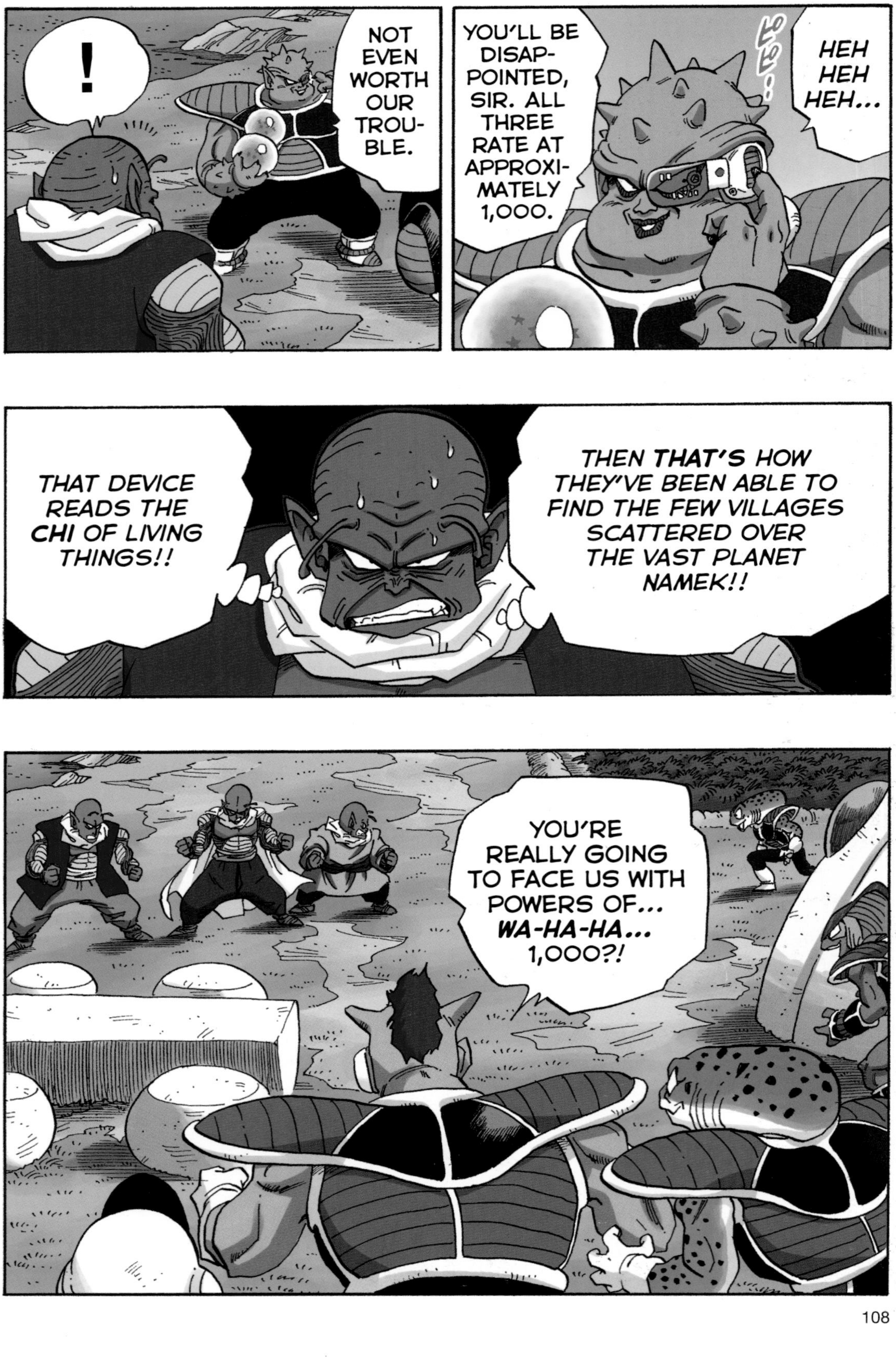

HEH HEH HEH...
YOU'LL BE DISAPPOINTED, SIR. ALL THREE RATE AT APPROXIMATELY 1,000.
NOT EVEN WORTH OUR TROUBLE.
!
THEN **THAT'S** HOW THEY'VE BEEN ABLE TO FIND THE FEW VILLAGES SCATTERED OVER THE VAST PLANET NAMEK!!
THAT DEVICE READS THE **CHI** OF LIVING THINGS!!
YOU'RE REALLY GOING TO FACE US WITH POWERS OF... **WA-HA-HA...** 1,000?!

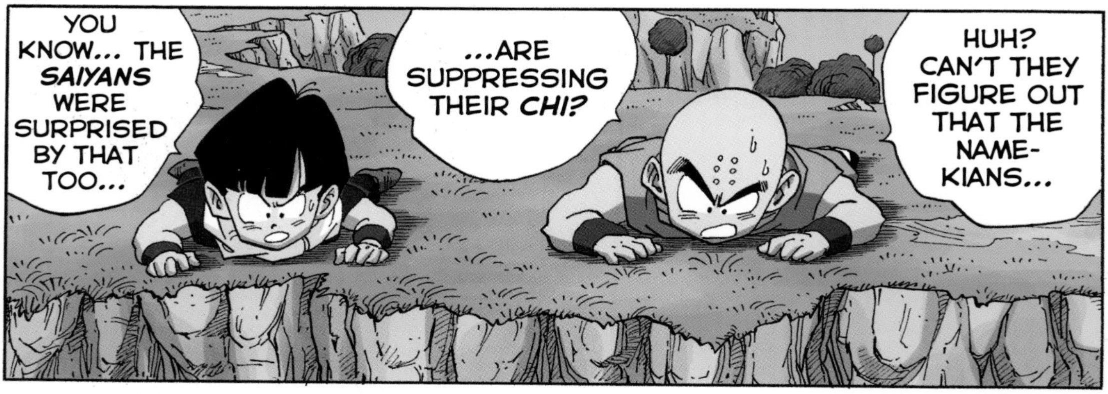
HUH? CAN'T THEY FIGURE OUT THAT THE NAME-KIANS...
...ARE SUPPRESSING THEIR *CHI?*
YOU KNOW... THE *SAIYANS* WERE SURPRISED BY THAT TOO...

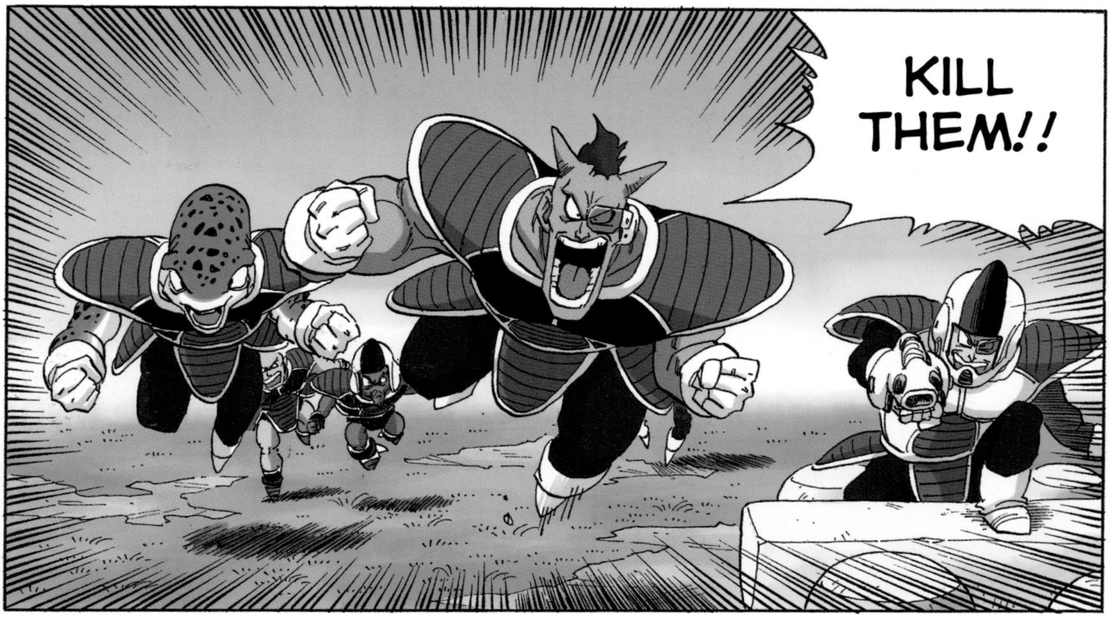
KILL THEM!!

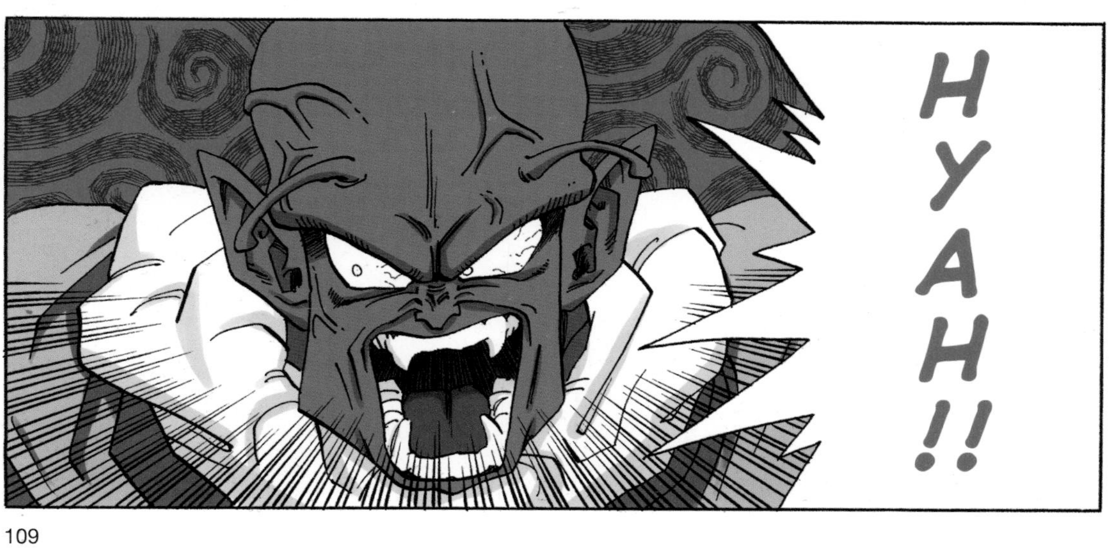
HYAH!!

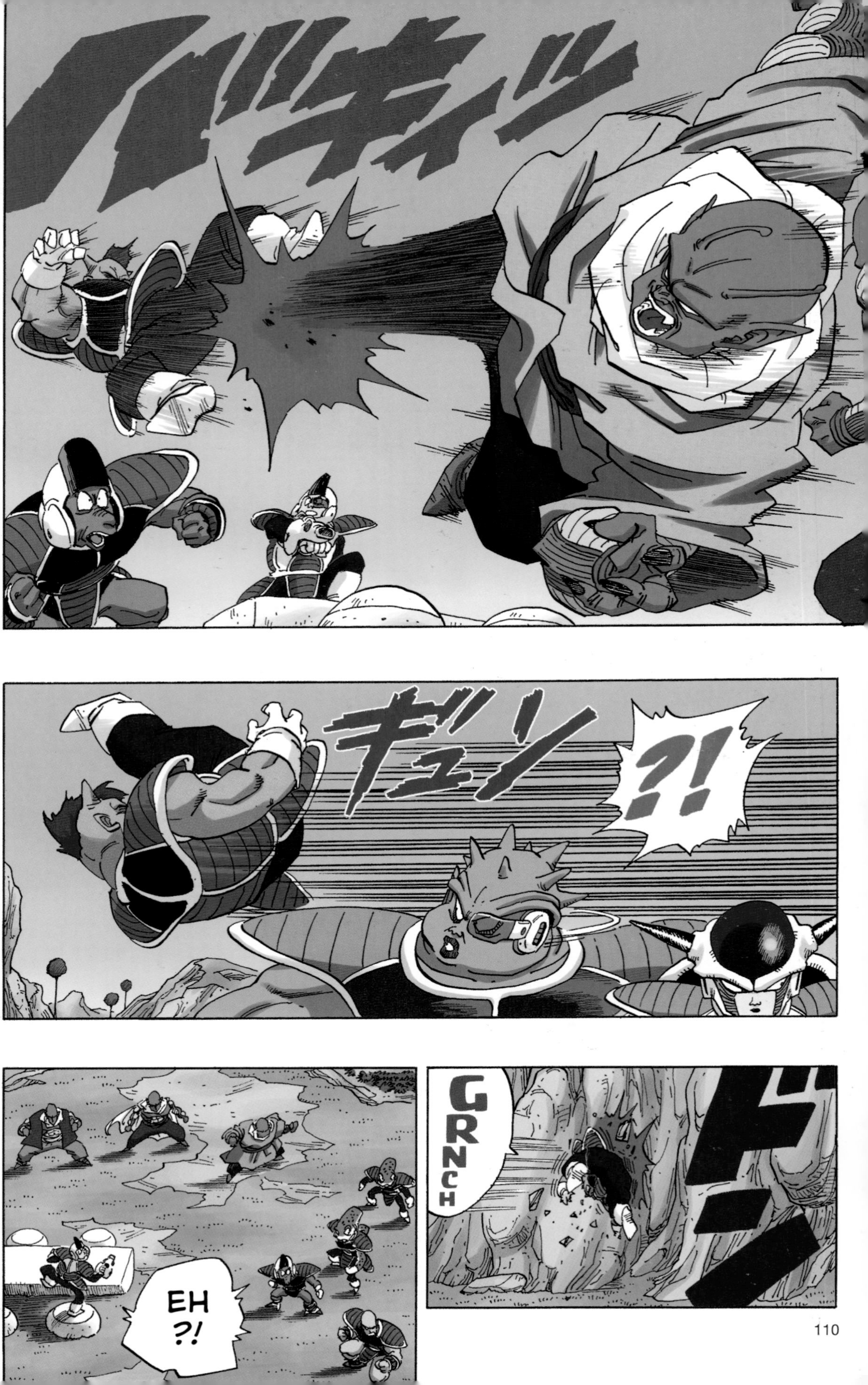

ギュン
?!
GRNCH
EH ?!

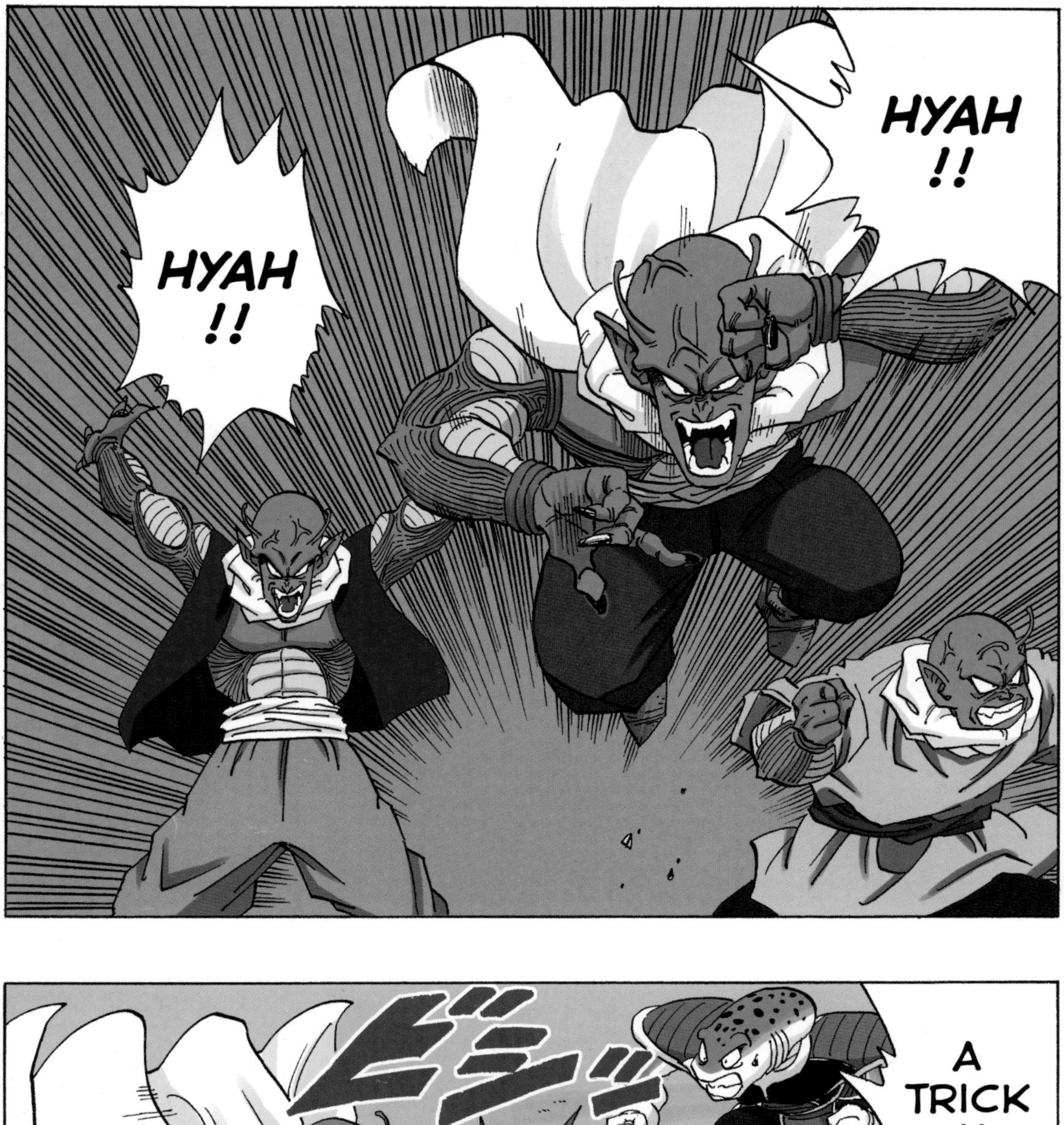
HYAH !!
HYAH !!

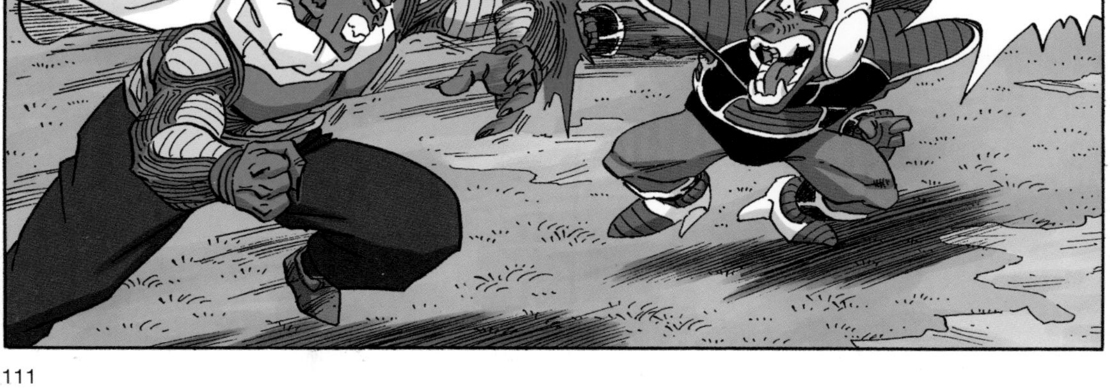
A TRICK !!

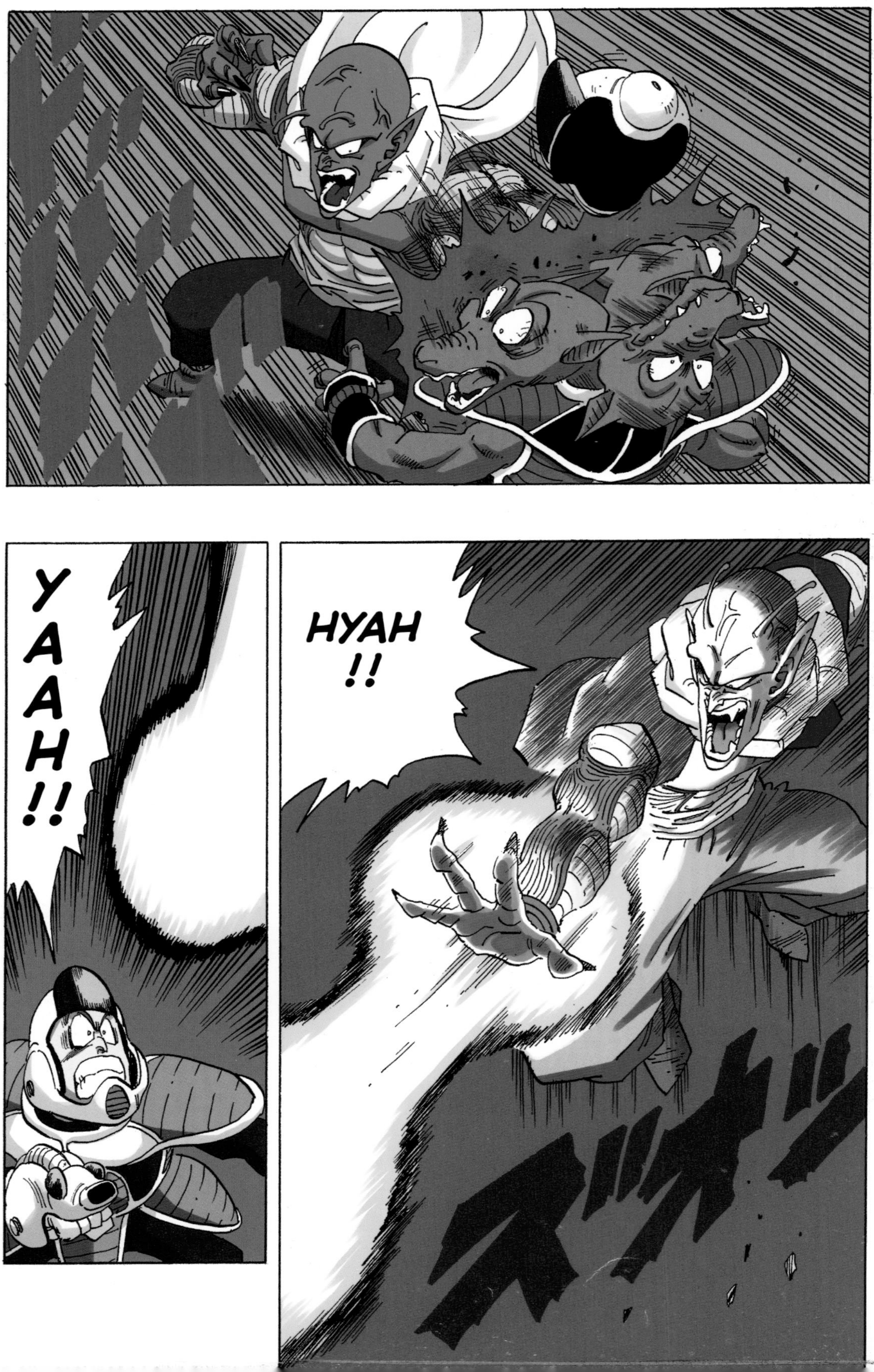
HYAH!!
YAAH!!

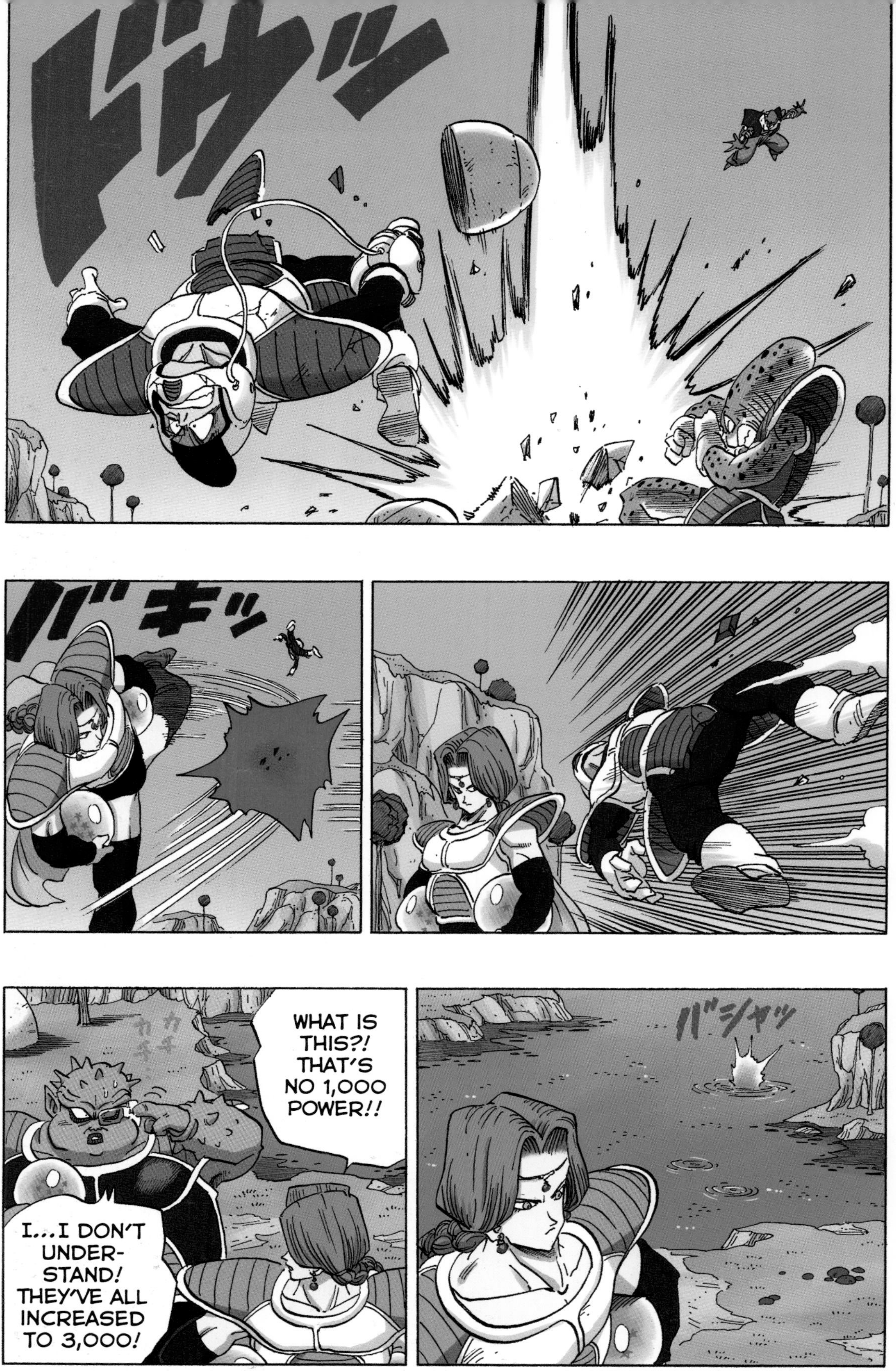
バキッ
バシャッ
カチ
カチ…
WHAT IS THIS?! THAT'S NO 1,000 POWER!!
I...I DON'T UNDER-STAND! THEY'VE ALL INCREASED TO 3,000!

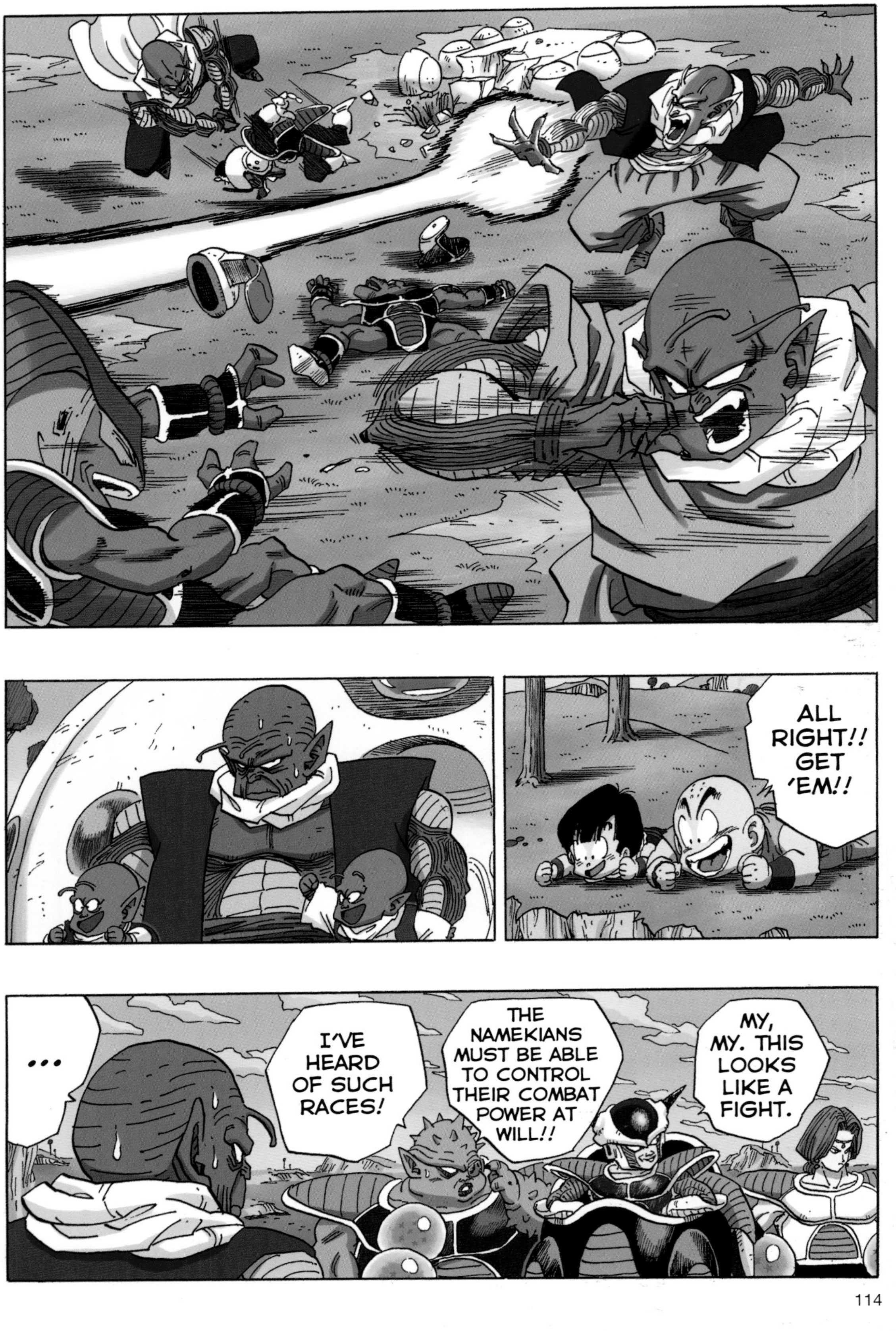
ALL RIGHT!! GET 'EM!!
MY, MY. THIS LOOKS LIKE A FIGHT.
THE NAMEKIANS MUST BE ABLE TO CONTROL THEIR COMBAT POWER AT WILL!!
I'VE HEARD OF SUCH RACES!
...

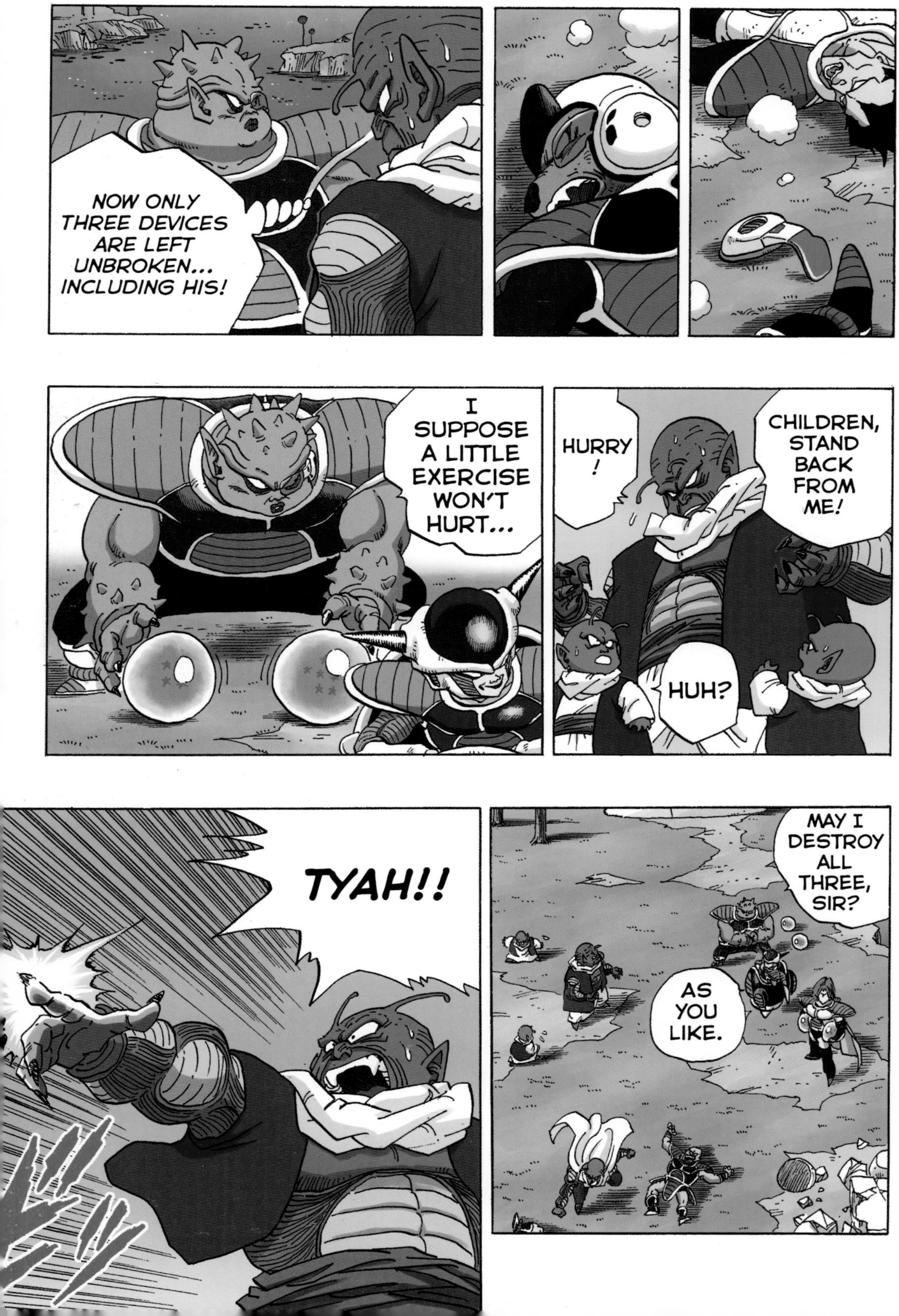
NOW ONLY THREE DEVICES ARE LEFT UNBROKEN... INCLUDING HIS!
CHILDREN, STAND BACK FROM ME!
HURRY!
HUH?
I SUPPOSE A LITTLE EXERCISE WON'T HURT...
MAY I DESTROY ALL THREE, SIR?
AS YOU LIKE.
TYAH!!

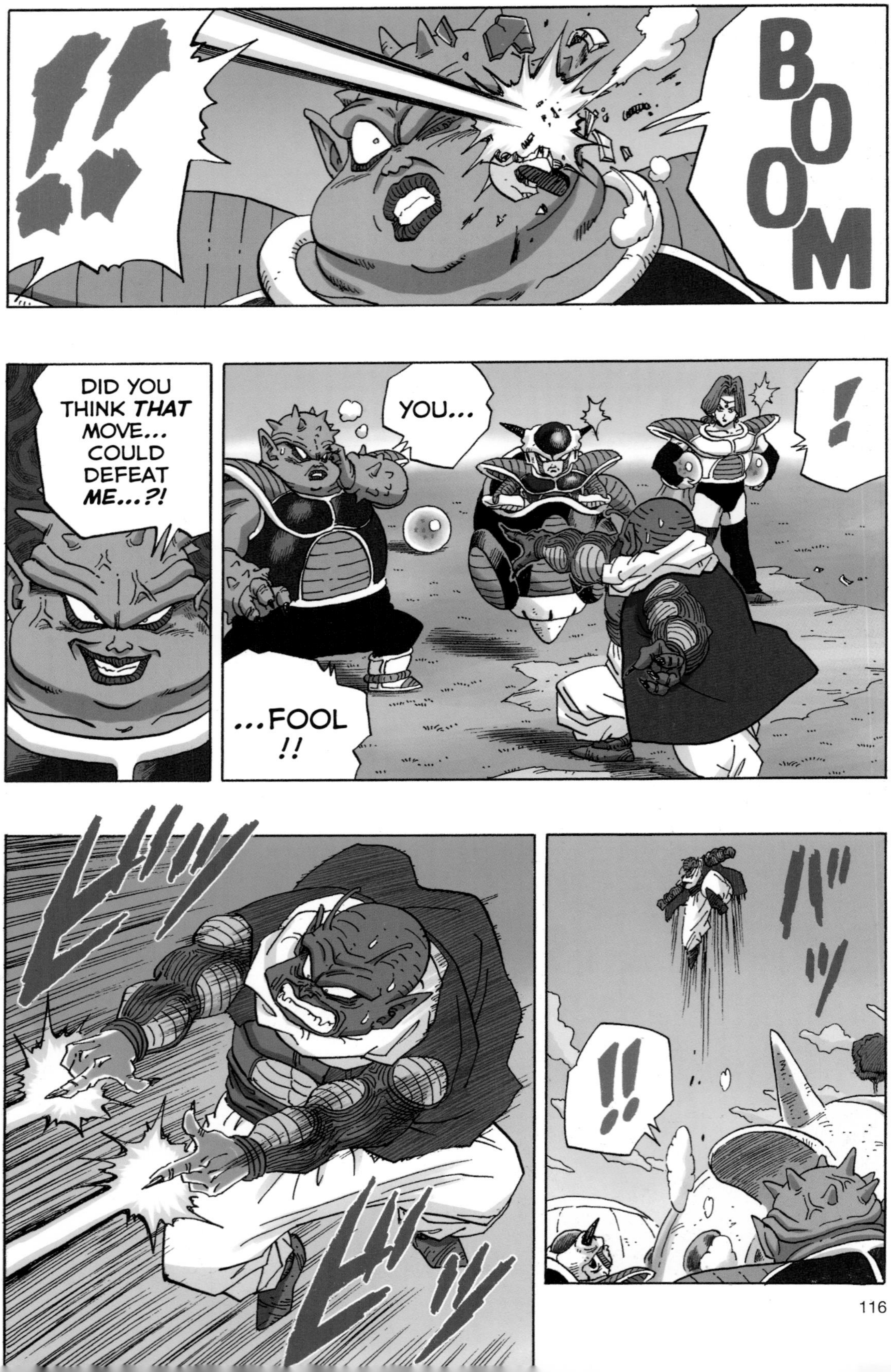
BOOM
!!
!
YOU...
...FOOL !!
DID YOU THINK *THAT* MOVE... COULD DEFEAT *ME...?!*
!!

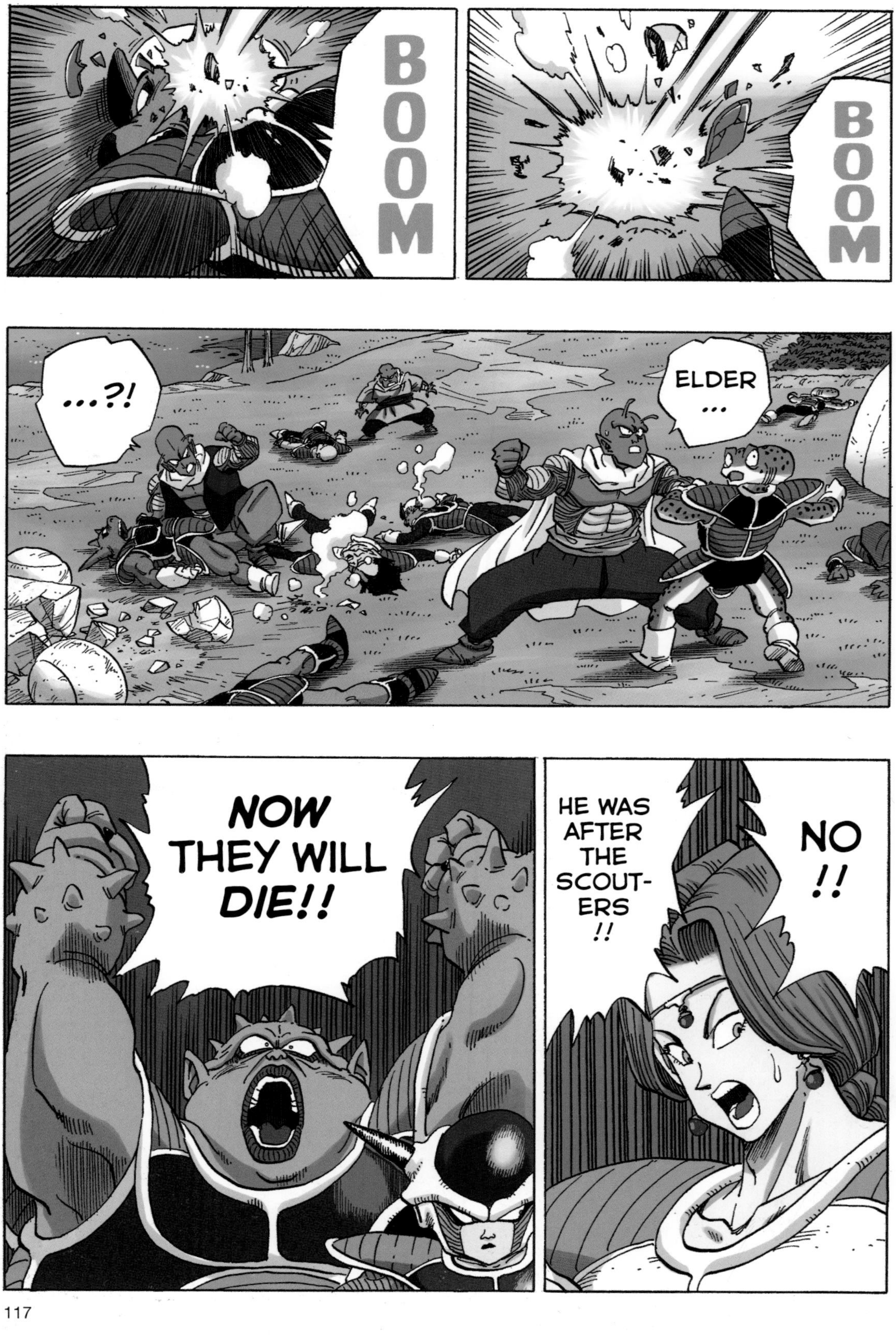
BOOM
BOOM
ELDER ...
...?!
NO !!
HE WAS AFTER THE SCOUTERS !!
NOW THEY WILL DIE!!

Chapter 9 • Ten Seconds of Death

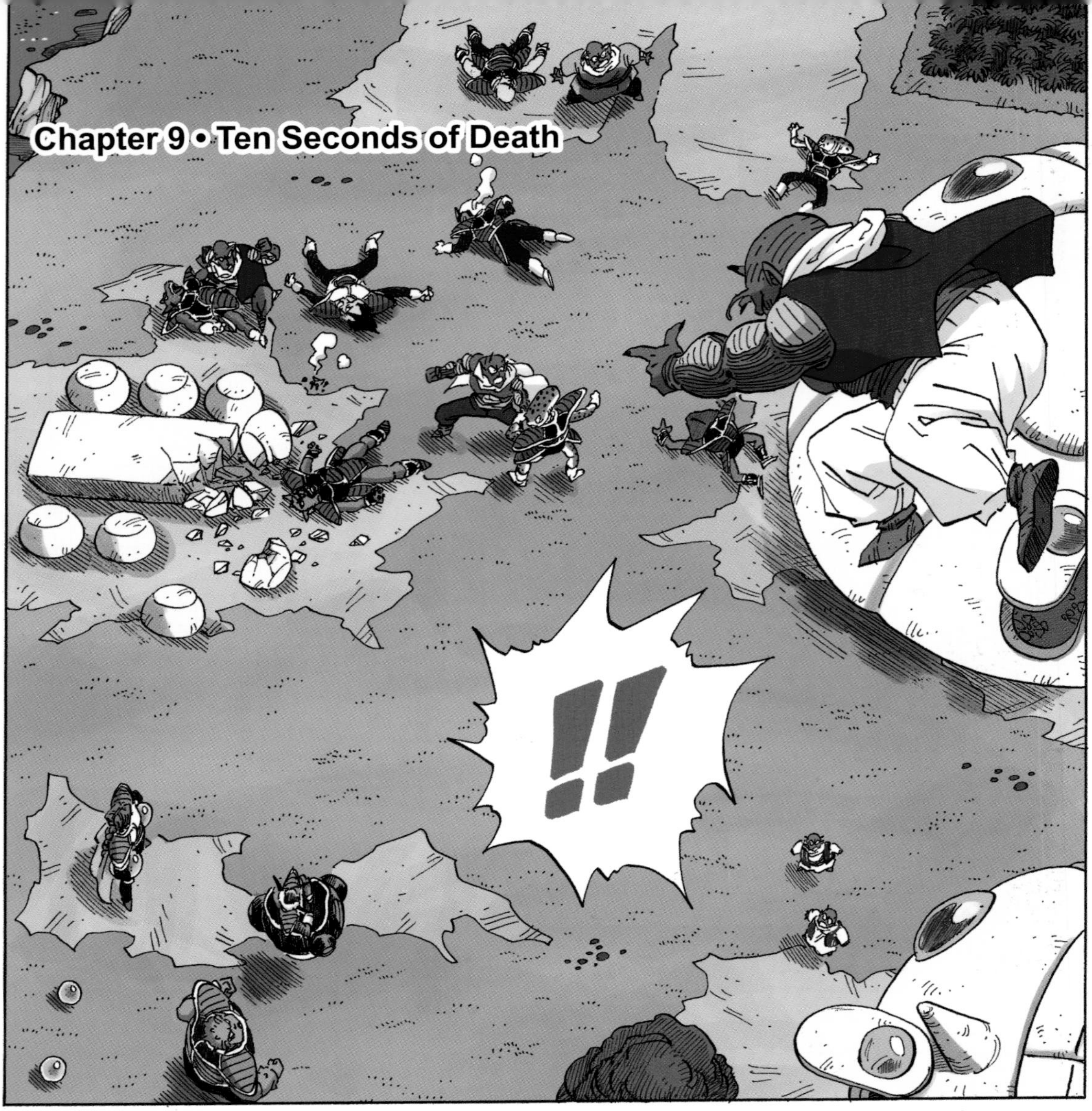
!!

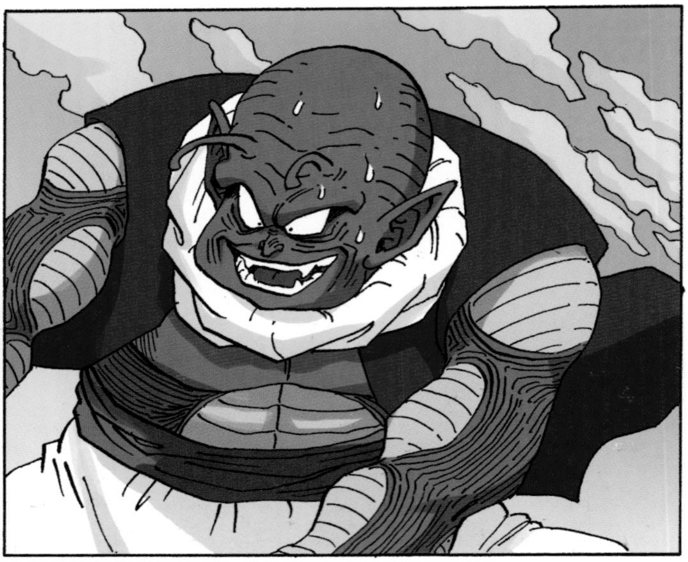

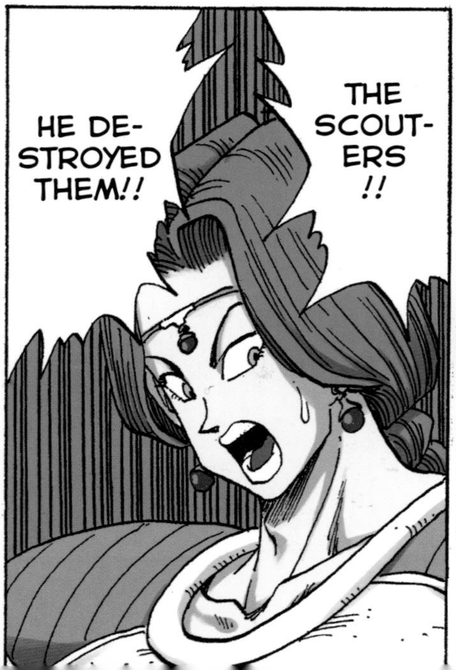
THE SCOUT-ERS!!
HE DE-STROYED THEM!!

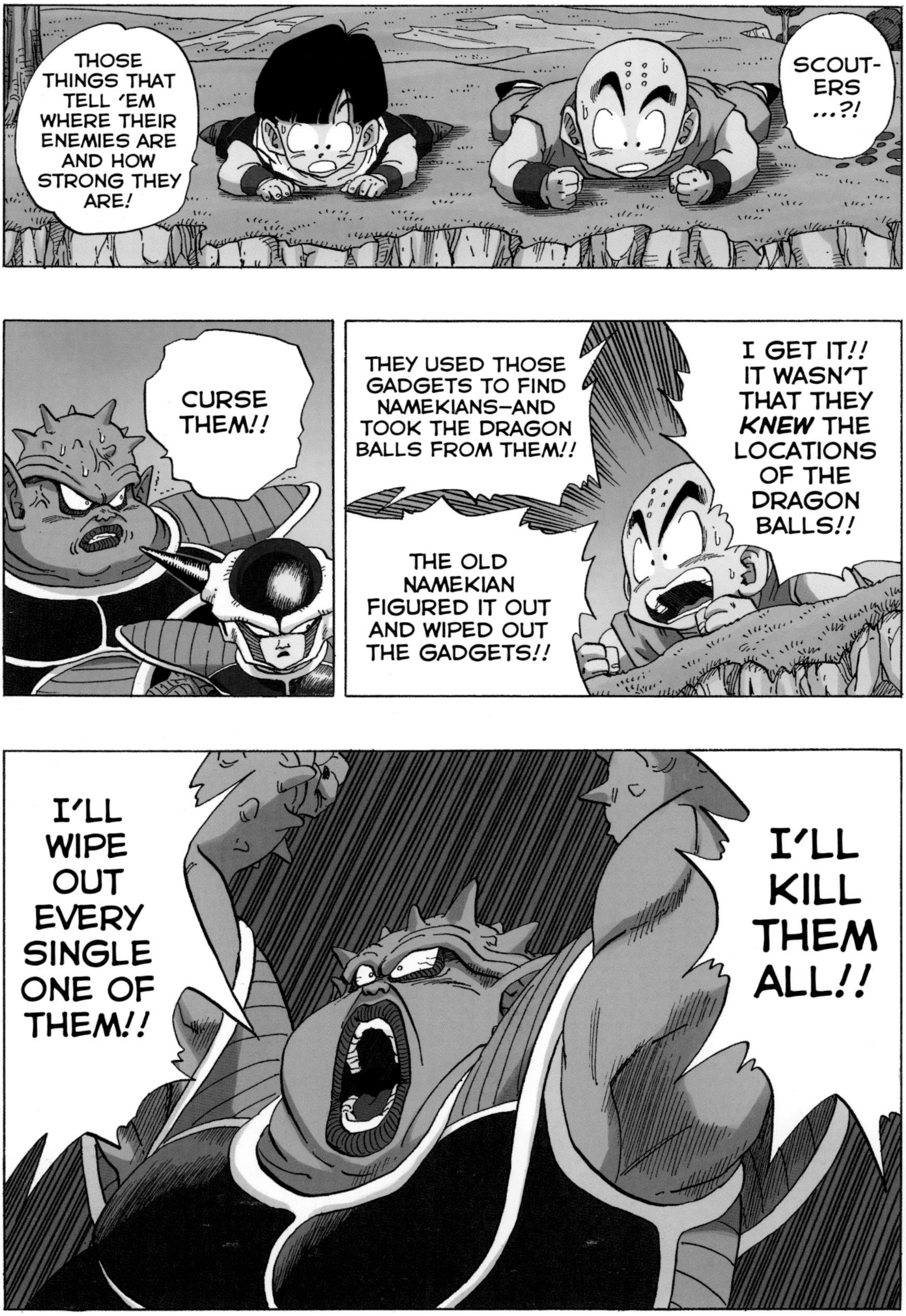
SCOUT-ERS ...?!
THOSE THINGS THAT TELL 'EM WHERE THEIR ENEMIES ARE AND HOW STRONG THEY ARE!
I GET IT!! IT WASN'T THAT THEY *KNEW* THE LOCATIONS OF THE DRAGON BALLS!!
THEY USED THOSE GADGETS TO FIND NAMEKIANS—AND TOOK THE DRAGON BALLS FROM THEM!!
THE OLD NAMEKIAN FIGURED IT OUT AND WIPED OUT THE GADGETS!!
CURSE THEM!!
I'LL KILL THEM ALL!!
I'LL WIPE OUT EVERY SINGLE ONE OF THEM!!

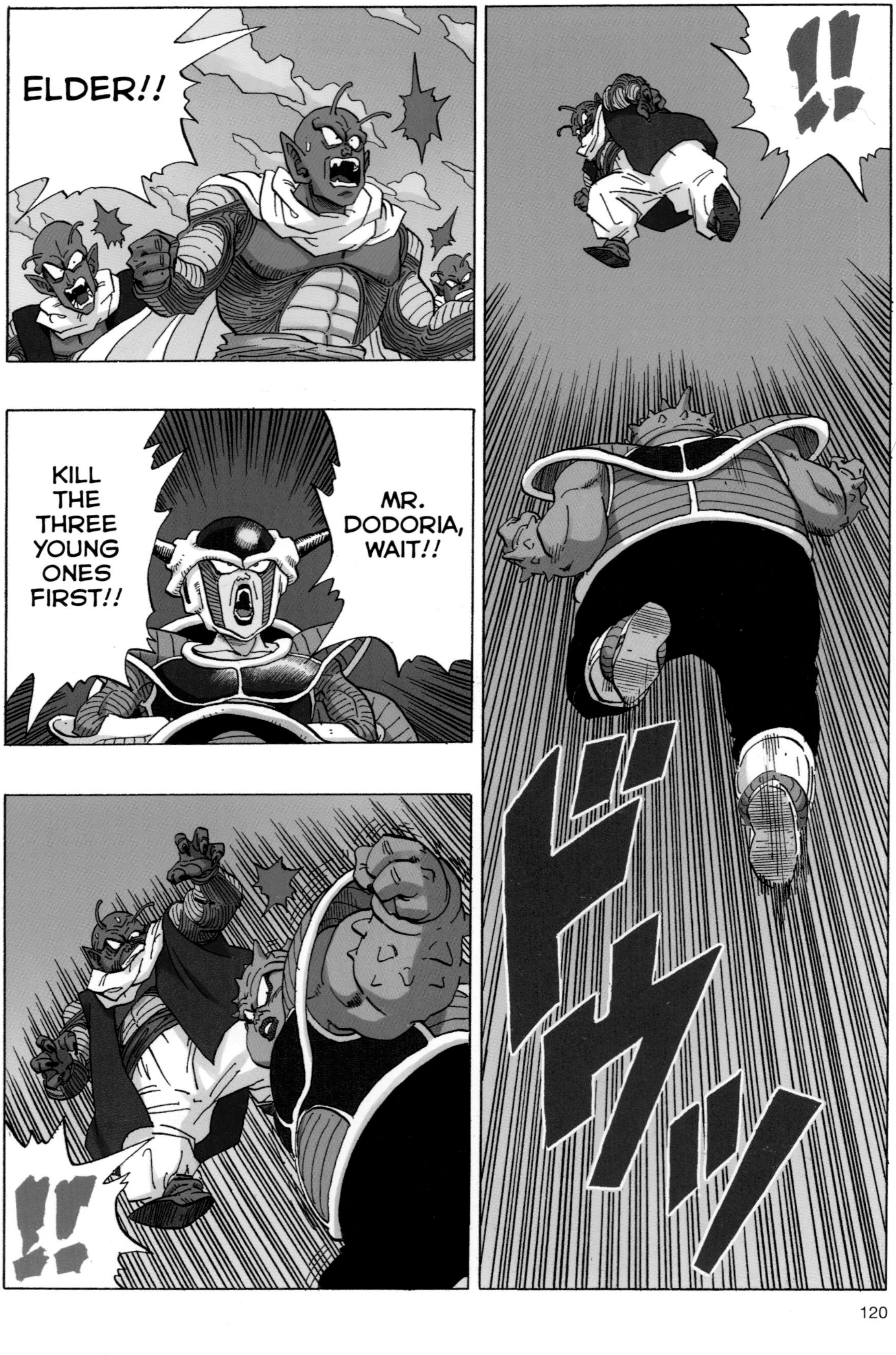
!!
ドゥッ
ELDER!!
MR. DODORIA, WAIT!!
KILL THE THREE YOUNG ONES FIRST!!
!!

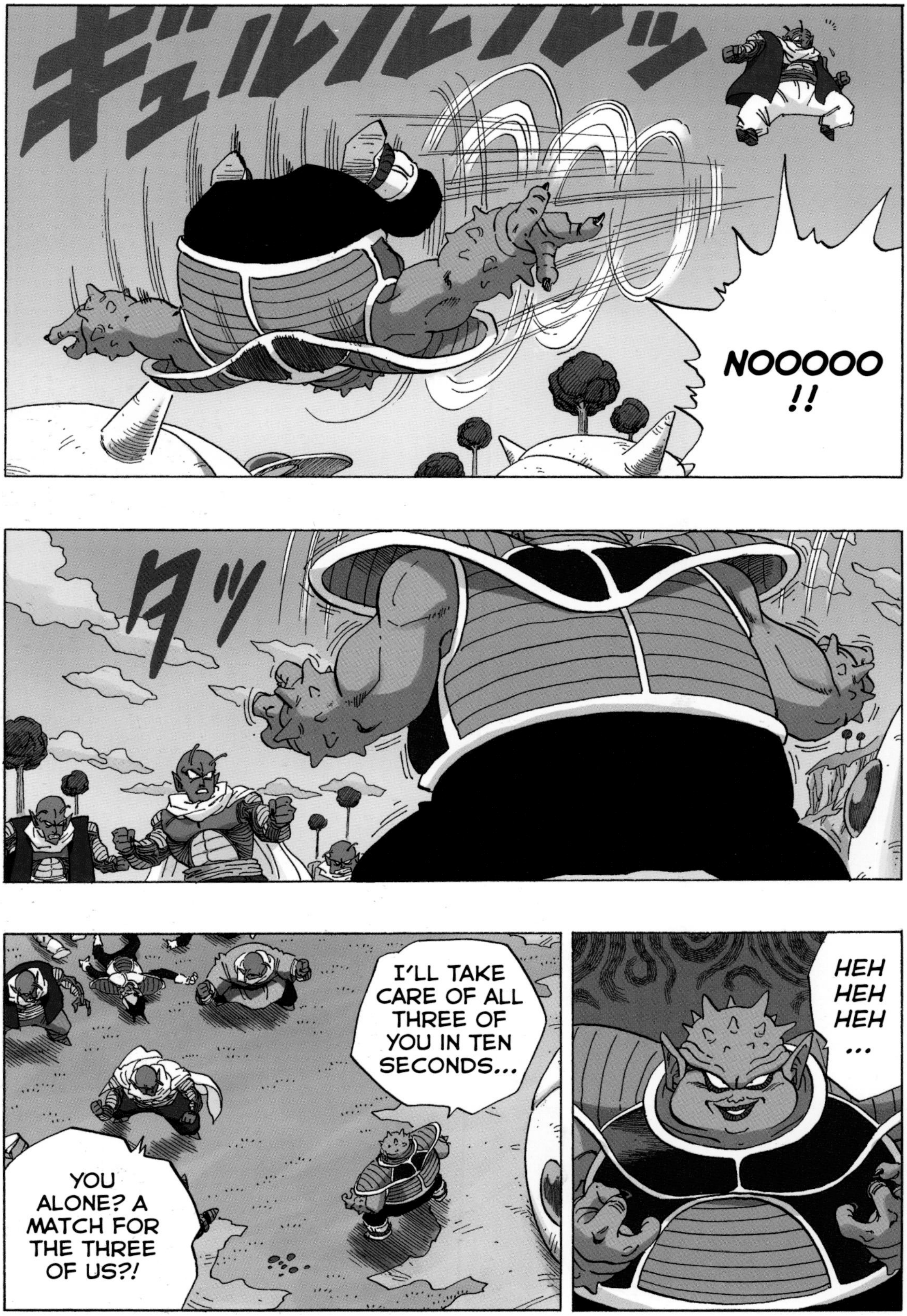
ギュルルルッ
NOOOOO !!
タッ
HEH HEH HEH ...
I'LL TAKE CARE OF ALL THREE OF YOU IN TEN SECONDS...
YOU ALONE? A MATCH FOR THE THREE OF US?!

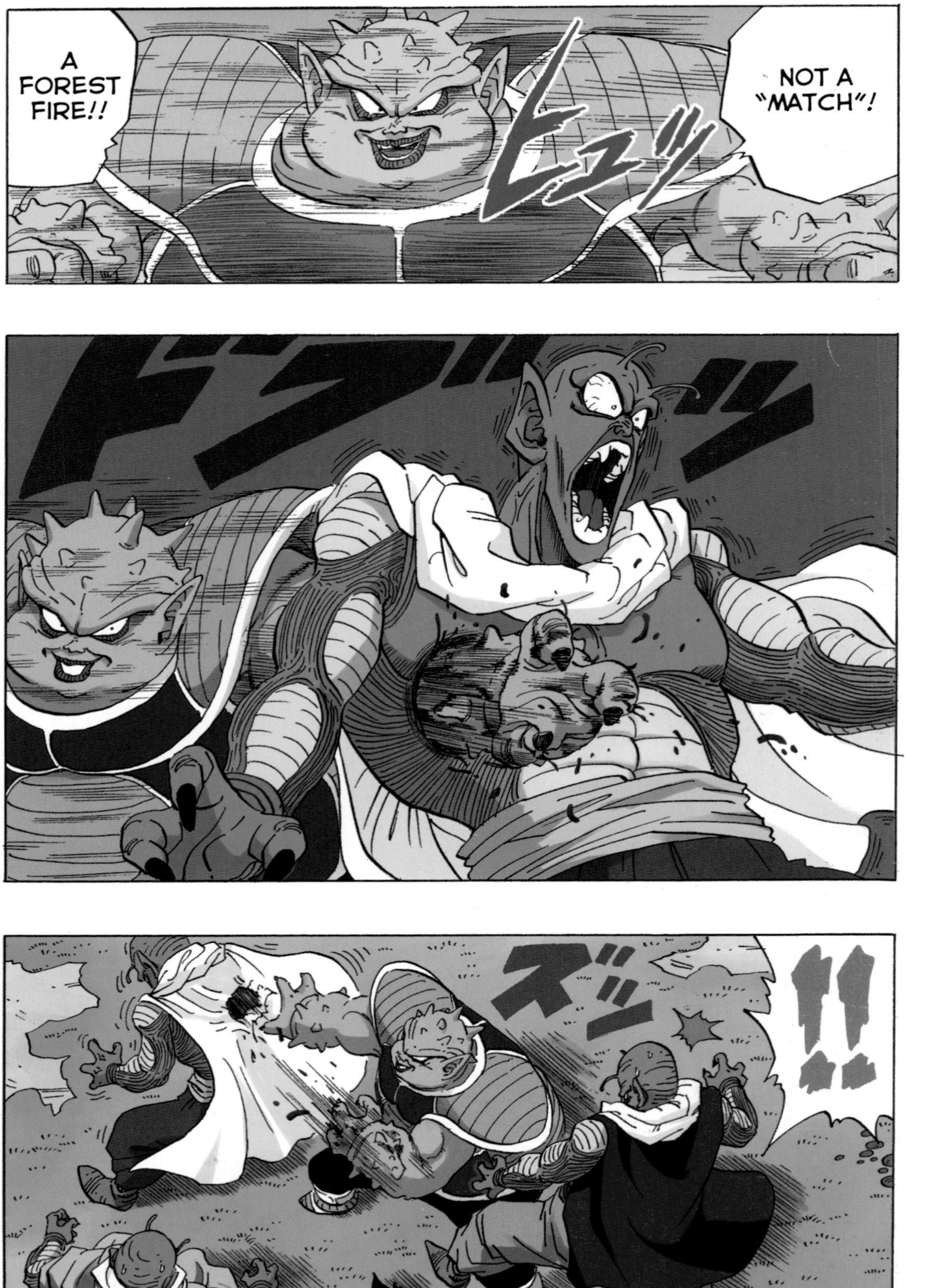
NOT A "MATCH"!
A FOREST FIRE!!
!!

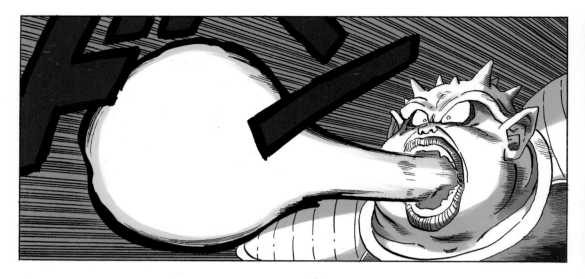

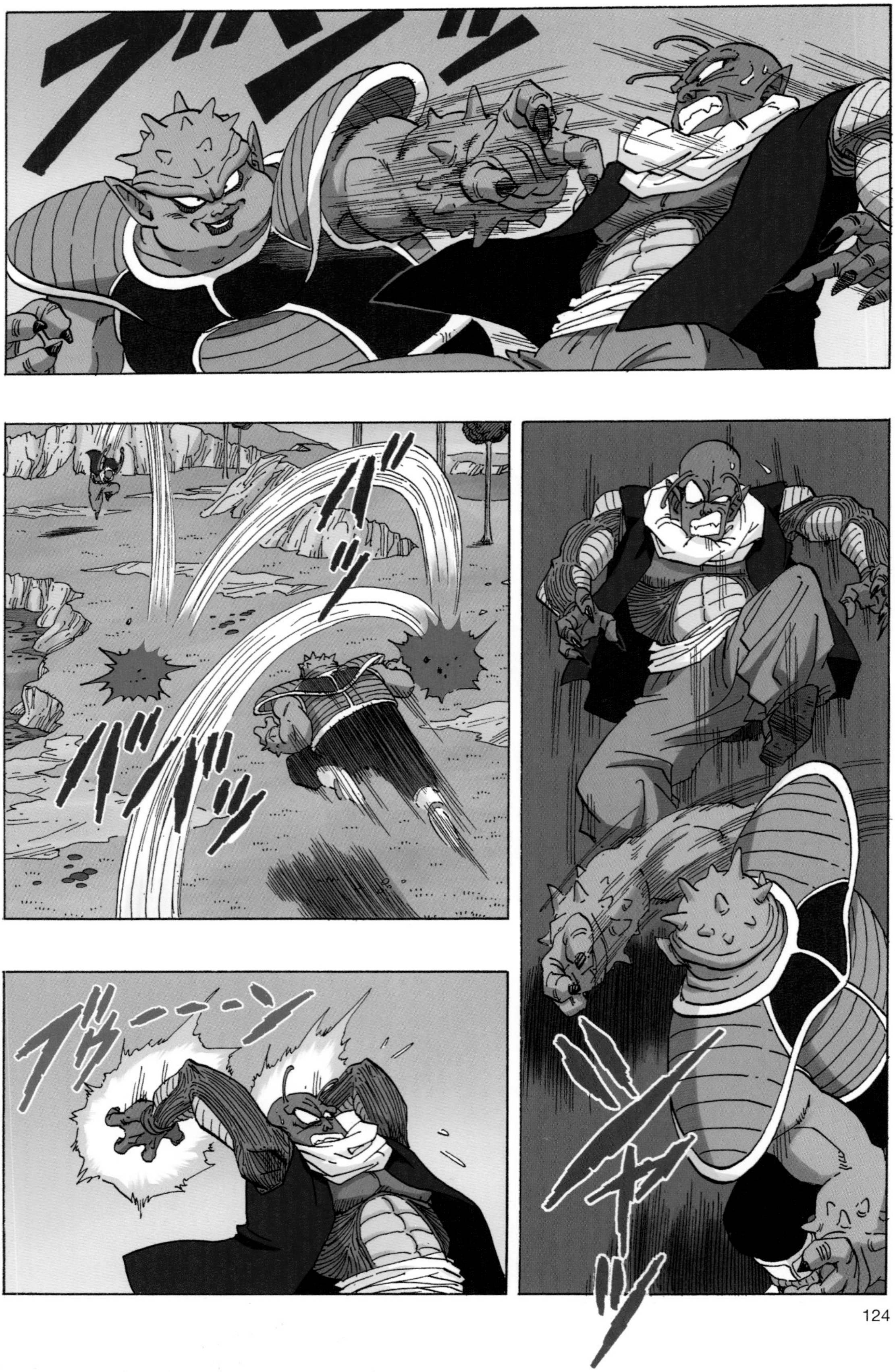
ブバンッ
ババッ
ブゥーーーン

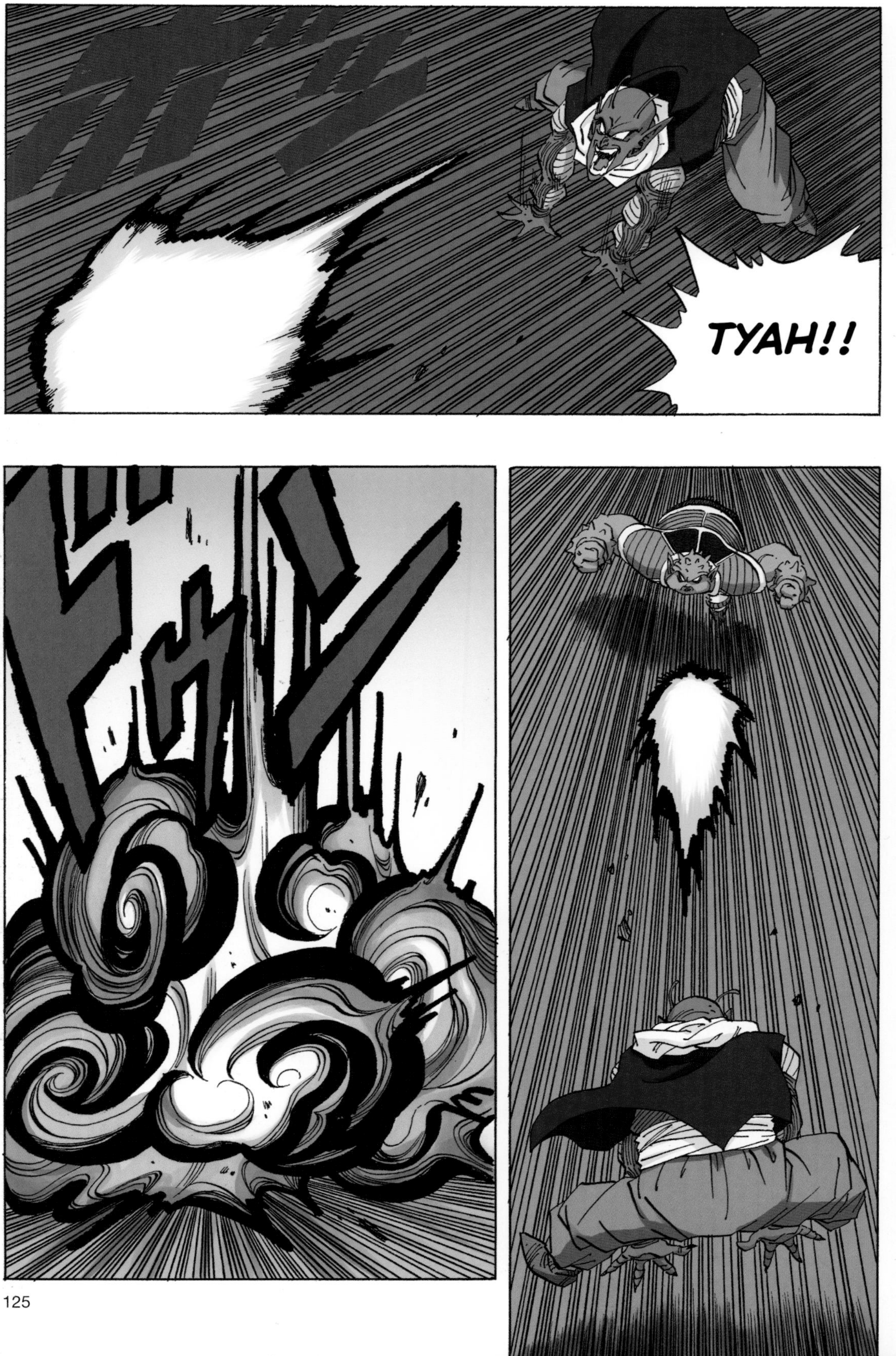
TYAH!!

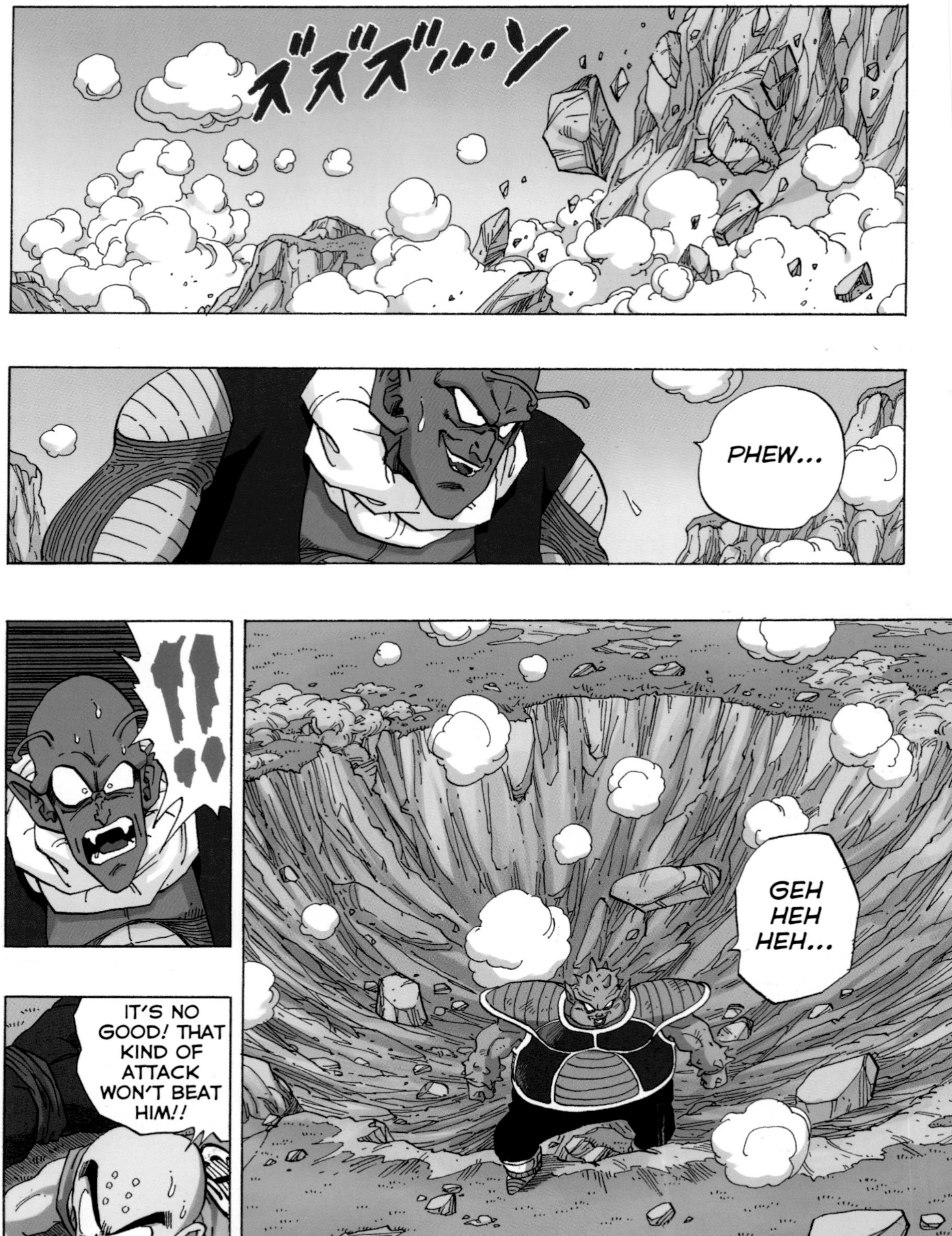
ズズズ...ン
PHEW...
GEH HEH HEH...
IT'S NO GOOD! THAT KIND OF ATTACK WON'T BEAT HIM!!

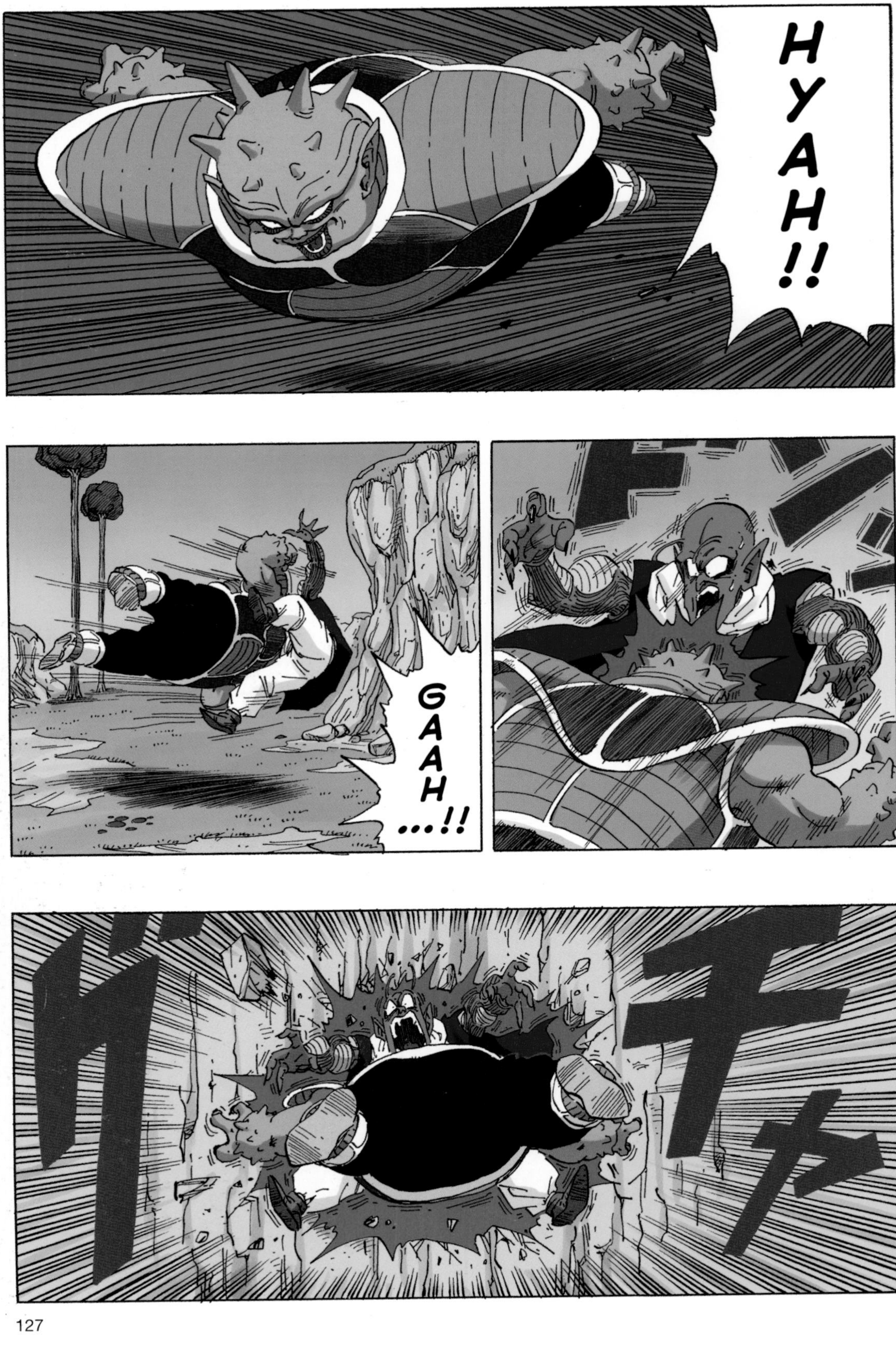
HYAH!!
GAAH...!!

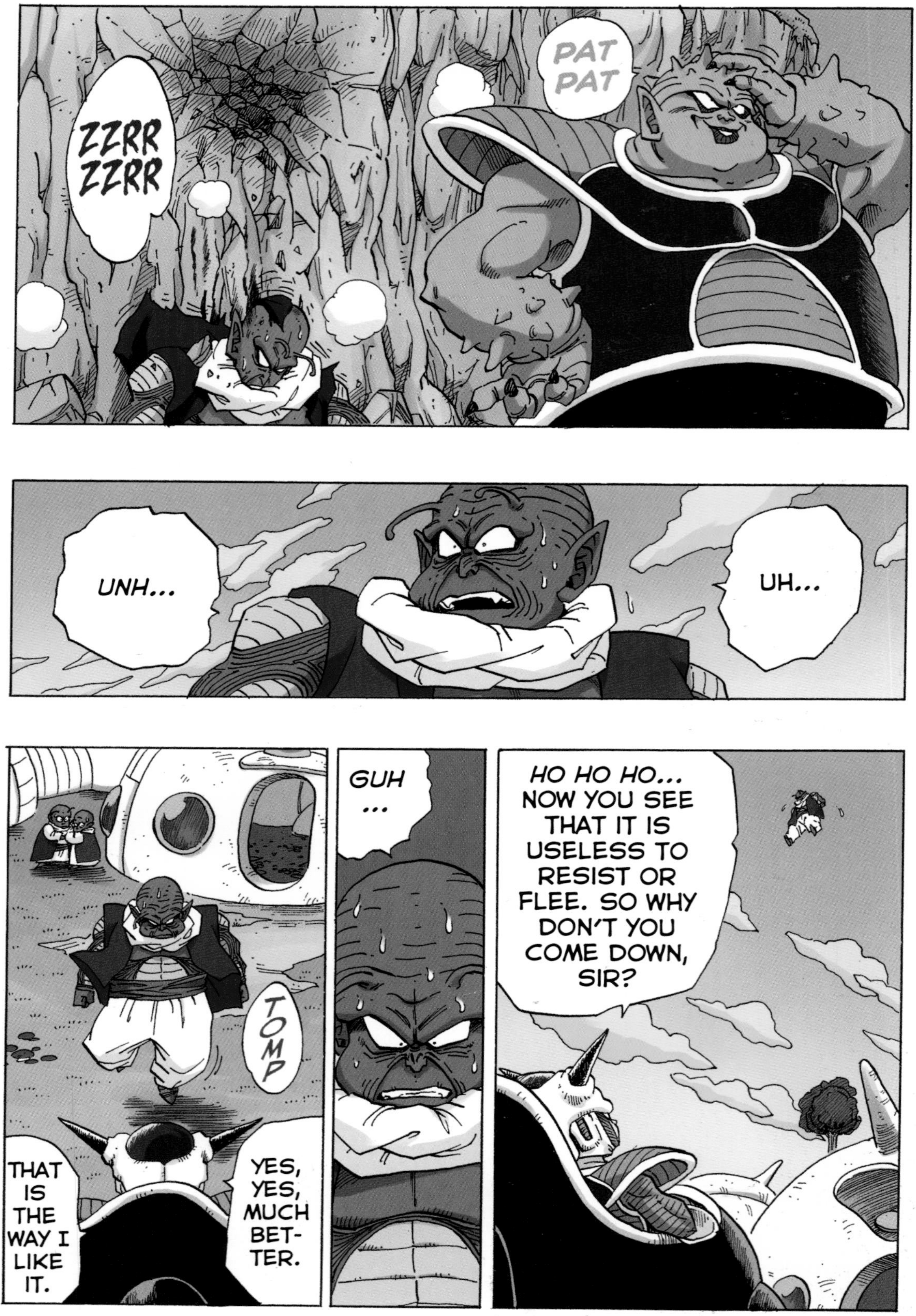
PAT PAT
ZZRR ZZRR
UH...
UNH...
HO HO HO... NOW YOU SEE THAT IT IS USELESS TO RESIST OR FLEE. SO WHY DON'T YOU COME DOWN, SIR?
GUH ...
TOMP
YES, YES, MUCH BETTER.
THAT IS THE WAY I LIKE IT.

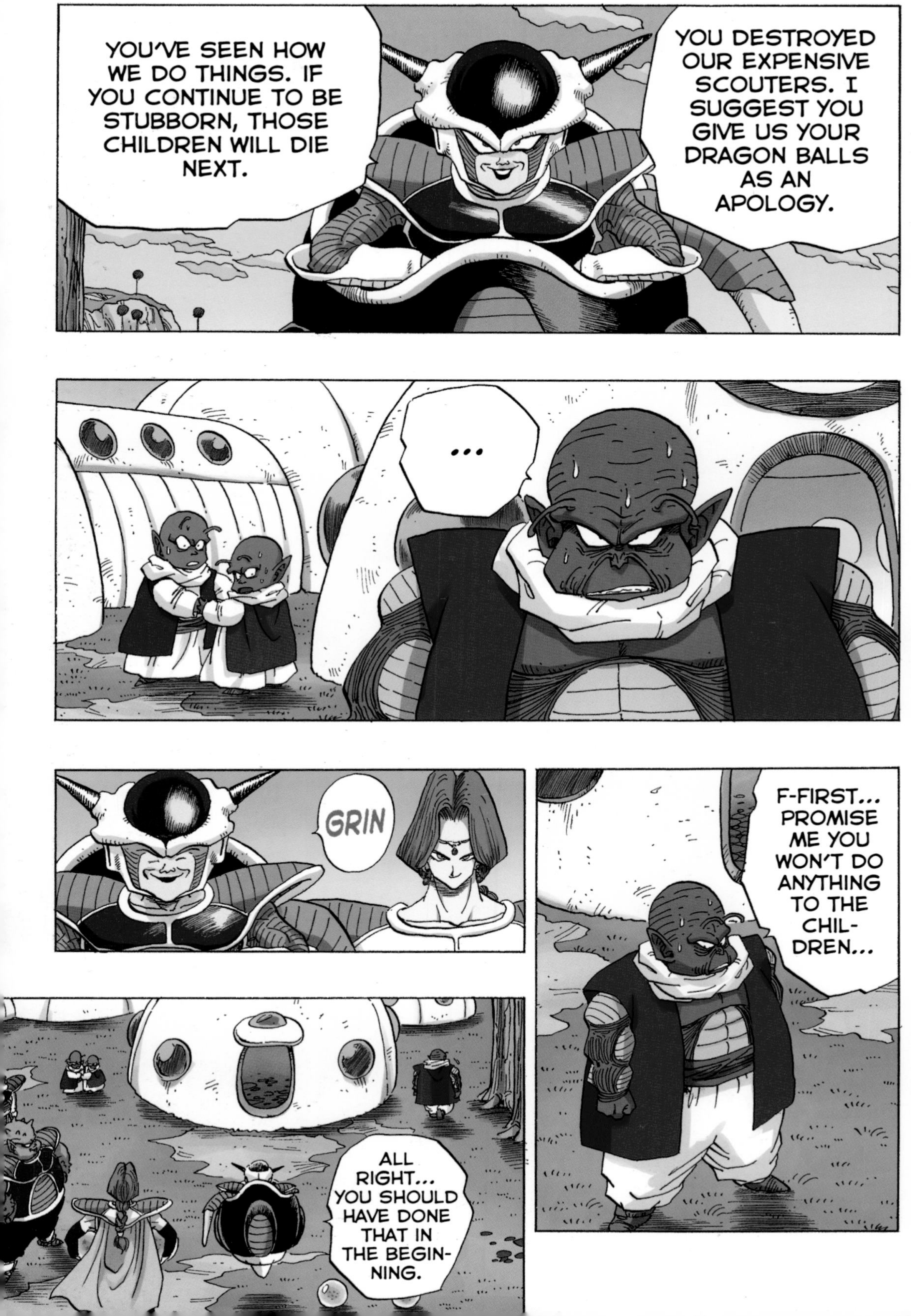
YOU DESTROYED OUR EXPENSIVE SCOUTERS. I SUGGEST YOU GIVE US YOUR DRAGON BALLS AS AN APOLOGY.
YOU'VE SEEN HOW WE DO THINGS. IF YOU CONTINUE TO BE STUBBORN, THOSE CHILDREN WILL DIE NEXT.
...
F-FIRST... PROMISE ME YOU WON'T DO ANYTHING TO THE CHIL-DREN...
GRIN
ALL RIGHT... YOU SHOULD HAVE DONE THAT IN THE BEGIN-NING.

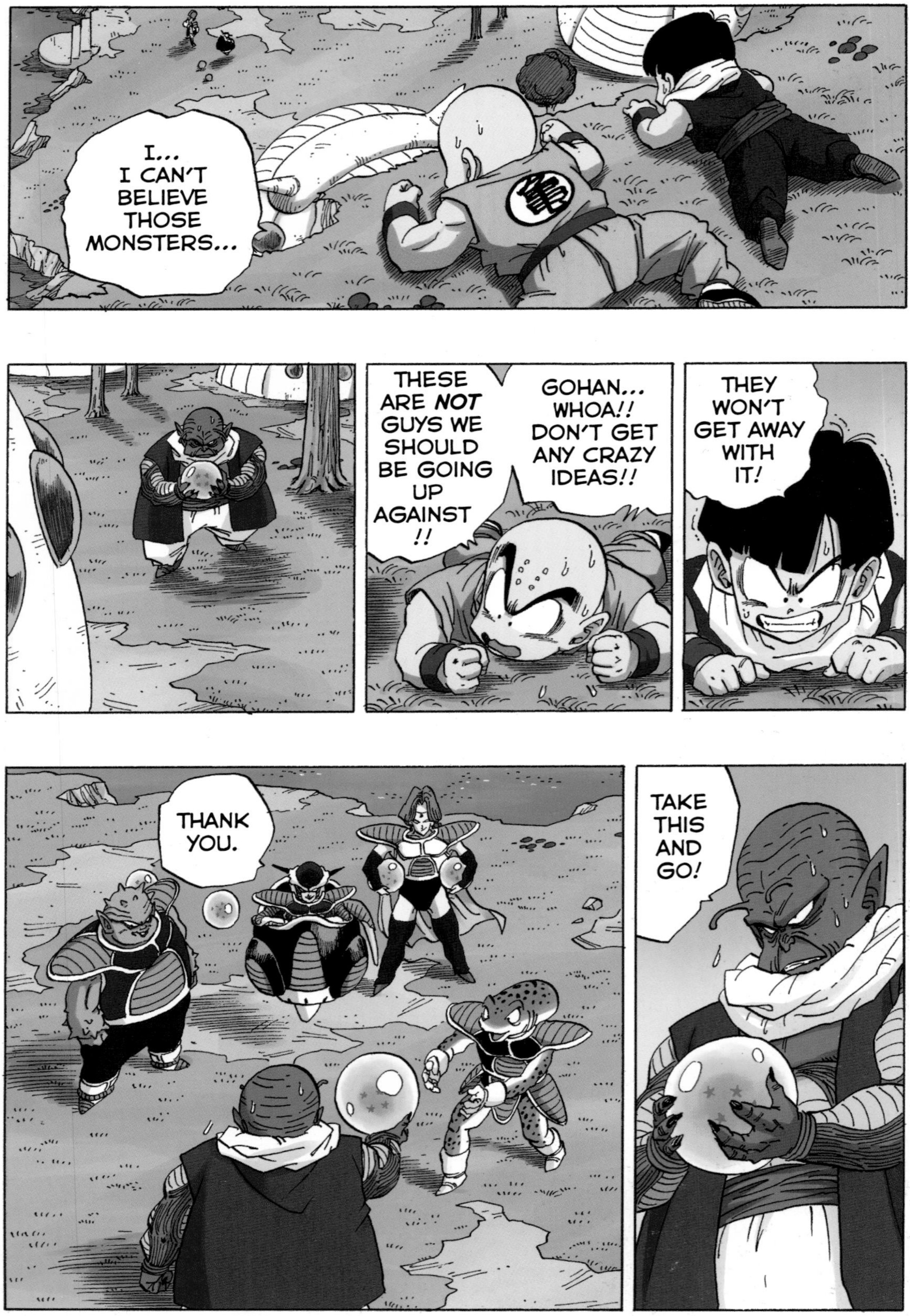
I... I CAN'T BELIEVE THOSE MONSTERS...
THEY WON'T GET AWAY WITH IT!
GOHAN... WHOA!! DON'T GET ANY CRAZY IDEAS!!
THESE ARE **NOT** GUYS WE SHOULD BE GOING UP AGAINST!!
TAKE THIS AND GO!
THANK YOU.

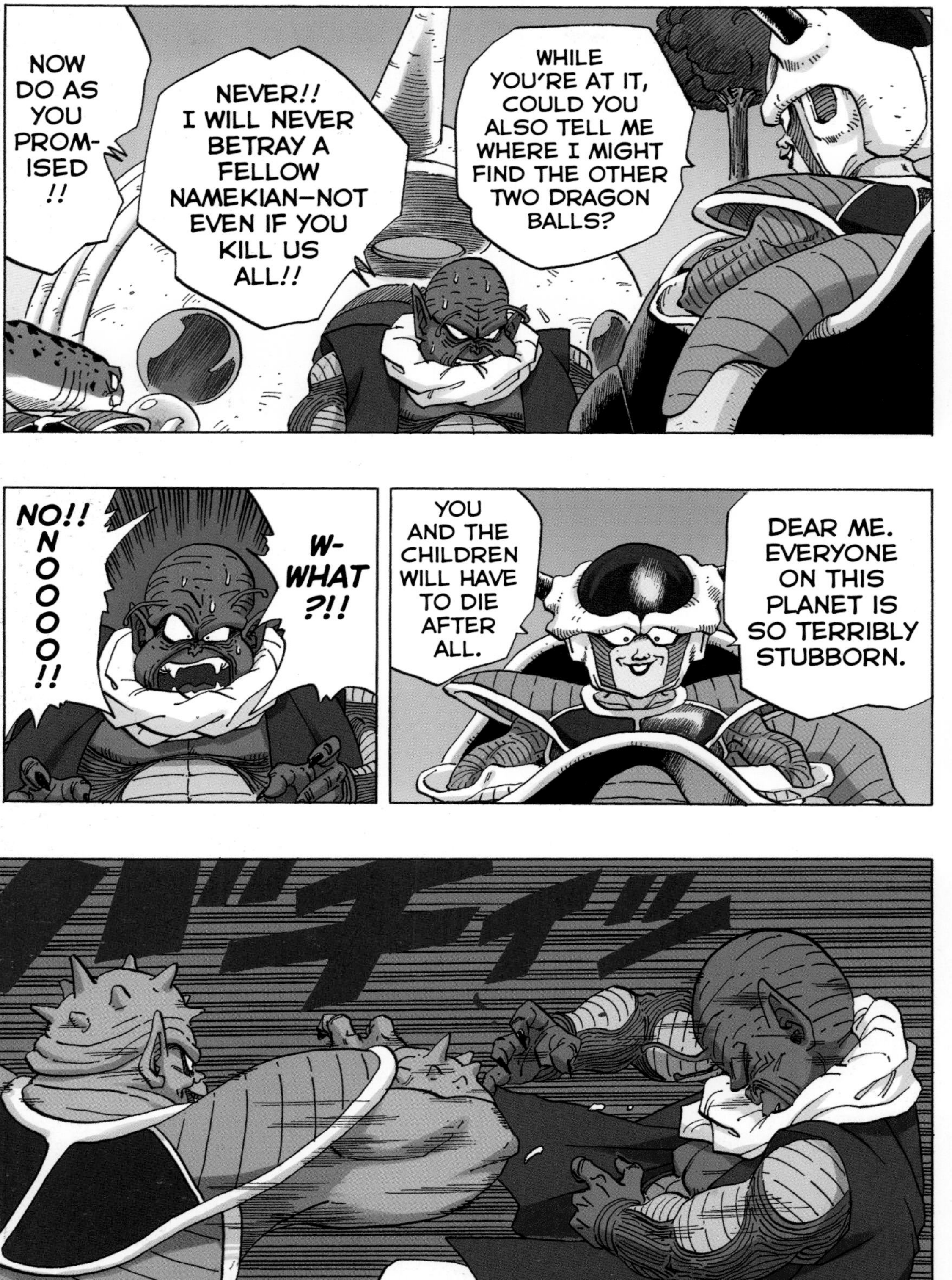

WHILE YOU'RE AT IT, COULD YOU ALSO TELL ME WHERE I MIGHT FIND THE OTHER TWO DRAGON BALLS?
NEVER!! I WILL NEVER BETRAY A FELLOW NAMEKIAN—NOT EVEN IF YOU KILL US ALL!!
NOW DO AS YOU PROM-ISED!!
DEAR ME. EVERYONE ON THIS PLANET IS SO TERRIBLY STUBBORN.
YOU AND THE CHILDREN WILL HAVE TO DIE AFTER ALL.
W-WHAT?!!
NO!! NOOOOOO!!

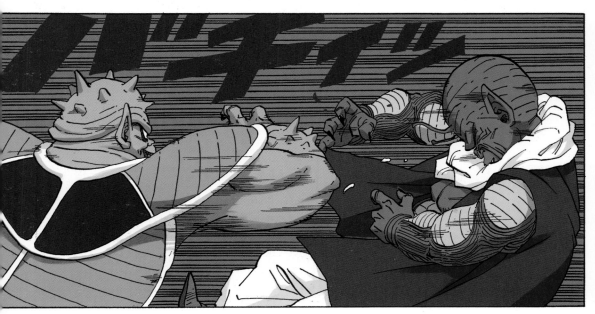

Chapter 10 • Son Gohan Snaps

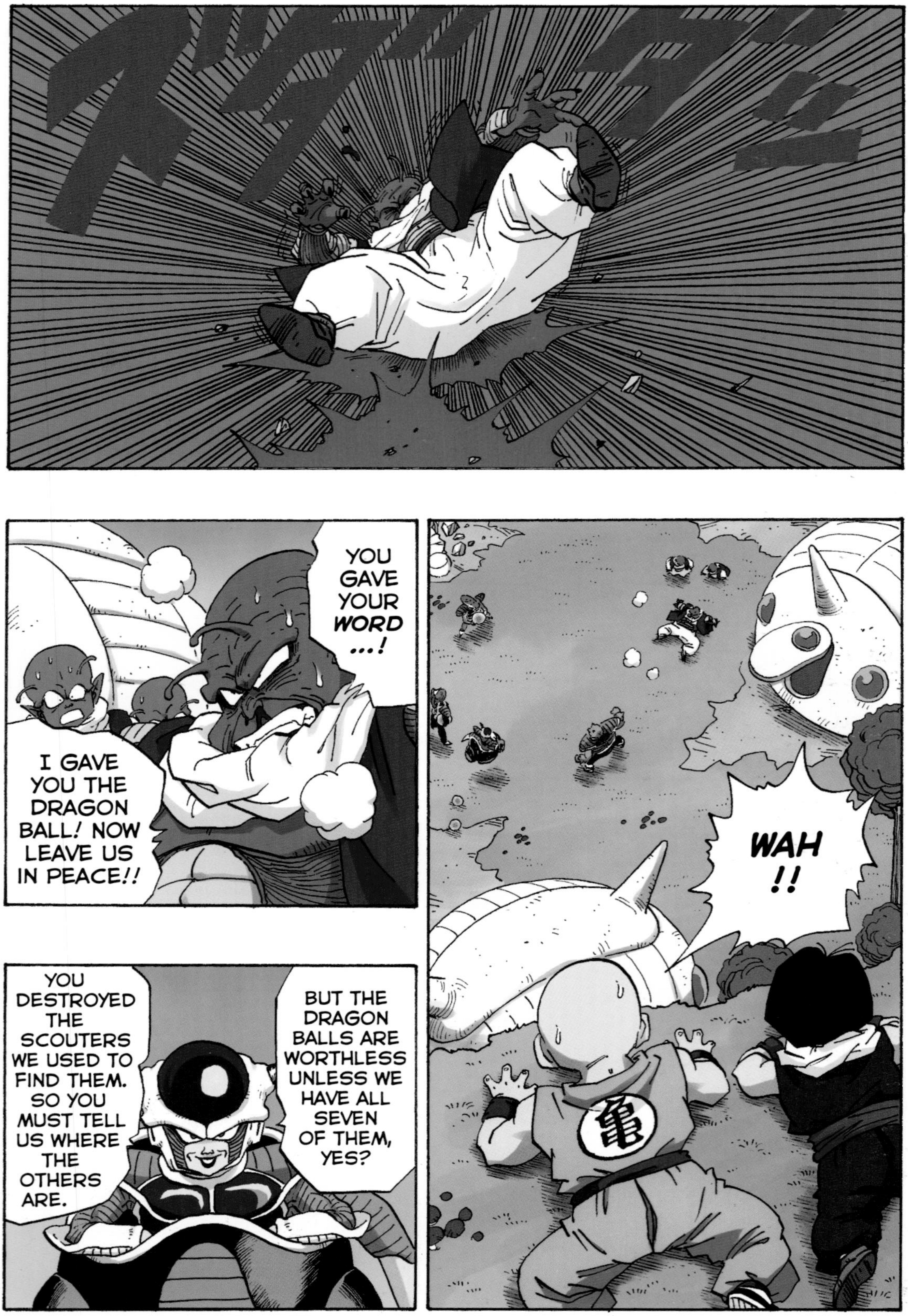
WAH !!
YOU GAVE YOUR WORD...!
I GAVE YOU THE DRAGON BALL! NOW LEAVE US IN PEACE!!
BUT THE DRAGON BALLS ARE WORTHLESS UNLESS WE HAVE ALL SEVEN OF THEM, YES?
YOU DESTROYED THE SCOUTERS WE USED TO FIND THEM. SO YOU MUST TELL US WHERE THE OTHERS ARE.

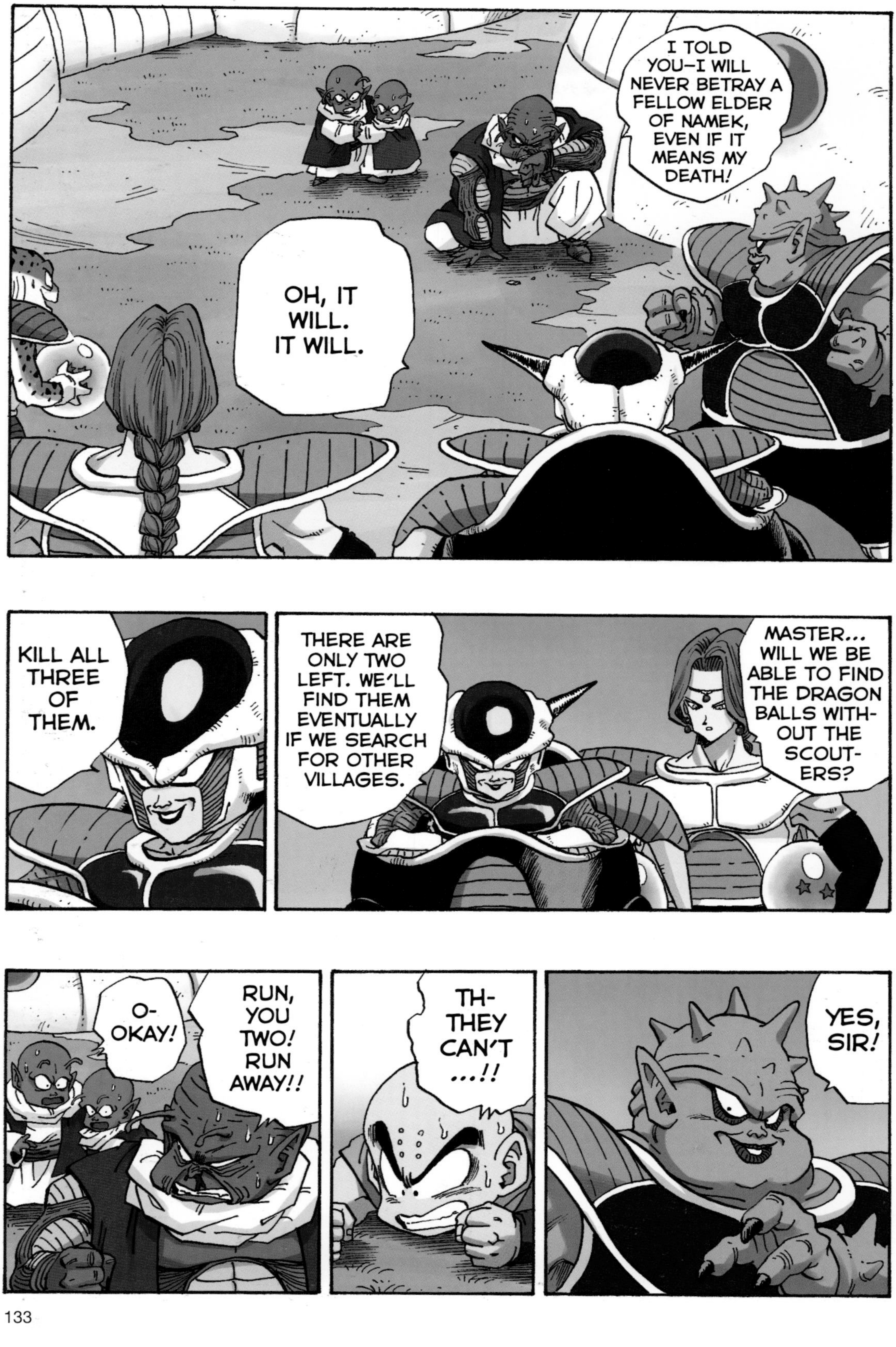
I TOLD YOU—I WILL NEVER BETRAY A FELLOW ELDER OF NAMEK, EVEN IF IT MEANS MY DEATH!
OH, IT WILL. IT WILL.
MASTER... WILL WE BE ABLE TO FIND THE DRAGON BALLS WITH-OUT THE SCOUT-ERS?
THERE ARE ONLY TWO LEFT. WE'LL FIND THEM EVENTUALLY IF WE SEARCH FOR OTHER VILLAGES.
KILL ALL THREE OF THEM.
YES, SIR!
TH-THEY CAN'T ...!!
RUN, YOU TWO! RUN AWAY!!
O-OKAY!

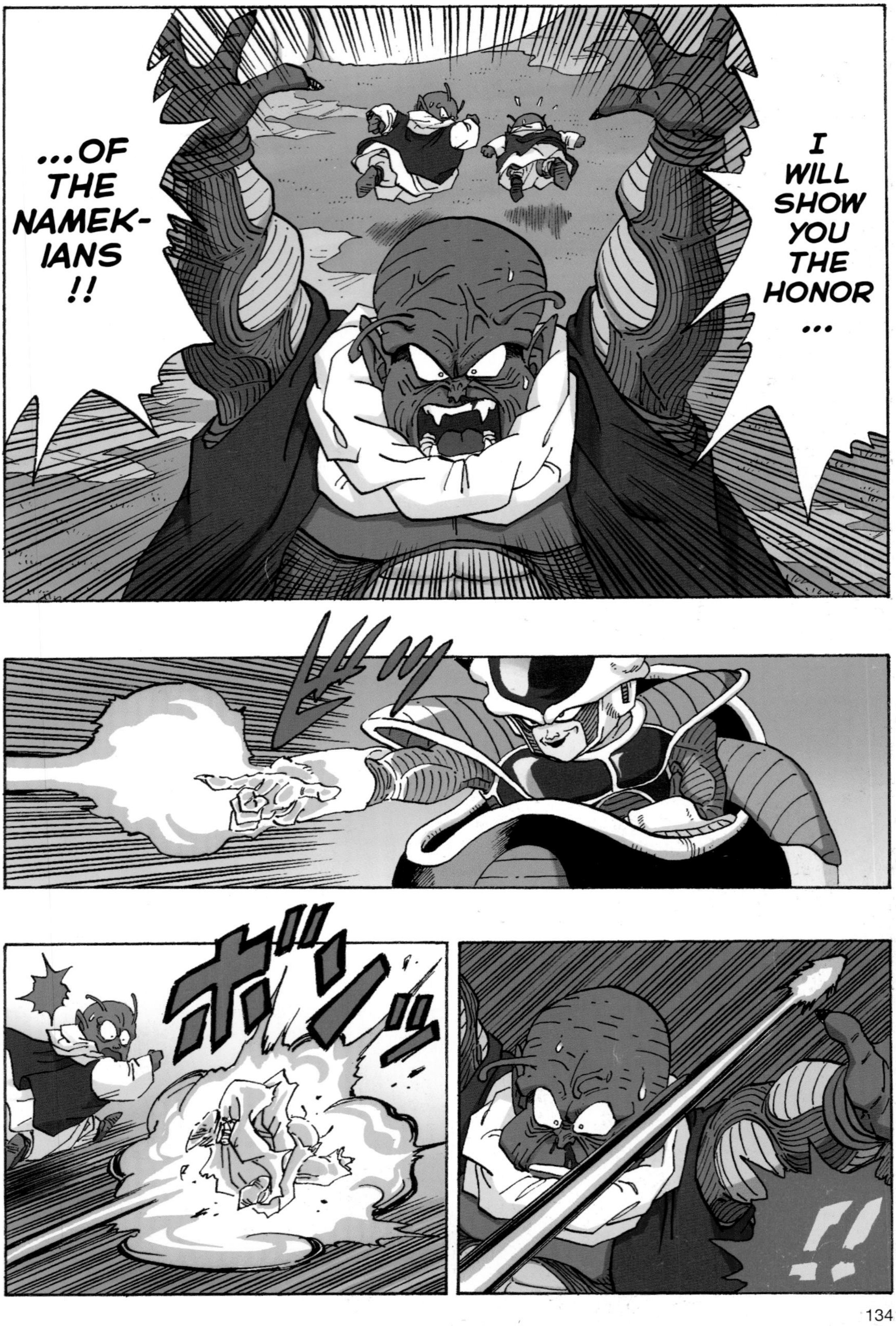
I WILL SHOW YOU THE HONOR...
...OF THE NAMEK-IANS!!
!!
ボンッ

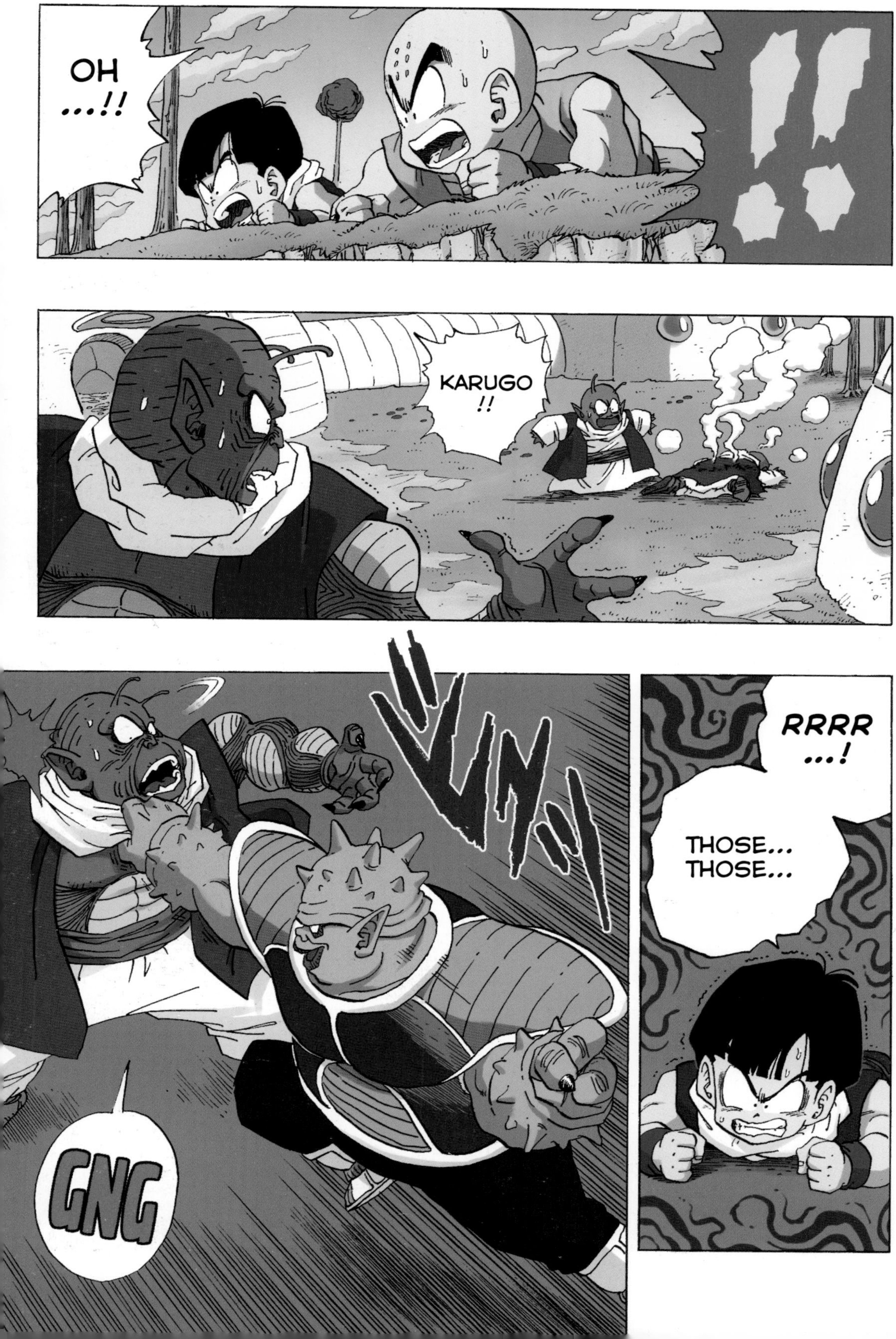
OH ...!!
KARUGO !!
RRRR ...!
THOSE... THOSE...
GNG

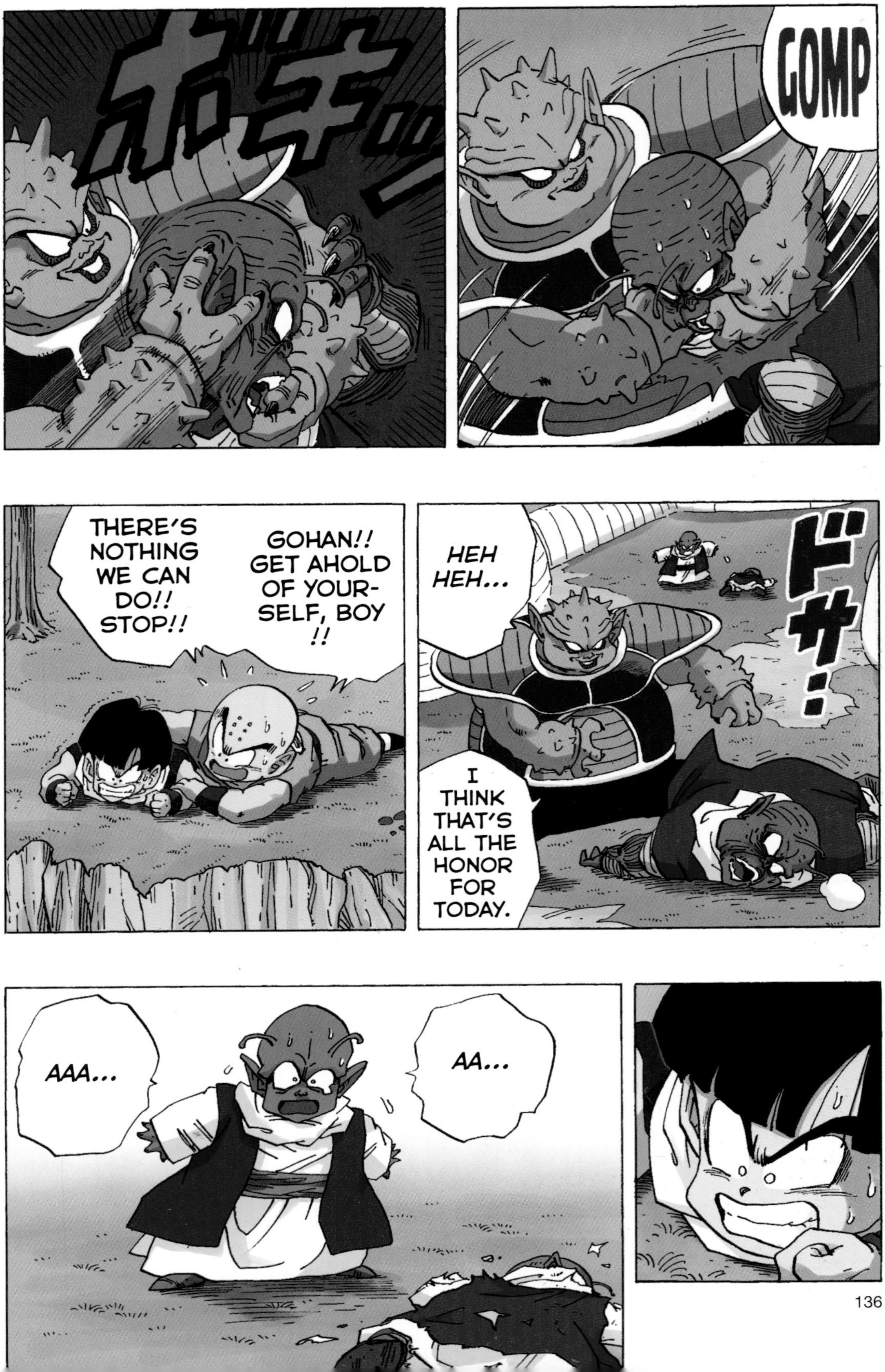
GOMP
HEH HEH...
I THINK THAT'S ALL THE HONOR FOR TODAY.
ドサ
GOHAN!! GET AHOLD OF YOUR-SELF, BOY !!
THERE'S NOTHING WE CAN DO!! STOP!!
AA...
AAA...

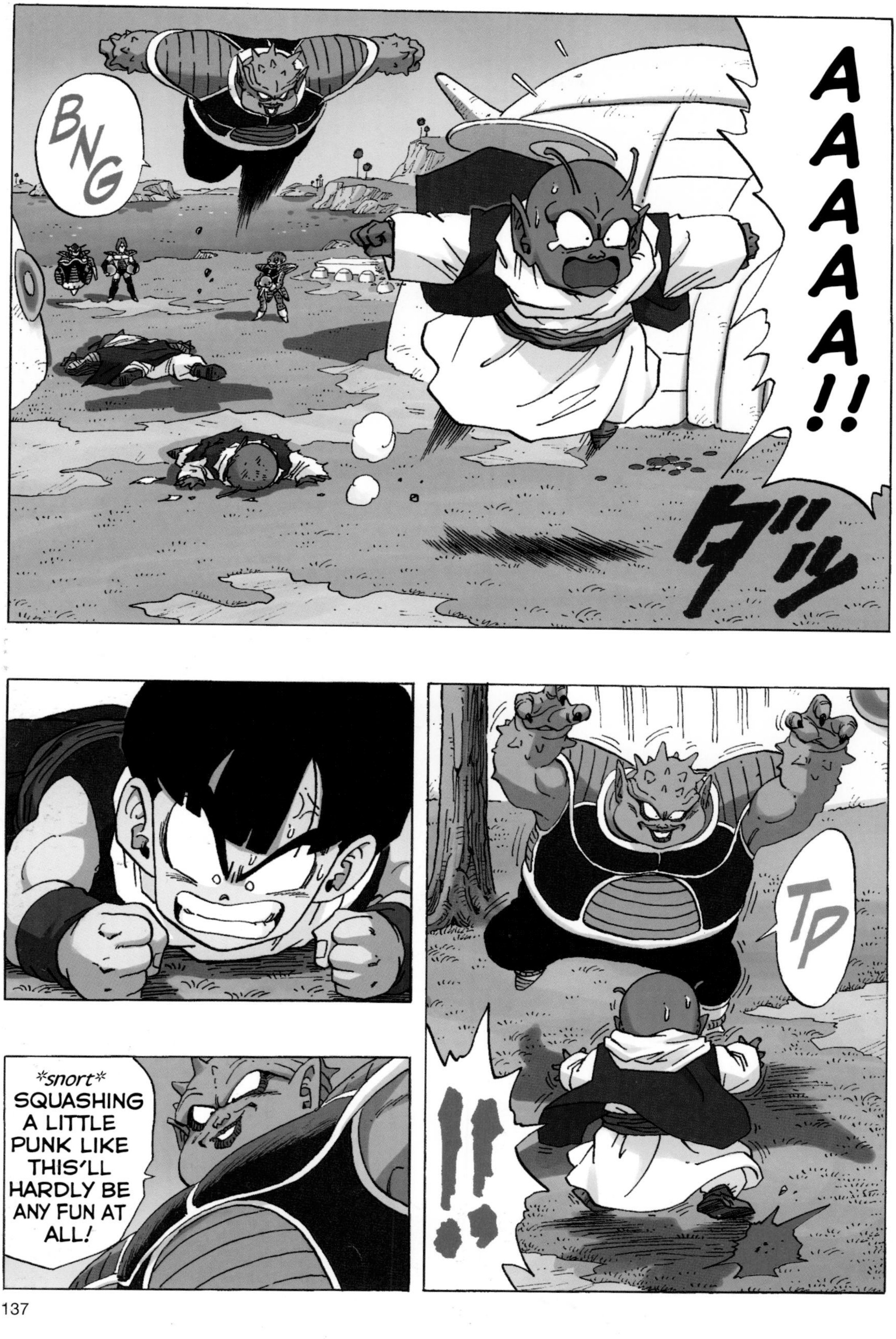
AAAAAA!!
BNG
ダッ
TP
!!
snort SQUASHING A LITTLE PUNK LIKE THIS'LL HARDLY BE ANY FUN AT ALL!

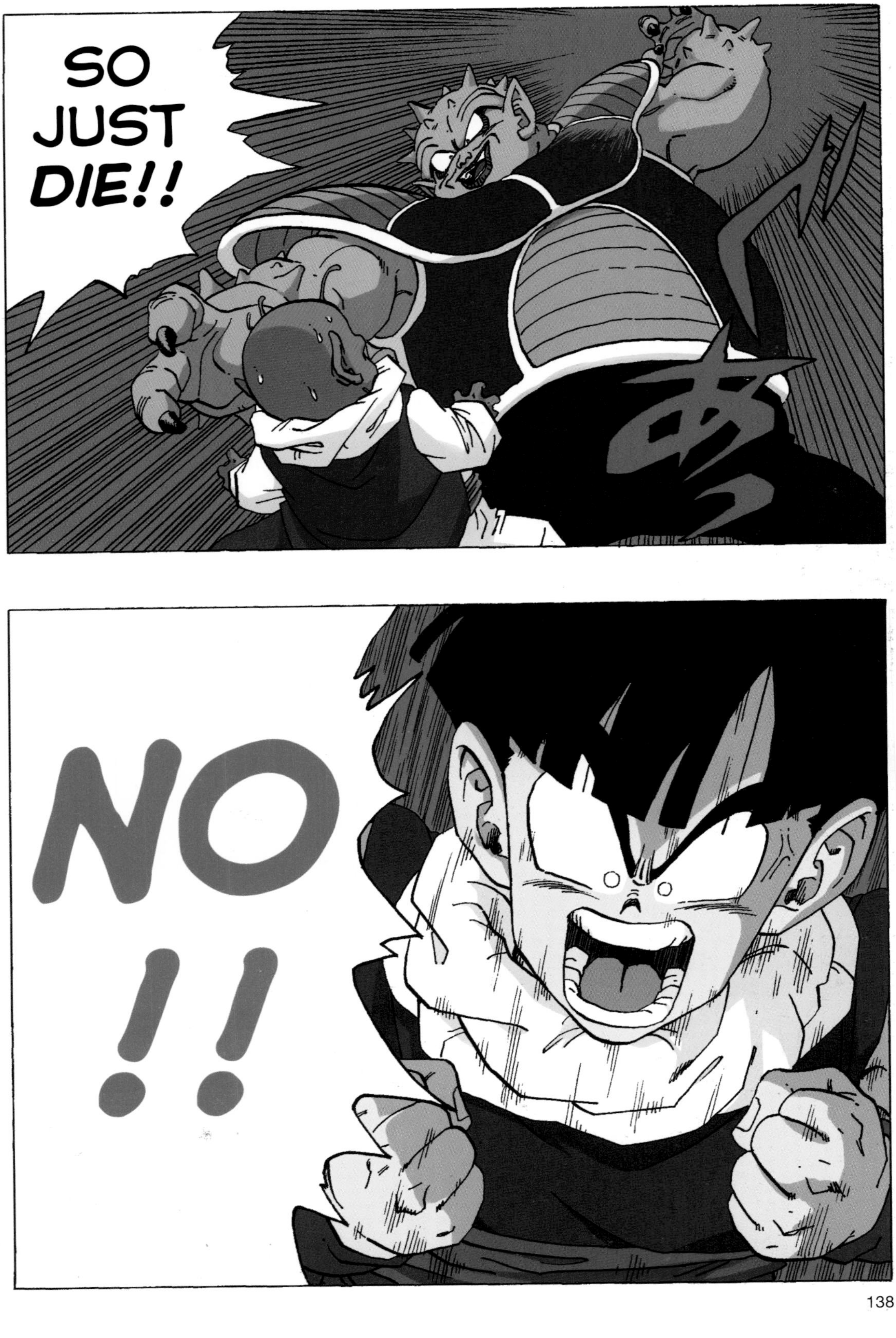
SO JUST DIE!!
NO!!

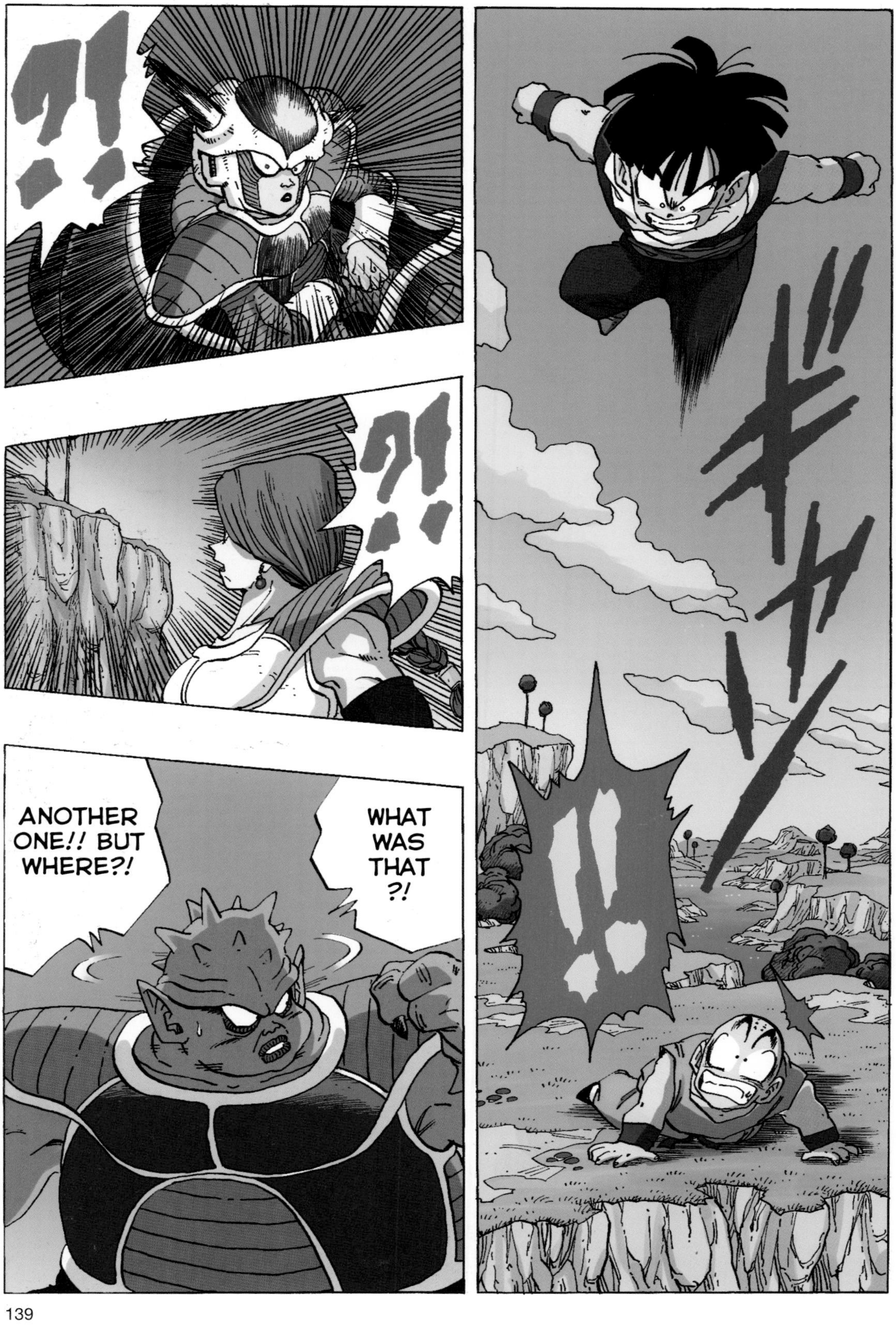
!!
?!
?!
WHAT WAS THAT?!
ANOTHER ONE!! BUT WHERE?!

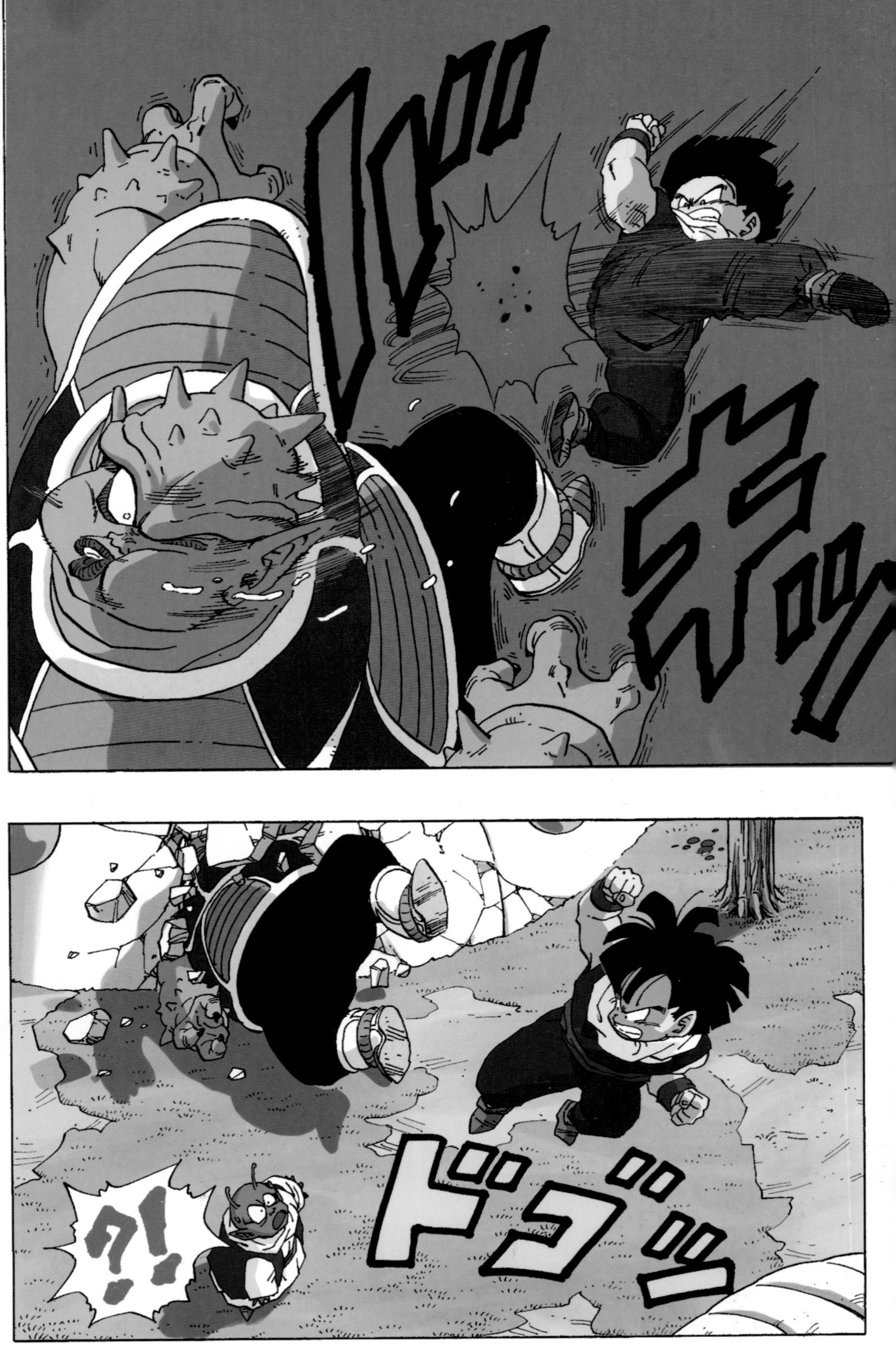
?!
ドゴッ

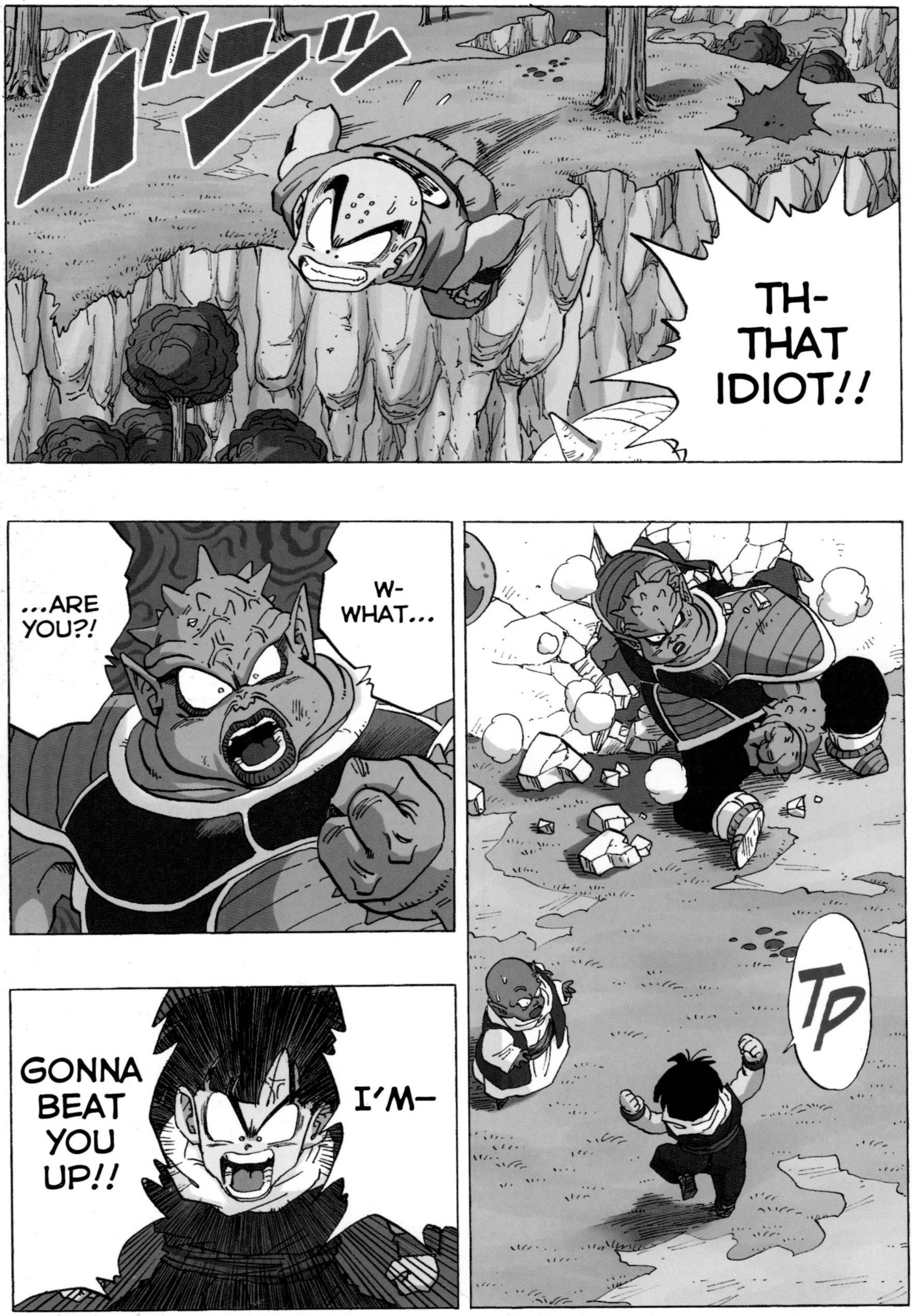
TH-
THAT
IDIOT!!
TP
W-
WHAT...
...ARE
YOU?!
I'M—
GONNA
BEAT
YOU
UP!!

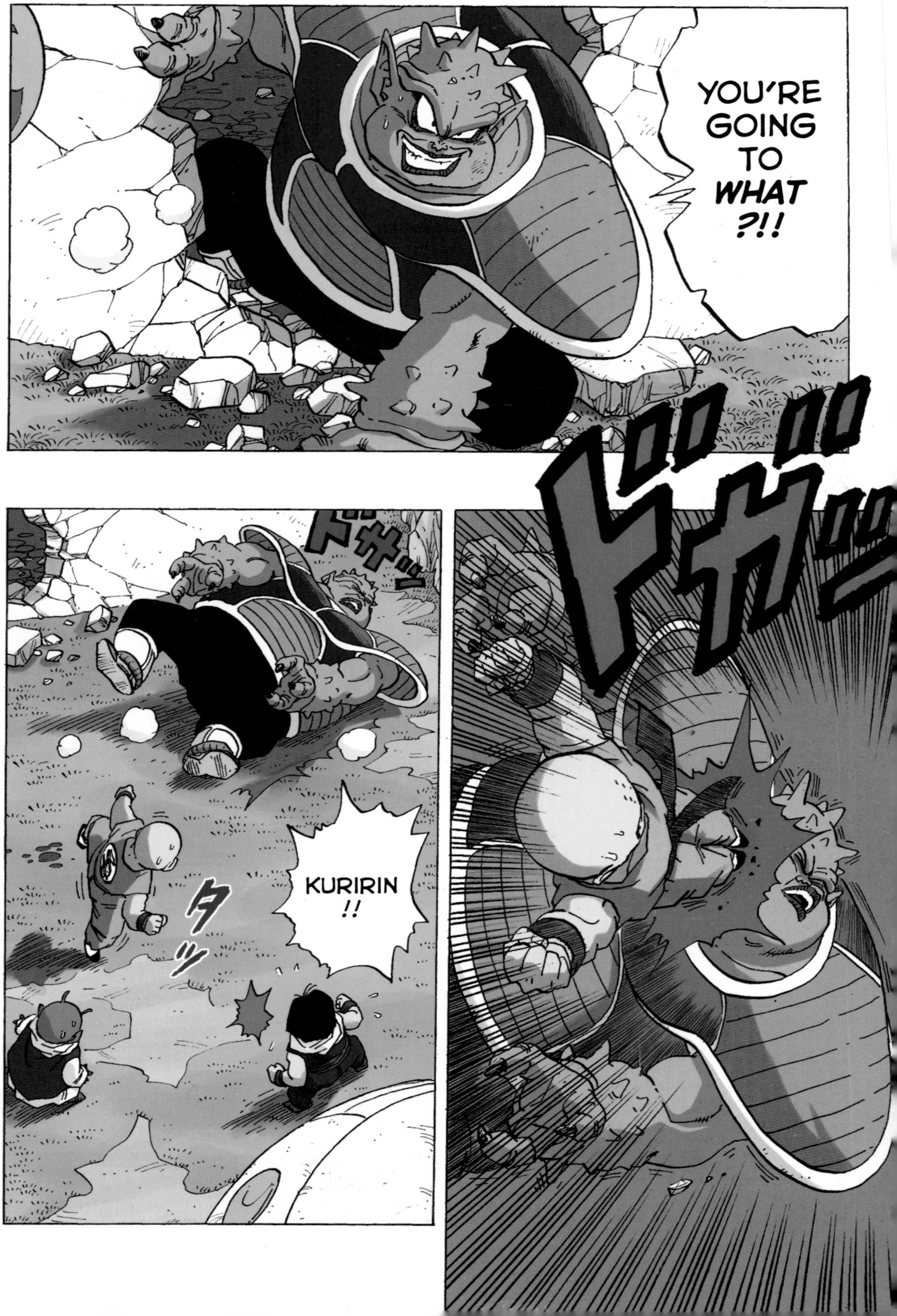
YOU'RE GOING TO *WHAT* ?!!
KURIRIN !!
タッ

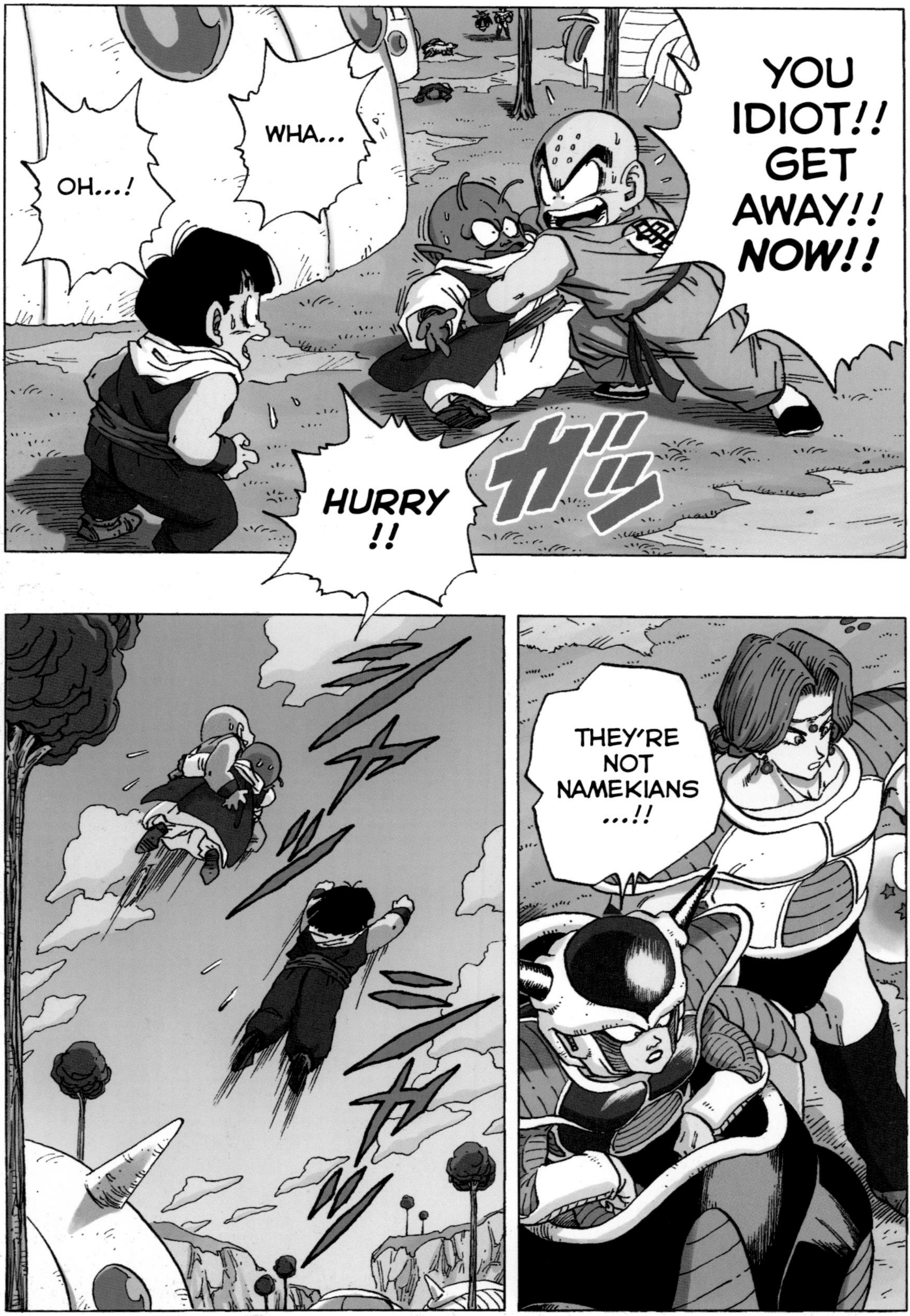
YOU IDIOT!! GET AWAY!! NOW!!
WHA...
OH...!
HURRY !!
ガッ
THEY'RE NOT NAMEKIANS ...!!

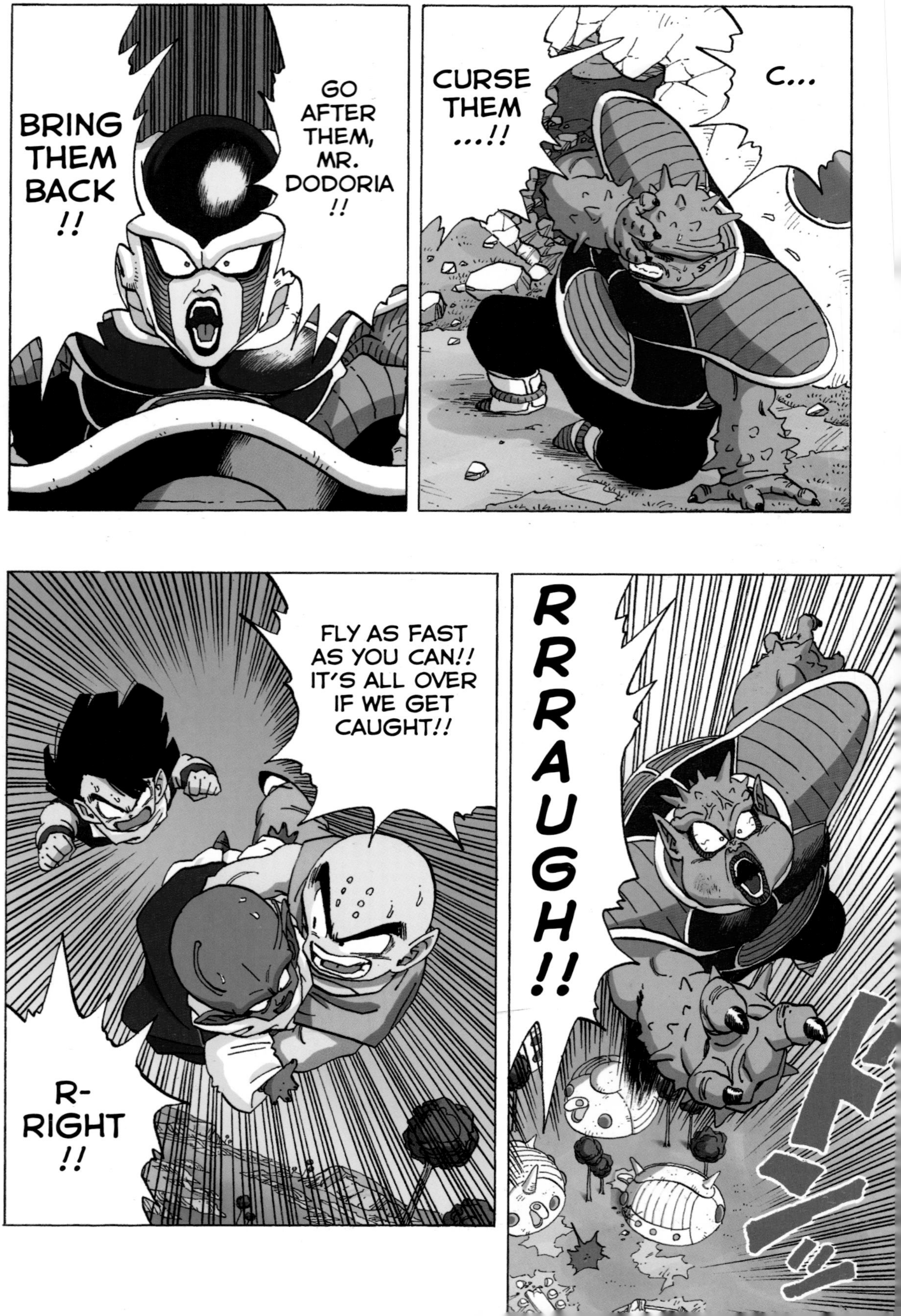
C...
CURSE THEM ...!!
GO AFTER THEM, MR. DODORIA!!
BRING THEM BACK!!
RRRAUGH!!
FLY AS FAST AS YOU CAN!! IT'S ALL OVER IF WE GET CAUGHT!!
R-RIGHT!!

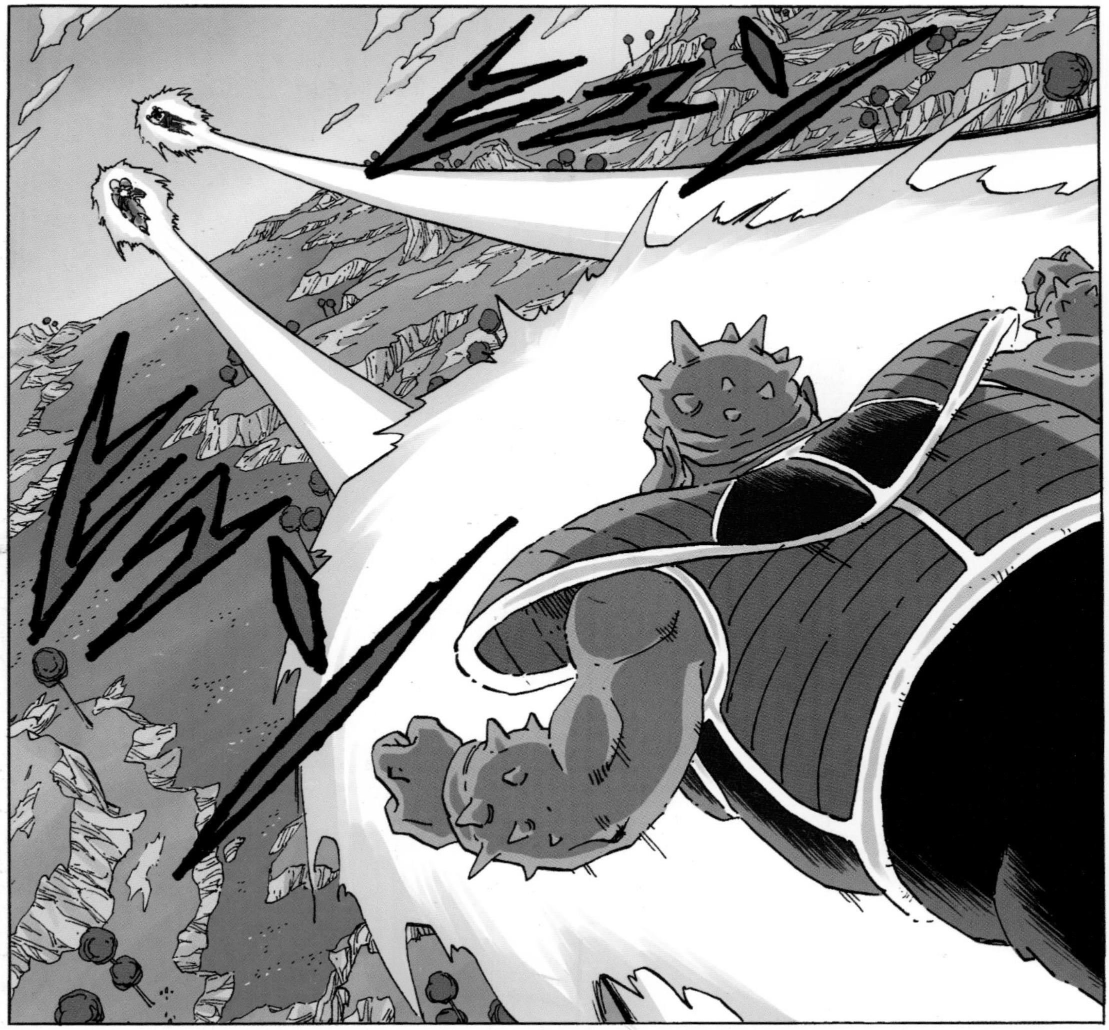

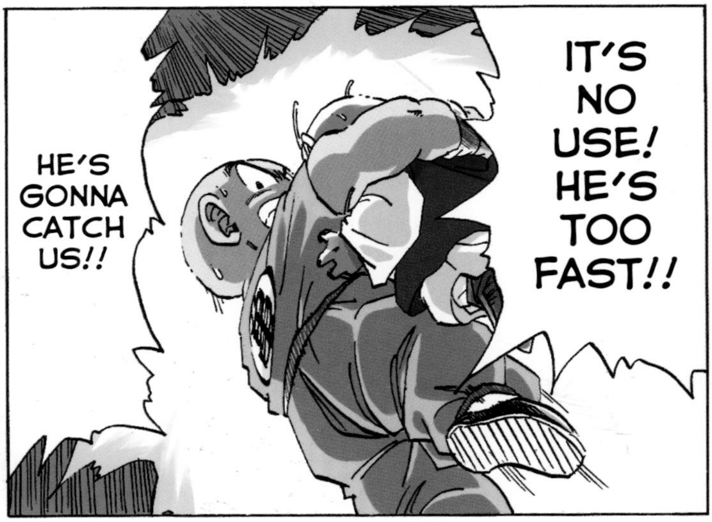

IT'S NO USE! HE'S TOO FAST!!
HE'S GONNA CATCH US!!

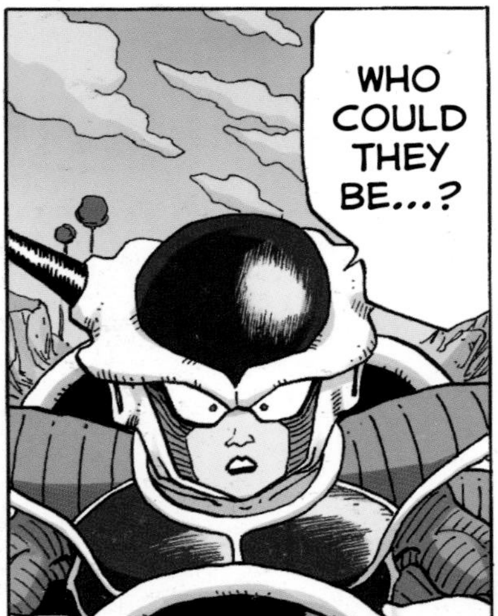

WHO COULD THEY BE...?

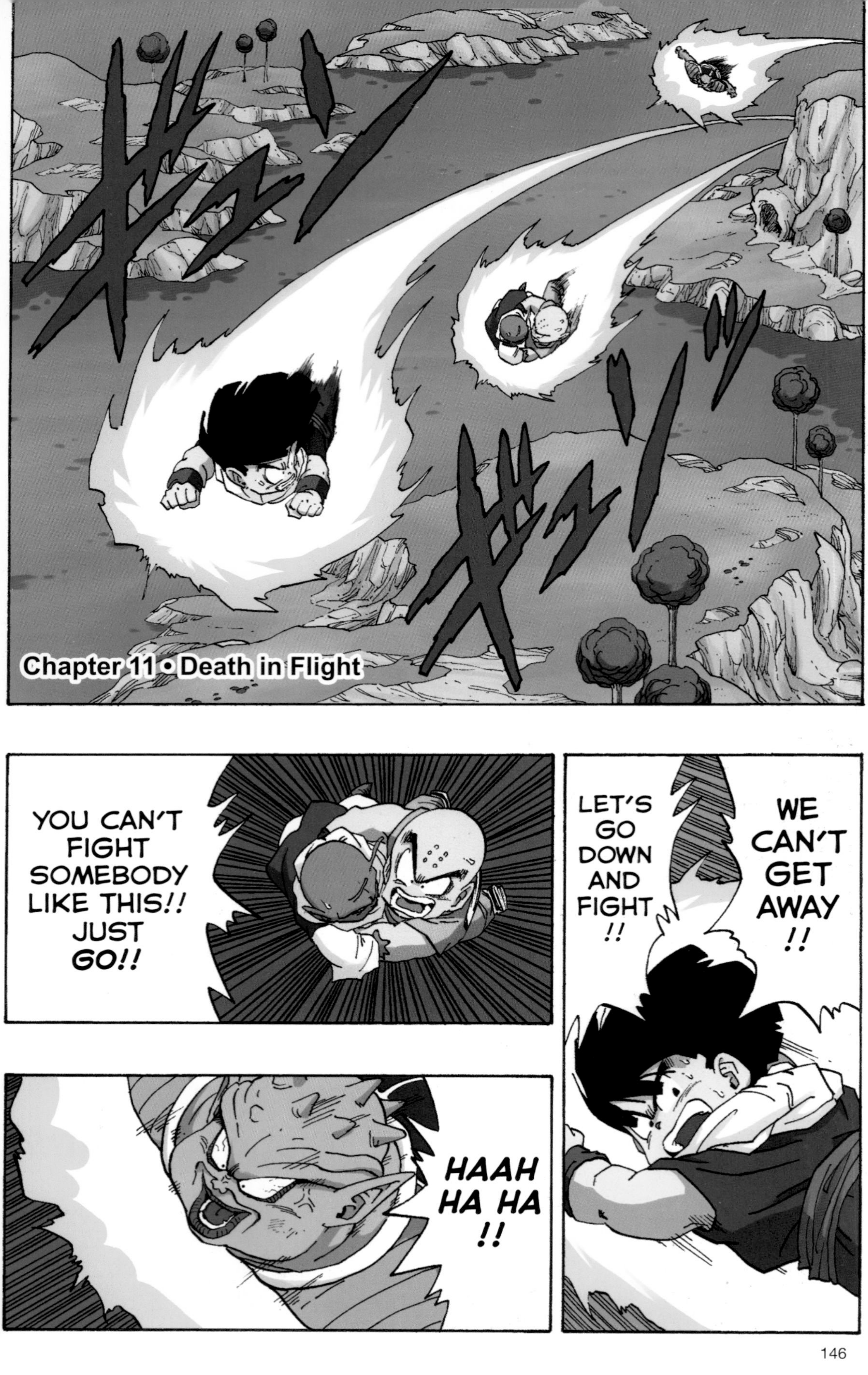
Chapter 11 • Death in Flight
WE CAN'T GET AWAY!!
LET'S GO DOWN AND FIGHT!!
YOU CAN'T FIGHT SOMEBODY LIKE THIS!! JUST GO!!
HAAH HA HA!!

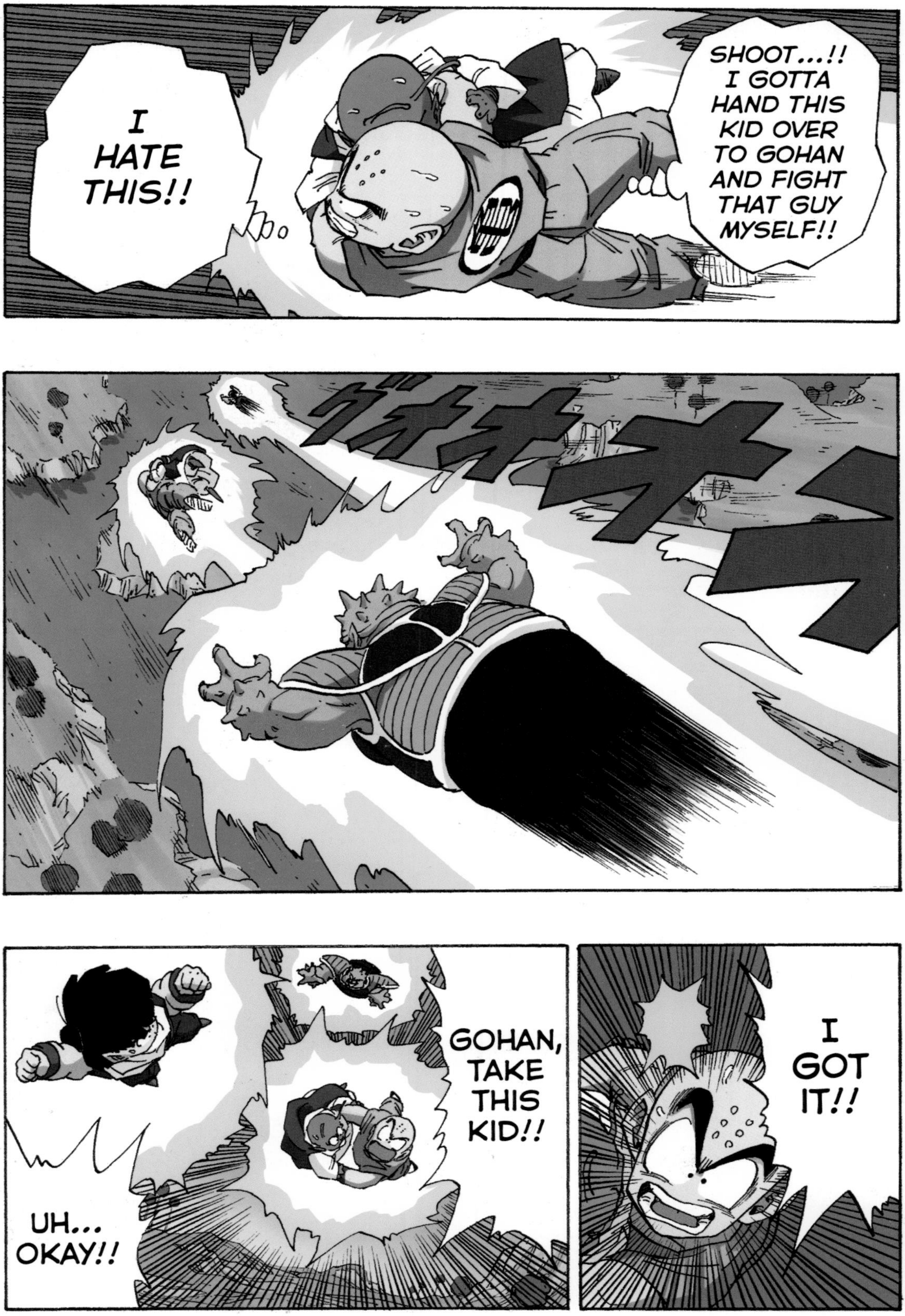
SHOOT...!! I GOTTA HAND THIS KID OVER TO GOHAN AND FIGHT THAT GUY MYSELF!!
I HATE THIS!!
I GOT IT!!
GOHAN, TAKE THIS KID!!
UH... OKAY!!

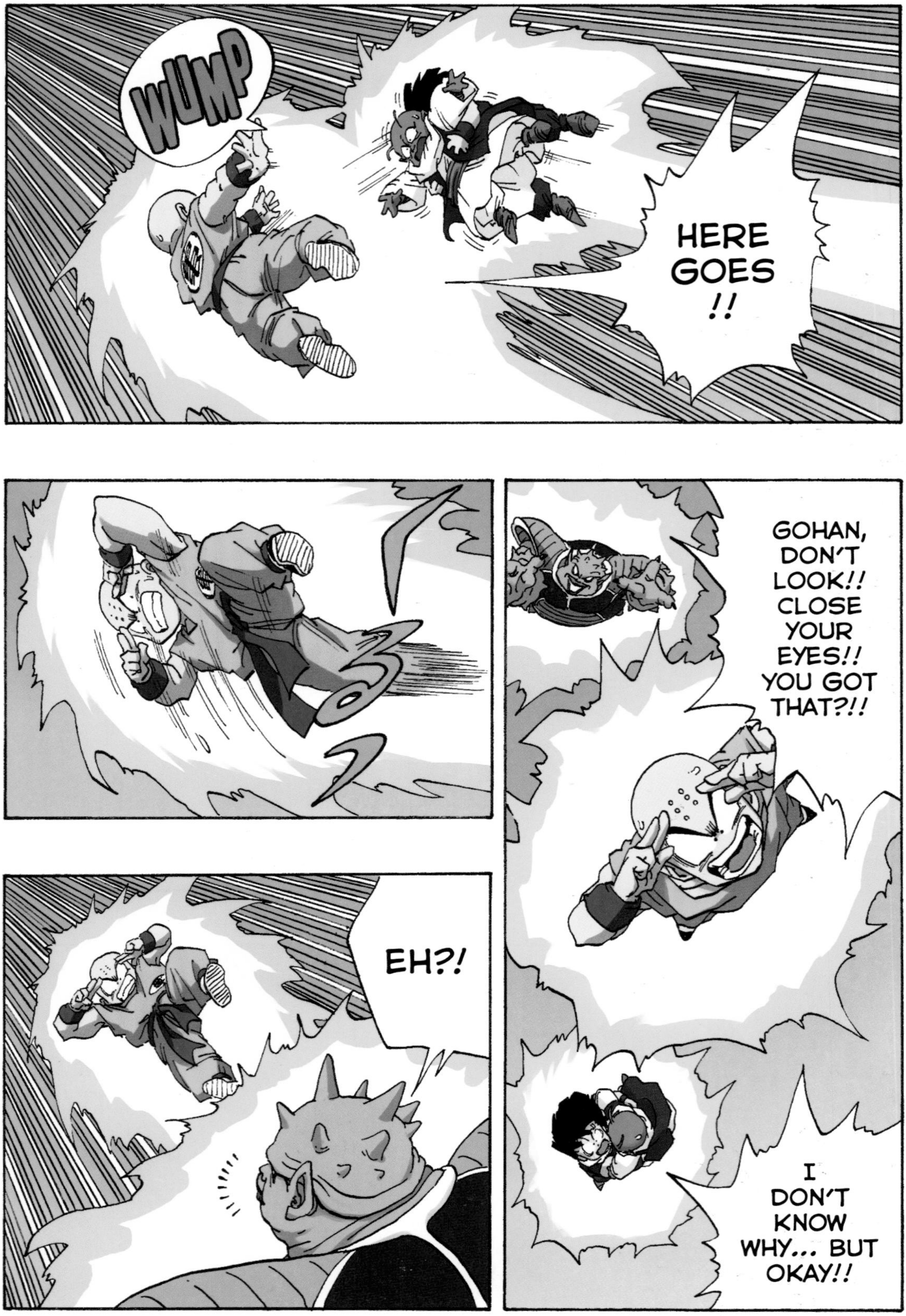
HERE GOES!!
WUMP
GOHAN, DON'T LOOK!! CLOSE YOUR EYES!! YOU GOT THAT?!!
I DON'T KNOW WHY... BUT OKAY!!
EH?!

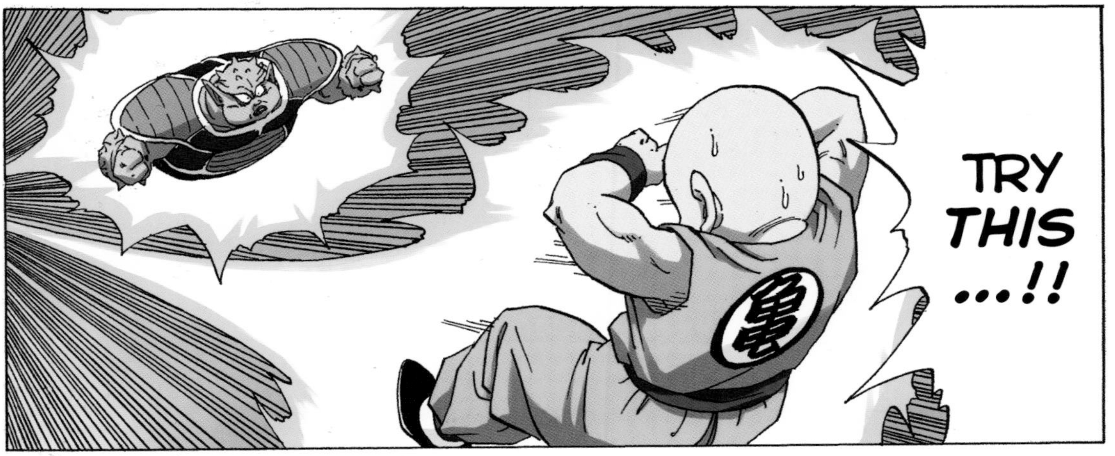
TRY THIS ...!!

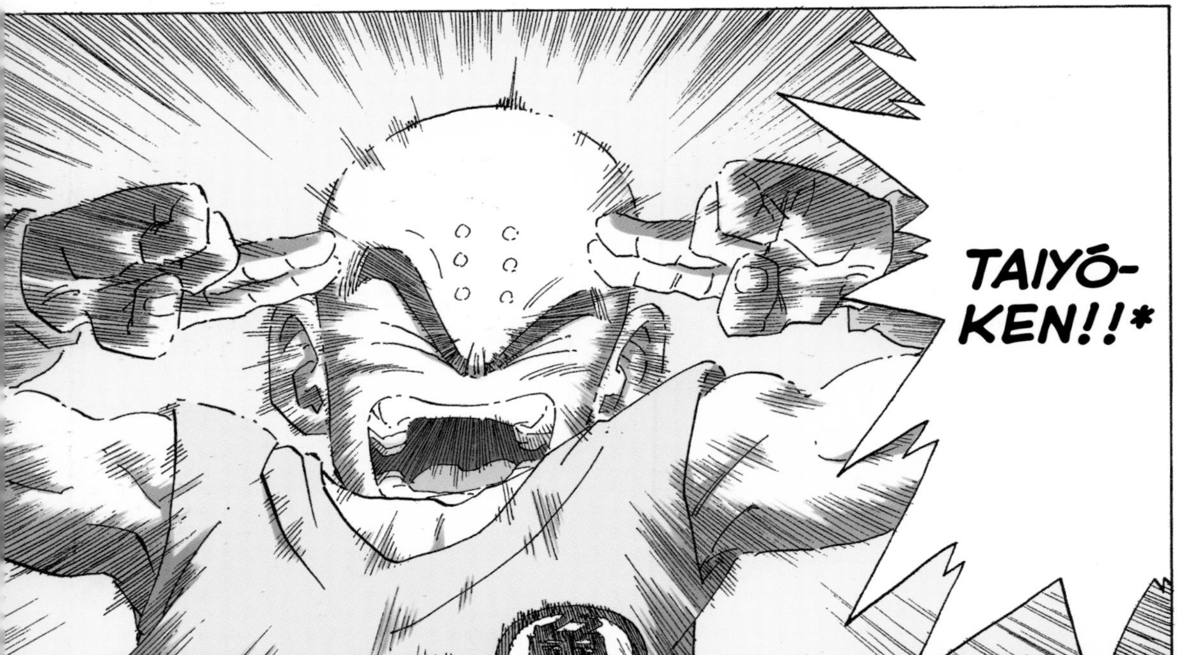
TAIYŌ-KEN!!*

*Fist of the Sun!

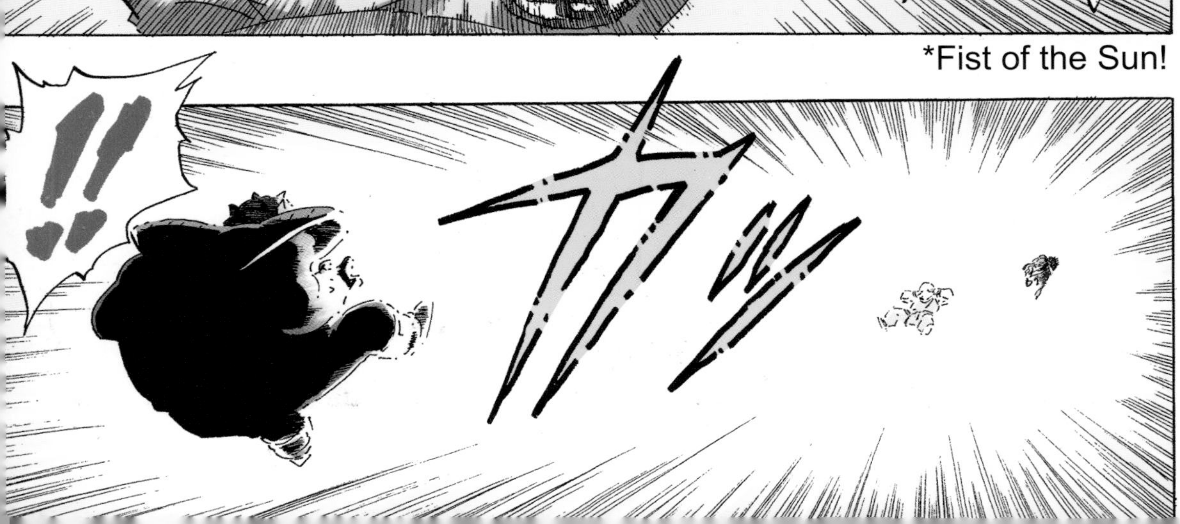
!!

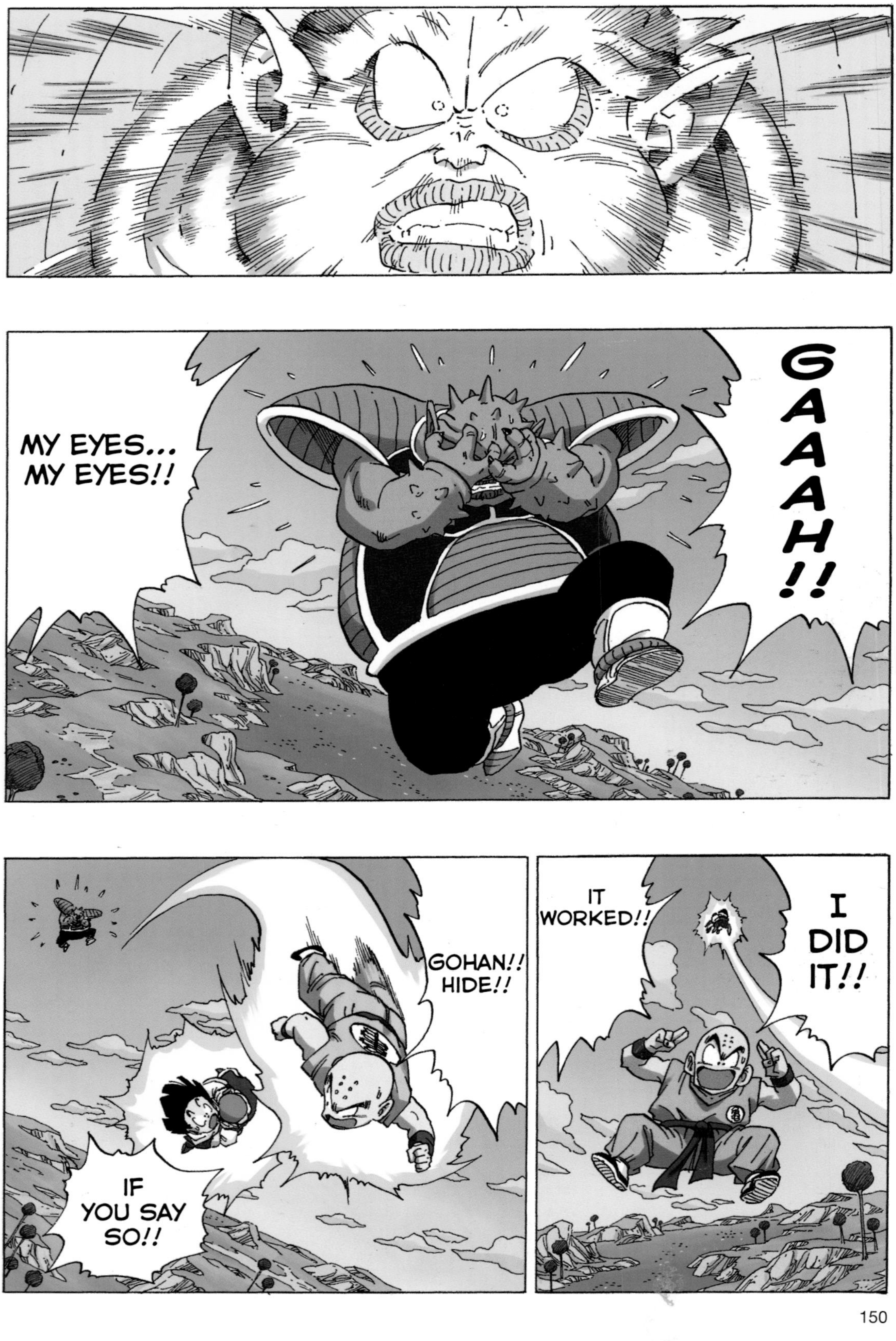
GAAAAH!!
MY EYES... MY EYES!!
I DID IT!!
IT WORKED!!
GOHAN!! HIDE!!
IF YOU SAY SO!!

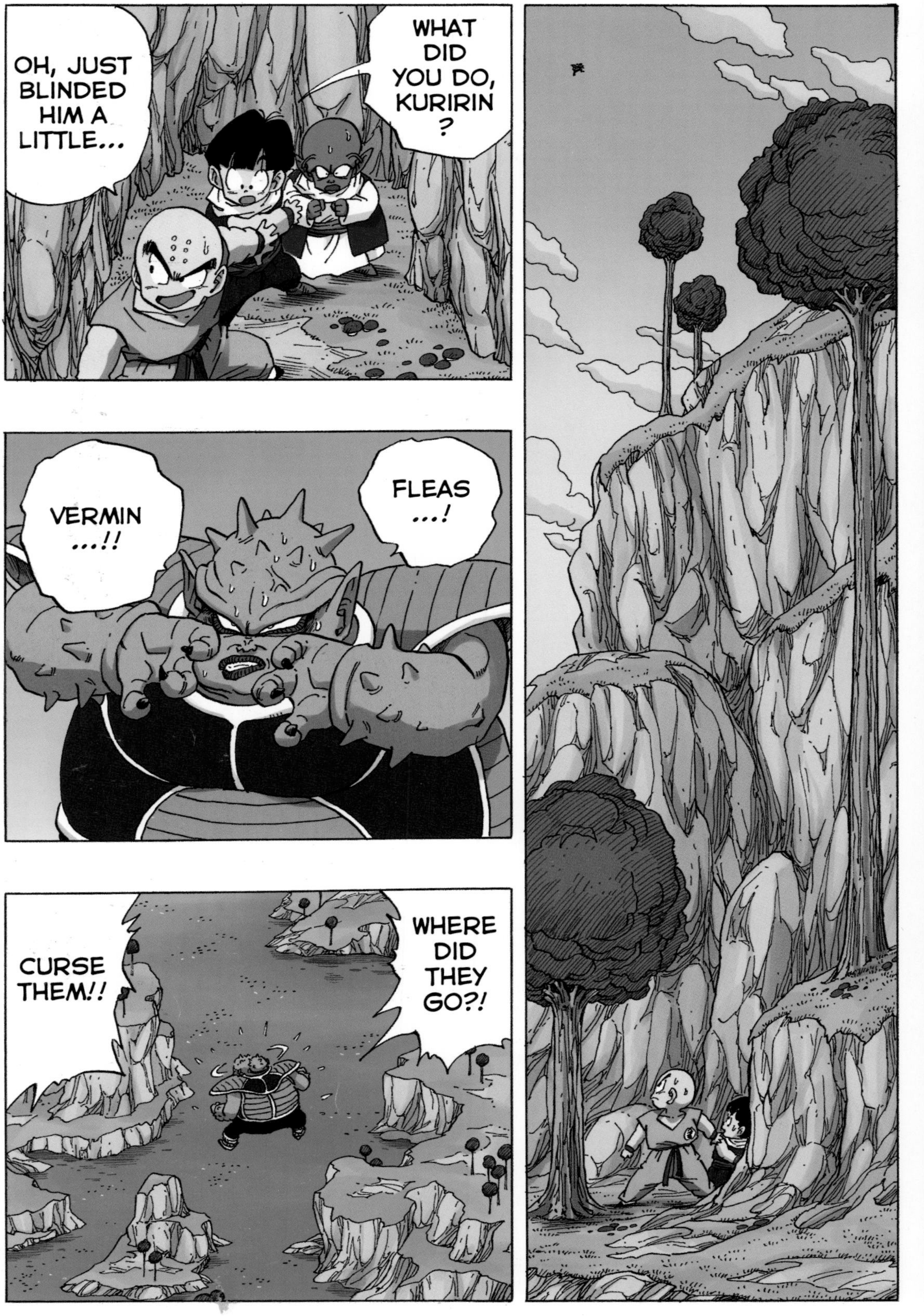
WHAT DID YOU DO, KURIRIN?
OH, JUST BLINDED HIM A LITTLE...
FLEAS ...!
VERMIN ...!!
WHERE DID THEY GO?!
CURSE THEM!!

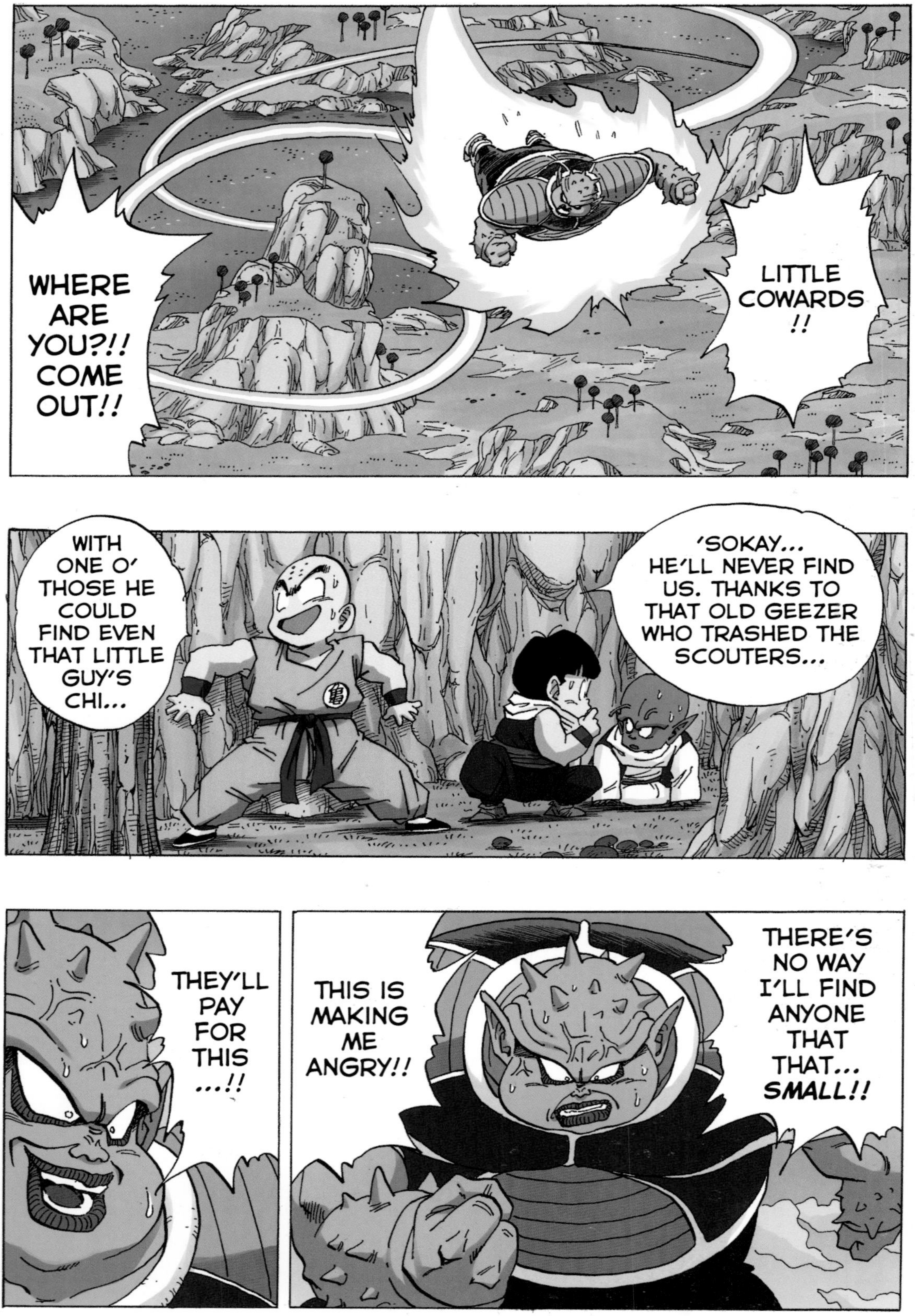
LITTLE COWARDS!!
WHERE ARE YOU?!! COME OUT!!
'SOKAY... HE'LL NEVER FIND US. THANKS TO THAT OLD GEEZER WHO TRASHED THE SCOUTERS...
WITH ONE O' THOSE HE COULD FIND EVEN THAT LITTLE GUY'S CHI...
THERE'S NO WAY I'LL FIND ANYONE THAT THAT... SMALL!!
THIS IS MAKING ME ANGRY!!
THEY'LL PAY FOR THIS ...!!

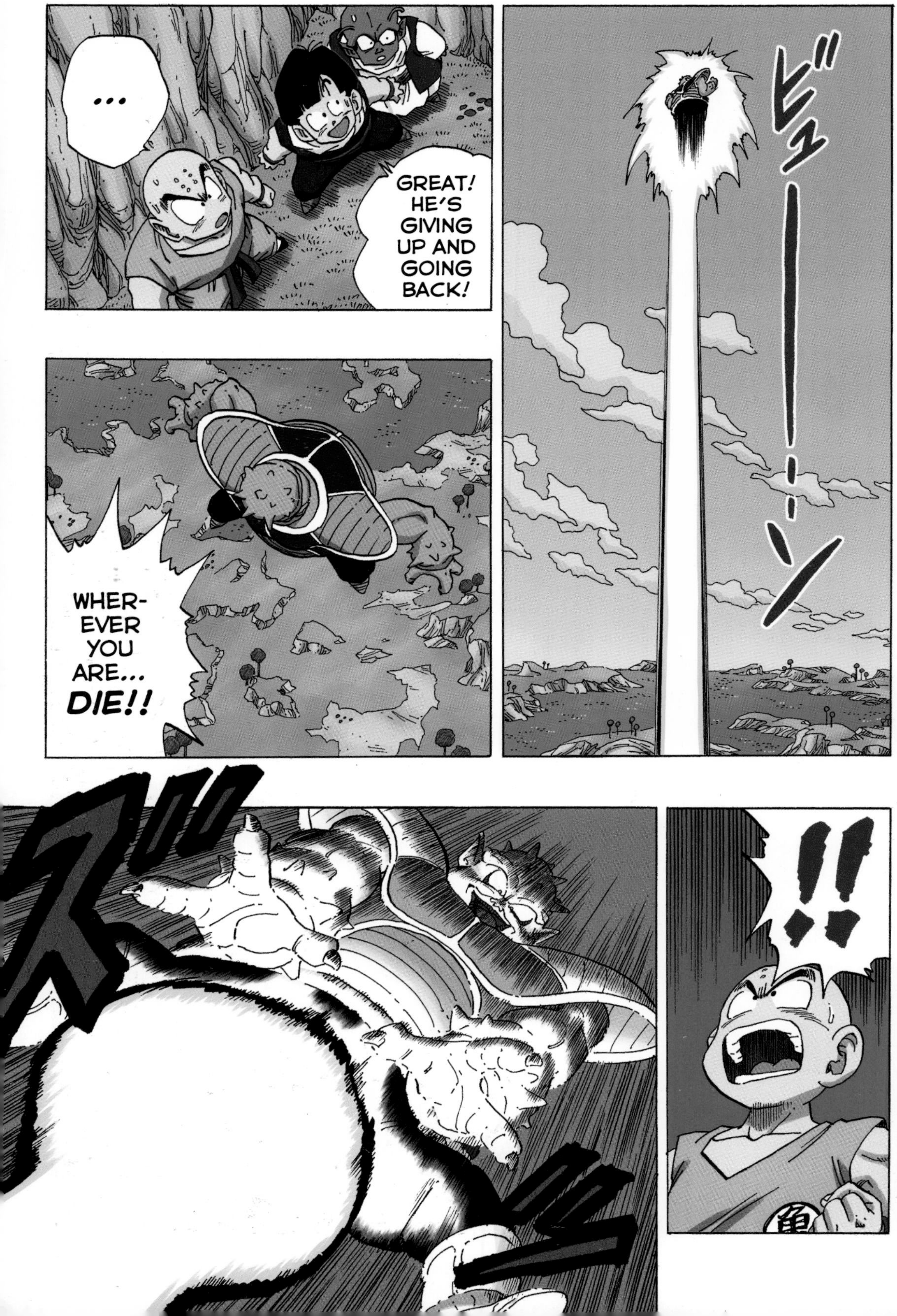
ビューーーン
GREAT! HE'S GIVING UP AND GOING BACK!
...
WHER-EVER YOU ARE... DIE!!
!!

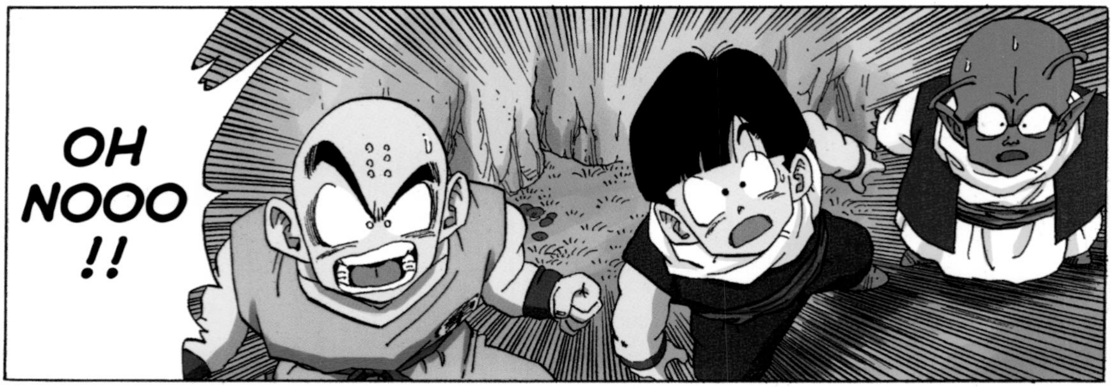
OH NOOO !!

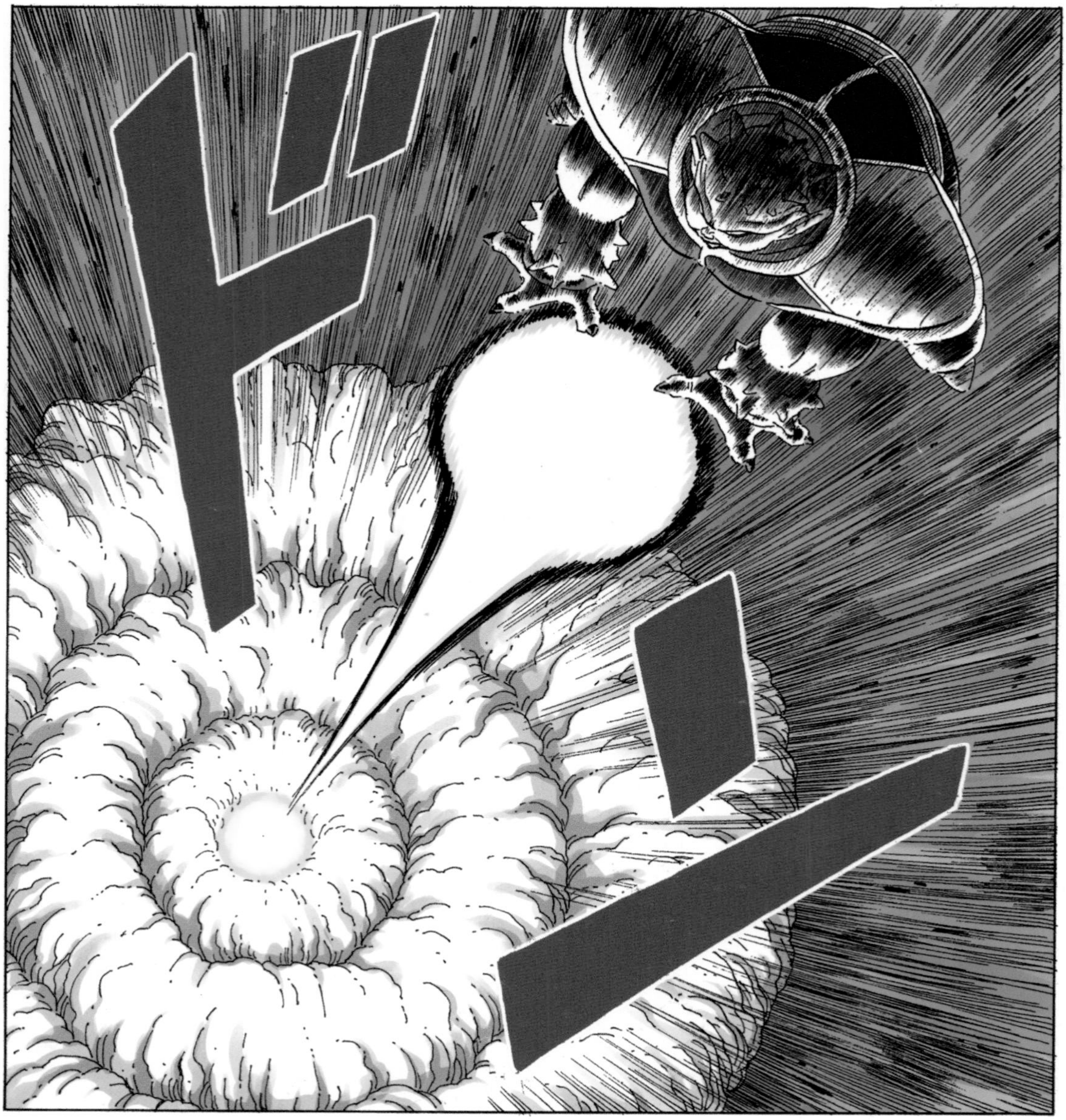
ドーン

グオッ
ズ・・・・・・ン

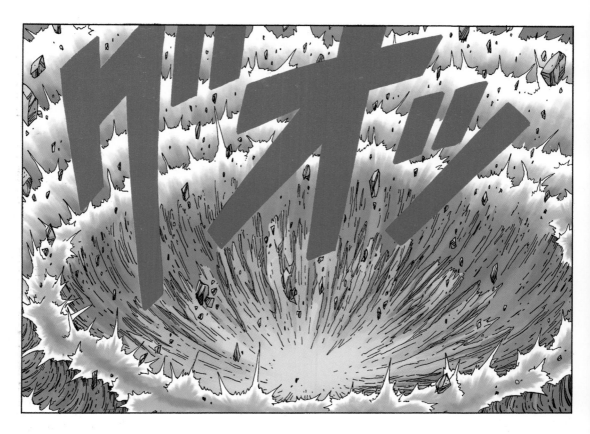

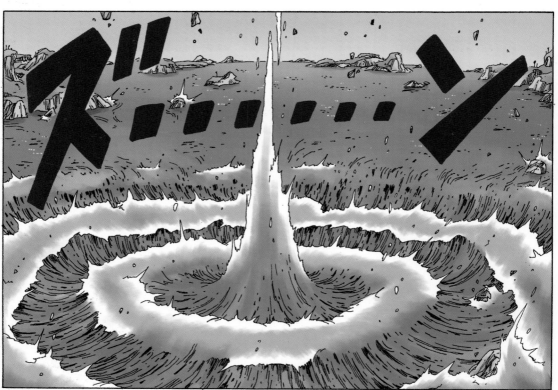

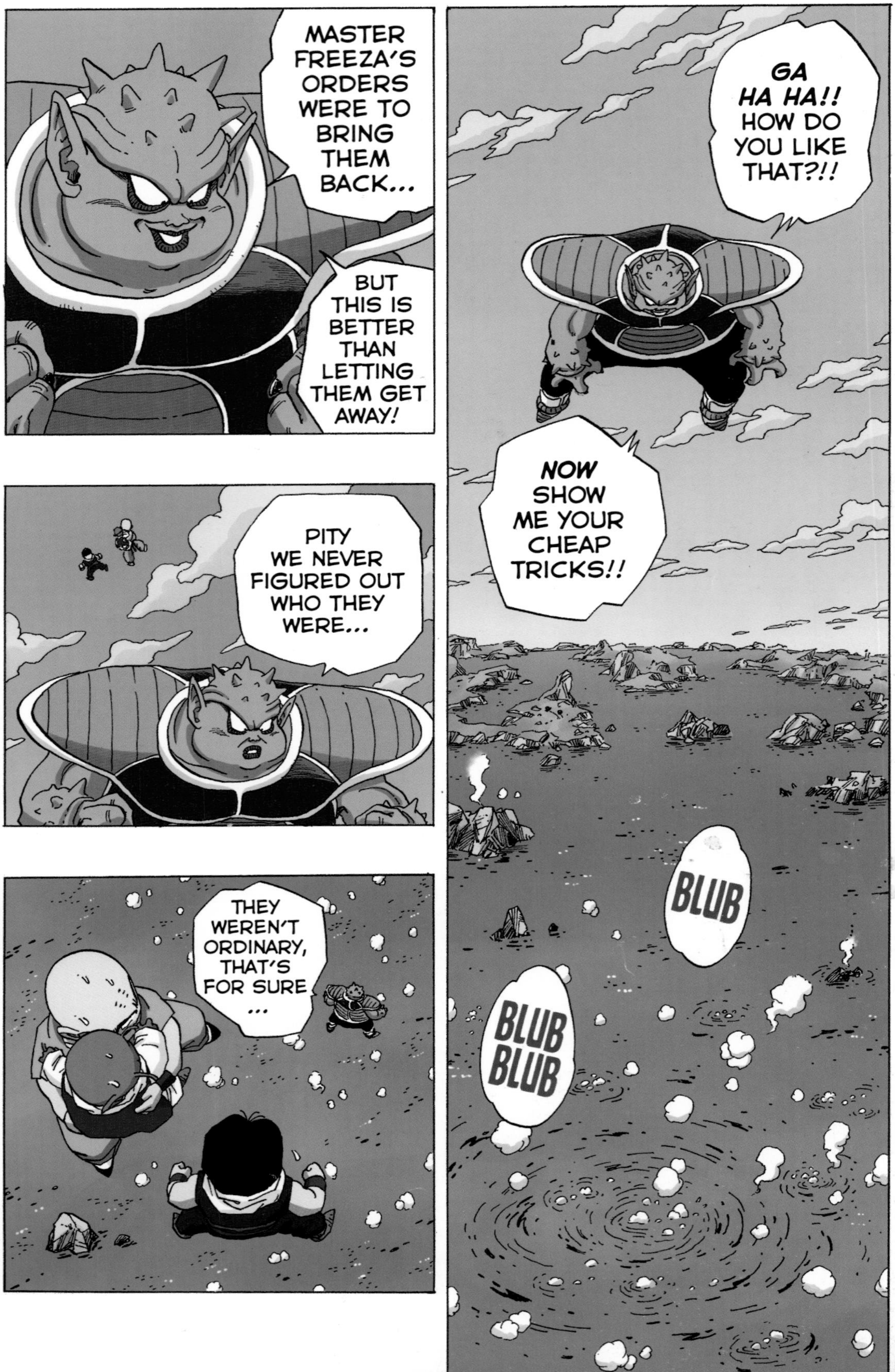
GA HA HA!! HOW DO YOU LIKE THAT?!!
NOW SHOW ME YOUR CHEAP TRICKS!!
BLUB
BLUB BLUB
MASTER FREEZA'S ORDERS WERE TO BRING THEM BACK...
BUT THIS IS BETTER THAN LETTING THEM GET AWAY!
PITY WE NEVER FIGURED OUT WHO THEY WERE...
THEY WEREN'T ORDINARY, THAT'S FOR SURE...

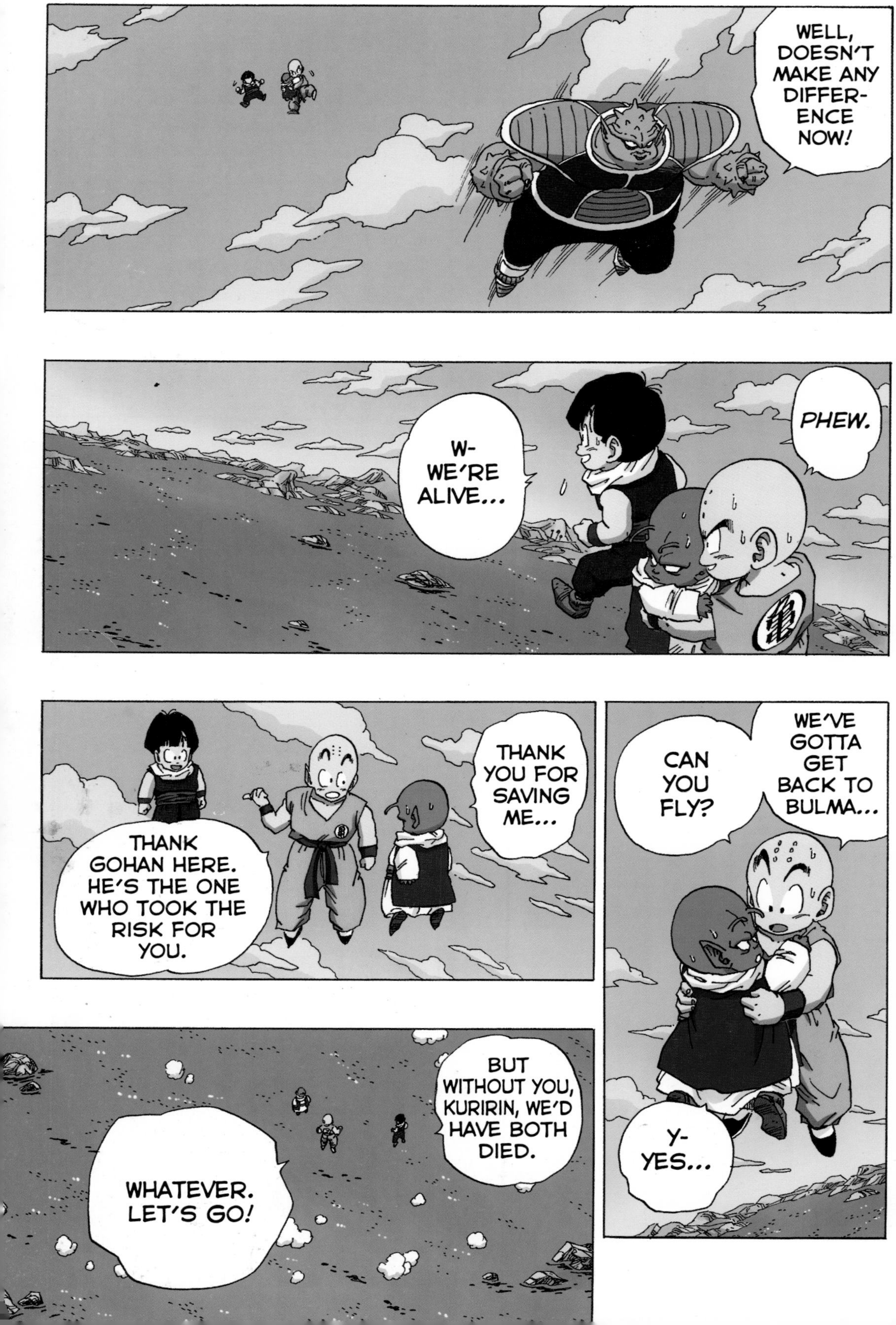
WELL, DOESN'T MAKE ANY DIFFERENCE NOW!
PHEW.
W- WE'RE ALIVE...
WE'VE GOTTA GET BACK TO BULMA...
CAN YOU FLY?
Y- YES...
THANK YOU FOR SAVING ME...
THANK GOHAN HERE. HE'S THE ONE WHO TOOK THE RISK FOR YOU.
BUT WITHOUT YOU, KURIRIN, WE'D HAVE BOTH DIED.
WHATEVER. LET'S GO!

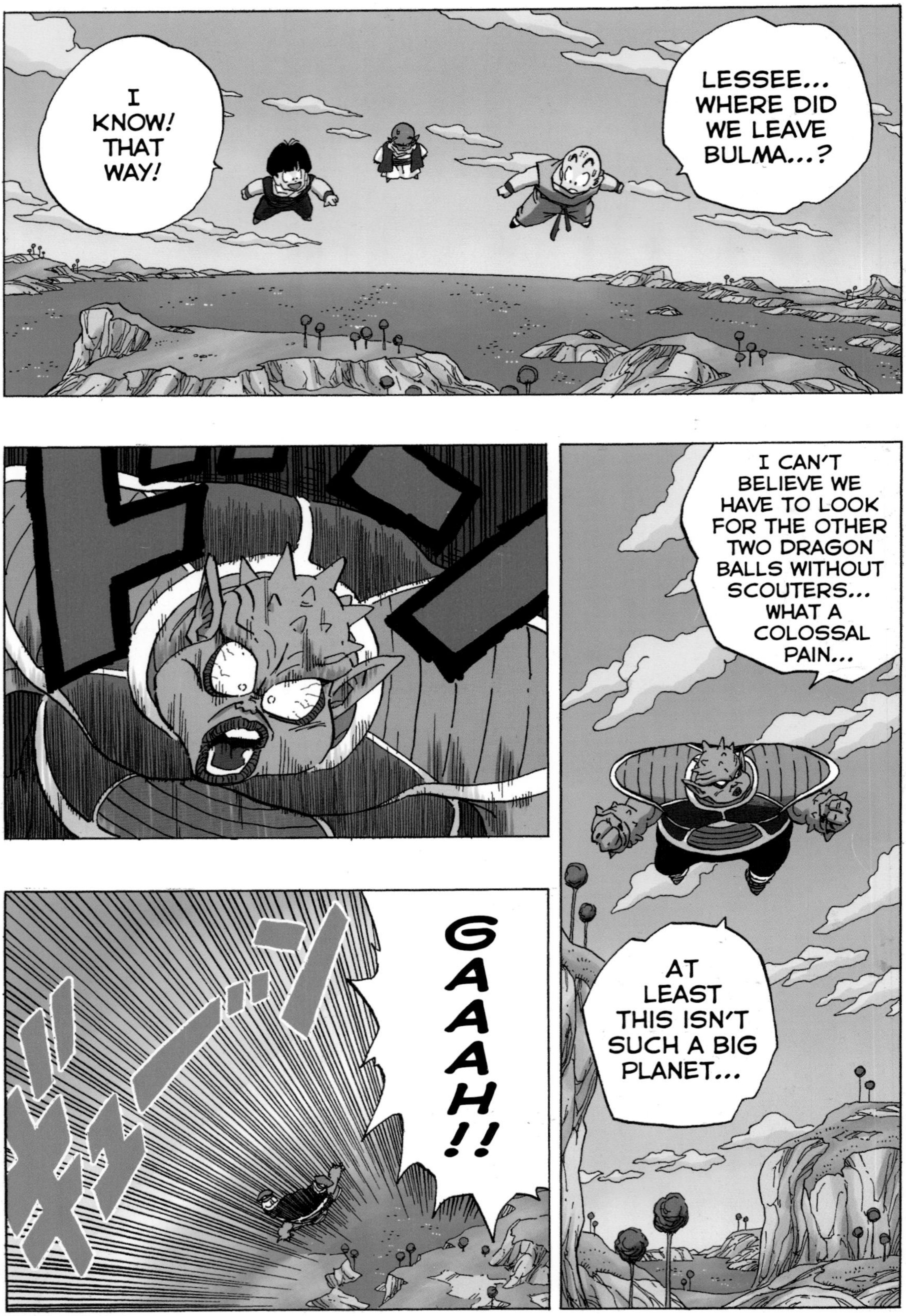
LESSEE... WHERE DID WE LEAVE BULMA...?
I KNOW! THAT WAY!
I CAN'T BELIEVE WE HAVE TO LOOK FOR THE OTHER TWO DRAGON BALLS WITHOUT SCOUTERS... WHAT A COLOSSAL PAIN...
AT LEAST THIS ISN'T SUCH A BIG PLANET...
GAAAAH!!

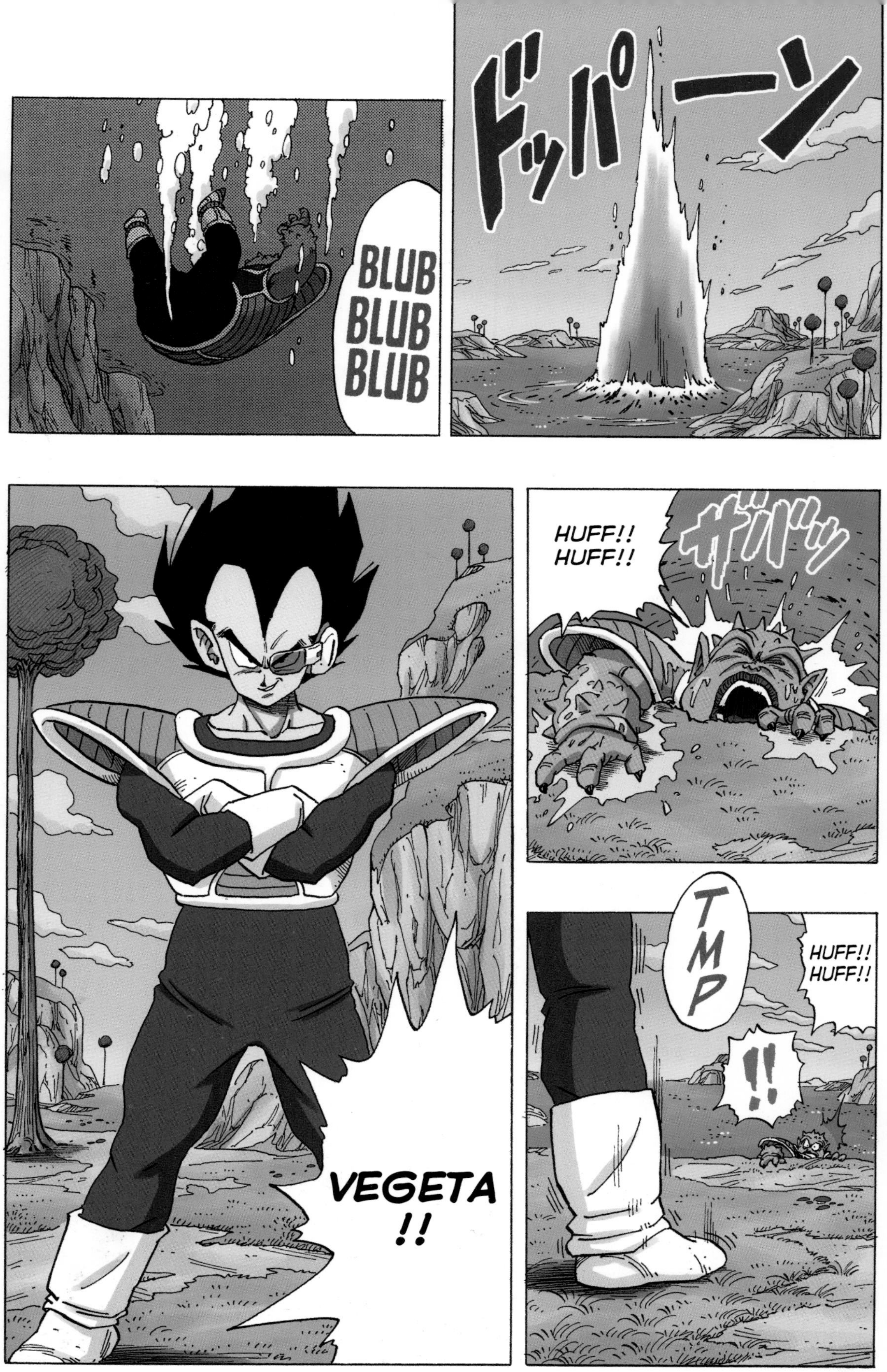
ドッパーン
BLUB BLUB BLUB
HUFF!! HUFF!!
ザバッ
TMP
HUFF!! HUFF!!
!!
VEGETA !!

Chapter 12 • Vegeta vs. Dodoria

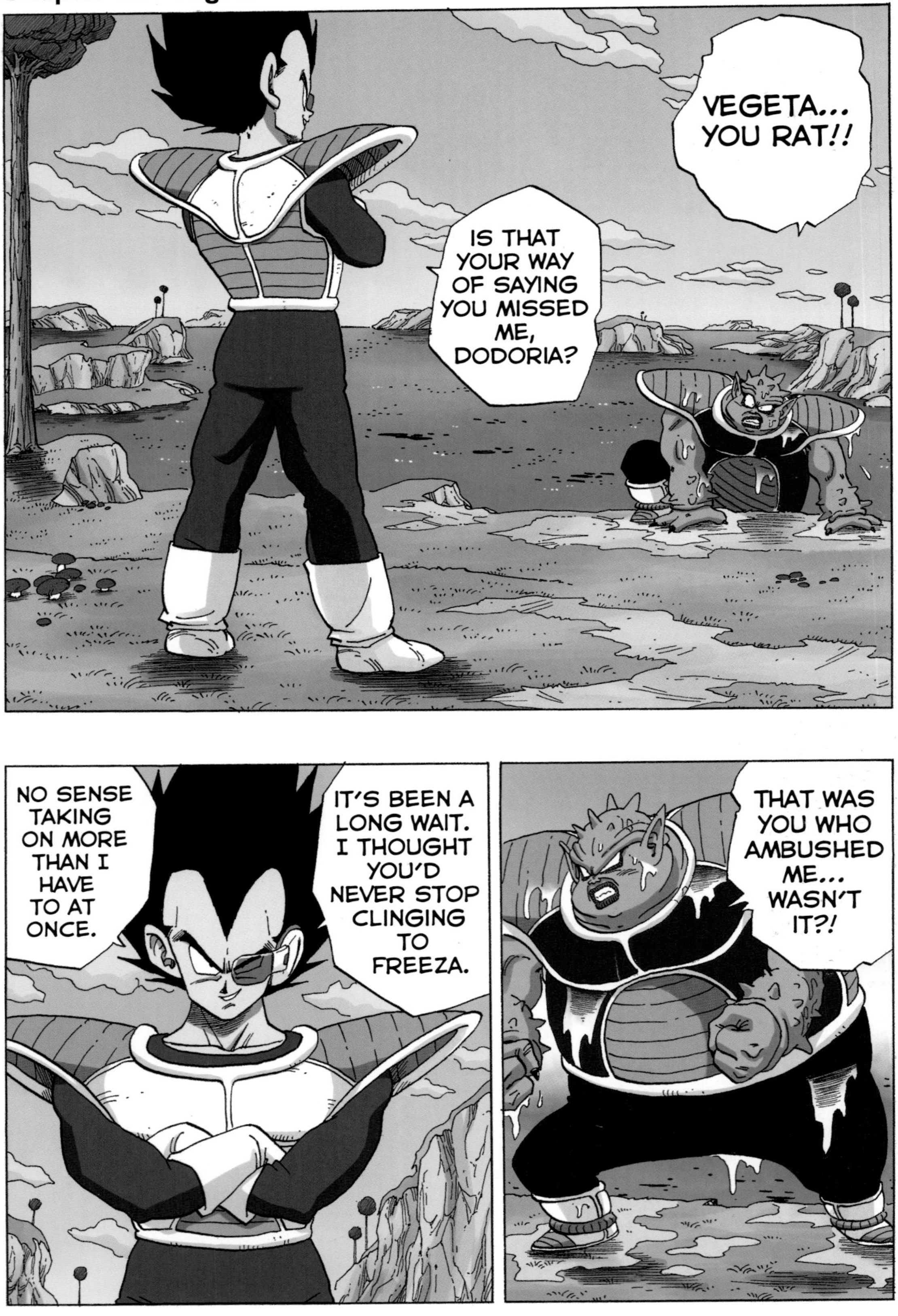
VEGETA... YOU RAT!!
IS THAT YOUR WAY OF SAYING YOU MISSED ME, DODORIA?
THAT WAS YOU WHO AMBUSHED ME... WASN'T IT?!
IT'S BEEN A LONG WAIT. I THOUGHT YOU'D NEVER STOP CLINGING TO FREEZA.
NO SENSE TAKING ON MORE THAN I HAVE TO AT ONCE.

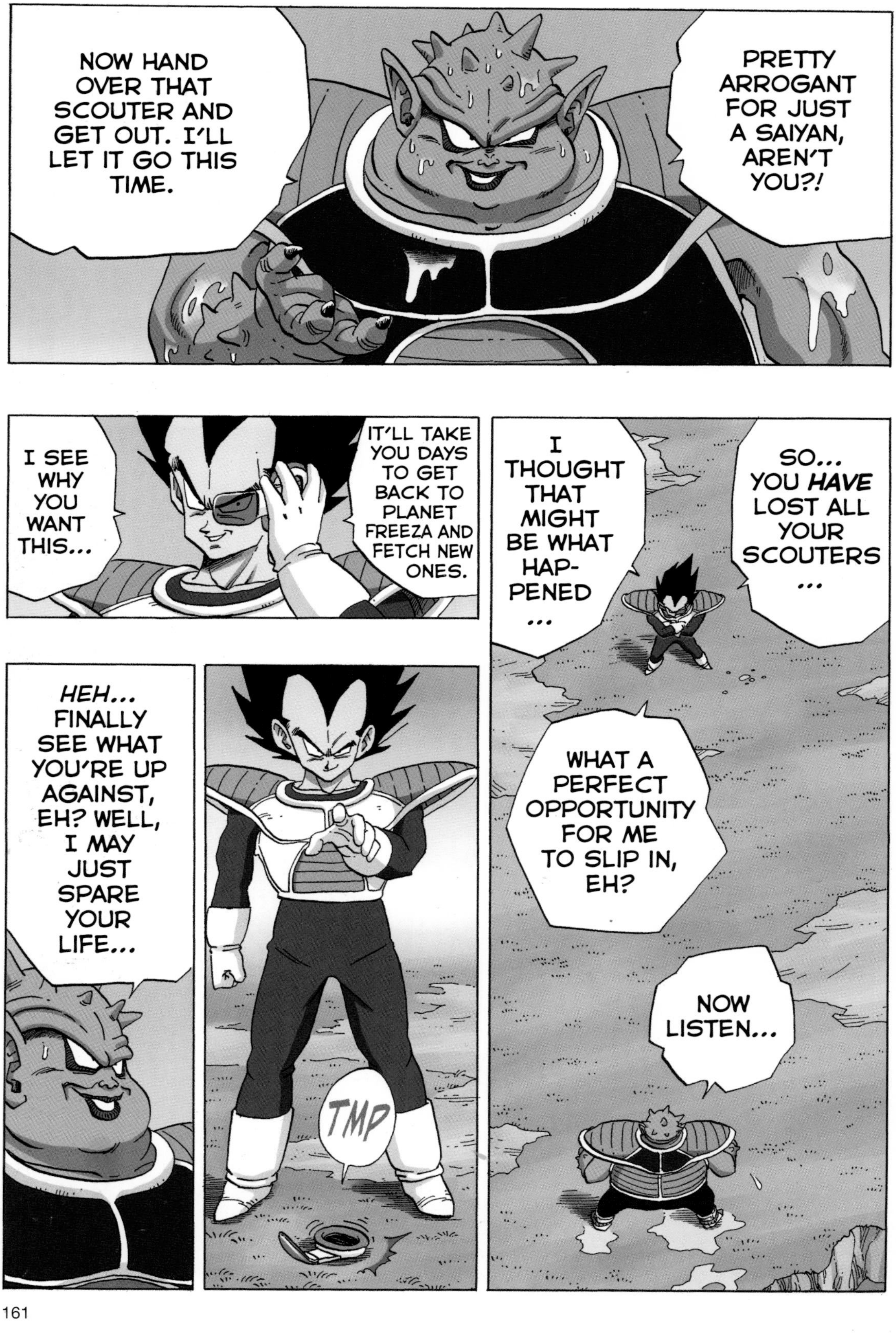
PRETTY ARROGANT FOR JUST A SAIYAN, AREN'T YOU?!
NOW HAND OVER THAT SCOUTER AND GET OUT. I'LL LET IT GO THIS TIME.
SO... YOU *HAVE* LOST ALL YOUR SCOUTERS...
I THOUGHT THAT MIGHT BE WHAT HAP-PENED...
WHAT A PERFECT OPPORTUNITY FOR ME TO SLIP IN, EH?
NOW LISTEN...
IT'LL TAKE YOU DAYS TO GET BACK TO PLANET FREEZA AND FETCH NEW ONES.
I SEE WHY YOU WANT THIS...
TMP
HEH... FINALLY SEE WHAT YOU'RE UP AGAINST, EH? WELL, I *MAY* JUST SPARE YOUR LIFE...

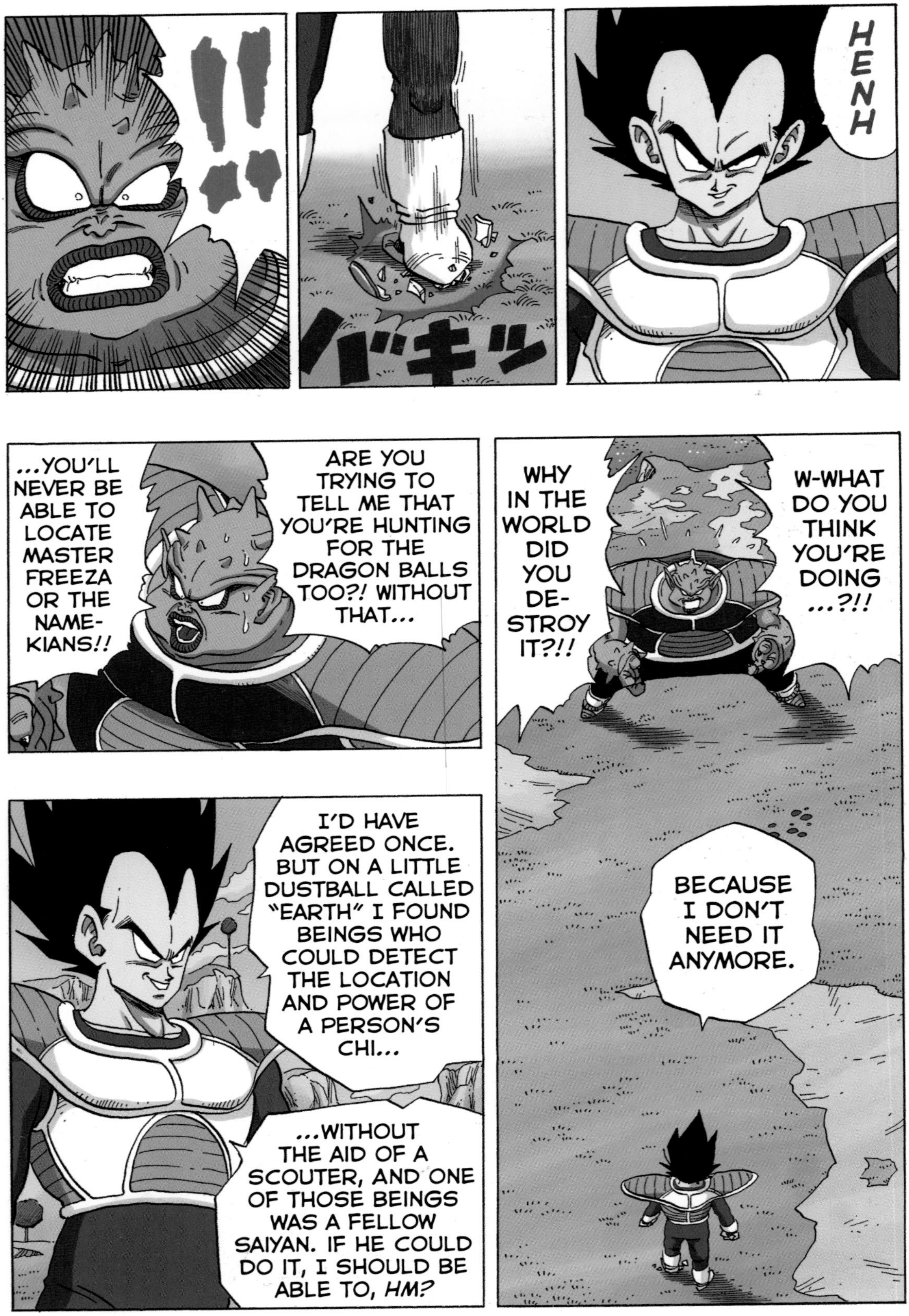
HENH
バキッ
!!
W-WHAT DO YOU THINK YOU'RE DOING ...?!!
WHY IN THE WORLD DID YOU DE-STROY IT?!!
BECAUSE I DON'T NEED IT ANYMORE.
ARE YOU TRYING TO TELL ME THAT YOU'RE HUNTING FOR THE DRAGON BALLS TOO?! WITHOUT THAT...
...YOU'LL NEVER BE ABLE TO LOCATE MASTER FREEZA OR THE NAME-KIANS!!
I'D HAVE AGREED ONCE. BUT ON A LITTLE DUSTBALL CALLED "EARTH" I FOUND BEINGS WHO COULD DETECT THE LOCATION AND POWER OF A PERSON'S CHI...
...WITHOUT THE AID OF A SCOUTER, AND ONE OF THOSE BEINGS WAS A FELLOW SAIYAN. IF HE COULD DO IT, I SHOULD BE ABLE TO, HM?

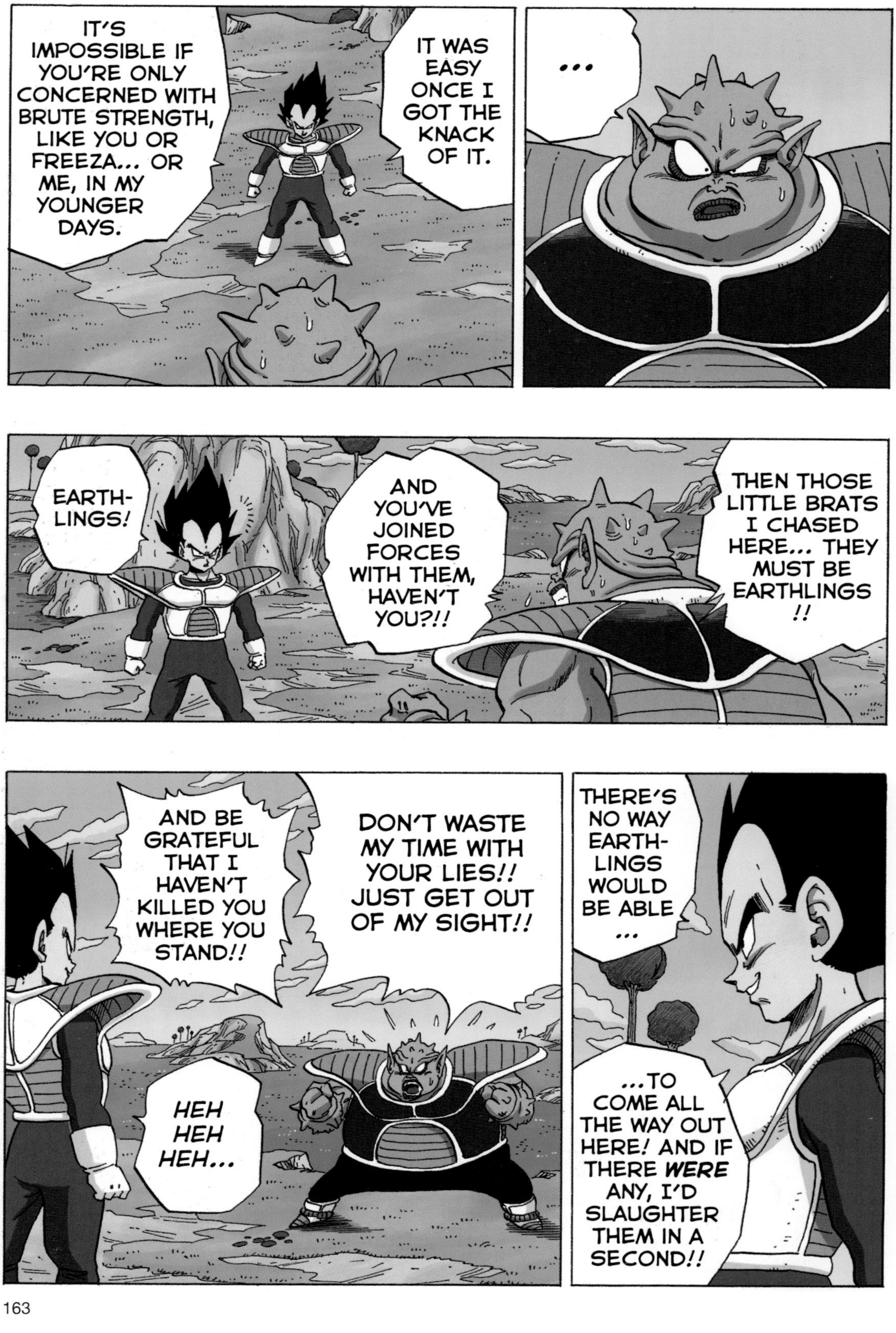
...
IT WAS EASY ONCE I GOT THE KNACK OF IT.
IT'S IMPOSSIBLE IF YOU'RE ONLY CONCERNED WITH BRUTE STRENGTH, LIKE YOU OR FREEZA... OR ME, IN MY YOUNGER DAYS.
THEN THOSE LITTLE BRATS I CHASED HERE... THEY MUST BE EARTHLINGS!!
AND YOU'VE JOINED FORCES WITH THEM, HAVEN'T YOU?!!
EARTH-LINGS!
THERE'S NO WAY EARTH-LINGS WOULD BE ABLE...
...TO COME ALL THE WAY OUT HERE! AND IF THERE *WERE* ANY, I'D SLAUGHTER THEM IN A SECOND!!
DON'T WASTE MY TIME WITH YOUR LIES!! JUST GET OUT OF MY SIGHT!!
AND BE GRATEFUL THAT I HAVEN'T KILLED YOU WHERE YOU STAND!!
HEH HEH HEH...

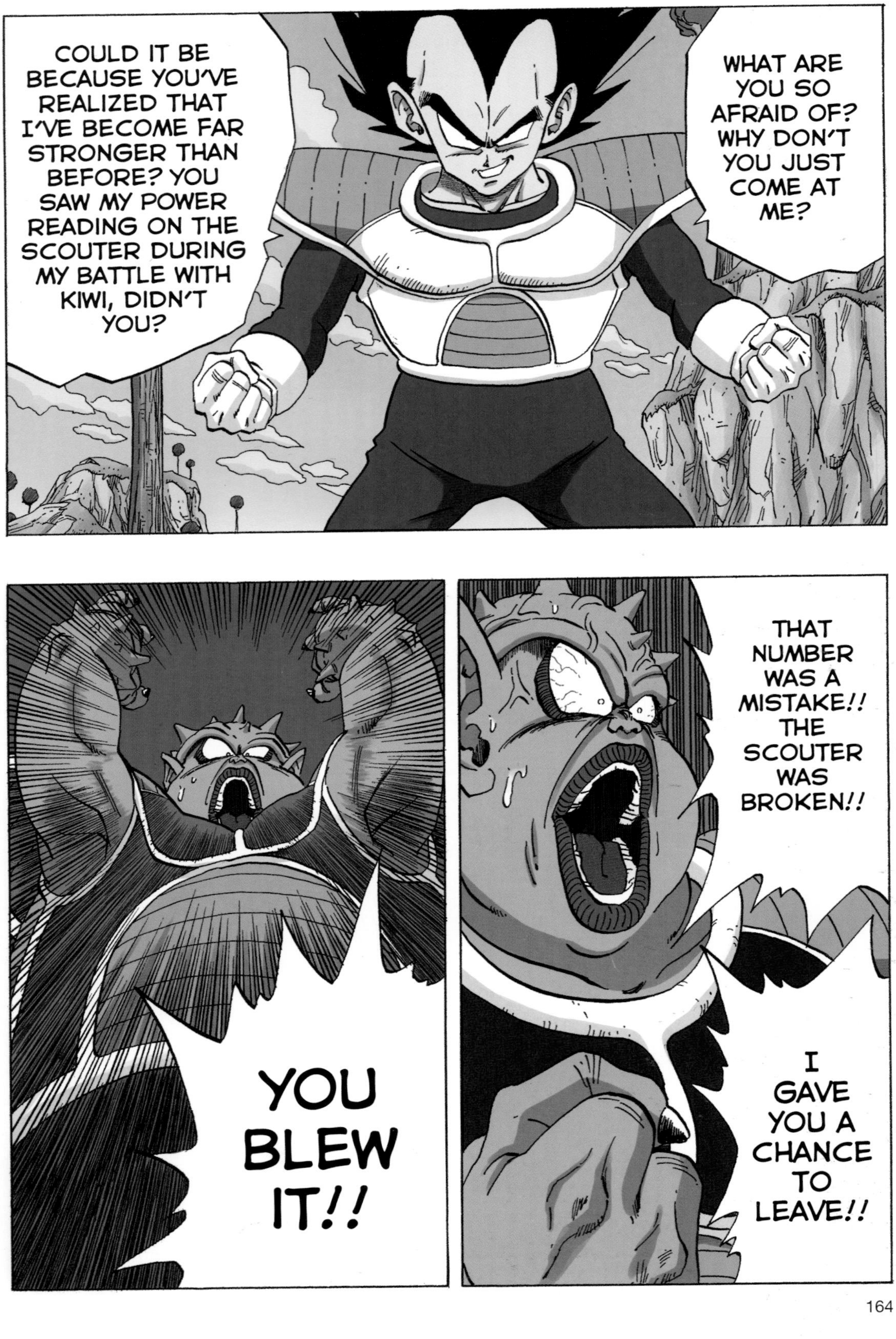
WHAT ARE YOU SO AFRAID OF? WHY DON'T YOU JUST COME AT ME?
COULD IT BE BECAUSE YOU'VE REALIZED THAT I'VE BECOME FAR STRONGER THAN BEFORE? YOU SAW MY POWER READING ON THE SCOUTER DURING MY BATTLE WITH KIWI, DIDN'T YOU?
THAT NUMBER WAS A MISTAKE!! THE SCOUTER WAS BROKEN!!
I GAVE YOU A CHANCE TO LEAVE!!
YOU BLEW IT!!

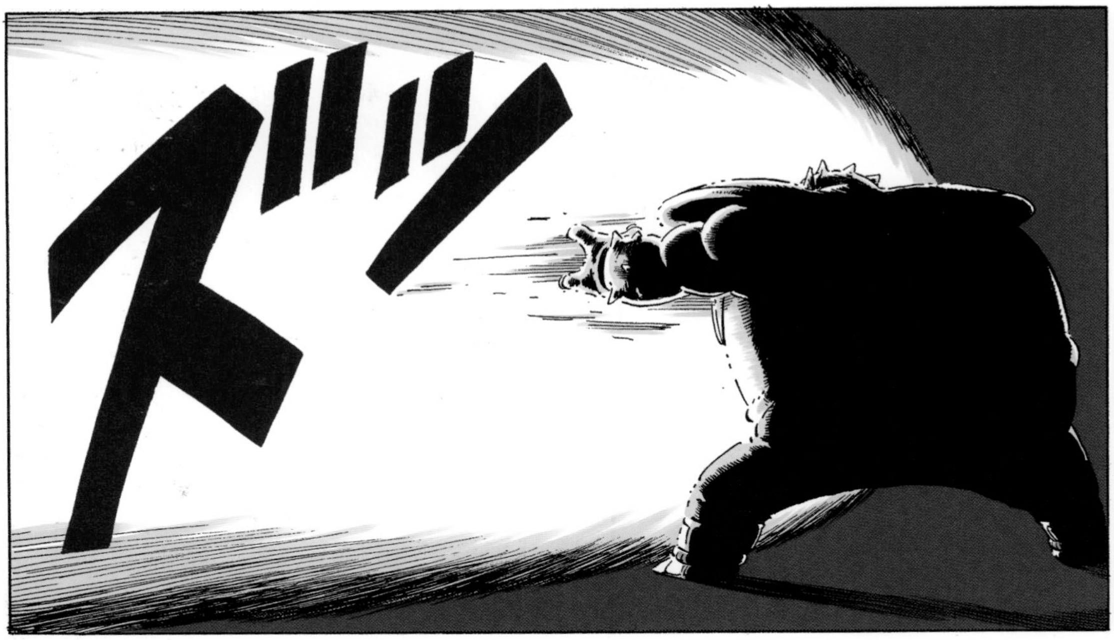
ズッ

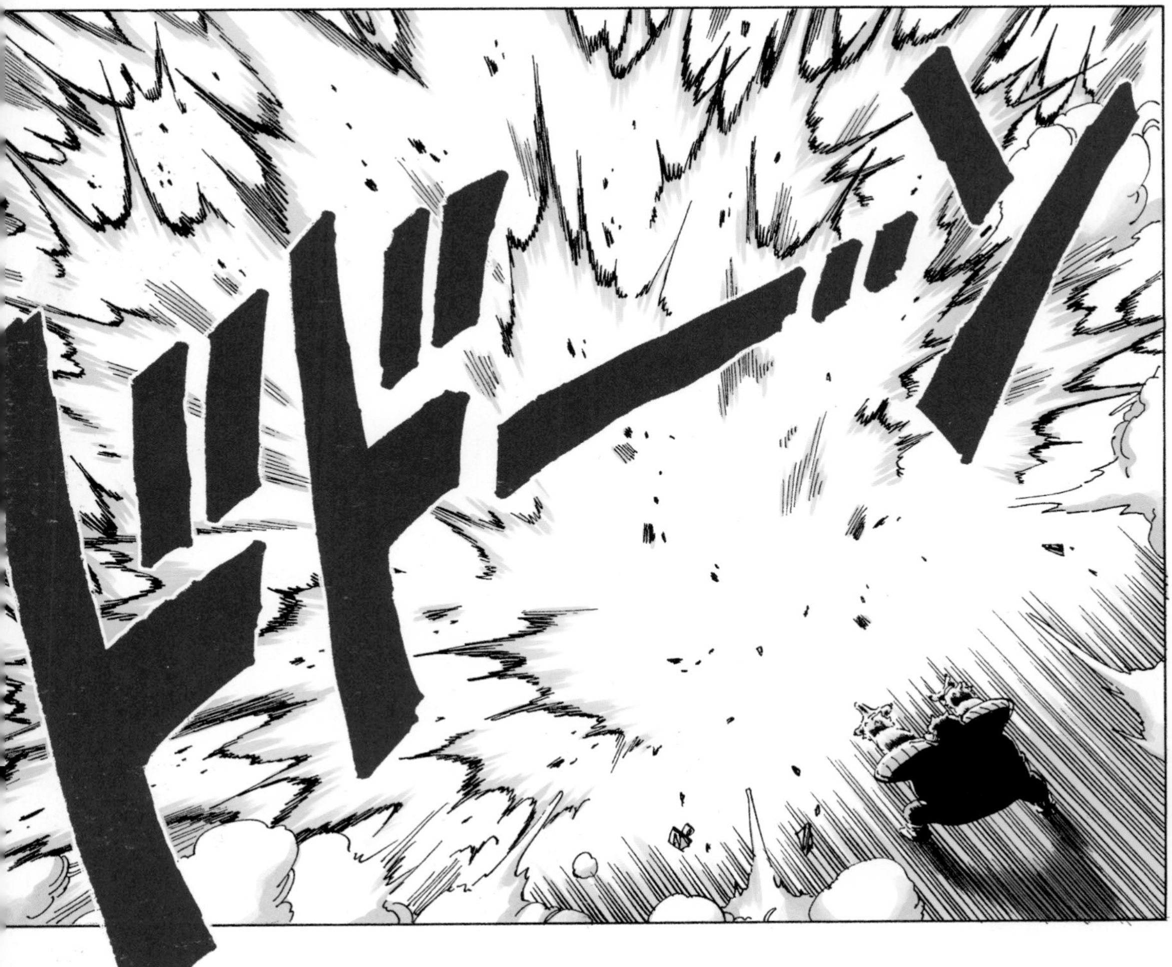
ドドーーッ

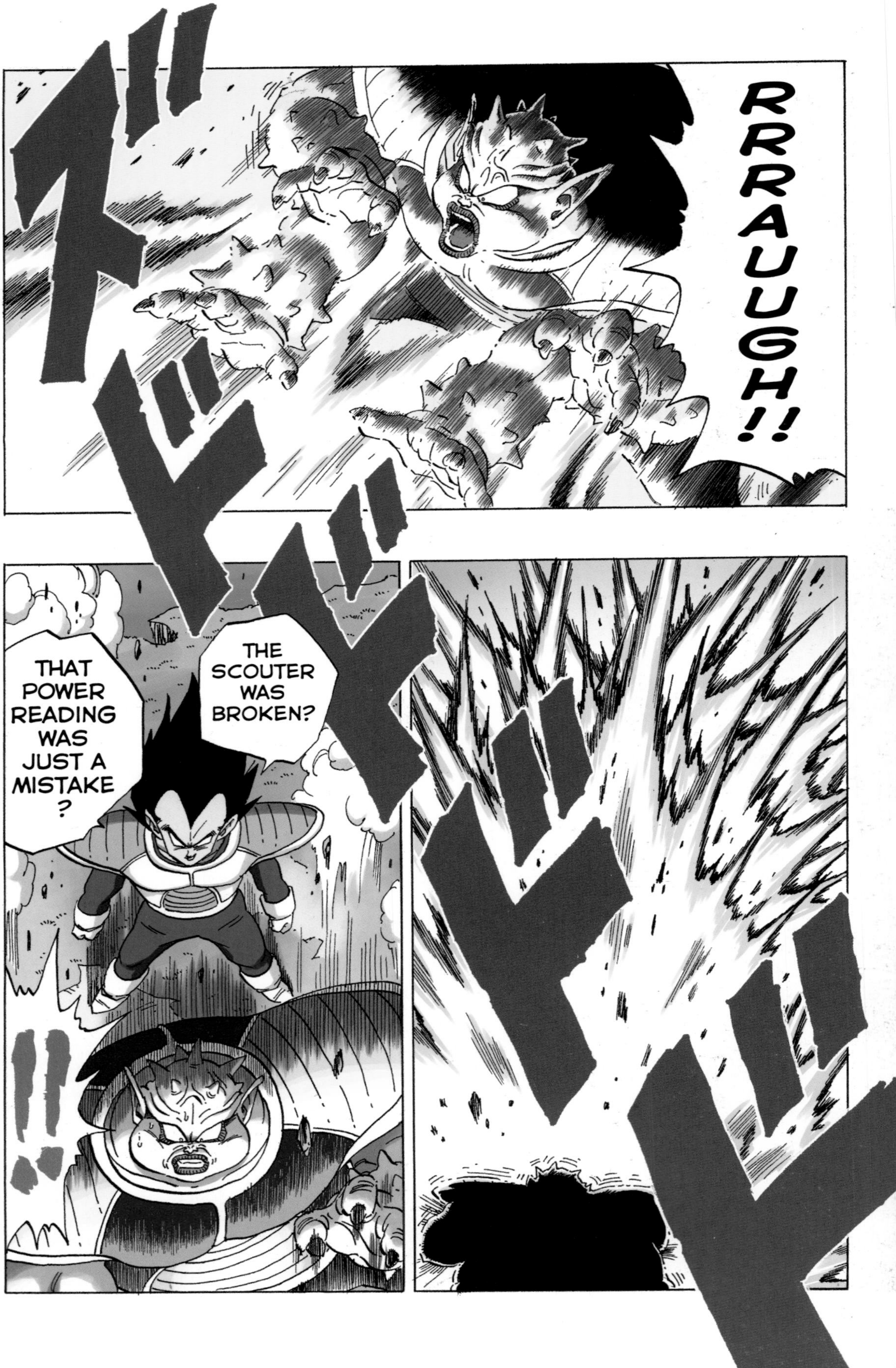
RRRAUUGH!!
THE SCOUTER WAS BROKEN?
THAT POWER READING WAS JUST A MISTAKE?
!!

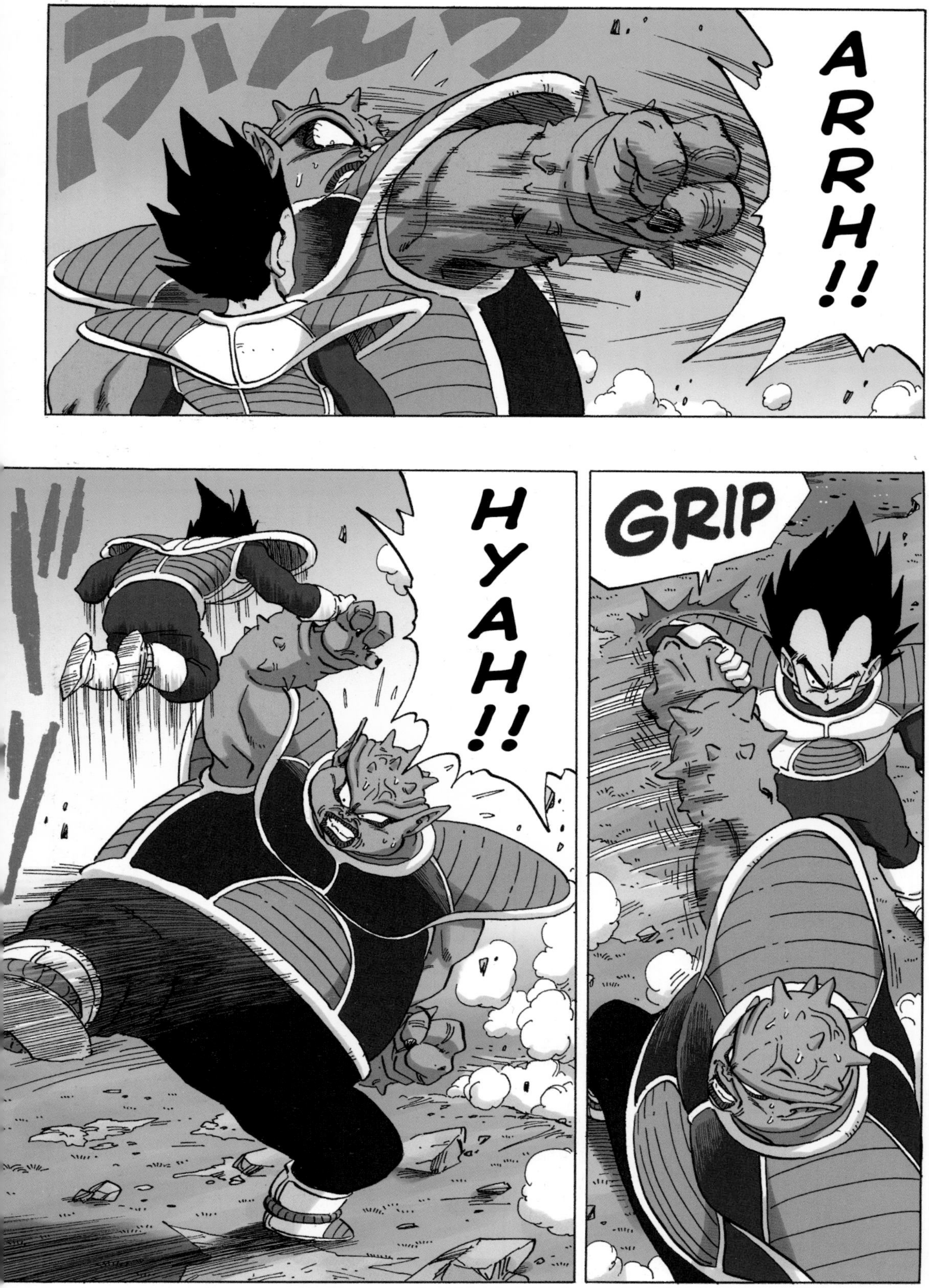
ARRRH!!
GRIP
HYAH!!

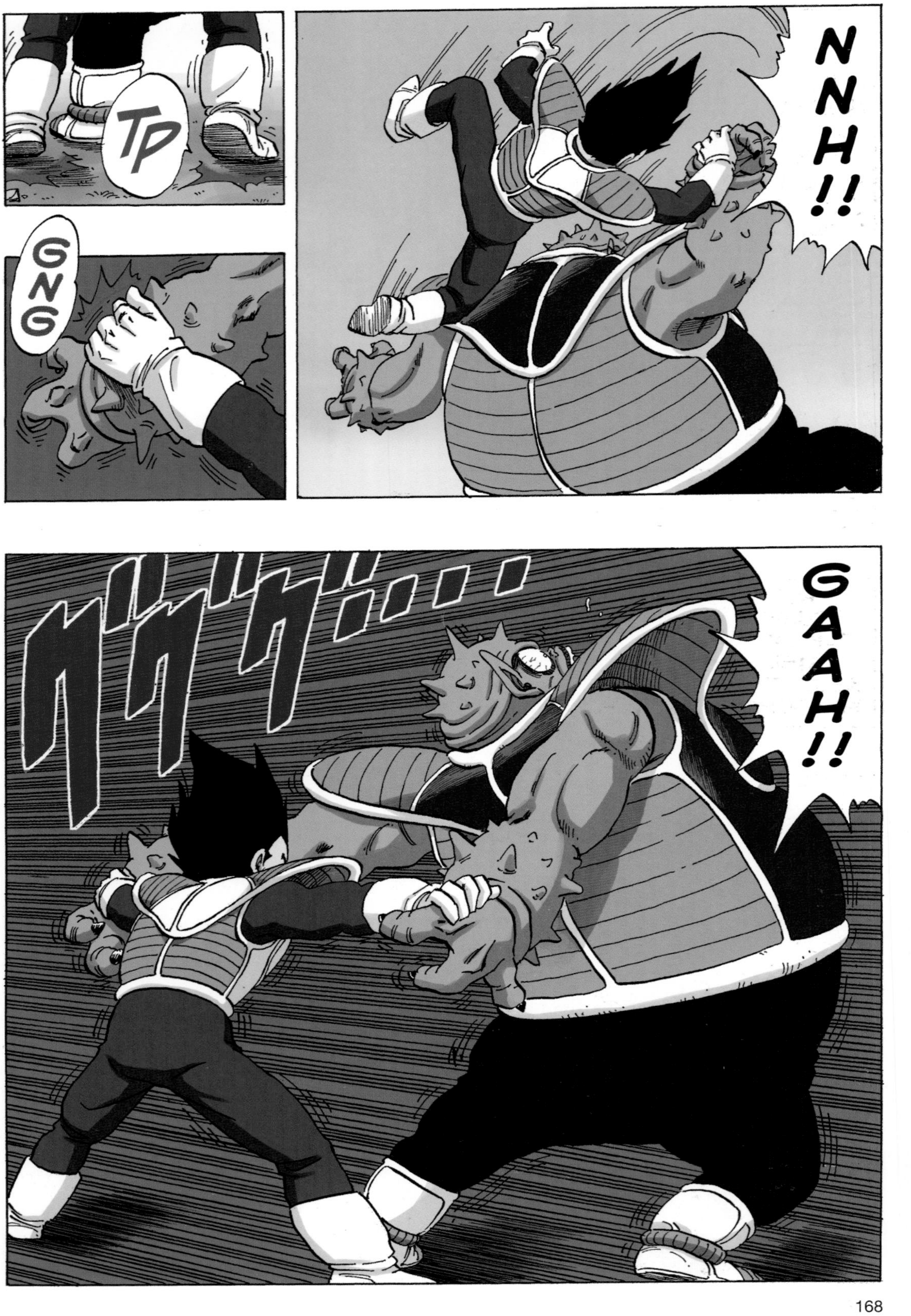
NNH!!
TP
GNG
GAAH!!
グググ....

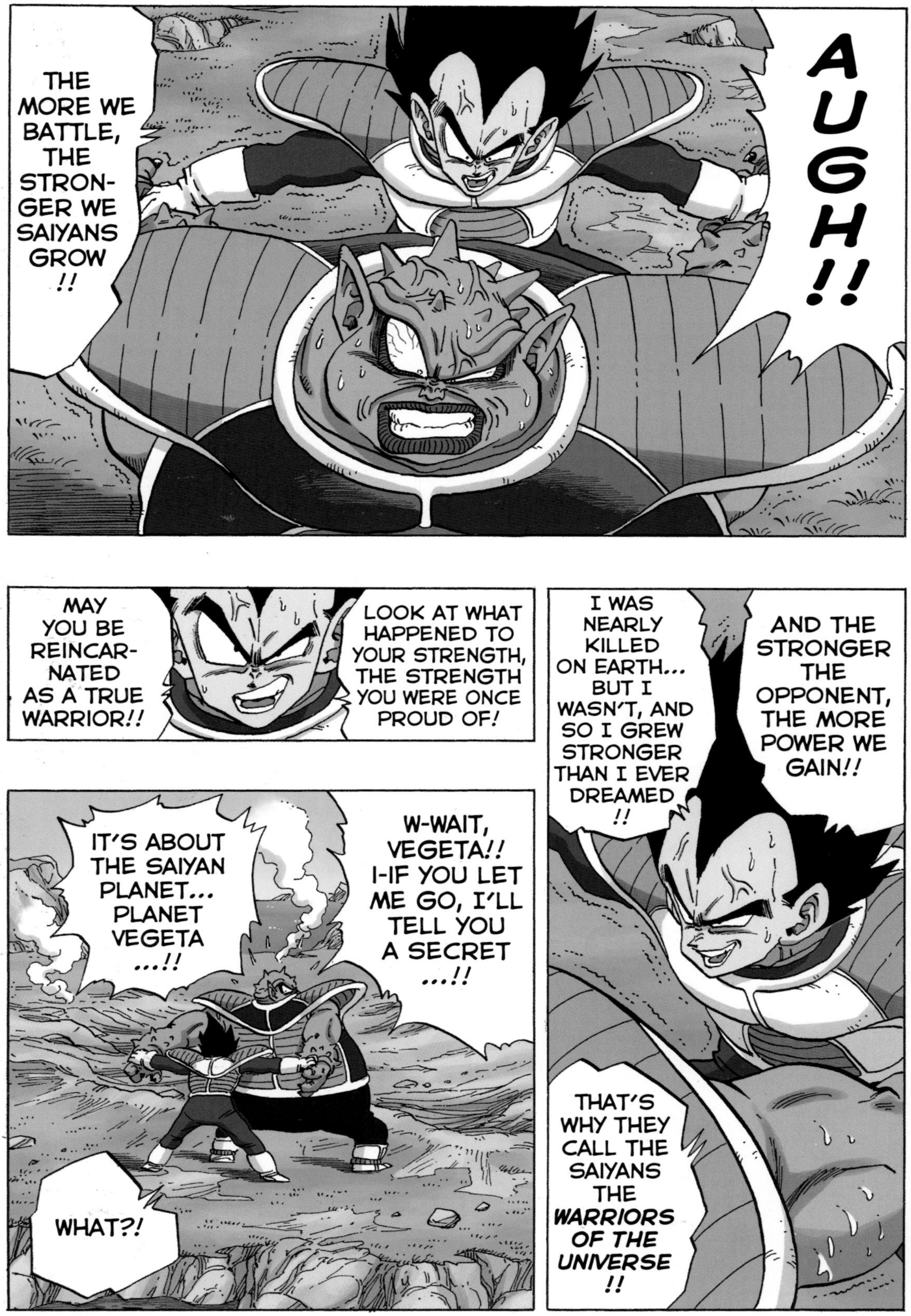
AUGH!!
THE MORE WE BATTLE, THE STRONGER WE SAIYANS GROW!!
I WAS NEARLY KILLED ON EARTH... BUT I WASN'T, AND SO I GREW STRONGER THAN I EVER DREAMED!!
AND THE STRONGER THE OPPONENT, THE MORE POWER WE GAIN!!
THAT'S WHY THEY CALL THE SAIYANS THE *WARRIORS OF THE UNIVERSE*!!
LOOK AT WHAT HAPPENED TO YOUR STRENGTH, THE STRENGTH YOU WERE ONCE PROUD OF!
MAY YOU BE REINCARNATED AS A TRUE WARRIOR!!
W-WAIT, VEGETA!! I-IF YOU LET ME GO, I'LL TELL YOU A SECRET...!!
IT'S ABOUT THE SAIYAN PLANET... PLANET VEGETA...!!
WHAT?!

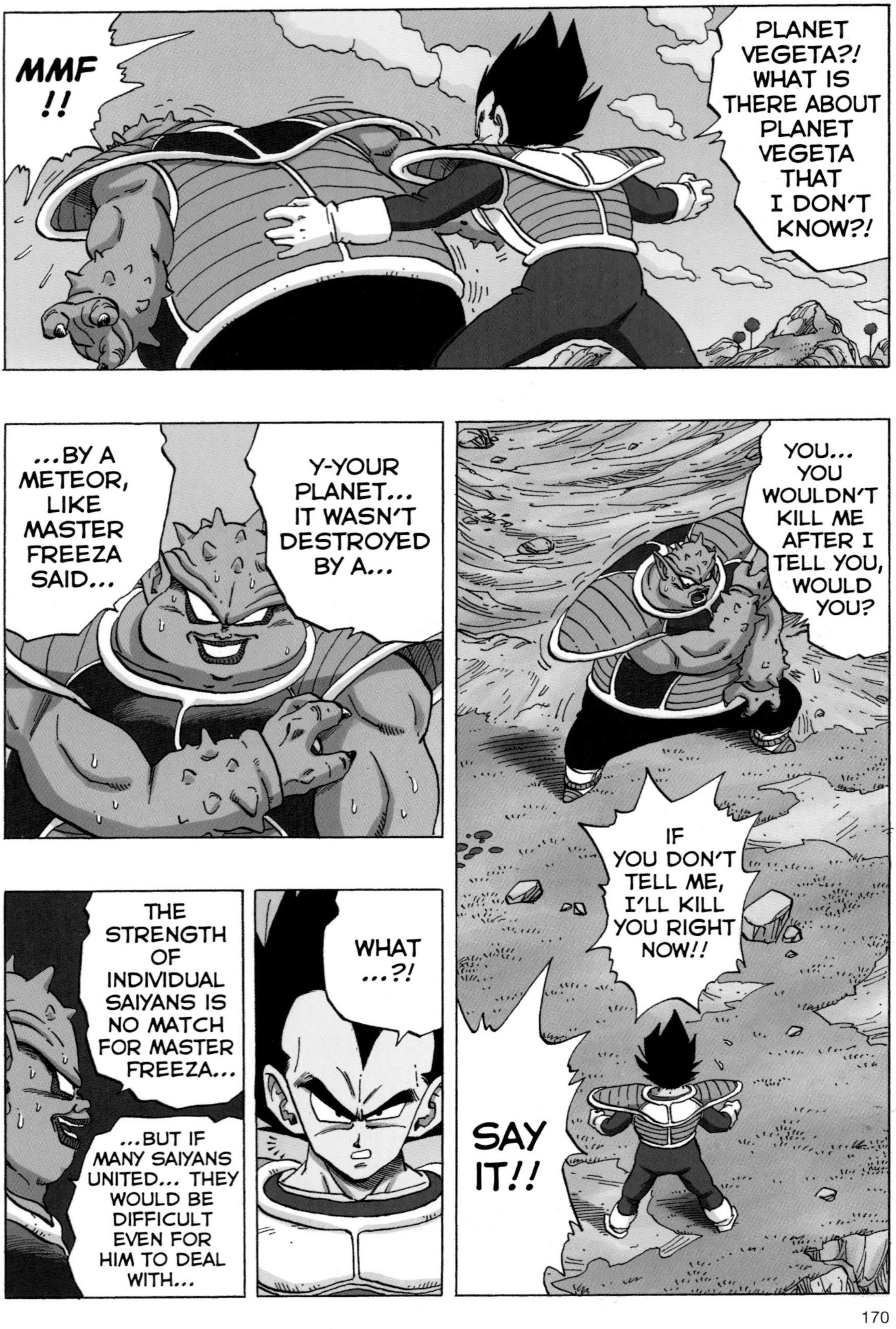
PLANET VEGETA?! WHAT IS THERE ABOUT PLANET VEGETA THAT I DON'T KNOW?!
MMF!!
YOU... YOU WOULDN'T KILL ME AFTER I TELL YOU, WOULD YOU?
IF YOU DON'T TELL ME, I'LL KILL YOU RIGHT NOW!!
SAY IT!!
Y-YOUR PLANET... IT WASN'T DESTROYED BY A...
...BY A METEOR, LIKE MASTER FREEZA SAID...
WHAT...?!
THE STRENGTH OF INDIVIDUAL SAIYANS IS NO MATCH FOR MASTER FREEZA...
...BUT IF MANY SAIYANS UNITED... THEY WOULD BE DIFFICULT EVEN FOR HIM TO DEAL WITH...

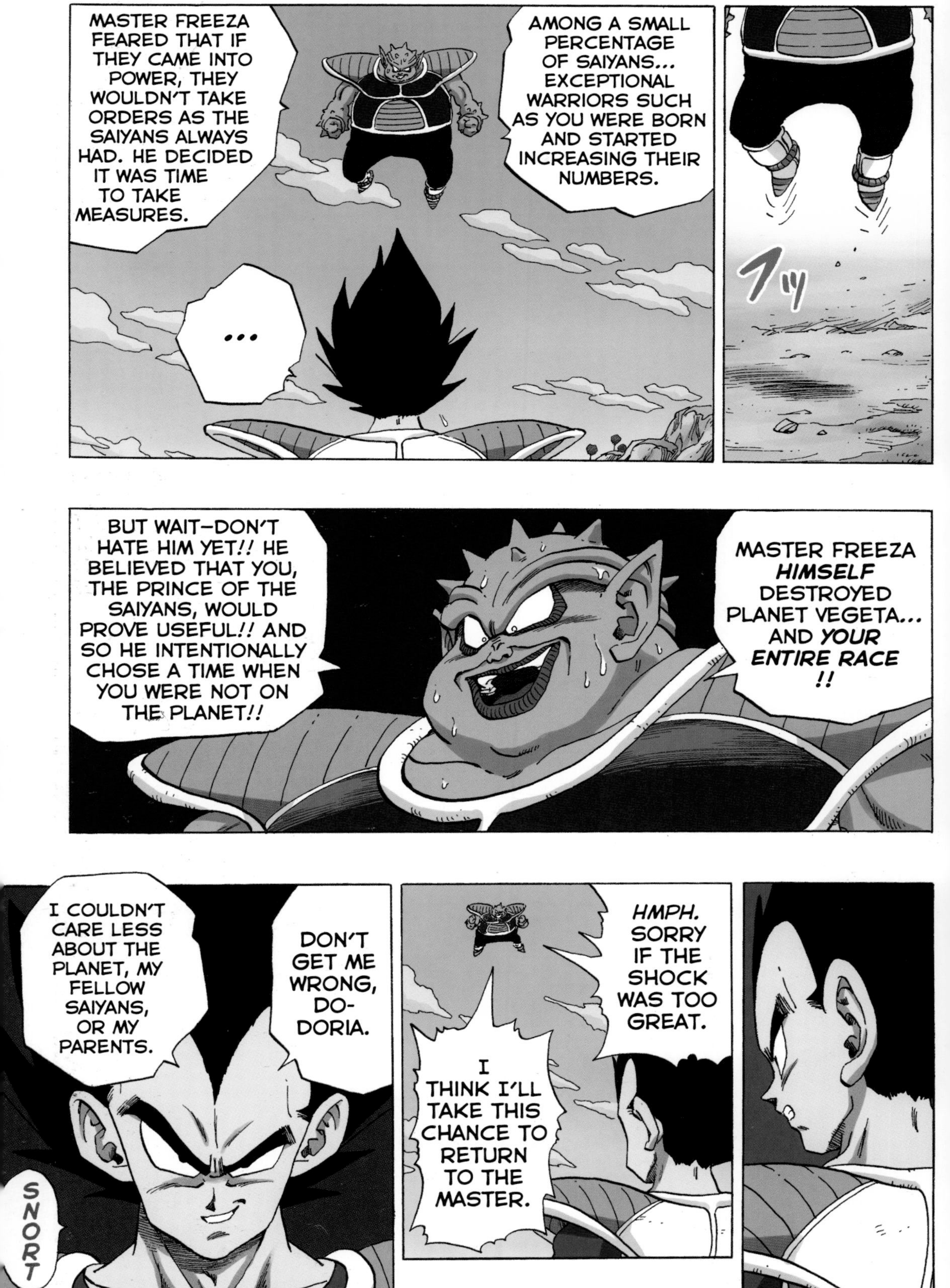
フッ
AMONG A SMALL PERCENTAGE OF SAIYANS... EXCEPTIONAL WARRIORS SUCH AS YOU WERE BORN AND STARTED INCREASING THEIR NUMBERS.
MASTER FREEZA FEARED THAT IF THEY CAME INTO POWER, THEY WOULDN'T TAKE ORDERS AS THE SAIYANS ALWAYS HAD. HE DECIDED IT WAS TIME TO TAKE MEASURES.
...
MASTER FREEZA *HIMSELF* DESTROYED PLANET VEGETA... AND *YOUR ENTIRE RACE* !!
BUT WAIT—DON'T HATE HIM YET!! HE BELIEVED THAT YOU, THE PRINCE OF THE SAIYANS, WOULD PROVE USEFUL!! AND SO HE INTENTIONALLY CHOSE A TIME WHEN YOU WERE NOT ON THE PLANET!!
HMPH. SORRY IF THE SHOCK WAS TOO GREAT.
I THINK I'LL TAKE THIS CHANCE TO RETURN TO THE MASTER.
DON'T GET ME WRONG, DO-DORIA.
I COULDN'T CARE LESS ABOUT THE PLANET, MY FELLOW SAIYANS, OR MY PARENTS.
SNORT

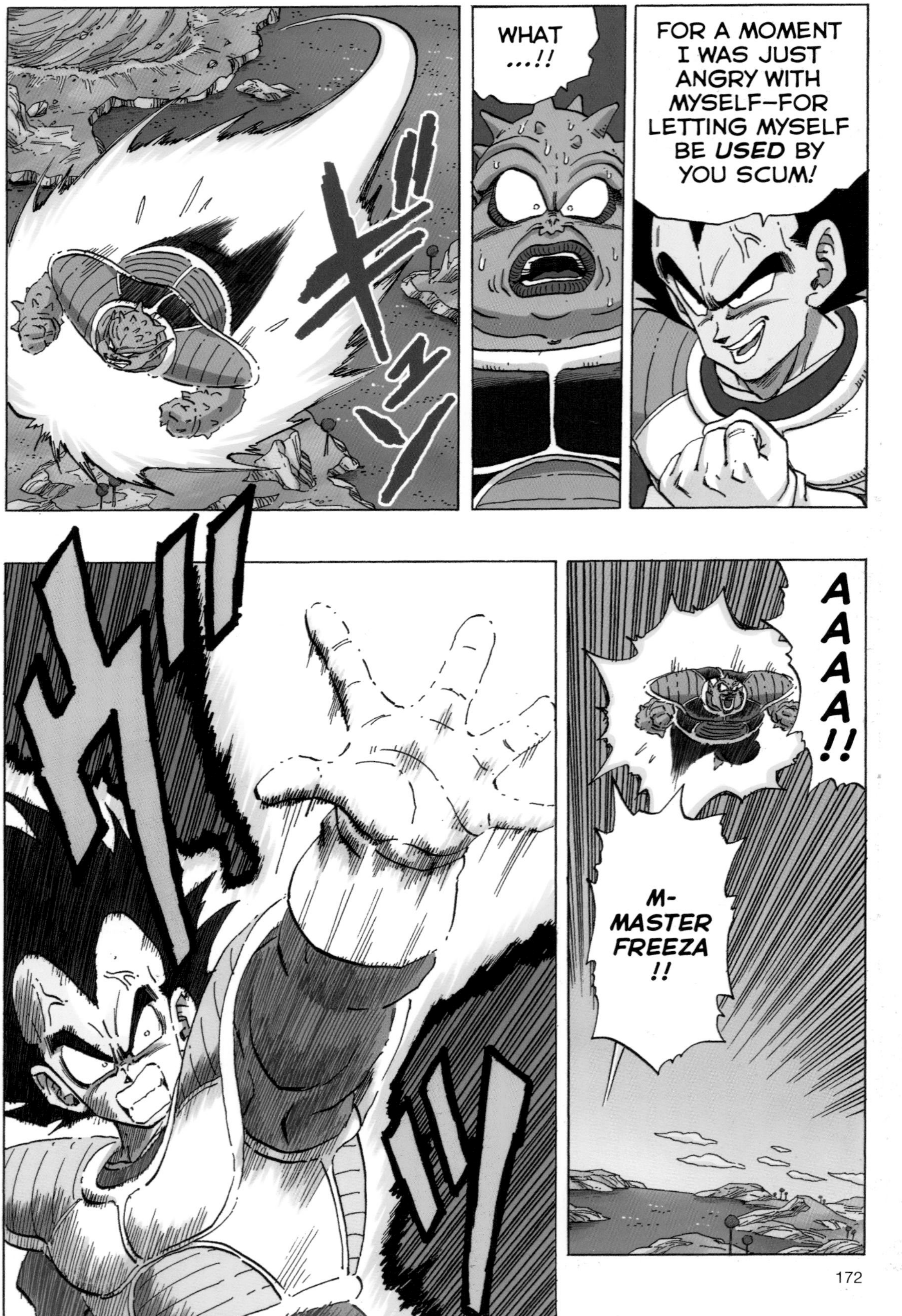
FOR A MOMENT I WAS JUST ANGRY WITH MYSELF—FOR LETTING MYSELF BE *USED* BY YOU SCUM!
WHAT ...!!
AAAAA!!
M-MASTER FREEZA !!

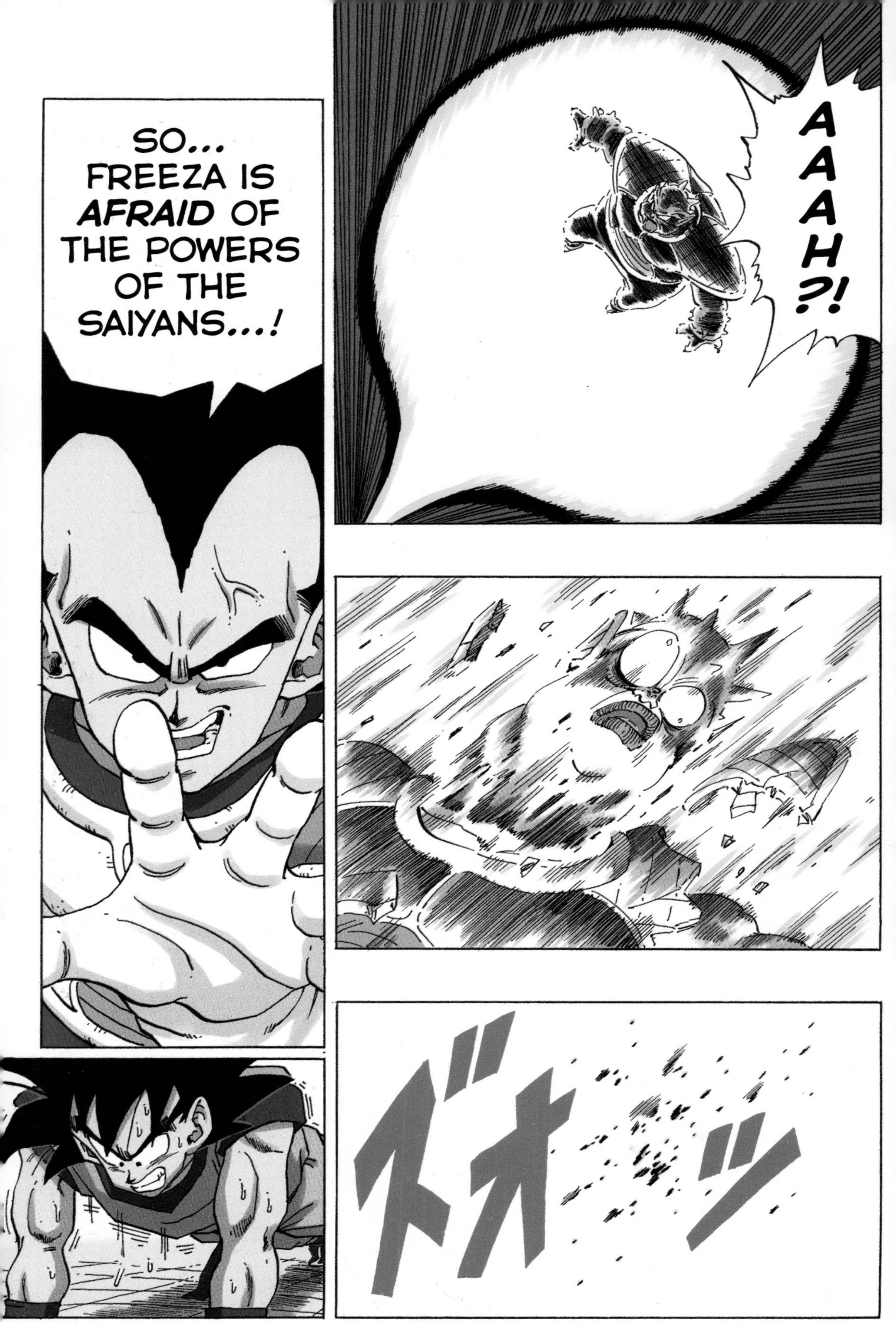
AAAAH?!
ズオッ
SO... FREEZA IS *AFRAID* OF THE POWERS OF THE SAIYANS...!

Chapter 13 • Hide and Seek

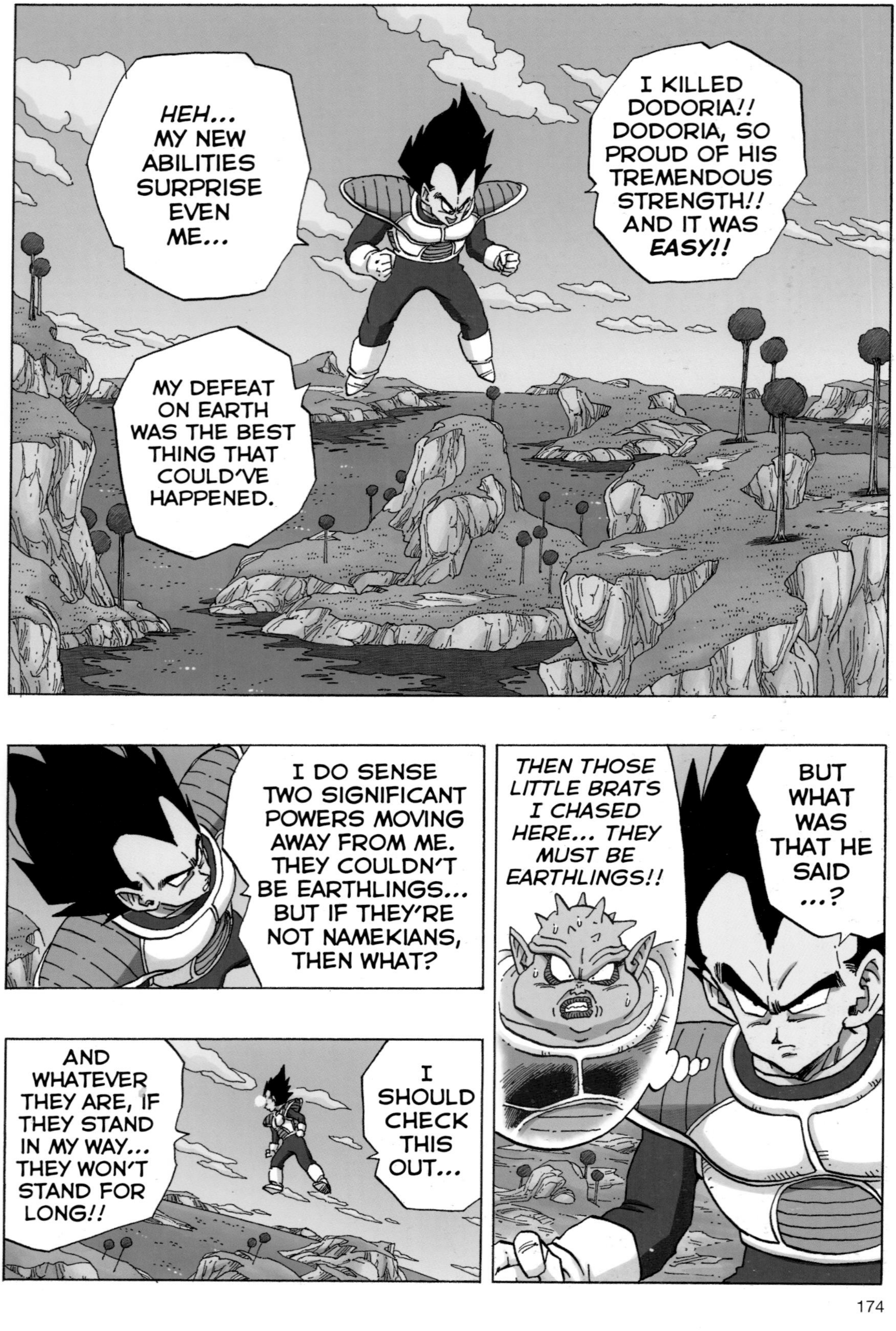

I KILLED DODORIA!! DODORIA, SO PROUD OF HIS TREMENDOUS STRENGTH!! AND IT WAS EASY!!
HEH... MY NEW ABILITIES SURPRISE EVEN ME...
MY DEFEAT ON EARTH WAS THE BEST THING THAT COULD'VE HAPPENED.
BUT WHAT WAS THAT HE SAID ...?
THEN THOSE LITTLE BRATS I CHASED HERE... THEY MUST BE EARTHLINGS!!
I DO SENSE TWO SIGNIFICANT POWERS MOVING AWAY FROM ME. THEY COULDN'T BE EARTHLINGS... BUT IF THEY'RE NOT NAMEKIANS, THEN WHAT?
I SHOULD CHECK THIS OUT...
AND WHATEVER THEY ARE, IF THEY STAND IN MY WAY... THEY WON'T STAND FOR LONG!!

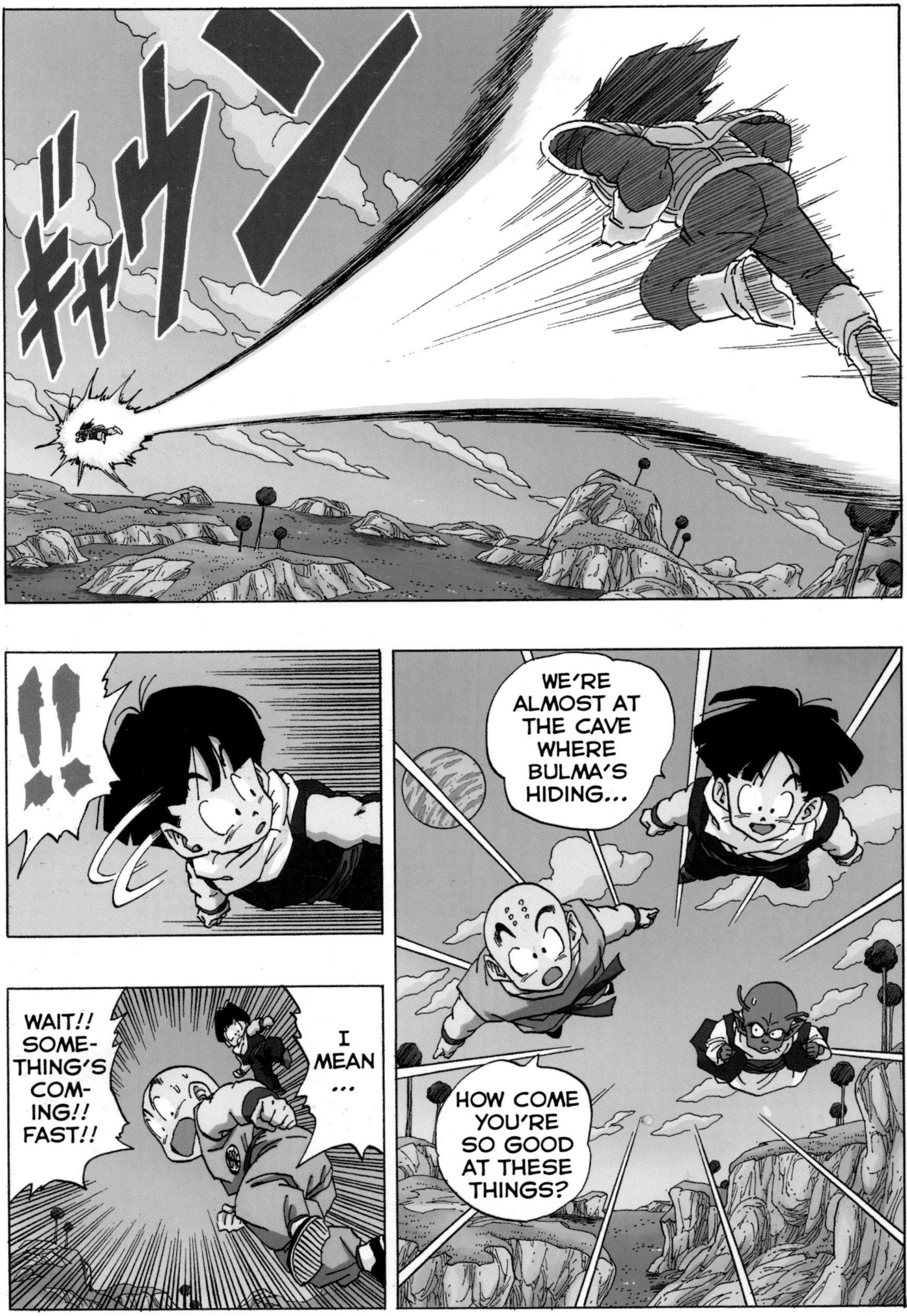
ギャウン
WE'RE ALMOST AT THE CAVE WHERE BULMA'S HIDING...
HOW COME YOU'RE SO GOOD AT THESE THINGS?
!!
I MEAN...
WAIT!! SOME-THING'S COM-ING!! FAST!!

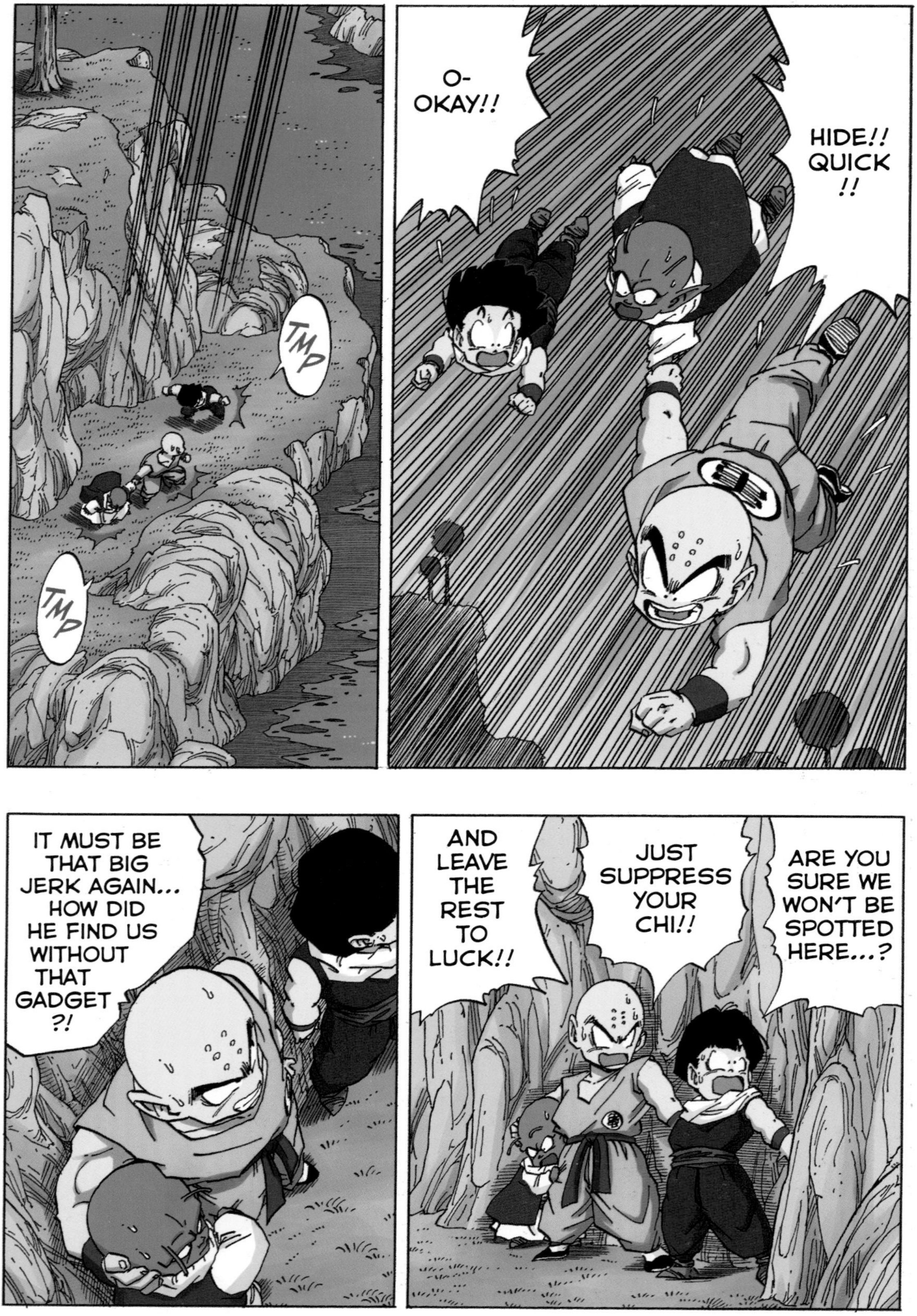
HIDE!! QUICK!!
O-OKAY!!
TMP
TMP
ARE YOU SURE WE WON'T BE SPOTTED HERE...?
JUST SUPPRESS YOUR CHI!!
AND LEAVE THE REST TO LUCK!!
IT MUST BE THAT BIG JERK AGAIN... HOW DID HE FIND US WITHOUT THAT GADGET?!

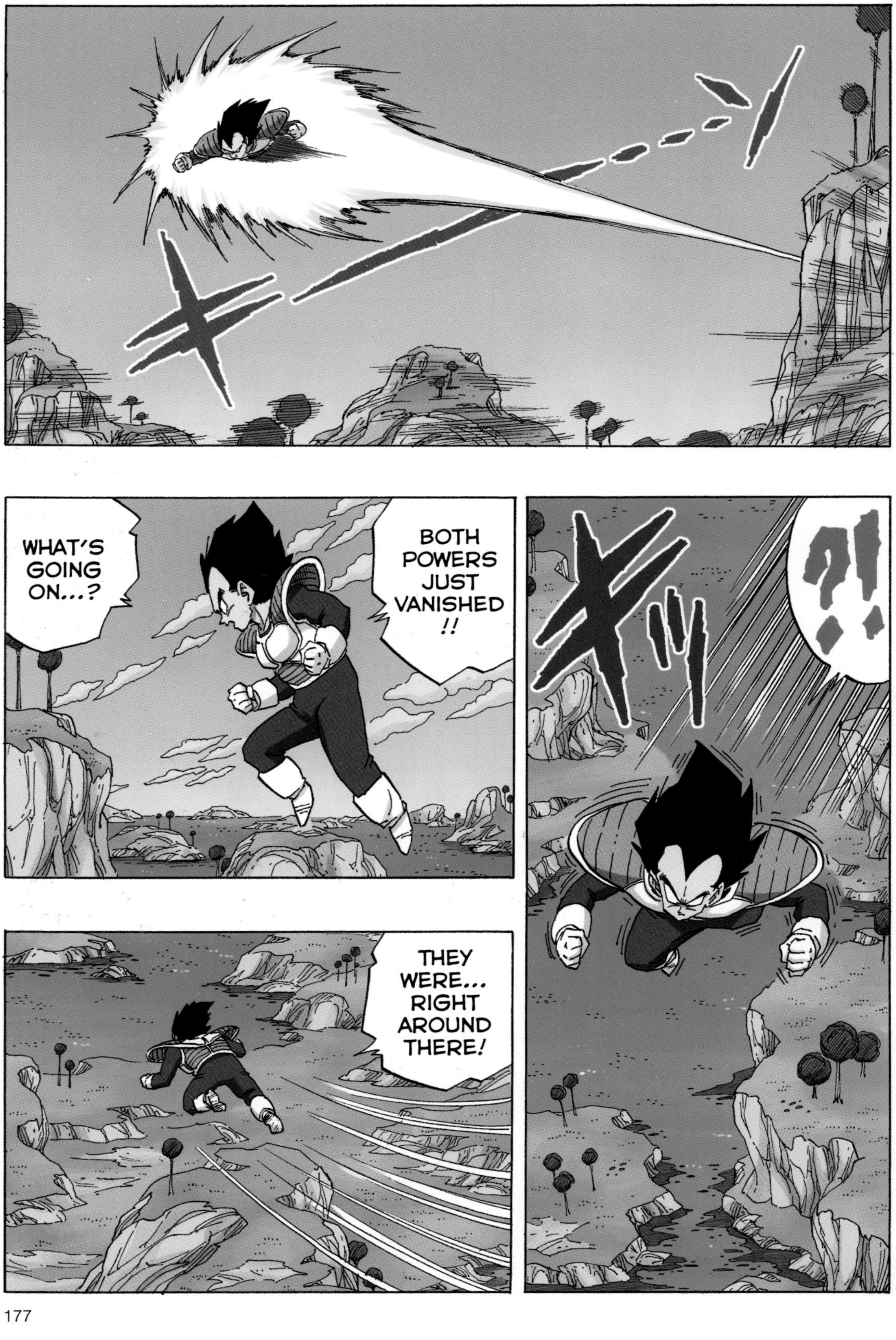
?!
BOTH POWERS JUST VANISHED!!
WHAT'S GOING ON...?
THEY WERE... RIGHT AROUND THERE!

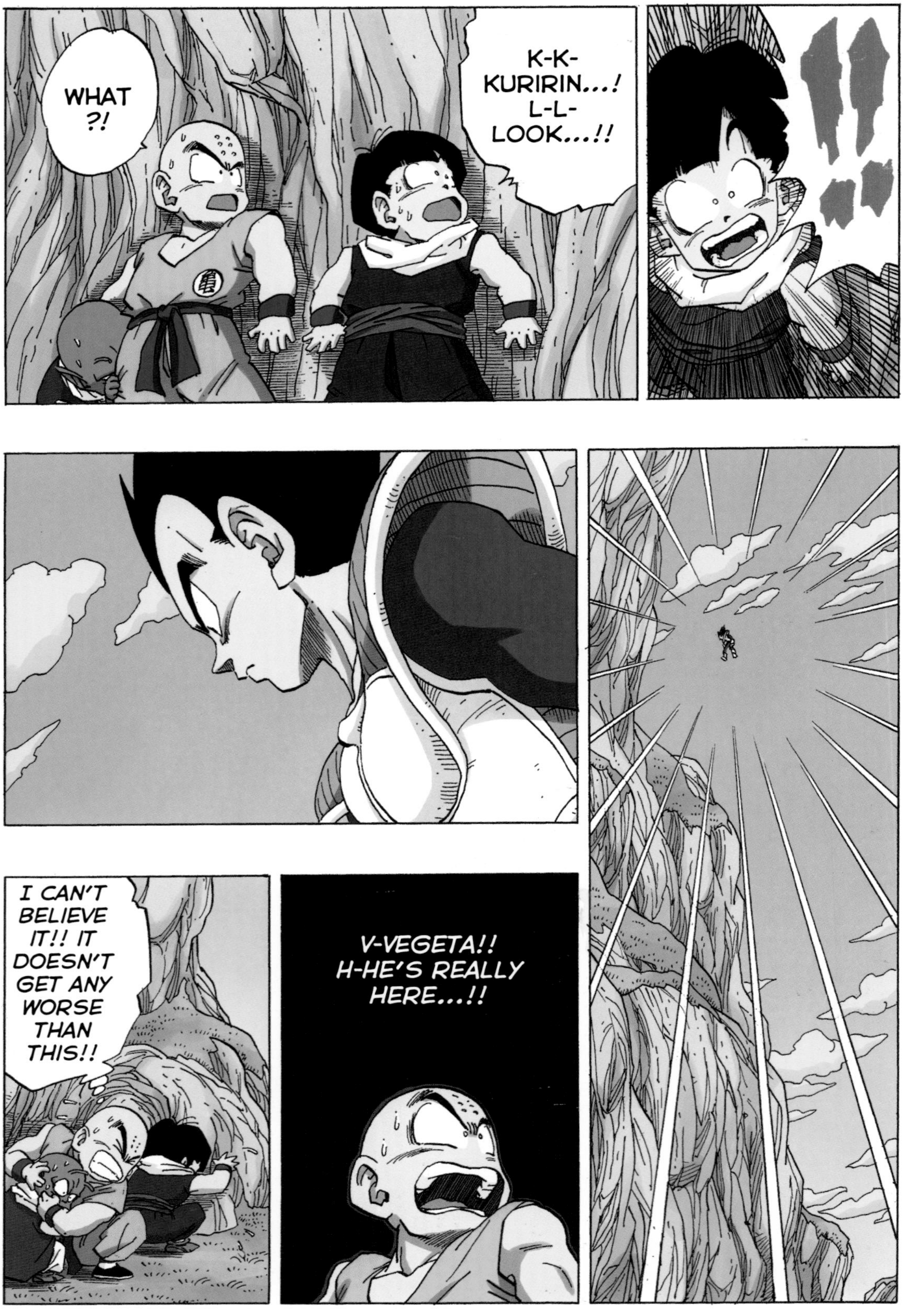
K-K-KURIRIN...! L-L-LOOK...!!
WHAT?!
V-VEGETA!! H-HE'S REALLY HERE...!!
I CAN'T BELIEVE IT!! IT DOESN'T GET ANY WORSE THAN THIS!!

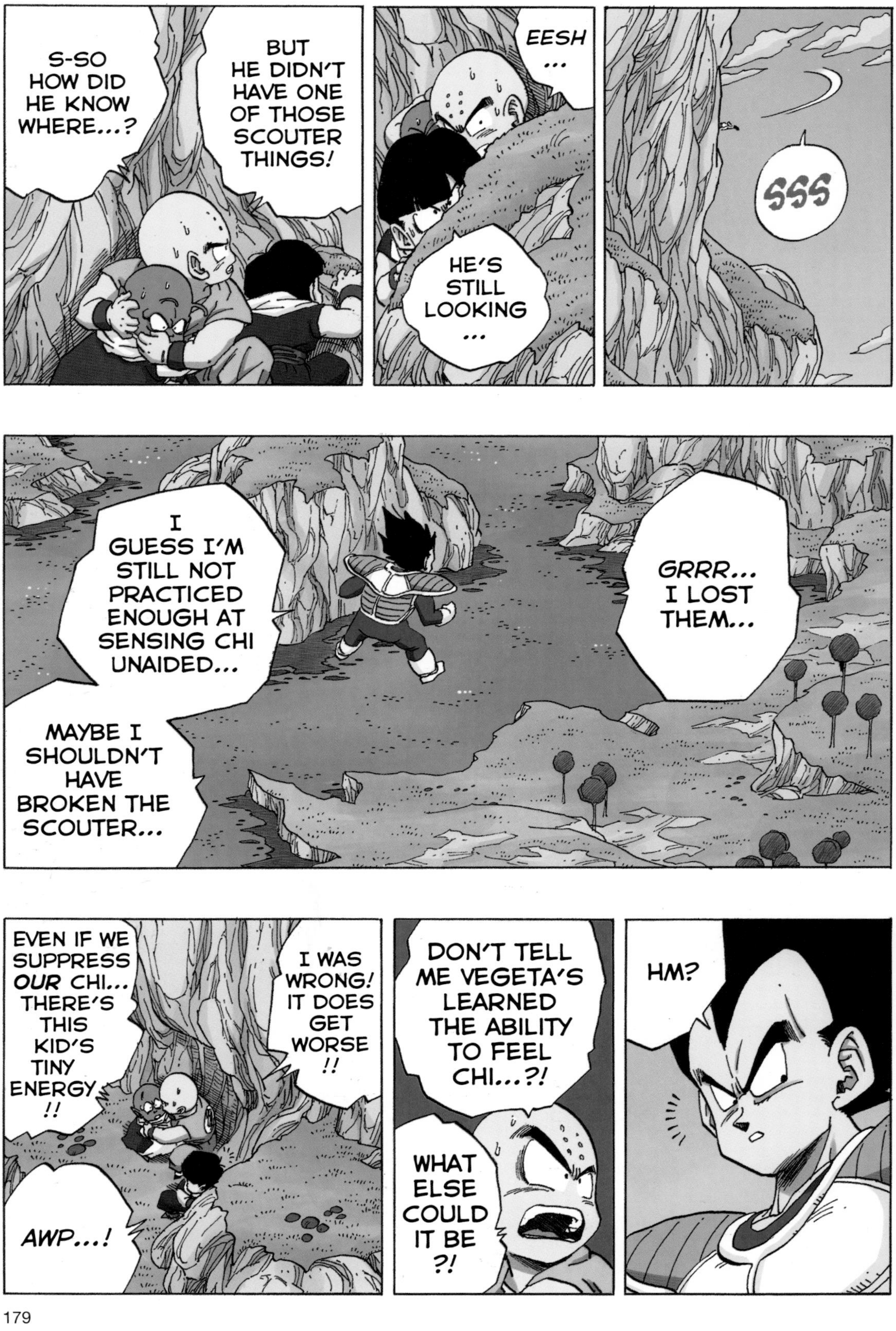
SSS
EESH ...
HE'S STILL LOOKING ...
BUT HE DIDN'T HAVE ONE OF THOSE SCOUTER THINGS!
S-SO HOW DID HE KNOW WHERE...?
GRRR... I LOST THEM...
I GUESS I'M STILL NOT PRACTICED ENOUGH AT SENSING CHI UNAIDED...
MAYBE I SHOULDN'T HAVE BROKEN THE SCOUTER...
HM?
DON'T TELL ME VEGETA'S LEARNED THE ABILITY TO FEEL CHI...?!
WHAT ELSE COULD IT BE ?!
I WAS WRONG! IT DOES GET WORSE !!
EVEN IF WE SUPPRESS *OUR* CHI... THERE'S THIS KID'S TINY ENERGY !!
AWP...!

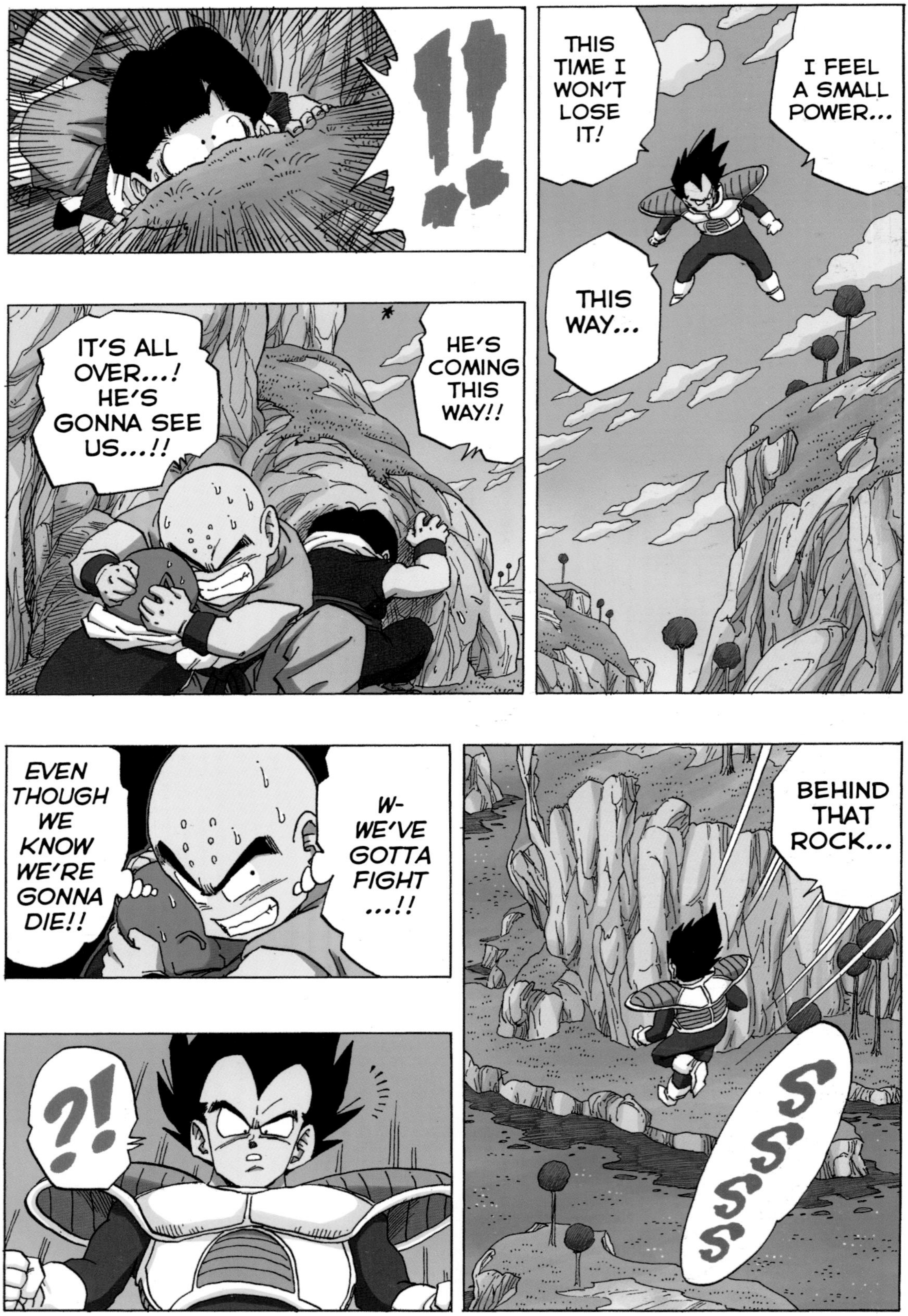
I FEEL A SMALL POWER...
THIS TIME I WON'T LOSE IT!
THIS WAY...
!!
HE'S COMING THIS WAY!!
IT'S ALL OVER...! HE'S GONNA SEE US...!!
BEHIND THAT ROCK...
SSSSS
W- WE'VE GOTTA FIGHT...!!
EVEN THOUGH WE KNOW WE'RE GONNA DIE!!
?!

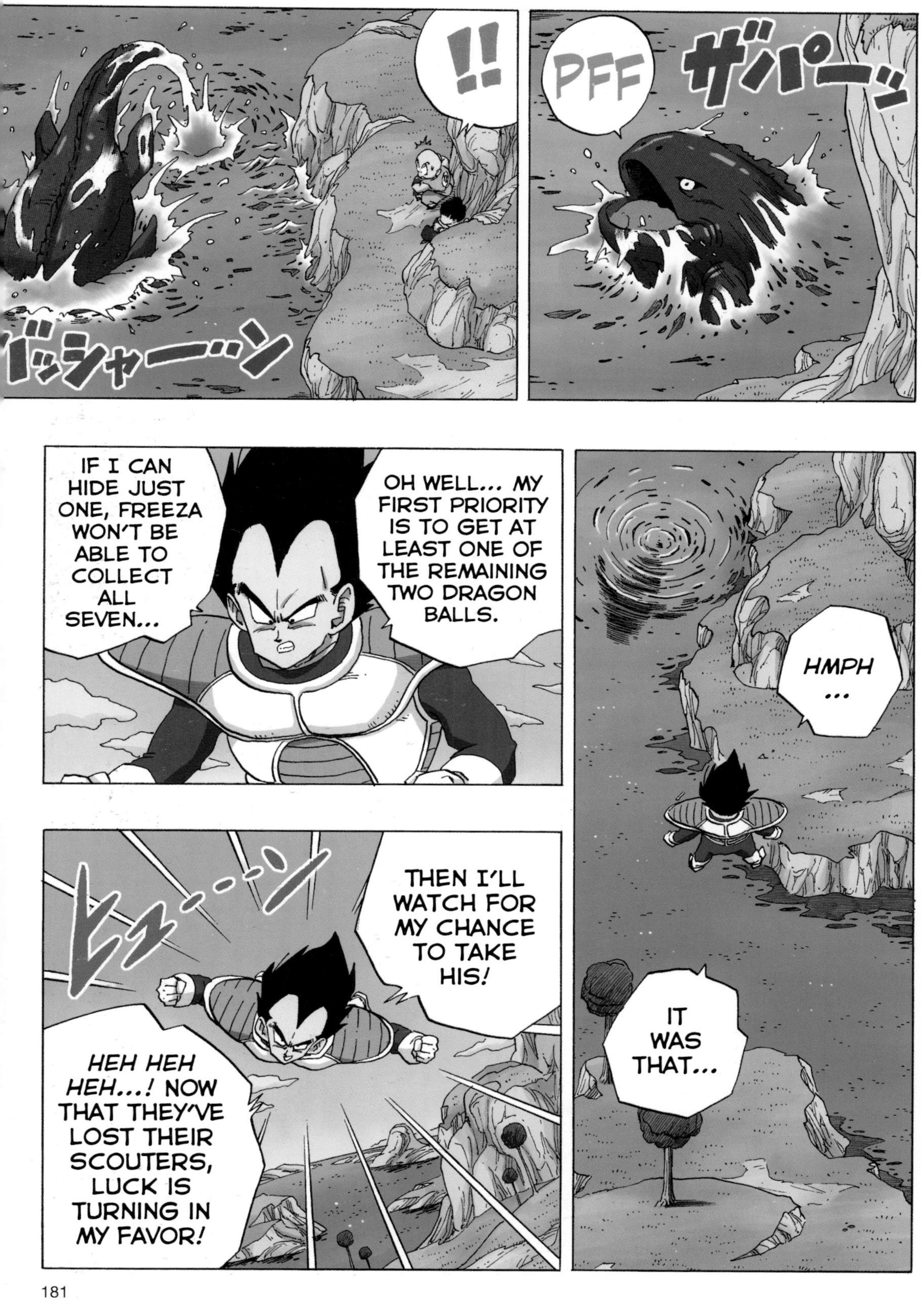
PFF
ザパーッ
!!
バッシャーーン
HMPH ...
IT WAS THAT...
OH WELL... MY FIRST PRIORITY IS TO GET AT LEAST ONE OF THE REMAINING TWO DRAGON BALLS.
IF I CAN HIDE JUST ONE, FREEZA WON'T BE ABLE TO COLLECT ALL SEVEN...
THEN I'LL WATCH FOR MY CHANCE TO TAKE HIS!
ヒューーン
HEH HEH HEH...! NOW THAT THEY'VE LOST THEIR SCOUTERS, LUCK IS TURNING IN MY FAVOR!

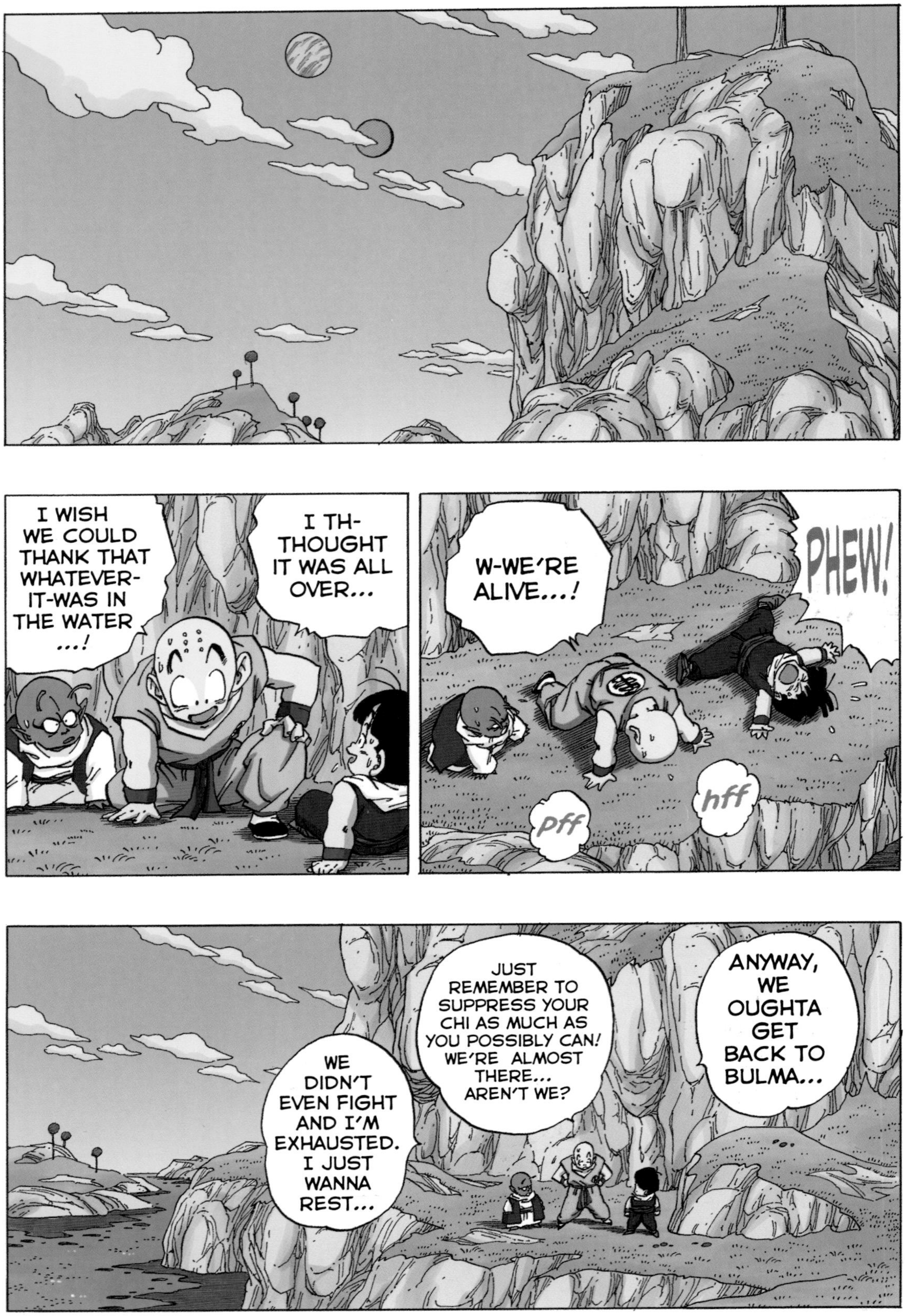
PHEW!
W-WE'RE ALIVE...!
hff
pff
I TH- THOUGHT IT WAS ALL OVER...
I WISH WE COULD THANK THAT WHATEVER-IT-WAS IN THE WATER ...!
ANYWAY, WE OUGHTA GET BACK TO BULMA...
JUST REMEMBER TO SUPPRESS YOUR CHI AS MUCH AS YOU POSSIBLY CAN! WE'RE ALMOST THERE... AREN'T WE?
WE DIDN'T EVEN FIGHT AND I'M EXHAUSTED. I JUST WANNA REST...

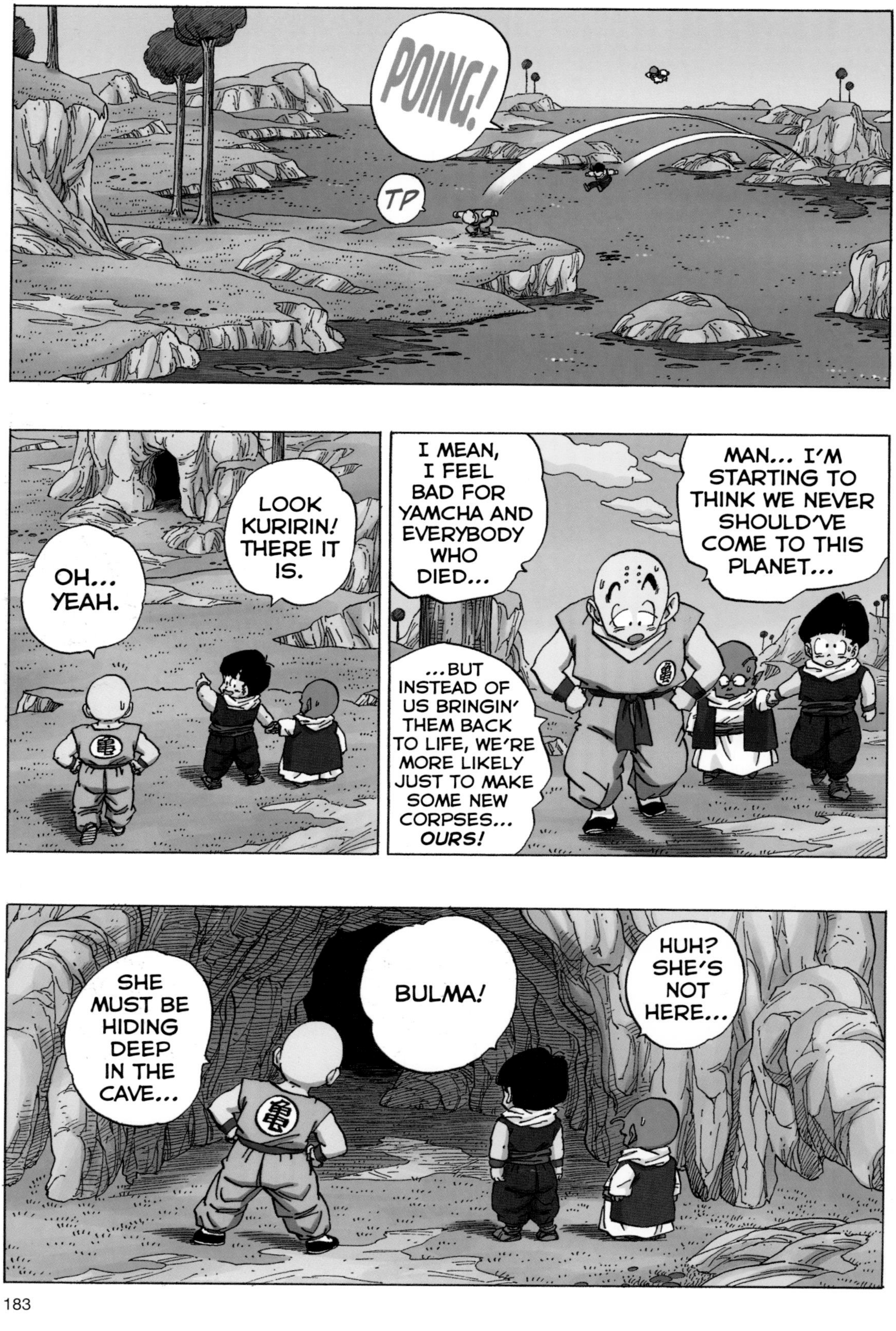
POING!
TP
MAN... I'M STARTING TO THINK WE NEVER SHOULD'VE COME TO THIS PLANET...
I MEAN, I FEEL BAD FOR YAMCHA AND EVERYBODY WHO DIED...
...BUT INSTEAD OF US BRINGIN' THEM BACK TO LIFE, WE'RE MORE LIKELY JUST TO MAKE SOME NEW CORPSES... *OURS!*
LOOK KURIRIN! THERE IT IS.
OH... YEAH.
HUH? SHE'S NOT HERE...
BULMA!
SHE MUST BE HIDING DEEP IN THE CAVE...

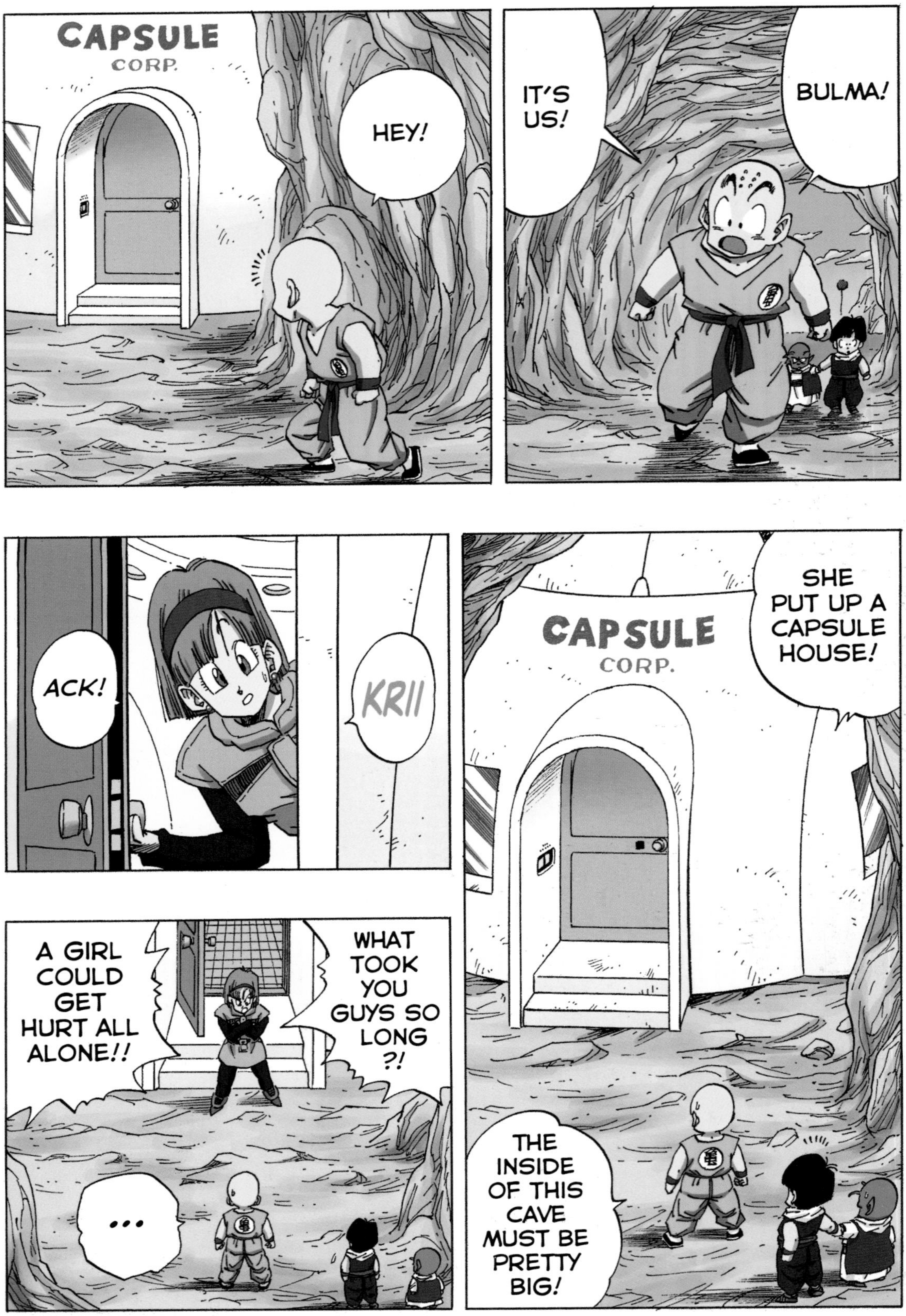
BULMA!
IT'S US!
HEY!
CAPSULE CORP.
SHE PUT UP A CAPSULE HOUSE!
CAPSULE CORP.
THE INSIDE OF THIS CAVE MUST BE PRETTY BIG!
KRII
ACK!
WHAT TOOK YOU GUYS SO LONG?!
A GIRL COULD GET HURT ALL ALONE!!
...

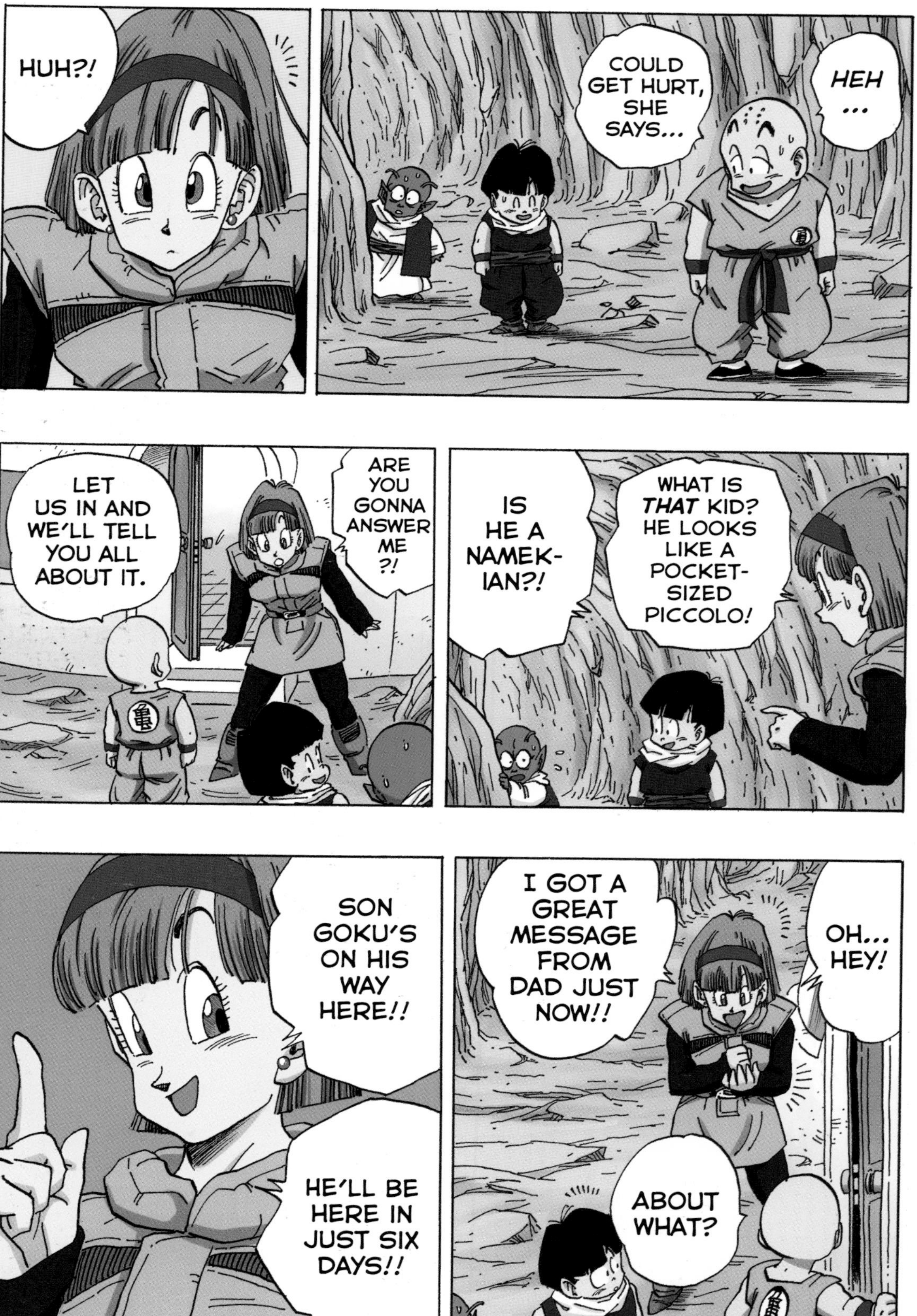
HEH...
COULD GET HURT, SHE SAYS...
HUH?!
WHAT IS *THAT* KID? HE LOOKS LIKE A POCKET-SIZED PICCOLO!
IS HE A NAMEK-IAN?!
ARE YOU GONNA ANSWER ME?!
LET US IN AND WE'LL TELL YOU ALL ABOUT IT.
OH... HEY!
I GOT A GREAT MESSAGE FROM DAD JUST NOW!!
ABOUT WHAT?
SON GOKU'S ON HIS WAY HERE!!
HE'LL BE HERE IN JUST SIX DAYS!!

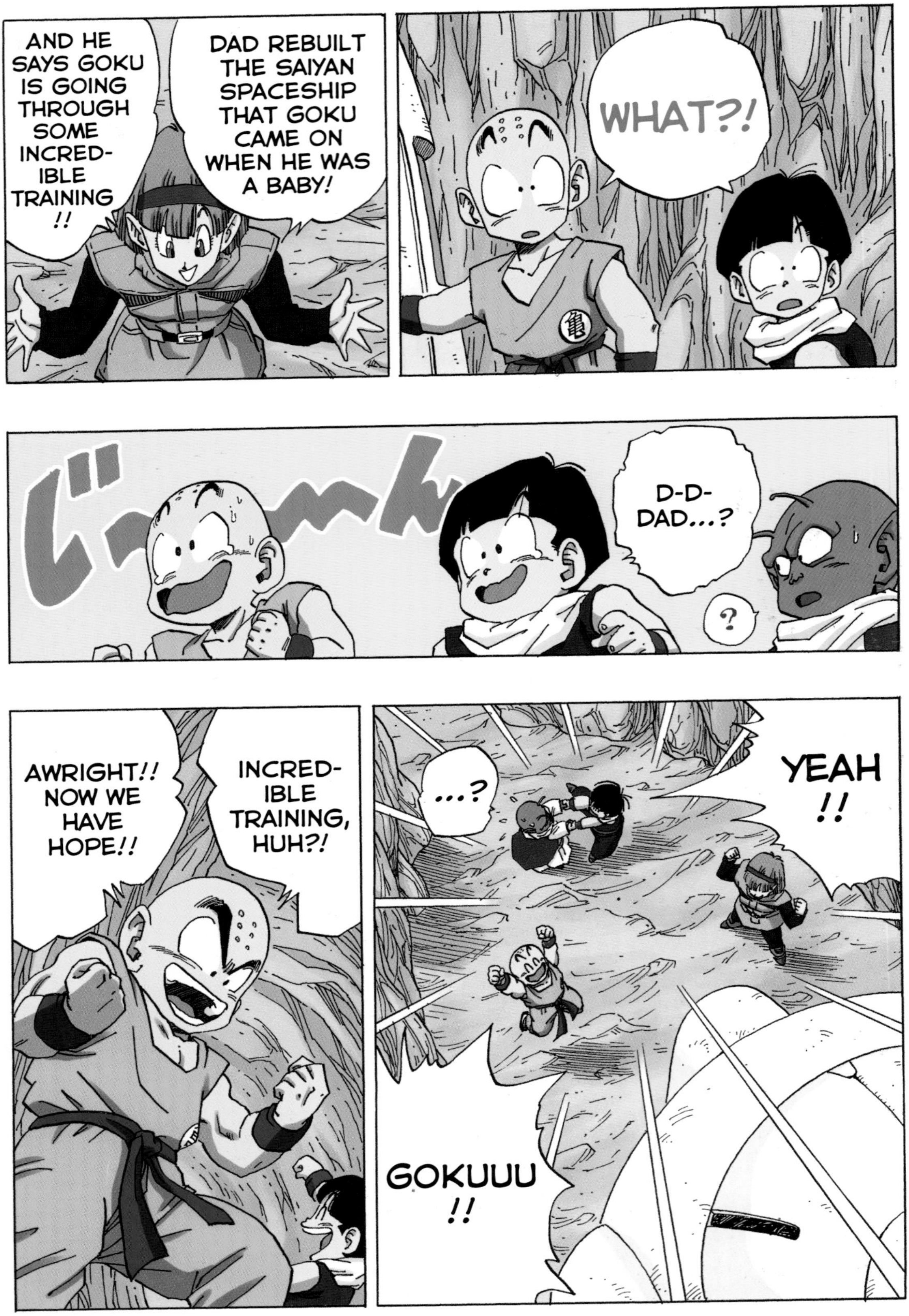
WHAT?!
DAD REBUILT THE SAIYAN SPACESHIP THAT GOKU CAME ON WHEN HE WAS A BABY!
AND HE SAYS GOKU IS GOING THROUGH SOME INCRED-IBLE TRAINING!!
?
D-D-DAD...?
じ〜ん
YEAH!!
...?
GOKUUU!!
INCRED-IBLE TRAINING, HUH?!
AWRIGHT!! NOW WE HAVE HOPE!!

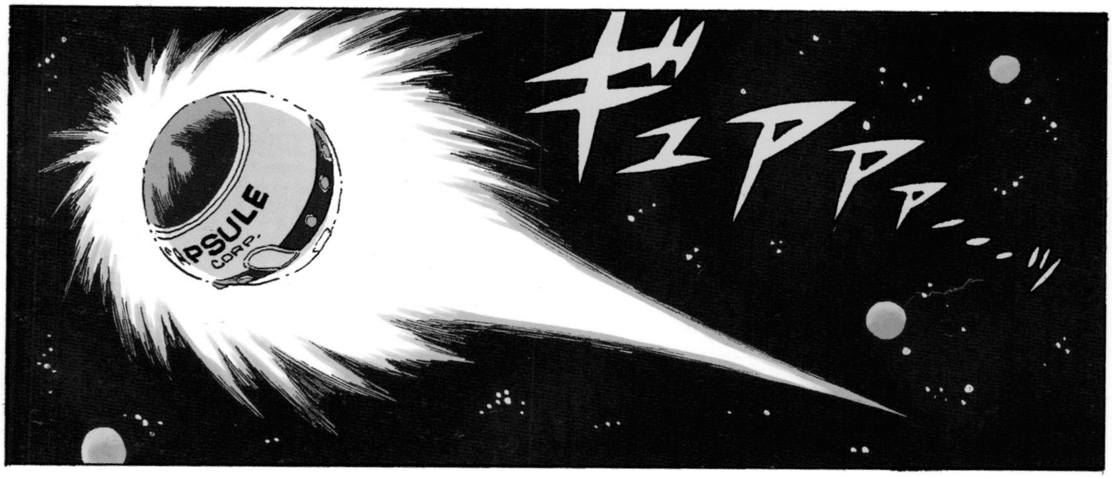

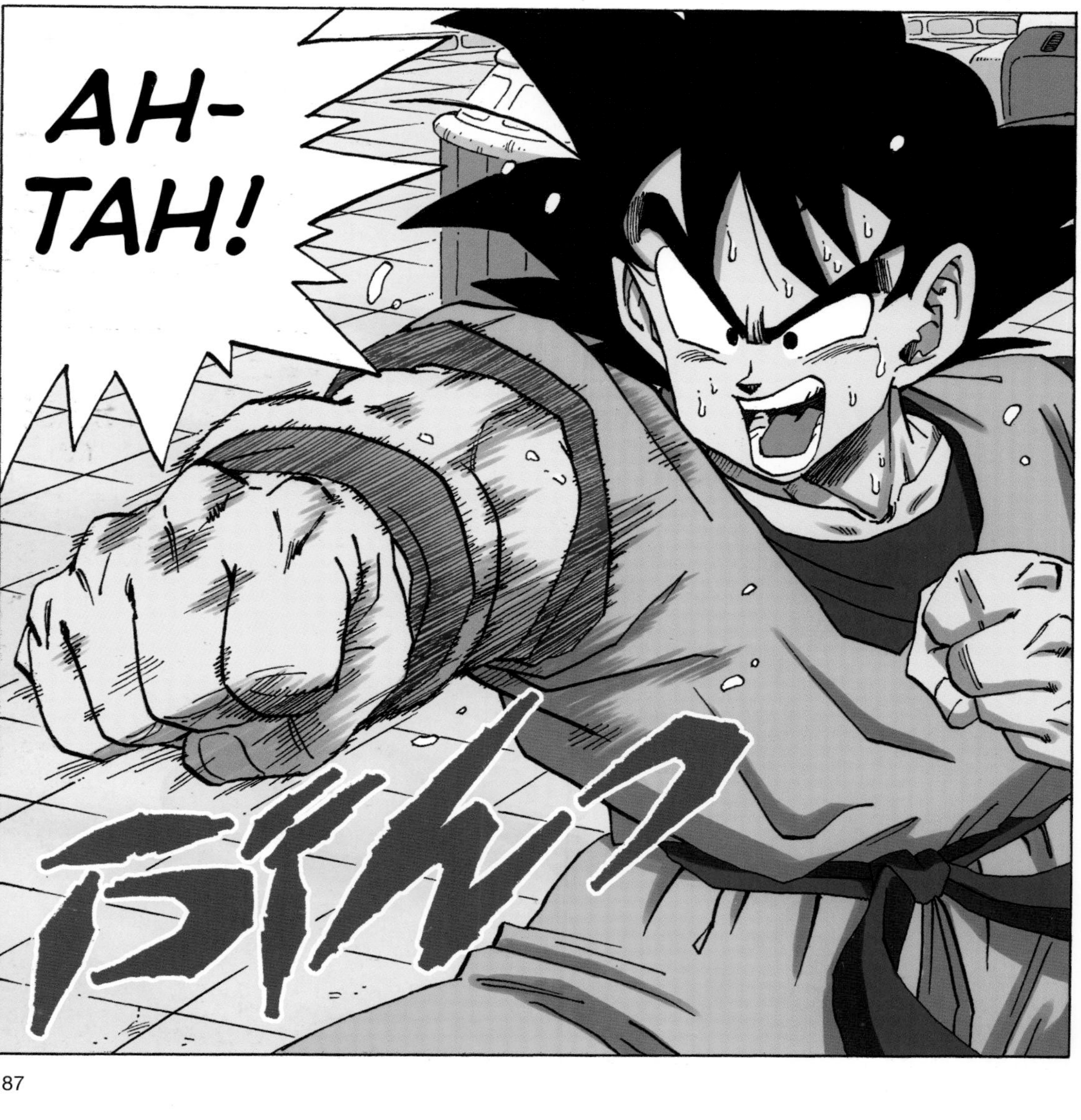
AH-TAH!

Chapter 14 • The Sixth Dragon Ball

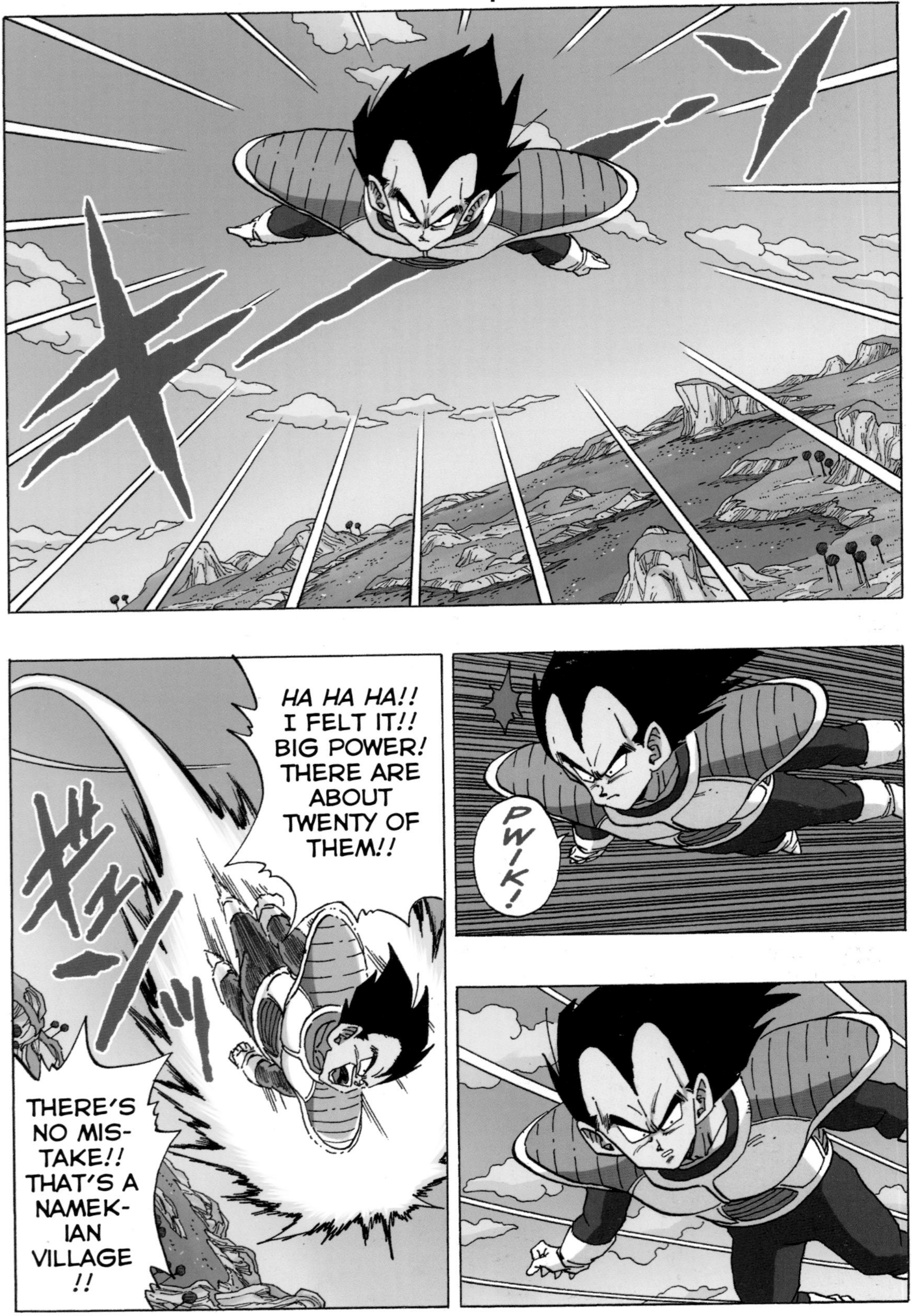
PWIK!
HA HA HA!! I FELT IT!! BIG POWER! THERE ARE ABOUT TWENTY OF THEM!!
THERE'S NO MIS-TAKE!! THAT'S A NAMEK-IAN VILLAGE !!

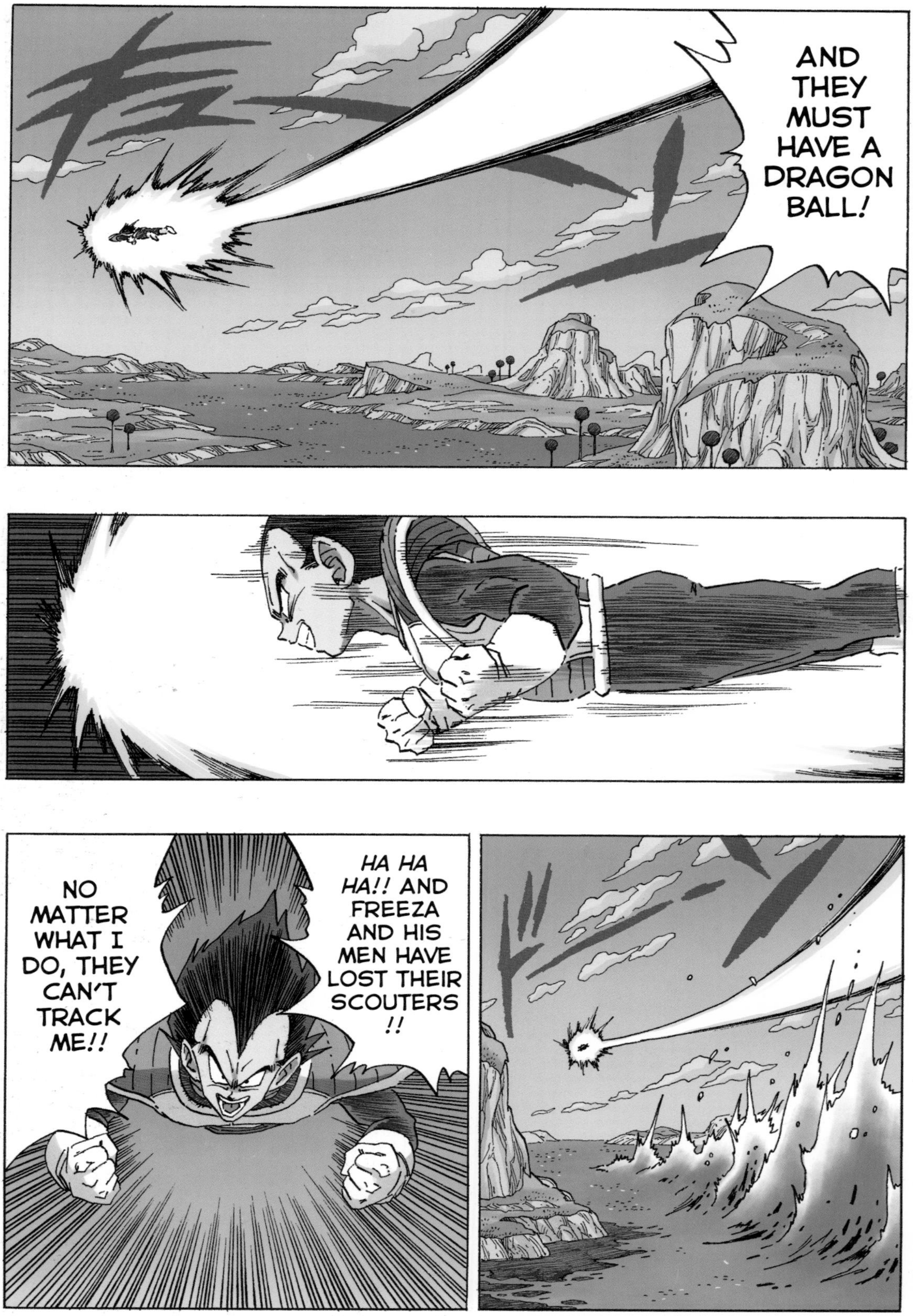
AND THEY MUST HAVE A DRAGON BALL!
HA HA HA!! AND FREEZA AND HIS MEN HAVE LOST THEIR SCOUTERS!!
NO MATTER WHAT I DO, THEY CAN'T TRACK ME!!

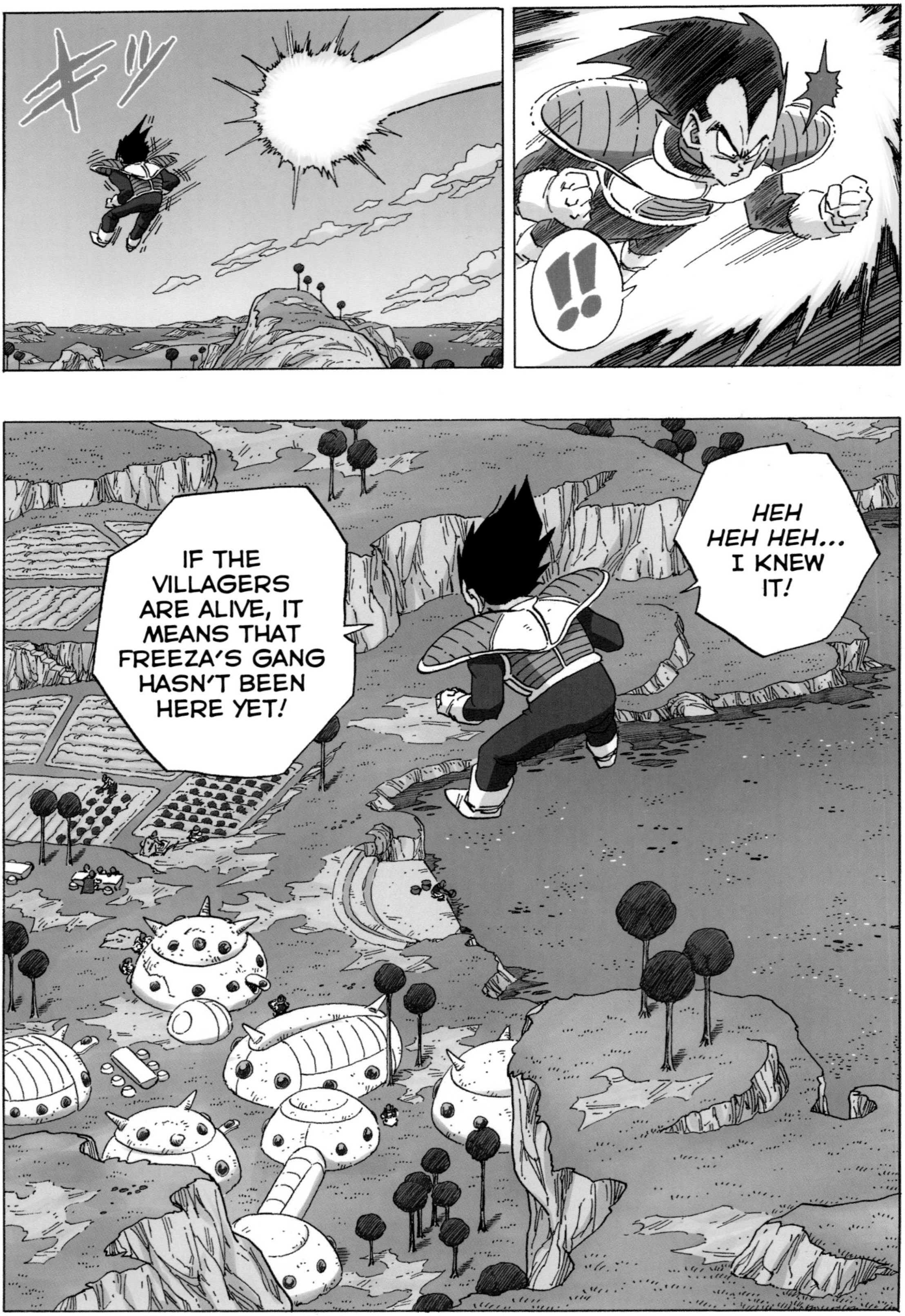
!!
ギッ
HEH HEH HEH... I KNEW IT!
IF THE VILLAGERS ARE ALIVE, IT MEANS THAT FREEZA'S GANG HASN'T BEEN HERE YET!

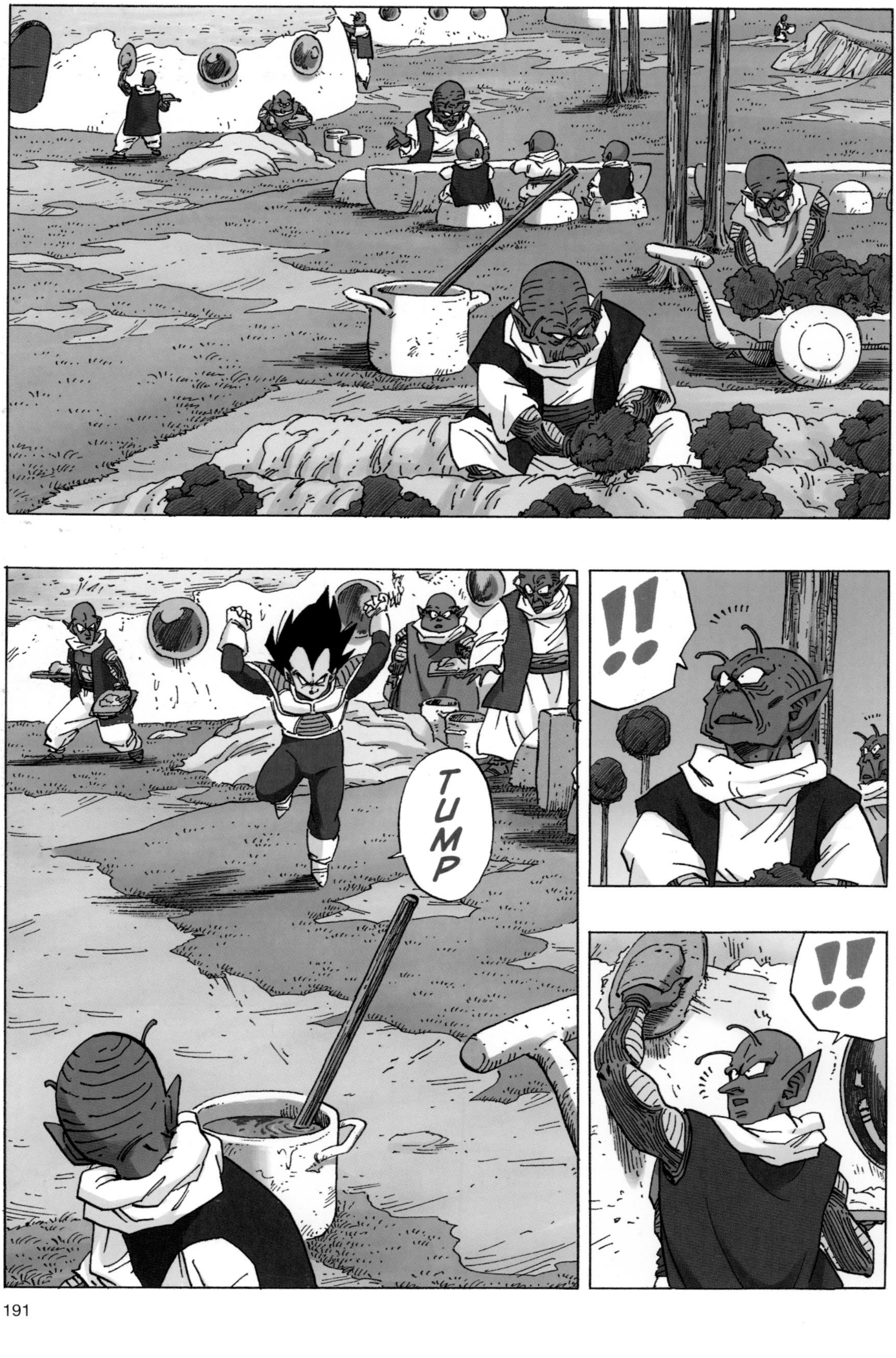
!!
!!
TUMP

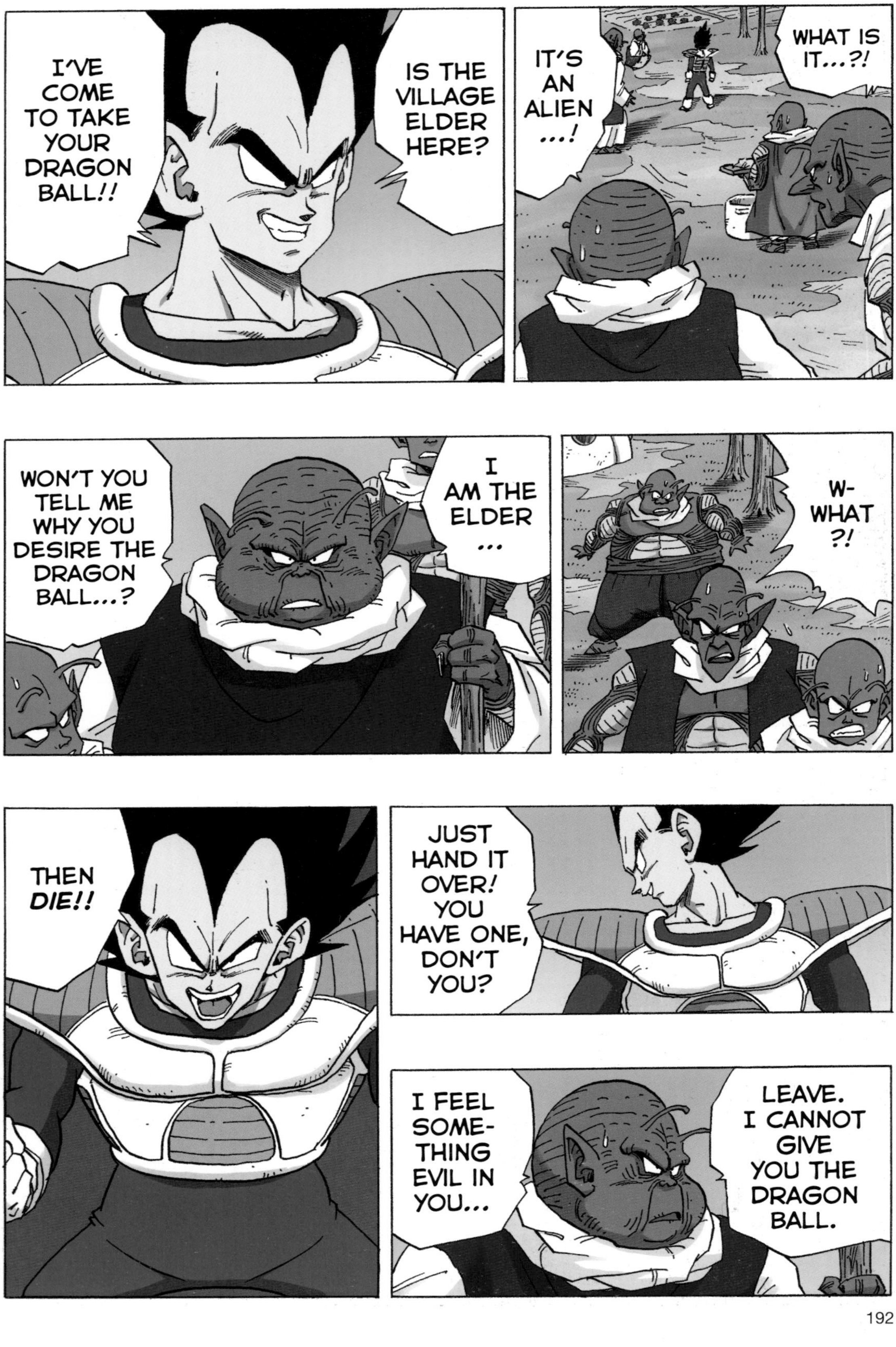
WHAT IS IT...?!
IT'S AN ALIEN...!
IS THE VILLAGE ELDER HERE?
I'VE COME TO TAKE YOUR DRAGON BALL!!
W-WHAT?!
I AM THE ELDER...
WON'T YOU TELL ME WHY YOU DESIRE THE DRAGON BALL...?
JUST HAND IT OVER! YOU HAVE ONE, DON'T YOU?
LEAVE. I CANNOT GIVE YOU THE DRAGON BALL.
I FEEL SOME-THING EVIL IN YOU...
THEN *DIE!!*

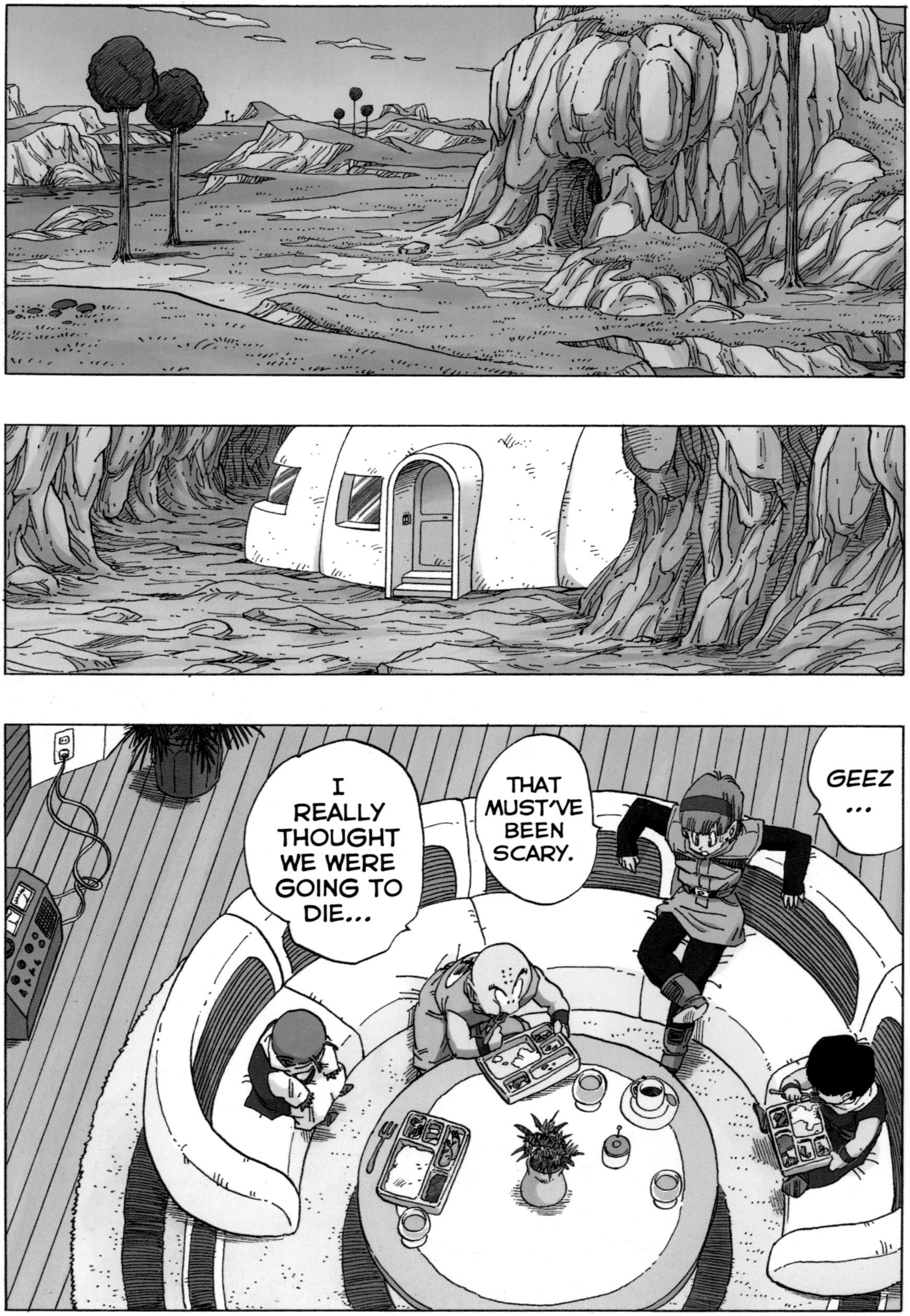
GEEZ ...
THAT MUST'VE BEEN SCARY.
I REALLY THOUGHT WE WERE GOING TO DIE...

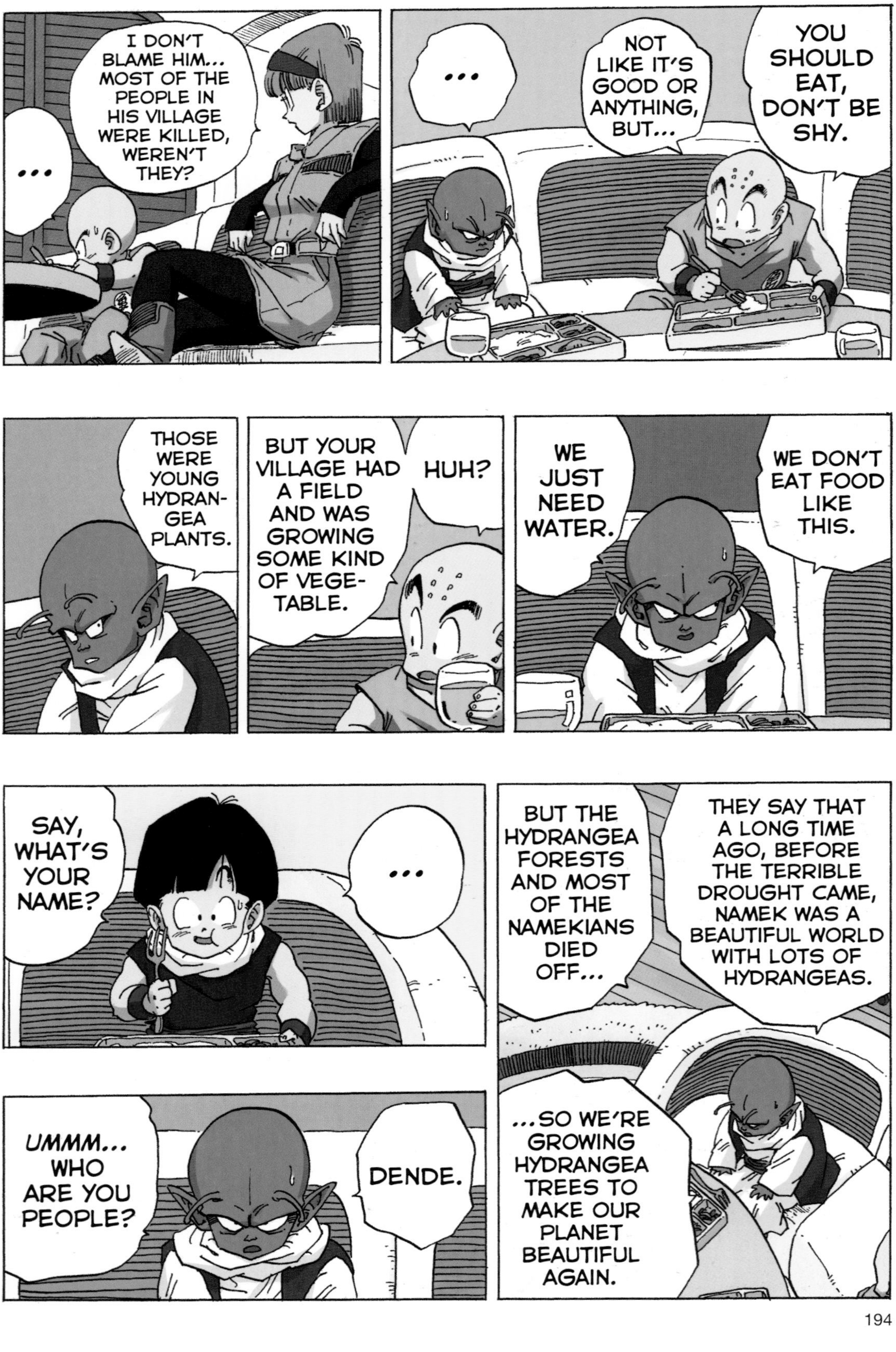
YOU SHOULD EAT, DON'T BE SHY.
NOT LIKE IT'S GOOD OR ANYTHING, BUT...
...
I DON'T BLAME HIM... MOST OF THE PEOPLE IN HIS VILLAGE WERE KILLED, WEREN'T THEY?
...
WE DON'T EAT FOOD LIKE THIS.
WE JUST NEED WATER.
HUH?
BUT YOUR VILLAGE HAD A FIELD AND WAS GROWING SOME KIND OF VEGE-TABLE.
THOSE WERE YOUNG HYDRAN-GEA PLANTS.
THEY SAY THAT A LONG TIME AGO, BEFORE THE TERRIBLE DROUGHT CAME, NAMEK WAS A BEAUTIFUL WORLD WITH LOTS OF HYDRANGEAS.
BUT THE HYDRANGEA FORESTS AND MOST OF THE NAMEKIANS DIED OFF...
...SO WE'RE GROWING HYDRANGEA TREES TO MAKE OUR PLANET BEAUTIFUL AGAIN.
SAY, WHAT'S YOUR NAME?
...
DENDE.
UMMM... WHO ARE YOU PEOPLE?

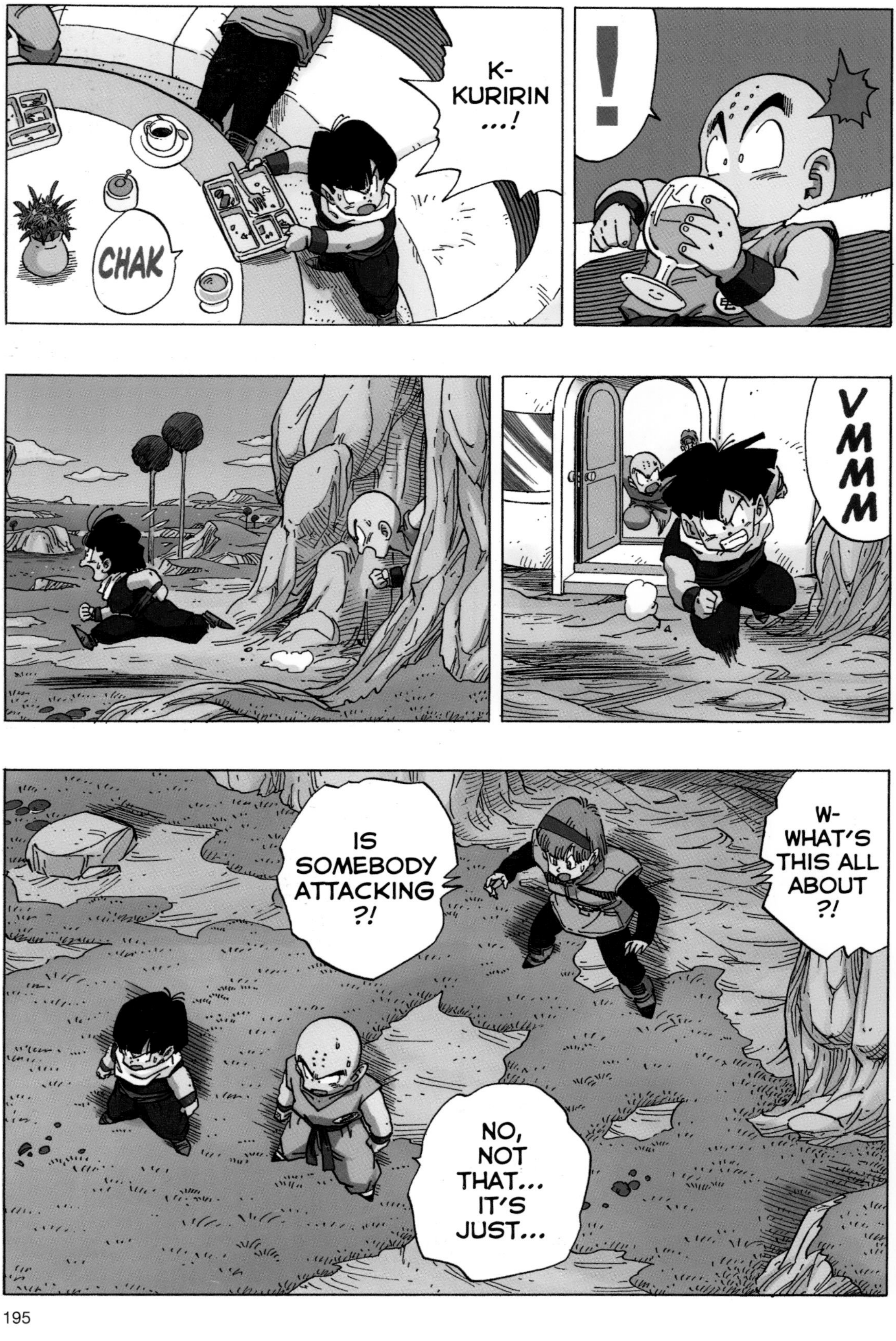
!
K-KURIRIN...!
CHAK
VMMM
W-WHAT'S THIS ALL ABOUT?!
IS SOMEBODY ATTACKING?!
NO, NOT THAT... IT'S JUST...

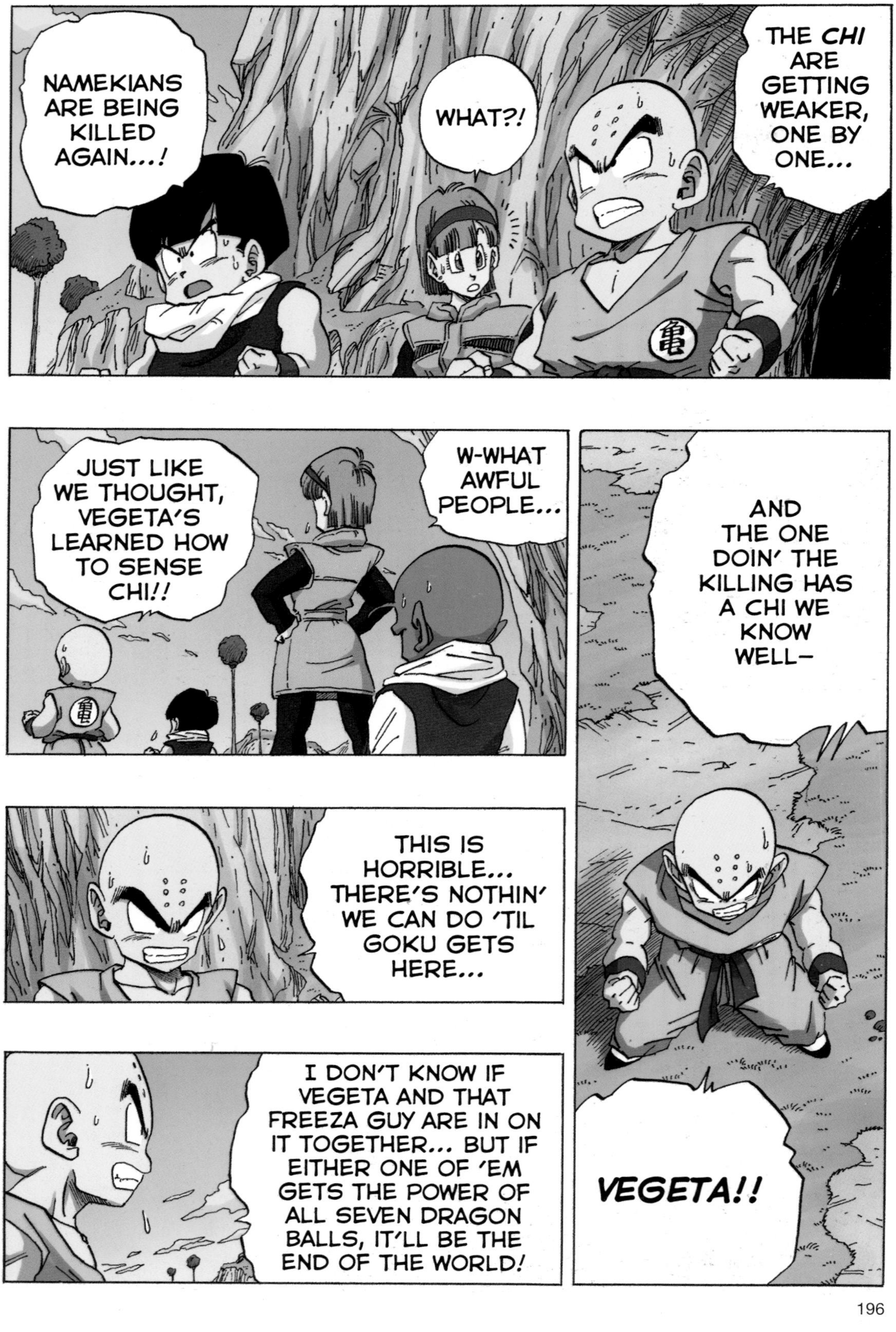
THE CHI ARE GETTING WEAKER, ONE BY ONE...
WHAT?!
NAMEKIANS ARE BEING KILLED AGAIN...!
AND THE ONE DOIN' THE KILLING HAS A CHI WE KNOW WELL—
VEGETA!!
W-WHAT AWFUL PEOPLE...
JUST LIKE WE THOUGHT, VEGETA'S LEARNED HOW TO SENSE CHI!!
THIS IS HORRIBLE... THERE'S NOTHIN' WE CAN DO 'TIL GOKU GETS HERE...
I DON'T KNOW IF VEGETA AND THAT FREEZA GUY ARE IN ON IT TOGETHER... BUT IF EITHER ONE OF 'EM GETS THE POWER OF ALL SEVEN DRAGON BALLS, IT'LL BE THE END OF THE WORLD!

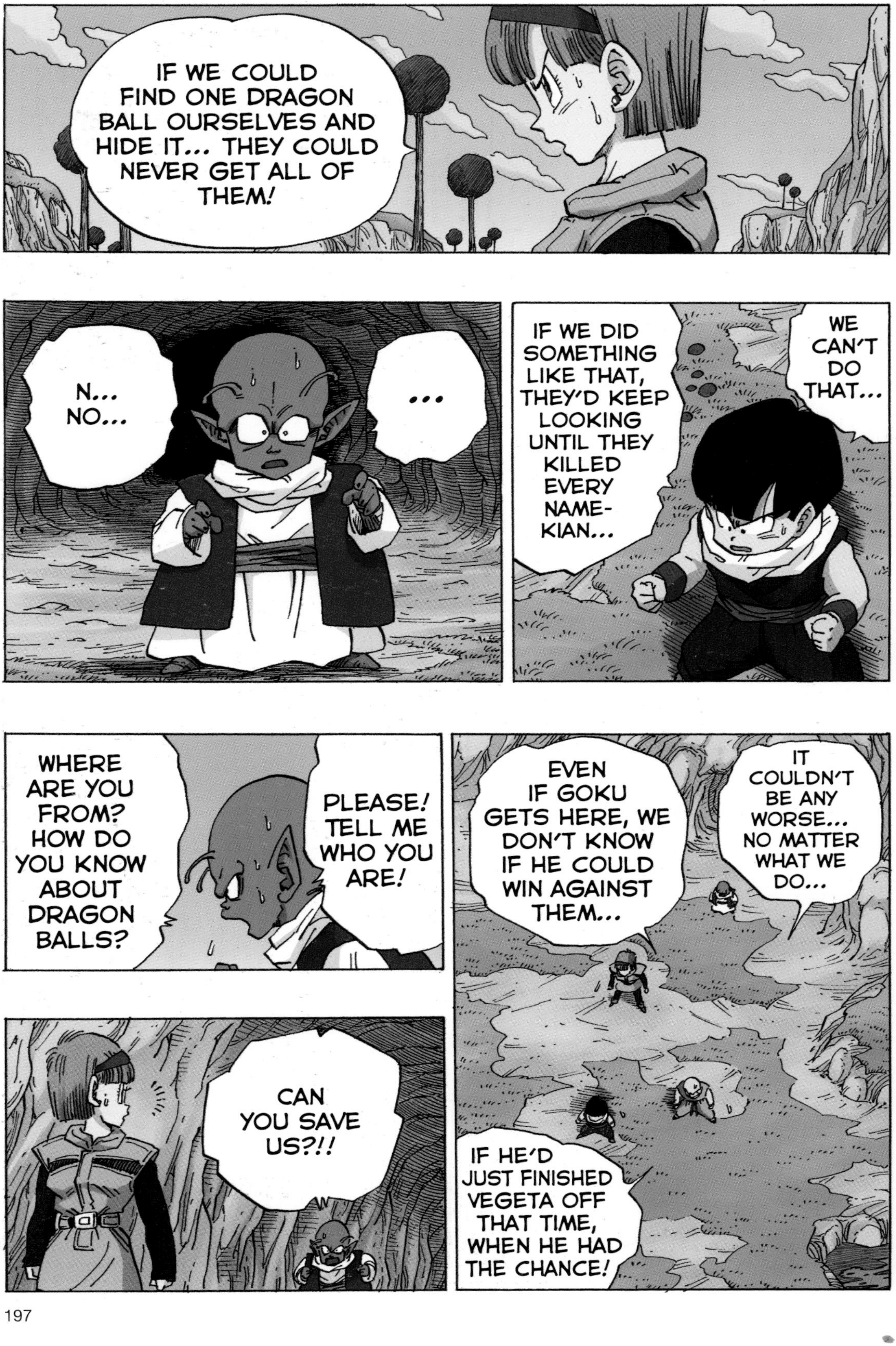
IF WE COULD FIND ONE DRAGON BALL OURSELVES AND HIDE IT... THEY COULD NEVER GET ALL OF THEM!
WE CAN'T DO THAT...
IF WE DID SOMETHING LIKE THAT, THEY'D KEEP LOOKING UNTIL THEY KILLED EVERY NAME-KIAN...
...
N... NO...
IT COULDN'T BE ANY WORSE... NO MATTER WHAT WE DO...
EVEN IF GOKU GETS HERE, WE DON'T KNOW IF HE COULD WIN AGAINST THEM...
IF HE'D JUST FINISHED VEGETA OFF THAT TIME, WHEN HE HAD THE CHANCE!
PLEASE! TELL ME WHO YOU ARE!
WHERE ARE YOU FROM? HOW DO YOU KNOW ABOUT DRAGON BALLS?
CAN YOU SAVE US?!!

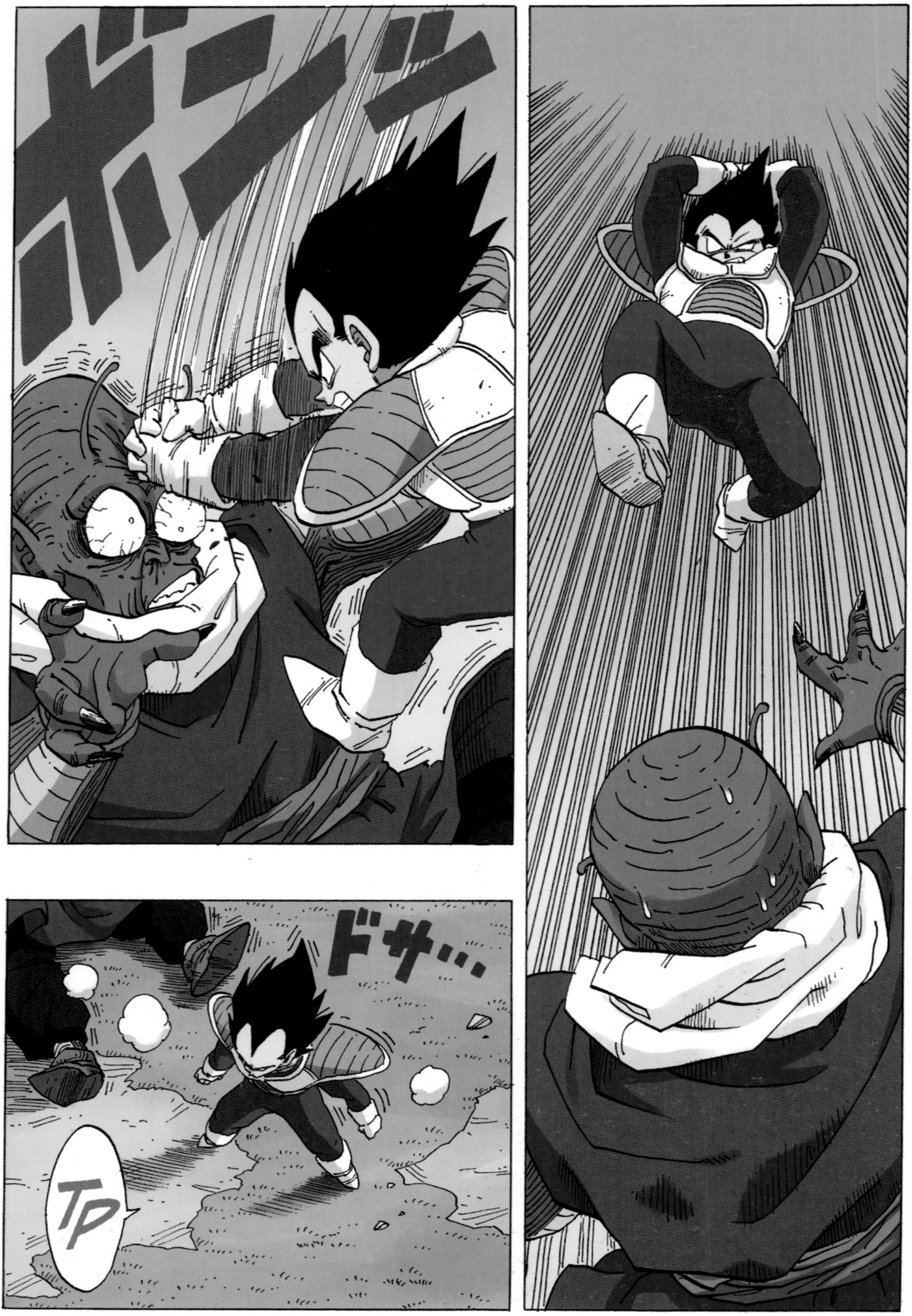
ドサ…
TP

LET ME ASK YOU AGAIN... WHERE IS THAT DRAGON BALL?!
THERE IS NOT EVIL *IN* YOU...
YOU *ARE* EVIL! YOU WILL NOT HAVE THE DRAGON BALL!!
SUCH A STUBBORN OLD GEEZER...
FINE, THEN, HAVE IT YOUR WAY. I'LL LOOK FOR IT MY-SELF...

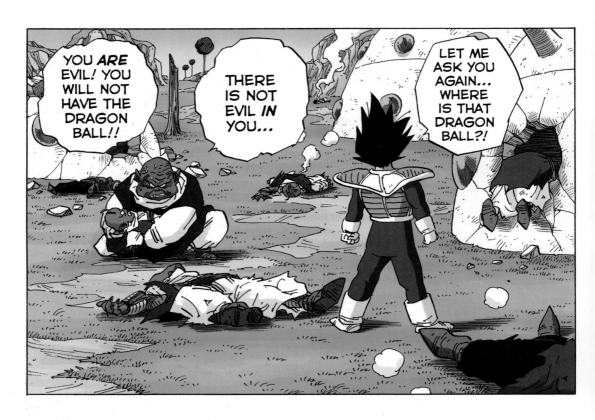

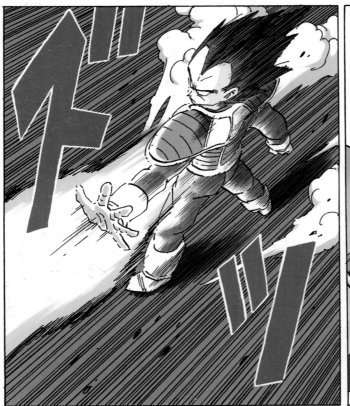

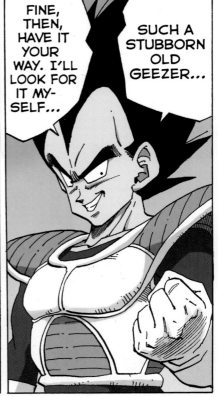

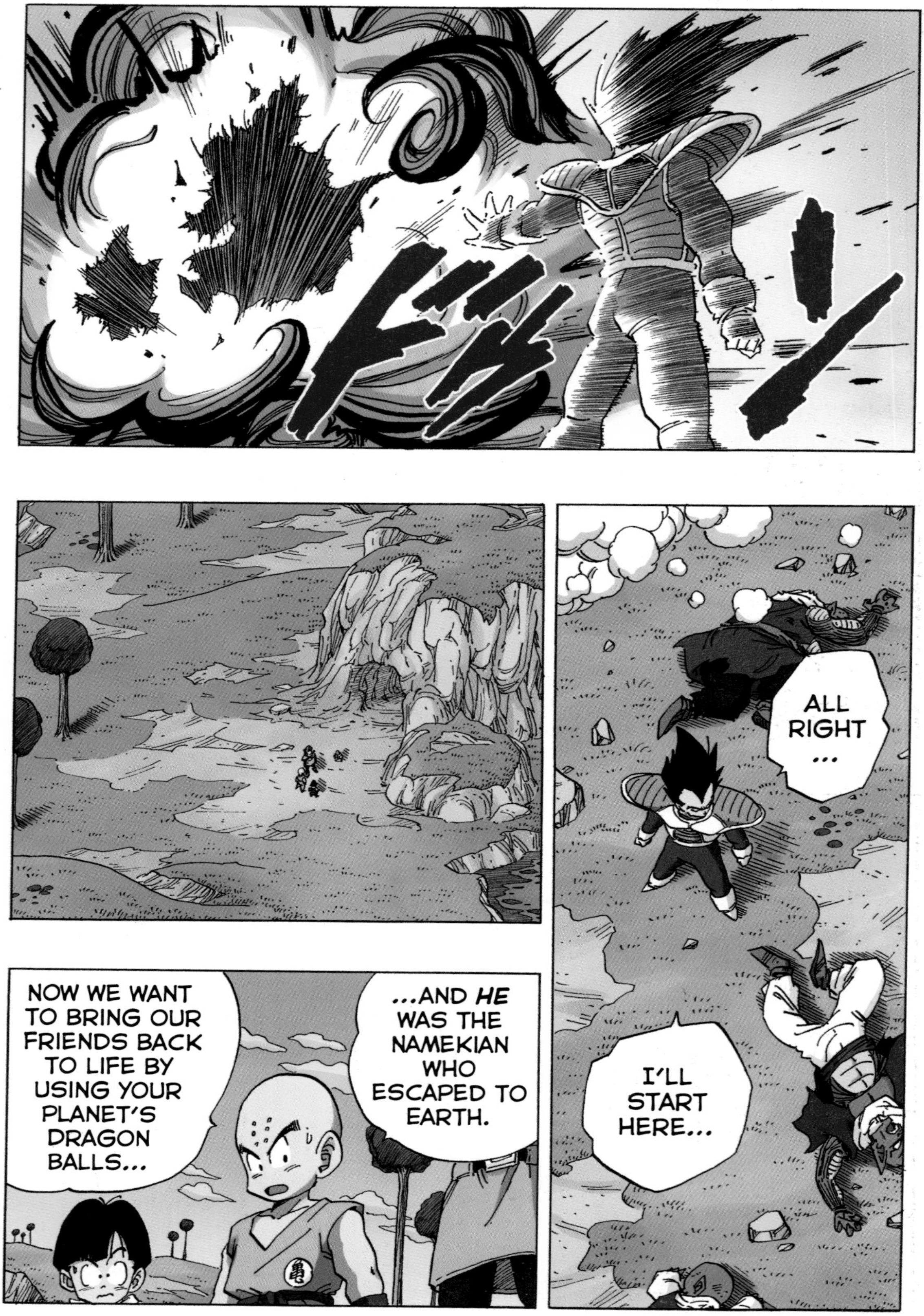
ALL RIGHT...
I'LL START HERE...
...AND *HE* WAS THE NAMEKIAN WHO ESCAPED TO EARTH.
NOW WE WANT TO BRING OUR FRIENDS BACK TO LIFE BY USING YOUR PLANET'S DRAGON BALLS...

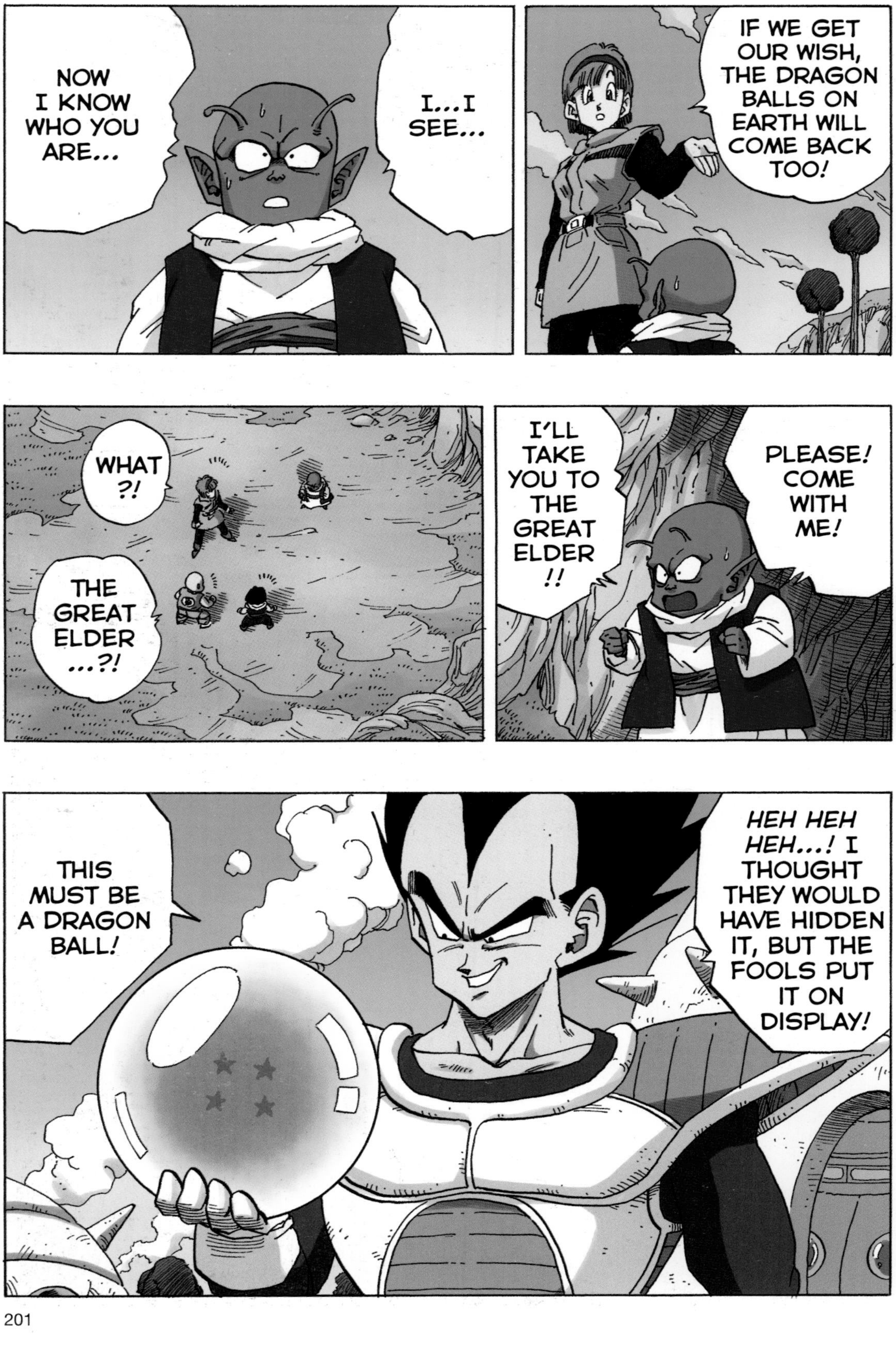
IF WE GET OUR WISH, THE DRAGON BALLS ON EARTH WILL COME BACK TOO!
I...I SEE...
NOW I KNOW WHO YOU ARE...
PLEASE! COME WITH ME!
I'LL TAKE YOU TO THE GREAT ELDER!!
WHAT?!
THE GREAT ELDER...?!
HEH HEH HEH...! I THOUGHT THEY WOULD HAVE HIDDEN IT, BUT THE FOOLS PUT IT ON DISPLAY!
THIS MUST BE A DRAGON BALL!

Chapter 15 • The Last Dragon Ball

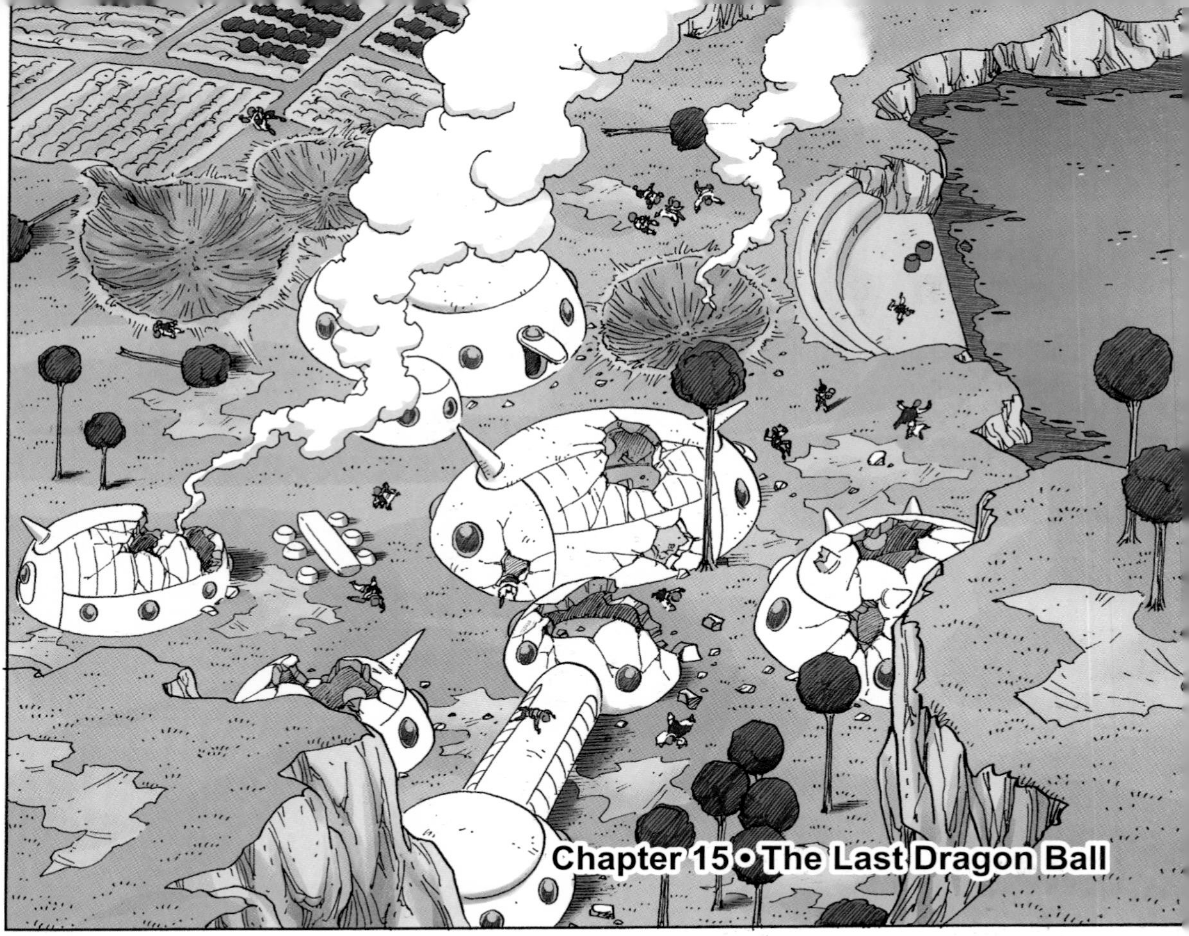

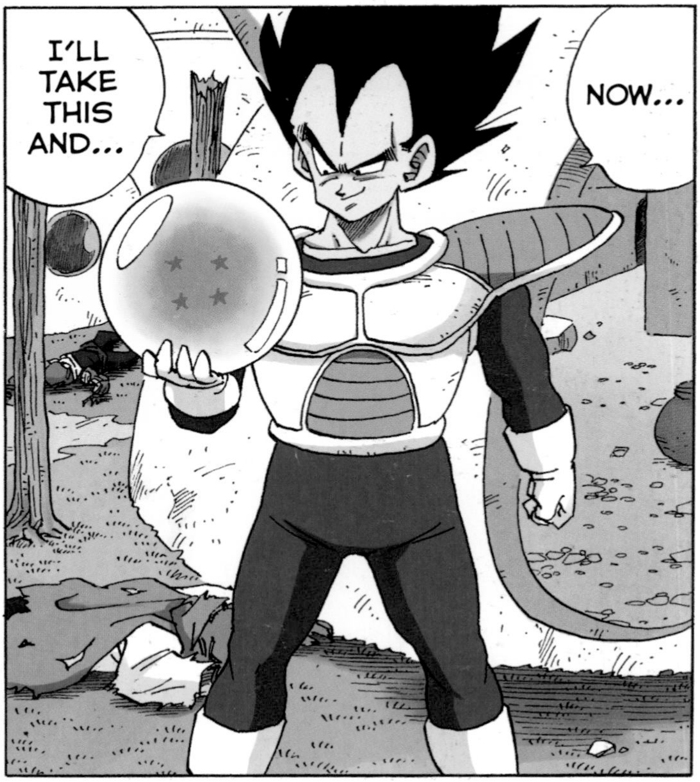
NOW...
I'LL TAKE THIS AND...

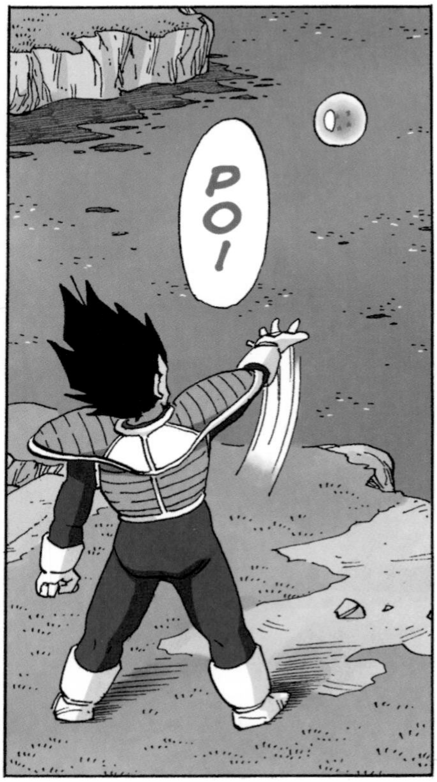
POI

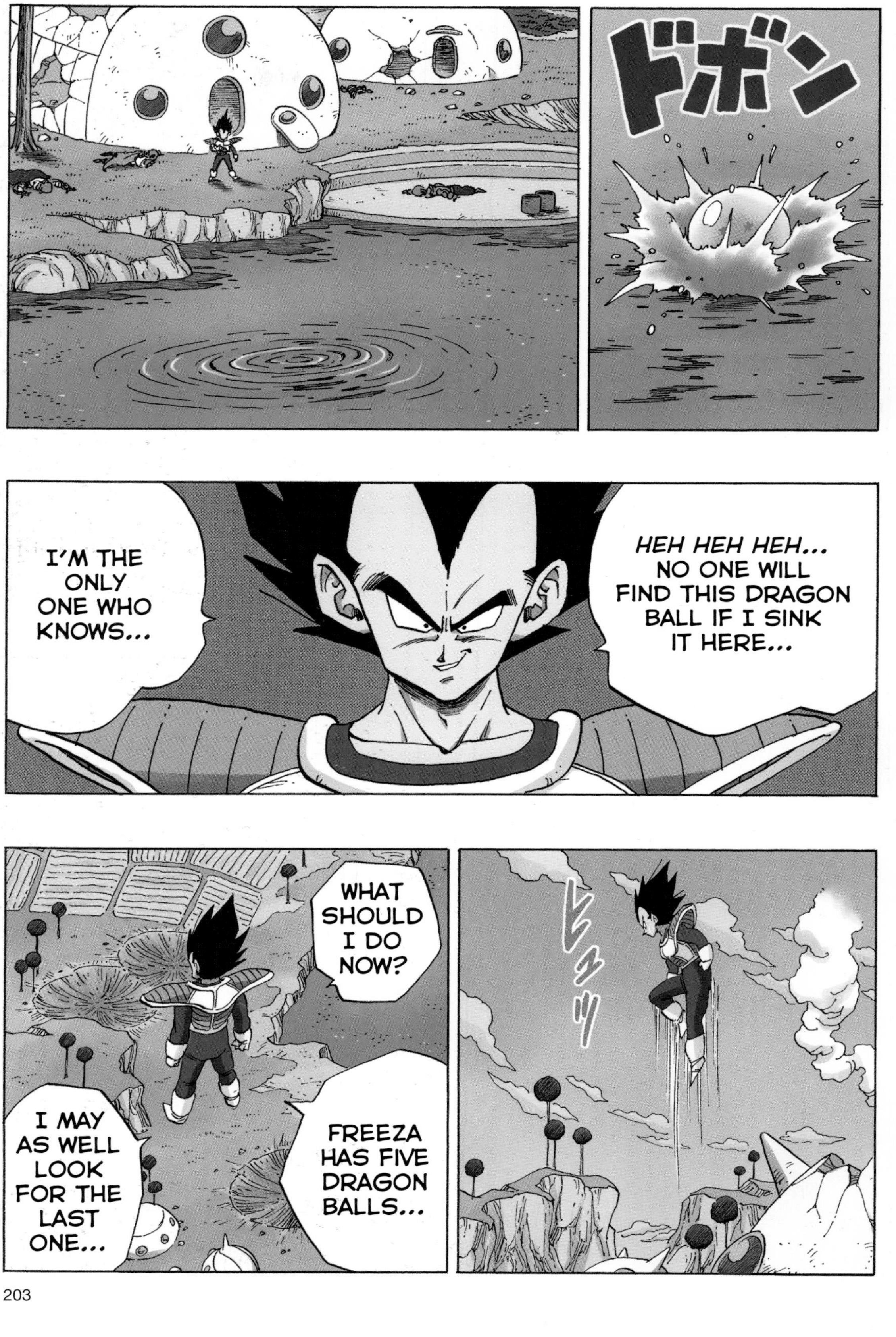
ドボン
HEH HEH HEH... NO ONE WILL FIND THIS DRAGON BALL IF I SINK IT HERE...
I'M THE ONLY ONE WHO KNOWS...
ヒュッ
WHAT SHOULD I DO NOW?
FREEZA HAS FIVE DRAGON BALLS...
I MAY AS WELL LOOK FOR THE LAST ONE...

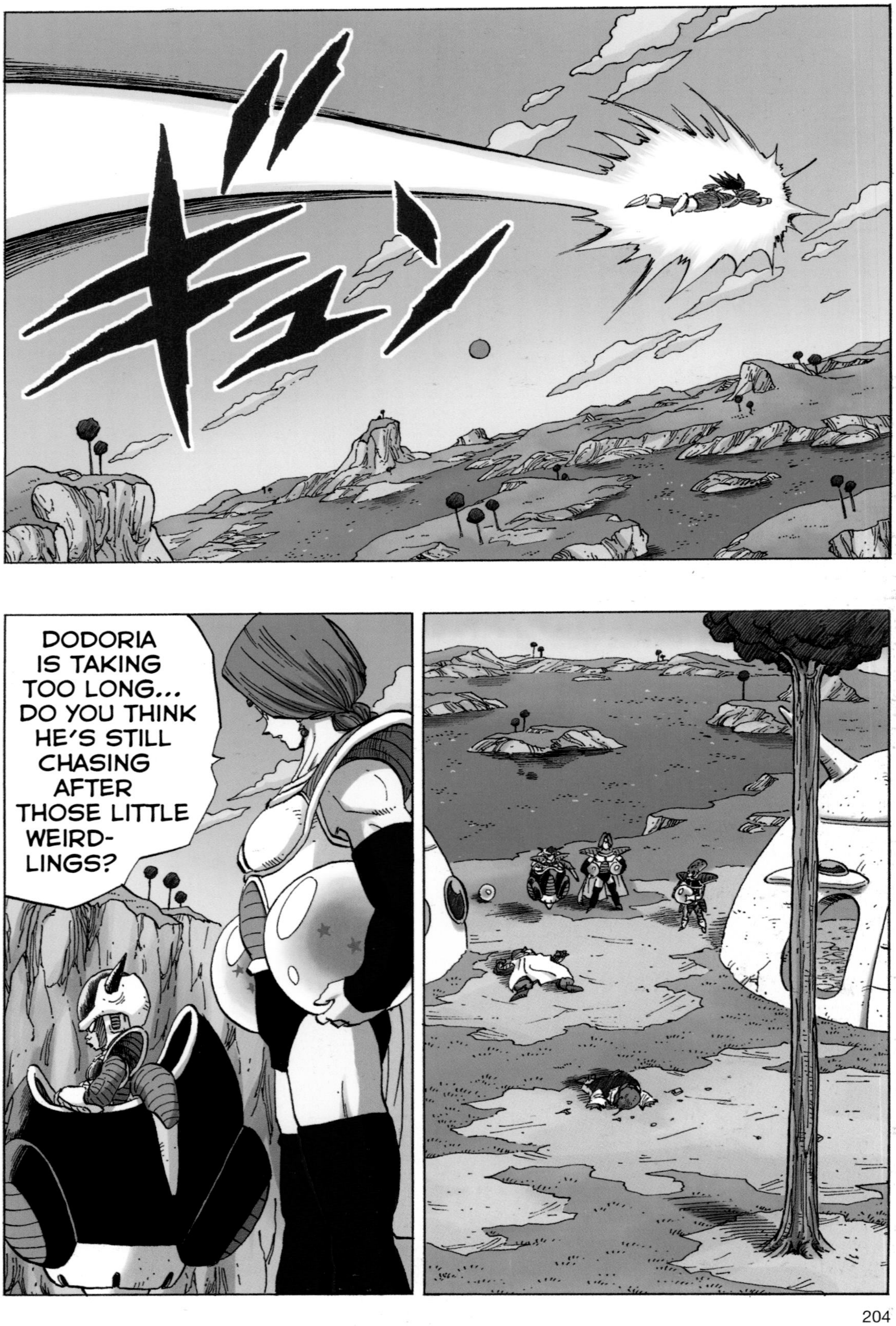
ギュン
DODORIA IS TAKING TOO LONG... DO YOU THINK HE'S STILL CHASING AFTER THOSE LITTLE WEIRD-LINGS?

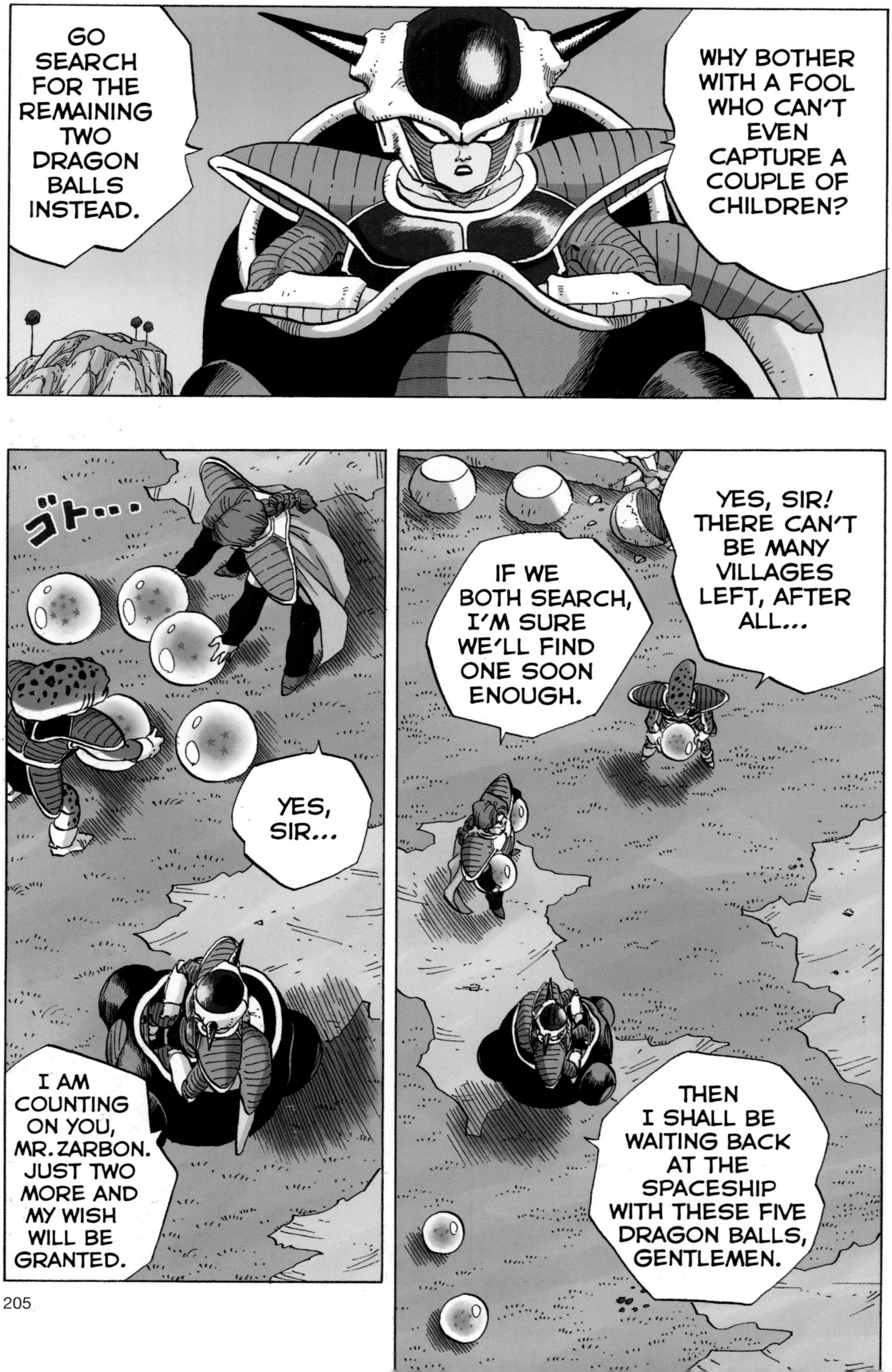
WHY BOTHER WITH A FOOL WHO CAN'T EVEN CAPTURE A COUPLE OF CHILDREN?
GO SEARCH FOR THE REMAINING TWO DRAGON BALLS INSTEAD.
YES, SIR! THERE CAN'T BE MANY VILLAGES LEFT, AFTER ALL...
IF WE BOTH SEARCH, I'M SURE WE'LL FIND ONE SOON ENOUGH.
THEN I SHALL BE WAITING BACK AT THE SPACESHIP WITH THESE FIVE DRAGON BALLS, GENTLEMEN.
ゴト…
YES, SIR...
I AM COUNTING ON YOU, MR. ZARBON. JUST TWO MORE AND MY WISH WILL BE GRANTED.

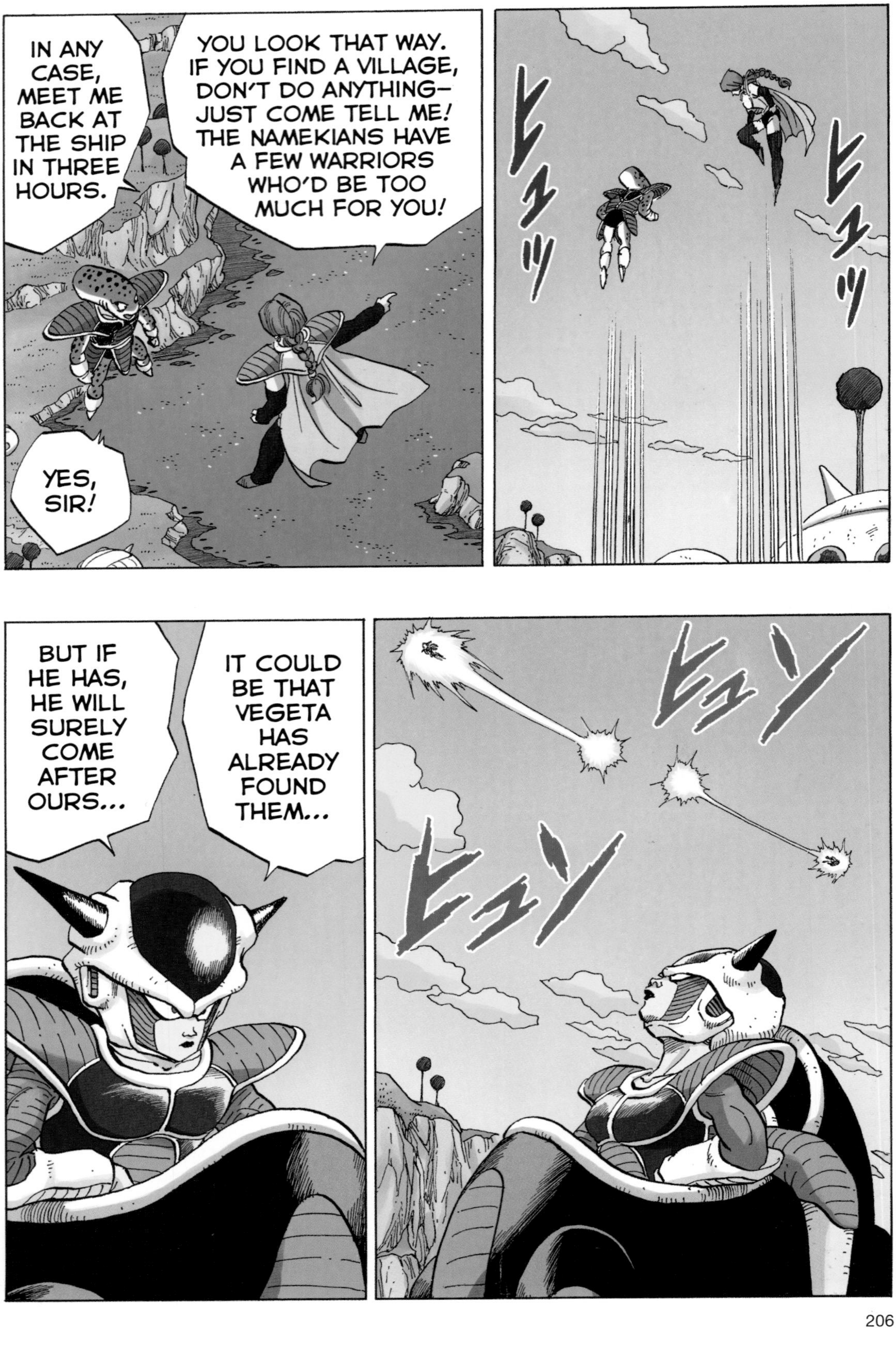
ヒュッ
ヒュッ
YOU LOOK THAT WAY. IF YOU FIND A VILLAGE, DON'T DO ANYTHING–JUST COME TELL ME! THE NAMEKIANS HAVE A FEW WARRIORS WHO'D BE TOO MUCH FOR YOU!
IN ANY CASE, MEET ME BACK AT THE SHIP IN THREE HOURS.
YES, SIR!
ヒュン
ヒュン
IT COULD BE THAT VEGETA HAS ALREADY FOUND THEM...
BUT IF HE HAS, HE WILL SURELY COME AFTER OURS...

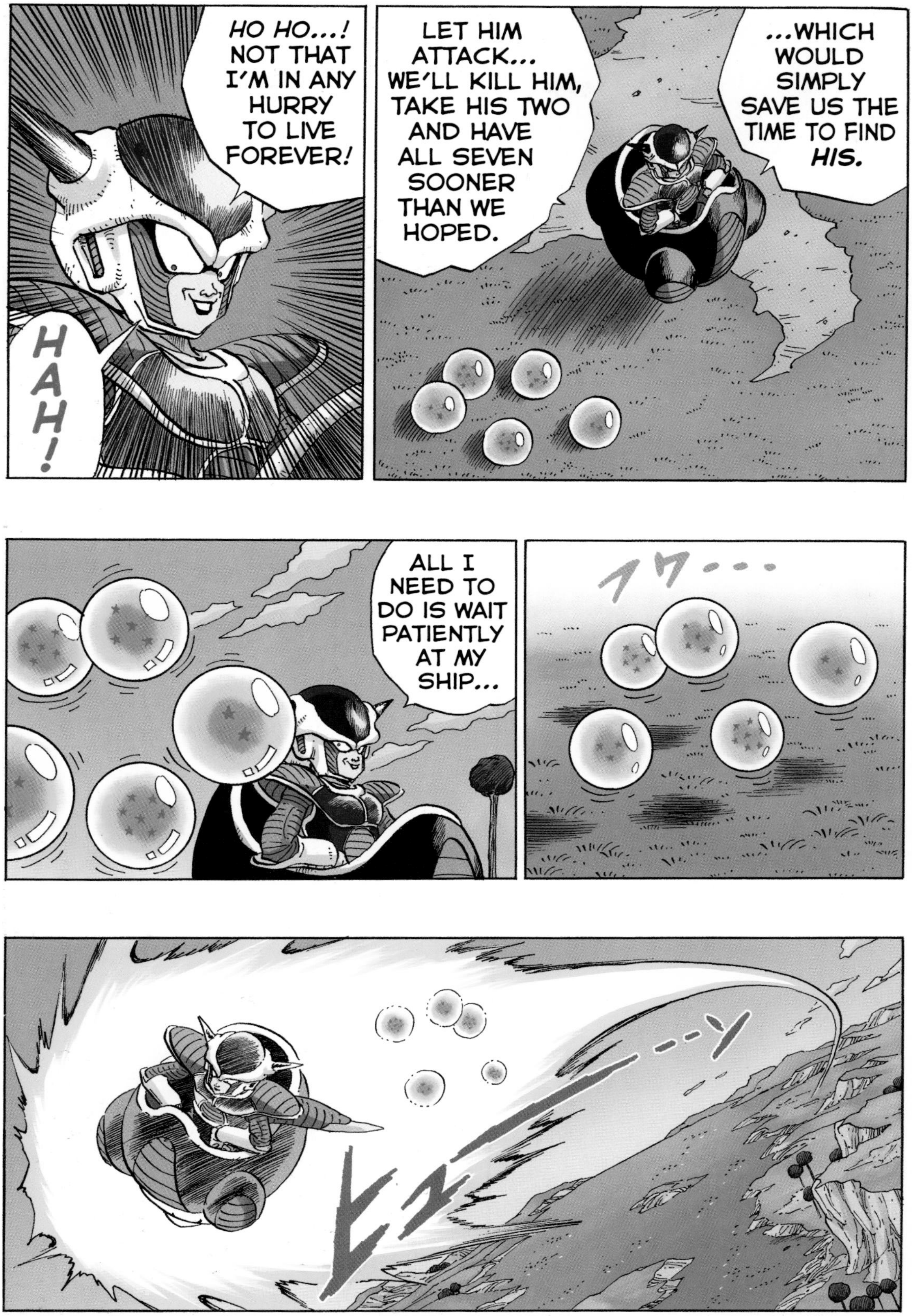

LET HIM ATTACK... WE'LL KILL HIM, TAKE HIS TWO AND HAVE ALL SEVEN SOONER THAN WE HOPED.
...WHICH WOULD SIMPLY SAVE US THE TIME TO FIND *HIS.*
HO HO...! NOT THAT I'M IN ANY HURRY TO LIVE FOREVER!
HAH!
フワ・・・
ALL I NEED TO DO IS WAIT PATIENTLY AT MY SHIP...
ヒューーン

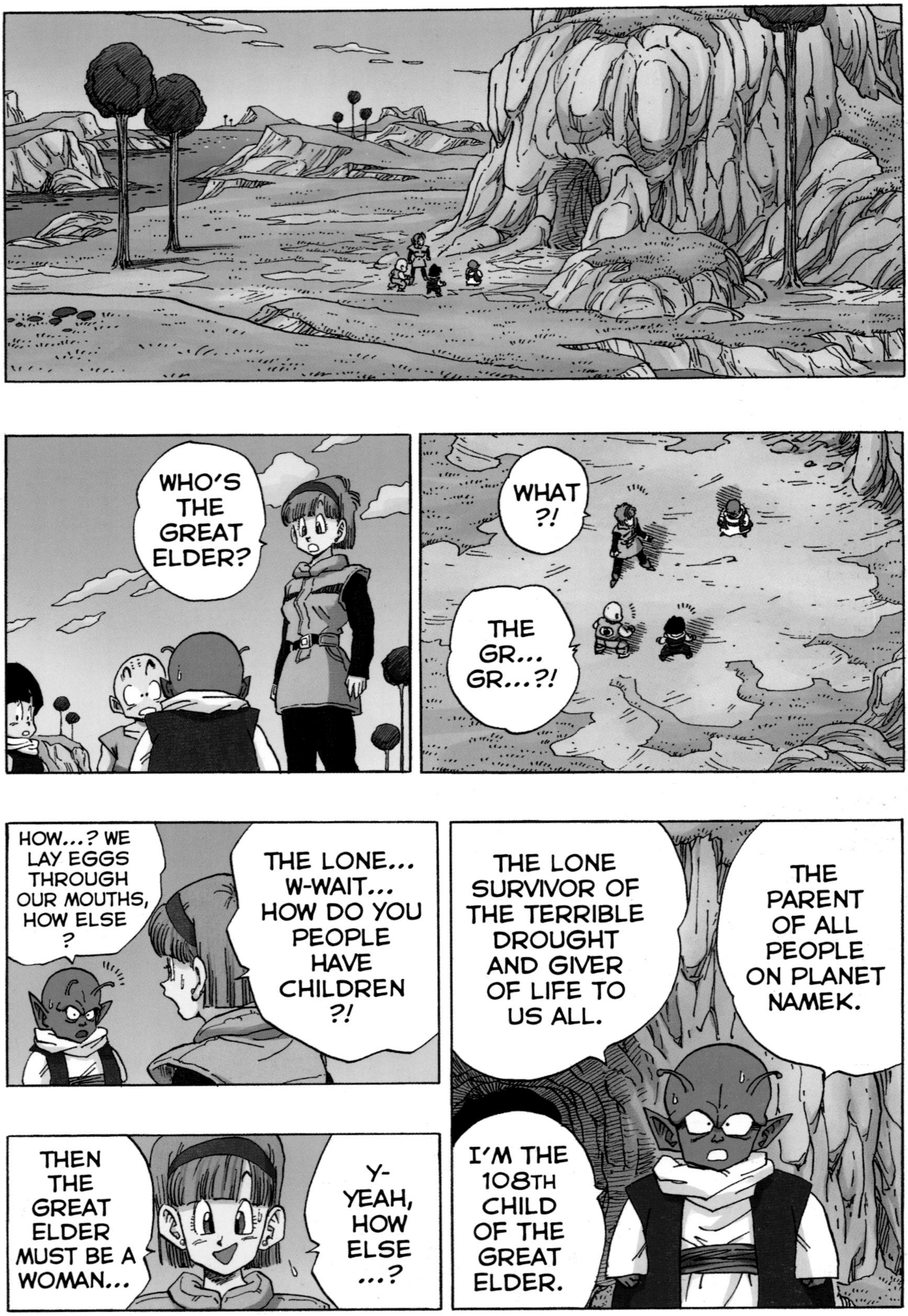
WHAT ?!
THE GR... GR...?!
WHO'S THE GREAT ELDER?
THE PARENT OF ALL PEOPLE ON PLANET NAMEK.
THE LONE SURVIVOR OF THE TERRIBLE DROUGHT AND GIVER OF LIFE TO US ALL.
I'M THE 108TH CHILD OF THE GREAT ELDER.
THE LONE... W-WAIT... HOW DO YOU PEOPLE HAVE CHILDREN ?!
HOW...? WE LAY EGGS THROUGH OUR MOUTHS, HOW ELSE ?
Y-YEAH, HOW ELSE ...?
THEN THE GREAT ELDER MUST BE A WOMAN...

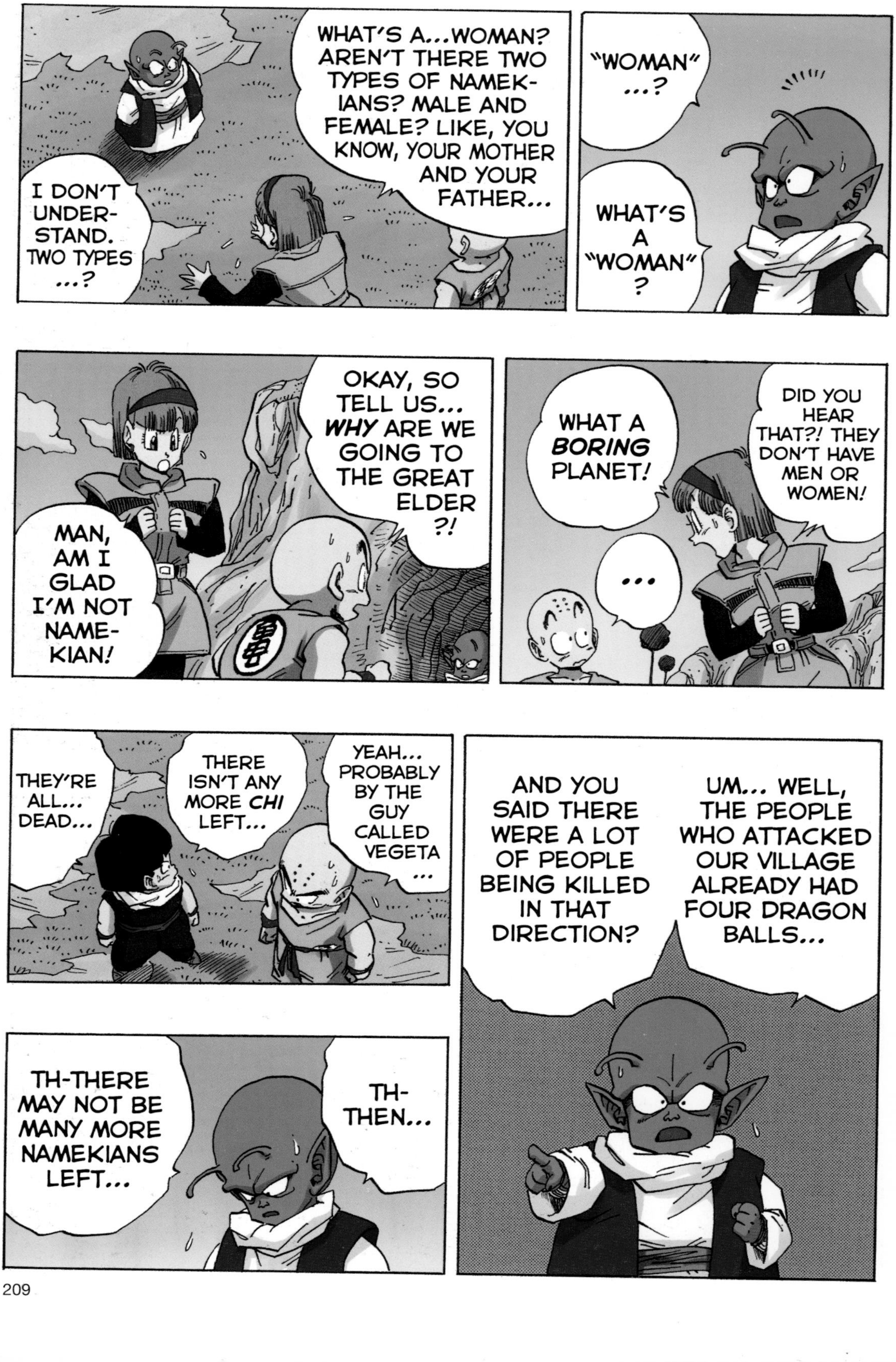
"WOMAN" ...?
WHAT'S A "WOMAN" ?
WHAT'S A...WOMAN? AREN'T THERE TWO TYPES OF NAMEKIANS? MALE AND FEMALE? LIKE, YOU KNOW, YOUR MOTHER AND YOUR FATHER...
I DON'T UNDERSTAND. TWO TYPES ...?
DID YOU HEAR THAT?! THEY DON'T HAVE MEN OR WOMEN!
WHAT A *BORING* PLANET!
...
OKAY, SO TELL US... *WHY* ARE WE GOING TO THE GREAT ELDER ?!
MAN, AM I GLAD I'M NOT NAMEKIAN!
UM... WELL, THE PEOPLE WHO ATTACKED OUR VILLAGE ALREADY HAD FOUR DRAGON BALLS...
AND YOU SAID THERE WERE A LOT OF PEOPLE BEING KILLED IN THAT DIRECTION?
YEAH... PROBABLY BY THE GUY CALLED VEGETA ...
THERE ISN'T ANY MORE *CHI* LEFT...
THEY'RE ALL... DEAD...
TH- THEN...
TH-THERE MAY NOT BE MANY MORE NAMEKIANS LEFT...

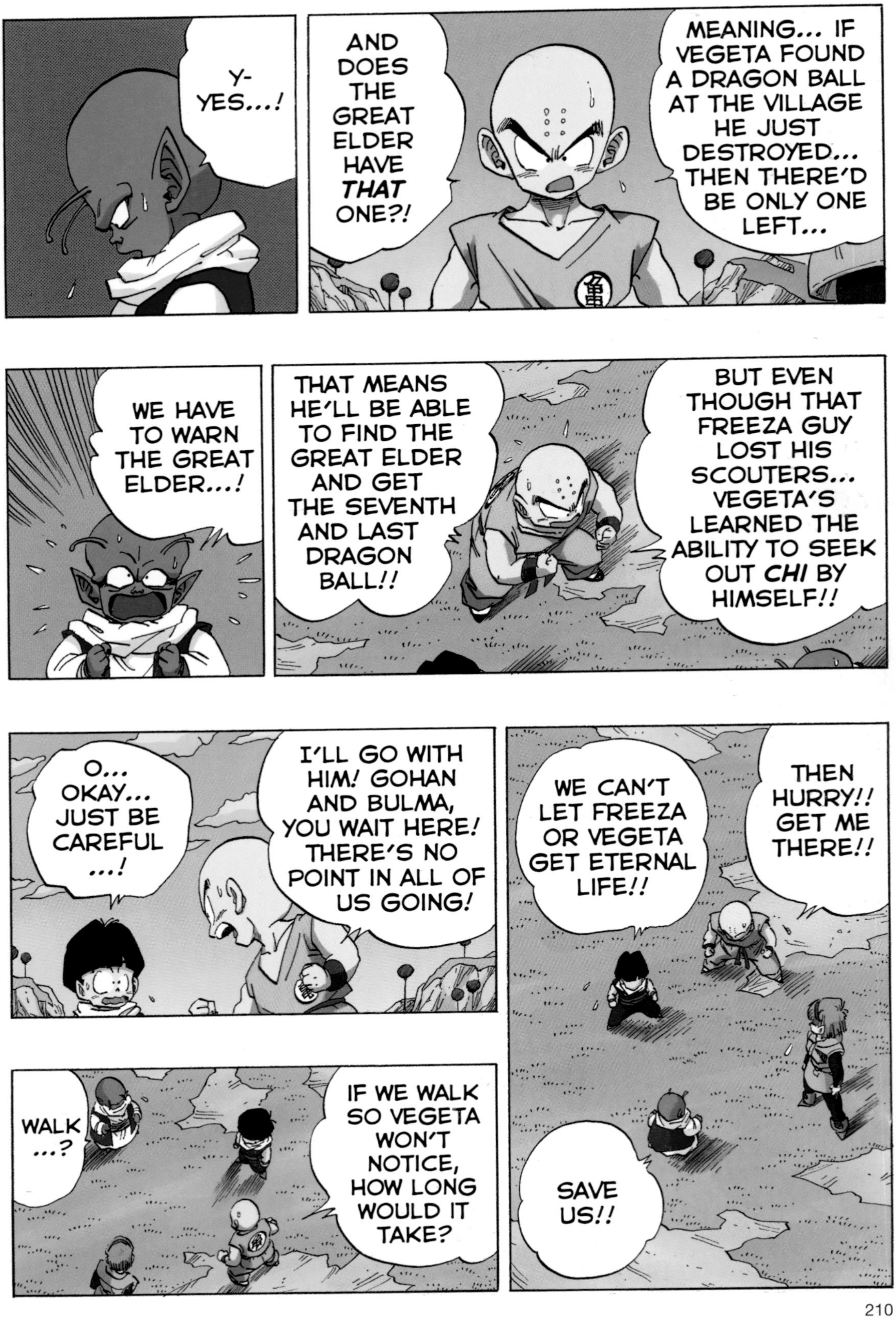
MEANING... IF VEGETA FOUND A DRAGON BALL AT THE VILLAGE HE JUST DESTROYED... THEN THERE'D BE ONLY ONE LEFT...
AND DOES THE GREAT ELDER HAVE *THAT* ONE?!
Y- YES...!
BUT EVEN THOUGH THAT FREEZA GUY LOST HIS SCOUTERS... VEGETA'S LEARNED THE ABILITY TO SEEK OUT *CHI* BY HIMSELF!!
THAT MEANS HE'LL BE ABLE TO FIND THE GREAT ELDER AND GET THE SEVENTH AND LAST DRAGON BALL!!
WE HAVE TO WARN THE GREAT ELDER...!
THEN HURRY!! GET ME THERE!!
WE CAN'T LET FREEZA OR VEGETA GET ETERNAL LIFE!!
SAVE US!!
I'LL GO WITH HIM! GOHAN AND BULMA, YOU WAIT HERE! THERE'S NO POINT IN ALL OF US GOING!
O... OKAY... JUST BE CAREFUL ...!
IF WE WALK SO VEGETA WON'T NOTICE, HOW LONG WOULD IT TAKE?
WALK ...?

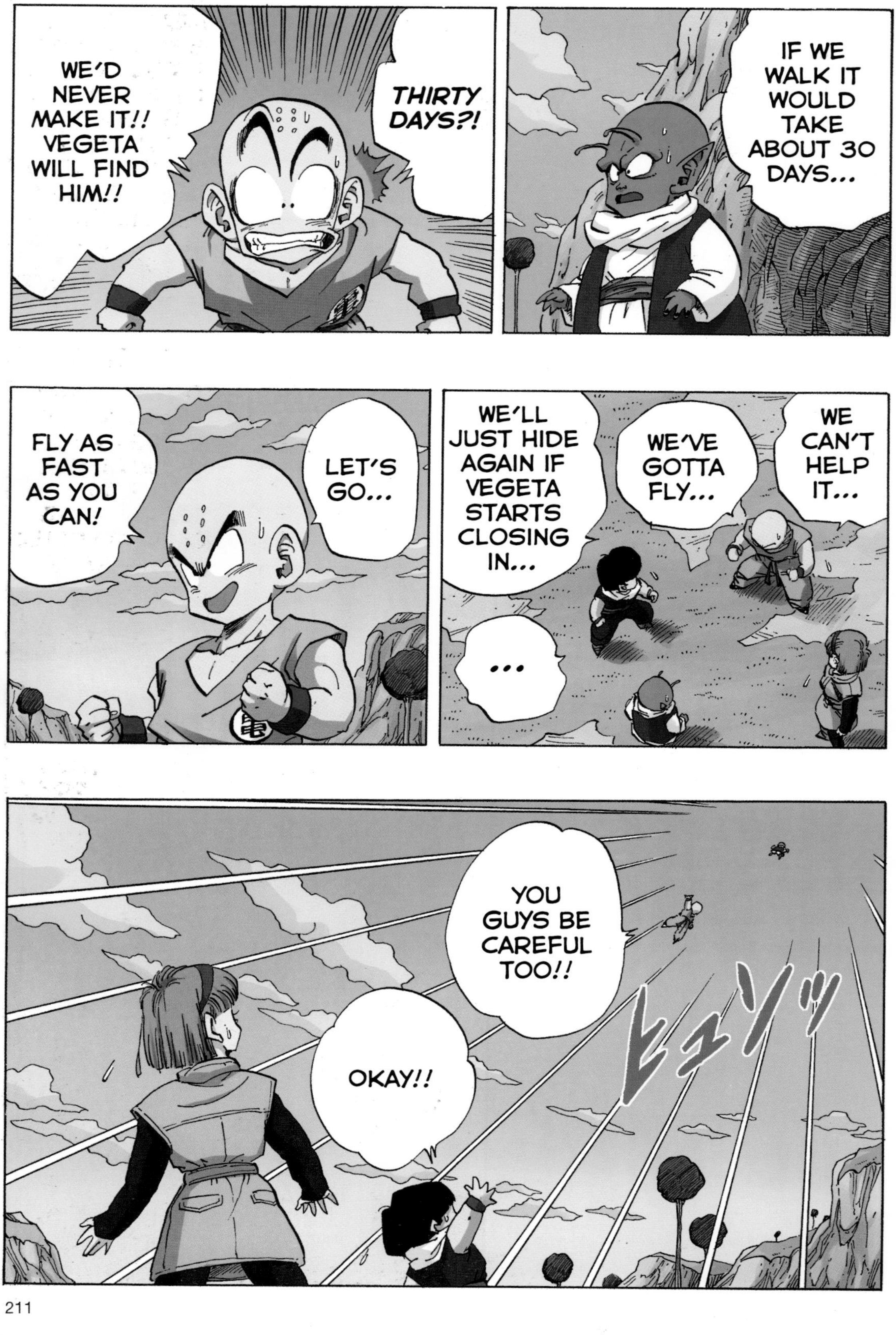
IF WE WALK IT WOULD TAKE ABOUT 30 DAYS...
THIRTY DAYS?!
WE'D NEVER MAKE IT!! VEGETA WILL FIND HIM!!
WE CAN'T HELP IT...
WE'VE GOTTA FLY...
WE'LL JUST HIDE AGAIN IF VEGETA STARTS CLOSING IN...
...
LET'S GO...
FLY AS FAST AS YOU CAN!
YOU GUYS BE CAREFUL TOO!!
ヒュンッ
OKAY!!

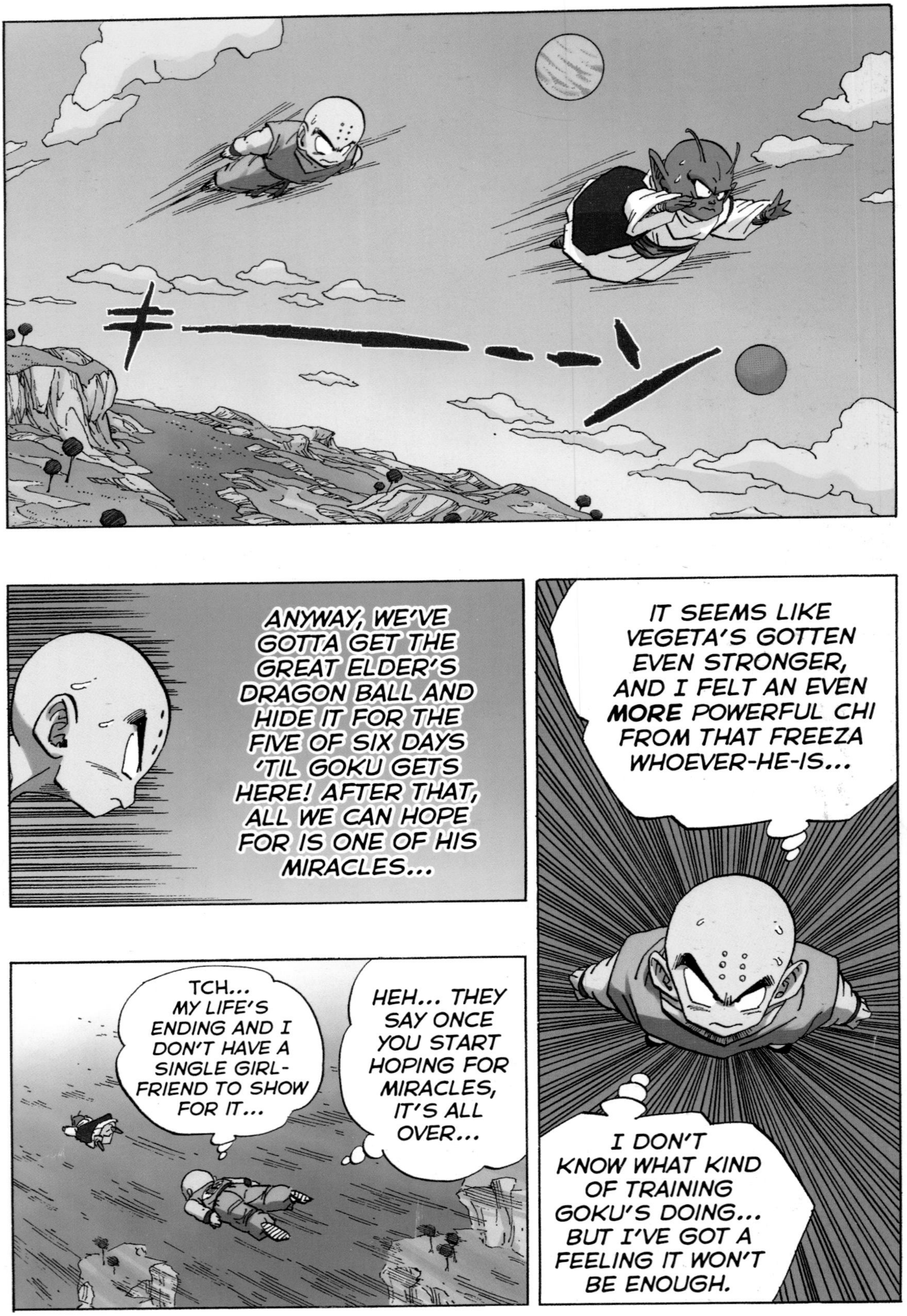
IT SEEMS LIKE VEGETA'S GOTTEN EVEN STRONGER, AND I FELT AN EVEN **MORE** POWERFUL CHI FROM THAT FREEZA WHOEVER-HE-IS...
I DON'T KNOW WHAT KIND OF TRAINING GOKU'S DOING... BUT I'VE GOT A FEELING IT WON'T BE ENOUGH.
ANYWAY, WE'VE GOTTA GET THE GREAT ELDER'S DRAGON BALL AND HIDE IT FOR THE FIVE OF SIX DAYS 'TIL GOKU GETS HERE! AFTER THAT, ALL WE CAN HOPE FOR IS ONE OF HIS MIRACLES...
HEH... THEY SAY ONCE YOU START HOPING FOR MIRACLES, IT'S ALL OVER...
TCH... MY LIFE'S ENDING AND I DON'T HAVE A SINGLE GIRL-FRIEND TO SHOW FOR IT...

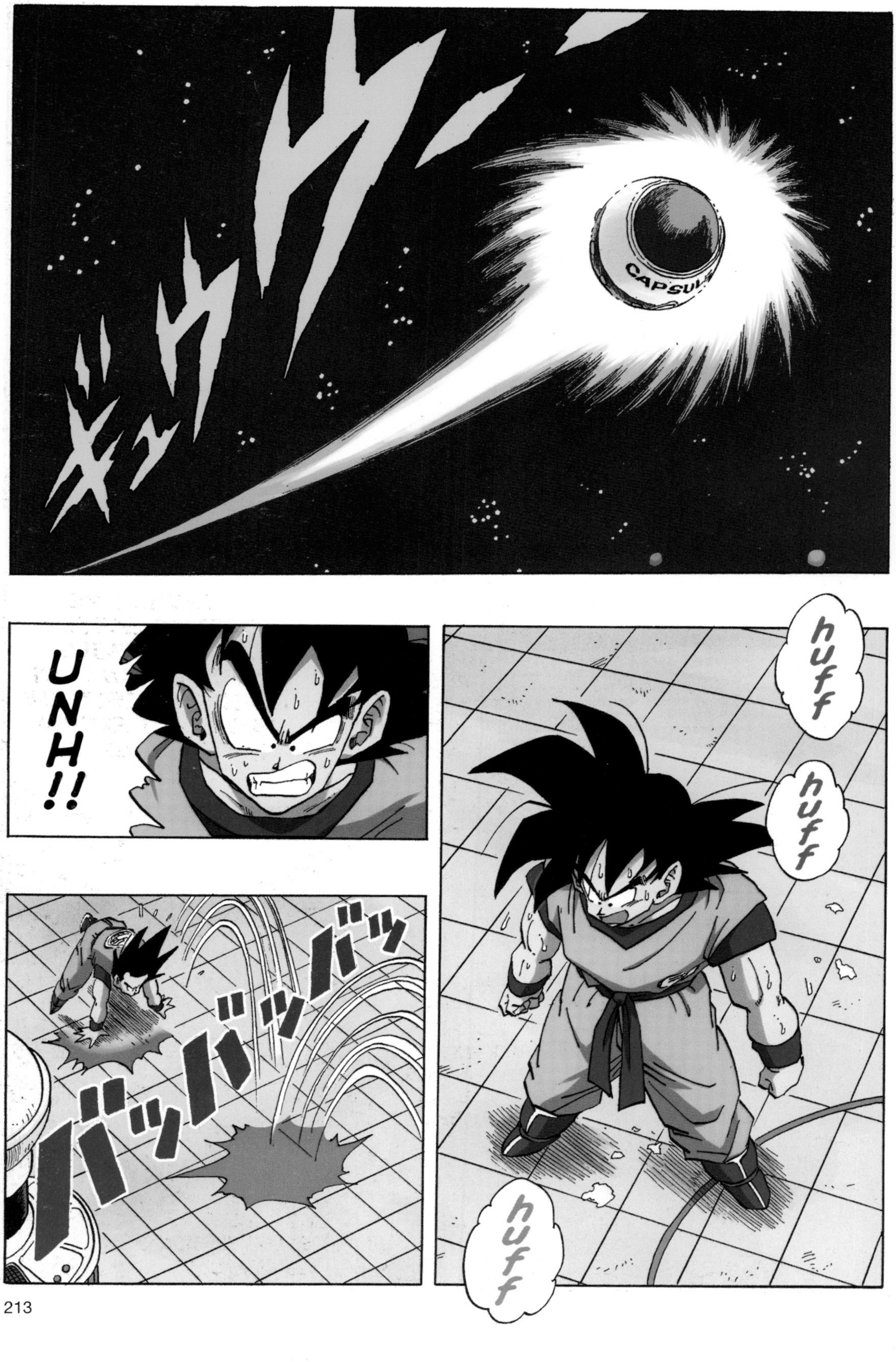
huff
huff
huff
UNH!!
バッバッバッ

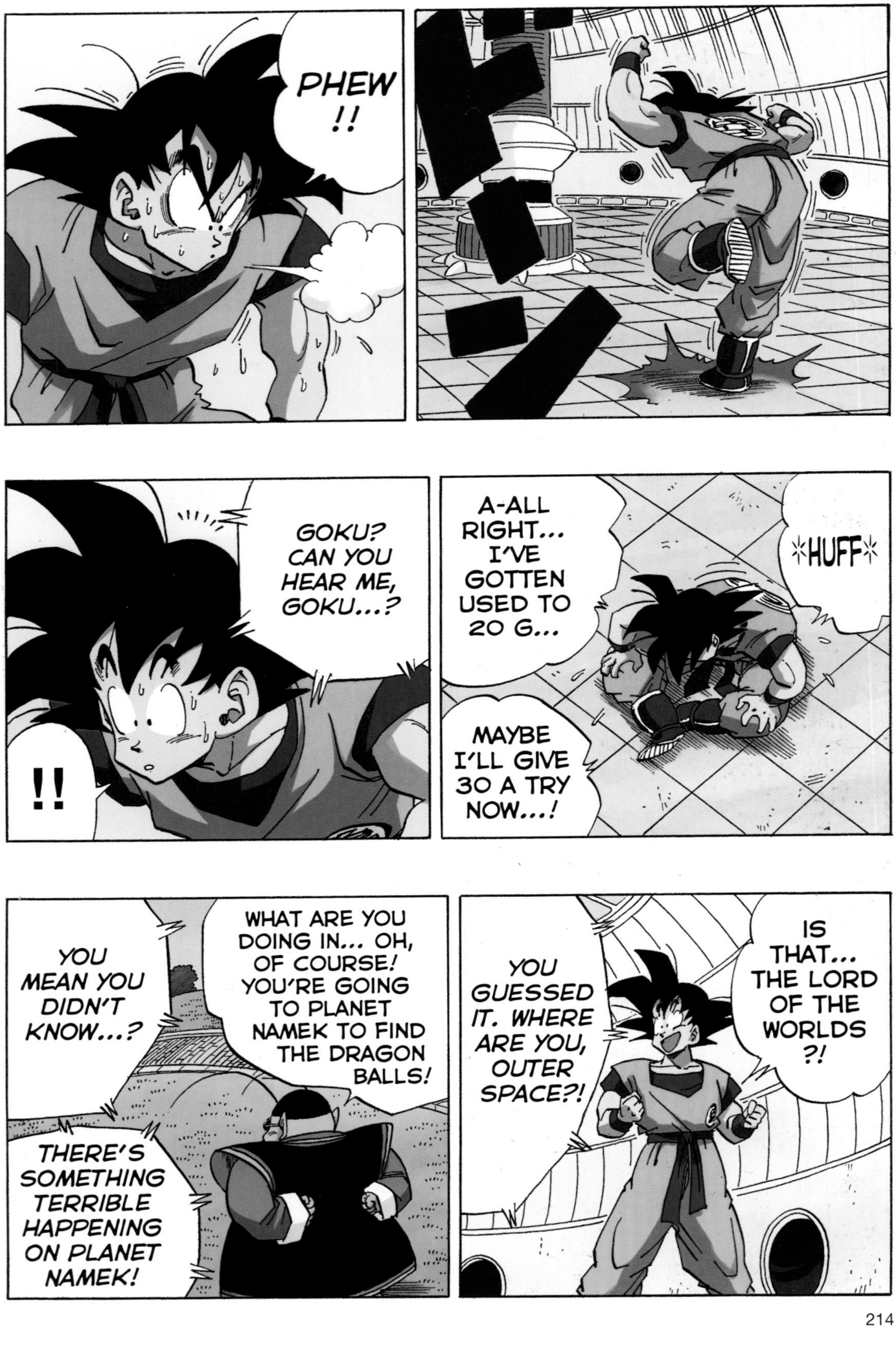
PHEW !!
HUFF
A-ALL RIGHT... I'VE GOTTEN USED TO 20 G...
MAYBE I'LL GIVE 30 A TRY NOW...!
GOKU? CAN YOU HEAR ME, GOKU...?
!!
IS THAT... THE LORD OF THE WORLDS ?!
YOU GUESSED IT. WHERE ARE YOU, OUTER SPACE?!
WHAT ARE YOU DOING IN... OH, OF COURSE! YOU'RE GOING TO PLANET NAMEK TO FIND THE DRAGON BALLS!
YOU MEAN YOU DIDN'T KNOW...?
THERE'S SOMETHING TERRIBLE HAPPENING ON PLANET NAMEK!

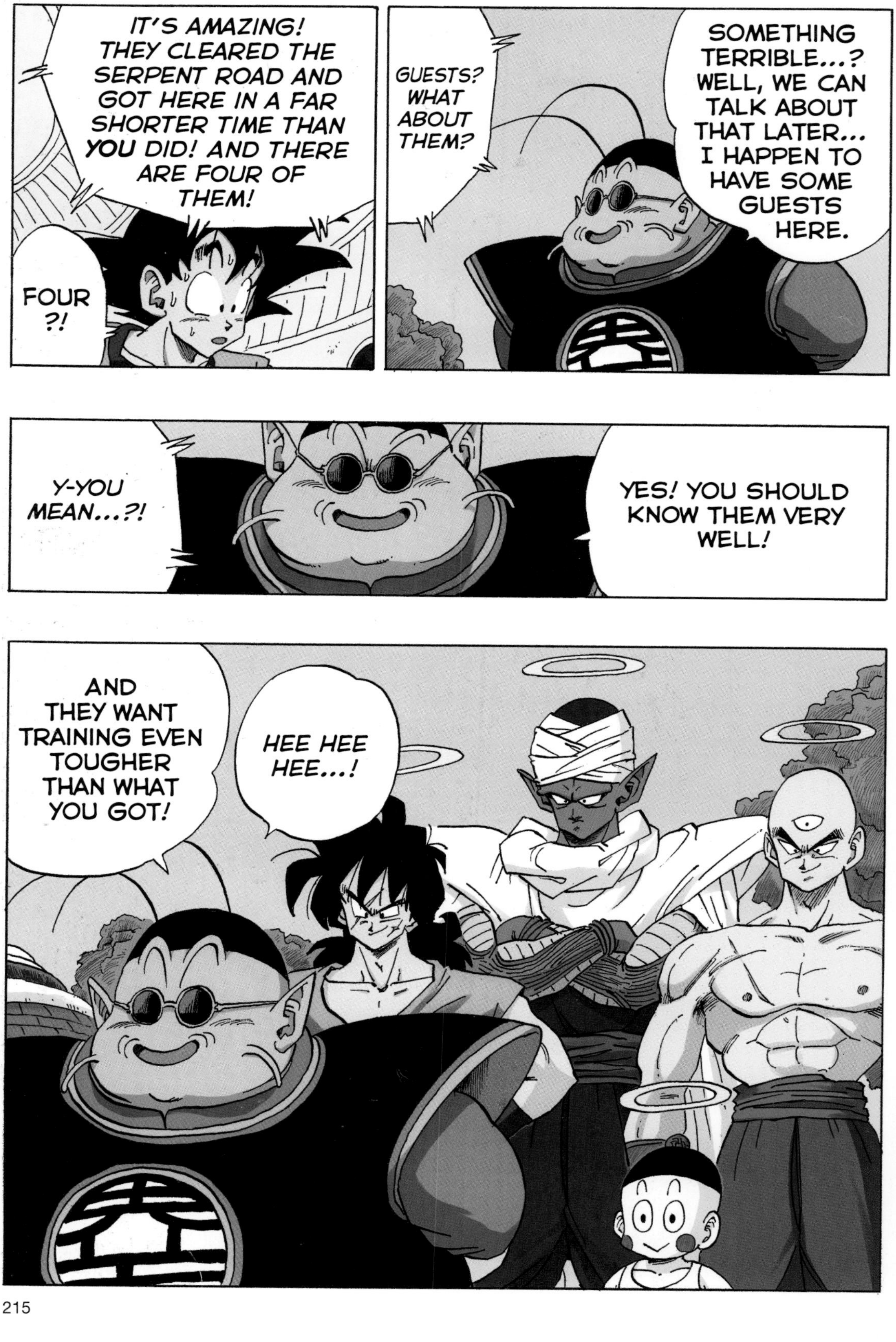
SOMETHING TERRIBLE...? WELL, WE CAN TALK ABOUT THAT LATER... I HAPPEN TO HAVE SOME GUESTS HERE.
GUESTS? WHAT ABOUT THEM?
IT'S AMAZING! THEY CLEARED THE SERPENT ROAD AND GOT HERE IN A FAR SHORTER TIME THAN YOU DID! AND THERE ARE FOUR OF THEM!
FOUR ?!
Y-YOU MEAN...?!
YES! YOU SHOULD KNOW THEM VERY WELL!
AND THEY WANT TRAINING EVEN TOUGHER THAN WHAT YOU GOT!
HEE HEE HEE...!

Chapter 16 • The Four Dead Heroes

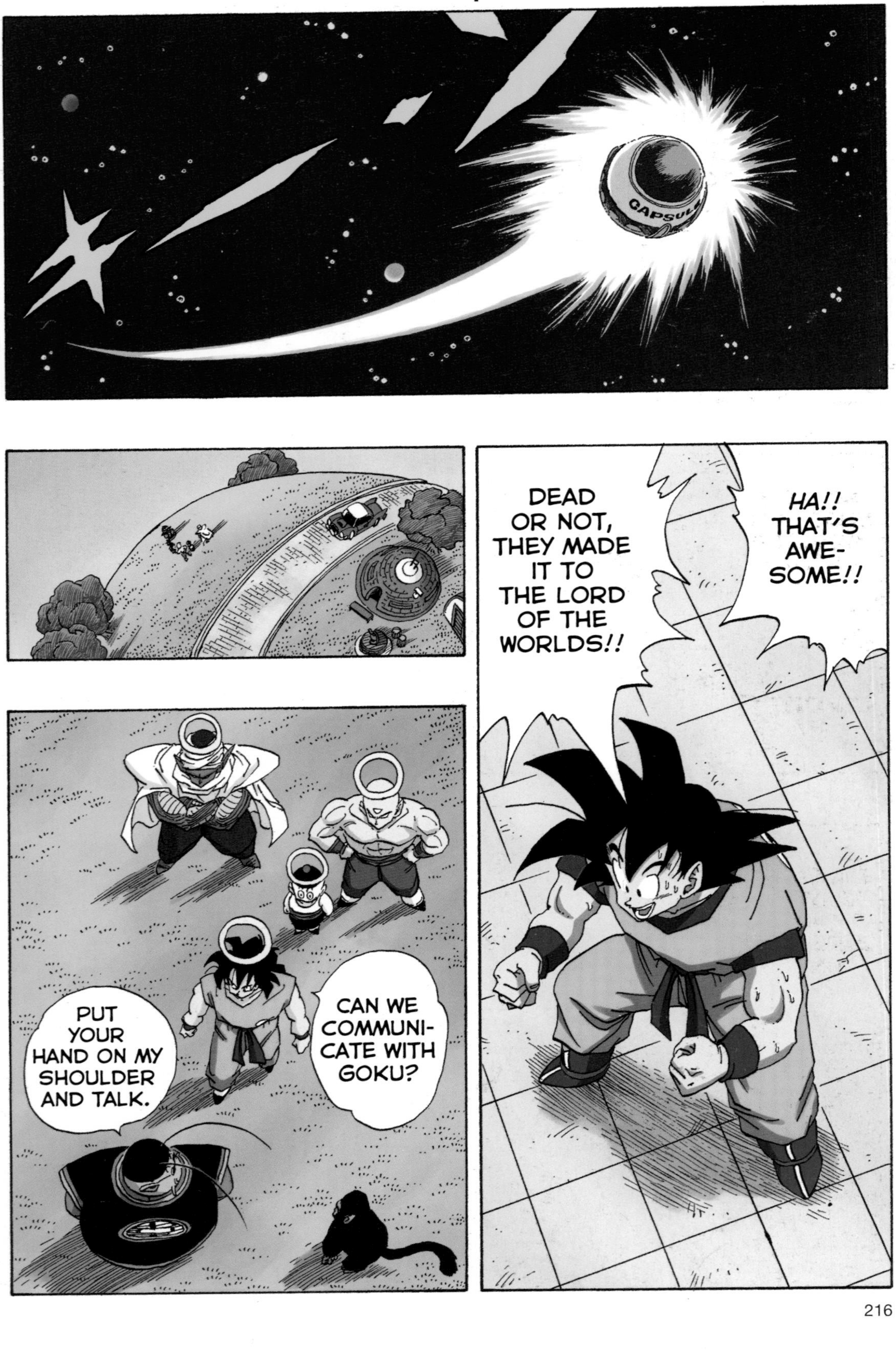
HA!! THAT'S AWESOME!!
DEAD OR NOT, THEY MADE IT TO THE LORD OF THE WORLDS!!
CAN WE COMMUNICATE WITH GOKU?
PUT YOUR HAND ON MY SHOULDER AND TALK.

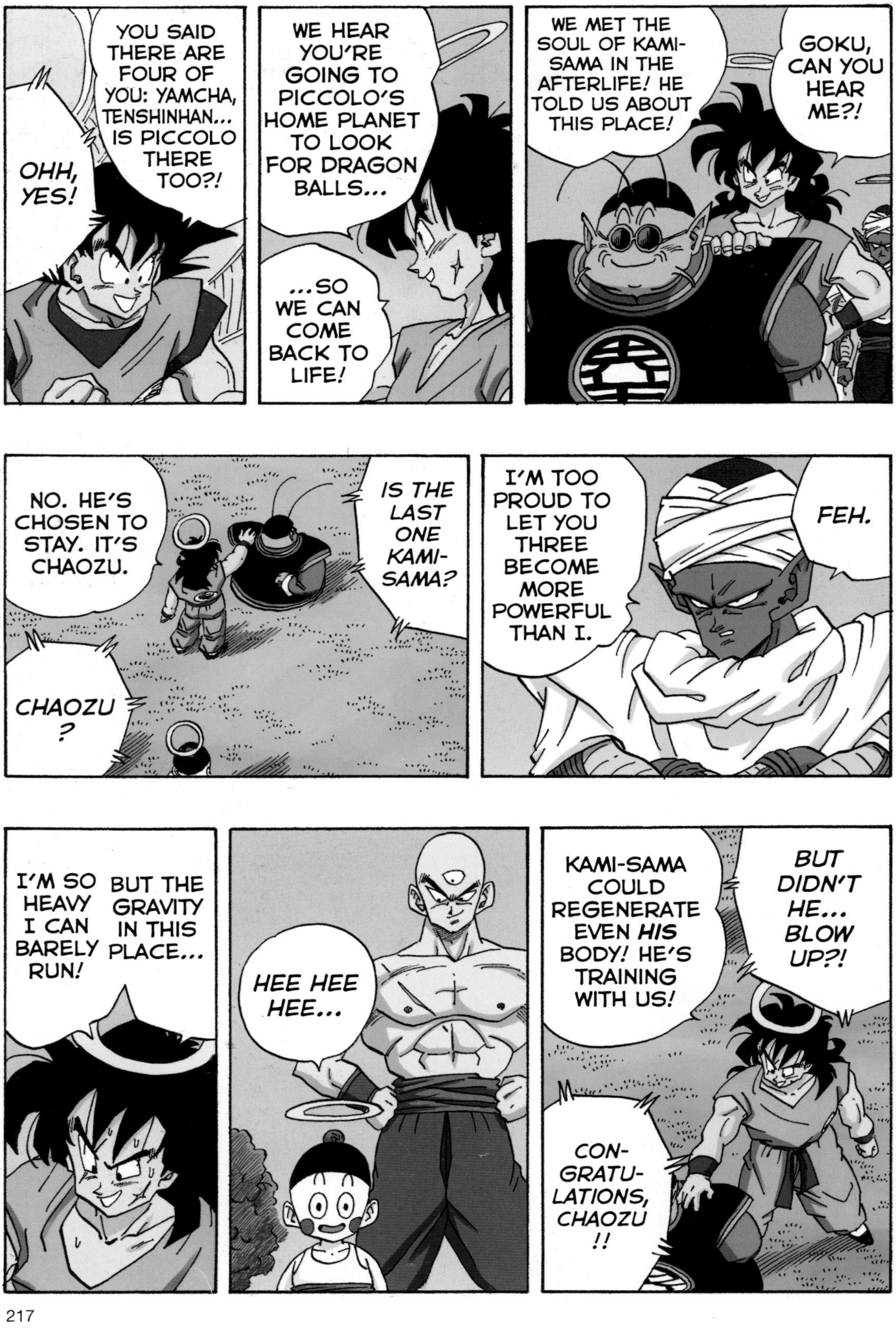
GOKU, CAN YOU HEAR ME?!
WE MET THE SOUL OF KAMI-SAMA IN THE AFTERLIFE! HE TOLD US ABOUT THIS PLACE!
WE HEAR YOU'RE GOING TO PICCOLO'S HOME PLANET TO LOOK FOR DRAGON BALLS...
...SO WE CAN COME BACK TO LIFE!
YOU SAID THERE ARE FOUR OF YOU: YAMCHA, TENSHINHAN... IS PICCOLO THERE TOO?!
OHH, YES!
FEH.
I'M TOO PROUD TO LET YOU THREE BECOME MORE POWERFUL THAN I.
IS THE LAST ONE KAMI-SAMA?
NO. HE'S CHOSEN TO STAY. IT'S CHAOZU.
CHAOZU?
BUT DIDN'T HE... BLOW UP?!
KAMI-SAMA COULD REGENERATE EVEN HIS BODY! HE'S TRAINING WITH US!
CONGRATULATIONS, CHAOZU!!
HEE HEE HEE...
BUT THE GRAVITY IN THIS PLACE...
I'M SO HEAVY I CAN BARELY RUN!

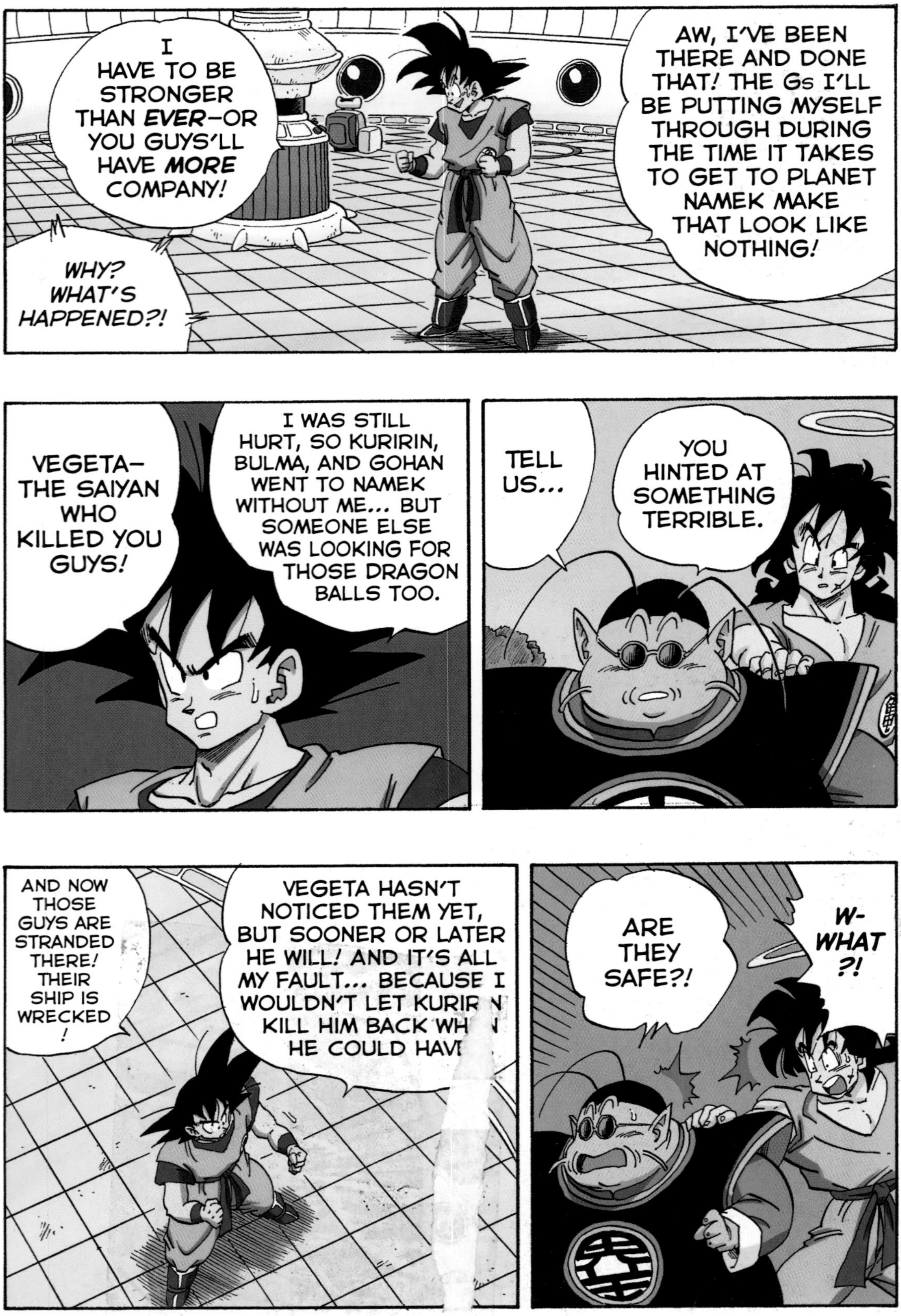
AW, I'VE BEEN THERE AND DONE THAT! THE Gs I'LL BE PUTTING MYSELF THROUGH DURING THE TIME IT TAKES TO GET TO PLANET NAMEK MAKE THAT LOOK LIKE NOTHING!
I HAVE TO BE STRONGER THAN EVER—OR YOU GUYS'LL HAVE MORE COMPANY!
WHY? WHAT'S HAPPENED?!
YOU HINTED AT SOMETHING TERRIBLE.
TELL US...
I WAS STILL HURT, SO KURIRIN, BULMA, AND GOHAN WENT TO NAMEK WITHOUT ME... BUT SOMEONE ELSE WAS LOOKING FOR THOSE DRAGON BALLS TOO.
VEGETA—THE SAIYAN WHO KILLED YOU GUYS!
W-WHAT?!
ARE THEY SAFE?!
VEGETA HASN'T NOTICED THEM YET, BUT SOONER OR LATER HE WILL! AND IT'S ALL MY FAULT... BECAUSE I WOULDN'T LET KURIR N KILL HIM BACK WH N HE COULD HAV
AND NOW THOSE GUYS ARE STRANDED THERE! THEIR SHIP IS WRECKED!

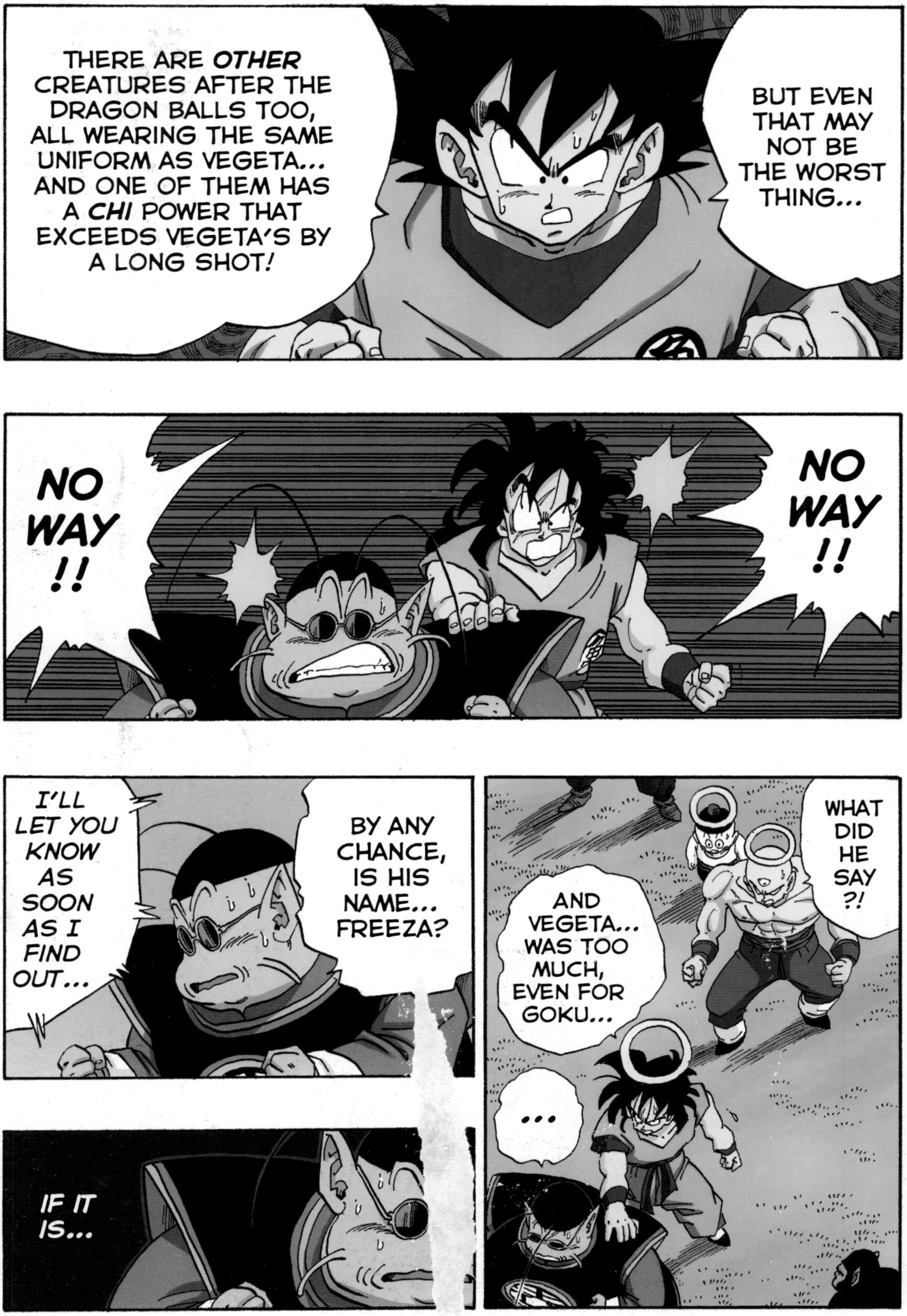
THERE ARE OTHER CREATURES AFTER THE DRAGON BALLS TOO, ALL WEARING THE SAME UNIFORM AS VEGETA... AND ONE OF THEM HAS A CHI POWER THAT EXCEEDS VEGETA'S BY A LONG SHOT!
BUT EVEN THAT MAY NOT BE THE WORST THING...
NO WAY!!
NO WAY!!
WHAT DID HE SAY?!
AND VEGETA... WAS TOO MUCH, EVEN FOR GOKU...
...
BY ANY CHANCE, IS HIS NAME... FREEZA?
I'LL LET YOU KNOW AS SOON AS I FIND OUT...
IF IT IS...

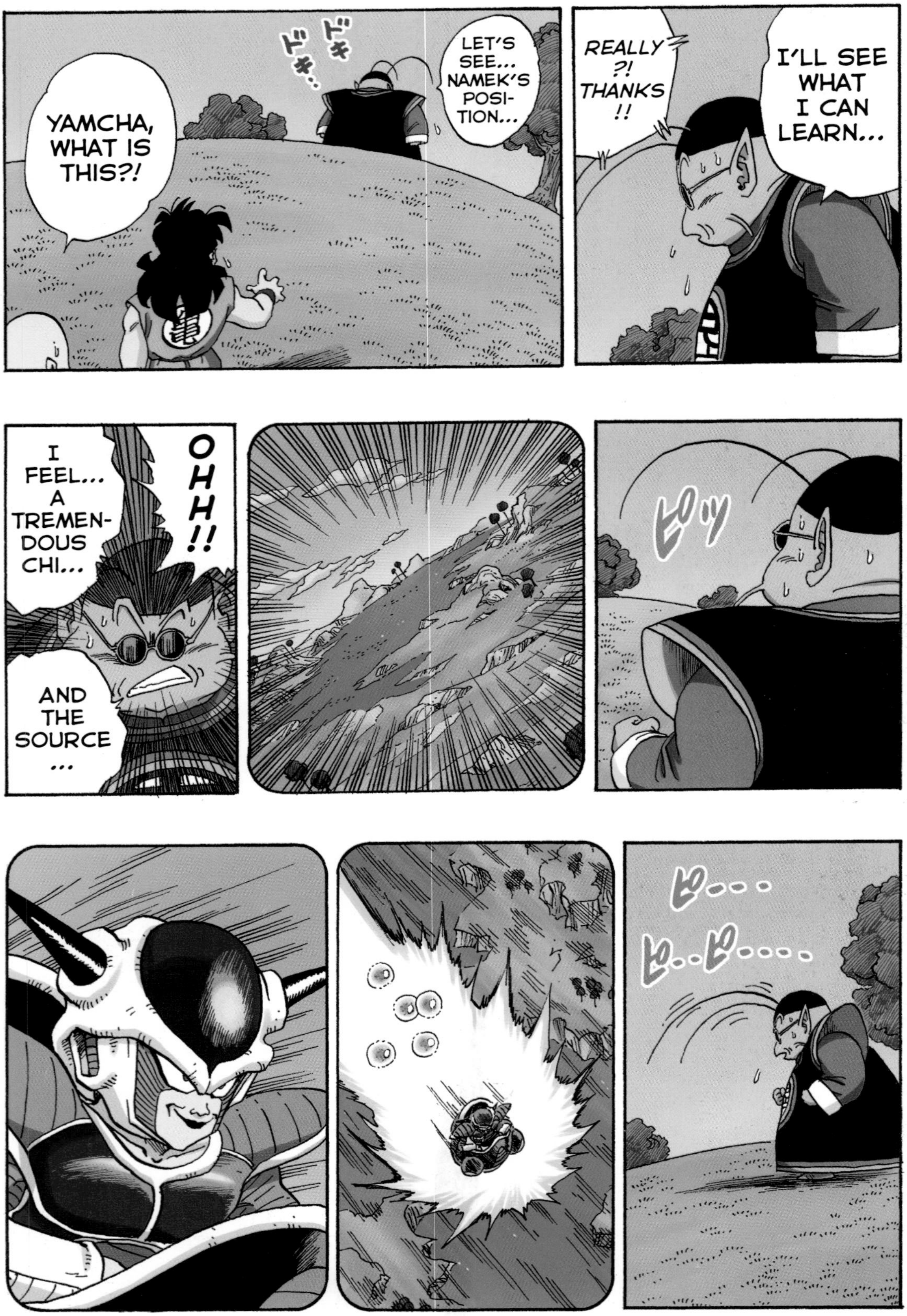
I'LL SEE WHAT I CAN LEARN...
REALLY?! THANKS!!
LET'S SEE... NAMEK'S POSITION...
ドキ ドキ..
YAMCHA, WHAT IS THIS?!
ピッ
OHH!!
I FEEL... A TREMENDOUS CHI...
AND THE SOURCE ...
ピ...
ピ..ピ....

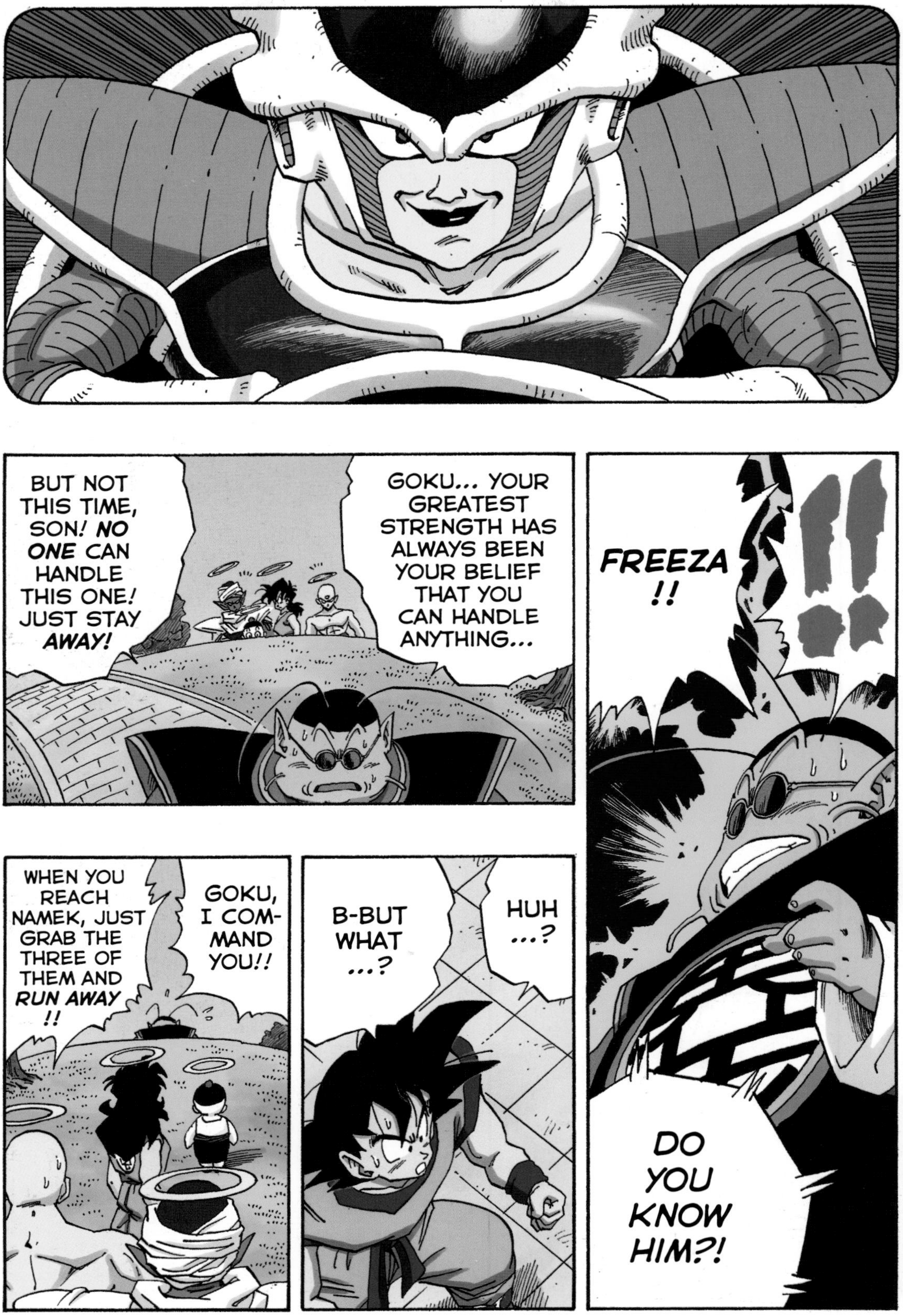
FREEZA !!
DO YOU KNOW HIM?!
GOKU... YOUR GREATEST STRENGTH HAS ALWAYS BEEN YOUR BELIEF THAT YOU CAN HANDLE ANYTHING...
BUT NOT THIS TIME, SON! NO ONE CAN HANDLE THIS ONE! JUST STAY AWAY!
HUH ...?
B-BUT WHAT ...?
GOKU, I COMMAND YOU!!
WHEN YOU REACH NAMEK, JUST GRAB THE THREE OF THEM AND RUN AWAY !!

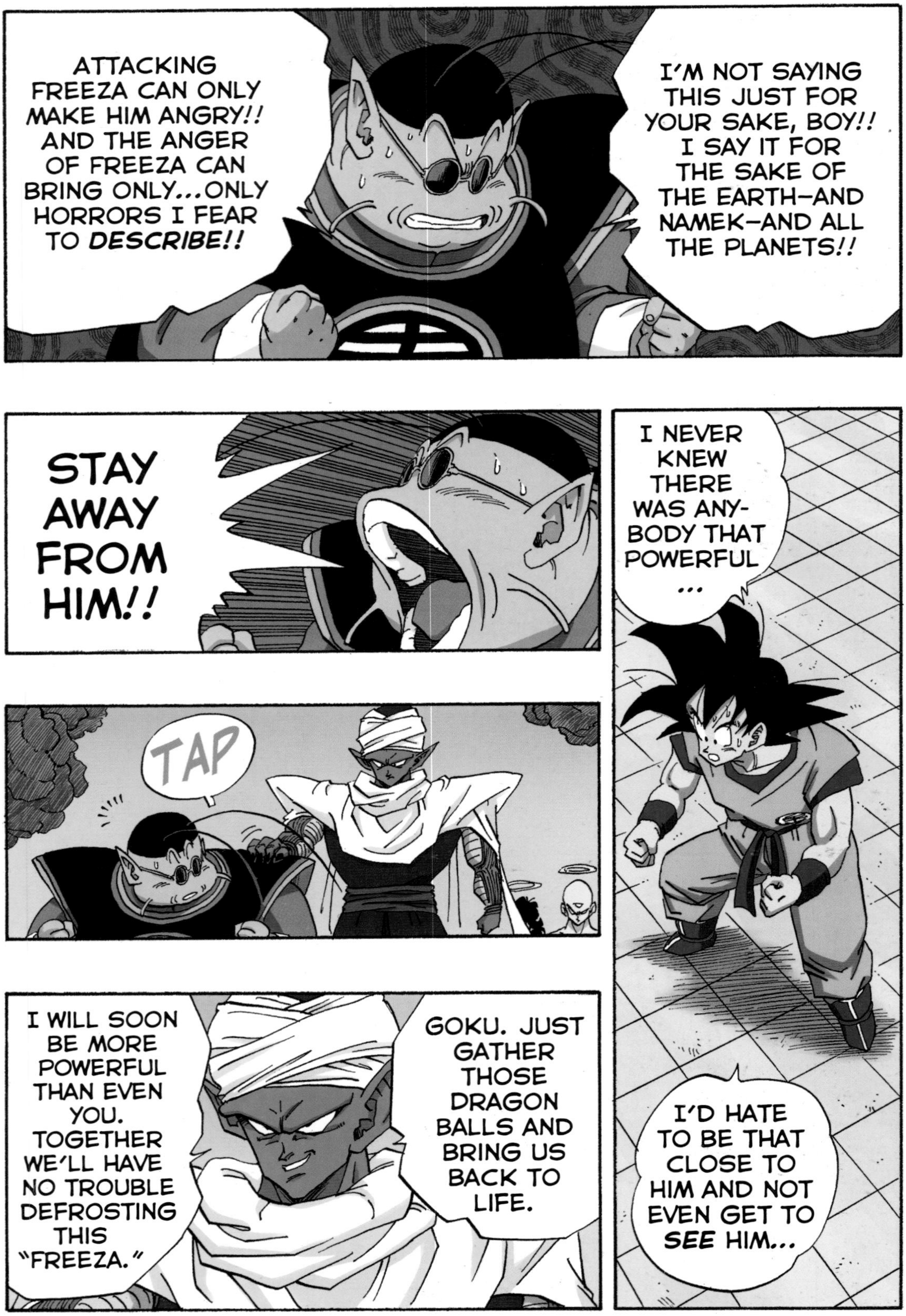
I'M NOT SAYING THIS JUST FOR YOUR SAKE, BOY!! I SAY IT FOR THE SAKE OF THE EARTH—AND NAMEK—AND ALL THE PLANETS!!
ATTACKING FREEZA CAN ONLY MAKE HIM ANGRY!! AND THE ANGER OF FREEZA CAN BRING ONLY...ONLY HORRORS I FEAR TO *DESCRIBE!!*
I NEVER KNEW THERE WAS ANY-BODY THAT POWERFUL ...
I'D HATE TO BE THAT CLOSE TO HIM AND NOT EVEN GET TO *SEE* HIM...
STAY AWAY FROM HIM!!
TAP
GOKU. JUST GATHER THOSE DRAGON BALLS AND BRING US BACK TO LIFE.
I WILL SOON BE MORE POWERFUL THAN EVEN YOU. TOGETHER WE'LL HAVE NO TROUBLE DEFROSTING THIS "FREEZA."

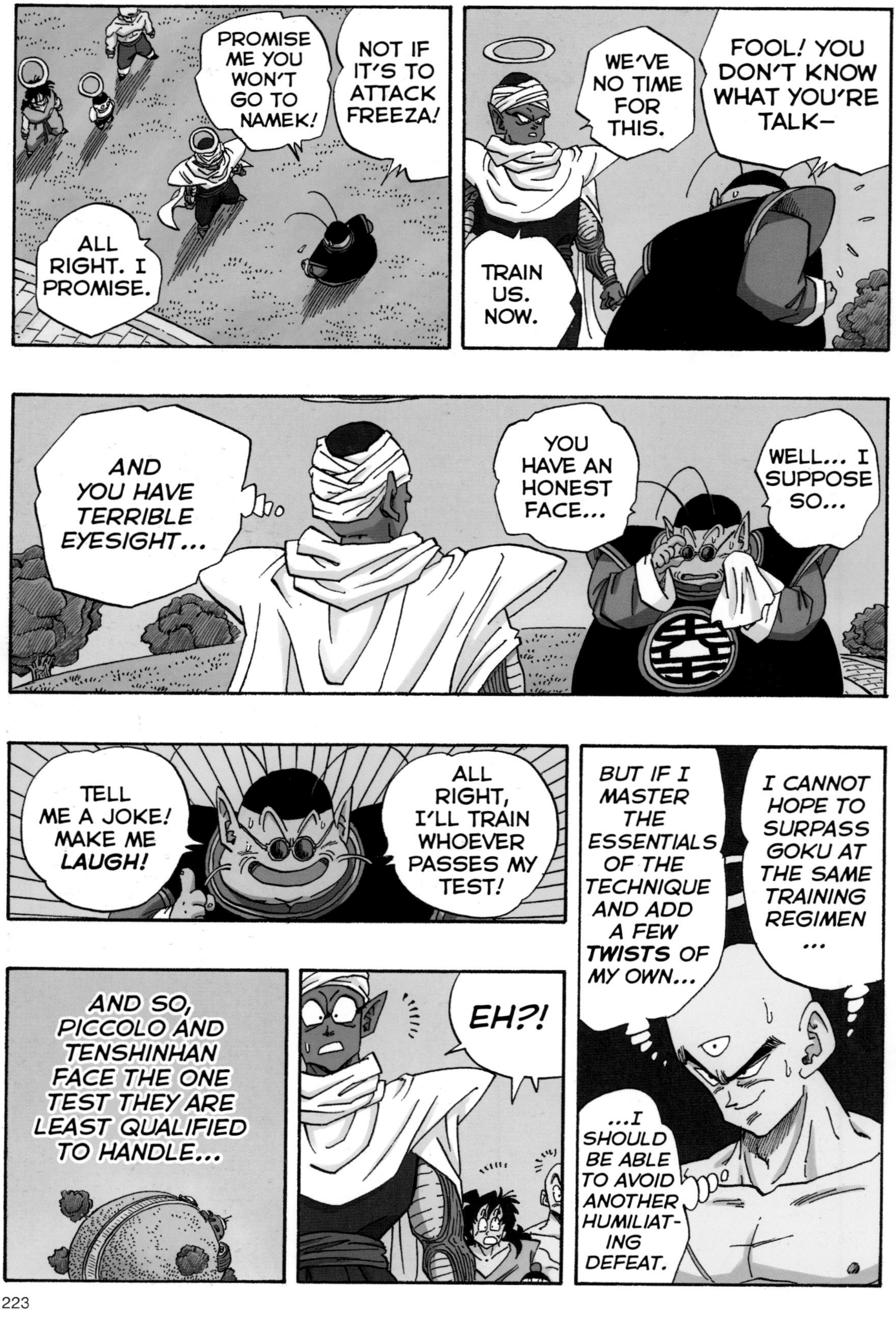
FOOL! YOU DON'T KNOW WHAT YOU'RE TALK—
WE'VE NO TIME FOR THIS.
TRAIN US. NOW.
NOT IF IT'S TO ATTACK FREEZA!
PROMISE ME YOU WON'T GO TO NAMEK!
ALL RIGHT. I PROMISE.
WELL... I SUPPOSE SO...
YOU HAVE AN HONEST FACE...
AND YOU HAVE TERRIBLE EYESIGHT...
I CANNOT HOPE TO SURPASS GOKU AT THE SAME TRAINING REGIMEN...
BUT IF I MASTER THE ESSENTIALS OF THE TECHNIQUE AND ADD A FEW TWISTS OF MY OWN...
...I SHOULD BE ABLE TO AVOID ANOTHER HUMILIATING DEFEAT.
ALL RIGHT, I'LL TRAIN WHOEVER PASSES MY TEST!
TELL ME A JOKE! MAKE ME LAUGH!
EH?!
AND SO, PICCOLO AND TENSHINHAN FACE THE ONE TEST THEY ARE LEAST QUALIFIED TO HANDLE...

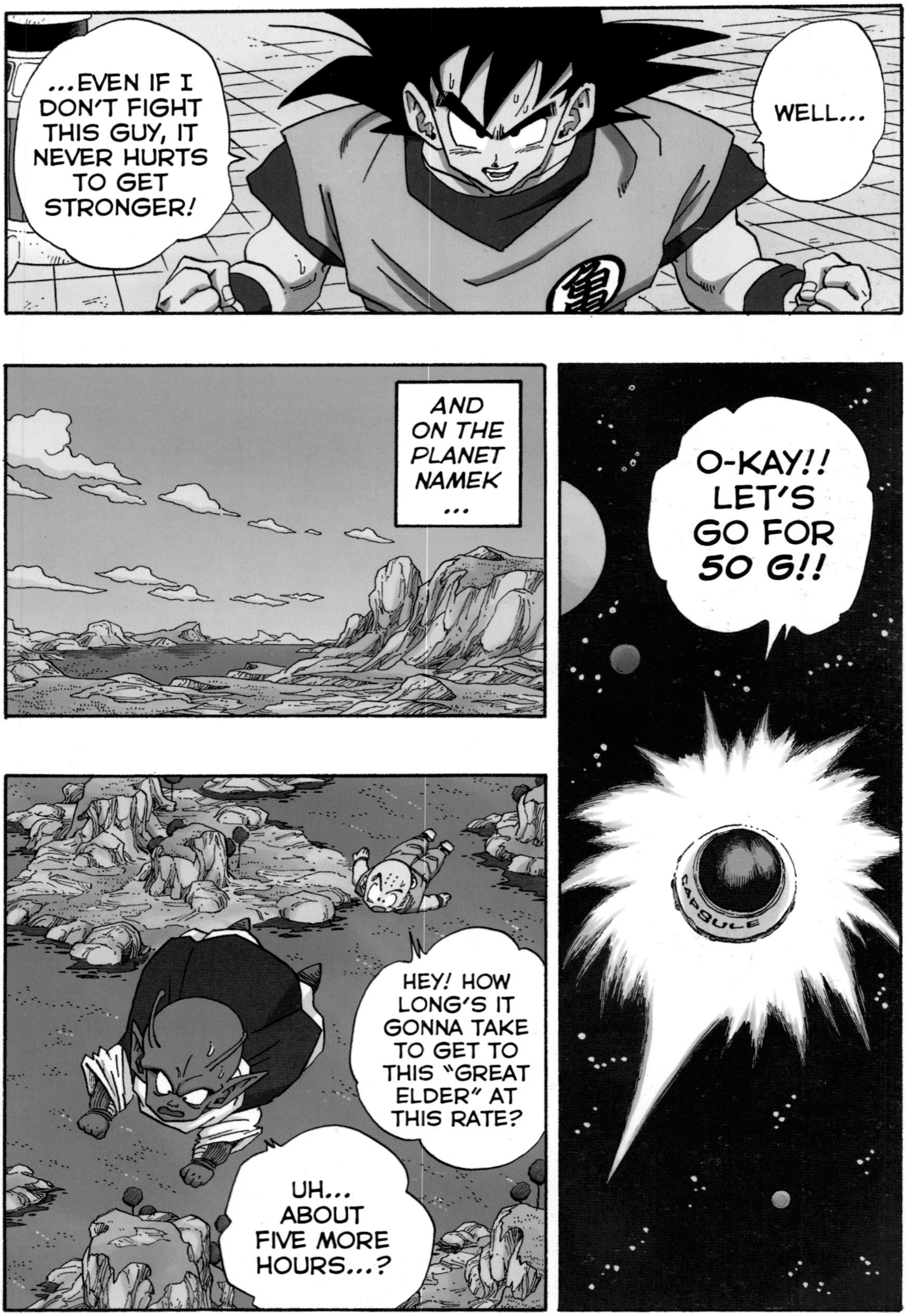
WELL...
...EVEN IF I DON'T FIGHT THIS GUY, IT NEVER HURTS TO GET STRONGER!
O-KAY!! LET'S GO FOR 50 G!!
CAPSULE
AND ON THE PLANET NAMEK ...
HEY! HOW LONG'S IT GONNA TAKE TO GET TO THIS "GREAT ELDER" AT THIS RATE?
UH... ABOUT FIVE MORE HOURS...?

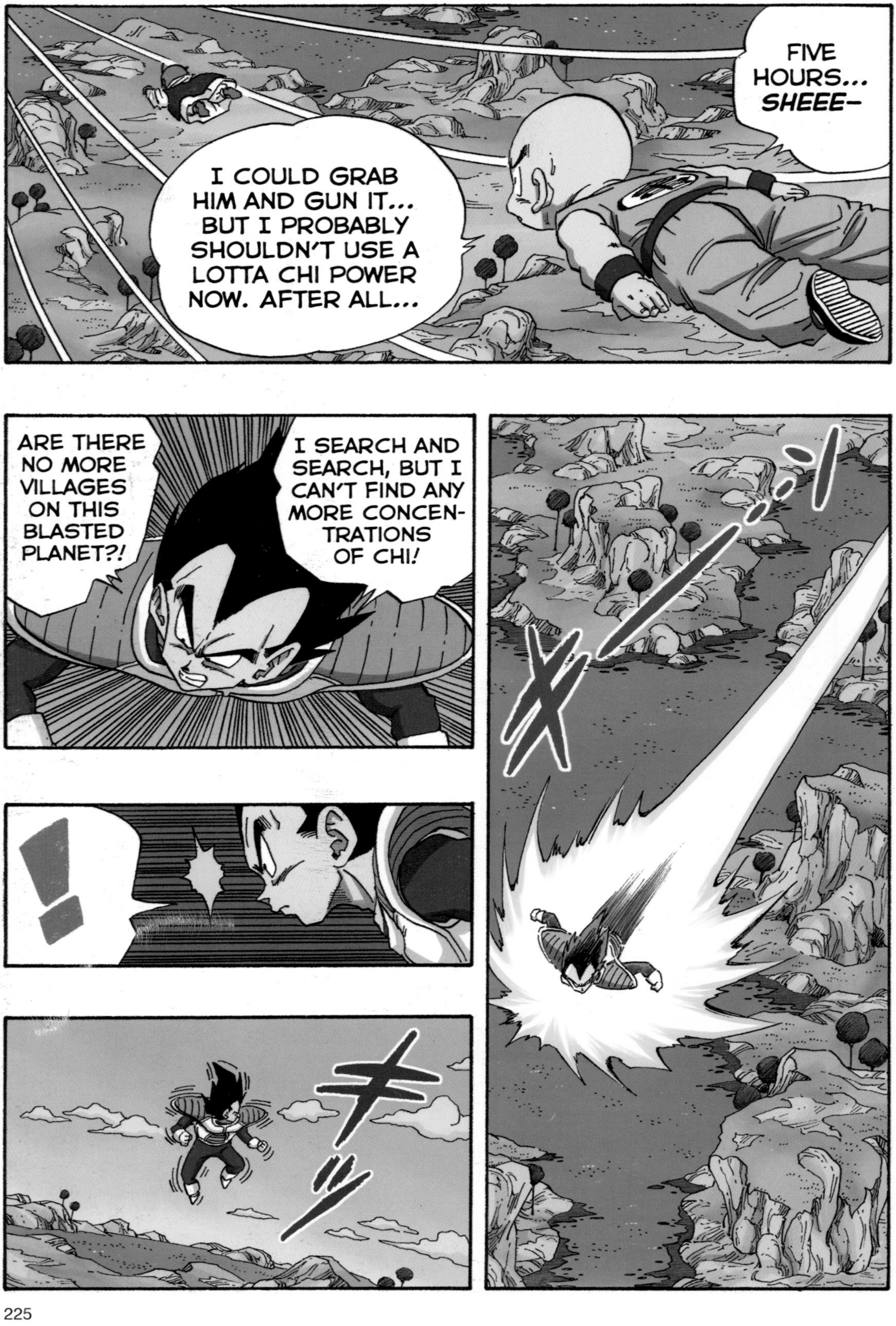
FIVE HOURS... SHEEE–
I COULD GRAB HIM AND GUN IT... BUT I PROBABLY SHOULDN'T USE A LOTTA CHI POWER NOW. AFTER ALL...
I SEARCH AND SEARCH, BUT I CAN'T FIND ANY MORE CONCENTRATIONS OF CHI!
ARE THERE NO MORE VILLAGES ON THIS BLASTED PLANET?!
!

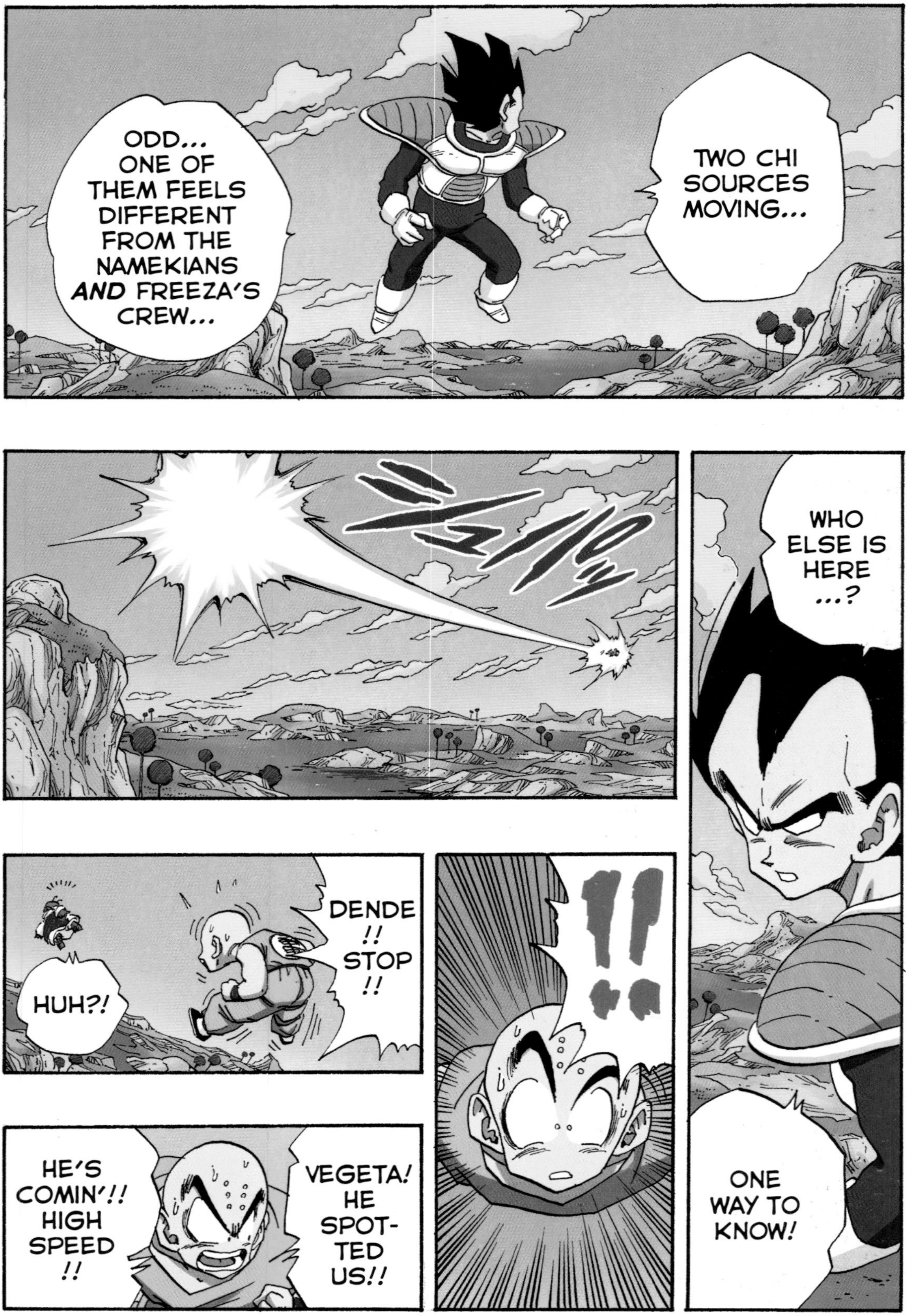
TWO CHI SOURCES MOVING...
ODD... ONE OF THEM FEELS DIFFERENT FROM THE NAMEKIANS *AND* FREEZA'S CREW...
WHO ELSE IS HERE ...?
ONE WAY TO KNOW!
!!
DENDE!! STOP!!
HUH?!
VEGETA! HE SPOT-TED US!!
HE'S COMIN'!! HIGH SPEED!!

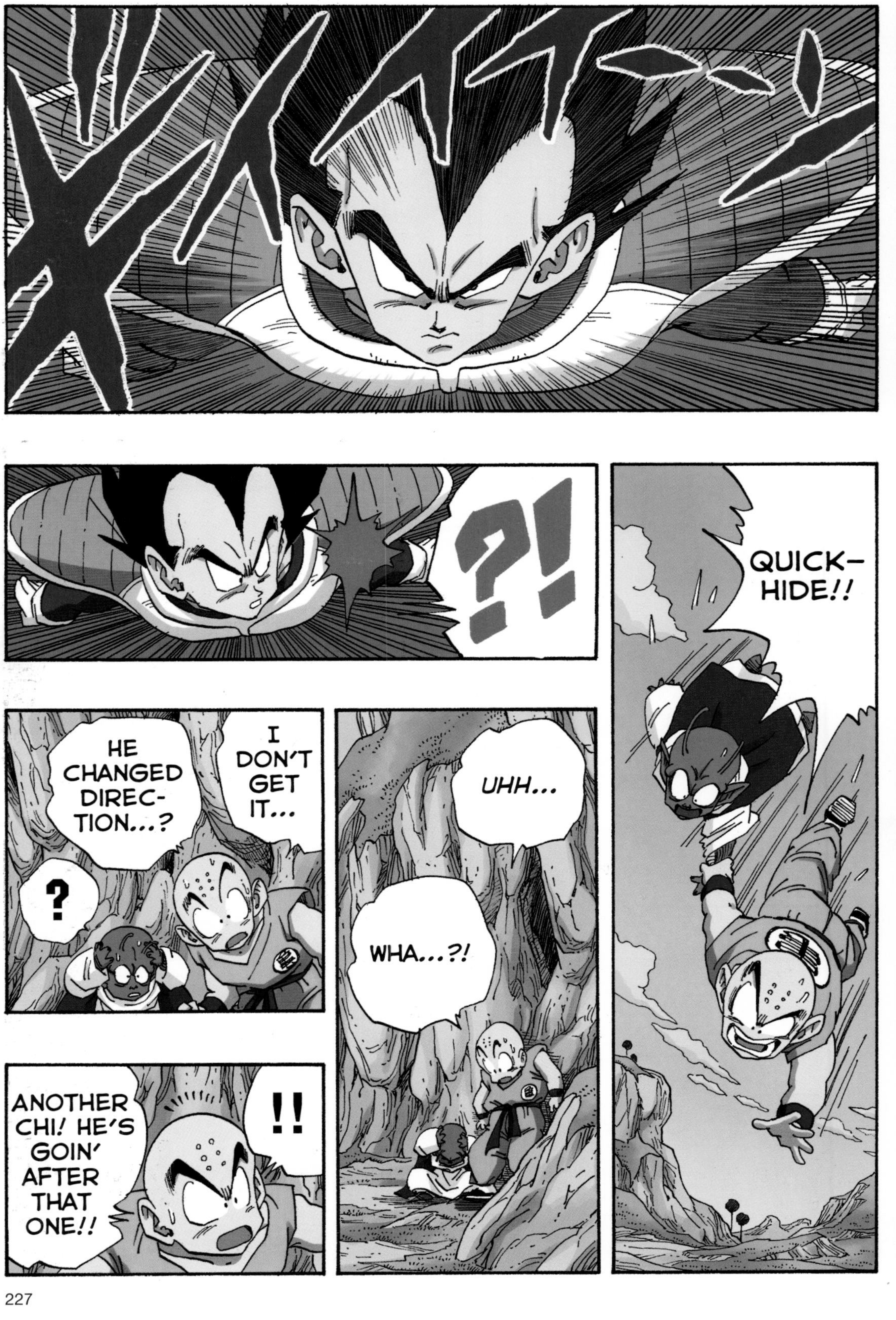

QUICK-HIDE!!
?!
UHH...
WHA...?!
I DON'T GET IT...
HE CHANGED DIREC-TION...?
?
!!
ANOTHER CHI! HE'S GOIN' AFTER THAT ONE!!

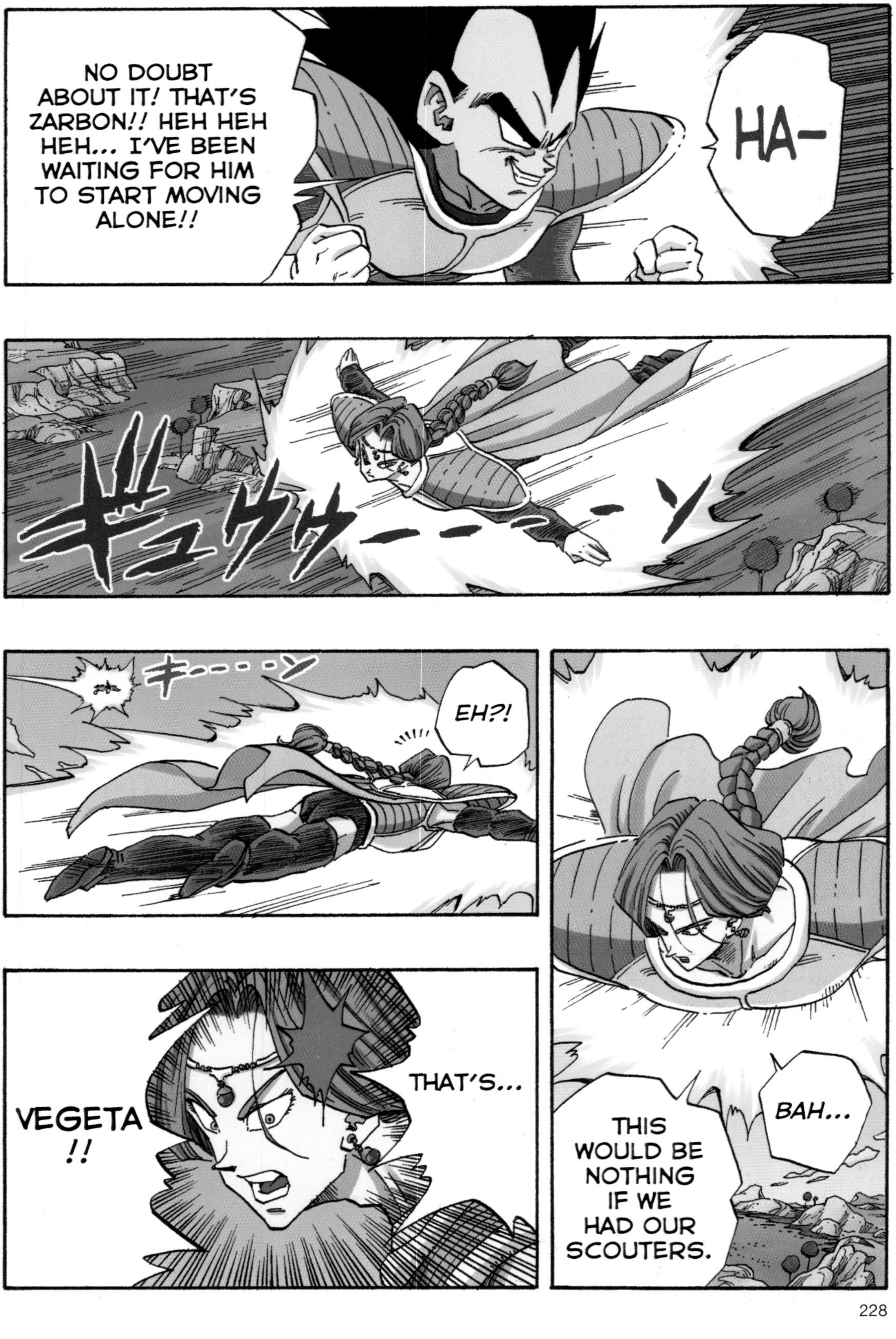
HA-
NO DOUBT ABOUT IT! THAT'S ZARBON!! HEH HEH HEH... I'VE BEEN WAITING FOR HIM TO START MOVING ALONE!!
ギュウウーーーン
BAH...
THIS WOULD BE NOTHING IF WE HAD OUR SCOUTERS.
EH?!
キーーーーン
THAT'S...
VEGETA!!

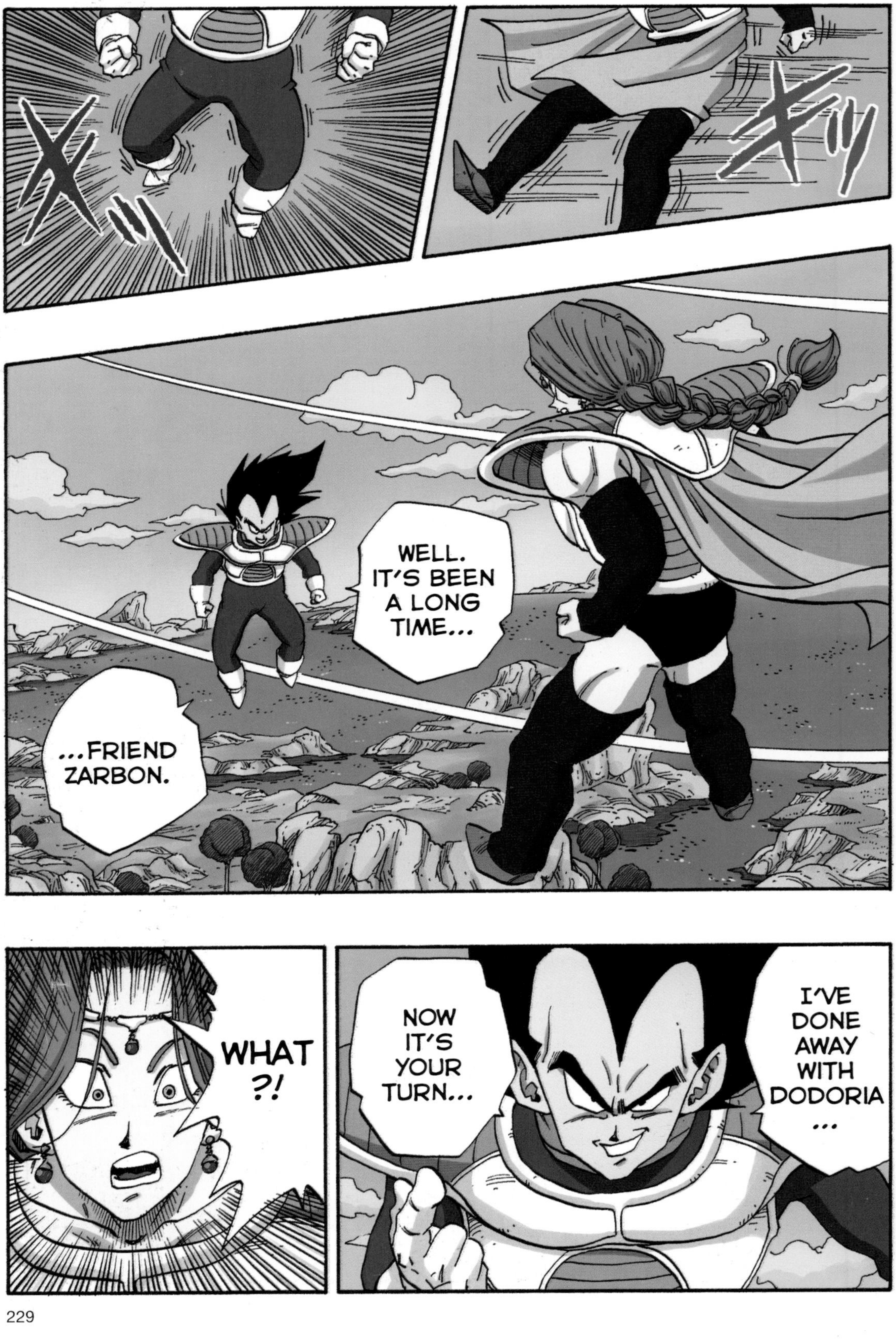
ギッ
ズッ
WELL. IT'S BEEN A LONG TIME...
...FRIEND ZARBON.
I'VE DONE AWAY WITH DODORIA ...
NOW IT'S YOUR TURN...
WHAT ?!

Chapter 17 • Vegeta vs. Zarbon

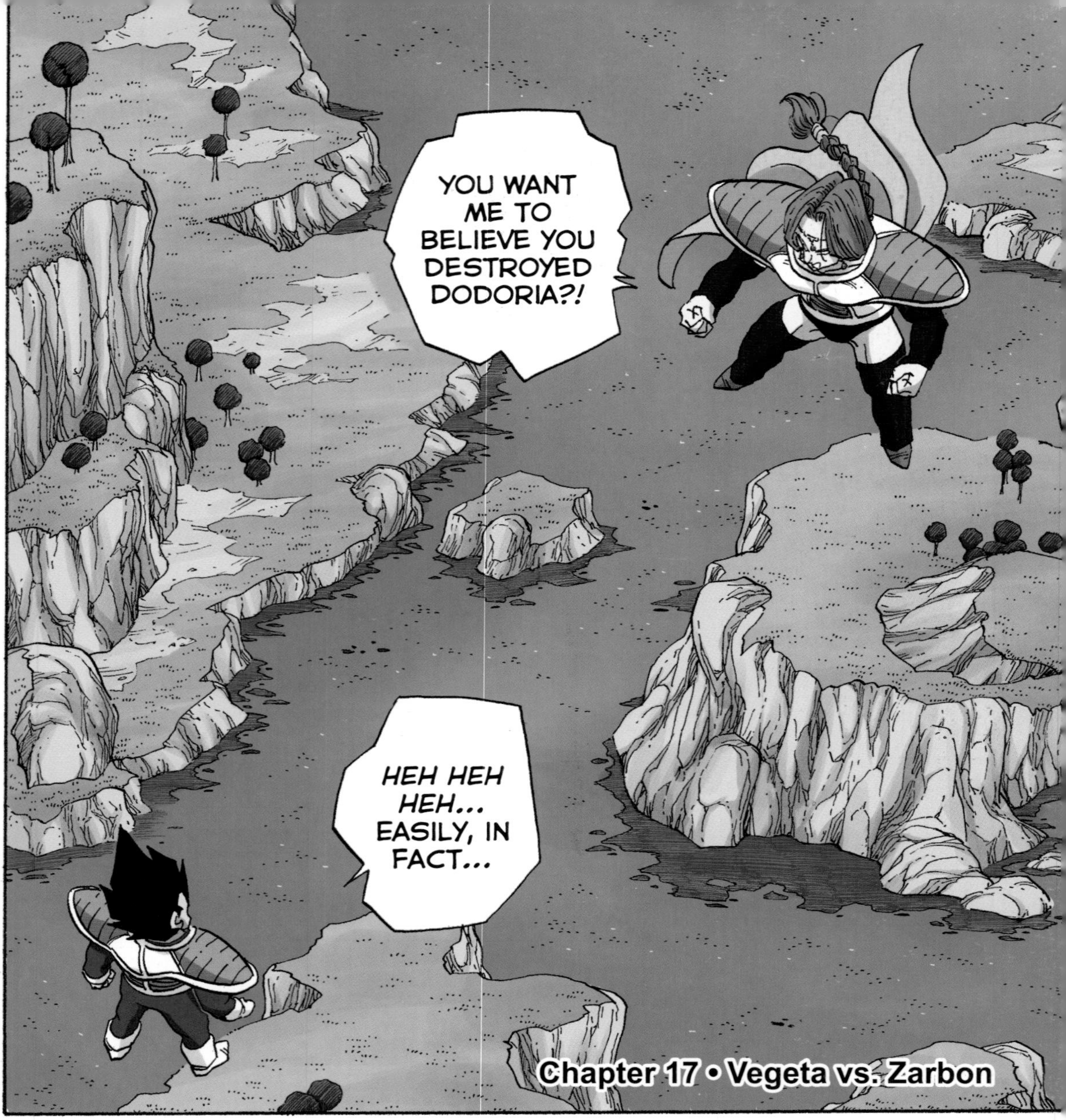
YOU WANT ME TO BELIEVE YOU DESTROYED DODORIA?!
HEH HEH HEH... EASILY, IN FACT...

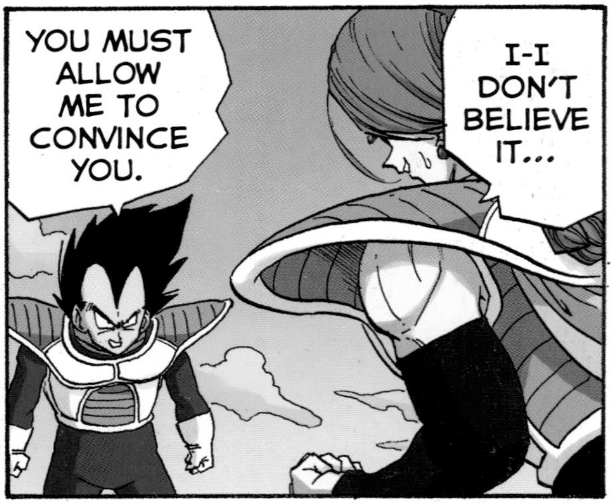
I-I DON'T BELIEVE IT...
YOU MUST ALLOW ME TO CONVINCE YOU.

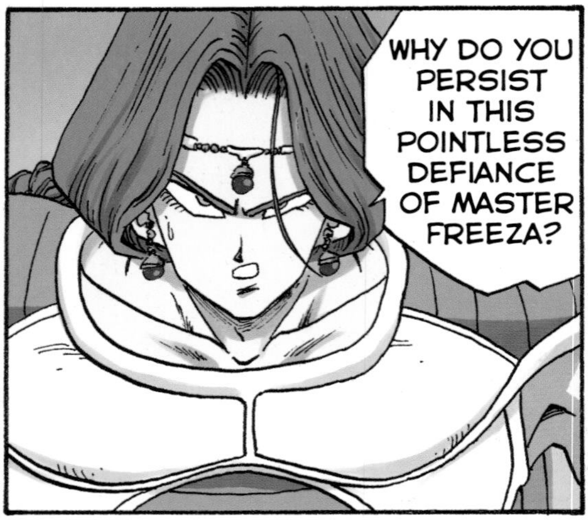
WHY DO YOU PERSIST IN THIS POINTLESS DEFIANCE OF MASTER FREEZA?

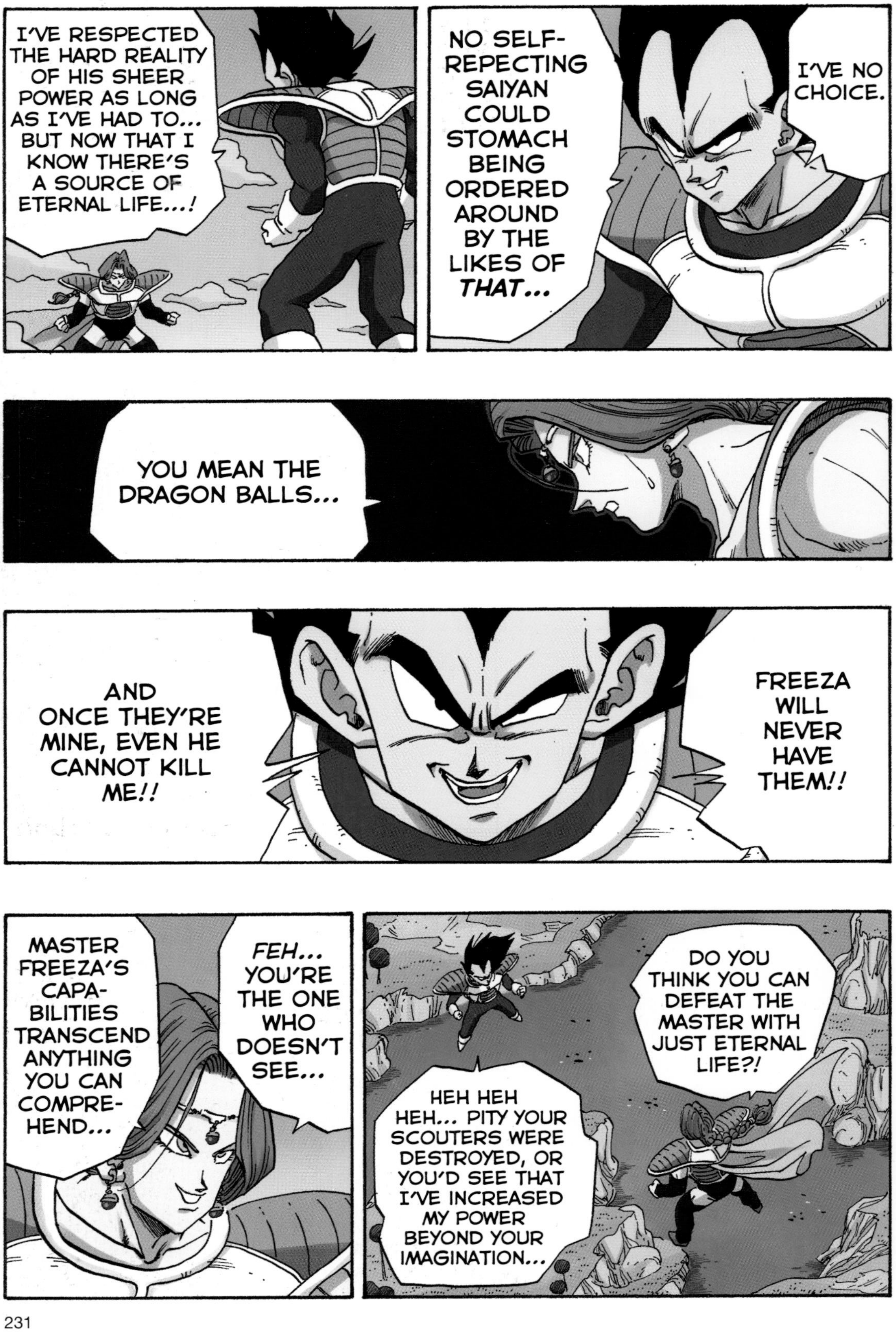
I'VE NO CHOICE.
NO SELF-REPECTING SAIYAN COULD STOMACH BEING ORDERED AROUND BY THE LIKES OF *THAT*...
I'VE RESPECTED THE HARD REALITY OF HIS SHEER POWER AS LONG AS I'VE HAD TO... BUT NOW THAT I KNOW THERE'S A SOURCE OF ETERNAL LIFE...!
YOU MEAN THE DRAGON BALLS...
FREEZA WILL NEVER HAVE THEM!!
AND ONCE THEY'RE MINE, EVEN HE CANNOT KILL ME!!
DO YOU THINK YOU CAN DEFEAT THE MASTER WITH JUST ETERNAL LIFE?!
HEH HEH HEH... PITY YOUR SCOUTERS WERE DESTROYED, OR YOU'D SEE THAT I'VE INCREASED MY POWER BEYOND YOUR IMAGINATION...
FEH... YOU'RE THE ONE WHO DOESN'T SEE...
MASTER FREEZA'S CAPA-BILITIES TRANSCEND ANYTHING YOU CAN COMPRE-HEND...

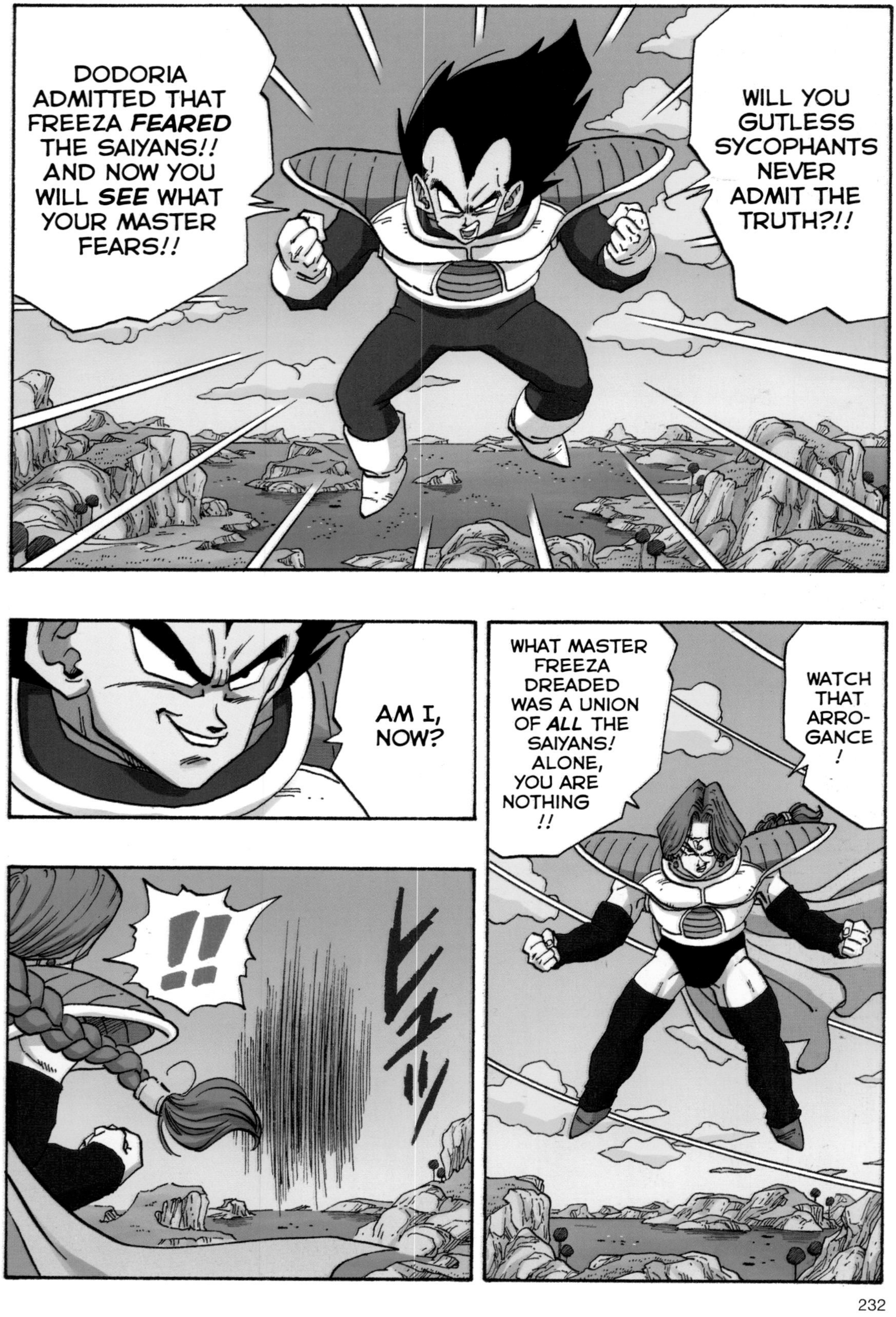
WILL YOU GUTLESS SYCOPHANTS NEVER ADMIT THE TRUTH?!!
DODORIA ADMITTED THAT FREEZA *FEARED* THE SAIYANS!! AND NOW YOU WILL *SEE* WHAT YOUR MASTER FEARS!!
WATCH THAT ARROGANCE!
WHAT MASTER FREEZA DREADED WAS A UNION OF *ALL* THE SAIYANS! ALONE, YOU ARE NOTHING!!
AM I, NOW?
!!
ヒュッ

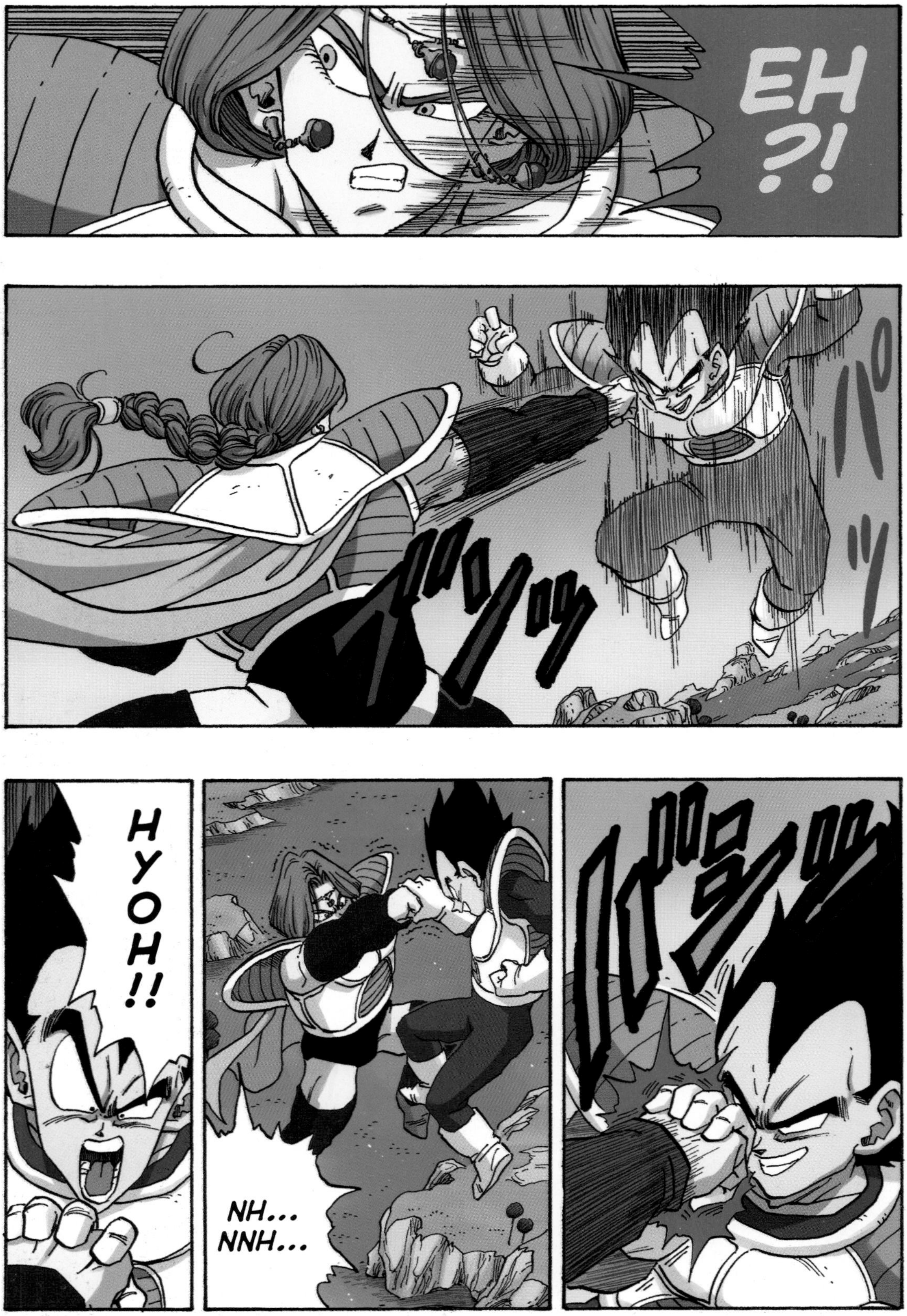
EH ?!
パッ
NH... NNH...
HYOH!!

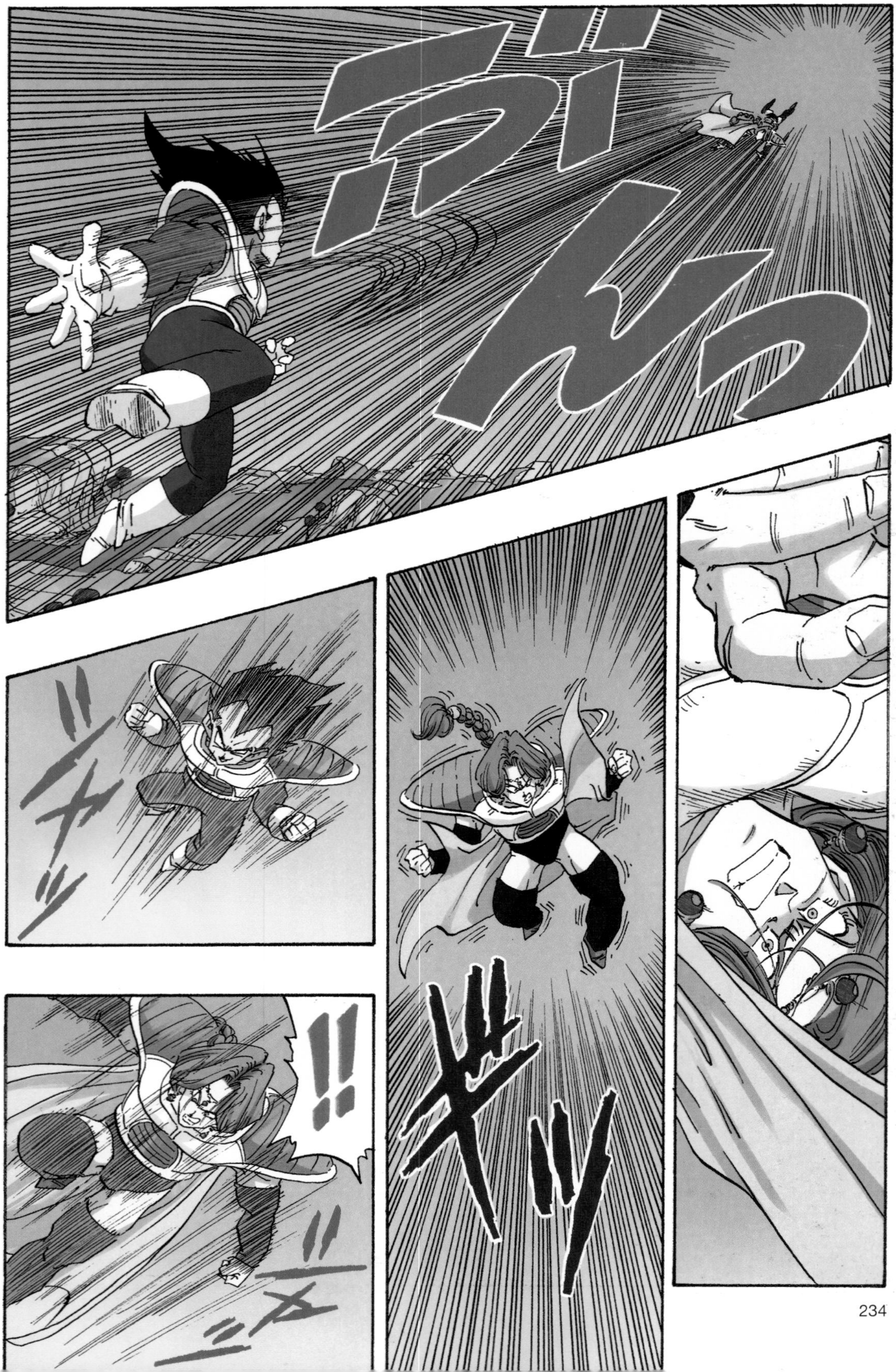
ギッ
!!

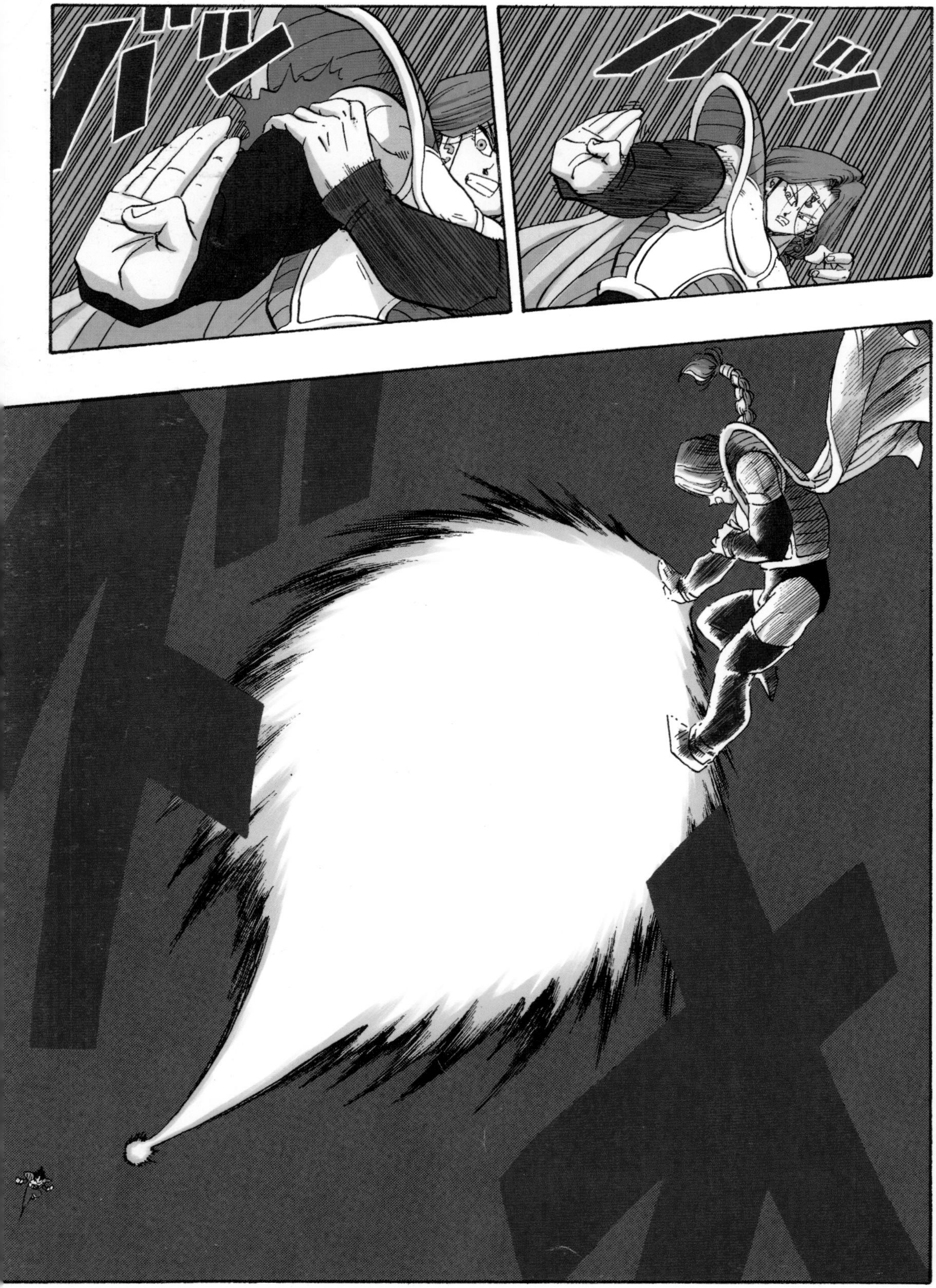

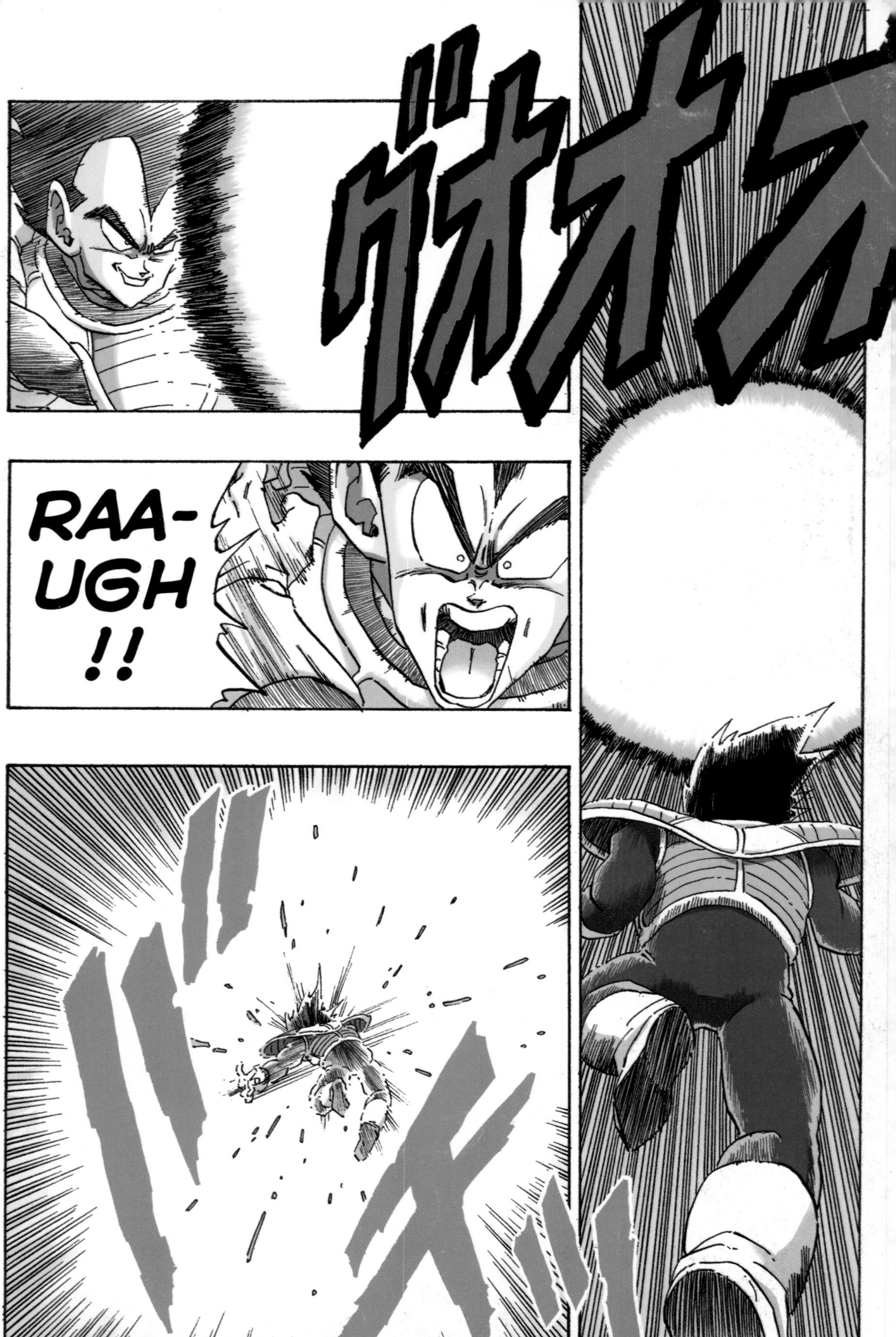
RAA-UGH!!

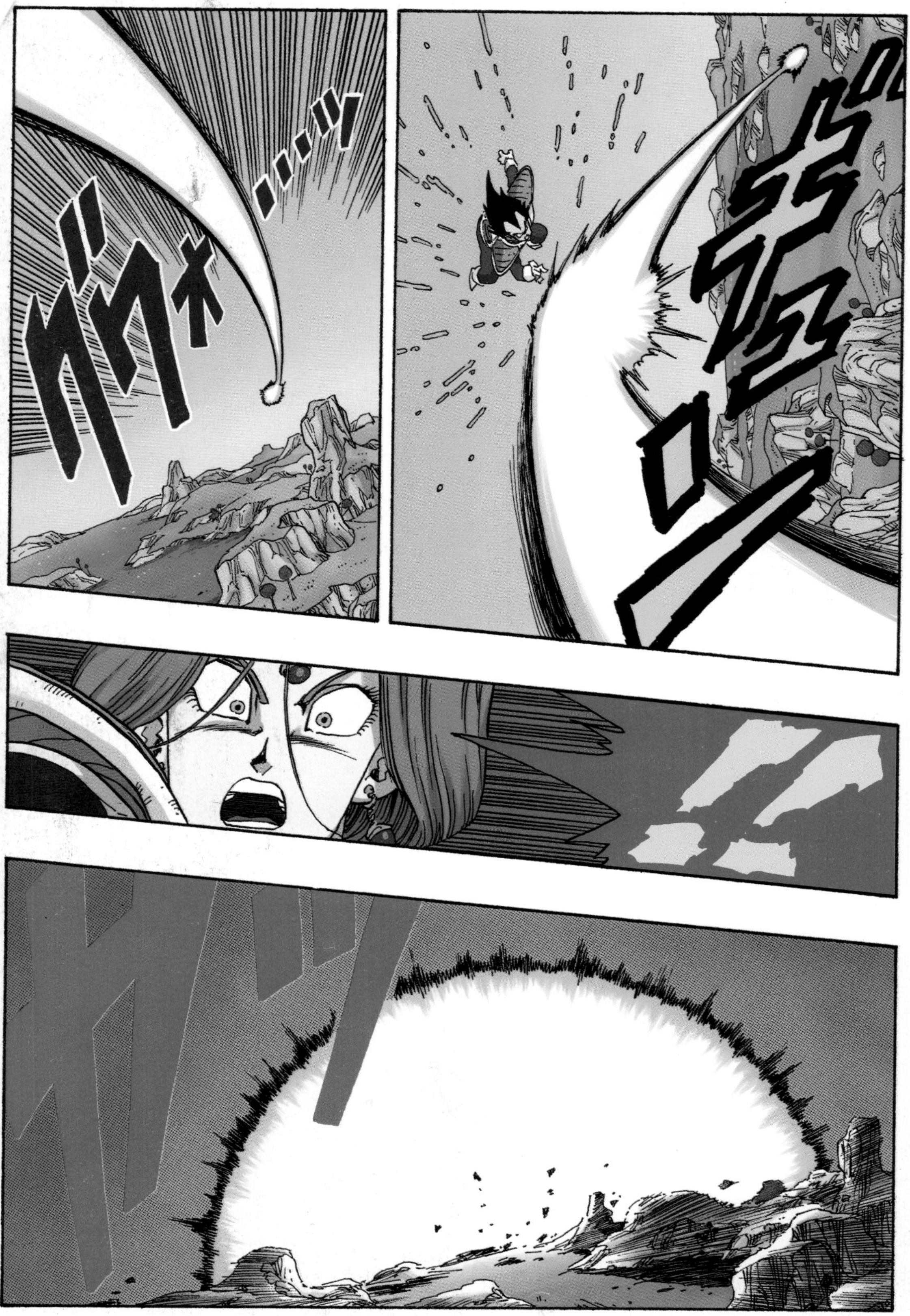

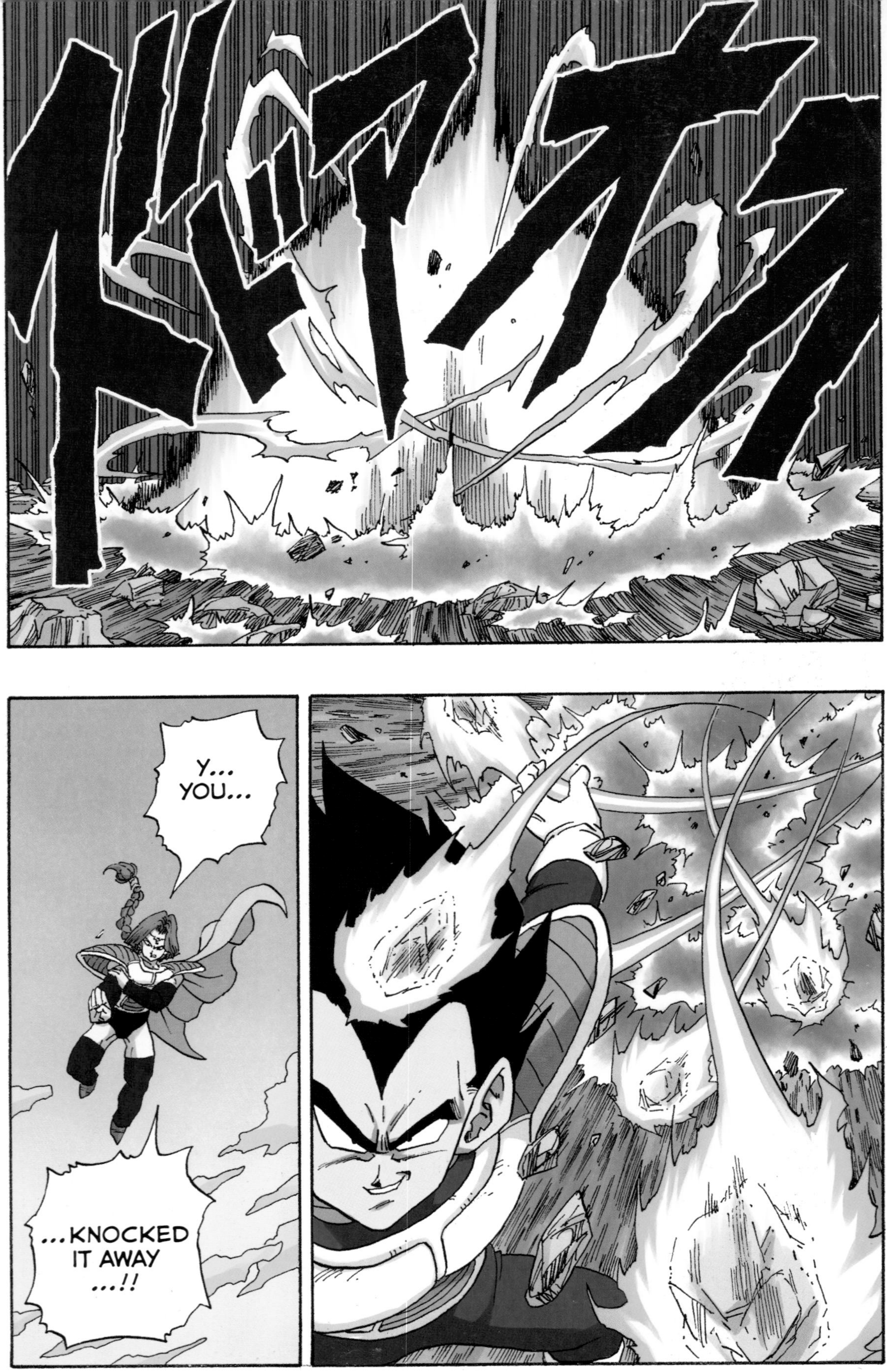
Y... YOU...
...KNOCKED IT AWAY ...!!

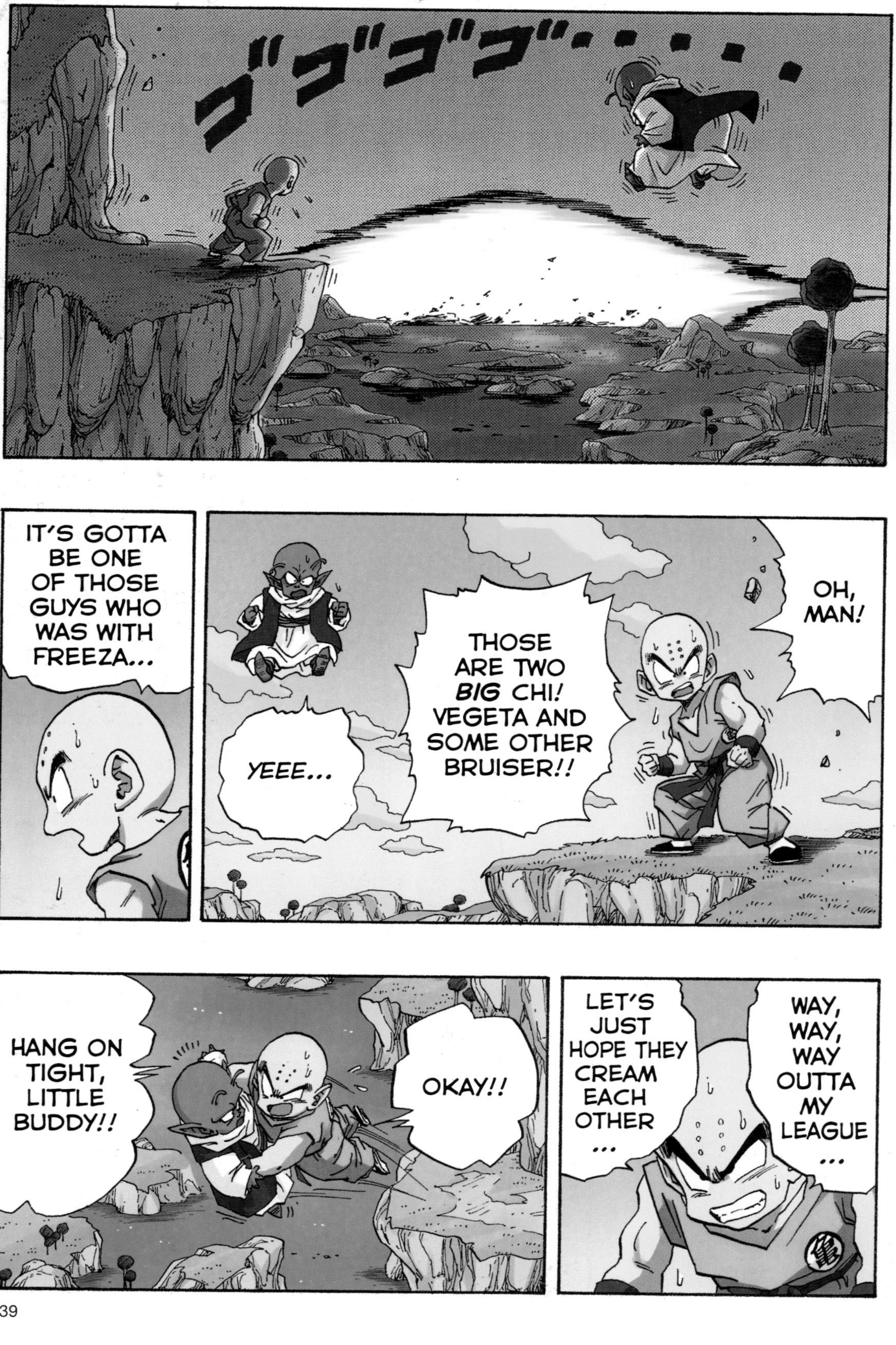
ゴゴゴゴ・・・・・
OH, MAN!
THOSE ARE TWO *BIG* CHI! VEGETA AND SOME OTHER BRUISER!!
YEEE...
IT'S GOTTA BE ONE OF THOSE GUYS WHO WAS WITH FREEZA...
WAY, WAY, WAY OUTTA MY LEAGUE...
LET'S JUST HOPE THEY CREAM EACH OTHER...
OKAY!!
HANG ON TIGHT, LITTLE BUDDY!!

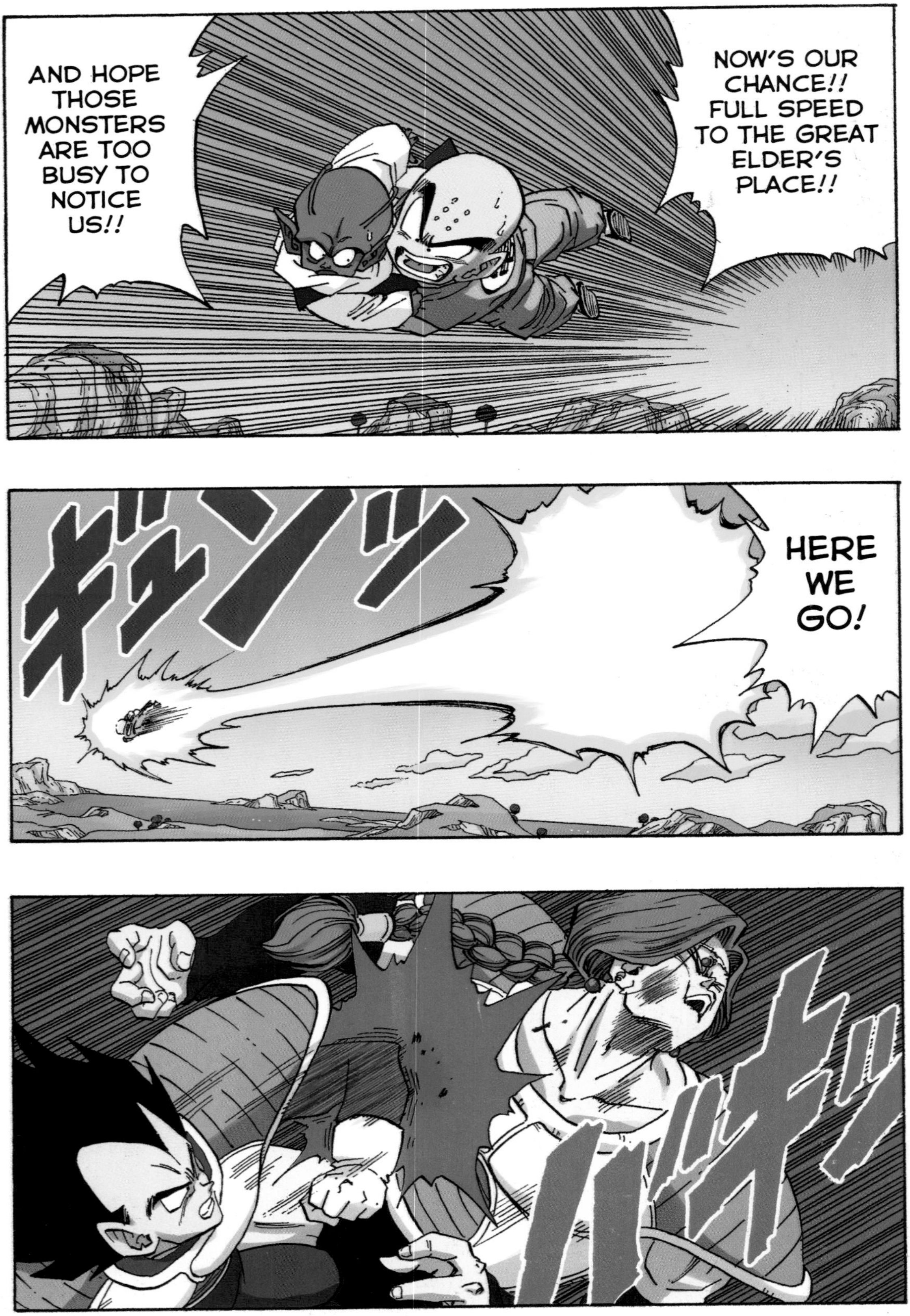
NOW'S OUR CHANCE!! FULL SPEED TO THE GREAT ELDER'S PLACE!!
AND HOPE THOSE MONSTERS ARE TOO BUSY TO NOTICE US!!
HERE WE GO!
ギュンッ
バキッ

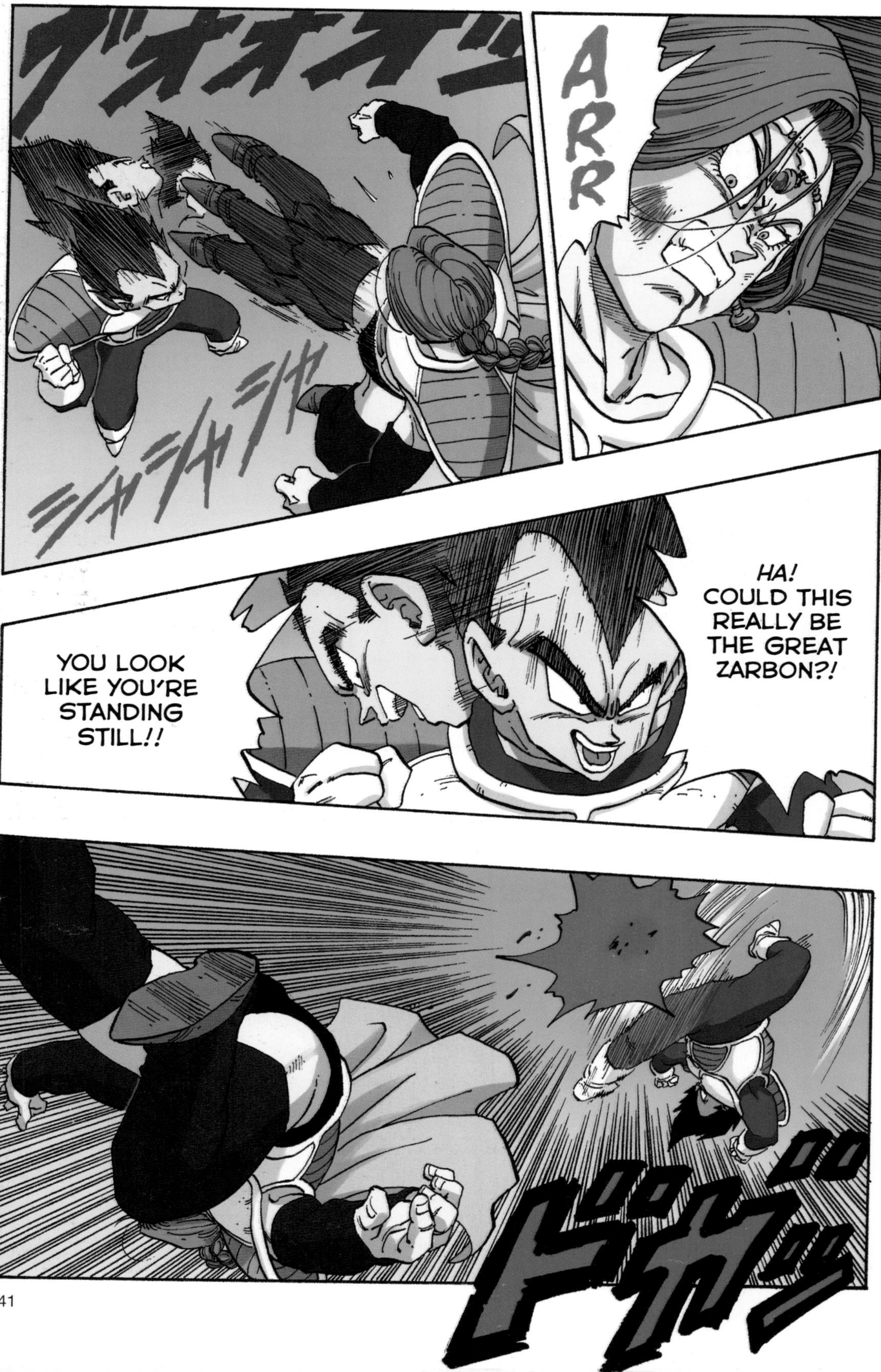
ARR
HA! COULD THIS REALLY BE THE GREAT ZARBON?!
YOU LOOK LIKE YOU'RE STANDING STILL!!

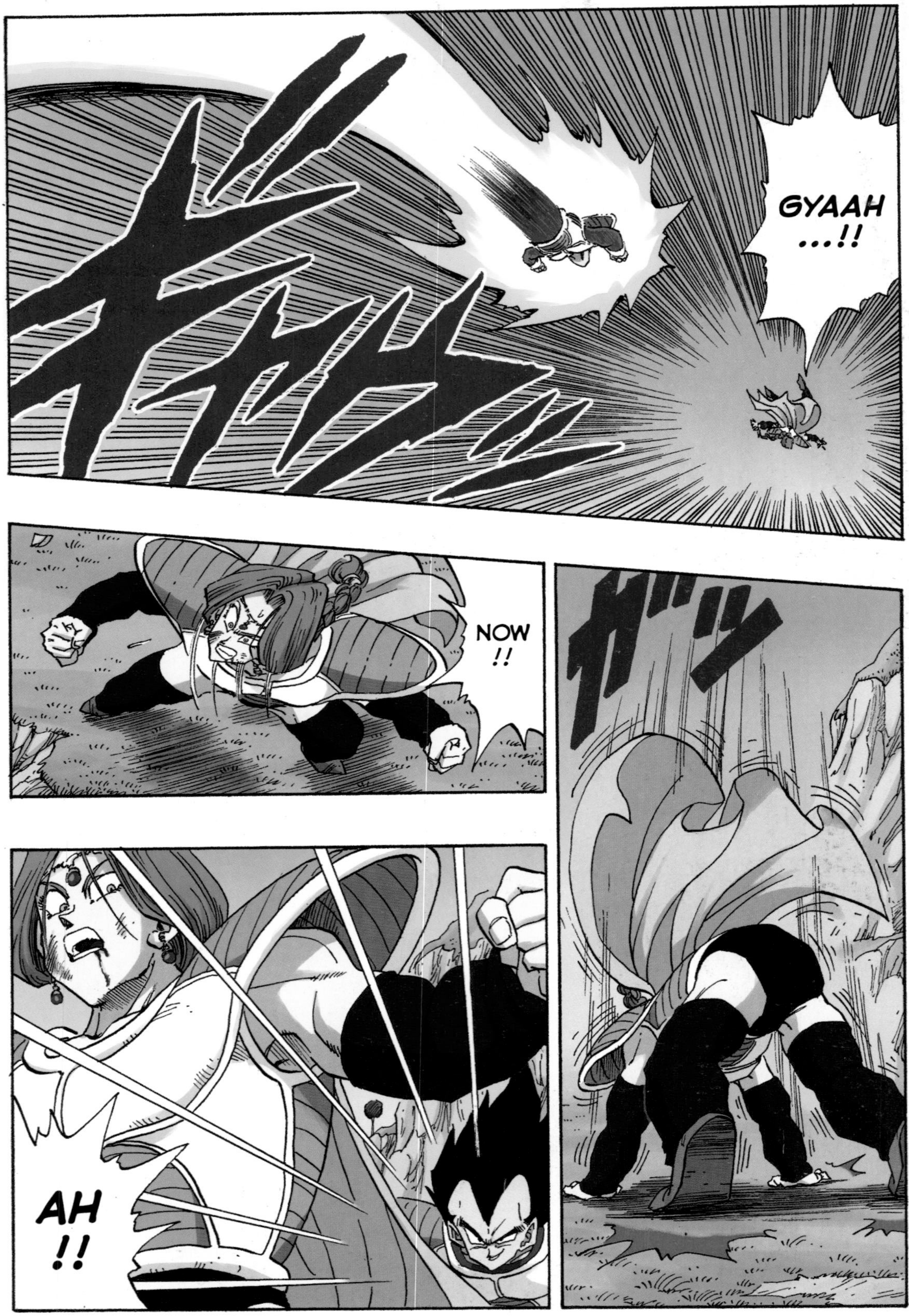
GYAAH ...!!
NOW !!
AH !!